WOMEN IN JAPANESE SOCIETY

WOMEN IN JAPANESE SOCIETY

An Annotated Bibliography of Selected English Language Materials

KRISTINA RUTH HUBER

*Chapters on Women Writers and
Women's Spoken Language by Kathryn Sparling*

HQ
1762
.H83x
1992
West

Bibliographies and Indexes in Women's Studies, Number 16

GREENWOOD PRESS
Westport, Connecticut • London

Library of Congress Cataloging-in-Publication Data

Huber, Kristina R.
    Women in Japanese society : an annotated bibliography of selected
English language materials / Kristina Ruth Huber.
        p.   cm.—(Bibliographies and indexes in women's studies,
ISSN 0742-6941; no. 16)
    "Chapters on women writers and women's spoken language by Kathryn
Sparling."
    Includes bibliographical references and index.
    ISBN 0-313-25296-3 (alk. paper)
    1. Women—Japan—History—Bibliography. 2. Women—Japan—Social
conditions—Bibliography. 3. Women authors, Japanese—Bibliography.
I. Sparling, Kathryn. II. Title. III. Series.
Z7964.J3H82   1992
[HQ1762]
016.30542'0952—dc20   92-15371

British Library Cataloguing in Publication Data is available.

Library of Congress Catalog Card Number: 92-15371
ISBN: 0-313-25296-3
ISSN: 0742-6941

First published in 1992

Greenwood Press, 88 Post Road West, Westport, CT 06881
An imprint of Greenwood Publishing Group, Inc.

Printed in the United States of America

The paper used in this book complies with the
Permanent Paper Standard issued by the National
Information Standards Organization (Z39.48-1984).

10 9 8 7 6 5 4 3 2 1

For

R. Grey Smith and Marjorie Hunt Smith

Jackson H. Bailey and Caroline A. Bailey

and

Evan Ira Farber and Hope Farber

—KH

Contents

Acknowledgments

This bibliography has been compiled with the help of many people including colleagues at St. Olaf, Earlham, and Carleton Colleges, and family and friends. Jackson Bailey, Forrest Brown, Evan Farber and Steven Nussbaum helped with its initial conception. Brenda Bankart, Marjorie Bingham, Joseph Grabill, Susan Gross, Steven Nussbaum and Eleanor Zelliot shared bibliographies compiled in the course of their work. Richard Bodman, Forrest Brown, Robert Entenmann, Evan Farber, Anne Imamura, Bruce Nordstrom and Bardwell Smith suggested materials as they came across them. Many of the above people as well as J. Randolph Cox shared hard-to-find items from their private collections.

This bibliography would have been impossible to compile without the professional commitment of the staffs of many libraries across the country. The primary library collections used were those of St. Olaf College, Carleton College, the University of Minnesota, Earlham College, the Library of Congress, Luther-Northwestern Seminary, and Bethel College and Seminary, and those accessed through the Minnesota state-funded PALS and MINITEX interlibrary loan systems.

The St. Olaf College Academic Computing Center was of tremendous assistance, as was the telephone support staff of the WordPerfect Corporation. Susan Baker of Greenwood Press provided technical assistance in a calm, patient, and sympathetic manner, while several editors provided encouragement. George Butler and Andrew Schub were able to shepherd the work to completion.

Robert Entenmann, Phyllis Larson, LaNelle Olsen, Jean Parker, Bardwell Smith and Marjorie Smith read the manuscript in part or in whole. Frank Joseph Shulman made helpful suggestions. R. Grey Smith edited the manuscript with the exception of the chapters on language and literature, and helped transform it into a cohesive, consistent work. As always, the responsibility for remaining errors is my own.

St. Olaf College supported a portion of this work by providing a Small Grant to cover the initial data base searching costs, a Faculty Development Summer Grant and sabbatical funding.

Sharon Sievers sent a letter of encouragement early in the project which confirmed the need for a bibliography like this. Jack and Cappy Bailey, George and Jane Silver, Evan and Hope Farber, and Jim and Helen Cope were always interested and supportive. Many St. Olaf, Carleton and Earlham colleagues heard more than they wanted to know about the agonies of bibliography compilation and made helpful suggestions. The attenders of Cannon Valley Friends Meeting, Jennifer Busa and members of my extended family were also very patient, supportive, and interested.

Above all, my children Katherine (age 5) and Elizabeth (age 11), and my husband Michael deserve the appreciation of all the users of this bibliography. Their support and sacrifice over the last seven years cannot be acknowledged adequately.

Kris Huber

I would like to express special appreciation to Martha Boyd and Jean Hayes, secretaries in the Department of Asian Languages and Literatures at Carleton College, and to student research assistant Julie Armstrong. I am also indebted to Professors Shigeru Tobita and Yoshinori Watabe of Chūō University for arranging visiting status for me at Chūō University in the summer of 1991, and to Chūō University for generous institutional support without which this project would have been difficult to complete.

Kathryn Sparling

Introduction

Purpose and Audience

As women have become a focus of popular and scholarly interest worldwide, increased attention to Japanese women has generated a rich profusion of studies and translations, especially over the past twenty years. This bibliography is an attempt at comprehensive coverage of that ever-expanding field. It surveys translations of original sources and 19th- and 20th-century materials in English on all aspects of the lives of Japanese women—from prehistory to the present—in the public, private, and professional spheres. There is also a chapter on the experiences of non-Japanese women in Japan.

This bibliography of English-language resources is intended primarily for an audience of undergraduates and teachers of undergraduates. It should serve as an overview of the wealth of resources available, and as a guide to selecting and evaluating materials of particular interest. We believe it will be useful to experts as well—to specialists in Women's Studies who seek grounding in Japanese Studies, or vice versa, and in fact to anthropologists, sociologists, historians, economists, literature scholars, etc. well acquainted with materials on Japanese women within their own disciplines who wish a broader view.

We hope too that this bibliography will offer a glimpse of the history and development of both scholarship and journalism on Japanese women. Materials published between 1841 and 1990 are included. They range in scope from a brochure prepared in Japan for the World's Columbian Exposition of 1893 and a contemporary *manga* [comic] version of *The Tale of Genji* to standard scholarly studies and translations.

Criteria for Inclusion

All materials found with women in Japan as a primary focus have been included. Materials with significant sections or chapters devoted to the topic have also been included. In addition, selected materials (which may appear to the reader to be of a more general nature but which set a context necessary for the study of Japanese women) have been listed (e.g. Doi's *Anatomy of Dependence* [#2] and Nakane's *Japanese Society* [#6]). Items covering the experiences of Japanese women outside Japan have not been covered.

Literature entries have been restricted to those written by Japanese women, and secondary scholarship about such works, with the exception of Tanizaki's *Makioka Sisters* [#136] which appears in the general chapter on Women's Place. We have excluded all other literary works by men in which women figure prominently (Arishima Takeo's novel *A Certain Woman* or third category "women" plays of the Nō theater). No secondary criticism on images of women or child birth, etc., in literature has been listed. (See Organization and Format section, below, for details on the literature chapters.)

All books, chapters in books, scholarly journal articles, published conference papers, and popular magazine articles meeting the above subject criteria were included. No newspapers, unpublished manuscripts, juvenile literature, or audiovisual materials have been considered. We were also unable to provide thorough coverage of university graduate department publications or small literary magazines. It has been assumed that relevant encyclopedias and dictionaries (e.g. *Kodansha Encyclopedia of Japan*) would be consulted by the user prior to the use of this bibliography. Dissertations have not been included because of easy access (both in print and electronically) via *Dissertation Abstracts*.

All materials found in this bibliography were verified through standard bibliographic verification procedures using at least one of the following: the *National Union Catalog*, the On-line Computer Library Center [OCLC], the Research Libraries Information Network [RLIN], the *Union List of Serials*, *New Serials Titles* or the *Minnesota Union List of Serials*. All items are available in the United States via regular interlibrary loan channels.

Materials published through December 1990 were included.

Sources Consulted

● *Bibliography of Asian Studies* ISSN:0067-7159

> The essential reference for the study of Japan. Includes many journals not covered in standard sources, chapters in edited books, and monographs. Covers 1941 to date; the 1986 edition was the latest published as of March 1992. Anyone wishing to update the listings in *Women in Japan* should start with the subsequent volumes.

● Electronic Databases

DIALOG	WILSONLINE
Books in Print	Readers Guide
Book Review Index	Humanities Index
Economic Literature Index	Social Sciences Index
ERIC	Business Periodicals Index
GPO Monthly Catalog	
Historical Abstracts	
LC MARC—Books	
MLA Bibliography	
PAIS International	
Philosopher's Index	
Population Bibliography	
PsychInfo (Psychological Abstracts)	
Religion Index One	
REMARC (pre-1900 through 1970-)	
SocialSci Search	
Sociological Abstracts	

● *Women Studies Abstracts*

● Previously published bibliographies on Japanese women and on Japanese literature

● Annual literature bibliographies published in *Japanese Literature Today* and *P.E.N. News*

• Privately compiled bibliographies of colleagues

• Reference lists from major books on Japanese women

• Reference lists from selected periodical articles

• Individual issues of periodicals not consistently indexed by standard sources or of such critical importance that a hand-search was warranted:

> *Ampo, Anthropological Linguistics, Armchair Detective, Bulletin of Concerned Asian Scholars, Chanoyu Quarterly, Chicago Review, Comparative Literature Studies, Concerned Theatre Japan, Contemporary Japan* (through the Occupation years only), *East, Ellery Queen Mystery Magazine, Harvard Journal of Asiatic Studies, Hudson Review, Japan Christian Quarterly, Japan Echo, Japan Interpreter, Japan Missionary Bulletin, Japan Quarterly, Japanese Journal of Religious Studies, Japanese Literature Today, Journal of Asian Studies, Journal of Japanese Studies, Journal of the Association of Teachers of Japanese, Japanese Women* (pre-World War II issues only), *Language and Speech, Language in Society, Language Sciences, Lingua, Literature East and West, Literary Review, Look Japan, Mangajin, Monumenta Nipponica, Mundus Artium, Prairie Schooner, Papers in Linguistics, P.E.N. News, Review of Japanese Culture and Society, Transactions of the Asiatic Society of Japan, Western Humanitites Review.*

• Suggestions of many colleagues.

Organization and Format

Chapters (unified by subject) are grouped, somewhat arbitrarily, into the different spheres in which women live their lives. The first section offers a plurality of perspective on the place and worth of women at home and in society. Large chapters are subdivided into sections. Within sections, entries are listed in order of author and then chronologically. If no author is identified, items are listed by title. In citations, standard United States bibliographic format is used throughout. Japanese format (family name first) is used for Japanese names in annotations. To avoid confusion, all surnames appear in upper case to assist those unfamiliar with Japanese names.

The literature portion is arranged differently in several respects. It has been divided chronologically into "premodern" and "modern," with the conventional arbitrary dividing line of 1868 (the date of the Meiji Restoration); and generically into "prose" (long and short fiction, drama, and literary essays) and poetry.

Modern prose entries are arranged and annotated by author. Some individual works are discussed briefly in the author annotations, but most are simply listed. The bulk of the modern prose items are fiction. Though there are many women among important modern playwrights (several women listed in the chapter for their fiction also wrote plays or television scenarios), drama by women has not, to our knowledge, been translated into English. Some literary essays by women have appeared in English translation, but they have not been sought systematically for inclusion here. Even though many writers of serious adult fiction began writing children's stores, we have reluctantly excluded fiction written primarily for children because the volume of such translations would exceed the limits of this work.

Because the authorship of premodern prose is often unknown or questionable, entries in that chapter have been listed under the Japanese title of the work (multiple translations made listing by English title impractical). "Prose" here arbitrarily refers to tales (*monogatari*), literary diaries (*nikki*), and miscellanies or essays (*zuihitsu*), even though all three are frequently studded with *waka* poetry. One piece of early literary criticism is also listed. There is no drama in this chapter.

Both modern and premodern poetry are arranged and annotated by poet. Listings include mainly "free verse" (sometimes called "Western-style poetry"), 17-syllable haiku, and the standard Japanese poetry form *waka* or *tanka*, which consists of five lines of 5,7,5,7,7 syllables respectively. There are also a few examples of poetry written in Chinese (*kanshi*), and the *sedōka* ("head-repeating" poem) of six lines of 5,7,7,5,7,7, an ancient form found only in the eighth-century anthology the *Man'yōshū*.

Each of the four literature chapters is divided into a main bibliography of primary literary texts written by women and a listing of secondary or critical works, books and articles *about* the primary texts. In all cases the main bibliography begins with an annotated list of anthologies in which many of the individual texts/poems are found. Later entries refer to these anthologies by author or compiler, listing entry number and page number of the translated item. Major anthologies have been listed here even when they contained very little written by women, partly to give the reader a sense of the changing state of the field.

The chapter on the spoken language is not comprehensive but is intended to offer a sampling of popular and scholarly approaches—linguistic, anthrolopological, pedagogical—to the relationship between women and language in Japan. It includes studies of special characterisitics of women's speech, including gesture, facial expression, and conversation strategy. It also lists books and articles on the language that the Japanese use to refer to women. This category includes lexical studies of everyday speech and popular slang related to women, plus pronoun usage and kinship terminology.

Sample Entries

Book

1095.[1] SIEVERS, Sharon L.[2] 1983.[3] *Flowers in Salt: The Beginnings of Feminist Consciousness in Modern Japan.*[4] Stanford:[5] Stanford University Press.[6] 240p.[7] Notes.[8] Index.[9] LCCN:82-60104.[10]

A study of women in the Meiji period with an emphasis on "the development of feminist consciousness" during that time. . . .[11]

Journal Article

1096. TSURUMI, E. Patricia. Apr./Jun. 1985. "Feminism and anarchism in Japan: Takamure Itsue, 1894-1964."[12] *Bulletin of Concerned Asian Scholars* 17(2):2-19.[13] 104 notes. ISSN:0007-4810.[14]

TSURUMI provides a lengthy and detailed bibliography of TAKAMURE Itsue, poet, anarchist, essayist, feminist, and historian. . . .

Translated Work (non-literary)

2. DOI, Takeo. 1973. *The Anatomy of Dependence.* [Translated by John BESTER.][15] Tokyo: Kodansha. 170p. [*Amae no kōzō.*[16] English.][17] 93 notes. LCCN:72-76297.

Translated Literary Work

1461. NAKAYAMA Chinatsu (1948-)[18]

Actress, essayist, fiction writer. Born in Kumamoto, Kyushu. Raised in Osaka, where she attended a children's theater school. . . . She began writing in 1970, and became an early activist in the women's movement, then in local politics. In 1980 she was elected a member of the lower house of the Diet, but lost her seat six years later. She has continued to write prolifically, both fiction and essays focusing on women's issues.[19]

> *Behind the Waterfall.* 1990. [Translated by Geraldine HARCOURT.] New York: Atheneum. 213p. LCCN:89-18437. Includes the following stories:
> "Good afternoon ladies." (pp. 111-213) [Misesu no afutanuun.]
> "The sound of wings." (pp. 47-110) [Haoto.]
> "Star time." (pp. 1-45) [Koyaku no jikan. 1980.][20]

1. Item numbers
   Used to identify citations in indexes and cross references.
2. Author
   Surname in capital letters; standard United States bibliographic format is used throughout (whether the author is American or Japanese).
3. Date of publication
   If the item has been republished, original date is given if known, and the date of the edition examined is given in brackets.
4. Title of work.
5. City of publication.
6. Publisher's name.
7. Number of pages. Or, if a chapter in an edited work, page numbers of chapter. (No effort has been made to ensure the inclusion of front matter in the total number of pages.)
8. References
   Given as "Notes," "Refs.," or "Bibl." If citations were numbered or easily counted, numbers are provided. "Notes" refers to footnotes or endnotes; "refs." to items in a bibliography; "bibl." has been used when references were unnumbered and it was impractical to count them.
9. Index
   Presence of an index in the work is indicated.
10. LCCN
    Library of Congress Card Number to assist with identification for interlibrary loan.
11. Annotation
    A brief summary of material included in the work is provided. All works were examined. References to Japanese names are made in Japanese style, i.e. surname first (in capital letters) with given name following.
12. Journal article
    Article title is in quotation marks.
13. Journal reference
    Following the name of the journal, the reference is in standard scholarly format: volume(number):pages.
14. ISSN
    The International Standard Serial Number is provided for identification purposes.
15. Translator
    Translators' names were noted if provided in the material. They appear in the Author/Editor/Translator Index.
16. Macrons
    Included in titles if used. Added to annotations when appropriate.

17. Uniform Title

    Title of a work in its original language; for identification purposes. "English" indicates the language into which it has been translated.

18. Date of Birth and Death

    Birth and death dates are provided as available. Living writers are indicated as in the example.

19. Annotation

    Annotations are provided for each individual writer. They are intended to assist with identification of the writer and to indicate experiences relevant to their writings.

20. Original Title and date of first publication

    The original Japanese title and date of first publication are provided if the information could be verified.

WOMEN'S PLACE

1

A Variety of Perspectives

General Context

1. BENEDICT, Ruth. 1946. *The Chrysanthemum and the Sword: Patterns of Japanese Culture.* Boston: Houghton Mifflin. 324p. Notes. Index. LCCN:46-11843. [Many editions.]

   Although BENEDICT was never able to visit Japan, her wartime study of patterns of Japanese culture became an enduring classic. Through a sympathetic juxtaposition of normative Japanese and American ideas and dispositions, she highlights the significance of issues such as hierarchy, proper place, and spiritual training in Japan. While not focusing on women per se, references to female roles and upbringing are found throughout the text. Her work, though always interesting, approaches culture in monolithic terms compared to more recent work on Japan by American anthropologists. [Annotation contributed by Steven NUSSBAUM, Earlham College.]

2. DOI, Takeo. 1973. *The Anatomy of Dependence.* [Translated by John BESTER.] Tokyo: Kodansha. 170p. 93 notes. LCCN:72-76297. [*Amae no kōzō.* English.]

   Although this work does not focus specifically on women, an understanding of DOI's concept of *amae* [dependence] is fundamental to an understanding of Japanese attitudes toward the female role in general and the mother role in particular. DOI's work is cited by many of the authors in this bibliography.

3. HANE, Mikiso. 1986. *Modern Japan: A Historical Survey.* Boulder: Westview. 450p. Bibl. Index. LCCN:86-7799.

   A general survey of Japanese history emphasizing the Tokugawa period to the present time. HANE has always been careful to include women in his studies [see also #17] and continues his efforts here. Although he does not discuss women's topics in depth, this work is very useful for defining context for major issues. Access through the index, especially for information on education, rights/subjugation, labor force, marriage, and prostitution.

4. "Japan." 1984. In: MORGAN, Robin, comp. and ed. *Sisterhood is Global: The International Women's Movement Anthology.* Garden City, NY: Anchor Press/Doubleday, pp. 376-382. No refs. LCCN:82-45332.

   In this encyclopedic volume, MORGAN has compiled statistical data and essays on the status of women over the world, country by country. The material on Japan includes sections on demography, government, economy, gynography [e.g. marriage, divorce, family, welfare, contraception, incest, sexual harassment, rape], "herstory," and mythography. See also HIGUCHI Keiko's accompanying essay [#73].

5. *Kojiki*. [Translated and introduced by Donald L. PHILIPPI.] 1968. Tokyo: University of Tokyo Press. 655p. Bibl. Index. LCCN:74-386152. [*Kojiki*. English.]

The *Kojiki* [*Record of Ancient Things*] is a collection of myth and history compiled in 712 C.E. It established the predominant clan of the time as the Imperial Family by tracing the clan's lineage to Amaterasu, the Sun Goddess. Many women figure in the events detailed, and clues to their roles and status are amplified in the footnotes supplied by PHILIPPI. An important reference point for Japanese feminists because of the portrayal of strong roles for women. [See also #7.]

6. NAKANE, Chie. 1970. *Japanese Society.* Berkeley: University of California Press. 157p. Bibl. LCCN:71-100021. [*Tateshakai no ningen kankei*. English.]

A seminal work on the vertical structure of relationships within Japanese society by a Japanese social anthropologist. Although she does not focus specifically on women, NAKANE's work is often viewed as fundamental to an understanding of Japanese society as a whole. A growing body of the literature is devoted to affirming or negating her theories.

7. *Nihongi: Chronicles of Japan from the Earliest Times to A.D. 697*. [Translated by W.G. ASTON; introduced by Terence BARROW.] 1972. Rutland, VT: Tuttle. 2 vol. Notes. Index. LCCN:70-152110. [*Nihon shoki*. English.]

Modeled on the Chinese dynastic histories, the *Nihongi* covers Japanese history and myth from the origin of the islands to the early Nara period. Probably completed in 720 C.E.; includes much of the same material as the *Kojiki* [see #5] but from different perspectives. Important to feminists for the same reasons.

8. NITOBE, Inazō. 1905. *Bushido: The Soul of Japan.* New York: G.P. Putnam's Sons. 203p. No refs. Index. LCCN:05-20750. [Many editions.]

In this oft-cited treatise on the feudal code called Bushido [The Way of the Samurai], NITOBE spends a chapter discussing the training and position of women. He stresses self-renunciation for the sake of family and the importance of mothers to the education of their sons.

Scholarly Works on Women's Identity

9. ACKROYD, Joyce. Nov. 1959. "Women in feudal Japan." *Transactions of the Asiatic Society of Japan* 3rd. series, 7:31-68. [Also cited as Asiatic Society of Japan. *Transactions*.] 112 notes.

A basic and oft-cited review of the changes in the status of women during the various stages of feudalism. ACKROYD's thesis, amply supported by examples and quotations from Japanese sources, is that the position of women declined as feudalism became more advanced.

10. BEARD, Mary. 1953. *The Force of Women in Japanese History.* Washington, D.C.: Public Affairs Press. 196p. No refs. LCCN:53-10839.

Probably the first comprehensive collection of materials on the history of Japanese women published in English. Includes brief biographical vignettes of women written by Japanese authors in the late 1930s at the urging of Baroness ISHIMOTO. BEARD has edited and updated the volume to include events through 1949. Often cited and well worth reading for its many descriptions of the lives of particular women.

11. BEAUCHAMP, Edward R. 1979. "The social role of Japanese women: Continuity and change." *International Journal of Women's Studies* 2(3):244-256. 37 notes. ISSN:0703-8240.

Compares women's roles and child rearing practices during Tokugawa Japan with those of contemporary Japan. Concludes that "the Tokugawa tradition has little to do with the social norms governing modern Japanese women," which "are the result of a complex mixture of economic changes, foreign influences and cultural tradition."

12. BINGHAM, Marjorie Wall and Susan Hill GROSS. 1987. *Women in Japan from Ancient Times to the Present.* [Edited by Janet DONALDSON.] St. Louis Park, MN: Glenhurst Publications. 317p. (*Women in World Area Studies.*) Notes & Bibl. LCCN:86-80572.

One in a series of textbooks on women designed to fill gaps in the secondary school curriculum. BINGHAM and GROSS provide a survey of women throughout Japanese history and include many quotations and photographs. Questions and group exercises are also provided. Susan PHARR and Gail Lee BERNSTEIN served as advisors for the project. (This text has also been used at the undergraduate level.)

13. DORE, Ronald P. 1978. *Shinohata: A Portrait of a Japanese Village.* New York: Pantheon Books. 322p. No refs. Index. LCCN:78-51791.

In this "memoir" of rural Japan aimed at the general reader but written by a renowned sociologist, DORE discusses the changes he has witnessed from his initial visit in 1955 through the 1960s. He specifically discusses the roles of women in his chapters entitled "Couples," "Wives, Husbands and Mothers," and "Growing-up," with other useful material scattered throughout the volume and accessible through the index.

14. ELLWOOD, Robert. Fall 1986. "Patriarchal revolution in ancient Japan: Episodes from the *Nihonshoki* Sūjin Chronicle." *Journal of Feminist Studies in Religion* 2(2):23-37. 13 notes. ISSN:8755-4178.

ELLWOOD reinterprets the *Nihonshoki* (a history of Japan written early in the 8th century C.E.) to provide an illustration of a society's transition from a basis in feminine spirituality to a male-based society. He provides justification for reversing the chronological order of two major rulers to show that a "patriarchal revolution" occurred between the reigns of Jingō ("a shamaness-queen who flourished around 200-270 C.E.") and Sūjin (a king "who probably [died] in the year 318").

15. FAUST, Allen K. 1926. *The New Japanese Womanhood.* New York: George Doran Co. 164p. Bibl. LCCN:26-13853.

A survey of women's status in Japan during the first quarter of the 20th century written by a male with 25 years of experience in Japan, during 13 years of which he served as president of Miyagi College [for Women] in Sendai. He sets the historical context and then describes education, new roles in industry, the arts, women and Japanese law, politics, "in society," and concludes by describing a few active feminists.

16. GEDDES, Margaret. Dec. 1977. "The status of women in post-war Japan: A critical examination of the contribution of the Occupation authorities towards raising the status of women in Japan." *Australian Outlook* 31(3):439-452. 54 notes. ISSN:0004-9913.

Using criteria developed by the New Women's Organization, GEDDES evaluates the change in status of Japanese women since World War II and analyzes the effect the Occupation had on these reforms. She provides historical and contemporary details on women's political participation and suffrage, opportunities for higher education, gender equality within the family, and women's working conditions.

17. HANE, Mikiso. 1982. *Peasants, Rebels, and Outcastes: The Underside of Modern Japan.* New York: Pantheon. 297p. Notes. Index. LCCN:81-18912.

HANE makes liberal use of diaries and eyewitness accounts to describe the lives of people in the lower levels of Japanese society, focusing especially on women in farming, textile factories, prostitution and mining, and women *burakumin* [outcastes]. Concentrates on the Meiji period through the 1930s with an epilogue to update the situation after World War II. Critiqued by TSURUMI in #2310.

18. HUNTER, Janet. 1989. *The Emergence of Modern Japan: An Introductory History Since 1853.* New York: Longman. 356p. Bibl. Index. LCCN:88-26634.

HUNTER devotes a chapter to a brief survey of women's history in the 20th century and a description of women's contemporary status. She emphasizes the difference between the *de jure* [legal] and *de facto* [actual] position of Japanese women, noting that the focus of the women's movement has been to "rebel against social customs and attitudes rather than legal discrimination," and that as long as women continue to be "satisfied with their role as good wives and wise mothers that potential will not be brought to bear on sexual inequalities and the gulf in status, role and influence between men and women will remain considerable."

19. ISHII-KUNTZ, Masako. Jul. 1989. "Collectivism or individualism? Changing patterns of Japanese attitudes." *Sociology and Social Research* 73(4):174-179. 28 refs. ISSN:0038-0393.

Questions the assumption that Japanese are collectivists, and finds that while data indicate that older males are collectivists, women and younger men are increasingly individualistic.

20. KATŌ, Ryōko. Spring 1989. "Japanese women: Subordination or domination?" *International Journal of Sociology of the Family* 19(1):49-57. 22 refs. ISSN:0020-7667.

Questions the image of Japanese women as "weak and helpless" noting that although economically dependent, the woman in her "maternal role" has had significant power as the primary care-giver which "is reinforced by emotional aspects of love and dependency."

21. KONDO, Dorinne. 1990. *Crafting Selves: Power, Gender, and Discourses of Identity in a Japanese Workplace.* Chicago: University of Chicago Press. 346p. Bibl. Index. LCCN:89-38547.

KONDO has combined an anthropological inquiry into the nature of self and self-definition for the Japanese, especially as seen in a *shitamachi* artisan community in Tokyo, with reflections on her own experiences as a Japanese American living in a Japanese community. Material on women is incorporated throughout the text; the chapter, "*Uchi*, Gender and Part-Time Work," focuses particularly on the women employed by the confectionery factory where KONDO worked.

22. KOYAMA, Takashi. 1961. *The Changing Social Position of Women in Japan.* Paris: UNESCO. 152p. Notes. LCCN:61-4577.

KOYAMA covers the change in the position of Japanese women, 1949-1959, from a sociological perspective. He focuses on institutional changes (legal, educational), and on changes for women in the family, in rural communities, and for working women. A final section discusses women and civic activities. The conclusions outline gains and problems. A densely-packed volume, especially useful for information on the 1950s.

23. KOYAMA, Takashi, Hachirō NAKAMURA, and Masako HIRAMATSU. 1967. "Japan." In: PATAI, Raphael. *Women in the Modern World.* New York: Free Press, pp. 290-314. Bibl. LCCN:67-12518.

A look at women's roles and status since World War II. KOYAMA and his colleagues first describe women's traditional roles and the concept of *ie* [household], and then state that the change in status thus far is due primarily to legal reforms (the Constitution), education, and support from mass media. However, the authors also note "the fundamental principle of sex equality has been put into practice without consideration for the many specific problems involved, and without sufficient preparation for handling them," and call for identification of actual problems and development of practical solutions.

24. LEBRA, Takie S. 1984. *Japanese Women: Constraint and Fulfillment.* Honolulu: University of Hawaii Press, 345p. Bibl. Index. LCCN:83-18029.

A thorough, well-documented ethnographic study which aims to be "an objective description of how women have lived and are living in Japan." Based on a sample of 57 women in a seaside resort town, the study defines and examines women's roles during various stages of the life cycle. LEBRA includes explicit descriptions of her methodology and many direct quotations from informants.

25. LEBRA, Takie Sugiyama. 1990. "The socialization of aristocratic children by commoners: Recalled experiences of the hereditary elite in modern Japan." *Cultural Anthropology* 5(1):78-100. 14 refs. ISSN:0886-7356.

While not focusing on women *per se*, LEBRA includes material discussing roles of elite women and daughters and female servants. She notes that the female servants made possible the aristocratic status of the family and served as surrogate mothers; includes descriptions of surrogate mothers by their charges.

26. LEHMANN, Jean-Pierre. 1982. *The Roots of Modern Japan.* New York: St. Martin's Press. 352p. Bibl. essay. Index. LCCN:82-743.

LEHMANN includes sections on the status of women in the Edo and Meiji eras in this work which delineates the cultural, economic, and political underpinnings of modern Japan. Recommended both for his succinct portrayal of women's status in Japan and for his comparisons with the status of women in Europe and elsewhere in Asia. Unfortunately he did not footnote his information, so one cannot pursue further his ideas.

27. LIFTON, Robert Jay. 1965. "Woman as knower: Some psychohistorical perspectives." In: LIFTON, Robert Jay, ed. *The Woman in America.* Boston: Houghton-Mifflin, pp. 27-51. 19 notes. LCCN:65-15157.

As a basis for his essay on the "potential for [women] possessing insight and wisdom," LIFTON describes 10th-century Japanese women as living one of three roles: nurturer [mother], temptress [geisha, prostitute], or knower [author, poet]. He suggests that Japanese women are currently under psychological stress as they struggle to become generalists and to fill all three roles.

28. McCLELLAN, Edwin. 1985. *Woman in the Crested Kimono: The Life of Shibue Io and her Family.* New Haven: Yale University Press. 200p. Notes. Index. LCCN:85-5359.

This literary work concerns the family of SHIBUE Io, "daughter of a merchant family in the 19th century and wife of a distinguished scholar-doctor of the samurai class." Most of the material is taken from the Japanese literary biography of her husband, SHIBUE Chūsai, written by MORI Ōgai.

29. MOLONY, Barbara. 1978. "Women and social and political change." In: WHITE, Merry I. and Barbara MOLONY, eds. *Proceedings of the Tokyo Symposium on Women.* Tokyo: International Group for the Study of Women, pp. 10-12. (Tokyo Symposium on Women, [1st], 1978.)

In this paper (an introduction to #1016 and #1159), MOLONY identifies possible catalysts for change in roles of women world-wide: internal pressures caused by increased participation in the work force and the development of feminist leaders; and external ideologies (e.g. the influence of the Allied Occupation forces in Japan).

30. MORRIS, Ivan. Mar. 1963. "Women of ancient Japan: Heian ladies." *History Today* 13(3):160-168. No refs. ISSN:0018-2753.

A general description of upper-class women in Heian Japan covering physical appearance, literary talents, legal rights, social roles, and their place in Japanese religion.

31. MORRIS, Ivan. 1972. *The World of the Shining Prince: Court Life in Ancient Japan.* New York: Knopf. 33p. Notes. Index. LCCN:64-12310.

Centering on the years 967-1068 C.E., MORRIS describes the culture in which upper-class women lived. In a chapter titled, "The Women of Heian and their Relations with Men," he covers women's physical features, their "low status in religion . . . [and] . . . favourable position in law," and rituals of courtship and marriage. He also outlines levels of wives (principal wives and concubines) and types of love-relationships. He illustrates his points with examples from *The Tale of Genji* by MURASAKI Shikibu and concludes his coverage of women with a chapter on her. [See #286 for a critique of MORRIS's views on marriage and #290 for MORRIS's response.]

32. NAKANE, Chie. Feb. 1975. "Women: A cross-cultural perspective." *PHP* 6(2):2-12. No refs. ISSN:0030-798X.

In this overview of women's status in general, NAKANE asserts that "in Japan a well-qualified woman, once admitted into an organization with the promise of promotion similar to that of her male colleagues, suffers much less discrimination than does a Western woman in the same situation."

33. NORBECK, Edward. 1976. *Changing Japan.* [Revised edition.] New York: Holt, Rinehart, Winston. 108p. (*Case Studies in Cultural Anthropology*). Bibl. LCCN:76-2709.

A useful overview of modern Japanese society from an anthropological perspective. NORBECK profiles both a rural fishing family and an urban family (a *salariiman* [white collar employee] and his family living in *danchi* [public housing]). Covers childbirth, family life, daily life, leisure hours, worship, and the future.

34. O'KELLY, Charlotte and Larry S. CARNEY. 1986. *Women and Men in Society: Cross-Cultural Perspectives on Gender Stratification.* Belmont, CA: Wadsworth. 336p. 157 notes. Index. LCCN:85-15391.

In their chapter, "Capitalist Industrial Society: Sweden and Japan," O'KELLY and CARNEY contrast Sweden's governmental commitment to the welfare state and to gender equality with Japan's traditional dependence on family for welfare and the effects of that dependence both on roles of women and on their status. They touch on historical background, employment prospects, education, family responsibilities, birth control and abortion, financial management, and violence against women.

35. OGATA, Sadako. 1977. "Women's participation in the modernization of Japan." *Studia Diplomatica* [Brussels] 30(3):205-212. No refs. ISSN:0770-2965.

A statement by Japan's Minister to the United Nations concerning both "women's position in traditional Japan" and the reality of women's current social status.

36. OKAMURA, Masu. 1973. *Women's Status.* Tokyo: International Society for Educational Information. 87p. (*Changing Japan*, no. 1.) No refs. LCCN:75-310661.

The first in a series of volumes "providing insights into the social and cultural ramifications of this country's unique development." OKAMURA focuses on the difference between women's legal status (equality) and status in practice ("many individual women will have to win on their own in the course of their daily lives"). Considers women at home, at work, in public life, and at school ("the real agent of an improved social position for women.").

37. PAULSON, Joy. 1976. "Evolution of the feminine ideal." In: LEBRA, Joyce, *et al. Women in Changing Japan.* Stanford: Stanford University Press, pp. 1-23. 67 notes. LCCN:75-33663.

A succinct description of the role of Japanese women from Amaterasu, the Sun Goddess, to the present. Special emphasis is given to the influence of religions (Buddhism and Confucianism) and war (World War II).

38. PHARR, Susan J. Apr. 1975. "Women in Japan today." *Current History* 68(404):174-176,183-184. 17 refs. ISSN:0011-3530.

Provides an overview of women's status historically, and describes trends for women in education, work, marriage, and political activity as of the mid-1970s.

39. PHARR, Susan J. 1976. "The Japanese woman: Evolving views of life and role." In: AUSTIN, Lewis, ed. *Japan: The Paradox of Progress.* New Haven: Yale University Press, pp. 301-327. (Seminar on the Future of Japan, Yale University, 1973.) Notes. LCCN:75-18163. [Later reprinted "in slightly different form" in CHIPP, Sylvia A. and Justin J. GREEN, eds. 1980. *Asian Women in Transition.* University Park: Pennsylvania State University Press, pp. 36-61. LCCN:79-20517.]

PHARR divides young Japanese women into three types: the "Neotraditionalists," who believe "the wife-mother role is primary . . . [and] . . . all other life activities should be subordinated to it;" the "New Women," who agree the "domestic role should be central . . . but . . . hold at the same time that women should be able to engage in numerous other activities not relating to the homemaker role; and the "Radical Egalitarians," who "reject traditional patterns of sex role allocations" and believe "women should feel free to play many roles simultaneously." PHARR provides historical context and includes descriptions of the women she interviewed. An excellent article, often cited in the literature.

40. PHARR, Susan J. 1977. "Japan: Historical and contemporary perspectives." In: GIELE, Janet Zollinger and Audrey Chapman SMOCK, eds. *Women: Roles and Status in Eight Countries.* New York: Wiley and Sons, pp. 217-255. Bibl. LCCN:76-39950.

PHARR provides an historical summary of roles and status, with descriptions of women's positions with respect to the legal system, occupations, the family, education, fertility and family planning, and "political action, volunteerism, and the women's movement."

41. REISCHAUER, Edwin O. 1988. *The Japanese Today: Change and Continuity.* Cambridge: Belknap Press. 426p. Bibl. Index. LCCN:87-14904.

In his chapter on women, REISCHAUER presents a succinct and unvarnished discussion of the position of Japanese women historically and currently. To those Westerners frustrated by a seeming lack of radicalism on the part of Japanese women concerning their position, he suggests that "Japanese women in recent decades have made such huge advances that they are still busy digesting them . . ."

42. RHIM, Soon Man. 1983. *Women of Asia: Yesterday and Today (India, China, Korea, Japan).* New York: Friendship Press. 141p. Notes. Index. LCCN:82-21053. [Earlier versions published in the *Journal of the Asiatic Society of Bangladesh* 23(2):99-132 (Aug. 1978) ISSN:0377-0540, and in *Asian Studies* 16:51-74 (1978).]

In a chapter titled "Status of women of Japan," RHIM provides a concise overview of women's status both historically and currently.

43. ROBINS-MOWRY, Dorothy. 1983. *The Hidden Sun: Women of Modern Japan.* Boulder: Westview Press. 394p. Bibl. Index. LCCN:82-20230.

Provides a solid introduction to the history of modern Japanese women; after providing historical context, covers social patterns, economic involvement, political activities, and interaction on a global level. ROBINS-MOWRY (the Women's Activities Officer at the United States Embassy, 1963-1969) describes her work as a "broad-brush study of the Japanese woman's attitudes and activities and their effect on herself, her society, and her country's policies." Extensive bibliography, chronology and list of women's organizations in the appendixes. More detailed than BINGHAM [#12]; those wishing a feminist interpretation should start with SIEVERS [#1167]. Reviewed by BOOCOCK in #2305 and by BUCKLEY in #2306.

44. SAKANISHI, Shio. Nov. 1956. "Women's position and the family system." *Annals of the American Academy of Political and Social Science* 308:130-139. [Also cited as the American Academy of Political and Social Science. *Annals.*] No refs. ISSN:0002-7162.

Reviews changes in women's status during the ten years following World War II including prostitution, family planning, education, employment, political participation, and legal rights.

45. SALAMON, Sonya. Fall 1973. "Stretching the limits of womanhood in contemporary Japan." *Journal of the Steward Anthropological Society* [Urbana] 5(1):68-82. [Also cited as Steward Anthropological Society. *Journal.*] 9 refs. ISSN:0039-1344.

Presents a case study of a woman pushing the boundaries of culturally defined roles for Japanese women and discusses in particular her experience of the loneliness of private "benchmarks" in role transitions.

46. SALAMON, Sonya. Autumn 1975. "The varied groups of Japanese and German housewives." *Japan Interpreter* 10(2):150-170. 16 notes. ISSN:0021-4450.

SALAMON suggests that NAKANE's description of group structures within Japanese society as hierarchical and static [see #6] does not fit when applied to women. SALAMON explores relationships among wives of Japanese executives incorporating much material from her 1973 article [#45], but also includes the experiences of other women as well. Discusses in detail the concept of *shin'yū* [longstanding intimate friend].

47. SMITH, Henry. 1980. "Consorts and courtesans: The women of *Shōgun*." In: SMITH, Henry, ed. *Learning from* Shōgun: *Japanese History and Western Fantasy*. Santa Barbara: University of California, Santa Barbara, Department of Asian Studies, pp. 99-112. Bibl. LCCN:81-172915.

In a book of essays intended to set correct historical context for James CLAVELL's novel *Shōgun*, SMITH gives background for the comments on women by the character Mariko, discusses several of the historical figures on which the female characters are based, and considers the concepts of love expressed in the novel. Specialized but useful for the nonspecialist who has read or is reading *Shōgun*.

48. SMITH, Robert J. Summer 1981. "Japanese village women: Suye-mura 1935-1936." *Journal of Japanese Studies* 7(2):259-284. 11 notes. ISSN:0095-6848.

A "preliminary report" based on the field notes of Ella Embree WISWELL and John EMBREE, later published in book form as *The Women of Suye Mura* [#50].

49. SMITH, Robert J. 1987. "Gender inequality in contemporary Japan." *Journal of Japanese Studies* 13(1):1-25. 44 notes. ISSN:0095-6848.

SMITH provides a thoughtful, perceptive and detailed review of inequalities in Japanese society based solely on gender and of changes which have occurred since World War II.

50. SMITH, Robert J. and Ella Lury WISWELL. 1982. *The Women of Suye Mura.* Chicago: University of Chicago Press. 293p. No refs. Index. LCCN:82-2708.

A journal of field research notes compiled in 1935 by Ella Lury WISWELL. She was at that time Ella EMBREE, wife of John EMBREE who wrote *Suye Mura: A Japanese Village* (Chicago: University of Chicago Press, [1939]. LCCN:40-1477.). SMITH and WISWELL's work is unique in that there are no other pre-World War II village studies focusing on women's lives. In addition, WISWELL was fluent in Japanese and able to converse and observe without an interpreter. Topics covered include the various stages of the life cycle, sex, interpersonal relationships, women's associations, and "The Handicapped, Misfits, Wanderers, and Witches." The work is discussed by NOLTE in #2308.

51. TAKAHASHI, Keiko. Dec. 1974. "Development of dependency in female adolescents and young adults." *Japanese Psychological Research* 16(4):179-185. 3 refs. ISSN:0021-5368.

Finds that the dependency motive for females remains strong from infancy to adulthood although the object of dependency (mother, girlfriend, boyfriend, spouse) changes with age.

52. TAKAMURE, Itsuye. Jul. 1938. "On A History of Japanese Women." *Japanese Women* 1(4):1-2. No refs. ISSN:0388-1369.

TAKAMURE briefly reflects on her five-volume scholarly history of Japanese women, the first "system[atic] and scholarly" "study of history from the woman's point of view." (Unfortunately, a complete English translation of this monumental effort is not readily available.)

53. TAKAMURE, Itsuye. Mar., May, & Jul. 1940. "A history of Japanese women." ["Rearranged" by Shigeri KANEKO.] *Japanese Women* 3(2):1,3-4; 3(3):2-3; 3(4):2. No refs. ISSN:0388-1369.

Briefly covers Japanese history from its mythological origins and Amaterasu, the Sun Goddess, through the reign of Genmyo Tenno [707-715 C.E.]. Although more detailed treatments concerning these periods are available, the excerpts included here are important because of the Japanese work from which they are taken: *A History of Women for 2600 Years* by TAKAMURE Itsuye. This was the first major, scholarly historical work to focus on Japanese women and was written by a Japanese woman.

54. TSURUMI, Kazuko. 1970. *Social Change and the Individual.* Princeton: Princeton University Press. 441p. Bibl. Index. LCCN:69-18073.

TSURUMI includes three chapters on women in her work. The first analyzes the socializing influences of family, management, labor unions, and writing circles on textile workers in Osaka. The second explores the impact of the war and Japan's defeat using as examples a soldier's mother and a soldier's wife, mothers of evacuated children, the mother of a child who died in Hiroshima, and other women. The final chapter deals with the mother role among middle-aged city and village women, and the role of mother-in-law among elderly agrarian women. All three chapters include lengthy excerpts from women's writings.

55. TSURUMI, Kazuko. 1979. *Women in Japan: A Paradox of Modernization.* Tokyo: Sophia University. 32p. (Institute of International Relations for Advance Studies on Peace and Development in Asia. *Research Papers. Series A,* 29.) 34 notes. LCCN:78-314916. [An earlier version of this paper appeared in the *Japan Foundation Newsletter* 5(1):2-7, Apr. 1977, ISSN:0385-2318. Reprinted in *PHP* 9(4):57-73, Apr. 1978, ISSN:0030-798X.]

In this lecture, TSURUMI points out that "modernization" in the mid-19th century had both positive and negative effects on women. Because it was essentially a "samuraization" of the total society, she contends the more egalitarian merchant and agrarian classes became patriarchal and hierarchical like the upper class, and lower-class women lost many privileges. But at the grassroots level, modern women are now reclaiming these freedoms.

56. UENO, Chizuko. Aug./Oct. 1987. "The position of Japanese women reconsidered." [With comments by D.P. MARTINEZ.] *Current Anthropology* 28(4):S75-S84. 20 refs. ISSN:0011-3204.

Asserting that interpretations of role and status of *jōmin* [ordinary people] cannot be based on texts written by or for the ruling class (e.g. *Onna Daigaku* [#126]), UENO reinterprets the history of common women's status. Discusses the traditionally respected position of *shufu* [female head of household (UENO's definition)] and notes the current paradox of retaining household authority while losing the "public power" (MARTINEZ's words) available to women earlier. Also describes the historical practice of having a village's post-puberty children live in dormitories which led to self-selected mates and gender-based support groups during pre-modern Japan. Commentary by MARTINEZ elucidates UENO's ideas.

57. WHITE, Merry I. and Barbara MOLONY, eds. 1978. *Proceedings of the Tokyo Symposium on Women.* Tokyo: International Group for the Study of Women. 214p. (Tokyo Symposium on Women, [1st], 1978.) No refs.

The outgrowth of a study group of Japanese, American, and Australian women researchers, this international symposium was the first of its kind in Japan, and focused primarily on Japanese women in the 20th century. Items annotated individually; for entry numbers see title index under *Proceedings of the Tokyo Symposium on Women.*

58. WHITE, Richard. 1976. "The Confucian ideal of womanhood." *Journal of the China Society* [Taipei] 13:67-73. [Also cited as China Society, Taipei. *Journal.*] 20 notes.

Uses the Chinese classic *Ku Lieh Nü Chuan*, a collection of "model women's biographies" written by the Confucian scholar LIU Shiang in the early Han Dynasty, to call into question STRAELEN's assertion in his *Japanese Woman Looking Forward* [#161] that "the opinion of Confucius about women was very bad . . . ." WILLIER suggests that uncritical use of STRAELEN and other sources has led to incorrect conclusions about the causes of a lowered status for Japanese women.

Japanese Women Speak

59. AKIYAMA, Yōko. Mar. 1974. "The hidden sun, women in Japan." *International Socialist Review* 35(3):16-24. 7 refs. ISSN:0020-8744.

A review of Japanese women's history aimed at "foreign sisters" to bridge "an information gap which disturbed our mutual understanding."

60. ANTRAM, Toshimi Kayahi. Winter 1990. "The programmed path." *Whole Earth Review* no. 9:78-79. No refs. ISSN:0749-5056.

A brief, rather bleak description of the typical path Japanese women follow through work and marriage by a woman who chose her own path by quitting her job and moving to the United States. Includes a short excerpt from a *manga* [comic] showing the pressures a young woman is under to marry.

61. BANDO, Mariko Sugahara. Mar. 1986. *Japanese Women: Yesterday and Today.* Tokyo: Foreign Press Center. 51p. (*About Japan Series*, no. 5.) No refs. [Published in Jul. 1977 as *The Women of Japan: Past and Present.* LCCN:80-451906.]

An overview of "the socio-economic changes affecting women's lives, as well as how their lives are changing . . . based . . . on objective data and thoroughly reliable opinion polls . . . ." Provides information on education, work, family life, attitudes, and political participation. Although not as comprehensive as *Japanese Women in Turmoil*, [#199], this useful summary may be easier to obtain.

62. BANZAI, Mayumi. 1979. *Stories (1925-1935) of a Japanese Grandma.* Tokyo: Hokuseido Press. 324p. No refs.

A Japanese woman records childhood memories of the late 1920s and early 1930s. Included are descriptions of family relationships, playing with friends, school and vacations.

63. BERNARD, Kyoko. Feb. 1978. "Women in Japan: Roles, rules and restrictions." *PHP* 9(2):61-71. No refs. ISSN:0030-798X.

Discusses possible causes for the lack of solidarity among Japanese women on issues of women's rights (e.g. role indoctrination, employment patterns, "structure of dependency").

64. CARTER, Aiko. 8 Mar. 1974. "On being a woman in Japan. Part 1: Forms of sex discrimination." *Japan Christian Activity News*, no. 499:1-4. No refs. ISSN:0021-4353. Reprinted in CARTER, Aiko. 1975. *On Being a Woman in Japan.* Tokyo: Femintern Press.]

A brief overview of four areas of sex discrimination: education, employment, abortion laws, and adoption practices. The author is a Japanese activist. [Part 1 of 4; see Author Index.]

65. CARTER, Aiko Yokoya. [1979.] "Japanese society and women." In: *Women in Asia: Working Together for Christ.* Japan: The Conference, pp. 49-78. 15 refs. (Christian Women's Conference, 1979, Japan.)

In this exploration of the historical basis for the status of contemporary Japanese women, CARTER discusses the development and effects of the *ie* [household] system and Buddhism, and the struggle for change in the 20th century. She concludes by outlining the varying foci within the contemporary women's movement and briefly reviews laws relating to women.

66. CHIKAP, Mieko. 1986. "I am an Ainu, am I not?" *Ampo: Japan-Asia Quarterly Review* 18(2/3):81-87. No refs. LCCN:77-612830.

An Ainu woman speaks eloquently at the NGO '85 Forum in Nairobi, Kenya, concerning her people and her identification as an Ainu.

67. CHIKAP, Mieko. 1989. "Long, cold winter—An Ainu childhood related." *Ampo: Japan Asia Quarterly Review* 20(4)/21(1):32-39. No refs. LCCN:77-12830.

This brief memoir focuses primarily on recollections of the author's brothers and male friends as they struggled with racism. A few memories of her own are included.

68. HARA, Kimi. Oct./Dec. 1951. "Women's status in modern society." *Contemporary Japan* 20(10/12):496-508. 13 notes. ISSN:0388-0214.

Describes the difficulty of making the transition from the traditional *ie* [household] system with its vertical structure to the horizontal system implemented in the Civil Code adopted after World War II. Comments on changes affecting women.

69. HASEGAWA, Michiko. Jun. 1984. "Equality of the sexes threatens cultural ecology." *Economic Eye* 5(2):23-26. 3 notes. ISSN:0389-0503.

Argues that passage of the United Nations Convention on the Elimination of All Forms of Discrimination Against Women would have a negative impact on Japanese culture and destroy the social ecology of role differentiation—"the various forms of mutual cooperation and support by which people sustain one another and perpetuate human life."

70. HATSUMI, Reiko. 1959. *Rain and the Feast of the Stars*. Boston: Houghton Mifflin. 215p. LCCN:58-9064.

Relates memories of a childhood in pre-World War II Japan from the perspective of a young girl. HATSUMI was one of several children in a well-to-do, aristocratic family. Most chapters deal with home life and tutors; one chapter describes her experiences at Sacred Heart School, in both the foreigner's section and the Japanese section.

71. HAYASHI, Fumiko. Jun. 1934. "About our modern women." *Contemporary Japan* 3(1):114-120. No refs. ISSN:0388-0214.

A description of Japanese women for Western readers by a female novelist.

72. HIGUCHI, Keiko. Jul./Sep. 1982. "Japanese women in transition." *Japan Quarterly* 29(3):311-318. No refs. ISSN:0021-4590.

A social critic on women's problems addresses reasons for change in women's roles (especially longer life expectancy and economics).

73. HIGUCHI, Keiko. 1984. "Japan: The sun and the shadow." [Translated by Akiko TOMII.] In: MORGAN, Robin, comp. and ed. *Sisterhood is Global: The International Women's Movement Anthology*. Garden City, NY: Anchor Press/Doubleday, pp. 382-388. Bibl. LCCN:82-45332.

In this anthology of essays on women's status world-wide, HIGUCHI (author of *Bringing Up Girls* [#74] and other works) summarizes the status of Japanese women through a series of anecdotal and revealing examples of women's experiences throughout the life cycle. She also explores the question of why most women are not angry with their status. See [#4] for the accompanying statistical data.

74. HIGUCHI, Keiko. 1985. *Bringing up Girls: Start Aiming at Love and Independence (Status of Women in Japan)*. [Translated by Akiko TOMII.] Kyoto: Shoukadoh Booksellers Press Co. 252p. No refs. [*Onna no ko no sodatekata*. English.]

HIGUCHI wrote this discussion on the status of women and the rearing of girls for a Japanese audience. It is filled with examples of social acculturation and HIGUCHI's ideas for coping with an 80-year life span, which by its length alone precludes total reliance on one's role as a mother for self-fulfillment.

75. IIJIMA, Aiko. Jun. 1975. "Where are we headed? A critical analysis of 30 years of 'woman's policy'." In: *Japanese Women Speak Out*. Tokyo: White Paper on Sexism—Japan Task Force, pp. 68-81. No refs. [Excerpted in *Quest: A Feminist Quarterly* 4(2):78-86, Winter 1978, ISSN:0098-955X.]

A concise outline of women's status since World War II by a member of the Asian Women's Congress to Fight Discrimination and Aggression. Beginning with government-initiated prostitution in anticipation of the Occupation Army's arrival, IIJIMA traces women's involvement in the peace movement and in labor unions, and the government's development of a "woman's policy" facilitating utilization of women in the labor force. She concludes with a summary of the women's liberation movement in the 1970s.

76. IKEGAME, Mieko. [1984.] "Sisters of the sun: Japanese women today." *Change International Reports: Women and Society*, no. 12. No refs. ISSN:0206-9037.

Discusses women's status since the Tokugawa era, focussing on societal structures (e.g. *ie* [household]), effects of modernization and militarism, prostitution, marriage and education.

77. IWAO, Sumiko. [1976?] "A full life for modern Japanese women." In: Nihonjin Kenkyūkai. *Text of Seminar on "Changing Values in Modern Japan."* Tokyo: Nihonjin Kenkyūkai (in association with the Asia Foundation), pp. 95-111. No refs. LCCN:78-312892.

IWAO presents a variety of statistical data in her discussion of how institutional changes since World War II have affected women's behavior and awareness. She focuses on "women's status in society," whether Japanese women are content, and the "kind of life led by Japanese women." Not as complete as *Japanese Women in Turmoil* [#199], but more available.

78. IWAO, Sumiko Furuya. 1981. "The feminine perspective in Japan today." In: GROSSBERG, Kenneth A., ed. *Japan Today.* Philadelphia: Institute for the Study of Human Issues, pp. 16-27. No refs. LCCN:81-1077.

In this record of panel discussions held during "Japan Today" celebrations in 1979 in the United States, IWAO gives a traditional description of Japanese women as "the most powerful person" in the home, and notes that "in the smooth running of the home, a woman can express her abilities." She also includes statistics suggesting that women would prefer to be reborn as a female.

79. IWAO, Sumiko. 10 Feb. 1983. "The Japanese woman in the 1980s: Today's well-educated matrons contradict the 'pretty doll' image." *Look Japan* (10 Feb. 1983):12-13. No refs. ISSN:0456-5339.

As indicated by her subtitle, IWAO reinterprets the "typical foreigner's view" of the status of Japanese women, pointing out Japanese women's high level of education, their control over family finances, and the growth in number of women employed. She predicts that women will not play active roles in "the [Japanese] political world" because of its "peculiar" conditions and that "part-time female workers will not [in the future] require high wages."

80. IWAO, Sumiko. Winter 1985. "Women yesterday and today." *Japan Echo* 12(4):49-50. No refs. ISSN:0388-0435.

The introduction to #398, #700, and #1028; discusses in general terms changes in women's status since the United Nations Decade for Women (1976-1985).

81. Japanese Woman's Commission for the World's Columbian Exposition. 1893. *Japanese Women.* Chicago: A.C. McClurg. 159p. plus 16p. pamphlet. No refs.

An in-depth survey of "the true condition of the Japanese woman, ancient and modern," prepared by various unidentified Japanese women for the 1893 World's Fair. The survey of political history provides brief biographical sketches beyond those found in most historical summaries. Other sections include women in literature, religion, domestic life, industrial occupations, and the arts. A summary chapter focuses on contemporary Meiji women with an emphasis on civic organizations and education. A separate pamphlet (bound in) lists the items of a lady's boudoir on display at the fair.

82. KAN, Shina. 14 Jun. 1950. "Japanese women move forward." *Far Eastern Survey* 19(12):122-124. 2 notes. ISSN:0362-8949.

An optimistic appraisal of women's progress in the areas of politics, government structure, and industry since the end of World War II.

83. KIRISHIMA, Yōko. Autumn 1975. "Liberation begins in the kitchen." *Japan Interpreter* 10(2):141-150. No refs. ISSN:0021-4450.

KIRISHIMA (described in the introduction as "one of the most outspoken, controversial and popular authors writing for and about contemporary Japanese women") justifies her decision to write a cookbook by arguing that to give up one's skills in cooking while pursuing traditional male skills in business will ultimately limit one's development and lead to the "traditionally feminine traits" of weakness and helplessness. [See also #421 for context.]

84. KITAZAWA, Yōko. Jun. 1975. "To be female and outcaste in Japan: Three generations of prejudice." In: *Japanese Women Speak Out.* Tokyo: White Paper on Sexism—Japan Task Force, pp. 134-141.

KITAZAWA, an economist, presents background information on the *burakumin* [the lowest social caste], made official during the Tokugawa era. She then provides a précis of *Three Generations of Japanese Women* by KOBAYASHI Hatsue (the third generation woman) which "expresses well the century of poverty, rural conventionalism, social discrimination . . . and sexism they faced and still struggle against as an all-female household."

85. KIYOOKA, Chiyono Sugimoto. 1936. *Chiyo's Return.* Garden City: Doubleday, Doran and Co. 338p. No refs. LCCN:35-27233.

In essence, a sequel to SUGIMOTO's *A Daughter of the Samurai* [#106], but written by SUGIMOTO's daughter, Chiyo. After ten years of schooling in America, Chiyo and her mother return to Japan for a year during which she rediscovers Japanese life and customs.

86. KIYOOKA, Chiyono Sugimoto. 1959. *But the Ships are Sailing, Sailing . . .* [Tokyo]: Hokuseido. 238p. No refs. LCCN:62-29225.

A personal narrative of the Occupation by the author of *Chiyo's Return* [#85] and the daughter of the author of *A Daughter of the Samurai* [#106]. KIYOOKA details her feelings toward the Emperor at the end of the War, her experiences working for the Occupation Forces, and her relationships with her family, including her mother and her husband, KIYOOKA Eiichi. (KIYOOKA Eiichi is the grandson of FUKUZAWA Yukichi and editor of *Fukuzawa Yukichi on Japanese Women. Selected Works* [#122].)

87. KOBAYASHI, Hatsue. Oct./Dec. 1976. "Grandmother, mother and myself." [Translated by Mie KONDAIBŌ.] *Japan Quarterly* 23(4):340-356. No refs. ISSN:0021-4590. [Onna sandai.]

An excerpt of a memoir concerning three generations of *burakumin* [Japan's lowest social caste] women. Discusses the author's family relationships, schooling, marriage, and struggle with poverty. Centers on the years preceding World War II and the War years. Introduced by #88.

88. KONDAIBŌ, Mei. Oct./Dec. 1976. "A search for new directions." *Japan Quarterly* 23(4):336-339. No refs. ISSN:0021-4590.

A lengthy introduction to #87, #114, and #424. Provides background on older single women, the *burakumin* [the lowest social caste], and Koreans living in Japan.

89. MAKIHARA, Kumiko. 1 Feb. 1990. "Japanese women: Rewriting tradition." *Lear's* 2(11):78-101. No refs. ISSN:0897-0149.

MAKIHARA summarizes the two roles most Japanese women must choose between: fulltime housewife or career woman. She notes alternative routes some have chosen and discusses the costs of all. For the general reader.

90. MAKIHARA, Kumiko. Fall 1990. "Who needs equality?" *Time* 136(19):35-36. No refs. ISSN:0040-781X. [Special Issue.]

MAKIHARA explains to the general reader why Japanese women might not prefer career equality with men, and outlines women's incentives to avoid becoming "dull corporate drones."

91. MATSUOKA, Yōko. 1952 [rep. 1973.] *Daughter of the Pacific*. Westport, CT: Greenwood Press. 245p. No refs. LCCN:72-12634.

The autobiography of a woman who was educated in Cleveland, Ohio, and at Swarthmore College before World War II and who lived in Japan during the War. An engaging and well-written memoir. MATSUOKA was well-traveled, attending various youth conferences and also the Pan-Pacific Women's Conference in Vancouver, Canada, with her mother, one of three official delegates.

92. MEGURO, Yoriko. 1983. "The role of women in Japanese society." In: COGAN, John J. and Donald O. SCHNEIDER, eds. *Perspectives on Japan: A Guide for Teachers*. Washington, D.C.: National Council for the Social Studies, pp. 48-60. 41 refs. LCCN:83-61859.

Summarizes women's roles with respect to "historical background and cultural constraints" and discusses work and the role of the housewife. Introductory.

93. MISHIMA, Sumie Seo. 1941 [rep. 1981]. *My Narrow Isle: The Story of a Modern Woman in Japan*. Westport, CT: Hyperion. 280p. No refs. LCCN:79-2945 and 41-3014.

This volume and the following [#94] comprise the autobiography of MISHIMA Sumie Seo. *My Narrow Isle* focuses on her childhood years in Osaka and Tokyo, including her years at Tsuda English College and Wellesley College, and her struggles to earn a living after her return to Japan prior to World War II.

94. MISHIMA, Sumie Seo. 1953 [rep. 1971]. *The Broader Way: A Woman's Life in the New Japan*. Westport, CT: Greenwood Press. 247p. No refs. LCCN:74-138596 and 53-6588.

This sequel to *My Narrow Isle* [#93] covers the late War years and the Occupation, with emphases on survival, use of her American education, and changes in the Japanese social structure. The two volumes together eloquently describe the problems young Japanese women who studied in the United States faced upon their return to Japan.

95. MISHIMA, Sumie Seo. Feb. 1941. "Tomorrow." *Asia* 41:99-100. No refs.

A Wellesley-educated Japanese woman reflects on her life after her return to Japan and laments the war effort which is affecting both Japanese relatives and Chinese friends.

96. MUKŌDA, Kuniko. Winter 1980. "Some thoughts on Japanese women." *Japan Echo* 7(4):123-124. No refs. ISSN:0388-0435.

Briefly compares Japanese and American women as seen through attitudes toward ordering and receiving restaurant meals.

97. NAKAMOTO, Hiroko. 1970. *My Japan, 1930-1951*. [As told to Mildred Mastin PACE.] New York: McGraw-Hill Book Company. 157p. No refs. LCCN:77-102459.

The autobiography of a woman who was 15 when the Hiroshima bombing occurred. She relates details about her childhood and schooling, and her experiences after the war up to the time she received a scholarship to study in the United States. Although PACE writes "for the young reader," this is a usable firsthand account.

98. NAKANO, Ann. 1986. *Japanese Women: A Century of Living History*. Adelaide [Australia]: Rigby. 142p. No refs.

Presents autobiographical sketches from 26 Japanese girls and women ranging in age from 11 to 103, including luminaries like KATŌ Shidzue and TABEI Junko as well as those less well known. Material on family backgrounds and life experiences is included.

99. NOJIRI, Yoriko. Jun. 1975. "Sexism in the process of socialization." In: *Japanese Women Speak Out.* Tokyo: White Paper on Sexism—Japan Task Force, pp. 62-63. No refs.

A brief report on "socialization into women's roles" with a list of discipline checkpoints (table manners, minding one's own clothing) for girls and boys, and on the "role of education in reinforcement of sexism" (e.g. the level to which women are educated).

100. "One woman's outcry." 1981. In: AOKI, Michiko Y. and Margaret B. DARDESS, comps. and eds. 1981. *As the Japanese See It: Past and Present.* Honolulu: University of Hawaii Press, pp. 250-253. No refs. LCCN:81-11526.

A young woman describes discrimination suffered as a *burakumin* [outcaste] in a letter to the editor of the *Asahi Shimbun* in 1955.

101. SAEGUSA, Saeko. 1966. "The independent woman in Japan." *East* 2(5):12-14. No refs. ISSN:0012-8295.

An essay by the editor of *Fujin Kōron*, a leading women's magazine, about problems associated with women's newly (since World War II) strengthened roles.

102. SAGA, Jun'ichi. 1987. *Memories of Silk and Straw.* [Translated by Garry O. EVANS.] Tokyo: Kodansha International. 258p. No refs. LCCN:86-45724.

A collection of oral histories recorded by the town physician which recount episodes in the lives of inhabitants of Tsuchiura, Ibaraki Prefecture, over the last century. The women profiled discuss geisha, midwives, infanticide, shopping by rickshaw, a strike at the girls' school, and their lives as wives and daughters.

103. SAKANISHI, Shio. Autumn 1963. "Education of a heathen: Position of women in the new Japan." *Michigan Quarterly Review* 2(4):249-255. No refs. ISSN:0026-2420.

The text of SAKANISHI's address upon receipt of an honorary degree at the University of Michigan in 1963. SAKANISHI reflects on her own education in Japan and the United States as well as on the gains and losses made by Japanese women since World War II.

104. SHIMOMURA, Mitsuko. Winter 1990. "Japan: Too much Mommy-san." *New Perspectives Quarterly* 7(1):24-27. No refs. ISSN:0893-7850.

A prominent newspaper editor discusses the changes in women's roles, as well as changes in Japanese society, as more women enter the work force. "Too much Mommy-san" refers to a description of the overcommitment to children by women who have no outside work and whose husbands are not at home. SHIMOMURA also outlines "what ought to be" the aim of Japanese feminists: to "slow down the economic momentum and scale back working time so fathers can spend time with their children."

105. SODEI, Takako. Spring 1985. "Sex role differentiation in Japan." *IHJ Bulletin* 5(2):5-11. No refs. [Journal also cited as *International House of Japan Bulletin.*] ISSN:0285-2608. Reprinted as: "Unequal opportunity: Sex-role differentiation in Japan." Aug. 1985. *Speaking of Japan* 56:6-16. ISSN:0389-3510.

A compact discussion of the roots of sex role differentiation in the home and at work presented to the College Women's Association of Japan in February, 1985.

106. SUGIMOTO, Etsu Inagaki. [c.1925]. *A Daughter of the Samurai.* New York: Doubleday, Page and Co. for the Japan Society. 314p. LCCN:26-11769.

An autobiography written by a woman growing up in the days following the Meiji Restoration. Details her life in a samurai-class family in the mountainous region of Japan, her education in Tokyo, and her married life in the United States. She returns to Japan as a widow with two children and lives as part of her husband's family until given permission to return to the United States. [See also #85 and #86.]

107. SUGISAKI, Kazuko. 1986. "From the moon to the sun: Women's liberation in Japan." In: IGLITZIN, Lynne B. and Ruth ROSS, eds. *Women in the World: 1975-1985, the Women's Decade*. [2nd edition, revised.] Santa Barbara: ABC-Clio, pp. 109-124. 19 notes. LCCN:85-6158.

After a brief history of women in Japan, SUGISAKI focuses on the postwar period and, more specifically, the United Nations Women's Decade. She discusses political activism (Mothers' Congresses, consumer movements), the culture center phenomenon, and possibilities for formal adult education.

108. TAKAYAMA, Hideko. 22 Jan. 1990. "The main track at last: As Japan's economy moves forward, women are just catching up." *Newsweek* 115(4):50-51. No refs. ISSN:0028-9604.

A brief, upbeat look at expanding opportunities for women in the areas of education and work.

109. TRAGER, James. 1982. *Letters from Sachiko: A Japanese Woman's View of Life in the Land of the Economic Miracle*. New York: Atheneum. 218p. Notes. Index. LCCN:82-45312.

Adaptations of letters written by three Japanese women to their sister, the wife of the author. The composite "Sachiko" comments in a chatty fashion on family matters and on her success as a saleslady for Noevir cosmetics. Reviewed by BOOCOCK in #2305.

110. UESHITA, Momo. 1970. "The status of women in Japan after the second World War." *Japanese Religions* 6(4):44-57. 7 notes. ISSN:0448-8954.

Summarizes changes in women's status since World War II, touching on politics, social movements, labor, education, family life, and prostitution.

111. WATANABE, Haruko K. and Yōko NUITA. 1978. "Japanese women pioneers." *Frontiers: A Journal of Women Studies* 3(3):55-62. No refs. ISSN:0160-9009.

A catalogue of videotapes highlighting Japanese women pioneers [see #112 for the project description]. Included are ANNO Kimiko, scientist; EGAMI Fuji, broadcast journalist; KATŌ Shizue, family planner; TAKADA Yuri, consumer movement activist; NOGAMI Yaeko, novelist; YAMATAKA Shigeri, a family services activist (who works with widows and with suicide prevention); MIBUCHI Yoshiko, family court judge; and ASAKA Fusa, medical case worker. Includes the complete transcript of their interview with ICHIKAWA Fusae, woman suffragist and long-time Diet member.

112. WATANABE, Haruko. 1980. "Toward an international women's video network: Recording women's history on video." *Feminist International* no.2:102-103. No refs. ISSN:0388-371X.

Describes the project she and NUITA Yōko undertook to videotape interviews with Japanese women pioneers and ten women chosen to "project a more dynamic image of women" and to make tapes available to an international audience. Women recorded include those described in #111 as well as KANEMATSU Sachiko, men's counselor; FUROSHIMA Atsuko, gynecologist; TAKAHASHI Ine, dairy farmer; ISHIHARA Ichiko, businesswoman; KASAI Masae, volleyball instructor; ISHITAKE Mitsue, storyteller; KOBAYASHI Noriko, nautical journalist; ŌKUBO Sawako, assemblywoman; TADE Minami, sculptor; and NAKANE Chie, social anthropologist.

113. YAMADA, Waka. 1937. *The Social Status of Japanese Women.* Tokyo: Kokusai bunka shinkōkai [Society for International Cultural Relations]. 19p. No refs. LCCN:38-8721.

YAMADA, a member of the Seitōsha [the Bluestockings] and columnist for the *Asahi Shimbun,* speaks to foreigners in this speech given at the Society for International Cultural Relations. She feels women have lost their treasured status and have declined to "mere drudges," and that a "woman's movement is necessary to bring out the real motherhood and womanhood that has been pushed into the dark cave of oppression." Her thesis is not that women's rights are necessary, but that in the ideal family situation they are not necessary because the male leader "in love and understanding looks after the welfare of his wife and family."

114. YAMAGUCHI, Fumiko. Oct./Dec. 1976. "Crossing over this sea." *Japan Quarterly* 23(4):357-362. No refs. ISSN:0021-4590.

YAMAGUCHI expresses her anguish as a child at being a member of the Korean minority in Japan and having an alcoholic father. She then relates her experiences in Korea as an adult on a visit to relatives with her mother. Item #88 serves as an introduction to this article.

115. YAMAJI, Yaeko. 1984. *The Diary of a Japanese Innkeeper's Daughter.* [Translated by Miwa KAI; edited and annotated by Robert J. SMITH and Kazuko SMITH.] Ithaca, NY: China-Japan Program, Cornell University. 180p. Index. (*Cornell University East Asia Papers,* no. 36. ISSN:8756-5293.)

The diary of an adopted daughter and only child of a Kyushu innkeeper written during the 1930s. YAMAJI notes happenings at the inn, activities of her pets, the weather, and other events of her daily life. The diary was brought to the United States by Ella and John EMBREE who stayed at the inn during their fieldwork [see #50].

116. YUASA, Rei. Feb. 1978. "Japanese women—still shackled by Confucianism?" [Translated by Dorothy TESSOHN.] *Feminist Japan* no. 4:3-8. [Also cited as 1(4):3-8.] 5 notes. ISSN:0386-197X.

YUASA speaks against Confucian ideals for women which are still accepted in Japanese society and illustrates her discussion with a description of Sony's work/study program for junior high school graduates. Also describes the application of Confucian values in *Onna Daigaku* [#126], and notes the various texts which reinforced these views through the Meiji period.

117. Y.W.C.A. [Young Women's Christian Association.] Nov. 1938. "Present status and main problems of Japanese women." *Japanese Women* 1(6):2-3. No refs. ISSN:0388-1369.

Briefly discusses women and economic life, women at home and their relation to the community, women and social work, women and "world relationships," and women and the church.

Japanese Men Speak

118. BLACKER, Carmen. 1964. *The Japanese Enlightenment: A Study of the Writings of Fukuzawa Yukichi.* Cambridge: Cambridge University Press. 186p. (University of Cambridge. *Oriental Publications,* no. 10.) Notes. Index. LCCN:64-1805.

FUKUZAWA Yukichi (1835-1901) was one of a group of Japanese scholars and philosophers who called for "a new view of man and his place in nature" to support the technological changes of the Meiji Restoration. BLACKER summarizes FUKUZAWA's views on women through a discussion of FUKUZAWA's *Shin Onna Daigaku,* a critique of *Onna*

Daigaku [#126] (the standard prescription for women's behavior at the time), in which he called for equality in marriage, property rights and education for women, and the intermixing of young people before marriage.

119. FUKUHARA, Rintarō. Oct./Dec. 1954. "Women, gods and letters." *Japan Quarterly* 1(1):87-91. No refs. ISSN:0021-4590.

A rather bizarre discussion on the "womanliness" of Japanese women.

120. FURUYA, Tsunatake. Jul./Sep. 1967. "Meiji women: Landmarks they have left." *Japan Quarterly* 14(3):318-325. No refs. ISSN:0021-4590.

A rambling discussion of several of the changes that the Meiji era brought to women: abolishment of eyebrow shaving and tooth blackening customs, and greater opportunity for education and social activism.

121. FUKUZAWA, Yukichi. 1976. "The equal numbers of men and women." In: *Meiroku Zasshi, Journal of the Japanese Enlightenment.* [Introduced and translated by William BRAISTED.] Cambridge: Harvard University Press, pp. 385-386. Notes. LCCN:76-27134.

In responding to the "noisy discussion" engendered by KATŌ's article on equal rights [see #127], FUKUZAWA (1875) suggests that rather than becoming enmeshed in definitions of rights, one must realize that the number of men and women in the world is roughly equal; and, therefore, each man should have only one female partner so as not to cause a surplus of men.

122. FUKUZAWA, Yukichi. 1988. *Fukuzawa Yukichi on Japanese Women: Selected Works.* [Translated and edited by Eiichi KIYOOKA; introduced by Keiko FUJIWARA.] [Tokyo]: University of Tokyo Press. 254p. 49 refs. Index. LCCN:88-149420.

A collection of works of FUKUZAWA Yukichi (1835-1901), "one of the first to speak out on women and their position in society" with the intent of upgrading their role. Focuses on four main areas: "marriage, physique, and legal and economic aspects." FUJIWARA's introduction, "In search of an ideal image of womanhood," provides biographical data and historical context.

123. HANE, Mikiso. 1984. "Fukuzawa Yukichi and women's rights." In: CONROY, Hilary, Sandra T.W. DAVIS, and Wayne PATTERSON, eds. *Japan in Transition: Thought and Action in the Meiji Era, 1868-1912.* Rutherford, NJ: Fairleigh Dickinson University Press, pp. 96-112. 69 notes. LCCN:82-48577.

Analyzes the ideas of FUKUZAWA Yukichi [1835-1901], a Meiji reformer who attacked traditional models for the treatment of women. FUKUZAWA criticized Buddhist and Confucianist values, and called for equality between men and women, preeminence of the husband-wife relationship within a family, monogamy, and better education for women. HANE places these then radical ideas in historical context and provides biographical data.

124. HOSHII, Iwao. 1986-1987. *The World of Sex: Perspectives on Japan and the West.* Woodchurch, Ashford, Kent: Paul Norbury Publications. Vol. 1-4. LCCN:88-134046, 88-134076, 88-134089,88-134099.

A four-volume set presenting from a global perspective a wide ranging survey of topics related to sexuality, parenting, and marriages. Brief discussions of Japan-centered topics such as "Women's Readiness to Work," "Women's Place in the Home?" and "Divorce in Japan," appear alongside "Suttee," "Alimony in Muslim Divorce," and "The Church and Remarriage."

125. INOUYE, Jukichi. 1911 [rep. 1985]. *Home Life in Tokyo.* London: KPI. 323p. No refs. LCCN:86-150612.

Another in the genre of "This is how the Japanese live," but with a twist—the author is a Japanese (male) sent by the Japanese government to England to be educated.   He comments in detail on women's dress, "toilet," and a woman's daily life (both servant and upper class) in turn-of-the-century Japan.

126.   KAIBARA, Ekiken [Ekken].   1905 [rep. 1979].   "Women and Wisdom of Japan." ["Greater Learning for Women."] [*Onna Daigaku*. English.] In: KAIBARA, Ekken. *The Way of Contentment and Women and Wisdom of Japan: Greater Learning for Women.* Washington, D.C.: University Publications of America.   46 p. [Items paged separately.] No refs. LCCN:79-65352.

This tract, first published in 1716, probably has had more effect on Japanese women than any other single piece of written material.   Given to girls at an early age, it instructed them on their place in life and their proper behavior.   For historical context when studying the role and status of Japanese women, this work is a necessity.   [Note: According to HIRONAKA Wakako, author of the article on *Onna Daigaku* in the *Kodansha Encyclopedia of Japan* (Tokyo: Kodansha, 1983.   8:108a. LCCN:83-80778.), the essay is attributed to KAIBARA because it is similar to his chapter "Women's Education" in his five-volume work on education.   However, it is also speculated that his wife, KAIBARA Tōken, may have adapted the text from Ekken's work.]

127.   KATŌ, Hiroyuki.   1976.   "Abuses of equal rights for men and women."   [Parts 1-2.]   In: *Meiroku Zasshi, Journal of the Japanese Enlightenment.*   [Translated and introduced by William BRAISTED.]   Cambridge: Harvard University Press, pp. 376-379.   Notes.   LCCN:76-27134.

KATŌ (an Enlightenment scholar) warns in 1875 of erring too far when considering the matter of equal rights and expresses concern that Japan will follow the example of Europe where "the rights of the wife seem rather to surpass those of the husband . . . ."   [See also #121 for the ongoing debate.]

128.   KUSAKA, Kimindō.   Jun. 1984.   "Do Japanese women want total equality?"   *Economic Eye* 5:19-21.   No refs.   ISSN:0389-0503.

KUSAKA provides a sensationalistic look at the deleterious effects of the women's liberation movement in the United States and a list of "tough choices" for Japanese women to consider before they finally decide whether total equality is appropriate for Japanese society as a whole.

129.   KUSAKA, Kimindo.   Spring 1989.   "The power of Japanese women."   *Economic Eye* 10(1):29.   ISSN:0389-0503.

KUSAKA makes much of distinguishing between status and power in this essay on the power of Japanese women, suggesting that since women already wield the power in the home that they leave men in control of the workplace.   He concludes by asserting that women who wish to be career employees (and who therefore will not have children) will not pass on their genetically-based temperaments, and will eventually disappear from the gene pool and thus society.

130.   MATSUNO, Tsuneyoshi.   1989.   *Wives of the Samurai: Their Eventful Lives During the Period of Civil Wars.*   New York: Vantage Press.   66p.   No refs.   LCCN:88-90233.

A non-scholarly narration of the stories of nine women from the Tokugawa period, including Oichi-no-kata, Nene Kitaho-mandokoro, Yodo-dono, HOSOKAWA Gracia, Houshun-in, YAMANOUCHI Kazutoyo's wife, Oan and Okiku, and HŌJŌ Masako.

131. NISHIKAWA, Jun. 1985. "Keynote speech." In: Asahi Shimbun. *Women in a Changing World*. Tokyo: Asahi Shimbun. 137p. (Asahi International Symposium, 1985, Tokyo.) No refs. LCCN:87-167893.

Analyzes the nature of Japanese sexual discrimination and Japan's Equal Rights in Employment Law. Notes the joint exploitation of women and men by Japan's industrial structure. Includes comments on the speech by Eleanor SMEAL (National Organization for Women), John IRVING (author), and NUITA Yōko (United Nations Commission on the Status of Women).

132. SATŌ, Kennosuke. 1930. *Amanojaku's Outspoken Comments*. Tokyo: Kenkyusha. 248p. No refs. LCCN:49-56828.

A collection of commentaries which appeared in the English edition of the *Osaka Mainichi* and *Tokyo Nichi Nichi* newspapers in the late 1920s. SATŌ, who used the pen name Amanojaku, muses about various topics including matrimony, double suicide, licensed prostitution, the nature of Japanese womanhood, and women's legislation. References to women are very brief and cursory, but they provide an example of what the foreign community was reading about Japanese women at the time.

133. SATŌ, Kennosuké. Sep. 1934. "The changing Japanese woman." *Contemporary Japan* 3(2):275-282. No refs. ISSN:0388-0214.

Describes the status of contemporary women as somewhere in between medieval women ("the chief champion of the status quo") and that of modern, 20th-century women. Quite generalized.

134. TAKADA, Masatoshi. Summer 1989. "Woman and man in modern Japan." *Japan Echo* 16(2):39-44. No refs. ISSN:0388-0435.

In an explanation of ways in which the gap between male and female roles in Japan is being bridged, TAKADA touches on the topics of fashion styles, men who cook and women with careers, the proliferation of household services available for purchase, new drinking patterns, and sexuality.

135. TAKASAWA, Keiichi. 1955. *Women of Japan*. [Tokyo]: Tokyo News Service. 93p. No refs. LCCN:57-413.

Short essays accompany the artist's sketches and paintings of women. Commentary focuses on items such as women and tobacco, scent, jealousy, "down-town mood," and "taxi dancers."

136. TANIZAKI, Jun'ichirō. 1957. *The Makioka Sisters*. [Translated by Edward G. SEIDENSTICKER.] New York: Knopf. 530p. LCCN:57-10311. [*Sasameyuki*. English.]

The story of a declining but well-respected Osaka merchant family in pre-World War II Japan. Through this work of fiction, TANIZAKI provides an eloquent and authentic portrayal of women, their roles, and their lives as part of an *ie* [household] during this time period. Focuses especially on the problem of arranging a marriage for a shy, 30-year-old woman, so that her younger sister can make formal her nonconformist relationship with a boyfriend.

137. TSUDA, Mamichi. 1976. "The distinction between husbands and wives (Fūfu Yūbetsu)." In: *Meiroku Zasshi, Journal of the Japanese Enlightenment*. [Translated and introduced by William BRAISTED.] Cambridge: Harvard University Press, pp. 277-279. Notes. LCCN:76-27134.

A condemnation of the traditional Asian philosophy of separate spheres for wives (the home) and husband (the outside) written by an Enlightenment scholar in 1874.

138. TSUDA, Mamichi. 1976. "Distinguishing the equal rights of husbands and wives." In: *Meiroku Zasshi, Journal of the Japanese Enlightenment.* [Translated and introduced by William BRAISTED.] Cambridge: Harvard University Press, pp. 435-436. Notes. LCCN:76-27134.

TSUDA draws a distinction between equal rights for men and women (political rights) and for husbands and wives (civil rights within the family) as part of the continuing discussion among Enlightenment scholars in 1875.

Official Views

139. AKIMOTO, Shunkichi. 1937. *Family Life in Japan.* Tokyo: Board of Tourist Industry. Japanese Government Railways. 86p. (*Tourist Library*, 17.) No refs. LCCN:38-11848.

Outlines the status of women in pre-World War II Japan from an official viewpoint. An intriguing blend of commentary—from a reinterpretation of the historical status of women in its best light to assurances that today's young bride need not fear a mother-in-law, "as it is the mother-in-law who will rather beg to be excused . . . ." Also includes a description of the "Girls' University . . . considered by some as a little too much of the blue-stocking variety," a reference to the *Seitōsha* (a feminist group of the early 20th century). Useful as an example of a pre-World War II Japan attempting to assert itself as progressive in its attitudes toward women.

140. FUJITA, Taki. 1954. *Japanese Women in the Postwar Years.* Tokyo: Nihon Taiheiyō Mondai Chōsakai. 13p. (Conference of the Institute of Pacific Relations, 12th, Kyoto, 1954.) (*Japan Supplementary Paper*, no. 1.) No refs.

FUJITA (Director of the Women's and Minor's Bureau of the Ministry of Labor) presents a variety of statistics throughout a discussion of women in the immediate postwar years (1949-1953). Includes numbers of voters, women legislators (world-wide comparison), and cases brought to the newly established Family Court, as well as statistics concerning employment, wages, union membership, and education.

141. Japan. Rōdōshō Fujin Shōnenkyoku. 1968-. *The Status of Women in Japan.* Tokyo: Women's and Minors' Bureau, Ministry of Labor. No refs. LCCN:87-642016 [series number]. [*Fujin no genjō*. English.]

An ongoing series of statistical reports documenting the condition of women in Japan. Typical topics include: politics, education, work, family life, rural women, social welfare, women's organizations, and the United Nations Decade for Women. (Annotation based on the 1983 edition.)

142. Japan. Rōdōshō. Fujin Shōnenkyoku. 1954. *Statistical Materials Relating to Japanese Women, No. 6.* Tokyo: Women and Minor's Bureau, Ministry of Labor. 29p. No refs.

A variety of general statistics from 1953 focused on women; topics include population, political activity, labor and wages, welfare (including public assistance), birth control, abortion and prostitution, judicature (family courts, human rights, imprisonment), agriculture, and household economy.

Non-Japanese Commentators, 1841 - 1943

143. ACKERMANN, Jessie. 1915. "The Ainu." In: JOYCE, T. Athol and N.W. THOMAS. 1915. *Women of all Nations.* New York: Funk and Wagnalls, 3:516-518. LCCN:18-18818.

A brief description of physical characteristics, the position of women in Ainu society, and the tattooing process. Includes two black and white photographs of Ainu women.

144. ARNOLD, Edwin. 1891. *Japonica.* New York: Charles Scribner's Sons. 128p. No refs. LCCN:04-19319.

ARNOLD began his career in Japan in 1870 as a teacher. In this work, he provides a rather rambling description of Japan on the occasion of his leave-taking. He discusses women, noting the "semi-angelic sweetness of Japanese wives" and "the family pride and singular absence of selfishness or greed which marks these Japanese women." He closes his volume with his hopes for "nobler laws and new recognition of the debt Japan owes to her gentle, patient, bright, and soft-souled womankind."

145. ARNOLD, Edwin. 1894 [rep. 1972]. *Wandering Words.* Freeport, NY: Books for Libraries. 372p. No refs. LCCN:75-39660.

In an essay titled "Love and Marriage," ARNOLD once again underscores the "semi-angelic" nature of Japanese women [see also #144]. He comments on the status of women and on the possibility that Christianity might improve that status.

146. BACON, Alice Mabel. 1919. *Japanese Girls and Women.* Boston: Houghton Mifflin. 478p. No refs. Index. [Many editions.]

A basic work cited by most authors referring to women after its original publication in 1891. BACON describes childhood, education, family roles, and life for different ranks of women. This edition contains revisions to the earlier one, including an additional chapter, "Ten Years of Progress."

147. BARBOUR, Katherine H. 1936. *Women of Japan; Prepared Especially for Business and Industrial Girls.* New York: The Womans Press. 85p. No refs. LCCN:36-17622.

A text for discussion by the Business and Industrial Girls section of the National Young Women's Christian Association [YWCA]; the first quarter consists of a discussion of "race"—the impossibility of defining racial groups and of allowing one group to claim superiority. The main portion of the text provides a brief history of Japanese women, a discussion of women as "economic assets," and an overview of various women's movements. The final chapter focuses on Japan as a world power and the pressures Japan is under as a country.

148. BEARD, Miriam. 1930. *Realism in Romantic Japan.* New York: MacMillan. 521p. No refs. LCCN:30-25633.

BEARD gives a very insightful picture of the changing roles of Japanese women and households in the late 1920s. She more than most Occidental writers at that time seems to understand in depth the traditional roots of women's status from both the male and female points of view. She discusses the way in which Japanese society might change, "not . . . campaigning or demanding as in the case of a more prosperous America . . . [but] . . . by a transformation in the national economy . . . [and through the vehicle of the housewife] . . . who hold[s] the power to convert or destroy Japanese culture at its root—the home."

149. BROWNELL, Clarence Ludlow. 1903. *The Heart of Japan: Glimpses of Life and Nature far from the Travellers' Track in the Land of the Rising Sun.* New York: McClure, Phillips and Co. 307p. No refs. LCCN:03-24241.

A travelogue containing a brief description of the female-ruled world of the *ama* [divers], an amusing portrayal of luckless males in a community of all-powerful women.

150. CHAMBERLAIN, Basil Hall. 1905 [rep. 1971]. *Japanese Things: Being Notes on Various Subjects Connected with Japan.* [Also cited as *Things Japanese . . .*] Rutland, VT: Tuttle. 568p. Notes. Index. LCCN:76-87791.

The section on "women (status of)" consists primarily of a translation of KAIBARA Ekken's *Onna Daigaku, The Greater Learning for Women* [see #126], which the author translates as *The Whole Duty for Women.* CHAMBERLAIN also notes that women are more equal to men in the lower classes than the upper.

151. CHIMNABAI II, Maharani of Baroda and S.M. MITRA. 1911. *The Position of Women in Indian Life.* New York: Longman, Green and Co. 358p. Bibl. Index. LCCN:81-900609.

In a work calling for an elevation in "woman's position in India's public life," the authors include a chapter on women in Japan for comparison. They feel that "Japanese women have not made progress in comparison with the advance of their men." The descriptions are typical of accounts of this period, except for a listing of women's occupations which relates their prowess as bill collectors and circulating library agents.

152. DIXON, William Gray. 1882 [rep. 1973]. *The Land of the Morning.* Wilmington: Scholarly Resources. 689p. No refs. LCCN:72-82093.

An account of four years in Japan by a British professor of the Imperial College of Engineering in Tokyo. Includes a very positive description of women's contribution historically and of their current status as of 1880, a physical description of ladies in general, and a brief mention of a meeting with the Empress and two princesses.

153. EMERSON, Ruth. 1916. *Japan Today.* New York: National Board of the YWCA of the United States of America. 60p. (*History of Women* [Woodbridge, CT: Research Publications] no. 7349.] Bibl.

Written by the "Secretary to Japan" of the [United States] National Board of the Young Women's Christian Association [YWCA], this item takes one on an in-depth tour emphasizing the lives of girls and women from all levels of society, with an eye as to what role the YWCA should play. Includes descriptions of "Christian factories," training classes for picture brides on their way to the United States, and the work of the YWCA in Japan.

154. GRIFFIS, William Elliot. 1876 [rep. 1973]. *The Mikado's Empire.* Wilmington: Scholarly Resources. 2 vol. No refs. Index. LCCN:72-82094.

The perceptive journal of a schoolmaster determined to give "the true picture of Japan" as of the 1870s. Although biased by his Western Christian values, he summarizes the societal views of women at the time in a chapter called "Position of Women." He lived in "the interior" (Fukui) and appears to have read Japanese, referring to a library of works on the duties of women, so that his observations may be more reliable than others of this period.

155. HOLLAND, Clive. 1915. "Japan." In: JOYCE, T. Athol and N.W. THOMAS. 1915. *Women of all Nations.* New York: Funk and Wagnalls, 3:489-515. LCCN:18-18818.

A typical, turn-of-the-century description of Japanese women in an encyclopedic treatment of women worldwide edited by two Fellows of the Royal Anthropological Institute. Includes physical and mental characteristics, dress, upbringing, home life, upper-class and working-class women, geisha, and work opportunities. Of most interest, perhaps, are the 21 black and white photographs of women from varied walks of life: Red Cross nurses, "tailoresses," hotel servants, fisherwomen, etc.

156. "The Japanese Empire." [A Special Issue.] Sep. 1936. *Fortune* 14(3):47-192. No refs. ISSN:0015-8259.

An introduction to the issue states that "in the apparent confusion of a civilization, three patterns may be discerned. A civilization is men, their ideas, and the way they make a living." Despite the masculine focus, many photographs show women in daily life, as geisha, as workers in textile mills, as a farmer's wife, and as *moga [modan gāru*—modern girl]. Especially given the date, an interesting portrait.

157. *Manners and Customs of the Japanese in the Nineteenth Century.* [With an introduction to the new edition by Terence BARROW.] 1841 [rep. 1973]. Rutland, VT: Tuttle, 298p. (*Harpers Family Library* no. 132.) No refs. LCCN:72-83676.

An introduction to Japan for English speakers "from the accounts of recent Dutch residents [of Deshima, the only trading port open to non-Japanese before the mid-19th century] in Japan, and from the German work of Dr. Ph[ilip] Fr[anz] von SIEBOLD." Pages 122-124 describe the condition of women in general terms; the tale of a faithful samurai wife during political troubles is also included (pp. 171-175).

158. MERE, Gerald. 1921/1922. "Japanese women, ancient and modern." *Transactions and Proceedings of the Japan Society, London* 19:2-29. No refs. LCCN:08-16048.

MERE notes that Westerners [at least as of the 1920s] "have been inclined to underestimate the influence of the Japanese woman" and proceeds to outline accomplishments of women from mythological times through the 1920s.

159. NEHRU, S.S. 1936. *Money, Men and Women in Japan.* Tokyo: Kokusai Shuppan Insatsusha. 222p. No refs.

A sweeping, hyperbolic description of Japanese women, of their gifts in the kitchen and factory, and as pearl divers. Dismisses reports of women working like "coolie[s]" on starvation wages, etc., because of the "wonderful physique" of the women in a factory he visited.

160. STEINER, Jesse F. 1943. *Behind the Japanese Mask.* New York: MacMillan. 159p. No refs. Index. LCCN:43-636.

A wartime work attempting to present "as clearly as possible the basic traits and characteristics of the Japanese people," which includes a chapter on women, marriage and morals. STEINER gives a traditional description of the subordinate role of the Japanese woman, with an emphasis on the family system and on mistresses.

161. STRAELEN, H.v. 1940. *The Japanese Woman Looking Forward.* Tokyo: Kyo Bun Kwan. 191p. Bibl. LCCN:41-16779.

Forwards by YASUI Tetsu (President, Women's Christian College of Japan) and KAWAI Michi (Keisen Girls' School) recommend this volume to those wishing "to study the influence of ethics, culture and religion upon the national characteristics and customs of Japanese womanhood," both in historical perspective and as of 1940. Father van STRAELEN, a Dutch Catholic, includes many comments from prominent Japanese women in his discussions of Buddhism and Confucianism and women, changes in women's status since the Meiji era, women and the family system, and women and the war. An oft-cited classic.

Non-Japanese Commentators, The Occupation to the Present

162. ARNOTHY, Christine. 1959. *Women of Japan.* London: Andre Deutsch. 96p. No refs. LCCN:62-26981.

In a brief 62 pages of text, the author describes Japanese women she met while on a visit. A variety of women appear, but descriptions are superficial. The remaining 30 pages are photographs, which might be of interest to students of the late 1950s in Japan.

163. BERGER, Michael. Spring 1976. "Japanese women—old images and new realities." *Japan Interpreter* 11(1):56-67. 8 notes. ISSN:0021-4450.

An insightful exposé of the outsiders' traditional stereotype of the Japanese woman as a "passive, male-dominated, childlike creature." With a liberal use of quotations from Westerners and Japanese informants, BERGER makes the case that "foreign women are among the strongest perpetuators of the 'weak Japanese woman' stereotype."

164. BRODERICK, Catherine. Oct./Dec. 1982. "[Opinion from abroad—5:] Japanese women, charming and changing." *Wheel Extended* 12(4):33-35. No refs. ISSN:0049-755X.

BRODERICK briefly discusses Japanese women's definitions of their role both historically and currently. She stresses that they "eschew the suggestion that they enter a board room with the ambition and zeal of a samurai . . . [but would rather continue to] . . . happily practice traditional roles which allow them to be behind-the-scenes pillars of society . . . ." Better recognition of the energy and talent contributed is the main goal.

165. BUCK, Pearl S. 1966. *People of Japan.* New York: Simon and Schuster. 255p. No refs. LCCN:66-20246.

A warm, nostalgic description of Japan, interspersed with memories of BUCK's visits. On pp. 73-104, BUCK (an American novelist) discusses the post-war Japanese woman as an example of change in Japan, and comments that change "is in the mind and spirit, she [the Japanese woman] knows now that she is a human being, not more than the man but certainly not less."

166. BURUMA, Ian. 1984. *Behind the Mask: On Sexual Demons, Sacred Mothers, Transvestites, Gangsters, and other Japanese Cultural Heroes.* New York: New American Library. 272p. [Uniform title: *A Japanese Mirror.*] Notes. Index. LCCN:85-2901.

BURUMA uses a nontraditional approach to describing Japanese women by using examples from films, novels, and TV shows which depict goddesses, "demon women," women in pornography, "doll-women" (e.g. department store ushers), and fantasy women.

167. CHRISTOPHER, Robert. 1983. *The Japanese Mind: The Goliath Explained.* New York: Linden Press. 352p. Bibl. Index. LCCN:82-25896. [Excerpted as "Japanese women wage a quiet revolution." May/Jun. 1981. *Asia: A Magazine for American Readers* 4(1):24-27,48,50-51. ISSN:0161-4355.]

CHRISTOPHER discusses what he sees as "a subtle but inexorable consensus-changing process concerning sexual roles" in Japan. In his chapter, "A Woman's Place," he profiles five women: MATSUDA Taeko, prominent in the construction industry; MORIYAMA Mayumi, a member of the House of Councillors; KAWAGUCHI Yoriko, a high level official with MITI (the Ministry of Trade and Industry); OCHIAI Ryō, Sony's highest ranking woman employee; and SHIMOMURA Mitsuko of the *Asahi News*, and reflects on the shape and speed of the change.

168. CONDON, Jane. 1985. *A Half Step Behind: Japanese Women of the '80s.* New York: Dodd, Mead and Co. 319p. Notes & Bibl. Index. LCCN:80-10147. [Excerpted in *Winds* [Japan Air Lines] Sept. 1986:45-50.]

A collection of interviews with Japanese women of various ages and occupations together with commentary by CONDON. The women relate details about family life, feminism, education, and work, revealing much about their status, roles, and outlook.

169. CONNER, John W. Winter 1985. "Differential socialization and role stereotypes in Japanese females." *Journal of Psychoanalytic Anthropology* 8(1):29-45. 7 notes and 19 refs. ISSN:0278-2944.

A summary of the traditional interpretation of the Japanese woman's role as wife and mother. Discusses the inner strength of women and the power inherent in their position. Stresses the concept of role complementarity within a family. Makes heavy use of standard sources.

170. COURDY, Jean-Claude. 1984. *The Japanese: Everyday Life in the Empire of the Rising Sun.* [Translated by Raymond ROSENTHAL.] New York: Harper and Row. 269p. No refs. Index. LCCN:80-5775. [*Les Japonais.* English.]

Brief description of women's independence socially and restricted status professionally (pp. 119-128). Relates discussions with several older, single women about their frustrations.

171. COWLEY, G.A. 1962. "Post-war changes in status of Japanese women." *Transactions of the International Conference of Orientalists in Japan* 7:27-34. [Also cited as International Conference of Orientalists in Japan. *Transactions* and as *Kokusai Tōhō Gakusha Kaigi Kiyō*.] No refs. ISSN:0538-6012.

A positive look at the changes in political and educational participation of Japanese women and their place in society in the 1950s.

172. CRESSY, Earl Herbert. 1955 [rep. 1975]. *Daughters of Changing Japan.* Westport, CT: Greenwood Press. 305p. No refs. LCCN:75-390.

In 1953, CRESSY advertised in Japan for young women willing to share parts of their life stories with him. Based on the manuscripts of ten, CRESSY composed this narrative covering several as they came of age from the 1930s through the early 1950s, dealing primarily with their role as women and romantic love versus arranged marriage.

173. FALLOWS, Deborah and Karen KASMAUSKI. Apr. 1990. "Japanese women." *National Geographic* 177(4):52-83. No refs. ISSN:0027-9358.

Describes a variety of Japanese women and also FALLOWS' attempts to fit into a Japanese neighborhood. As in other *National Geographic* articles, the pictures relate a large portion of the story, and KASMAUSKI's photographs of both typical and unusual women are striking.

174. GIBNEY, Frank. May 1975. "Those exotic (erotic) Japanese women." *Cosmopolitan* (May 1975):181. No refs. ISSN:0010-9541.

Despite its title, this is a reasonable summary of women's status in the mid-1970s. GIBNEY profiles three young women and then sets overall context. For the general reader.

175. GIBNEY, Frank. 1985. *Japan: The Fragile Superpower.* [Second revised edition.] New York: New American Library. 430p. No refs. Index. LCCN:85-21577.

Within a larger section on the concept of *amae* [dependence], GIBNEY describes three Japanese women (a bar hostess, an advertising copy writer, and a university graduate and mother) to illustrate the "three faces of the Japanese Eve." Strengths within home and family are stressed.

176. HAYASHI, Yuriko and Masako NAKAMURA. Nov. 1976. "Men and women in Japan." *PHP* 7(11):64-75. No refs. ISSN:0030-798X.

Jane HARVEY, Rebecca COLEMAN, and Martha MULKIN, three American women of varying ages and marital and vocational status, discuss together the situation of Japanese women, touching on such topics as the "man-to-woman relationship," the mother-child relationship, and Japanese women and their work.

177. HIBBARD, Esther L. Jan. 1966. "Japanese women today: A panel discussion." *Japan Christian Quarterly* 32(1):3-14. No refs. ISSN:0021-4361.

Topics for discussion cover the changes since World War II in dating and marriage, money, education, and work. It is interesting to note that, for this mid-1960s panel, the American women are introduced by their husbands' names (e.g. Mrs. Mark Peattie) rather than by their own.

178. HUNTINGTON, Robert M. 1968. "Comparison of western and Japanese cultures." *Monumenta Nipponica* 23(3/4):475-484. 25 notes. ISSN:0027-0741.

HUNTINGTON includes in his general comparison a brief discussion of the inferior status of female newborns and women in Japan.

179. "Japanese women: A world apart." 14 May 1988. *Economist* 307(7550):19-22. No refs. ISSN:0013-0613.

A brief but pithy summary of women's status in Japan as of 1988, with an emphasis on business/work force involvement. Includes a section on the impact of the 1986 Equal Employment Opportunities Law. Useful as a current overview from a Western perspective.

180. KILMER, Renée M. and Thomas F. LANNIN, Jr. Dec. 1989. "Introduction." *Review of Japanese Culture and Society* 3(1):iv-vii. No refs. ISSN:0913-4700.

Summarizes the contents of this special issue on women and the family and justifies the publication of the material by noting that "struggles with cultural change and internationalization make discussions of the family essential to the on-going discourse of feminism in Japan." Papers included in this volume were given at the First Conference of the Pacific Rim Consortium on Women's Studies: The Japan-U.S. Conference on Women and the Family, held 28-30 March 1989 in Saitama, Japan. [See also #253, #265, #348, #359, #380, #716 & #989.]

181. LAURIA, Alma. 1989. "The position of women in Japanese economy and society." *Revista International di Scienze Economiche e Commerciali* 36(12):1141-1149. No refs. ISSN:0035-6751.

LAURIA summarizes the lack of opportunity for women in the Japanese workplace despite the 1986 Equal Employment Opportunity Law and provides statistics showing satisfaction with the *status quo* on the part of most men and women. She outlines reasons encouraging part-time employment and points out notable exceptions to the rule, *e.g.*, DOI Takako and several entrepreneurs.

182. METRAUX, Daniel A. Winter 1987. "Frustration in a chauvinist society: Japanese women today." *Journal of the National Association for Women Deans, Administrators, and Counselors* 50(2):27-31. 6 refs. ISSN:0094-3460.

An introductory article (note journal audience) summarizing the plight of Japanese women as regards their status as married women, and their lack of opportunities to express themselves through meaningful careers.

183. MOERAN, Brian. May 1989. "Homo harmonicus and the Yenjoy girls: Production and consumption of Japanese myths." *Encounter* 72(5):19-24. No refs. ISSN:0013-7073.

Likens the Japanese experience to a film, where women define the individual frames and the men provide the action within. A very visual article, sprinkled with Japanese phrases, which addresses the question of change in women's status in recent years.

184. MOOREHEAD, Caroline. 20/27 Dec. 1984. "The women of Japan." *New Society* 70(1148):453-455. No refs. ISSN:0028-6729.

A feminist critique of Japanese society and its roles for women with many individual examples. Begins with the adverse reaction awaiting TABEI Junko on her return from her successful conquest of Mount Everest and ends with an elderly television character, Oshin, who has gained material success through business acumen.

185. O'REILLY, Jane O. 1 Aug 1983. "Women: A separate sphere." [Reported by Alan TANSMAN.] *Time* 122(5):68-69. No refs. ISSN:0040-781X.

A brief but densely written overview of women's status for the general reader.

186. POWELL, Bill, Hideko TAKAYAMA, and Dorian BENKOIL. 10 July 1989. "The end of the affair? Behind the furor about Uno's 'geisha problem' is Japan's new woman." *Newsweek* 114(2):22. No refs. ISSN:0028-9604.

Uses societal condemnation of Prime Minister UNO Sōsuke's past affair with a geisha to indicate the changing status of women in Japan.

187. REDMAN, Vere. Jun. 1962. "Modern Japanese women." *Bulletin of the Japan Society of London* no.37:12-17. [Also cited as Japan Society, London. *Bulletin.*] No refs. ISSN:0021-4701.

REDMAN addresses primarily the "look" of Japanese women, how circumstances have changed for women since World War II, and compares British women with Japanese women. His conclusion: ". . . that modern Japanese women generally look very nice, generally are very nice, and contain in their number some quite real people."

188. RICHIE, Donald. 1987. *Different People: Pictures of Some Japanese.* New York: Kodansha. 204p. No refs. LCCN:87-81681.

Rather than write a memoir, RICHIE chose to gather vignettes he had written about individual people who impressed him in some way. Fifteen women are profiled, including KUROYANAGI Tetsuko (a television personality [see #1104]), YAMADA Isuzu (an actress) and ODA Mayumi (a print artist).

189. RIGGS, Lynn and Barbara YATES. Feb. 1984. "Speaking their minds." *PHP* (Feb. 1984):36-43. No refs. ISSN:0030-798X.

Two Americans share their observations on Japanese women and the possibilities for change in their role and status.

190. ROBINS, Dorothy B. Mar. 1965. "Nylons and Japanese women." *AAUW Journal* 58(3):106-108,148. No refs. ISSN:0001-0278. [Reprinted in *Japan Christian Quarterly* 32(1):15-18, Jan. 1966. ISSN:0021-4361.]

ROBINS, writing while working for the United States Information Service, relates questions Japanese women are asking themselves and visitors at various women's centers. Topics include violence in the media, volunteer work, family relations, child rearing, and working women.

191. SHARMA, Kalpana. Dec. 1989. "Women of Japan." *World Press Review* 3(12):70. No refs. ISSN:0195-8895.

An Indian journalist comments on social and employment restrictions faced by Japanese women.

192. SHELDON, Gerard P. 1989. *Gentle Ways in Japan: A Photographic Study of the Familiar.* Tiburon, CA: Saville Photo Arts Publishing. 228p. No refs. LCCN:89-90649.

HELDON includes a chapter on women, with photographs portraying women of various ages and vocations. His captions are rather euphoric, *e.g.*, "women in Japan may exhibit that inner radiance interwoven with various shades of beauty not only in their smile, but in a serene, gentle, almost ephemeral aura, often apparent until late in life."

193. SPENCE, Elizabeth. Mar. 1956. "What place women in postwar Japan?" *Independent Woman* 35:4-5,27. [Also cited as *National Business Woman*.] No refs. ISSN:0027-8831.

SPENCE, a civilian with the Occupation Forces, reflects on the new opportunities for women in Japan and the struggle they face to change attitudes.

194. STEVENS, John. Oct. 1988. "Wives and goddesses." *PHP Intersect* (Oct. 1988):46. No refs. ISSN:0910-4607.

In this short and superficial commentary, STEVENS attempts to debunk Western stereotypes of "the Japanese wife," but merely provides others.

195. TAYLOR, Jared. 1983. *Shadows of the Rising Sun: A Critical View of the Japanese Miracle.* New York: William Marrow. 336p. Notes. Index. LCCN:83-9915.

TAYLOR includes a chapter on sex and sex roles in this critique of Japan.

Polls and Attitudinal Surveys

196. AZUMA, Hiroshi and Keiko KASHIWAGI. 1987. "Descriptors for an intelligent person: A Japanese study." *Japanese Psychological Research* 29(1):17-26. 4 refs. ISSN:0021-5368.

Male and female college students and mothers of female students were asked to describe an intelligent person. Females thus described were rated high in social competence and the language arts. Male student responses showed more sex-role differentiation.

197. BANKART, Brenda B. Jan. 1985. "Japanese attitudes toward women." *Journal of Psychology* 119(1):45-51. 15 refs. ISSN:0022-3980.

The short version of the Attitudes toward Women Scale [AWS] was translated into Japanese, amended slightly for cultural consistency, and then administered to Japanese college men and women and to married women with children to determine attitudes toward women's roles in society. BANKART concludes that Japanese men and married women are more conservative than college women; Japanese men are most traditional overall.

198. De VOS, George and Hiroshi WAGATSUMA. 1961. "Value attitudes toward role behavior of women in two Japanese villages." *American Anthropologist* 63:1204-1230. 34 refs. ISSN:0002-7294. [Reprinted in De VOS, George A. 1975. *Socialization for Achievement: Essays on the Cultural Psychology of the Japanese.* Berkeley: University of California Press, pp. 110-130. LCCN:78-132420.]

Examines attitudes toward social status and roles of women in two rural villages. By means of the Thematic Apperception Test [TAT], determines that a farm village is still very inclined toward "traditional samurai-influenced values" while the fishing village is "relatively free from emphasis on these roles." A widely-cited study.

199. Hakuhōdō Institute of Life and Living. 1984. *Japanese Women in Turmoil.* Tokyo: The Institute. 399p. (*Changing Lifestyles in Japan*, 2) No refs. LCCN:85-213426.

Aimed at those interested in marketing to Japanese women, this volume "reports on changes women are going through and the kinds of anxieties they are experiencing in the process of making changes in their lives." It includes an extensive compilation of statistics and quotations from a variety of Japanese women by age and occupational status on topics such as how best to raise children, the possibility of war, adjusting to marriage, finances, balancing roles, violence, and society as a whole.

200. HAYASHI, Chikiyo. [1976?] "Changes in Japanese thought during the past twenty years." In: Nihonjin Kenkyūkai. *Text of Seminar on "Changing Values in Modern Japan."* Tokyo: Nihonjin Kenkyūkai (in association with the Asia Foundation), pp. 3-57. No refs. LCCN:78-312892.

Reports on an ongoing survey of Japanese national character. This paper is the source of an oft-cited statistic on the number of women who would like to be reborn as women (up from 27% to 51% over "the last 20 years"). Otherwise, nothing particular to women.

201. INAGAKI, Tomoko. 1967. "A cross-cultural study of the feminine role concept between Japanese and American college women." *Psychologia* 10(3/4):144-154. 14 refs. ISSN:0033-2852.

INAGAKI differentiates between the role concepts of "other-oriented" and "self-oriented." She finds that Japanese women are primarily "other-oriented" but are shifting to "self-oriented," while American women are primarily "self-oriented" but shifting to a third state in which "other-oriented" is achieved by developing one's own personality. The major differences between Japanese and American women are "in attitudes toward the husband and children and society."

202. INOMATA, Satoru and Elliot McGINNIES. Sep. 1970. "Social attitudes among Japanese and American teenagers: 1. Girls." *Psychologia* 12(2/3):88-101. 2 refs. ISSN:0033-2852.

Surveys 2010 girls between the ages of 11 and 18 about self-perceptions, future plans, family life, and friendship and dating patterns. Data are compared with those gathered in a 1956 survey of American girls.

203. "Is the Japanese woman's place in the home?" 1 Dec. 1978. *Japan Report*, p. 8. No refs. ISSN:0021-4604.

Briefly reports on a November 1977 poll of "highly educated" Japanese in which respondents were questioned about views on "limiting women to household roles," women's education, inheritance laws, and retention of premarital surnames.

204. Japan. Gaimushō. 1975. *Status of Women in Modern Japan—Report on Nationwide Survey.* [Tokyo]: Ministry of Foreign Affairs. 48p. No refs.

Presents results of a detailed government survey concerning life purpose, marriage, employment, old age, and society. For women identified as farmers' wives, the study provides further detailed data on their work, health care, and problems of old age.

205. Japan. Naikaku Sōri Daijin Kanbō. Apr. 1977. *Report on Survey of Opinion Leaders on Women's Problems in Japan.* [Tokyo]: Foreign Press Center. 32p. No refs. LCCN:79-311149.

"Opinion leaders" from government, industry and the mass media are surveyed about the probable role of women during the next ten years (the United Nations Women's Decade), and about changes which should be initiated by new government policies. Topics covered include education, employment, social and political participation, and the family. Data are often compared with data from surveys of women and the general public.

206. *Opinion Poll on Women.* Feb. 1977. [Tokyo]: Foreign Press Center. 22p. No refs. LCCN:80-497065.

Presents results of a survey conducted in August 1976 designed to "ascertain women's opinion about their social status and their participation in social activities with a view to providing data and information for the formulation of future government policies and programs covering women's problems." Questions focus primarily on work, education and government policies.

207. SHIMA, Yōko. 1980. "Male-female differences in a cross-cultural feminist analysis." *Feminist International* no.2:97-99. No refs. ISSN:0388-371X.

SHIMA surveyed Japanese and American college students to determine "attitudes toward feminism, . . . sex differences, and the effects of sex differences on their self-images."

208. SUGIYAMA, Meiko. 1978. "The present state of housewives' consciousness in Japan: Results of public opinion polls." In: WHITE, Merry I. and Barbara MOLONY, eds. *Proceedings of the Tokyo Symposium on Women.* Tokyo: International Group for the Study of Women, pp. 115-132. (Tokyo Symposium on Women, [1st], 1978.) 4 notes.

SUGIYAMA provides data showing that over the last 30 years women have come to be more likely to express an opinion on social and political issues and are "advocat[ing] a stronger role for women." Also presents data on choice of an "ideal home," career and family choices, and education of children.

209. SUGIYAMA, Meiko. Jan. 1984. "A woman's place in society: Comparative attitudes in Japan, West Germany, and the United States." *Behaviormetrika* no. 15:55-75. No refs. ISSN:0385-7417.

SUGIYAMA compares data from personal interview surveys from Japan, West Germany, and the United States concerning "A) sexual relations between men and women; B) marriage for women; C) jobs for women; D) possibility of divorce; E) sharing housework; and F) husband's right to final decision."

210. UENODA, Setsuo. Aug. 1939. "Japanese women: A modern appraisal." *Contemporary Japan* 8(6):774-782. No refs. ISSN:0388-0214.

Reports on, and interprets results of, a survey run by *Fujin Gahō,* "a leading women's periodical" which questioned "young women" about women's suffrage, working after marriage, marrying for love, importance of potential spouse's income, and suitability of remarriage for young widows.

211. "What Japanese women want as seen in recent survey statistics." 1980. *Feminist International* no.2:116-119. No refs. ISSN:0388-371X.

Presents data from a survey of OLs ["office ladies"] on married life and of working women on reasons for working and associated problems. Especially useful because it suggests various interpretations of the data by providing context for the questions.

212. "Young women in Tokyo and New York: A survey picture of their lives." Jun. 1973. *PHP* 4(6):46-50. No refs. ISSN:0030-798X.

Briefly presents results of a poll conducted by Teijin (a textiles manufacturer) concerning interest in social issues, attitudes toward men, happiest times, and interest in life.

Women as Depicted in Art and the Mass Media

213. COALDRAKE, William H. 1978. "Images of women in Momoyama and early Edo period *Fūzoku Ga*—social and stylistic perception." In: WHITE, Merry I. and Barbara MOLONY, eds. *Proceedings of the Tokyo Symposium on Women.* Tokyo: International Group for the Study of Women, pp. 67-79. (Tokyo Symposium on Women, [1st], 1978.) 24 notes & 18 refs.

Examines the portrayal of women in *Fūzoku ga* paintings ["paintings of manners and customs"] of Momoyama and early Edo times (ca. 1570-1670). COALDRAKE discusses roles of women, women's status, and the possibility that women were artists of these paintings.

214. COOK, Schura. Mar. 1988. "Aspects of pornography in Japan." *Women's World* no. 17:28-29. No refs. LCCN:90-656110.

A report on a meeting at the Shinjuku Women's Information Center. KIMURA Rima's presentation on pornography and the resultant discussion is summarized. Submitted by the International Feminists of Japan.

215. DESSER, David. 1988. *Eros Plus Massacre: An Introduction to the Japanese New Wave Cinema*. Bloomington: Indiana University Press. 239p. Notes, bibl., filmography. Index. LCCN:87-45245.

In his survey of 1960s New Wave film, DESSER devotes a chapter to the image of women in Japanese society as seen on film, particularly through the films of directors MIZOGUCHI Kenji, KUROSAWA Akira, KINOSHITA Keisuke, IMAI Tadashi, MASUMURA Yasuzō, SHINDO Kaneto, IMAMURA Shōhei, ŌSHIMA Nagisa and others. Detailed descriptions of important films are included.

216. *The Feminine Image: Women of Japan*. [Includes an abstract of an essay by Sanna Saks DEUTSCH. Essay and catalogue by Howard A. LINK.] 1985. Honolulu: Honolulu Academy of Arts. 146p. Bibl. LCCN:85-17755.

Portrays the depiction of women in Japanese art from the Neolithic arts of the Jōmon period through 1868. The introductory essay by DEUTSCH duplicates general material found more easily elsewhere; however, the collection of materials is unique. The photographs of the exhibition items are accompanied by LINK's catalogue notes and a written description. Contextual essays introduce each of five groupings of materials.

217. "Genre paintings of women during a period of peace." Apr. 1985. *East* 21(2):40-43. No refs. ISSN:0012-8295.

Reproductions of two paintings, "Bath-house Girls" and "Weavers and Dyers," from the 17th century with descriptions of their historical context.

218. HOAAS, Solrun. Feb. 1978. "Women in the arts and the media speak out." *Feminist Japan* no. 4:55-58. [Also cited as 1(4).] No refs. ISSN:0386-197X.

A conversation between HIDARI Sachiko (film actress), ATSUMI Ikuko (poet), TOMIYAMA Taeko (artist), and NASU Machiko (scenario writer). Topics include portrayal of women in films and *ukiyo-e*, women poets, and human rights.

219. IDE, Sachiko. Feb. 1978. "Language, women and mass media in Japan." *Feminist Japan* no. 4:22-24. [Also cited as 1(4).] No refs. ISSN:0386-197X.

Discusses two broad implications of male-dominated mass media: the treatment of women (e.g. using first names as with a child rather than surnames as with an adult male), and the lack of women's perspectives in the content.

220. Idobata Group. Jun. 1975. "Sexism in children's picture books—An interim report." In: *Japanese Women Speak Out*. Tokyo: White Paper on Sexism—Japan Task Force, pp. 51-61. No refs.

Children's books published in 1973-1974 which were favorably reviewed by major newspapers and/or received major awards were surveyed for sexist bias by Idobata, a women's consciousness-raising group. Twenty-one titles are discussed on the basis of four criteria: sex roles, masculinity and femininity, mother roles, and women's occupations.

221. KILBURN, David. 4 Dec. 1989. "New magazines seek Japanese women." *Advertising Age* 60(52):S6. No refs. ISSN:0001-8899.

Briefly discusses new magazines aimed at "working women . . . with disposable income." Provides sample circulation statistics and advertisement rates.

222. LEDDEN, Sean and Fred FEJES. Summer 1987. "Female gender role patterns in Japanese comic magazines." *Journal of Popular Culture* 21(1):155-176.   19 notes. ISSN:0022-3840.

LEDDEN uses LEBRA's [#1183] three categories of gender role specification to analyze women's roles as portrayed in *manga* [comics]. Provides many examples and illustrations from *manga*.

223. LOVEDAY, Leo and Satomi CHIBA. 1981. "At the crossroads: The folk ideology of femininity in the Japanese comic." *Communications* 7(2/3):135-150. 27 refs. ISSN:0341-2059.

Through their examination of *manga* [comics] aimed at women, the authors perceive the "folk ideology of femininity" as at a crossroads of value maintenance ("self-sacrificing mother") and value shift ("romaniticized sex role deviancy").

224. ["Manga."] Oct. 1990. *Mangajin* 1(4):20-81. No refs. ISSN:1051-8177.

This special issue [1(4)] of *Mangajin* focuses on *manga* [comics] for and about women [see also #615]. This section includes excerpts from *OL Shinka-ron* by AKIZUKI Risu, *Pocket Story* by MORI Masayuki, *Obatarian* by HOTTA Katsuhiko, *Dai-Tōkyō Binbō Seikatsu Manyuaru* by MAEKAWA Tsukasa, and *Top wa Ore da!!* by TORII Kazuyoshi.

225. MATSUI, Yayori. Feb. 1978. "Contempt for women and Asians in the Japanese press." [Translated by Chiko WATANABE and Diane L. SIMPSON.] *Feminist Japan* no. 4:12-14. [Also cited as 1(4).] No refs. ISSN:0386-197X.

A female reporter for the *Asahi Shimbun* decries the lack of interest on the part of her male colleagues concerning social and women's issues, including the *kisaeng* [prostitution] tourist trade in Korea.

226. MELLEN, Joan. Nov. 1975. "The husbandless patriarchy: Men and women in the Japanese film." *PHP* 6(11):63-74. ISSN:0030-798X.

Discusses the roles of men and women in various Japanese films and shows how they portray "the strength of patriarchy and the concomitant belief that there are two kinds of women, the "wife" and the "loose woman."

227. MELLEN, Joan. 1976. *The Waves at Genji's Door: Japan through its Cinema.* New York: Pantheon Books. 463p. Bibl. Index. LCCN:76-9592.

MELLEN wishes through this study to place "the Japanese film . . . in its historical, social and political context." She includes much material on women, their image on film, and how their role in society is portrayed.   One chapter focuses on KUROSAWA's interpretation of women in particular. Although her American feminist attitudes permeate her interpretation to an extent, this is a very useful and detailed look at a view of Japanese women otherwise not well covered in English.

228. MULHERN, Chieko. Feb. 1985. *Japanese TV Drama by, for and about Women.* East Lansing: Michigan State University, Office of Women in International Development. 6p. (*WID Forum*, no. 85-III) No refs. ISSN:0888-7772.

MULHERN discusses the housewife orientation of Japanese television, with illustrations of show titles and plot summaries. She then describes a long-running, highly popular series, "Oshin," written and produced by Japanese women.

229. MURAMATSU, Yasuko. Apr./Jun. 1986. "For wives on Friday: Women's roles in TV dramas." *Japan Quarterly* 33(2):159-163. No refs. ISSN:0021-4590.

On the basis of content analyses of women's roles in television dramas in 1974 and 1984, MURAMATSU discusses female characters and their role transitions from satisfied family members to rebellious pioneers.

230. NUITA, Yōko. [1980?] "Impact of audio visual media on socio-cultural behaviour of women in Japan." In: *The Influence of Audio-Visual Media on the Socio-Cultural Behaviour of Women: Two Examples, Japan and Canada.* [Paris]: UNESCO. 78p. (*Cultural Development Documentary Dossier*, 17.) Notes. LCCN:81-169736.

A thorough report which considers the image of women presented on radio and television, and attitudes toward women performers and female staff members of broadcasting companies. NUITA also examines the impact of television and radio on women in a country where 93% of the people watch television daily, and housewives watched an average of almost five hours per day in 1975. Useful statistics.

231. OGI, Masahiro. 1966. "Virgins and the house of the rising sun: The image of the Japanese woman in films." *East* 2(5):23-27. No refs. ISSN:0012-8295.

A Japanese film critic analyzes three main female character types in Japanese cinema: the mother, the passionate woman, and the chaste virgin and discusses actresses who have filled particular roles illustrating the above types.

232. RICHIE, Donald. "Women in Japanese cinema." In: RICHIE, Donald. 1987. *A Lateral View: Essays on Contemporary Japan.* Tokyo: Japan Times, pp. 139-143. No refs. LCCN:88-191246.

In this brief 1976 essay, RICHIE discusses the Japanese film literature "which reflects with undismayed clarity just what it means to be a woman in Japan."

233. SCHODT, Frederick. 1983. *Manga! Manga! The World of Japanese Comics.* Tokyo: Kodansha International. 260p. Bibl. Index. LCCN:82-48785.

In a chapter titled "Flowers and Dreams," SCHODT discusses the art work and topics of girls' comics, and the entrance of women to the world of cartoonists.

234. STEVENSON, John. 1986. *Yoshitoshi's Women.* Boulder: Avery Press. 94p. Bibl. LCCN:86-70867.

Reproductions of an 1888 woodblock print series, including representations of housewives, court ladies, prostitutes, waitresses and geisha. STEVENSON's text provides historical context as well as an interpretation of the items in the prints themselves.

235. SUZUKI, Midori. Winter 1985. "Portrayal of families and gender roles in Japan's TV advertising." *Japan Christian Quarterly* 51(1):19-23. No refs. ISSN:0021-4361.

In an analysis of television commercials portraying families, SUZUKI (Foundation for Children's Television) found that, although settings are modern, values are traditionally patriarchal and Confucian. Includes data on portrayal of mothers (settings, activities).

236. TRACEY, David. Dec. 1988. "Dutiful heroines." *PHP Intersect* (Dec. 1988):12-13. No refs. ISSN:0910-4607.

Briefly looks at the roles of women as portrayed in the Japanese cinema, especially in *haha mono* ["mother films"]. Also notes director ITAMI Jūzō's film, "A Taxing Woman", describing it as a "feminist film of sorts."

237. TSUJI, Nobuo. May 1989. "Women of the baths." *Journal of Japanese Trade and Industry* 8(3):34-35. No refs. ISSN:0285-9556.

Provides a reproduction of a painting of *yuna* [female bath attendants] done around 1630. A brief discussion accompanies the painting.

238. "Women in advertising." Aug. 1988. *Journal of the American Chamber of Commerce in Japan* 25(8):58-60. ISSN:0002-7847.

Highlights ten advertising posters from 1926-1953 which featured women and mirror "the social values . . . of the times . . . ." Short descriptions of all ten provided along with the photographs.

Other

239. AKIYAMA, Carol and Nobuo AKIYAMA. 1976. *Changing Roles of Women and Men.* New York: Regents. 63p. No refs. LCCN:76-379091.

An English language text with essays for discussion written by United States Peace Corps language consultants. Aimed at a Japanese audience, topics include the family, marriage and divorce, and working women.

240. BALL, Jena. Nov. 1990. "Home is a strange place." *Intersect* 6(11):25-27. ISSN:0910-4607.

Describes the "special problems" faced by Japanese women raised abroad as they return to Japanese schools and enter the workforce.

241. CHERRY, Kittredge. Sep. 1985. "Superstition and the sexes." *PHP Intersect* (Sep. 1985):44,46. No refs. ISSN:0910-4607.

Briefly discusses the folk superstitions concerning particular ages which are "dangerous" (age 33 for a woman), and the banning of women from "mountains and other 'holy places.'"

242. DAVIDSON, Martin C. Jun. 1977. "A girl dreams in Tokyo." *PHP* 8(6):76-83. No refs. ISSN:0030-798X.

Profiles several young women in Tokyo and discusses their aspirations, either before, or in lieu of, marriage.

243. HIGUCHI, Chiyoko. 1973. *Her Place in the Sun: Women Who Shaped Japan.* ["English version by" Sharon RHOADS.] Tokyo: East Publications. 184p. No refs.

Originally a collection of sketches published in *East* aimed at the general reader. Included are: Izumo no Okuni, HOSOKAWA Gracia, Oichi no Kata, Chacha (Yodogimi), Kasuga no Tsuboné, Kazu no Miya, YOSANO Akiko, and two women described by the seventeenth century writer of popular fiction IHARA Saikaku. [See author index for the original articles.]

244. HUNT, Chester L. Mar. 1965. "Female occupational roles and urban sex ratios in the United States, Japan, and the Philippines." *Social Forces* 43(3):407-417. 25 notes. ISSN:0037-7732.

HUNT hypothesizes that the more advanced industrially, the higher the ratio of women to men in urban areas. Discusses the reasons why this is not the case in 1960s Japan.

245. ISHIDA, Eiichirō. Oct./Dec. 1957. "The island of women." *Japan Quarterly* 4:454-460. No refs. ISSN:0021-4590.

Provides an anthropological perspective on the myths concerning Hachijō-jima, supposedly inhabited by women only. Discusses commonalities with the Amazon myth of the West as well as stories from other traditions.

246. KANAMARU, Eiko. 1980. "Chronology." [Translated by Michiko SHIGA.] *Feminist International* no.2:120-122. No refs. ISSN:0388-371X.

A list of events occurring from July 1977 through November 1979 of interest to women. Includes conferences and special achievements (e.g. establishment of a women's printing firm and the qualification for a United States commercial pilot's license by a Japanese woman).

247. *Life of the Japanese Woman Today, Compiled from Contributions by the Teaching Staff of the Tokyo Higher Normal School for Women.* 1937. Tokyo: Kenkyusha. 61p. No refs. LCCN:72-223164.

Describes four main aspects of the life of Japanese women in the 1930s: the home, domestic education, vocation, and social (and political) activities. The latter section includes a list of all women's organizations in Tokyo with descriptions of their purpose and activities.

248. MAKI, John M., ed. 1972. *We the Japanese: Voices from Japan.* New York: Praeger. 221p. Bibl. Index. LCCN:75-121849.

A collection of items translated from various young people's magazines, books, and government publications. Those related to girls cover dating etiquette, career guidance, and a brief sketch on a girls' karate club. Unfortunately, the selections seem to reinforce stereotypes (men's careers include industrial design, international commerce, construction, television, and advertising; women's are social welfare work, commercial design, and modeling), but the editorial comments help with perspective.

249. "Men and women's war and peace." Summer 1980. *East* 16(9/10):5-9. No refs. ISSN:0012-8295.

A rambling commentary on men who were in World War II and women today. A few undocumented statistics on the number of women who do not wish to marry, number of divorces, and the observation that *nō* audiences are growing as women have more leisure time. Supposedly a follow-up to "Women in red Fairlady Zs" [#255].

250. Nihon Kōtsū Kōsha. 1957. *The Japanese Woman: A Pictorial.* Tokyo: C.E. Tuttle for the Japan Travel Bureau. 116p. No refs. LCCN:57-12841.

A rather superficial but intriguing look at Japanese women of the 1950s. After the "standard" geisha section, the work includes pictures of women at work, leisure, and with their children. The range of pictures included reveals the variety of women's interests (from striptease acts to skiers, *ama* [diving women], and "office ladies" on a company trip).

251. "Only virgins can be raped." Mar. 1988. *Women's World* no. 17:28-29. No refs. LCCN:90-656110.

Reports on Japanese social and legal attitudes toward rape, and describes the types of calls received by the Tokyo Rape Crisis Center's hotline. The title of the article refers to the fact that "under Japanese law, the rape of a virgin is a more serious offence."

252. ŌTSUKA, Eiji. Spring 1989. "Teen-age fans of the 'Sweet Emperor.'" *Japan Echo* 16(1):65-68. No refs. ISSN:0388-0435.

Explores the popularity of the dying emperor among school-aged girls, concluding that they see in his ". . . frailty and isolation an exalted image of themselves, insulated by a protective wall of virginal sweetness from the ultracapitalist society that threatens to destroy them."

253. SERIZAWA, Motoko. Dec. 1989. "Aspects of an aging society." [Translated by Motoko HORI.] *Review of Japanese Culture and Society* 3(1):37-46. 4 notes. ISSN:0913-4700.

SERIZAWA uses data gathered from surveys and a telephone hotline service for seniors to point out problems senior citizens face: problems with spouses, including the desire for divorce; changing relationships with children; legal issues; and the needs of caregivers.

254. SUGAWARA, Mariko, Setsuko KITAMURA and Nao MOROTA. 1983. "Chronology concerning Japanese women." In: MURAMATSU, Yasuko, ed. *Women and Work: Working Women and their Impact on Society.* Tokyo: International Group for the Study of Women, pp. 231-236. (Tokyo Symposium on Women, 2nd, 1983. *Proceedings.*) 5 notes. LCCN:84-187204.

Lists various occurrences during the period 1868-1983 affecting Japanese women.

255. "Women in red Fairlady Z's." 1980. *East* 16(5/6):52-53. No refs. ISSN:0012-8295.

Ostensibly a short commentary on the strides women have taken since World War II, but actually a negative statement focusing primarily on the crimes newly independent women are committing, how the position of the father has been eroded by women's growing dominance in the family, and the (assumed) "mortification" of male students at the 34% of colleges and universities which have female valedictorians this year. Short and superficial, but unusual in content. [See also #249.]

WOMEN IN THE PRIVATE SPHERE

2

Women at Home:
Marriage, Mothering
and Homemaking

Marriage and Divorce

256. ARKOFF, Abe, Gerald MEREDITH, and Shinkurō IWAHARA. Dec. 1964. "Male dominant and equalitarian attitudes in Japanese, Japanese-American and Caucasian-American students." *Journal of Social Psychology* 64:225-229. 15 refs. ISSN:0022-4545.

In the view of these authors, Japanese male college students exhibit a "male dominant" attitude toward marriage and female college students have "equalitarian" attitudes toward marriage.

257. BJORKSTEN, Oliver J.W. 1984. "Current marital trends and outcome of marriage counseling in Japan: 1982." *Journal of Sex and Marital Therapy* 10(2):123-136. 14 notes. ISSN:0092-623X.

Provides statistics and basic interpretations of data on marriage and divorce in the United States and Japan. Also includes a brief discussion on Japanese women's reasons for divorce.

258. BLACKER, Carmen. 1958/1959. "Fukuzawa Yukichi on family relationships." *Monumenta Nipponica* 14(1):40-60. 40 notes. ISSN:0027-0741.

An overview of FUKUZAWA Yukichi's views on parent-child and husband-wife relationships. This Enlightenment scholar of the Meiji period strongly rejected the Confucian traditions which resulted in a lowly status for women. BLACKER explains FUKUZAWA's critique of *Onna Daigaku* [see #126] clearly, and then outlines FUKUZAWA's prescription for a new vision of the role of women in Japan. Although not recent, this is a basic article for the study of transition of women's roles.

259. BLOOD, Robert O. 1967. *Love Match and Arranged Marriage: A Tokyo-Detroit Comparison.* New York: Free Press. 264p. Bibl. Index. LCCN:67-12511.

A study of Japanese marriages based on data from the late 1950s. Drawing on comments from interviewees, BLOOD first describes various types of relationships and then attempts to answer two questions: "What are the differential consequences after marriage of the new and old systems of mate-selection in Japan?" and "Are the effects of internal and external forces on marriage the same in Tokyo and Detroit?"

260. CORNELL, Laurel L. Winter 1984. "Why are there no spinsters in Japan?" *Journal of Family History* 9(4):326-339. 26 refs. ISSN:0363-1990.

Explores possible reasons for the lack of unmarried women in traditional Japan, and concludes that there were no roles for unmarrieds (e.g. as professionals, as domestics, or in religion) and that no economic barriers to marriage existed.

261. CORNELL, Laurel L. May 1989. "Gender differences in remarriage after divorce in Japan and the United States." *Journal of Marriage and the Family* 51(2):457-463. 24 refs. ISSN:0022-2445.

Provides statistics to show that Japanese women who divorce are less likely than Japanese men or than American women to remarry. Notes that many Japanese women do not wish to remarry and briefly explores possible reasons for this attitude.

262. CORNELL, Laurel L. Summer 1990. "Peasant women and divorce in preindustrial Japan." *Signs: Journal of Women in Culture and Society* 15(4):710-732. 54 notes. ISSN:0097-9740.

By the use of village population registers, CORNELL reinterprets the consequences of divorce for peasant women in preindustrial Japan and concludes that divorce came early in the marriage; that it was not usually the result of barrenness; that the consequences were fairly benign in terms of "depriving a woman of a valued social role, subjecting her to economic hardship, [or] imperiling her children;" and that most women remarried soon after their divorce.   CORNELL compares these consequences to those of divorce for contemporary women and concludes that divorce is much more costly for women today.

263. DAVIDSON, Martin C. Jul. 1977. "Living alone together—Marriage in Japan." *PHP* 8(7):74-81. No refs. ISSN:0030-798X.

Describes the daily activities of young married women in Tokyo and the "separate but busy routines" married couples develop.

264. EDWARDS, Walter Drew. 1989. *Modern Japan through its Weddings: Gender, Person and Society in Ritual Portrayal*. Stanford: Stanford University Press. 173p. Bibl. Index. LCCN:88-28619.

A thorough and detailed study of the wedding ritual in contemporary Japan, providing historical context and a comparison of *miai kekkon* [marriages resulting from arranged introductions] and *ren'ai kekkon* [marriages resulting from "love matches"]. EDWARDS discusses the "actors," including bride, groom, families and go-between, the engagement process, wedding planning, and the ceremony itself. EDWARDS also explores extensively the issues of gender and society as seen through this coming of age ritual.

265. FUJIEDA, Mioko. Dec. 1989. "Some thoughts on domestic violence in Japan." [Translated by Julianne DVORAK.] *Review of Japanese Culture and Society* 3(1):60-66. 15 notes & 6 refs. ISSN:0913-4700.

FUJIEDA notes that "domestic violence" in Japan is defined as children's violence/rebellion against parents.   She describes the lack of data on sexual violence against women, outlining societal assumptions about relationships between the sexes and pointing out that a low divorce rate may lead to incorrect assumptions about the amount of spousal abuse which occurs in Japan.

266. FUKUTAKE, Tadashi. 1967/1974. *Japanese Rural Society*. [Translated by R.P. DORE.] Tokyo: Oxford University Press/Tokyo: University of Tokyo Press. 230p. Bibl. Index. LCCN:67-8869/74-81989. [*Nihon nōson shakairon*. English.]

In his chapter on the *ie* [household] system and farm life, FUKUTAKE describes the traditional role of a bride and her transition to matriarch in rural, pre-World War II Japan.

267. HAYAMI, Akira. 1987. "Another *fossa magna*: Proportion marrying and age at marriage in late 19th century Japan." *Journal of Family History* 12(1/3):57-72. 17 notes & 12 refs. ISSN:0363-1990.

Concludes that there were two patterns of marriage in late 19th-century Japan: "one of early marriage in eastern Japan and one of late marriage in western Japan." Provides possible reasons for the differentiation.

268. HENDRY, Joy. 1981/1986. *Marriage in Changing Japan: Community and Society.* New York: St. Martin's Press / Rutland, VT: Tuttle. 274p. Bibl. Index. LCCN:81-9376.

An anthropological study of marriage undertaken in a Kyushu community during the 1970s. HENDRY provides the historical and geographical context and then describes in detail the structure of households, the mechanics of making a match, the betrothal, and the wedding. She goes on to discuss childbirth, attainment of adulthood, and house building as rituals connected to the marriage process.

269. HENDRY, Joy. 1987. "Marriage and the family in modernising Japan." *Saeculum* 38(1):4-18. No refs. ISSN:0080-5319.

A detailed study of family and marriage with the intent of determining continuity and change since the Meiji period, and of gauging the effect of Western influence on marriage practices. HENDRY includes data on the "wider position" of women in society, on divorce and remarriage, and on cohabitation by unmarried couples.

270. HOSODA, Hisako. 1979. *Altair and Vega: Loving Memories of a Marriage to Hiromu Hosoda.* [Translated by Susanne ANDERSON.] [City unknown]: Hosoda Book Fund. 330p. No refs. LCCN:79-128321. [*Myōtoboshi.* English.]

A biography of HOSODA Hiromu, a prominent career officer during World War II and later in the Ground Self-Defense Forces. The work was written by his wife and includes a large amount of material on their relationship. (According to HOSODA, Altair and Vega are sometimes called the "husband and wife" stars.)

271. "I just called to say I love you?" Jan./Feb. 1989. *East* 24(5)49. No refs. ISSN:0012-8295.

Relates the story of a husband-beating wife.

272. ITAMOTO, Yōko. 1988. "Advice to the lonely: Marriage is self-affirmation." *Japan Echo* 15(Special Issue):34-40. No refs. ISSN:0388-0435.

Beginning with a description of the problems rural marriage brokers have attracting young women to the country, ITAMOTO (head of the Marriage Consultation Office of Nippon Seinenkan) analyzes the different approaches young men and women take when seeking partners and makes recommendations to men and their families for positive change.

273. IWAHARA, Shinkurō. 1964. "Marriage attitudes in Japanese college students." *Psychologia* 7(3/4):165-174. 3 refs. ISSN:0033-2852.

A technical study to determine if attitudes toward marriage "were a function of sex, prestige, age, and environment" using the Jacobson's Marriage Attitude Scale. Subjects came from both women's and coeducational institutions.

274. "Japan is a man's country." 1964. *East* 1(3):34-37. No refs. ISSN:0012-8295.

A very bitter response to AUMENT, 1964 [#2247], focusing on the change in this Japanese woman's husband on their return to Japan from a several year posting in Europe where her husband "did in Rome what the Romans do." [See #307 for her husband's comments.]

275. KAN, Kikuchi. Jan. 1940. "Women and marriage." *Contemporary Japan* 9(1):55-60. No refs. ISSN:0388-0214.

Expresses the concern that higher education has a negative impact on a woman's success in marriage. Describes appropriate skills to be cultivated (e.g. cooking, cleanliness, and skillful clothing selection).

276. KANEKO, Shigeri. Mar. 1938. "On some phases of the problem of marriage." *Japanese Women* 1(2):1-2. No refs. ISSN:0388-1369.

SHIGERI (of the League for the Protection of Motherhood) points out the inconsistencies between women's newer views of marriage (love match, "housekeepers") and the traditional Civil Code. The situation is exacerbated by men leaving for the (Chinese) front as partners in "unofficial matches." She concludes by calling for a review of the marriage laws.

277. KAWATA, Satoshi. Apr./Jun. 1985. "Wedding extravaganzas." *Japan Quarterly* 32(2):168-173. No refs. ISSN:0021-4590.

Describes the various options available to women and men for matchmaking services and weddings. In 1984, the cost of a wedding and setting up housekeeping averaged $26,400, with the bride and her family contributing just less than one half the cost. Suggests that huge weddings are a mother's "last momentous undertaking and thus the complexity of the ceremonies continues to expand."

278. KRISHER, Bernard. 7 Jun. 1971. "Sob sisters." *Newsweek* 77(23):50,52. No refs. ISSN:0028-9604.

KRISHER reports that the type of replies provided to wives with concerns in the *Yomiuri* [*Newspaper*] advice column is generally "*shikata ga nai*" [it can't be helped] and "be patient." Contrasts the replies of Ann LANDERS and the *Yomiuri* team to the letter of a love-struck high school student.

279. KUMAGAI, Fumie and Gearoid O'DONOGHUE. Summer 1978. "Conjugal power and conjugal violence in Japan and the U.S.A." *Journal of Comparative Family Studies* 9(2):211-222. 20 refs. ISSN:0047-2328.

Based on a survey of high school students concerning the interaction of their parents, KUMAGAI and O'DONOGHUE conclude that there is a "high level of conjugal violence in both societies" and that the level of violence by Japanese and American husbands and American wives is similar, but lower for Japanese wives.

280. KUMAGAI, Fumie. Spring 1979. "Social class, power and husband-wife violence in Japan." *Journal of Comparative Family Studies* 10(1):91-105. 29 refs. ISSN:0047-2328.

KUMAGAI concludes that social class has little impact on the amount of conjugal violence in Japan. In addition, women hold dominant positions in family decision making, and the rate of conjugal violence is low compared with the United States.

281. KUMAGAI, Fumie. Spring 1983. "Changing divorce in Japan." *Journal of Family History* 8(1):85-108. 35 refs. ISSN:0363-1990.

KUMAGAI surveys divorce in Japan from 1882-1983, concentrating on the 1960s to date. Includes reasons for divorce, duration of marriage up to the divorce, regional differentiation, rate of remarriage, and her projections for future divorce rates.

282. LEBRA, Takie. Spring 1978. "Japanese women and marital strain." *Ethos* 6(1):22-41. 7 notes and 8 refs. ISSN:0091-2131.

LEBRA suggests and defines a new typology for describing Japanese marriages as "structured or unstructured" (to replace arranged or love marriages). She then discusses many examples of marital strain as revealed to her by 54 women between the ages 31-80.

283. LOUIS-FREDERIC. 1972. *Daily Life in Japan at the Time of the Samurai, 1185-1603.* [Translated by Eileen M. LOWE.] London: Allen and Unwin. 256p. *(Daily Life Series,* v.17.) Bibl. & Notes. Index. LCCN:73-152660.

In a comprehensive survey of medieval Japan from a predominantly male perspective, LOUIS-FREDERIC does include several pages on aristocratic and warrior-class women while discussing love and marriage.

284. "Lump it, lady." Feb. 1989. *Harper's Magazine* 278(1665):24,26. No refs. ISSN:0017-789X.

Reprints an advice column from the 29 July 1988 *Yomiuri Shimbun* where a woman seeks counsel about whether to divorce her husband.

285. MASUDA, Kōkichi. Jan./Apr. 1975. "Bride's progress: How a *yome* becomes a *shūtome.*" *Journal of Asian and African Studies* 10(1/2):10-19. 14 refs. ISSN:0021-9096.

Based on responses from 1660 *yome* [wife of the inheriting son in a household/daughter-in-law] in a 1971 survey, MASUDA identifies four stages of a married woman's progress in the hierarchy of the household: the honeymoon/transition stage where the bride becomes a member of the new household, cutting ties with her own; motherhood; middle-age, where the loyalties of her children shift from her mother-in-law to her; and the assumption of full responsibilities of the *shūtome* [wife of the head of household/mother-in-law].

286. McCULLOUGH, William H. 1967. "Japanese marriage institutions in the Heian Period." *Harvard Journal of Asiatic Studies* 27:103-167. 6 notes. ISSN:0073-0548.

McCULLOUGH focuses on marriage practices among "the courtier class at Kyoto during the 10th, 11th, and 12th centuries," by describing the conditions for marriage, the location of marital residences, inheritance, and the selection and divorce of spouses. A basic and oft-cited study; McCULLOUGH includes a critique of MORRIS's descriptions in *The World of the Shining Prince* [#31]. [See also #290 and #305 for critiques of this article.]

287. MINATOYA, Lydia Yuriko and Yoshimitsu HIGA. Apr. 1988. "Women's attitudes and behaviors in American, Japanese and cross-national marriages." *Journal of Multicultural Counseling and Development* 16(2):45-62. 20 refs. ISSN:0090-5461.

MINATOYA and HIGA surveyed Japanese women married to Japanese, Japanese women married to Americans, and American women married to Americans concerning attitudes toward marriage, child rearing, and family life. Data provided; all persons resided in Okinawa.

288. MOFFAT, Susan. 17 Dec. 1990. "Real estate's role as Tokyo cupid." *Fortune* 122(15):15. ISSN:0015-8259.

A brief description of *Spa!* magazine's column, "Look for a Tokyo Girl with a House," which profiles wealthy single women who will inherit property in Tokyo.

289. "Monologues of a Tokyo couple." Jun. 1988. *East* 24(1):15-17. No refs. ISSN:0012-8295.

Presents the hypothetical thoughts of two spouses complaining about the attitudes of the other. The woman comes across as self-centered and parasitic of her husband.

290. MORRIS, Ivan. Spring 1968. "Marriage in the world of Genji." *Asia* no.11:54-77. No refs.

MORRIS wrote this description of marriage in Heian Japan in reaction to McCULLOUGH's critique [#286] of MORRIS's views in his *The World of the Shining Prince* [#31]. He includes a definition of marriage appropriate to Heian Japan, a discussion of marital residence and the various levels of wives (e.g. principal wife, concubine), and then compares this system of marriage with those of the West.

291. MOSK, Carl. Spring 1980. "Nuptiality in Meiji Japan." *Journal of Social History* 13(3):474-489. 25 notes. ISSN:0022-4529.

MOSK focuses on age of first marriage and rates of marriage. He also analyzes the data in light of Malthusian and Neo-Malthusian models in protoindustrial societies (Western Europe and Japan).

292. "Mrs. Kaifu's open house." 30 Sep. 1989. *Economist* 312(7622):34. No refs. ISSN:0013-0613.

Comments very briefly on the trials of being a political wife in Japan, using Mrs. KAIFU's protests over having to move to the official residence of the Prime Minister.

293. ŌHASHI, Terue. 1980. "The marriageable age." [Translated by Vera MACKIE.] *Feminist International* no.2:3-4. No refs. ISSN:0388-371X.

Deplores the societal pressure encouraging/forcing marriage by age 25, and cites the factors which contribute to a 94% marriage rate for those over 30.

294. ŌMACHI, Tokuzō. 1963. "Ashiire-kon, putting-one's-feet-in-marriage." In: DORSON, Richard M., ed. *Studies in Japanese Folklore.* Bloomington: Indiana University Press, pp. 251-266. (*Indiana University Folklore Series*, no. 17). Notes. LCCN:63-62500.

Ashiire-kon is described as an "archaic marriage form reflecting an intermediate stage in the change from a matrilocal to a patrilocal system" as practiced on To-shima in the Izu Islands. At age 15 young people move to dormitories and choose their spouses. The woman then works for the man's family but the couple sleep in the woman's home. Upon retirement of the man's parents to a retirement home, the couple take over the household.

295. PLATH, David W. 1980. *Long Engagements: Maturity in Modern Japan.* Stanford: Stanford University Press. 235p. Notes. LCCN:79-65181.

PLATH explores the adult years as depicted in Japanese novels and through four case studies compiled while doing research in the Hanshin area (between Kobe and Osaka). He discusses *The Makioka Sisters* [#136] and *A Man in Ecstacy* as portrayals of women's experiences, and presents the stories of two middle aged women, a traditional *yome* [wife of the inheriting son in a household/daughter-in-law], and a woman who is determined "to continue her career as a television producer."

296. SALAMON, Sonya. Jan./Apr. 1975. "'Male chauvinism' as a manifestation of love in marriage." *Journal of Asian and African Studies* 10(1/2):20-31. 16 refs. ISSN:0021-9096.

SALAMON focuses on that time in the marital relationship after the first child is born, while the wife is a full-time homemaker, and the work-related responsibilities of the husband are growing. She explores the development of *teishu kampaku* [more or less equivalent to "petty tyrant" behavior] on the part of husbands. Although it is defined as blatant male chauvinism by most female Western observers, SALAMON shows how it is more likely a culturally acceptable expression of dependent love and masculinity.

297. SALAMON, Sonya. Nov. 1977. "Family bounds and friendship bonds: Japan and West Germany." *Journal of Marriage and the Family* 39(4):807-820. 39 refs. ISSN:0022-2445.

In her broader discussion on the structure of married persons' relationships with family members and with persons outside the immediate family, SALAMON describes friendship patterns of Japanese married women. Includes an explanation of the *shin'yū* [longstanding intimate friend].

298. SONO, Ayako. 1985. "Behind every great man." *Journal of Japanese Trade and Industry* 1985(3):53. No refs. ISSN:0285-9556.

SONO, a Christian novelist, comments briefly on Japanese men's expressions of fondness for their wives.

299. SUENO, Akira. 1977. *Entrepreneur and Gentleman: A Case History of a Japanese Company.* Rutland, VT: C.E. Tuttle. 249p. No refs. LCCN:76-51611. [*Waga Shōkon ni Kui Nashi.* English.]

In this Japanese businessman's autobiography, SUENO [of Showa Boeki] discusses his personal philosophy and business practices. He includes a short section on how a manager "should utilize the talents of his wife" at the different stages of a company's development (pp. 111-113).

300. SUGAWARA, Makoto. Mar./Apr. 1970. "How gentle the Japanese wife? The psychology behind Japan's domestic life." *East* 6(2):6-13. No refs. ISSN:0012-8295.

Discusses changes in the husband-wife relationship in the 20 years following World War II, suggesting that the defeat caused such contempt for men on the part of wives that they became "education mamas," putting all their hopes in their sons. For the general reader.

301. TAMURA, Naomi. 1893. *The Japanese Bride.* New York: Harper and Brothers, 92p. (*Harper's Black and White Series.*) [*History of Women* [Woodbridge, CT: Research Publications], reel 609, no.4843.] No refs. LCCN:13-12918.

Intended to provide "a glimpse of our homelife," including its "dark side," so that readers may "compare the homes under Buddhist influence with the homes under the influence of Christianity." TAMURA discusses the rationale for marriage, courting, the wedding and honeymoon, and family life following marriage.

302. TANABE, Seiko. Jul. 1988. "The marriage game." *PHP Intersect* (Jul. 1988):44-45. No refs. ISSN:0910-4607.

TANABE (a novelist) expresses her views on Japanese marriages, especially "commuter" marriages.

303. "To be able to marry or not, that is the question." Jul./Aug. 1989. *East* 25(2):26-27. No refs. ISSN:0012-8295.

A brief article on the lack of potential brides for unmarried men. Includes statistics.

304. WAGATSUMA, Hiroshi and George De VOS. Fall 1962. "Attitude towards arranged marriage in rural Japan." *Human Organization* 21(3):187-200. 16 notes. ISSN:0018-7259.

WAGATSUMA and De Vos use an analysis of the effects of legal change of marriage laws on social attitudes as "a methodological exercise on the use of projective techniques in measuring attitudinal aspects of social change." Data on both rural and urban women's attitudes toward marriage, either arranged or love-match, is included in the discussion.

305. WAKITA, Haruko. Winter 1984. "Marriage and property in premodern Japan from the perspective of women's history." [Translated and introduced by Suzanne GAY.] *Journal of Japanese Studies* 10(1):73-99. 66 notes. ISSN:0095-6848.

WAKITA uses official documents and literary sources in her "overview of the historiography on patriarchal authority and the subordination of women." Three major issues are discussed: "the establishment of patriarchal authority among the aristocracy in Nara and Heian times, and how it affected marriage and inheritance practices; divided inheritance and virilocal marriage practices common among warriors during the Kamakura period; and the position of women among the common people . . . in premodern society." Disagreements with McCULLOUGH's theories [#286] are explained.

306. "Wedding bills." Apr. 1989. *PHP Intersect* (Apr. 1989):4. No refs. ISSN:0910-4607.

Briefly notes statistics on wedding costs for 1988.

307. "Without our women Japan could not be a man's country." 1964. *East* 1(3):37-38. No refs. ISSN:0012-8295.

The male response to #274. The husband of "Anonymous" firmly believes that women control the finances and the household and describes the Japanese woman as "a ripe fruit with a hard kernel: she is soft on the outside but firm indeed inside."

308. YOSHIDA, Ritsuko. Apr./Jun. 1990. "Getting married the corporate way." *Japan Quarterly* 37(2):171-175. No refs. ISSN:0021-4590.

Provides a brief overview of matchmaking historically and contemporary corporate introduction services. Notes that more men than women are unmarried and puts the cause on overly selective women who are able to be "picky" given their financial independence. Calls for shorter work weeks to allow women and men the leisure to meet naturally.

309. YUZAWA, Yasuhiko. 1990. "Recent trends of divorce and custody in Japan." *Journal of Divorce* 13(3):129-141. No refs. ISSN:0147-4022.

Although focusing primarily on a description of divorce categories and statistical changes in the divorce rate, YUZAWA demonstrates that more mothers are receiving custodial rights for children than previously.

Wives of Non-Japanese Men

310. HEARN, Setsuko Koizumi. 1918 [rep. 1978]. *Reminiscences of Lafcadio Hearn*. [Translated by Paul Kiyoshi HISADA and Frederick JOHNSON.] Folcroft, PA: Folcroft Library Editions. 87p. No refs. LCCN:78-16202.

A brief story concerning Lafcadio HEARN (who came to Japan in 1891) written by his Japanese wife. HEARN did much writing about Japan in English, and this item gives glimpses of a Japanese woman's reactions to living with a foreigner who described himself as one who had "nothing Western about me."

311. OKAMOTO, Adele Marie. 1949. *Two Go Together*. Kyoto: Bunseido. 324p. No refs. LCCN:75-304500. [*Dōgyō ni-nin*. English.]

An autobiography/biography of a young woman and her mother. OKAMOTO presents the story of her Japanese mother's marriage and subsequent estrangement, her own upbringing, and her eventual unification with her German father. The settings shift from Southeast Asia to Japan and to Europe; no political details or chronologies are presented for context.

Mothering

312. AIDA, Yūji. Aug. 1971. "What Japanese mothers have lost." *PHP* (Aug. 1971):28-30. No refs. ISSN:0030-798X.

A World War II veteran grieves for the old-style mother and asserts that today's women "have lost the halo image in the eyes of their husbands and children."

313. AZUMA, Hidemi. Jun. 1975. "A child's death—The beginning of struggle for daycare." In: *Japanese Women Speak Out.* Tokyo: White Paper on Sexism—Japan Task Force, pp. 17-25. No refs.

The story of a mother who placed her child in an unlicensed, for-profit daycare center due to lack of space at government-sponsored centers. The child died on a day when there were only four staff members to care for 54 children. She summarizes her efforts to reform the daycare situation in Japan.

314. BANKART, Brenda. 1989. "Japanese perceptions of motherhood." *Psychology of Women Quarterly* 13(1):59-76. 20 refs. ISSN:0361-6843.

BANKART surveyed mothers and male and female university students using the Motherhood Inventory (MI). She concludes that the male students supported traditional views of a woman's role as mother, mothers believed a woman's "greatest fulfillment was associated with mothering," and university women "recognized the importance and hard work of mothering, but were less likely to perceive it as the primary source of women's fulfillment." Data on attitudes toward premarital pregnancy, adoption, and abortion included.

315. BANKART, C. Peter and Brenda M. BANKART. 1985. "Japanese children's perceptions of their parents." *Sex Roles* 13(11/12):679-690. 9 refs. ISSN:0360-0025.

Children in Morioka and Tokyo were asked a variety of questions concerning their parents (e.g. who takes you to the doctor, helps with science homework, laughs with you, etc.), to determine "what effect, if any, Japanese mothers'. . . [employment] . . . has on their children's perceptions of parental roles." In a sample with 46% of mothers working, the "data did not reveal any differences in the perceptions of mothers' roles. . . ."

316. CAUDILL, William and David W. PLATH. Nov. 1966. "Who sleeps by whom? Parent-child involvement in urban Japanese families." *Psychiatry* 29(4):344-366. 37 notes. ISSN:0033-2747. [Reprinted in LEBRA, Takie Sugiyama and William P. LEBRA, eds. 1974. *Japanese Culture and Behavior: Selected Readings*. Honolulu: University of Hawaii Press, pp. 277-312. LCCN:73-78978.]

Outlining seven stages in the nuclear family cycle, CAUDILL and PLATH show that parents usually sleep jointly with one or more of their children until parents are in their late 40s; and that the pattern is based on the "nurturant aspects of family life" and a "de-emphasis of its sexual aspects."

317. CAUDILL, William and Helen WEINSTEIN. Feb. 1969. "Maternal care and infant behavior in Japan and America." *Psychiatry* 32(1):12-43. 38 refs. ISSN:0033-2747. [Reprinted in LEBRA, Takie Sugiyama and William P. LEBRA, eds. 1974. *Japanese Culture and Behavior: Selected Readings*. Honolulu: University of Hawaii Press, pp. 225-276. LCCN:73-78978.]

Analyzes the type of interaction Japanese and American mothers have with their three- to four-month-old infants. For Japanese mothers, the authors further distinguish the type and duration of interaction of mothers in families with independent businesses vs. salaried families.

318. CAUDILL, William. 1972. "Tiny dramas: Vocal communication between mother and infant in Japanese and American families." In: LEBRA, William P., ed. *Transcultural Research* *in Mental Health.* Honolulu: University of Hawaii Press, pp. 25-48. (*Mental Health Research in Asia and the Pacific,* vol. 2.) Bibl. LCCN:69-19283.

This study shows that American mothers talk more to their babies and Japanese mothers do more "lulling" of their babies. It examines the possible effects that mother's pace of life and response by mothers to infant vocalization may have on these findings.

319. CHUNG, Byung-ho. Autumn 1988. "Labor-market demand for working mothers and the evolution of [the] day care system in Japan." *International Journal of Sociology of the Family* 18(2):233-247. 75 refs. ISSN:0020-7667.

CHUNG traces the demand for part-time workers since World War II and the parallel need for daycare centers. She briefly describes four, including one for *burakumin* children and one for Japanese children of Korean ancestry. She discusses how methods of socialization (via daycare) for one in four preschoolers differs from socialization within the family primarily by the mother.

320. CONROY, Mary, *et al.* Jun. 1980. "Maternal strategies for regulating children's behavior: Japanese and American families." *Journal of Cross-Cultural Psychology* 11(2):153-172. 36 refs. ISSN:0022-0221.

Contrasts the way Japanese and American mothers respond to hypothetical situations in which their children misbehave. In general, Japanese mothers use "feeling-oriented appeals" while American mothers rely on "their authority as mothers." Discusses the cultural contexts for the mothers' responses.

321. DURRETT, Mary Ellen, Midori OTAKI, and Phyllis RICHARDS. Jun. 1984. "Attachment and the mother's perception of support from the father." *International Journal of Behavioral Development* 7(2):167-176. [Also cited as *I J B D. International Journal . . .*] 24 refs. ISSN:0165-0254.

Using the Strange Situation Procedure, DURRETT, *et al.*, have determined that mothers of "securely attached infants" indicate greater spousal support than those of "anxiously attached/avoidant or . . . /resistant infants." Although relationships may differ from those of American couples, they conclude that "adequacy of mothering seems to be influenced by the support perceived by the mother and family context."

322. DURRETT, Mary Ellen, *et al.* Feb. 1986. "Mother's involvement with infant and her perception of spousal support, Japan and America." *Journal of Marriage and the Family* 48(1):187-194. 35 refs. ISSN:0022-2445.

Builds on their earlier study [#321] by adding comparative American data and new data from a Home Observation for Measurement of the Environment Inventory [HOME]. The conclusion that perceived spousal support is directly related to mothers' involvement with their infants remains unchanged.

323. ETŌ, Jun. 1979. "The breakdown of motherhood is wrecking our children." *Japan Echo* 6(4):102-109. No refs. ISSN:0388-0435.

ETŌ (a literary and social critic) decries the lack of mothering available to children under six, especially for those of middle-class mothers who do not work because of financial necessity. Explores means to bring mothers back into the home (e.g. withholding salary during pre-children years to provide a "salary" while mothering).

324. FOGEL, Alan, Sueko TODA, and Masatoshi KAWAI. May 1988. "Mother-infant face-to-face interaction in Japan and the United States: A laboratory comparison using 3-month-old infants." *Developmental Psychology* 24(3):398-406. 34 refs. ISSN:0012-1649.

FOGEL, *et al.*, observed mother interactions with three-month-old infants finding that in Japan, where indirectness is an important part of verbal communication, mothers "used a greater variety of nonverbal stimulation (facial expression and looming) and more often used touching than did American mothers."

325. FRAGER, Robert. 1972. "Jewish mothering in Japan." *Sociological Inquiry* 42(1):11-17. 14 refs. ISSN:0038-0245.

Provides a (serious) comparison of mothering techniques of Jewish and Japanese women, emphasizing the "tremendous warmth, love, and supportiveness of their children," the inducement of guilt feelings in children for the amount of suffering undertaken, and complimentarity of roles for men and women with women being respected for their nurturing abilities.

326. FUJITA, Mariko. Winter 1989. "'It's all mother's fault': Childcare and the socialization of working mothers in Japan." *Journal of Japanese Studies* 15(1):67-91. 32 notes. ISSN:0095-6848.

Details the "cultural ideology of motherhood" prevalent in contemporary Japan and discusses its impact on mothers with preschool children in daycare. FUJITA outlines daycare teachers' criticisms of mothers (mothers are selfish by choosing to work, they take advantage of teachers, and they are inexperienced at child raising), and discusses acculturation problems of young children returning from a stay abroad. She supplements her scholarly research with personal observations as both an overseas returnee and as a mother of a preschooler in daycare.

327. GARFINKEL, Perry. Sep. 1983. "The best 'Jewish mother' in the world." *Psychology Today* 17(9):56-60. No refs. ISSN:0033-3107.

Discusses the success of the Japanese educational system and the role played in that success by Japanese mothers.

328. HARTLEY, Shirley Foster. Summer 1970. "The decline of illegitimacy in Japan." *Social Problems* 18(1):78-91. 62 refs. ISSN:0037-7791.

Describes the sharp decline in birth rates of illegitimate children from 1900 (8.8% of total births) to 1964 (1.6 births per thousand). Explores reasons for the high earlier rate (primarily public recognition of concubinage) to the very low rate in the 1960s.

329. HESS, Robert D., *et al.* 1980. "Maternal expectations for mastery of developmental tasks in Japan and the United States." *International Journal of Psychology* 15(4):259-271. 26 refs. ISSN:0020-7594.

HESS and his colleagues asked Japanese and American mothers of five year olds to identify behaviors that they expected of their children before age four, between ages four and six, and after age six. They conclude that "Japanese mothers tended to be concerned about skills that show self-control, compliance with adult authority, and social courtesy in interactions with adults."

330. "Home economics." Aug. 1988. *PHP Intersect* (Aug. 1988):5. No refs. ISSN:0910-4607.

Briefly notes the results of a poll of housewives on the type of household tasks their daughters are assigned (cleaning up after meals, helping prepare meals, etc.). No data analysis provided.

331. HORTON, Mack. 1980. "Reactionaries on the shelf: Advice to Japanese mothers by 'gentleman amateurs'." *Feminist International* no.2:28-31. No refs. ISSN:0388-371X.

Describes best-selling (Japanese) books on child-raising techniques. Focusing on two popular male authors (HAMAO Minoru and KAWAKAMI Gentarō), HORTON points out their lack of credentials, their "Neo-Neo-Confucian" values, and their heavily negative impact on gender role equality issues. Translations from the books illustrate HORTON's points.

332. IMAMURA, Anne E. Summer 1986. "Back to basics: The family and the school in Japan." *Issues in Education* 4(1):52-64. 26 notes. ISSN:0747-6043.

The point of the article is that the United States cannot adopt Japanese educational practices (which rely heavily on maternal participation) separate from their cultural context. IMAMURA uses excerpts of interviews with members of the Association of Foreign Wives of Japanese to illustrate her rationale. These mothers of children in the Japanese school system discuss both the expectations of the school for their participation as mothers and their own feelings toward their intercultural children's education.

333. IMPOCO, Jim. 24 Dec. 1990. "Motherhood and the future of Japan." *U.S. News and World Report* 109(25):56-57. No refs. ISSN:0041-5537.

Describes possible causes for an all-time low birthrate of 1.57 per woman as of 1989: housing shortages, the cost of raising children, and women's desire to work. Notes initial corporate and governmental response to the problem.

334. KASHIWAGI, Keiko, Hiroshi AZUMA, and Kazuo MIYAKE. 1982. "Early maternal influences upon later cognitive development among Japanese children: A follow-up study." *Japanese Psychological Research* 24(2):90-100. 10 refs. ISSN:0021-5368.

KASHIWAGI, *et al.*, conclude that their results "suggest that environmental and maternal factors determine child's development not only in early age but also constitute long term and cumulative effect upon later cognitive development."

335. KAWAKITA, Noriko. Jun. 1983. "Don't look at frogs." *PHP* 14(6):68-70. No refs. ISSN:0030-798X.

A brief recitation of "old wives" tales concerning mothers-to-be. For the general reader.

336. KITAHARA, Michio. Spring 1989. "Incest—Japanese style." *Journal of Psychohistory* 16(4):445-450. 9 refs. ISSN:0145-3378.

A review essay providing details from two Japanese-language books on incest: *Misshitsu no haha to ko* [Mother and Child in the Closed Room] by KAWANA Kimi (Tokyo: Ushio Shuppan Sha, 1984) and *Kinjirareta Sei* [Forbidden Sex] by TAKAHASHI Mutsuo (Tokyo: Ushio Shuppan Sha, 1984). Provides tables of data from hot-lines (e.g. phone calls dealing with incest, relationships of persons involved in incest, and decisive incidents leading to mother-son incest). The essay discusses these and other data in depth and concludes that the books are "important because they shed light on the nature of the mother-son relationship in Japan in its extreme form. . . . "

337. KITANO, Harry H.L. Aug. 1964. "Inter- and intragenerational differences in maternal attitudes toward child rearing." *Journal of Social Psychology* 63(2):215-220. 4 refs. ISSN:0022-4545.

Concludes that intergenerational differences in maternal child rearing attitudes exist in Japan and that intragenerational attitudes are similar in Japan and the United States.

338. KOBAYASHI, Fukuko. Feb. 1978. "Motherhood in Japan: Myth and reality." *Feminist Japan* no. 4:19-21. [Also cited as 1(4).] No refs. ISSN:0386-197X.

With non-specific references to the work of BENEDICT, NAKANE, DE VOS (all in this bibliography) and Betty FRIEDAN, KOBAYASHI explores the "Japanese Cult of Motherhood" and speculates about the possibility for change.

339. KURACHI, Akemi. Sep. 1984. "Reactions to an incident involving a child in school: A comparison of Japanese and American mothers and teachers' reactions." *Journal of Cross-Cultural Psychology* 15(3):321-336. 23 refs. ISSN:0022-0221.

Concludes that Japanese and American mothers would react quite differently to a hypothetical incident involving their child and the classroom teacher.

340. KUROMARU, Shoshirō. Nov. 1973. "Changes in Japanese mother-child separation anxiety in Japan [1963-1972]." *Journal of Nervous and Mental Disease* 157(5):339-345. 3 refs. ISSN:0022-3018.

Focuses solely on children's behavior which has become increasingly independent during the years studied; neglects any analysis of "mothering style" which might affect the behavior.

341. LANHAM, Betty B. 1966. "The psychological orientation of the mother-child relationship in Japan." *Monumenta Nipponica* 21(3/4):322-333. 20 notes. ISSN:0027-0741.

LANHAM uses reported conversations between mothers and children to illustrate her perceptions of Japanese child-rearing techniques in the early 1960s, especially use of persuasion and inducement of shame rather than scolding or physical punishment.

342. MASUMOTO, Miss. Mar. 1967. "The new role of the Japanese wife and mother." *Journal of Family Welfare* 13(3):58-61. No refs. ISSN:0022-1074.

Considers work as a new role which mothers have undertaken, and alludes to resultant family problems in a general way. MASUMOTO ends with a description of the ideal Japanese citizen.

343. MORIKAWA, Hiromi, Nancy SHAND, and Yorio KOSAWA. Jun. 1988. "Maternal speech to prelingual infants in Japan and the United States." *Journal of Child Language* 15(2):237-256. 37 refs. ISSN:0305-0009.

MORIKAWA, *et al.*, compare Japanese and American mothers' verbal interactions with three-month-old infants and note cultural differences (e.g. Japanese mothers use indirect speech styles and Americans are more direct).

344. MORSBACH, Gisela, *et al.* May 1983. "The occurrence of 'maternity blues' in Scottish and Japanese mothers." *Journal of Reproductive and Infant Psychology* 1(1):29-35. 26 refs. ISSN:0264-6838.

MORSBACH and her colleagues analyze the lower occurrence of post-partum depression among Japanese mothers.

345. MORSBACH, Gisela. Jun. 1983. "Attitudes and experiences of Japanese mothers concerning the period of childbirth." *Psychologia* 26(2):73-85. 13 refs. ISSN:0033-2852.

MORSBACH interviewed 63 new Japanese mothers concerning their attitudes toward recent trends in childbirth practices in Great Britain (some of which have also been adopted in Japan), e.g. hospital birth, drug-free childbirth, husband's presence at the birth, and spontaneous vs. induced labor.

346. NAKAMURA, Masanao. 1976. "Creating good mothers." In: *Meiroku Zasshi, Journal of the Japanese Enlightenment.* [Translated and introduced by William BRAISTED.] Cambridge: Harvard University Press, pp. 401-404. Notes. LCCN:76-27134.

A call by an Enlightenment scholar in 1875 for the education of daughters in order to create fine mothers and, also, for adequate prenatal care to enable the development of strong children.

347. NISHIYAMA, Yayoi. 1980. "The hidden world of women parturition huts in Japan." *Feminist International* no.2:64-66. No refs. ISSN:0388-371X.

A general description of huts for childbirth in the Wakasa Bay area and of local customs concerning their use.

348. OCHIAI, Emiko. Dec. 1989. "The modern family and Japanese culture: Exploring the Japanese mother-child relationship." [Translated by Masako KAMIMURA.] *Review of Japanese Culture and Society* 3(1):7-15. 9 notes. ISSN:0913-4700.

Questions the general applicability of the "modern family" (which emphasizes the mother-child relationship) as a theoretical concept when analyzing Japanese or Western society. Argues that the Japanese mother-child relationship is not, as often is claimed, unique to Japan, or an "unchanging foundation of Japanese culture."

349. OGATA, Kazuko. Spring 1971. "Mothers and the textbook controversy." [Translated by B. TUCKER.] *Japan Christian Quarterly* 37(2):80-82. No refs. ISSN:0021-4361.

Reports on the book, *Kyōkasho o kangaeru: Hahaoya-tachi no kenkyū kara* [*Thinking about Textbooks—From a Study by Mothers*], written to document tendencies towards nationalism and militarism as revealed through the Ministry of Education's textbook policies.

350. SANO, Toshiyuki. 1983. "Behavior patterns of mother and child in separation and greeting at a Japanese day nursery." *Jinruigaku Zasshi. Journal of the Anthropological Society of Nippon* 91(3):435-454. [Also cited as *Journal of the Anthropological Society of Nippon.*] 20 refs. ISSN:0003-5505.

Based on observations of mother-child interaction during dropoff and pickup at a day nursery, SANO concludes that mother/female child interaction is more physical (hugs, etc.) than mother/male child interaction.

351. SATŌ, Kinko. 1982. "Is your mother nice to you?" *Japan Echo* 9(Special Issue):32-40. 1 note. ISSN:0388-0435.

Concludes that a survey of children and mothers in Japan, Korea, Thailand, the United States, Britain, and France "reveals Japanese mothers to be inward-looking, self-contained, and pessimistic, and with very little sense of allegiance or responsibility to family, school, community, nation, or religion." (Only 63.9% of Japanese children think their mothers are nice; all other nations were above 95%.)

352. SCHOOLER, Carmi and Karen C. SMITH. Feb. 1978. " '. . . and a Japanese wife.' Social structural antecedents of women's role values in Japan." *Sex Roles* 4(1):23-41. 12 refs. ISSN:0360-0025.

Based on a 1972 survey of mothers of elementary school-aged children in the Kobe area, SCHOOLER and SMITH show that Japanese women think of themselves as mothers and persons before wives. Also discussed are ranking of husbands' perceptions of their roles, important "qualities and values" for "fulfilling the role of wife," spousal relations, and division of household duties.

353. SHAND, Nancy. Feb. 1985. "Culture's influence in Japanese and American maternal role perception and confidence." *Psychiatry* 48(1):52-67. 39 refs. ISSN:0033-2747.

Contrasts the influence of a long-standing culture (Japan's) on maternal role perception and confidence with that of a newer, more disparate culture (that of the United States). Data was gathered through questionnaires and drawings from first time mothers in their last trimester of pregnancy.

354. SIMONS, Carol. Mar. 1987. "They get by with a lot of help from their *kyoiku mamas*." *Smithsonian* 17(2):44-53. No refs. ISSN:0037-7333.

Describes the roles of mothers in the educational process. For the general reader.

355. SMITH, Karen C. and Carmi SCHOOLER. Aug. 1978. "Women as mothers in Japan: The effects of social structure and culture on values and behavior." *Journal of Marriage and the Family* 40(3):613-620. 25 refs. ISSN:0022-2445.

SCHOOLER and SMITH explore the possibility of a trend toward individualism in Japanese society based on their data concerning maternal role perception. They discuss role priorities, the "ideal mother" image, and child rearing practices.

356. SODEI, Takako. Winter 1982. "Family stability in an age of working women." *Japan Echo* 9(4):94-102. No refs. ISSN:0388-0435.

SODEI debunks the myths that working mothers have children with higher delinquency rates and that their divorce rate is higher, and expresses sympathy to the state of chronic fatigue of most working women. Concludes by stating starkly that because of the increasing number of elderly to be cared for, Japan must choose between a welfare state with working women and higher taxes, or a family-based society where women assume care responsibilities.

357. TAKADA, Toshiko. Aug. 1971. "The joy of creating." *PHP* (Aug. 1971):13-15. No refs. ISSN:0030-798X.

One of Japan's "outstanding poetesses" comments on the importance of mothers raising young children themselves, but emphasizes that afterwards "a woman should get out in society and work at her own life."

358. TAKAHASHI, Keiko. Mar. 1986. "Examining the strange-situation procedure with Japanese mothers and 12-month-old infants." *Developmental Psychology* 22(2):265-270. 26 refs. ISSN:0012-1649.

Within this study focusing primarily on infants' reactions to strangers and strange situations, TAKAHASHI briefly contrasts the Japanese mother role with that of the American mother role, noting that Japanese mothers very rarely leave their infants, even with other close family members.

359. TAKAHASHI, Michiko. Dec. 1989. "Working mothers and families." [Translated by Tamon ARAI.] *Review of Japanese Culture and Society* 3(1):21-30. 10 notes. ISSN:0913-4700.

TAKAHASHI discusses in detail the effect mothers' employment has on families, including difficulties faced by working mothers of small and school-age children. She concludes that, because the number of mothers in the work force will continue to increase, it is irrelevant to discuss whether effects on children are positive or negative. Rather "what should be discussed is the type of family life and family cooperation that is necessary in order that mothers' employment may have a positive effect. . . ."

360. TAKAHASHI, Shigehiro. May 1977. "Child-murder/mother-suicides in Japan." *PHP* 8(5):61-76. No refs. ISSN:0030-798X.

Discusses thoroughly the phenomenon of child-murder/mother-suicides, providing an analysis of historical context, motives, and societal structure contributing to such actions. Includes statistics. (Article more scholarly than typically found in this journal.)

361. TAKENAGA, Nobuyuki. 1983. "Working mothers and their children in Japan, with special reference to three surveys on schoolchildren, teachers and mothers." In: MURAMATSU, Yasuko, ed. *Women and Work: Working Women and their Impact on Society.* Tokyo: International Group for the Study of Women, pp. 56-64. (Tokyo Symposium on Women, 2nd, 1983. *Proceedings.*) No refs. LCCN:84-187204.

TAKENAGA surveyed mothers, their school-aged children, and the teachers of their children to determine the effect of working on children's activities and school performance. The concerns of working mothers are discussed.

362. TAKUMA, Taketoshi and Masami OHINATA. 1979. "The transition of the Japanese mother's way of thinking about child-rearing." *Tōhoku Psychologia Folia* 38(1/4):130-143. 5 refs. ISSN:0040-8743.

TAKUMA and OHINATA investigated the attitudes toward, and methods of, childbearing and child rearing of college-educated women who were mothers during times of social change (the 1930s, early 1950s, and 1970) to determine if such change made an impact on those attitudes or methods.

363. TAMURA, Tomoko. 1981. "I want to work, but . . ." [Translated by Hiroko KATAOKA.] In: AOKI, Michiko Y. and Margaret B. DARDESS, eds. *As the Japanese See it: Past and Present.* Honolulu: University Press of Hawaii, pp. 164-167. No refs. LCCN:81-11526.

A succinct description of one housewife's conflict over her desire to work and the demands of two young children and housework.

364. TANAKA, Masako. 1986. "Maternal authority in the Japanese family." In: De VOS, George A. and Takao SOFUE, eds. *Religion and Family in East Asia.* Berkeley: University of California Press, pp. 227-236. 9 refs. LCCN:86-6925. (Originally published as *Senri Ethnological Studies,* no. 11. ISSN:0387-6004.)

TANAKA explores the contradictory views of women as passive and obedient, and as wielders of power at home. She argues that society claims "motherhood alone can legitimize a woman," that men are dependent on women for all personal care while women are dependent on men because they must have someone for whom to care. Motherhood becomes a "sacred role of life-giver and care-giver . . . the sacred quasi-religious myth of motherhood," and although women have little jural authority in the household, their moral authority is great.

365. TANAKA, Masako. 1987. "The myth of perfect motherhood: Japanese women's dilemma." In: ECK, Diana L. and Devaki JAIN. 1987. *Speaking of Faith: Global Perspectives on Women, Religion, and Social Change.* Philadelphia: New Society Publishers, pp. 75-83.

TANAKA delineates three reasons for highly-trained Japanese women's choice of the "privileged secruity of being mother-wife" over meaningful work outside the home: dependence of the male on the wife as "sole care-giver," the responsibility of the wife and mother as "life-giver" (in the absence of a "Creator God") and the responsibility of the woman to provide the link between past and future generations of the family.

366. TOBIN, Joseph J., David Y. WU, and Dana H. DAVIDSON. 1989. *Preschool in Three Cultures: Japan, China and the United States.* New Haven: Yale University Press. 238p. Bibl. Index. LCCN:88-20904.

In their study of Komatsudani, a Japanese preschool, TOBIN and his colleagues explored questions of mother teacher interaction including who is teaching children to read, what is the division of impartation of social skills, and how young mothers are supported and socialized. Teachers' work lives are also discussed.

367. UEYAMA, Michiko. May 1939. "On the day nursery." *Japanese Women* 2(3):1-2. No refs. ISSN:0388-1369.

Provides statistics on numbers of childcare centers, children served, and number of staff for 1924-1939. Also gives numbers of seasonal nurseries (in agricultural areas, etc.), 1930-1939.

368. WHITE, Merry. 1987. *The Japanese Educational Challenge: A Commitment to Children.* New York: Free Press. 210p. Notes. Index. LCCN:86-29503.

Includes a chapter "Learning at Mother's Knee" which details the role of Japanese mothers in the education of their children, focusing on the preschool years. Other references to mother-child relationships are scattered throughout the text.

369. WHITE, Merry. 1988. *The Japanese Overseas: Can They Go Home Again?* New York: Free Press. 179p. 237 refs. Index. LCCN:87-33836.

In this study of Japanese families returning from an occupation-related stay abroad, WHITE analyzes "problems of membership and identity" and "the effects of the overseas sojourn on [members'] participation in meaningful groups and institutions." It is the woman who "manages [the family's] readjustment to Japan" and through her "chief role as mother . . . direct[s] her children's scholastic progress." WHITE includes case studies in her analyses.

370. WHITE, Merry. Summer 1987. "The virtue of Japanese mothers: Cultural definitions of women's lives." *Daedalus* 116(3):149-163. 16 notes. ISSN:0011-5260.

A succinct appraisal of the status of Japanese women as defined within the Japanese cultural context: "it is by her mothering that [a Japanese woman] is known and valued." White assists the American observer in breaking out of an American ethnocentric perspective and in gaining a balanced view of women's roles and social fulfillment in Japan.

371. YAMAGUCHI, Hirotsugu. Apr. 1989. "Congruence of causal attributions for school performance given by children and mothers." *Psychological Reports* 64(2):359-363. 6 refs. ISSN:0033-2941.

YAMAGUCHI studied junior high school students and their mothers to compare "the attributions of children with mothers' attributions and children's predictions of their mother's attributions for children's school performances."

372. YASUKAWA, Yoriko. 1981. "Baby hotel, Japan's 'outlaw' nurseries." *UNICEF News* 107(1):24-25. No refs. ISSN:0379-2854.

YASUKAWA describes the opening of private childcare facilities due both to the lack of government facilities and to the inflexible hours of those available. Because they are unregulated, the quality varies and public demand for government control is rising.

The Larger Family

373. CAMPBELL, Ruth and Elaine M. BRODY. Dec. 1985. "Women's changing roles and help to the elderly: Attitudes of women in the United States and Japan." *Gerontologist* 25(6):584-592. 28 refs. ISSN:0016-9013.

CAMPBELL and BRODY explore attitudes of three generations of women toward responsibility for care of elderly family members, and the effect of women's changing lifestyles on availability for such care in both the United States and Japan.

374. FREED, Anne O. 1990. "How Japanese families cope with fragile elderly." *Journal of Gerontological Social Work* 15(1-2):39-56. 39 refs. ISSN:0163-4372.

FREED presents case studies and a review of both the American and Japanese literature on coping strategies for dealing with elderly parents. She notes that given more working women, the advent of the nuclear family, and restrictive living conditions, traditional methods of elder-care are no longer possible but that new strategies are not yet developed sufficiently. Coping mechanisms delineated include obligation, anger, martyrdom, religion, passivity, community supports, and reframing.

375. HAMABATA, Matthews Masayuki. 1990. *Crested Kimono: Power and Love in the Japanese Business Family.* Ithaca, NY: Cornell University Press. 191p. Notes & bibl. Index. LCCN:89-46173.

In this ethnographic study of upperclass business families, HAMABATA details the role of women family members in the interworkings of various male-run enterprises. He focuses particularly on the maintenance of the *ie* [household] and its businesses through marriage, the interconnectedness of businesses through women's natal kinship and social networks, and the strength of indebtedness relationships in the interweaving of the corporate world of Japan.

376. HANI, Setsuko. 1948. *The Japanese Family System, as Seen from the Standpoint of Japanese Women.* Tokyo: Nihon Taiheiyo Mondai Chosakai. 41p. (*Pacific Studies Series.*) No refs. LCCN:50-3340. [Excerpted in LIVINGSTON, Jon, Joe MOORE, and Felicia OLDFATHER, eds. 1973. *Imperial Japan, 1800-1945.* New York: Pantheon, pp. 424-431. (*The Japan Reader, 1.*) LCCN:73-7015.]

A discussion of the traditional Japanese *ie* [household] system taken from several Japanese sources. Pointing out the absence of individual rights, HANI focuses on marriage and divorce and on the borrowing ahead on salaries of female house members sent by their families to work as geisha or in factories. Hope for change through the implementation of the new constitution is expressed.

377. HAUSER, William B. 1986. "Why so few?: Women household heads in Osaka chōnin families." *Journal of Family History* 11(4):343-351. 11 refs. ISSN:0363-1990.

HAUSER examined the records of 1507 Osaka *chōnin* ["urbanite"] families from 1707-1872. Noting the reasons that female succession is unusual, even with the probability of family extinction, he goes on to discuss the reasons for its extreme rarity after 1730, hypothesizing that the merchant guilds were attempting to curtail the number of licensed businesses.

378. HAYAMI, Akira. Spring 1983. "The myth of primogeniture and impartible inheritance in Tokugawa Japan." *Journal of Family History* 8(1):3-29. 28 refs. ISSN:0363-1990.

Analyzes population registers from the village of Nishijo covering the years 1773-1869, and determines that "women frequently headed households, especially when their husbands departed temporarily as migrants." Discusses the possible reasons for this exception to the Meiji Civil Code.

379. "In-law frictions." May 1988. *PHP Intersect* (May 1988):4. No refs. ISSN:0910-4607.

Briefly provides the results of a poll of mothers-in-law concerning areas of disagreement with their son's wives. Main areas of concern were tradition, customs, and education of grandchildren. No data analysis provided.

380. ISHIDA, Akira, ed. Dec. 1989. "Women and the family: Post-family alternatives." [Japanese portions translated by Julianne DVORAK.] *Review of Japanese Culture and Society* 3(1):79-95. 10 notes. ISSN:0913-4700.

A panel discussion culminating a symposium on women and the family in which TOMIOKA Taeko, UENO Chizuko, MIZUTA Noriko, Miriam M. JOHNSON and Myra STROBER discuss the form families may take in the future and the effect these forms will have on the roles of women. The discussion is facilitated by OGINO Miho. For associated articles see #180, #253, #265, #348, #359, #716 & #989.

381. ISONO, Fujiko. Mar. 1964. "The family and women in Japan." *Sociological Review* 12(1):39-54. No refs. ISSN:0038-0261.

ISONO analyzes the change of women's status prior to and after World War II, especially through changes in the *ie* [house/family] system. Writing in the early 1960s, she is quite optimistic (e.g. "women now enjoy almost complete equality with men under the law, even including equal pay") but not blind to the problems associated with the transition.

382. KAMO, Yoshinori. Fall 1990. "Husbands and wives living in nuclear and stem family households in Japan." *Sociological Perspectives* 33(3):397-417. 22 refs. ISSN:0731-1214.

Based on a survey of couples in Tokyo with school-aged children, this technical article analyzes family living arrangements, discusses resource exchanges and attitudes toward filial responsibility, and concludes that the husband is most happy living with his in-laws while the wife is least happy with her in-laws.

383. KITAZAWA, Yōko. 1986. "An ageing society: Who will bear the burden?" *Ampo: Japan-Asia Quarterly Review* 18(2/3):55-64. No refs. LCCN:77-12830.

Calling aging "the biggest concern of women over forty in Japan today," KITAZAWA provides detailed discussion and data on the aging problem and criticizes the Nakasone government for "dumping" the problem on women through their "home-based welfare policy."

384. KODAMA, Kayoko. Spring 1983. "Problems for women in rapidly aging society." *Japan Christian Quarterly* 49(2):68-74. 10 notes. ISSN:0021-4361.

A personal account of the sacrifice and frustration involved in caring for elderly parents-in-law. KODAMA includes contextual materials (statistics and descriptions of government policy). [Introduced by #390.]

385. KUME, Ai. Sep. 1956. "Status of women and the family system." *United Asia* 8:247-251. No refs. ISSN:0041-7173.

An examination of the traditional family system which was legally abolished in 1947 but continues to exist. KUME is concerned that the upcoming revision of the Constitution might include a return to a legal *ie* [house/family] system. (The proposed revision was not made.)

386. MORGAN, S. Philip and Kiyosi HIROSIMA. Apr. 1983. "The persistence of extended family residence in Japan: Anachronism or alternative strategy?" *American Sociological Review* 48(2):269-281. 36 refs. ISSN:0003-1224.

An in-depth examination of extended families in Japan which suggests that women are more likely to have more children and work outside the home with this arrangement. Presents results of a 1978 survey which show that few involved in this setting wish to break up the arrangement.

387. ODA, Yoshihiko. Oct. 1977. "Three mothers-in-law in Japan." *PHP* 8(10):61-69. No refs. ISSN:0030-798X.

Provides three examples of mother-in-law/daughter-in-law interactions focused on problems of living in the same household.

388. WALTHALL, Anne. Spring 1990. "Family ideology of the rural entrepreneurs." *Journal of Social History* 23(3):463-483. 70 notes. ISSN:0022-4529.

While focusing primarily on the familial structure among rural artisan and merchant families during the nineteenth century, WALTHALL includes material on education of girls, the practice of sending girls out to be trained by other families, women's involvement in business, women's pilgrimages and travels, and women's relationships within their families.

389. WATANABE, Kazuhiro. 1980. "The war between wife and mother-in-law." *Japan Echo* 7(Special issue):21-29. No refs. ISSN:0388-0435.

WATANABE paints a rather stark, bleak picture of wife/mother-in-law relationships (e.g. "They take the opposite sides on every question") in this translation of a 1977 article written for a Japanese audience.   Discusses roles of husbands in easing frictions, recommends adopting the attitude of separate families under the same roof, and suggests several ways of implementing same.

390. WILLIAMS, Mary Tatem. Spring 1983. "A trilogy of women's voices: Introduction." *Japan Christian Quarterly* 49(2):67-68. No refs. ISSN:0021-4361.

WILLIAMS focuses primarily on changes in family relationships for women in her introduction to three articles, #384, #440 & #1120.

391. "Women had high status in old Japan." 1976. *East* 12(6):11-12. No refs. ISSN:0012-8295.

A report on the work of Dr. MAEDA Taku on inheritance patterns in the Tohoku and northern part of the Kantō District before the Meiji period. Based on family registers and genealogies, he concludes that headship of families usually passed to the first-born child. Although *East* is by no means scholarly, this brief précis may be useful.

392. YAMANAKA, Hideko (Eiko). 1981. "Looking after my father-in-law: In retrospect." [Translated by Hiroko KATAOKA.] In: AOKI, Michiko Y. and Margaret B. DARDESS, eds. *As the Japanese See it: Past and Present.* Honolulu: University Press of Hawaii, pp. 161-164. No refs. LCCN:81-11526.

The author relates her experience caring for her partially paralyzed father-in-law, and ends with pleas for homes for the aged, for lifelong hobbies and for savings to enable the elderly to grow old without worry.

Homemaking

393. ABE, Yōko. 1979. "Housewives at the helm." *Japan Echo* 6(4):93-101. No refs. ISSN:0388-0435.

ABE discusses the impact of refrigerators and other appliances on traditional housewives and outlines the variety of activities housewives now undertake to cultivate themselves physically and mentally. Her conclusion is that middle-aged men are no longer heads of their households—their wives have taken over the management.

394. BEN-ARI, Eyal. Feb. 1990. "A bureaucrat in every Japanese kitchen." *Administration and Society* 21(4):472-492. 54 refs. ISSN:0095-3997.

In this technical article discussing "coproduction schemes" as a local governmental administrative strategy, BEN-ARI uses the example of a new garbage disposal and recycling system implemented in a Japanese city which relied in part on incorporating the traditional housewife/mother role in the system and the participation of local women's associations.

395. CHAPMAN, Christine. Feb. 1984. "The mask behind the smile." *PHP* (Feb. 1984):20-27. No refs. ISSN:0030-798X.

CHAPMAN reports on the demise of the "myth of the contented housewife" as seen through the publication of SAITO Shigeo's *Tsumatachi no shishuki* [*Wives in the Autumn of Life*].

396. FUKAYA, Masashi. 1978. "Socialization and sex-roles of housewives." In: WHITE, Merry I. and Barbara MOLONY, eds. *Proceedings of the Tokyo Symposium on Women.* Tokyo: International Group for the Study of Women, pp. 133-149. (Tokyo Symposium on Women, [1st], 1978.) No refs.

In her survey of full time housewives with elementary school-aged children, FUKAYA specifically questioned women about their capabilities as housewives, their sense of happiness, and their sense of social involvement. Includes the data from which her conclusions are drawn.

397. GOTŌ, Aki. Winter 1982. "Where are Japanese housewives heading?" *Japan Echo* 9(4):103-111. No refs. ISSN:0388-0435.

A rather dismal look at the emptiness of the lives of women over 35 and the breakdown of the family where old and young suffer the whims of spoiled, middle-aged couples.

398. HIGUCHI, Keiko. Winter 1985. "Women at home." *Japan Echo* 12(4):51-57. No refs. ISSN:0388-0435.

HIGUCHI looks at changes in women's status in the post-World War II period, questioning whether these changes "actually expand women's human rights or merely increase housewives' prerogatives." [For an introduction to this article, see #80.]

399. IMAMURA, Anne E. 1978. "The active housewife: Continuity and change in the status of shufu." *Transactions of the International Conference of Orientalists in Japan* no.23:85-98. [Also cited as *Kokusai Tōhō Gakusha Kaigi Kiyoo.*] 14 notes & 6 refs. ISSN:0538-6012.

IMAMURA defines five varieties of "active" housewives, all of whom hold in common the absolute commitment to the fulfillment of her role as *shufu* [keeper of the home] but pursue outside interests on a secondary level. [For a fuller discussion of the same data see #400].

400. IMAMURA, Anne E. 1978. "The active urban housewife: Structurally induced motivation for increased community participation." In: WHITE, Merry I. and Barbara MOLONY, eds. *Proceedings of the Tokyo Symposium on Women.* Tokyo: International Group for the Study of Women, pp. 88-114. (Tokyo Symposium on Women, [1st], 1978.) 23 notes & 7 refs.

Provides a thorough discussion of each stage in the housewife life cycle, discusses the effect of housing type on outside activities, and presents five typologies for categorizing purposes of outside activities: the need to get out, development of useful skills for post-child rearing years, community service, personal betterment, and development of life purpose after child rearing. [For a briefer version of the same data see #399].

401. IMAMURA, Anne E. 1980. "New life styles for housewives." *Japan Echo* 7(Special Issue):30-41. No refs. ISSN:0388-0435.

Basically the same paper as #400 with the addition of a short comparison between Japanese and American housewives. References appear only in #400.

402. IMAMURA, Anne E. Jan./Feb. 1985. "A window on her world: The relevance of housing type for the urban Japanese housewife." *Ekistics* 52(310):34-44. 17 refs. ISSN:0013-2942. [Reprinted in VAN VLIET, William, ed. *Women, Housing and Community*. Brookfield, VT: Avebury, 1988, pp. 73-97. LCCN:89-121.]

Although based on the same data as her earlier papers [#399-#401], IMAMURA places more emphasis on description of housing types (including photos and floor plans) and the effect of housing environment on "patterns of interaction in the wider community." Includes women living in owned houses, owned condominiums, rented houses, rented apartments, *danchi* [public housing], and company or government housing. Especially useful for those unfamiliar with the urban Japanese setting.

403. IMAMURA, Anne E. 1987. *Urban Japanese Housewives: At Home and in the Community.* Honolulu: University of Hawaii Press. 193p. (*Studies of the East Asian Institute, Columbia University.*) Bibl. Index. LCCN:86-27262.

A sociological study of housewives living in a *danchi* [public housing] complex in Saitama City, a Tokyo suburb, in 1977-1978. IMAMURA describes the community setting, the housewives and their "life course," and their activities within and outside their homes—from culture classes to civic participation. She then presents five summary role types illustrated by descriptions of individual women: home is best, long-range planner, civic activist, searcher for meaning, and personal education.

404. IMAMURA, Anne E. Apr. 1987. "The Japanese urban housewife: Traditional and modern social participation." *Social Science Journal* 24(2):139-156. 28 notes. ISSN:0035-7634.

In this technical sociological discussion concerning community participation by wives of white-collar and professional men, IMAMURA analyzes the effect of industrialization and urbanization on family and community structures in Japan. She also includes descriptions of some organizations to which women belong.

405. JALALI-ROMANOVSKY, Ulrike. 1988. "Self-assessment and consciousness of housewives: A case study on women in Nagano and Shizuoka. In: NISH, Ian, ed. 1988. *Contemporary European Writing on Japan: Scholarly Views from Eastern and Western Europe.* Kent, England: Paul Norbury Publications, pp. 120-125. No refs. LCCN:88-193026.

Compares ages, educational background, employment background, current work status, outside activities, satisfaction with current status, reasons for choosing outside work or not, and feelings of inferiority toward spouses for housewives (both full-time and those with outside jobs) from Nagano and Shizuoka.

406. Japan. Ministry of International Trade and Industry. Information Industry Section. Oct./Dec. 1982. "Technopia, May 1990." *Japan Quarterly* 29(4):437-444. No refs. ISSN:0021-4590.

In this fictional account of a *salariiman* [white collar employee] and his family in 1990, several pages are devoted to "Mrs. SUZUKI" and her life. The wife/mother role appears unchanged but technical advances have been made which make her life easier.

407. "Japanese wives hold few illusions but keep firm grip on purse strings." Jul. 1983. *Business Japan* 28:13-14. No refs. ISSN:0300-4341.

A short review of the results from the International Comparative Survey of Women's Problems conducted by the Prime Minister's Office, Women's Affairs Section, which confirms that Japanese women's view of their role as inside the home remains strong.

408. KAMIMURA, Yoshihiro. Sep./Oct. 1984. "Don't do it yourself: Japan's new 'convenience business.'" *Journal of Japanese Trade and Industry* 1984(5):31-33. No refs. ISSN:0285-9556.

Briefly discusses *benri-ya* [convenience businesses] serving a market for "convenience services of an extremely simple nature that housewives could manage themselves" (e.g. shopping, cleaning, food preparation). Suggests the high proportion of working women have changed their concept of time either by choosing other more appealing activities or by being aware of what their labor is worth (i.e. "time is money").

409. KUBOTA, Kyōko. Jan./Mar. 1986. "Alcoholism and the housewife." *Japan Quarterly* 33(1):54-58. No refs. ISSN:0021-4590.

Concentrating on women in their 30s and 40s, KUBOTA profiles three women alcoholics who drink for escape. She concludes by expressing her concern for women in their 20s who are increasingly being identified as alcoholics. She places the underlying cause of female alcoholism as women's place in Japanese society.

410. KURITA, Yasuyuki. 1978. "Urban life seen through household possessions." *Japan Echo* 5(4):114-123. No refs. ISSN:0388-0435.

A survey run by KURITA explored number and type of possessions in apartments of various sizes. He comments on the role of women in these households as reflected by the types of materials owned.

411. LEBRA, Takie Sugiyama. Summer 1980. "Autonomy through interdependence: The Housewives Labor Bank." *Japan Interpreter* 13(1):133-142. 3 notes. ISSN:0021-4450.

A sociological analysis of the Housewives Labor Bank, an organization enabling women to work for each other and to receive assistance as desired. While LEBRA focuses primarily on issues of dependence, autonomy, and interdependence as revealed through this system, she also provides details on the actual workings of the bank.

412. "Mrs. Japan: A profile." 1980. *Japan Pictorial* 3(1):1-7. No refs. ISSN:0388-6115.

KUMANO Michiyo serves as an example of a Japanese housewife, "a modern, middle-class housewife and mother who seems to know what she wants out of life."

413. SHAILER, Mary Jacinta. Jun. 1972. "The danchi wives and community building." *Japan Missionary Bulletin* 26(5):287-290. No refs. ISSN:0021-4531.

SHAILER briefly notes the isolation and loneliness of most *danchi* [public housing] women and calls for community organization with the aim of social service.

414. TAKAHASHI, Sachiko. 1986. "Weary wives—A glance into Japanese homes through 'Wives of a Kingdom' and 'Housewives Autumn'." *Ampo: Japan-Asia Quarterly Review* 18(2/3):65-69. No refs. LCCN:77-12830.

Provides insight into the frustrations and dilemmas of wives of *salariiman* [white collar employees], especially those living in company-owned housing. Uses as illustrations the books "Wives of a Kingdom" by KINOSHITA Ritsuko (a "social commentary" discussing the suppression of private life "for the sake of the company") and "Housewives Autumn" by SAITO Shigeo ("a piece of social reportage" discussing alcoholism among wives of company employees).

415. UENO, Chizuko. Apr./Jun. 1987. "Genesis of the urban housewife." *Japan Quarterly* 34(2):130-142. No refs. ISSN:0021-4590.

UENO traces the social position of common women (village or peasant wives) through their metamorphosis into urban housewives, discussing the role of *shufu* [female head of house] in agricultural areas, the custom of segregating young men and women by age in group homes in southwestern Japan, the traditionally high rate of divorce, the institution of patriarchal *ie* [family/household] concept for all levels of society during the Meiji period, and the "samurai-zation" of the family system. Within the modern time frame, she discusses the dual roles and burdens of working women and shows how some women are overcoming the social isolation of nuclear family housewives by their community participation and social activism.

416. VOGEL, Suzanne H. 1978. "The professional housewife." In: WHITE, Merry I. and Barbara MOLONY, eds. *Proceedings of the Tokyo Symposium on Women.* Tokyo: International Group for the Study of Women, pp. 150-155. (Tokyo Symposium on Women, [1st], 1978.) No refs.

VOGEL defines the job of the Japanese housewife as "a profession of mothering" and "a woman's lifetime employment." With these definitions firmly in place, she proceeds to caution American women about comparing women's status in the two countries, pointing out that the life-time commitment to family (women) or company (men) makes equal demands on each, that the autonomy and power of the Japanese housewife in her realm is greater than that of an American homemaker, and while totally dependent financially, the Japanese wife is not dependent on her husband emotionally.

417. VOGEL, Suzanne H. Winter 1978. "Professional housewife: The career of urban middle class Japanese women." *Japan Interpreter* 12(1):16-43. 19 notes. ISSN:0021-4450.

In this detailed study, VOGEL explains the segregation of roles in Japanese society and observes that the "Japanese housewife sees her place as the center of the family and her function as mothering" (i.e. nurturing). Describes training for this role, and the responsibilities and functions of the role during both the peak of the career (the child rearing years) and the retirement years. Also discusses ways in which the profession of housewife is changing. The article will assist Westerners in interpreting the role from a Japanese perspective.

418. "Yen and women" 17 Jun. 1989. *Economist* 311(7607):93. No refs. ISSN:0013-0613.

Briefly discusses investment strategies of Japanese women and notes new strategies of banks to attract their investment dollars.

Single Women

419. GOMI, Yuriko. Mar. 1939. "The home for mothers and children in need." *Japanese Women* 2(2):1-2. No refs. ISSN:0388-1369.

Describes group accommodation arrangements for single women (widows, divorcées, or abandoned women) and their dependents which provide low-cost housing and daycare to enable mothers to earn a living.

420. MATSUMOTO, Nancy. Oct. 1988. "Women who don't need men." *PHP Intersect* (Oct. 1988):42-43. No refs. ISSN:0910-4607.

Describes older women who are choosing independent lives rather than remaining with retired husbands or remarrying if a widow.

421. MURRAY, Geoffrey. Sep. 1976. "Marriage: Passport to an easy life?" *PHP* 7(9):35-44. No refs. ISSN:0030-798X.

A thoughtful representation of the views of KIRISHIMA Yōko, a journalist, writer, and "unwed" mother of three children. [Provides a useful background for #83.]

422. PERRY, Linda L. Jan./Apr. 1975. "Being socially anomalous: Wives and mothers without husbands." *Journal of Asian and African Studies* 10(1/2):32-41. 13 refs. ISSN:0021-9096. [Reprinted in PLATH, David, ed. *Adult Episodes in Japan.* Leiden: Brill, 1975, pp. 32-41. LCCN:76-362108.]

PERRY discusses how men are defined by their occupations and women by their spouses. If a woman's spousal link is broken, some women can retain their social position by renewing ties with fathers or relying on adult sons. If a woman is independent, her income level is probably quite low, as is her social status.

423. SATŌ, Yōko, *et al.* 1983. "Work and life of single women of the post-war generation." In: MURAMATSU, Yasuko. *Women and Work: Working Women and their Impact on Society.* Tokyo: International Group for the Study of Women, pp. 199-216. (Tokyo Symposium on Women, 2nd, 1983. *Proceedings*.) No refs. LCCN:84-187204.

Surveys "not yet married" (i.e. single) women born immediately after World War II to determine attitudes toward marriage and work. After comparing data to that of other countries in Asia and the West, the authors build a model of single women's attitudes toward work.

424. SHIOZAWA, Miyoko and Tomiko SHIMADA. 1976. "Documentary on postwar women living alone." *Japan Quarterly* 23(4):363-377. No refs. ISSN:0021-4590.

Presents the stories of three women who reached marriageable age during World War II and never married. Discusses the problems these women face as they reach retirement age. [Introduced by #88.]

425. SODEI, Takako and Michiko NAOI. 1978. "The life of Japanese divorcees and widows." IN: WHITE, Merry I. and Barbara MOLONY, eds. *Proceedings of the Tokyo Symposium on Women.* Tokyo: International Group for the Study of Women, pp. 184-188. (Tokyo Symposium on Women, [1st], 1978.) No refs.

Reports briefly on a survey of widows and divorcées. Provides statistics. [Conclusions more fully developed in #426.]

426. SODEI, Takako. 1985. "The fatherless family." *Japan Quarterly* 32(1):77-82. No refs. ISSN:0021-4590.

Discusses problems faced by widows or divorcées with respect to finances, household management, child rearing, and education of children.

427. YAMASHITA, Katsutoshi. Oct./Dec. 1986. "Divorce, Japanese style." *Japan Quarterly* 33(4):416-420. No refs. ISSN:0021-4590.

YAMASHITA describes the increase in the divorce rate and outlines reasons for the change. Also notes the increase in "non-divorce divorces" and "retirement divorces." He reports from a woman's perspective, having found most divorced men unwilling to discuss their experiences.

428. YOSHIHIRO, Kiyoko. Jul./Sep. 1987. "Interviews with unmarried women." *Japan Quarterly* 34(3):305-309. No refs. ISSN:0021-4590.

Briefly discusses the lives of women who remain single by choice: their desire for careers, social pressures to marry, and the position of single mothers.

Other

429. DOLAN, Jr., Edward F. and Shan FINNEY. 1983. *The New Japan.* New York: Franklin Watts. 118p. Bibl. Index. LCCN:83-6600.

In a chapter titled "Japan at Home: The Woman of the House," DOLAN provides a rather superficial and upbeat description of women, concluding that "she remains loyal to the ancient concept of the wife and mother as the heart of the home . . . a deeply rooted tradition, perhaps so deeply rooted as to be instinctual." The authors have written many works "for young people" but have no background on Japan.

430. DORE, R.P. 1958. *City Life in Japan: A Study of a Tokyo Ward.* Berkeley: University of California Press. 472p. Notes. LCCN:59-16060.

One of the basic anthropological studies on Japan. Focuses on a Tokyo neighborhood. While women are not discussed as a separate group at any length, the sections on family and spousal relations contain useful material on the status and role of city women in the early to mid-1950s.

431. FUSE, Akiko. Summer 1981. "Role structure of dual career families." *Journal of Comparative Family Studies* 12(3):329-336. 15 refs. ISSN:0047-2328.

In this examination of families of male and female primary school teachers, FUSE discusses the role of wives in relation to family decision making, to time management and task allocation, and to types of social interaction.

432. HASHIMOTO, Mitsuru. Oct. 1986. "*Ie*, the world women make: Toward an interpretive sociology." *Journal of Family History* 11(4):353-370. 3 refs. ISSN:0363-1990.

HASHIMOTO presents the stories of two women from a street in the shopping district of Kyoto. One "built a household in her own generation" and has passed it on to her children; the other married into an old family with a wealth of tradition to learn. Covering approximately 40 years, provides details on the role of women in business (in this case pickles and catering) pre-War, during the War, and since World War II.

433. HILGER, M. Inez. 1971. *Together with the Ainu: A Vanishing People.* Norman: University of Oklahoma Press. 223p. Bibl. Index. LCCN:70-145504.

A study of the "remnant of Ainu culture in a matrix of Japanese culture." Includes sections on husband-wife relationships, tattooing of women, and childbirth.

434. KIMURA, Shosaburō. May 1978. "Married women: Weak link in Japan's family." *PHP* 9(5):57-72. No refs. ISSN:0030-798X.

KIMURA castigates women who no longer "work silently" but talk and criticize, or "s-mother" their children.

435. KINOSHITA, Kameki. Nov. 1962. "Girl's day in folk art." *Oriental Economist* 30(625):650-651. No refs. ISSN:0030-5294.

Introduces the types of dolls displayed on Girl's Day (on or around 3 March).

436. KUMAGAI, Fumie. Feb. 1984. "The life cycle of the Japanese family." *Journal of Marriage and the Family* 46(1):191-204. 30 refs. ISSN:0022-2445.

Documents the changing Japanese family, noting especially later marriage, early and short periods of childbearing, and an extended post-parental period. Provides comparative data for the United States and Canada, and discusses the impact of the above changes on the lives of women.

437. LEBRA, Takie Sugiyama. Oct. 1979. "The dilemma and strategies of aging among contemporary Japanese women." *Ethnology* 18(4):337-353. 14 refs. & 8 notes. ISSN:0014-1828.

LEBRA analyzes aging strategies through her continuing focus on autonomy and reciprocal dependence [see #411]. Because of changes in family structure, elderly women now strive for independence through economic independence and mental and physical health. They also work toward bonds involving intra- and extra-domestic interdependence.

438. NAOI, Michiko. 1980. "Report on elderly women." [Translated by Roslyn HAYMAN.] *Feminist International* no.2:23-26. No refs. ISSN:0388-371X.

A short but in-depth summary of the status of elderly women, covering economic, physical and psychological problems, and the impact of changing family structure on the care of the elderly.

439. VOGEL, Ezra F. 1971. *Japan's New Middle Class: The Salary Man and his Family in a Tokyo Suburb.* Berkeley: University of California Press. 299p. Bibl. Index. LCCN:63-21263.

In this classic work documenting the rise of the *salariiman* [white collar employees], VOGEL includes wives and mothers in most of his work, focusing in particular on the mother's role in preparing future *salariiman* [white collar employees] for school entrance exams, the wife's interactions in the home community, the structure of the family (mother and children vs. father), division of labor in the home (including a housewife's typical daily schedule), roles of women within the household, and child rearing.

440. YAGI, Kimiko. Spring 1983. "Forming new role relationships in the family." *Japan Christian Quarterly* 49(2):79-81. No refs. ISSN:0021-4360.

Calls for more equal relationships within the family and recommends equal education for women as the vehicle. [Introduced by #390.]

441. YANAGIDA, Kunio. 1957. *Japanese Manners and Customs in the Meiji Era.* [Translated by Charles S. TERRY.] Tokyo: Ōbunsha. 335p. (*A Cultural History of the Meiji Era (1868-1912)*, Vol. 4). No refs. Index. LCCN:59-8764.

YANAGIDA's chapter on the life of women discusses women and work, women's education, childbirth, and changes in village marriage customs (e.g. from the practice of young women living in associations separate from their parents and with relative freedom to choose mates, to the more often discussed arranged match and subsequent debased daughter-in-law role). Descriptive and general rather than analytical.

3

Health

Anthropometry and Body Mechanics

442. KŌHARA, Yukinari. Dec. 1972. "Motor performance and strength of the woman diver (Ama)." *Journal of Human Ergology* 1(2):157-165. 15 refs. ISSN:0300-8134.

Using 1958 data, KŌHARA compares *ama* [women divers] and farm women for agility and strength.

443. NISHIMURA, Kunio. 10 Sep. 1985. "The female figure." *Look Japan* (10 Sep. 1985):28. No refs. ISSN:0456-5339.

A very brief report concerning changes in women's measurements, noting a trend toward a "cylindrical shape."

444. RAHN, Hermann. 1965. "The physiological stresses of the ama." In: RAHN, Hermann and Tetsurō YOKOYAMA, eds. *Physiology of Breath-hold Diving and the Ama of Japan.* Washington, D.C.: National Academy of Sciences, National Research Council. *Publication* 1341, pp. 113-137. 16 refs. LCCN:65-62909.

An introductory overview of the working conditions of the *ama* [women divers] and the physiological changes their bodies undergo.

445. RAHN, Hermann and Tetsurō YOKOYAMA, eds. 1965. *Physiology of Breath-hold Diving and the Ama of Japan.* Washington, D.C.: National Academy of Sciences, National Research Council. *Publication* 1341. 369p. Refs. LCCN:65-62909.

Proceedings of a conference covering both general physiology and specific studies (e.g. mechanics of chest wall, body fluid volumes). [For annotations of individual papers, see #444, #447, #472, #794, #796 and #801.]

446. TAKAHASHI, Eiji. Apr. 1986. "Secular trend of female body shape in Japan." *Human Biology* 58(2):293-301. 9 refs. ISSN:0018-7143.

Uses Röhrer's Index to determine that the body shape of 18-year-old female junior college students in Sendai has become slimmer since the 1950s. Nutritional and activity pattern influences are discussed.

447. TATAI, Kichinosuke and Kyōko TATAI. 1965. "Anthropometric studies on the Japanese ama." In: RAHN, Hermann and Tetsurō YOKOYAMA, eds. *Physiology of Breath-hold Diving* *and the Ama of Japan.* Washington, D.C.: National Academy of Sciences, National Research Council. *Publication* 1341, pp. 71-83. 17 refs. LCCN:65-62909.

Surveys anthropometric studies taken since 1929 which compare data on *ama* [women divers] to other sectors of the population, and notes trends in change of body size in both.

Fertility

448. HANLEY, Susan B. and Kōzō YAMAMURA. 1977. *Economic and Demographic Change in Preindustrial Japan, 1600-1868.* Princeton: Princeton University Press. 410p. Bibl. Index. LCCN:77-71983.

HANLEY and YAMAMURA disagree with the standard Marxist interpretation "that during the last century and a half of the Tokugawa period the economy failed to grow." They argue instead that the economy grew during this period and that "population growth was controlled by a variety of methods [e.g. late marriage, abortion, infanticide, restricting marriage to the successor of the family] . . . the major reason . . . [being] . . . to enjoy a rising standard of living." They discuss population control at length in Chapter 9.

449. HANLEY, Susan B. 1979. "The Japanese fertility decline in historical perspective." In: CHO, Lee-Jay and Kazumasa KOBAYASHI, eds. *Fertility Transition of the East Asian Populations.* Honolulu: University of Hawaii Press, pp. 24-48. (*Monographs of the Center for Southeast Asian Studies, Kyoto University; English Language Series*, no.13.) 11 notes & 31 refs. LCCN:78-27219.

Argues that "completed families" before 1869 more "resembled their modern counterparts in size than those at the turn of the century . . . [which were] . . . unusual in the past few hundred years." Includes charts on birth and death rates, average age at first marriage for women, and typical life cycle of Japanese women. Also discusses methods of population control in villages during the Tokugawa era.

450. HAYAMI, Akira. 1985. "Rural migration and fertility in Tokugawa Japan: The village of Nishijo, 1773-1868." [Translated by Susan B. HANLEY and Laurel CORNELL.] In: HANLEY, Susan B. and Arthur P. WOLF, eds. *Family and Population in East Asian History.* Stanford: Stanford University Press, pp. 110-132. Notes. LCCN:83-40283.

With a focus on *dekasegi* ["leaving home to work"], HAYAMI provides figures on villagers who migrated to and from the village of Nishijo by sex, age, landholding status, and destination, with women leaving more often than men primarily because of the textile industry. He then goes on to analyze the influence of *dekasegi* on fertility and to compare fertility figures with those of other small towns in the same area.

451. "Japan: 7 in 10 married women want no more children; fertility falls." Jan./Feb. 1980. *Family Planning Perspectives* 12(1):52-53. 1 ref. ISSN:0014-7354.

Report on the results of the 1974 Japan Fertility Survey. In addition to discussing the numbers of women wishing no more children (by age and current family status), the article also presents figures on contraceptive use.

452. MORGAN, S. Philip, Ronald R. RINDFUSS, and Allan PARNELL. Mar. 1984. "Modern fertility patterns: Contrasts between the United States and Japan." *Population and Development Review* 10(1):19-40. 52 refs. ISSN:0098-7921.

Contrasts fertility patterns in the United States and Japan, explaining that Japan's patterns are based on "features of the Japanese economy and prevailing family structure and sex roles."

453. MOSK, Carl. 1983. *Patriarchy and Fertility: Japan and Sweden, 1880-1960.* New York: Academic Press. 320p. Bibl. Index. LCCN:82-4064.

Provides a study of the "economy and demography of the household within . . . [the] . . . patriarchal stem family system, and the implications of these two household factors for the long-term evolution of fertility." A brief section on marriage and the status of women in Japan is included. Quite technical, but basic for those interested in fertility studies.

Family Planning and Childbirth

454. COLEMAN, Samuel. Jan. 1981. "The cultural context of condom use in Japan." *Studies in Family Planning* 12(1):28-39. 42 notes. ISSN:0039-3665.

Examines social factors which may contribute to a very high rate of condom use (75.9%) among "contracepting married women." The effect of women's roles and status, as well as the "intensely private" nature of contraception for Japanese, are discussed. Also described is the role that door-to-door selling of condoms by older married women may play in this use rate.

455. COLEMAN, Samuel. 1983. *Family Planning in Japanese Society: Traditional Birth Control in a Modern Urban Culture.* Princeton: Princeton University Press. 261p. Bibl. Index. LCCN:83-42552.

A detailed study of family planning focusing on abortion and contraception, and the ways in which birth control methods are selected. Includes case studies of four couples and examples of anti-abortion cartoons.

456. FRANZ, Margaret-Mary and Motoko CHIBA. Jan./Feb. 1980. "Abortion, contraception, and motherhood in post-war Japan and the United States." *International Journal of Women's Studies* 3(1):66-75. 45 notes. ISSN:0703-8240.

Although sharing a goal of low birth rates, Japan and the United States have reached it by markedly different methods. FRANZ and CHIBA compare abortion practices and attitudes, and patterns of contraceptive use.

457. FUKASAKU, Mitsusada. Autumn 1975. "Psychology of infanticide." *Japan Interpreter* 10(2):205-208. No refs. ISSN:0021-4450.

Discusses the case of an Osaka woman who killed her third, fourth, fifth and sixth children in the early 1970s. Compares this current case with historical traditions and speculates on its causes.

458. KAKU, Kanae. 1975. "Were girl babies sacrificed to a folk superstition in 1966 in Japan?" *Annals of Human Biology* 2(4):391-393. 6 refs. ISSN:0301-4460.

Traditionally, girls born in the *hinoe-uma* [Fire-horse Year] were believed to be ill-fated and female infanticide was practiced. Because of the availability of birth control and abortion, it was expected that mortality rates for baby girls would not rise in 1966 (the most recent *hinoe-uma*). However, KAKU found that the "early neonatal mortality rates of accidents and violence for baby girls was indeed higher than other years and higher than for baby boys in 1966."

459. KATŌ, Shidzue. Oct. 1984. *A Fight for Women's Happiness: Pioneering the Family Planning Movement in Japan.* [Edited by Julie C. MacKENZIE.] Tokyo: Japanese Organization for International Cooperation in Family Planning. 121p. (*JOICFP Documentation Series* 11.) No refs. LCCN:85-244383.

After summarizing her early life and marriage to Baron ISHIMOTO, KATŌ focuses on her efforts to establish a birth control movement in Japan and her activities in the Japanese women's movement. Written when the author was 88.

460. McCOOEY, Christopher. Jul. 1985. "Abortion: Last resort, first choice." *PHP Intersect* (Jul. 1985):8-11,40. No refs. ISSN:0910-4607.

Reports on the use of abortion as a birth control measure, and provides statistics.

461. MURAMATSU, Minoru and Jean van der TAK. 1978. "From abortion to contraception—The Japanese experience." In: DAVID, Henry P., *et al*, eds. *Abortion in Psychosocial Perspective: Trends in Transnational Research.* New York: Springer, pp. 145-167. Bibl. LCCN:78-7784.

Documents the change from the use of abortion to limit family size to the use of contraceptives (primarily condoms) and sterilization. Includes statistics on the number of women with abortion experience and a brief description of condom marketing aimed at the female consumer.

462. NAGANO, Yoshiko. Summer 1973. "Women fight for control: Abortion struggle in Japan." *Ampo: Japan-Asia Quarterly Review* no. 17:14-20. No refs. LCCN:77-612830. Also published in *Japanese Women Speak Out* (#1180), pp. 85-90.

Reports on governmental attempts to change the Eugenics Protection Law by eliminating the economic hardship clause permitting abortion, increasing the number of abortions in cases of possible handicapped fetuses, and implementing counseling to lower the childbearing age. An appendix, "Where is the Pill?," discusses the nonavailability of the Pill to Japanese women for birth control purposes.

463. PATON, Tom. Spring 1974. "The unwanted pregnancy in Japan." *Japan Christian Quarterly* 40(2):93-101. 1 note. ISSN:0021-4361.

Discusses options for both early and late pregnancies and explains the Japanese cultural context for problems with adoption, foster care, and illegitimacy. Also provides a list of social service agencies with addresses and phone numbers.

464. POMMERENKE, Millicent. 1958. *Asian Women and Eros.* New York: Vantage. 337p. Bibl. LCCN:58-10182.

In 1954 the author accompanied her physician husband on a tour of India and Japan designed "to introduce certain Western concepts of obstetrics and gynecology . . . in an effort to help these countries cope with their population problems." Presents her concerns about the status of women and the problems of legalized abortion as a birth control method but reveals a fair amount of cultural bias.

465. POMPE VAN MEERDERVOORT, J.L.C. 1970. *Doctor on Desima.* [Translated by Elizabeth P. WITTERMANS and John Z. BOWERS.] Tokyo: Sophia University. 144p. Notes. Index. LCCN:72-116597. [*Vijf jaren in Japan.* English. Selections.]

A translation of selections from POMPE VAN MEERDERVOORT's *Vijf Jaren in Japan*, written while stationed on the trading island of Deshima from 1857-1863. The editors have included his comments on the childbirth practices he was able to observe in his position as a Dutch naval surgeon.

466. STANDLEE, Mary W. 1959. *The Great Pulse: Japanese Midwifery and Obstetrics through the Ages.* Rutland, VT: Tuttle. 192p. Notes. Index. LCCN:59-5994.

A compilation of "birth customs" beginning with mythical times and continuing through the Occupation. Describes current practices stressing midwives' roles and techniques, with an emphasis on natural childbirth.

467. TANABE, Seiko. Jul. 1985. "Let's get some things straight." [Translated by Geraldine HARCOURT.] *PHP Intersect* (Jul. 1985):41. No refs. ISSN:0910-4607.

In this translation of a 1982 article, TANABE (popular novelist and social critic) speaks out against proposed revisions to the Eugenic Protection Law which details conditions under which abortions are permitted.

468. UCHIDA, Yasuo. Feb. 1978. "Aspects of family planning in Japan." *Feminist Japan* no. 4:25-27. [Also cited as 1(4).] 4 refs. ISSN:0388-197X.

Briefly summarizes the birth control options available to women, provides statistics on birth rates and abortions, and notes the amount of male dominance in the most widely used prevention methods: condoms and the rhythm method.

469. YOSHIOKA, Yayoi. 1928. "The prevention of infant mortality in Japan today." In: *Women of the Pacific.* Honolulu: Pan Pacific Union, pp. 117-119. (Pan-Pacific Women's Conference, 1st, Honolulu, 9-19 August 1928.) No refs.

A female physician describes protective legislation designed to lower maternal and infant mortality (i.e. Factory Laws of 1922 and the Health Insurance Act) and provides a table listing organizations undertaking health education work.

Illness and Disease

470. FUKAZAWA, Michiko. Jan. 1977. "A child of wealth and growth: A case of *anorexia nervosa* in Japan." *Transactional Analysis Journal* 7(1):73-76. No refs. ISSN:0362-1537.

A case study of a 64-pound, 23-year-old woman who faced high expectations from her father. A short report.

471. FUKUDA, Kazuhiko, *et al.* 1980. "Hysteria and urbanization." *Folia Psychiatrica et Neurologica Japonica* 34(4):413-418. 9 refs. ISSN:0015-5721.

The authors suggest that "a loss of traditional sociocultural ties in the urbanizing process . . . [might] . . . increase the risk of hysteria [among women]."

472. HARASHIMA, Susumu and Shigeno IWASAKI. 1965. "Occupational diseases of the ama." In: RAHN, Hermann and Tetsurō YOKOYAMA, eds. *Physiology of Breath-hold Diving and the Ama of Japan.* Washington, D.C.: National Academy of Sciences, National Research Council. *Publication* 1341, pp. 85-98. 7 notes. LCCN:65-62909.

Surveys various diseases to which *ama* [women divers] are susceptible, as well as work habits following childbirth and causes of death.

473. LOCK, Margaret. 1987. "Protests of a good wife and wise mother: The medicalization of distress in Japan." In: NORBECK, Edward and Margaret LOCK, eds. *Health, Illness and Medical Care in Japan.* Honolulu: University of Hawaii Press, pp. 130-157. 71 refs. LCCN:87-10753.

LOCK describes both the "somatization of distress," especially in women and in children's illnesses blamed on their mothers. She sets these illnesses in an overall context of social change and notes that with the "medicalization of private distress and suffering . . . [comes] . . . public knowledge and . . . scrutiny," ultimately resulting in a change in status for women.

474. MUKAI, Takayo. 1989. "A call for our language: Anorexia from within." *Women's Studies International Forum* 12(6):613-638. Bibl. ISSN:0277-5395.

A detailed account of one woman's personal history and experience with anorexia. Includes childhood memories, descriptions of her attraction to anorexia, poetry describing her feelings and the details of her spontaneous recovery.

475. NOJIRI, Yoriko. Jun. 1975. "Women's occupational diseases." In: *Japanese Women Speak Out.* Tokyo: White Paper on Sexism—Japan Task Force, pp. 14-16. No refs.

A brief, non-medical discussion of "inflammation of the tendon sheath and cervical syndrome" common to telephone operators, cashiers, key-punchers, and typists; includes three brief case histories and notes problems in determining illness etiology given women's brief employment histories.

476. SONODA, Kyōichi. 1988. *Health and Illness in Changing Japanese Society.* Tokyo: University of Tokyo Press. 170p. Bibl. Index.

Includes material on smoking habits among female nursing students as well as a brief and general discussion on working women and the family.

477. TONAI, Shūji, *et al.* Dec. 1989. "Illness behavior of housewives in a rural area in Japan: A health diary study." *Culture, Medicine and Psychiatry* 13(4):405-417. 18 refs. ISSN:0165-005X.

Health diaries were used with 28 housewives in rural Japan to study incidence of illness over a four week period as well as strategies of care, *e.g.,* consulting a physician, consulting an acupuncturist, administering self-care (lying down and self-medication with household drugs or folk medicine).

478. YOSHIOKA, Yayoi. 1928. "Health work for women in industry in Japan." In: *Women of the Pacific.* Honolulu: Pan-Pacific Union, pp. 147-151. (Pan-Pacific Women's Conference, 1st, Honolulu, 9-19 August 1928.) Refs.

Provides statistics on the health status of female textile workers for the early 1920s, and calls for an effort to end tuberculosis among them, especially by shortening work hours and improving dormitory conditions.

Menopause

479. LOCK, Margaret. Mar. 1986. "Ambiguities of aging: Japanese experience and perceptions of menopause." *Culture, Medicine, and Psychiatry* 10(1):23-46. 44 refs. ISSN:0165-005X.

LOCK investigated attitudes toward, and experiences of, menopause among 1283 Japanese women from various occupations and income levels. She reports overall acceptance of menopause as part of the life cycle and low symptomology. Three case studies are included.

480. LOCK, Margaret. Dec. 1987. "The selfish housewife and menopausal syndrome in Japan." *Working Paper [on Women in International Development]* no. 154. 15p. 52 refs. ISSN:0888-5354.

LOCK reviews the Japanese discussion concerning the ideal woman and the appropriate role of the housewife as seen in *nihonjinron* ["essays on being Japanese"]. She notes contradictions caused by insistence on total commitment to family members (spouse and children) who are absent most of the time. She focuses particularly on menopausal syndrome and its use as an indicator of the ills associated with the growth of individualism and its concurrent problems of self-interest and lack of self-discipline.

481. LOCK, Margaret. Feb. 1988. "New Japanese mythologies: Faltering discipline and the ailing housewife." *American Ethnologist* 15(1):43-61. 79 refs. ISSN:0094-0496.

In her continuing work on menopause in Japan, LOCK discusses attempts by Japanese physicians to "medicalize" menopause. She also describes the growing number of syndromes (e.g. kitchen syndrome, apartment neurosis, and school-refusal syndrome) defined and attributed to changes in Japanese family structure and especially the role of women.

482. ROSENBERGER, Nancy. 1986. "Menopause as a symbol of anomaly: The case of Japanese women." In: OLESEN, Virginia L. and Nancy Fugate WOODS, eds. *Culture, Society and Menstruation.* Washington, D.C.: Hemisphere Publishing Corporation, pp. 15-24. 2 refs. LCCN:86-3066.

ROSENBERGER has done extensive questionnaire work on attitudes of Japanese men and women toward menopause, a traditional symbol of transition and anomaly. She presents these findings and also discusses the approaches of physicians and Chinese practitioners to the problems.

483. ROSENBERGER, Nancy R. 1987. "Productivity, sexuality, and ideologies of menopausal problems in Japan." In: NORBECK, Edward and Margaret LOCK, eds. *Health, Illness and Medical Care in Japan.* Honolulu: University of Hawaii Press, pp. 158-188. 27 refs. LCCN:87-10753.

ROSENBERGER explores attitudes of women in rural areas, provincial cities, and Tokyo toward menopause and examines ways in which women use menopausal symptoms as a reinforcement of their importance within family structures or as a period of transition toward activities for self-fulfillment.

Sex and Sexual Attitudes

484. IWAWAKI, Saburō and H.J. EYSENCK. Mar. 1978. "Sexual attitudes among British and Japanese students." *Journal of Psychology* 98(2):289-298. 5 refs. ISSN:0022-3980.

IWAWAKI and EYSENCK conclude that female Japanese students rarely think about sex and have little knowledge of "sexual problems" (as of the mid-1970s).

485. LEVY, Howard S. 1971. *Sex, Love and the Japanese.* Washington, D.C.: Warm-Soft Village Press, 91p. Notes. LCCN:76-159291.

LEVY provides information on physical changes in the Japanese woman, Japanese versus Western sexual practices, sexual attitudes and practices historically, and prostitution. Included are excerpts from six Japanese magazine articles dealing with sexual matters.

486. "Sexual behavior in Japan: Girls outperform boys." Summer 1983. *Journal of Popular Culture* 17(1):135-136. No refs. ISSN:0022-3840.

Reports on a survey by the Japan Society on Sex Education showing that high school and college age Japanese girls are more sexually active than boys. Includes comments by OCHIAI Keiko, SUGAWARA Mariko, MITSU Moriko and MIYA Yoshiko.

Suicide

487. BRYANT, Taimie L. Spring 1990. "*Oya-ko shinjū*: Death at the center of the heart." *UCLA Pacific Basin Law Journal* 8(1):1-31. 92 notes. ISSN:0884-0768.

A solid analysis of the concepts of *oya-ko shinjū* [parent-child suicide], *kogoroshi* [infanticide] and *haha-ko shinjū* ["mother-child"/"center of the heart" (death)]. BRYANT examines the legal status of those committing *oya-ko shinjū*, discusses two case studies of mothers killing their children but not committing suicide successfully, and two cases of paternal infanticide.

488. CECCHINI, R. M. May 1975. "Modern society and Japanese women." *Japan Missionary Bulletin* 29(4):207-214. 6 refs. ISSN:0021-4531.

CECCHINI analyzes suicide data for women (1947-1973) and speculates that many of the deaths are attributable to the transition to a "matriarchal nuclear family" which is solely dependent on a male provider, and to the difficulties of women who face family crises of divorce, accident, or death of that provider.

489. CECCHINI, Rose Marie. 1976. "Women and suicide." In: LEBRA, Joyce, *et al. Women in Changing Japan*. Stanford: Stanford University Press, pp. 263-296. 26 notes. LCCN:75-33663.

A thorough study of suicide providing statistics and an analysis of the causal effects of role conflict among Japanese women. Also provides data from "suicidal thought survivors."

490. HEADLEY, Lee A. 1983. "Japan. Part II. Inochi no denwa." In: HEADLEY, Lee A., ed. *Suicide in Asia and the Near East*. Berkeley: University of California Press, pp.45-58. No refs. LCCN:82-45913.

As an appendix to #496, HEADLEY includes statistics on calls concerning suicide to a lifeline telephone service, "Inochi no denwa," from 1975-1979.   Statistics are broken down by gender.

491. HIGUCHI, Chiyoko. Feb. 1972. "The price of loving: The path to double suicide." *East* 8(2):24-29. No refs. ISSN:0012-8295.

HIGUCHI tells the stories of two 17th-century couples who "broke the rules in their loves." The episodes are taken from IHARA Saikaku's *Five Women Who Loved Love*.

492. IGA, Mamoru, Joe YAMAMOTO, and Thomas NOGUCHI. Winter 1975. "Vulnerability of young Japanese women and suicide." *Suicide* 5(4):207-222. 14 refs. ISSN:0360-1390.

Determines role conflict and vulnerability of personality as the main causes of extremely high rates of suicide among young Japanese women. Compares rates of Tokyo and Kyoto-Osaka women, and provides psychological and historical contexts for their conclusions.

493. IGA, Mamoru. 1986. *The Thorn in the Chrysanthemum: Suicide and Economic Success in Modern Japan*. Berkeley: University of California Press. 231p. Notes. Index. LCCN:85-24504.

In his chapter on female suicides, IGA describes personality characteristics of suicide attempters (i.e. impetuous, ostentatious, explosive, compulsive), "precipitating causes" (i.e. illness and physical defects, family problems, marital problems and affairs), and discusses in detail the cultural contexts of sexual prejudice, financial insecurity, role conflict and ethnic prejudice. Other references to women occur throughout the work.

494. "The Japanese woman's tragic option." Jul. 1976. *Human Behavior* 5(7):73. No refs. ISSN:0046-8134.

Within an ongoing column titled "Death," a commentary suggests several reasons for "excessive suicide statistics" for Japanese women compared with those of other countries: conflicts between old and new ways, and lack of success in marriage or failure to marry.

495. KAWANISHI, Yūko. Spring 1990. "Japanese mother-child suicide: The psychological and sociological implications of the *Kimura* case." *UCLA Pacific Basin Law Journal* 8(1):32-46. 48 notes. ISSN:0884-0768.

KAWANISHI summarizes research on the concept of the mother-child relationship (which includes the Japanese idea of a mother's ego extending to include those of her children) and discusses the nature of suicide as a "culturally established method of communication" in Japan in order to provide context for the understanding of a Japanese woman's attempt to drown herself and her children in Los Angeles in 1985. Although the incident occurred outside Japan, the bulk of the text refers to the phenomenon when it occurs in Japan.

496. TATAI, Kichinosuke. 1983. "Japan. Part I." In: HEADLEY, Lee A. *Suicide in Asia and the Near East.* Berkeley: University of California Press, pp. 12-45. 28 refs. LCCN:82-45913.

While not focusing on women in particular, TATAI provides a summary article bringing together "all the material on suicide in Japan presently available," including many statistics detailing women's attempted and successful suicides.

Other

497. "Life expectancy of Japanese women now longer than 80 years." Oct. 1985. *East* 21(5):30. No refs. ISSN:0012-8295.

A very brief note marking the change in life expectancy. Also mentions the need for Japanese society to prepare for an octogenarian society.

498. NAKANO, Keiko. Oct. 1990. "Type A behavior, hardiness and psychological well-being in Japanese women." *Psychological Reports* 67(2):367-370. 15 refs. ISSN:0033-2941.

NAKANO provides a brief, technical report on reactions to "hassles" (not specified) by 107 college women, including both Type A and non-Type A women.

499. SEGAWA, Kiyoko. 1963. "Menstrual taboos imposed upon women." In: DORSON, Richard M., ed. *Studies in Japanese Folklore.* Bloomington: Indiana University Press, pp. 239-250. (*Indiana University Folklore Series*, no. 17). Notes. LCCN:63-62500.

Describes menstrual taboos, focusing on the use of special huts or isolated rooms and on cleansing rituals. Brief mention is also made of celebrations surrounding first menstruation of girls.

4

Religion and Spirituality

Buddhism and Shinto

500. AOYAMA, Hiroshi. Nov./Dec. 1970. "In the beginning: The birth of the Japanese gods." *East* 6(6):14-27. No refs. ISSN:0012-8295.

A summary of the Japanese creation myth, designed for the general reader. Includes section on Amaterasu, the sun goddess and "the direct ancestor of the Imperial Family."

501. BLACKER, Carmen. 1975. *The Catalpa Bow: A Study of Shamanistic Practices in Japan.* London: Allen and Unwin. 376p. Bibl. Index. LCCN:76-353814.

BLACKER reports in depth on shamans, men and women who believe(d) themselves capable of communicating with supernatural inhabitants of "the other world," and of healing and clairvoyance. Chapter 6 focuses on the historical shamans beginning with the Shinto *miko* ["powerful sacral woman"] and Chapter 7 discusses current shamanic mediums, including *kyōso* [founders of new religious sects]. Other references to women occur throughout the text.

502. BROOKS, Anne Page. 1981. "*Mizuko kuyō* and Japanese Buddhism." *Japanese Journal of Religious Studies* 8(3-4):119-147. 45 refs. ISSN:0304-1042.

BROOKS defines the practice of *mizuko kuyō* [services for aborted, miscarried, or stillborn children] within the Japanese Buddhist tradition. Describes the historical context, its contemporary popularity, and Buddhist views on abortion.

503. CECCHINI, Rose Marie. Feb. 1970. "Dialogue with a Buddhist nun on life after death." *Japan Missionary Bulletin* 24(1):44-48. No refs. ISSN:0021-4531.

CECCHINI (a Catholic nun) reminisces very briefly on her interaction with a Buddhist nun from Kawaragahama Temple and shares the nun's comments on death. The bulk of the article discusses CECCHINI's theological preparations for the next interview with the nun.

504. CHERRY, Kittredge. Jul. 1985. "Seeking sexual balance as the gods intended." *PHP Intersect* (Jul. 1985):44-45. No refs. ISSN:0910-4607.

Describes the work of Aiko CARTER [see Author/Translator/Editor Index] and others to re-establish sexual equality in Christianity and Buddhism, as well as to infuse more spirituality into the feminist movement.

505. DAVIS, Winston. 1980. *Dojo: Magic and Exorcism in Modern Japan.* Stanford: Stanford University Press. 332p. Notes. Index. LCCN:79-64219.

In his study of Sūkyō Mahikari [True-Light Supra-Religious Organization], one of the Japanese "new religions," DAVIS devotes a chapter to the spiritual experiences of women. He describes the physical, psychological, and/or spiritual ailments of eight women and the exorcism practiced on each.

506. ELLWOOD, Robert S. Aug. 1967. "The Saigū: Princess and priestess." *History of Religions* 7(1):35-60. 34 notes. ISSN:0018-2710.

A thorough study of the office of Virgin Priestess at the Grand Shrine of Ise, which traces its history through its demise in the 14th century. ELLWOOD bases his descriptions on an ancient text, the *Engishiki*, a "bureaucratic manual of Heian times," and quotes from it heavily.

507. FUJIKAWA, Asako. 1964. *Daughter of Shinran.* Tokyo: Hokuseido. 60p. Bibl. LCCN:68-130472.

A biography of Kakushin-ni (1224-1283), the youngest daughter of the founder of the Shin sect of Buddhism. She was considered "'Patron Mother' of [Jodo] Shinshu and . . . was virtually responsible for the founding of Honganji, the head temple of Shinshu at Kyoto."

508. FUJITA, Taki. Jul. 1939. "The spiritual life of Japanese women." *Japanese Women* 2(4):1-2. No refs. ISSN:0388-1369.

FUJITA describes the traits of Japanese women of the 1930s: piety, patriotism, self-sacrifice, dedication to children, and love of nature. Any Westernization is totally superficial, and "our spiritual, moral and philosophical traditions . . . developed since the dawn of our race still continue to be guiding principles of Japanese women of to-day."

509. GROSJEAN, Yasuko Morihara. Sep. 1988. "From Confucius to feminism: The Japanese woman's quest for meaning." *Ultimate Reality and Meaning* 11:166-182. 16 refs. ISSN:0709-549X.

Provides both a historical and current prospective on women's potential for reflection on, or direction of, life meaning and self-fulfillment. GROSJEAN explores how the Confucian concept of family prohibited women from developing a self-concept and lists four areas in which women must make major efforts: a) family (old traditions strong despite new laws, b) work (possibility of fulfillment through careers), c) language (developing new gender-equal vocabulary), and d) communication (in relationships and the mass media). She explores the shortcomings of Buddhism and Shinto for assistance on this quest for self-meaning and discusses how experience with western culture and/or Christianity has assisted Japanese feminists.

510. GUTHRIE, Stewart. 1988. *A Japanese New Religion: Risshō Kōsei-kai in a Mountain Hamlet.* Ann Arbor: University of Michigan, Center for Japanese Studies. 245p. (*Michigan Monograph Series in Japanese Studies*, no. 1) Bibl. Index. LCCN:86-33446.

In the chapter, "Six Members and an Interpretation," GUTHRIE presents short profiles of three female members of Risshō Kōsei-kai, a Nichiren movement in an unidentified farming village on Honshu.

511. HARDACRE, Helen. Sep. 1979. "Sex-role norms and values in Reiyūkai." *Japanese Journal of Religious Studies* 6(3):445-460. 4 refs. ISSN:0304-1042.

Reiyūkai, one of Japan's "new religions" (founded 1925), takes a conservative stance on the role of women and actively discourages the working of women anywhere but in the home. HARDACRE explores the mechanisms the Society uses to convince members of the appropriateness of this stance and the techniques adopted to enforce compliance.

512. HARDACRE, Helen. Jun./Sep. 1983. "The cave and the womb world." *Japanese Journal of Religious Studies* 10(2/3):149-176. 12 refs. ISSN:0304-1042.

HARDACRE describes the ritual ascent of the Oku-no-In peak of the Ōmine-san Shugendō site in Nara prefecture and argues that the rite has different meanings for men and women; i.e. that for women the experience of climbing through a cave symbolizing a womb is a "return to the source" that men cannot experience. She provides historical context for, and a psychological analysis of, the ritual. [Introduced by #529.]

513. HARDACRE, Helen. 1984. *Lay Buddhism in Contemporary Japan: Reiyūkai Kyōdan*. Princeton: Princeton University Press. 267p. Bibl. Index. LCCN:83-43075.

In Chapter 6 of her study of Reiyūkai Kyōdan [Society of Friends of the Spirits], HARDACRE discusses the role of women in the Society and considers the effect of the religion on their role within the family.

514. HARDACRE, Helen. 1986. *Kurozumikyō and the New Religions of Japan*. Princeton: Princeton University Press. 212p. Bibl. Index. LCCN:85-43287.

In a study of Kurozumikyō, one of the Shinto "new religions" founded in 1814, HARDACRE briefly surveys women's roles within the organization. She attributes the success of the active branch churches to the presence of female ministers who serve as counselors, and notes the involvement of lay women in projects of the churches.

515. HOPKINSON, Deborah. Winter, Spring and Summer 1979. "Women and Kamakura Buddhism: Dōgen's 'Raihai Tokuzui.'" *Kahawai: Journal of Women and Zen* 1(1):6-10, 1(2):9-10, 1(3):3-4. No refs. ISSN:0737-8335.

Describes the life of DŌGEN Zenji (1200-1253), a Zen Buddhist monk who accepted women students from 1233-1242. Parts two and three include HOPKINSON's translation of "Raihai Tokuzui," a chapter in his *Shōbōgenzō* which reveals his egalitarian attitudes toward women.

516. HOSHINO, Eiki and Dōshō TAKEDA. 1987. "Indebtedness and comfort: The undercurrents of *mizuko kuyō* in contemporary Japan." [Translated by Paul L. SWANSON.] *Japanese Journal of Religious Studies* 14(4):305-320. 14 refs. ISSN:0304-1042.

Explores the appeal of *mizuko kuyō* [Buddhist services for aborted, miscarried or stillborn children] and compares the occurrence of, and attitudes toward, abortion and infanticide in contemporary and Edo ("traditional") Japan. Explains how *mizuko kuyō* fits the "pattern of contemporary religious activity," and includes statistics.

517. IGETA, Midori. Jun./Sep. 1983. "The image of woman in sermons—Anju in 'Sanshō Dayū.'" [Translated by W. Michael KELSEY.] *Japanese Journal of Religious Studies* 10(2/3):247-272. 8 refs. ISSN:0304-1042.

IGETA discusses the psychological aspects of the use of heroines in traditional religious literature by analyzing the story of Anju in *Sanshō Dayū*. [Introduced by #529.]

518. KAMATA, Hisako. 1966. "Daughters of the gods: Shaman priestesses in Japan and Okinawa." In: *Folk Cultures of Japan and East Asia*. Tokyo: Sophia University Press, pp. 56-73. (*Monumenta Nipponica Monographs*, no.25). Notes. LCCN:72-183667.

Documents the differences in shaman roles and functions in various locations in Japan and Okinawa, both historically and as of this writing.

519. KANEKO, Sachiko and Robert E. MORRELL. Jun./Sep. 1983. "Sanctuary: Kamakura's Tōkeiji Convent." *Japanese Journal of Religious Studies* 10(2/3):195-228.   30 refs. ISSN:0304-1042.

KANEKO and MORRELL provide great detail on the history of the Tōkeiji Convent and its reputation for women's sanctuary, both political and social.   They outline divorce procedures and discuss many women prominent in the temple's founding and governance. [Introduced by #529.]

520. KING, Sallie B. Spring 1988. "Egalitarian philosophies in sexist institutions: The life of Satomi-san, Shinto miko and Zen Buddhist nun." *Journal of Feminist Studies in Religion* 4(1):7-26. 17 notes. ISSN:8755-4178.

KING has provided here a thoughtful and scholarly analysis of the "puzzle" caused by an examination of religious traditions with "egalitarian, nonsexist, optimistic philosophies" which are "embedded in obviously sexist institutions." Excerpts from the autobiography of SATOMI Myōdō, an intensely spiritual woman who attained "advanced levels of competence" in two major Japanese religions (Shinto and Zen Buddhism) illustrate KING's points. [See #537 for the complete translation.]

521. KITAMURA, Mariko. Spring 1980. "The best way is to keep away from them: Kamo no Chōmei's views of women in the *Hosshinshū*." *Journal of Asian Culture* 4:1-20. 3 notes and 20 refs. ISSN:0162-6795.

Illustrating her theory with translations of Buddhist spiritual "tales," KITAMURA concludes that Kano no Chōmei's view of women as represented in his *Hosshinshū* (circa 1210 C.E.) suggests that "if even such woeful creatures as women can attain enlightenment, then surely men can do it."

522. KUBO, Katsuko. 1982. *Reflections: In Search of Myself.* [Translated by Charles J. O'DROBINAK.] Tokyo: Sangaku Publishing Co. 199p. No refs. LCCN:84-220569. [*Hotoke o Motomeru Kokoro*. English.]

Using selections from her journal as a basis for her essays, KUBO here explores her spiritual journey: her intense searching for a meaning to life as a teenager, her reactions to authors like HESSE and TOLSTOY, and her ultimate centering in Reiyūkai Buddhism. She describes her religion as "a Buddhism that deals with raising children and afternoon television shows, . . . a way of coming to terms with ourselves, . . . a catalyst for creating a new and better person."

523. MATSUBARA, Hiroshi. Oct. 1976. "Women who serve the gods." *East* 12(9/10):12-19. No refs. ISSN:0012-8295.

A description of the daily routine of *miko* [maidens who serve at Shinto shrines]. For the general reader.

524. MATSUBARA, Hiroshi. Dec. 1976. "Women who are gods." *East* 13(1/2):6-12. No refs. ISSN:0012-8295.

A description (for the general reader) of the *noro* of Okinawa, elderly women who officiate at religious festivals and who are traditionally believed to be "deities in the shape of human beings."

525. MATSUBARA, Hiroshi. Oct. 1977. "Women who speak with the dead." *East* 13(11/12):73-78. No refs. ISSN:0012-8295.

A look at *itako* [women who commune with the dead]. For the general reader.

526. MORRELL, Robert E. Spring 1980. "Mirror for women: Mujū Ichien's *Tsuma kagami.*" *Monumenta Nipponica* 35(1):45-50. 22 notes. ISSN:0027-0741.

Introduces the ideas of MUJŪ Ichien (1226-1312), a Buddhist monk, who wrote on the "right behavior" for women in his *Tsuma kagami* [*Mirror for Women*].

527. NAKAMURA, Kyōko Motomochi. 1980. "No women's liberation: The heritage of a woman prophet in modern Japan." In: FALK, Nancy Auer and Rita M. GROSS. *Unspoken Worlds: Women's Religious Lives in Non-Western Cultures.* San Francisco: Harper and Row, pp. 174-190. Notes. LCCN:79-2989.

NAKAMURA discusses the role of women in leadership positions in the "new religions" and outlines problems inherent for women who succeed to leadership positions. Illustrates her theories with the example of KITAMURA Sayo, founder of the Tensho-kotai-jingukyo Movement, providing biographical data and spiritual beliefs.

528. NAKAMURA, Kyōko. Sep./Dec. 1981. "Revelatory experience in the female life cycle: A biographical study of women religionists in modern Japan." *Japanese Journal of Religious Studies* 8(3/4):187-205. 31 refs. ISSN:0304-1042.

Surveys the lives of ten female "religionists" focusing primarily on the effect of tradition in their lives, the nature of their revelatory experiences, and the effect of their work on their families. Nakamura illustrates her theories with the example of FUKATA Chiyoko (1887-1925).

529. NAKAMURA, Kyōko. Jun./Sep. 1983. "Women and religion in Japan: Introductory remarks." *Japanese Journal of Religious Studies* 10(2/3):115-121. No refs. ISSN:0304-1042.

Introduces a special issue on women and religion in Japan by focusing on the impact of women's studies on the discipline of religion, and the paucity of female researchers in this field. [Provides context for #512, #517, #519, #542, #543, #545.]

530. NAKANO, Ann. Aug. 1983. "Modern priestess." *PHP* 14(8):71-75. No refs. ISSN:0030-798X.

Sketches out a day in the life of SHIMURA Setsuko, a Shinto priestess.

531. NAKAYAMA, Shozen. 1961. "Woman's position viewed by Tenrikyō." *Tenri Journal of Religion* 3:8-12. No refs. ISSN:0495-1492. [Also published in *The Proceedings of the International Congress of Orientalists* 1963, 5:398-401 (International Congress of Orientalists, 25th, Moscow, 1960.)]

Delineates the views of women and women's roles as reflected in Tenrikyō religion and illustrates ways in which these views are implemented in the present activities of the Church.

532. NAYLOR, B. Christina. 1988. "Buddhas or bitches: Nichiren's attitude to women." *Religious Traditions* 11:63-76. 33 notes. ISSN:0156-1650.

Uses examples from the Lotus Sutra and others to illustrate the thesis that Nichiren's general attitude toward women was quite negative.

533. OHTANI, Yoshiko. 1970. *Eshin-Ni; the Wife of Shinran Shonin.* [Translated by Taitetsu UNNO and Alice UNNO.] Kyoto: Honpa Hongwanji. 53p. Bibl. LCCN:75-503907.

Provides translations of ten letters written by ESHIN Ni (1182-1268), thought to be the wife of SHINRAN Shonin, the founder of Shin Buddhism and one of the first priests to marry. The scholarly debate concerning SHINRAN's possible wife/wives is thoroughly reviewed, and the letters are annotated.

534. "The prophet of Tabuse." 1981. In: AOKI, Michiko Y. and Margaret B. DARDESS, comps. and eds. 1981. *As the Japanese See It: Past and Present*. Honolulu: University of Hawaii Press, pp. 250-253. No refs. LCCN:81-11526.

An excerpt from the official biography of KITAMURA Sayo (1900-1967), in which she foretells the atomic bombings and the end of World War II. KITAMURA was the founder of the Dancing Religion, and believed a Shinto deity spoke through her.

535. RODD, Laurel Rasplica. 1979. "Nichiren's teachings to women." *Selected Papers in Asian Studies*, new series, no.5, 20p. 18 notes. LCCN:84-7541.

RODD reviews general attitudes of Buddhist teachings toward women historically, and then shows how NICHIREN (1222-1282) was more supportive of women. Includes translations of sutras to illustrate her points.

536. SATHER, Jeanne and Kazue SUZUKI. Jul. 1985. "Cashing in on remorse." *PHP Intersect* (Jul. 1985):19-21. No refs. ISSN:0910-4607.

Describes the phenomenon of *mizugo* services [Buddhist services for aborted fetuses]. Interviews MIURA Domyo, a priest active in promoting these services, and others, both supportive and critical of the practice. (See *mizuko kuyō* in the Subject Index.)

537. SATOMI, Myōdō. 1987. *Passionate Journey: The Spiritual Autobiography of Satomi Myōdō*. [Translated and annotated by Sallie B. KING.] Boston: Shambhala. 212p. Bibl. LCCN:86-28057.

SATOMI Myōdō (1896-1978) writes of her search for The Way during her tumultuous life which included an unwed pregnancy, mental health difficulties, training as a Shinto *miko* [shrine maiden], and finally, progression through Zen training. KING provides a commentary including a section on women in Japanese religions. [See also #520.]

538. SMITH, Bardwell. 1988. "Buddhism and abortion in contemporary Japan: *Mizuko kuyō* and the confrontation with death." *Japanese Journal of Religious Studies* 15(1):3-24. 16 refs. ISSN:0304-1042.

SMITH expands the discussion of *mizuko kuyō* [Buddhist services for aborted, miscarried or stillborn children] to focus on the contemporary context for abortion and *mizuko kuyō*. Details the lack of choice in contraceptives, the effect of the private nature of abortion on the grieving process, perceptions of abortion as cause for later "personal and social misfortune," the impact of the "steady deterioration of traditional ancestral bonds," and the role of ritual in the healing process. SMITH also notes that while the ritual of *mizuko kuyō* may assist women in the grieving process, the underlying societal causes for large numbers of abortions are not being addressed.

539. SMITH, Bardwell. Winter 1990. "Research on abortion and grieving in Japan." *CWAS [Committee on Women in Asian Studies] Newsletter* 8(2):4-5. 2 refs. ISSN:0738-3185.

SMITH briefly describes *mizuko kuyō* and his current research with Elizabeth HARRISON on the topic. [See #538 for a fuller description of his research.]

540. SMITH, Robert J. 1974. *Ancestor Worship in Contemporary Japan*. Stanford: Stanford University Press. 266p. Bibl. Index. LCCN:74-82780.

Although SMITH does not focus specifically on women, women appear in the discussion, both in the role of ancestor and in the role of those paying respects.

541. SMYERS, Karen A. Jul. 1983. "Women and Shinto: The relation between purity and pollution." *Japanese Religions* 12(4):7-18. 33 notes. ISSN:0448-8954.

A short review of women's position in Shinto both historically and currently.

542. TAKAGI, Kiyoko. Jun./Sep. 1983. "Religion in the life of Higuchi Ichiyō." *Japanese Journal of Religious Studies* 10(2/3):123-147. 9 refs. ISSN:0304-1042.

TAKAGI provides both a secular and a spiritual biography of HIGUCHI Ichiyō [1872-1896], one of Japan's first prominent modern women authors. Based on an examination of her diaries, TAKAGI concludes HIGUCHI's religious experience was primarily intellectual. [Introduced by #529.]

543. TAKEMI, Momoko. Jun./Sep. 1983. "'Menstruation sutra' belief in Japan." [Translated by W. Michael KELSEY.] *Japanese Journal of Religious Studies* 10(2/3):229-247. 11 refs. ISSN:0304-1042.

Analyzes the various Japanese versions of the "Bowl of Blood" sutra, the sutra "which teaches the way of salvation for women who have fallen into Hell because of the pollution of blood." [Introduced by #529.]

544. THELLE, Notto R. Jul. 1983. "Women in society and religion." *Japanese Religions* 12(4):38-55. 14 notes. ISSN:0448-8954.

A review article covering LEBRA's *Women in Changing Japan* [#688], TANAKA's *This Kind of Woman* [#1424], and others. Included here for its English language summary of OKANO Haruko's *Die Stellung der Frau in Shinto* [*The Status of Women in Shinto*. (Harrassowitz, 1976)]. THELLE provides a brief discussion of women in Buddhism, the "new religions," and very briefly touches on the Christian church in Japan.

545. UCHINO, Kumiko. Jun./Sep. 1983. "The status elevation process of Sōtō sect nuns in modern Japan." *Japanese Journal of Religious Studies* 10(2/3):177-194. 12 refs. ISSN:0304-1042. Reprinted in: ECK, Diana L. and Devaki JAIN. 1987. *Speaking of Faith: Global Perspectives on Women, Religion, and Social Change.* Philadelphia: New Society Publishers, pp. 75-83.

A unique discussion focusing on Buddhist nuns of the Sōtō sect and their status within Buddhism and the larger secular society. UCHINO surveys nuns' status from the founding of the sect in the 13th century by Dōgen who believed women could attain Buddhahood, through times of severely low status during feudalism to more modern times where questions concerning who can become a nun and the role of the nun are discussed. Also discusses changes in the status of priests' wives. [Introduced by #529.]

546. YOSHIDA, Teigo. 1990. "The feminine in Japanese folk religion: Polluted or divine?" In: BEN-ARI, Eyal, Brian MOERAN, and James VALENTINE, eds. *Unwrapping Japan: Society and Culture in Anthropological Perspective.* Honolulu: University of Hawaii Press, pp. 58-77. 42 refs. LCCN:89-35666.

Explores the differences in attitudes toward women in the fishing villages of the "southwestern archipelago," where men are minor participants or are excluded from religious rituals, from the majority of Japanese fishing villages where women are considered polluted and are prohibited from boarding ships or traveling to certain locations, especially during menstruation or pregnancy.

Christianity

547. BOXER, C.R. 1934/1935. "Hosokawa Tadaoki and the Jesuits, 1587-1645." *Transactions and Proceedings of the Japan Society of London* 32:79-119. [Also cited as Japan Society, London. *Transaction and Proceedings.*] 54 notes. LCCN:08-16048.

This article on the husband of HOSOKAWA Gracia contains Portugese accounts of her conversion, her influence on her husband, and the story of her death.

548. CHO, Kiyo Takeda. Jul. 1959. "Japan's first Christian love letters: A glimpse at the correspondence of Danjo and Miyako Ebina." [Translated by Sobi AIKAWA.] *Japan Christian Quarterly* 25:212-218. No refs. ISSN:0021-4361.

A translation of correspondence between two Christians, EBINA Danjo and YOKOI Miyako, in 1882 when Christianity was still forbidden.

549. De FOREST, Charlotte B. 1923. *The Woman and the Leaven in Japan.* West Medford, MA: Central Committee on the United Study of Foreign Missions. 224p. Notes. Index. LCCN:23-9565.

Written as a text for adult Sunday Schools in the United States, this book describes Japanese Christian women—what their life as young women is like, their educational possibilities (including descriptions of individual schools and educators), successful occupational opportunities, and fields for Christian endeavors. The author grew up in Japan, spoke Japanese, and at the time of writing this text was president of Kobe College [for Women].

550. FLETCHER, Grace Niles. 1967. *The Bridge of Love.* New York: Dutton. 220p. No refs. LCCN:67-11377. [Also published as *Love is the Bridge.*]

The biography of HITOTSUYANAGI Maki (b. 1884) and HITOTSUYANAGI Merrell (1880-1964; formerly William Merrell VORIES), a Christian couple who founded the Omi Brotherhood. Maki, the daughter of Japanese nobility, studied in the United States and lived with Alice BACON [see #146]. Returning to Japan and "holding out" from marriage until she met Merrell at age 35, Maki devoted her life to their work in education, with the *eta* [Japan's lowest social caste], and their Christian community. This is one of the better "missionary biographies," although neither of the HITOTSUYANAGIs were technically missionaries.

551. HARA, T. 1922. "Prison gate work." *Christian Movement in Japan, Korea, and Formosa* 1922:191-197. No refs. LCCN:16-23733.

A Christian prison worker relates the tale of Miss K., a petty thief and drunkard who reformed under the care of the worker's family because she was given work, food, and secure lodgings.

552. HASHIKAWA, Masao. Spring 1984. "Broadcasting the resurrection: My daughter Takatsuka Hatsumi." [Translated by Harold EIMON.] *Japan Christian Quarterly* 50(2):83-85. No refs. ISSN:0021-4361.

A father's brief memoir of TAKATSUKA Hatsumi (1943-1981), a Christian woman who died of leukemia at age 38.

553. HIGUCHI, Chiyoko. May 1971. "In dedication to a foreign god: The story of Hosokawa Gracia." *East* 7(5):32-38. No refs. ISSN:0012-8295.

A brief, fictionalized biography for the general reader of HOSOKAWA Gracia, born AKECHI Tamako [1563-1600].

554. KAWAI, Michi and Ochimi KUBUSHIRO. 1934. *Japanese Women Speak: A Message from the Christian Women of Japan to the Christian Women of America.* Boston: The Central Committee on the United Study of Foreign Missions. 204p. Bibl. Index. LCCN:34-2882.

A survey of Japanese Christian women by a graduate of Bryn Mawr, the General Secretary of the Japanese National Young Women's Christian Association [YWCA] for 20 years, and at the time of writing, founder and principal of the Keisen Girls' School [see #1102 and #1103]. She discusses the Christian movement in Japan, education for women, and profiles 12 women, both career women and homemakers. A final chapter discusses women's peace efforts. KUBUSHIRO covers social work in Japan, from deaf-oral work to the Women's Christian Temperance Union [WCTU], as well as opportunities for further social reform. Although other surveys of this nature exist, this is written by Japanese women active in the fields discussed.

555. LAURES, Johannes. 1959. *Two Japanese Christian Heroes: Justo Takayama Ukon and Gracia Hosokawa Tamako.* Tokyo: Bridgeway Press. 128p. No refs. LCCN:58-14205.

An account of the life of HOSOKAWA Gracia Tamako (1563-1601) aimed at the general reader and consisting of selected translations from the author's scholarly work published in German. The Lady Gracia was both Japanese and Catholic at a time when political struggles made life difficult and tenuous; her story is one of a courageous woman who lived according to her ideals.

556. MATSUMURA, Akiko. Spring 1974. "Christ and the women of Japan." *Japan Christian Quarterly* 40(2):58-60. No refs. ISSN:0021-4361.

MATSUMURA questions whether Japanese women truly want independence, i.e. independence based on a positive view of self-worth (not a typical message for women in Japan). She shares her own early life and attitudes before Christianity assisted her to see herself as important.

557. MATSUZAWA, Kazuko, *et al.* Winter 1985. "Church women and the media: Results of a survey." [Translated by George L. OLSON.] *Japan Christian Quarterly* 51(1):24-29. No refs. ISSN:0021-4361.

A survey was conducted among 999 female members of the Japan Evangelical Lutheran Church about their mass media preferences and their attitudes toward social action and life-styles. The authors conclude that "in comparison to [Japanese] women in general, . . . these Christians make their own choices about the media, are more actively involved in social activities, and are less apt to support the values associated with the traditional Japanese family style."

558. MAYA, H. Winter 1982. "My story: One woman's response." *Japan Christian Quarterly* 48(1):11-20,61. 16 notes. ISSN:0021-4361.

A woman reacts to middle-age and discusses her reflections in light of Christianity and Carl Jung.

559. MIURA, Ayako. 1977. *The Wind is Howling.* [Translated and abridged by Valerie GRIFFITHS.] Downers Grove, IL: Intervarsity Press, 190p. No refs. LCCN:77-74845. [Michi ariki. English.]

Termed "an autobiographical journey from Nihilism to Christianity," this is MIURA's account of her postwar years—her struggles with tuberculosis and her search for meaning. It is a love story as well, relating her love for two men, one a tuberculosis patient who died, and MIURA Mitsuyo, whom she married.

560. MULHERN, Chieko. 1980. "Hosokawa Gracia: A model for Mariko." In: SMITH, Henry, ed. *Learning from* Shōgun: *Japanese History and Western Fantasy.* Santa Barbara: University of California, Santa Barbara, Department of Asian Studies, pp. 62-70. Bibl. LCCN:81-172915.

Intended for those who have read James Clavell's *Shōgun* and wish to separate historical characters from the necessities of the plot. MULHERN provides a portrait of HOSOKAWA Gracia (Mariko), her family, and her husband Tadaoki.

561. NORMAN, Gwen, W.H.H. NORMAN, and Gwen SUTTIE. 1967. *Japan Profiles; Ten Portraits of Contemporary Japanese Christian Men and Women.* [Toronto]: United Church of Canada, Division of Congregational Life & Work, Committee on Education for Mission. 120p. No refs. LCCN:68-105185.

This collection of biographical sketches was written by three missionaries of the United Church of Canada with extensive Japanese experience. The four women presented (ONO Kunjiro, KIKUTA Sumie, SEKIYA Ayako, and OTSUKA Noyuri) are committed Christians and active in social reform.

562. NUDING, Barbara and Richard MERRITT. Jan. 1965. "Praising our Lord in the dance." *Japan Christian Quarterly* 31(1):29-34. No refs. ISSN:0021-4361.

Interviews HANAYAGI Futaba, who uses the Hanayagi style of classical dance to interpret Christian themes for various denominations of Christian churches.

563. OKUDA, Akiko. 1986. "Women's liberation in Japan and Japanese Christianity." *Modern Churchman* new series 28(4):3-8. No refs. ISSN:0026-7597.

OKUDA notes that Christianity, in its beginnings in Japan, supported development of the individual (and therefore individual women), and discusses why it eventually "came to embrace the traditional social structures embodied in the 'good wife, wise mother' ideology." She calls for women to find ways to "increase the genuine quality of human life" by "being women who are doing theology" and by being socially and politically active.

564. POWLES, Cyril. Jan. 1966. "Christianity and women in Japan: Some historical notes." *Japan Christian Quarterly* 32(1):32-36. 4 notes. ISSN:0021-4361.

POWLES focuses on three areas of early Christian activity in regards to women's status: husband-wife relations, prostitution, and betterment of factory working conditions.

565. POWLES, Marjorie A. Winter 1987. "Japanese women and the church." *Japan Christian Quarterly* 53(1):5-14. 2 notes. ISSN:0021-4361.

Evaluates the status of Japanese women at the end of the United Nations Women's Decade in general, and then focuses specifically on women in the Nippon Seikōkai [Japanese Anglican Church], including women in the church hierarchy, roles of pastors' wives, and activities of laywomen.

566. REEDY, Jitsuko. Fall 1980. "Shizuko Wakamatsu." *Japan Christian Quarterly* 46(4):215-220. 19 notes. ISSN:0021-4361.

A brief biography of WAKAMATSU Shizuko (pen name of SHIMADA Kashiko, d. 1896), a Christian, poet, prolific translator of children's books, writer for *Jogaku Zasshi* [Women's Journal], wife, and mother of four children. [See Author/Translator/Editor Index for access to her literary works.]

567. RICH, Elaine Sommers. Spring 1974. "Japan's World Council President, Kiyoko Takeda Cho." *Japan Christian Quarterly* 40(2):106-108. No refs. ISSN:0021-4361.

Provides biographical details and insight into the philosophy of CHŌ Kiyoko, Asian President of the World Council of Churches.

568. SAITŌ, Aiko. Autumn 1986. "The role of housewives in the work of evangelization." *Japan Missionary Bulletin* 40(3):203-206. No refs. ISSN:0021-4531.

Expresses consternation at listening to men discuss the "role of housewives in the work of evangelization" in a recent church meeting. Calls for "a revolution in women's consciousness of their own spirituality" and for greater involvement of laywomen in the larger problems of society.

569. TAHARA, Yoneko. 1976. *Yoneko, Daughter of Happiness*. [As told to Bernard PALMER.] Chicago: Moody Bible Institute. 173p. No refs. LCCN:76-19009.

The story of a young Japanese woman who attempted suicide after the death of her mother. TAHARA lost both legs and an arm by jumping in front of a train; she relates the story of her recovery, conversion to Christianity and her marriage.

570. TAYLOR, Arch B. Spring 1974. "Liberation for women: A biblical view." *Japan Christian Quarterly* 40(2):61-70. 9 notes. ISSN:0021-4361.

Decries the conservative trend in attitudes towards equality of women which the Christian Church in Japan has taken. Using his own biblically-based interpretations, Taylor counters the arguments of "sexist church leaders" who are relying on "misinterpret[ed]" and mistranslat[ed]" biblical passages, and calls for a reconsideration of "the role of Christian education for women in modern Japan."

571. TAYLOR, Margaret Hopper. Spring 1974. "It doesn't have to be like that." *Japan Christian Quarterly* 40(2):88-92. 3 notes. ISSN:0021-4361.

Details the gap between equality provided for by legislation and the actual circumstances of women in the areas of education, employment, and marriage. Provides a number of suggestions by which Christians can bridge this gap.

572. TSUDA, Ume. Apr. 1913. "The ideal womanhood as a factor in missionary work: III. Japanese women, and the problems of the present day." *International Review of Missions* 2:291-304. No refs. ISSN:0020-8582.

After pointing out the problems of a period of rapid modernization during which people voice new ideas about roles for women but are not willing to put them into practice, TSUDA calls for more educational opportunities for women and for the adoption of Christian values. Christianity "places woman on the level with man, her individuality and worth in herself is recognized and full scope is given to her powers."

573. TSURU, Toshiko. Jul. 1963. "Memories of my mother." *Japan Christian Quarterly* 29(3):176-180. No refs. ISSN:0021-4361.

A Japanese Christian woman reflects on the life of her mother, also a Christian, who lived from 1887-1937.

574. TSUZUKIBASHI, Naoko. Winter 1986. "Sharing the message of Christ: The experiences of one housewife." [Translated by David PADRNOS.] *Japan Missionary Bulletin* 40(4):249-254. No refs. ISSN:0021-4531.

A Catholic housewife shares her frustrations and joys with "indirect evangelization" as seen through her daily and church-related activities.

575. WAGNER, C. Peter. Summer 1984. "Housewives are Japan's ripe harvest." *Japan Christian Quarterly* 50(3):167-169. No refs. ISSN:0021-4360.

Suggests that focusing the Church's evangelistic message on urban housewives rather than the family as a whole will result in a "ripe harvest" of new members.

576. WAKAMATSU, Shizuko. Fall 1980. "Selected writings of Shizuko Wakamatsu from the *Japan Evangelist*." [Compiled by John W. KRUMMEL.] *Japan Christian Quarterly* 46(4):221-227. No refs. ISSN:0021-4360.

Three articles published in the 1895 volume of the Japan Evangelist by WAKAMATSU Shizuko ("Mrs. Kashi IWAMOTO") reflect her thoughts on women's roles (that with a victorious end to the Sino-Japanese Conflict women may again further their education), the place of a wife within the *ie* [family/household], and women's contributions to religion historically.

577. "Women and changing church structures in Japan." Spring 1986. *Japan Missionary Bulletin* 40(1):23-32. No refs. ISSN:0021-4531.

Presents the results of a survey conducted by a "committee of Sisters, sponsored by the Women Major Superiors' Association of Japan . . . on women and structures in the Japanese [Catholic] Church." The views of both lay and religious women were solicited; questions focused on "experienced discrimination and level of interest in women's concerns; participation in Church structures . . .; perceptions of women's present position and role in the Church; and priority concerns for the Christian community." Although much less detailed than some may wish, the results represent a distinct group of women.

578. "Women and pastoral tasks." May 1975. *Japan Missionary Bulletin* 29(4):215-219. No refs. ISSN:0021-4531.

A brief discussion of the role lay women should play in the Japanese Catholic Church. For readers of Japanese, the complete text appears in the same issue.

579. YAMAMOTO, Kimiyo. 1957. "Toward a Christian nation: Women's work." In: STEVENS, Dorothy A., ed. *Voices from Japan: Christians Speak.* Philadelphia: Judson Press, pp. 51-53. No refs. LCCN:57-8339.

A very brief description of [Japanese] Baptist women's efforts, within and outside the church.

580. YOUNG, Richard Fox. Winter 1989. "Abortion, grief and consolation: Prolegomena to a Christian response to *mizuko kuyō. Japan Christian Quarterly* 55(1):31-38. 9 notes. ISSN:0021-4361.

After considering *mizuko kuyō* [Buddhist services for aborted, miscarried or stillborn children] from the context of traditional Japanese views of the *mizuko* ["water child"], the *mizuko*'s ability to affect the situation of "parents" or "siblings" after death, and of the Buddhist concepts of death, YOUNG calls for a Christian response to those suffering from abortion or miscarriage concerns.

5

Fashion, Leisure, Sports

Fashion

581. BUMILLER, Elisabeth. Dec. 1990. "In a society where dates were once set to change clothes. . . ." *Vogue* 180(12):147,150,154,156. No refs. ISSN:0042-8000.

Discusses the strong trend toward conformity in Japanese women's fashions as seen through three "distinct subgroups": *body-con* [body-conscious office ladies], *shibu-kaji* [Shibuya casual students and yuppies], and *ojōsan* [wealthy conservative dressers who follow the leadings of KAWASHIMA Kiko, the wife of Prince Aya].

582. CASAL, U.A. May 1966. "Japanese cosmetics and teeth blackening." *Transactions of the Asiatic Society of Japan*, 3rd. series, 9:5-27. [Also cited as Asiatic Society of Japan. *Transactions*.] 50 notes.

Covers patterns of powdering the face and neck, use of rouge, shaving of eyebrows, and blackening of teeth.

583. CASAL, U.A. Oct. 1969. "Combs in Japan (and some mythological reflections)." *Bulletin of the Japan Society of London* no.59:8-12. [Also cited as Japan Society, London. *Bulletin*; also cited as 4(6):8-12.] No refs. ISSN:0021-4701.

Emphasizes primarily the place of combs in myths, but also discusses briefly the use of combs by women throughout Japanese history.

584. CHERRY, Kittredge. Jun. 1984. "Designer with a difference." *PHP* 15(6):53-57. No refs. ISSN:0030-798X.

Describes the work of KINOSHITA Yukiko, a stroke victim and now designer of clothing for the handicapped.

585. "Chiyo Tanaka, queen of the fashion world." Summer 1959. *Who's Who in Japan* 3:13-18. 2 refs. LCCN:77-200599.

A description of TANAKA Chiyo, a renowned dress designer and the "Dress Designer to Her Majesty, the Empress of Japan." Provides a biographical sketch, TANAKA's views on "random subjects," and two brief critiques of her work.

586. "Courtesans, queens and office girls: A short history of hair styles." 1966. *East* 3(2):27-30. No refs. ISSN:0012-8295.

A brief recounting of "the connection between some major changes in Japan's civilization and the hair styles of its women." The conclusion: "It is good to watch women in postwar Japan enjoying their free mode of life and doing their hair just as they like."

587. DAN, Ino. 1935. *Catalogue of a Collection of Hair Ornaments, Pouches and Toilet Articles used by Japanese Women: The Collection of Baron Ino Dan.* Tokyo: [privately published]. 16p. No refs. LCCN:42-44522.

2A brief description of hairdressing by women and a listing of the various items collected by Baron DAN Ino with descriptions.

588. DE LOS RIOS, Astrid. Apr. 1989. "Head appeal." *PHP Intersect* (Apr. 1989):38-43. No refs. ISSN:0910-4607.

In an article discussing innovative ways in which hair salons attract customers, DE LOS RIOS briefly describes popular hair styles for women.

589. HEARN, Lafcadio. 1894. *Glimpses of Unfamiliar Japan*, Vol. 2. Boston: Houghton Mifflin. 356p. No refs. Index.

HEARN, a writer and teacher who lived for many years in Japan in Japanese style, includes among his various essays and stories a description of the dressing of women's hair.

590. "International stylist: Mme. Hanae Mori." 1973. *Japan* 11(1):22-26. No refs. LCCN:86-648185.

Incorporating ideas from the kimono into designs for modern women's dress is the aim of MORI Hanae, an internationally recognized fashion designer.

591. "Japanese women and cosmetics." Jul. 1981. *East* 17(7/8):16-20. 3 notes. ISSN:0012-8295.

A rather rambling and superficial look at the use of cosmetics by both men and women.

592. K., H. [KON, Hitarō.] Jul./Aug. 1969. "Mirror, mirror on the wall." *East* 5(4):18-27. No refs. ISSN:0021-8295.

An article for the general reader surveying images of women from the Yamato period to the present. Also discusses hair styles and use of cosmetics.

593. LEGGE, Trudy. Dec. 1981. "Shizue Takizawa—Just a robe and a sash." *PHP* 12(12):39-45. No refs. ISSN:0030-798X.

Describes the life and work of TAKIZAWA Shizue, a "kimono teacher" and designer.

594. "Makeup methods and utensils of Edo period women." Aug. 1987. *East* 23(3):29-33. No refs. ISSN:0012-8295.

Explains the methodology and meaning of teeth blackening, the powdering of faces and necks, the use of rouge, and scenting techniques.

595. MATSUBARA, Hiroshi. Apr. 1978. "Women who arrange hair." *East* 14(5/6):69-74. No refs. ISSN:0012-8295.

Profiles NAKAMURA Yae, one of the few traditional hairdressers who arrange the elaborate coiffures of geisha.

596. McCLAIN, James L. Winter 1987. "Mr. Itō's dance party." *Wilson Quarterly* 11(5):154-160. ISSN:0363-3276.

Within his discussion of a "crisis of cultural identity" occurring in 1887, McCLAIN briefly describes the masquerade ball hosted by Prime Minister ITŌ Hirobumi and his wife, a supporter of the Ladies Costume Society which encouraged the wearing of western dress. McCLAIN argues that this ball (with Japanese women in costume) touched off the conservative backlash and a return to traditional values.

597. MURRAY, Geoffrey. Dec. 1976. "The world of Hanae Mori—Fashion designer." *PHP* 7(12):35-44. No refs. ISSN:0030-798X.

Presents the story of MORI Hanae and describes her impact on the fashion world of Japan.

598. NAKAMURA, Yoshio. 1966. "What makes a woman beautiful?" *East* 2(5):15-22. No refs. ISSN:0012-8295.

Examines historical definitions of feminine beauty from Heian times to the present. For the general reader.

599. ŌYAMA, Shigeo. Oct./Dec. 1987. "A little revolution in kimonos." *Japan Quarterly* 34(4):405-409. No refs. ISSN:0021-4590.

Describes a new fashion trend in kimonos appealing to younger working women. Bushoan-brand kimono sets feature kimonos in new, easy-care fabrics, sold in a package with all the accessories needed, in stores with dressing rooms, at an affordable price, all marketed with a new fashion image.

600. "Padded bras give shape—and hope." Apr. 1989. *PHP Intersect* (Apr. 1989):29. No refs. ISSN:0910-4607.

Notes the recent availability of special bras imported from the United States for persons who have had a breast removed.

601. SAKATANI, Shiroshi. 1976. "Female decorations." In: *Meiroku Zasshi, Journal of the Japanese Enlightenment.* [Translated and introduced by William BRAISTED.] Cambridge: Harvard University Press, pp. 269-274. Notes. LCCN:76-27134.

Discusses the appropriateness of "decoration" as the principal purpose of women, focusing primarily on the new hairstyles as of 1874 (free-hanging hair).

602. SHIMADA, Tomiko. Jul./Sep. 1962. "Clothing habits." *Japan Quarterly* 9(3):352-363. No refs. ISSN:0021-4590.

A detailed look at changes in women's dress focusing on changes during the post-World War II period, but including a survey of styles since 1884. Also includes a discussion of the influence of dressmaking schools on the adoption of Western clothing and statistics on the amount of clothing owned and on fabric consumption.

603. TRUCCO, Terry. Jan./Feb. 1984. "The butterfly spreads its wings." *Journal of Japanese Trade and Industry* 1984(1):40-43. No refs. ISSN:0285-9556.

An interview with MORI Hanae, fashion designer and "successful female tycoon," about the growth of her company and the place of Japan in the international fashion world.

604. YAMANAKA, Norio. 1982. *The Book of Kimono*. Tokyo: Kodansha. 139p. No refs. Index. LCCN:82-80649.

Describes in meticulous detail the making of kimono and methods of wearing them, including movement and proper posture.

605. "Yukiko Hanai." 1989. *Japan Pictorial* 12(3):20-21. No refs. ISSN:0388-6115.

A very brief introduction to HANAI Yukiko, a Japanese fashion designer.

Leisure

606. ABE, Tsuyako. Oct./Dec. 1956. "Middle-aged women." *Japan Quarterly* 3(4):492-495. No refs. ISSN:0021-4590.

An essay discussing how women in their forties and fifties now remain active in society rather than becoming elderly non-participants.

607. "Adding spice to daily life." 1981. *Japan Pictorial* 4(3):9-16. No refs. ISSN:0388-6115.

A description of the types of activities middle-aged women are undertaking as a result of increased leisure time.

608. BRADY, Kate. 1980. "From fantasy to reality: Magazines for women." *Feminist International* no.2:5-8. 3 notes. ISSN:0388-371X.

Delineates the types of magazines aimed at women of different ages and status levels, and discusses their major messages. She notes all materials are edited by men, avoid hard news, and progress on a fantasy-to-reality continuum based on readers' ages.

609. CHERRY, Kittredge. Mar. 1985. "Little magazines link women." *PHP Intersect* (Mar. 1985):43. No refs. ISSN:0910-4607.

A very brief discussion of small feminist journals including *Onna kara onna e* [*From Woman to Woman*], *Onna no hangyaku* [*Female Revolt*], *Danchi no onna* [*Females of the Housing Complex*], and *Feminist Forum*.

610. FUJIHISA, Mine. [1983.] "A woman's view of the automobile: Have cars made women more independent?" *Wheel Extended* 13(4):24-26. No refs. ISSN:0049-755X.

FUJIHISA, a female broadcast critic and lecturer at three Japanese universities, asserts that automobiles have contributed more to the liberation of Japanese women "than all the rhetoric" and notes that women gain a sense of control and independence while driving.

611. IKEGAMI, Chizuko. Jan./Mar. 1981. "The changing life-style of the Japanese woman." *Wheel Extended* 10(3):14-20. No refs. ISSN:0049-755X.

Declaring it to be an "age of millions of housewife students," IKEGAMI discusses the success of cultural centers in the role of continuing education for women and outlines the problems faced by housewives past their mothering years.

612. KANO, Mikiyo. 1986. "Remolding Tennoism for modern Japan." *Ampo: Japan-Asia Quarterly Review* 18(2/3):24-29. No refs. LCCN:77-612830.

Discusses the role played by women's magazines in an attempt to revitalize the Emperor's role in Japan. Also notes the return to importance of a young woman's lineage and family status over ability or personal characteristics as a primary qualification for marriage.

613. KILBURN, David. 4 Sep. 1989. "Ad sexism protests stir Japanese shops." *Advertising Age* 60(38):21. ISSN:0001-8899. Summarized as: "Sexist ads draw increasing ire from Japanese women, force ad agency response." Nov./Dec. 1989. *Media Report to Women* 17(6):6. ISSN:0145-9651.

Notes that both top advertising agencies, Dentsu and Hakuhodo, have set up departments to educate staff on discrimination issues. Mentions briefly several ad campaigns which met with protest from women's groups.

614. KON, Hidemi. 1940. "Women's journals in Japan." *Contemporary Japan* 9(8):1166-1172. No refs. ISSN:0388-0214.

A short description of women's magazines (including *Shufu no Tomo* [*Housewife's Companion*], *Fujin Kurabu* [*Women's Club*], and *Fujin Kohron* [*Review for Women*]) by a man who strongly believes that self-sacrifice is women's traditional value.

615. LEDOUX, Trish. Oct. 1990. "Ladies' manga." *Mangajin* 1(4):14-19. No refs. ISSN:1051-8177.

Describes both *shōjo manga* ["little girl comics"] and *manga* catering to the adult women's market. Includes brief excerpts from *Watashi ga mama yo* [*I'm a Mama!*], and *Ma ni au ka mo shirenai* [*It Might be in Time*]. [See also #224.]

616. MATSUOKA, Yōko. Oct./Dec. 1954. "A column for women." *Japan Quarterly* 1(4):117-120. No refs. ISSN:0021-4590.

Reports on a regular column in the *Asahi Shimbun*, "Hitotoki," which publishes letters of social and political commentary by women. Examples of topics discussed and excerpts from letters are included.

617. Nihon Keizai Shimbun. Jan. 1988. "[Data box:] For single women only." *Look Japan* 33(382):30. No refs. ISSN:0456-5339.

A brief (one paragraph) announcement of the "first" single women's club, "The Fountains," located in Osaka.

618. PLIMPTON, Jack. 16 Aug. 1982. "Magazines slug it out for Japan women." *Advertising Age* 53:39. No refs. ISSN:0001-8899.

A brief description of the women's magazine market, especially the 20-30-year-old age group.

619. SCHREIBER, Mark. Apr. 1989. "Freeked at last." *PHP Intersect* (Apr. 1989):6. No refs. ISSN:0910-4607.

Notes the appearance of a new magazine for working women, *Freeker*.

620. SHAILER, Mary Jacinta. Jun. 1972. "The danchi wives and their leisure time." *Japan Missionary Bulletin* 26(5):284-286. No refs. ISSN:0021-4531.

Based on a 1971 survey in Nara Prefecture, SHAILER reports on the lack of positive relationships between neighbors living in *danchi* [public housing] and lack of involvement in outside activities, either cultural or social-service oriented.

621. STERNBERG, Ronald. Feb. 1990. "Hanako girls." *Intersect* 6(2):12. ISSN:0910-4607.

Describes the typical reader of *Hanako*, a magazine for "office ladies," and notes its overwhelming success at marketing for its advertisers.

622. SUGIMOTO, Sonoko. Jan. 1974. "How Japanese women have survived." *PHP* 5(1):15-17. No refs. ISSN:0030-798X.

SUGIMOTO (a novelist) suggests that women find an activity outside the home to make life worth living. She suggests typing braille books, organizing volleyball teams, etc.

623. "A Tokyo girl." Aug. 1988. *East* 24(2):16-18. No refs. ISSN:0012-8295.

Presents the hypothetical thoughts of a 16-year-old Tokyo girl and of her relatives and friends. The young woman comes across as self-centered and frivolous.

624. TRUCCO, Terry. 10 Sep. 1984. "Japan: Magazines salute 'modern' woman." *Advertising Age* 55:54,60. ISSN:0001-8899.

Briefly describes new women's magazines including *Travail*, *Sophia* and *25ans*, which appeal to the working woman (but support the traditional view that women should "retire" after marriage or childbirth).

625. "The working girl's guide." 1 Dec. 1989. *Asiaweek* 15(48):30. No refs. ISSN:1012-6244.

A brief profile of *Hanako*, a women's magazine appealing to single women in their twenties with "about $350 a month to spend in discretionary ways" before they marry. The main focus of the publication is consumerism.

Sports

626. CRAFT, Lucille. Mar. 1988. "When titans crash: Women's pro wrestling." *PHP Intersect* (Mar. 1988):25-28. No refs. ISSN:0910-4607.

Introduces the sport of women's professional wrestling, noting its appeal to teenaged girls and their strong following of its stars. Sponsors consider the matches as a portrayal of "the clashing of good and evil," involving "ordinary-looking girls . . . [which] . . . inspires young females who are wrestling with their own adolescent problems."

627. "For the love of mountains." 1989. *Japan Pictorial* 12(1):14-16. No refs. ISSN:0388-6115.

Profiles TABEI Junko, a female mountain climber and the first woman to scale Mt. Everest.

628. "Glamor girl of bowling—Ritsuko NAKAYAMA." 1971. *Japan* 1971(1):31-34. No refs. LCCN:86-648185.

Describes the career of Japan's first woman professional bowler.

629. MAKINO, Noriko. 1980. "The changing role of sport in women's lives." [Translated by Heather GLASS.] *Feminist International* no.2:70-72. No refs. ISSN:0388-371X.

Traces the development of women's sports and physical education since 1870. Discusses the philosophies underlying each.

630. McCREERY, Ruth. May 1983. "Petticoat pilot." *PHP* 14(5):58-64. No refs. ISSN:0030-798X.

Profiles NOZOKI Yae, founder of the Japan Women's Association of Aeronautics and a pilot since 1937.

631. "Midori and her triple axel." 1989. *Japan Pictorial* 12(3):23. No refs. ISSN:0388-6115.

A very brief profile of ITŌ Midori, the first Japanese figure skater to take a gold medal in the world figure skating championships.

632. NAKANO, Ann. Jun. 1984. "Junko Tabei: Mountaineer." *PHP* (Jun. 1984):74-78. No refs. ISSN:0030-798X.

NAKANO interviews TABEI Junko, mother, piano and English teacher, and the first woman to scale Mt. Everest.

633. NISHIMURA, Kunio. 10 Oct. 1985. "Masako Izumi: 88°-40' N, 58°-00' W: Her very own North Pole." *Look Japan* (10 Oct. 1985):25. No refs. ISSN:0456-5339.

Profiles IZUMI Masako, an actress who led an expedition to 150 kilometers short of the North Pole.

634. POWERS, Elizabeth. 1976. "Women in sports." In: LEBRA, Joyce, *et al. Women in Changing Japan.* Stanford: Stanford University Press, pp. 255-262. 1 note. LCCN:75-33663.

Discusses the structure of women's sports and the options available to those who wish to participate. Notes especially the emphasis on volleyball, made popular by the Hitachi Electric Company team which won an Olympic gold medal. Amateur participation is available to housewives through the Mamasan Volleyball Association. Also mentions other female sports figures (e.g. TABEI Junko who scaled Everest, and CHIBA Ginko and HITOMI Kinue, both Olympic champions).

635. ROBIN-TANI, Marianne and Noriyasu TANI. Aug. 1989. "Wild cats." *[PHP] Intersect* (Aug. 1989):front cover, 19-21. No refs. ISSN:0910-4607.

A report on Japan's first all-female football team, composed of employees of Osaka Kogin, a credit union.

636. SAYLE, Murray. Dec. 1975. "Junko Tabei—Small lady, big mountain." *PHP* 6(12):44-52. No refs. ISSN:0030-798X.

Profiles TABEI Junko, the first woman to successfully scale Mt. Everest.

637. "Tennis thorough-bred." 1989. *Japan Pictorial* 12(2):24-25. No refs. ISSN:0388-6115.

A brief note (and picture) concerning SAWAMATSU Naoko, the first Japanese to win the JAL Super Junior Tennis championship women's single title.

638. "Women pilots answer call of blue skies." 1968. *Japan* 1968(1):11-13. No refs. LCCN:86-648185.

Briefly profiles SAKATA Minae, a private pilot, and discusses her flying experiences.

6

Women as Consumers

639. "All-women purchasing mission." 1985. *Journal of Japanese Trade and Industry* 1985(5):63. No refs. ISSN:0285-9556.

A brief note that a team of five women was sent to Europe in search of household goods to be displayed at a JETRO [Japan External Trade Organization] exhibition.

640. ASAKAWA, Sumikazu. Jun. 1989. "Japan and the body-conscious consumer." *PHP Intersect* (Jun. 1989):36-39. No refs. ISSN:0910-4607.

ASAKAWA anticipates the young woman consumer "will serve as a model for the sophistication of Japanese consumer spending" and describes the type of products appealing to her.

641. AZUMA, Asō. Oct. 1985. "Some reflections on the shopping patterns of Japanese housewives." *East* 21(5):38-39,42-43,45. No refs. ISSN:0012-8295.

A rather derogatory commentary concerning the author's wife and her food purchasing habits. He does discuss her options of purchase (local shopkeepers, supermarkets, or food co-ops) and the social interactions which occur during her trips.

642. BAMBA, Tomoko. Apr./Jun. 1979. "The 'office ladies' paradise: Inside and out." *Japan Quarterly* 26(2):241-247. No refs. ISSN:0021-4590.

What begins as a review of young women's purchasing power and trends finishes as a reflective piece on the employment status of women and the overarching issues of marriage and child rearing. Includes some statistics on office ladies' buying and traveling habits.

643. BURTON, Jack. 14 Jan. 1985. "Women in Japan: A growing force." *Advertising Age* 56:40. No refs. ISSN:0001-8899.

A brief note on the "marketing clout" of Japanese women. Suggests the market for convenience items will grow as more women join the work force. Based on data from #199.

644. De MENTE, Boye and Fred Thomas PERRY. 1967. *The Japanese as Consumers: Asia's First Great Mass Market.* New York: Walker-Weatherill. 256p. Bibl. Index. LCCN:68-13566.

Drawing heavily on Japanese language sources, De MENTE and PERRY briefly discuss Japanese housewives as consumers, emphasizing the changes in life style made possible by electric rice cookers and synthetic fibers in particular. They also comment on how and where housewives shop.

645. "Exhibition of American and European products recommended by working women." Nov. 1985. *Focus Japan* 12(11):6. No refs. ISSN:0388-0311.

Announces the upcoming exhibition of products recommended by working women of Europe and the United States, and chosen by a team of five Japanese working women.

646. FIELDS, George. 1980. "The Japanese housewife: A marketing appraisal." In: NORBURY, Paul and Geoffrey BOWNAS, eds. *Business in Japan: A Guide to Japanese Business Practice & Procedure*. [Revised Edition.] Boulder: Westview, pp. 76-81. No refs. LCCN:80-51364.

A superficial discussion of the spending and saving habits of "the Japanese housewife." Contains the standard information about her roles as family banker and shopper.

647. FIELDS, George. 1983. *From Bonsai to Levi's: When West Meets East, an Insider's Surprising Account of How the Japanese Live*. New York: MacMillan. 213p. No refs. Index. LCCN:83-22196.

Originally written in Japanese for a Japanese audience, the book's intent is to relate "what puzzled and confounded the Western marketer in Japan." In Chapters 3 and 4, FIELDS, an Australian market researcher born and educated in Japan, explains the role and attitudes of the Japanese housewife as a financier and consumer, and further delineates differences in purchasing styles "pre- and post-marriage."

648. FIELDS, George. Nov. 1985. "Let the seller beware: Marketing to Japanese consumers." *Speaking of Japan* 6(59):17-23. No refs. ISSN:0389-350.

Within a general discussion of marketing in Japan, FIELDS briefly discusses the current force of the Japanese housewife in the consumer market and indicates that changes in her role will strongly effect marketing styles for consumer goods in the future.

649. "Japanese women buyers will tour U.S. trade fairs in October [1984]." 3 Sep. 1984. *Business America* 7(18):15. No refs. ISSN:0190-6275.

Announces the specific trade fairs the Women's Trade Mission will attend and provides an address for further information.

650. KITAZUME, Yukiko. 1979. "Why Japanese women buy costly imported handbags." *Japan Echo* 6(4):110-116. No refs. ISSN:0388-0435.

An essay which focuses primarily on pricing policies and the import market. KITAZUME ("a housewife") then speculates briefly on the nature of fads and the appeal of imported items to Japanese women.

651. MacMASTER, Norman. Jun. 1987. "'Kimono Revolution' makes for interesting times." *Journal of the American Chamber of Commerce in Japan* 24:49,51,53-54. No refs. ISSN:0002-7847.

MacMASTER warns marketers against considering Japanese women as a homogeneous group. Instead he divides them into four groups: career women, just-a-job women, currently-not-working-but-plan-to-work women, and stay-at-home women. He then describes the types of products appealing to each.

652. OGURA, M. May 1986. "Women's power." *Tokyo Business Today* (May 1986):16-18. No refs. ISSN:0911-7008.

OGURA reminds marketers that "women have become the single dominant force in Japan's consumer society" and illustrates his point with examples of successful merchandise.

653. S., J.V. Dec. 1984. "Women with a mission." *American Import/Export Management* 101(Dec. 1984):unpaged. No refs. ISSN:0279-4470.

Quotes ISHIHARA Ichiko, managing director of Takashimaya (a large department store chain), on the types of items for which she and other members of the JETRO buying mission were searching during their stay in the United States.

654. UCHIMURA, Kei. 1990. "Brushing up market for young women." *Journal of Japanese Trade and Industry* 9(3):25-26. No refs. ISSN:0285-9556.

Describes the latest trend in consumerism for young working Japanese women as the "brushing up market." Seen as a backlash to materialist consumerism which has dominated the spending of women in the 1980s, "brushing up" is defined as a search for "spiritual affluence" through finishing schools such as the John Robert Powers School.

655. U.S.-Japan Trade Study Group. 1981. *Japanese Women as U.S. Consumers.* Tokyo: JETRO [Japan External Trade Organization]. 86p. No refs.

The results of an extensive survey of Japanese women living, or who have lived, in the United States, concerning the categories and brands of American products purchased while in the United States, those items brought back to Japan (or desired once back in Japan), and those items bought as gifts. Highest on the lists were household goods (e.g. pans, towels, tableware), electrical appliances (e.g. mixers, irons), furniture, food, and cosmetics. Provides detailed lists of raw data, rationale for decisions, and housewives' suggestions for promoting American goods in Japan.

656. "Women creating a new wave in distribution: Part II. C'est La Vie, a department store for women only." Oct./Dec. 1982. *Wheel Extended* 12(4):24-26. No refs. ISSN:0049-755X.

The Takashimaya Department Store chain developed a specialty store aimed at women in their middle twenties and staffed it primarily with women (80% female management). It opened in Tachikawa City in 1982.

657. "The world's #1 customer." Oct. 1989. *Business Tokyo* 3(8):cover,25-29. No refs. ISSN:0914-0026.

Discusses the wealth of young Japanese women with statistics on how various groups (high school students, college women, single working women, young mothers, and middle aged women) spend their money. Outlines types of products which have appealed to these groups.

WOMEN IN THE PUBLIC SPHERE

7

Women Earning a Living

Overviews

658. AYAKAWA, Masako and Keiko SATŌ. Jan./Mar. 1983. "The growing female labor force: Its impact on the Japanese economy." *Japanese Finance and Industry* (Jan./Mar. 1983):36-39. [Also cited as *Japanese Finance and Industry: Quarterly Survey*.] No refs. ISSN:0385-2369.

An overview of changes in the labor force: outlines reasons for rising employment of women, the impact of their employment on household budgets and the labor market, and the potential changes required in the current economic structure as a result. Although short, a useful sketch.

659. BOWMAN, Mary Jean. 1983. "Women and the Japanese economic performance." In: WEISBROD, Burton and Helen HUGHES, eds. *Human Resources, Employment and Development. Vol. 3: The Problems of Developed Countries and the International Economy.* New York: St. Martin's Press, pp. 250-273. (International Economic Association World Congress, 6th, Mexico City, 1980. *Proceedings*.) 3 notes. LCCN:82-23163.

Explores "economic and educational activities of Japanese women since 1955" by analyzing employment by age cohort, delineating economic influences affecting women's participation in the labor force, and outlining effects of education on labor force participation.

660. BOWMAN, Mary Jean and Machiko OSAWA. 1986. *Developmental Perspectives on the Education and Economic Activities of Japanese Women.* [Washington, D.C.: Office of Educational Research and Improvement]. 17 refs. SuDocs No.:ED 1.310/2:271400.

Analyzes employment of Japanese women using cohort age-group data, discusses possibilities and limits within the current employment market, and explores the relationship between educational status and employment. Includes statistical data.

661. BURTON, Margaret E. 1918. *Women Workers of the Orient.* West Medford, MA: The Central Committee of the United Study of Foreign Mission. 240p. Bibl. Index. LCCN:18-8972.

Designed as a textbook for Christian women of North America, it includes sections on Japan focusing primarily on the conditions in textile factories, but also briefly covers women in business, teachers, writers, physicians and nurses, and the efforts of women's groups including the Red Cross and the Patriotic League. Most of the information is available in more recent treatments, but it may be interesting to read a contemporary account.

662. CARNEY, Larry S. and Charlotte G. O'KELLY. 1990. "Women's work and women's place in the Japanese economic miracle." In: WARD, Kathryn, ed. 1990. *Women Workers and Global Restructuring*. Ithaca, NY: Cornell University, School of Industrial and Labor Relations, ILR Press, pp. 113-145. (*Cornell International Industrial and Labor Relations Report*, 17.) 21 notes. LCCN:89-71699.

CARNEY and O'KELLY survey the role of women in the Japanese work force beginning with the Meiji period (1868-1912) and continuing through the post-World War II labor force to the present. Included are definitions and numbers for sections of the peripheral labor force, an examination of the policies used to exclude women from the main labor force (*e.g.*, the Equal Employment Opportunity Law), and projections for the future.

663. COLE, Robert E. and Ken'ichi TOMINAGA. 1976. "Japan's changing occupational structure and its significance." In: PATRICK, Hugh and Larry MEISSNER, eds. *Japanese Industrialization and its Social Consequences*. Berkeley: University of California Press, pp. 53-95. (Conference on Japanese Industrialization and its Social Consequences, University of Washington, 20-24 Aug. 1973.) Bibl. LCCN:75-7199.

In this technical survey of occupational structure, data on women are included in the section discussing pre-World War II Japan. Tables present figures on the percentage of women in the manufacturing sector, the transition of female factory workers to clerical workers, and comparative statistics on female factory workers in selected other countries.

664. "The current labor shortage and its prospects: Improvement likely over the medium term." Mar./Apr. 1990. *Fuji Economic Review* (Mar./Apr. 1990):5-13. No refs. LCCN:89-649273.

In its prognosis of the future labor supply, the Fuji Research Institute Corporation calls for parental leaves, expansion of child-care facilities, reemployment of women with prior training, and better conditions for part-time work (both through company offerings and by amending the tax exemption for two-income households).

665. ENGEL, John W. 1988. "Japanese and American housewives' attitudes toward employment of women." *Journal of Social Behavior and Personality* 3(4):363-371. 20 refs. ISSN:0886-1641.

ENGEL surveyed 200 Japanese and American housewives and concludes that, although none of the women questioned would be "happy as full-time housewives," both the Americans and Japanese thought it was an essential role while one had young children. American women seemed more sure of their ability to handle both home and work after children reached school age.

666. ERNST, Angelika. 1987. "A comparison of the position of women in the labour markets of Japan and West Germany." In: BERGMANN, Joachim and Shigeyoshi TOKUNAGA, eds. *Economic and Social Aspects of Industrial Relations: A Comparison of the German and Japanese Systems*. Frankfurt: Campus Verlag, pp. 95-116. 16 refs.

Taking an institutional rather than a cultural approach to an exploration of the position of women in the labor market, ERNST assumes only "gradational rather than fundamental differences" between Japan and Germany. She explores socioeconomic factors affecting employment and the labor market for women in both countries.

667. FRUIN, Mark. 1980. "Peasant migrants in the economic development of nineteenth-century Japan." *Agricultural History* 54(2):261-277. 17 refs. ISSN:0002-1482.

Although FRUIN discusses women only briefly, he does provide data which show that unmarried 19th-century women, especially lower class women, moved often for work and that marriage and childbirth were delayed.

668. FUKAO, Tokiko. Oct./Dec. 1982. "The expanding role of women in Japanese society." *Wheel Extended* 12(4):2-8. No refs. ISSN:0049-755X.

A "profile [of] the working Japanese female" based on statistics from the 1981 Labor White Paper.

669. FURUGORI, Tomoko. 1980. "Recent changes in the labor force: Behavior of women in Japan, a time-series analysis." *Keio Economic Studies* 17(1):51-69. 11 refs. ISSN:0022-9709.

In a technical study of the female labor force, FURUGORI considers its sensitivity to cyclical changes in the economy and to fluctuations in husbands' income. Includes many statistics.

670. FUSE, Akiko. 1978. "The state and problems of housewives' work in contemporary Japan." In: WHITE, Merry I. and Barbara MOLONY, eds. *Proceedings of the Tokyo Symposium on Women.* Tokyo: International Group for the Study of Women, pp. 156-183. (Tokyo Symposium on Women, [1st], 1978.) No refs.

FUSE provides statistics on working women and discusses the reasons for the increase in the number of employed women. She also considers the problems of child care and housework.

671. GREEN, Gretchen. Oct. 1989. "Women in Japan's labor force." *Journal of the American Chamber of Commerce in Japan* 26:21-22, 24-26,28,92. No refs. ISSN:0002-7847.

Summarizes women's position in the labor force including the effect of traditional societal values, employment patterns, and barriers to management roles. Discusses possibilities for change facilitated by entrepreneurial opportunities, the aging labor force, highly-educated women demanding better compensation, and the impact of non-Japanese firms becoming more competitive by hiring Japanese women. Includes statistics.

672. GULICK, Sidney L. 1915. *Working Women of Japan.* New York: Missionary Education Movement of the United States and Canada. 162p. No refs. LCCN:15-19437.

GULICK undertakes a description of the several categories of working women in an attempt to understand the effect of industrialization on them. He notes that BACON [#146] focuses primarily on higher and upper-middle classes while he discusses farmers, silk workers, wives and daughters of merchants and artisans, *komori* [baby-tenders], domestics, hotel and tea-house girls, factory workers, geisha and prostitutes. He then provides a description of the Matsuyama Working Girls' Home as an example of what can be done to ameliorate some of the harsher conditions of factory work.

673. HAYASHI, Hiroko. 1985. "Japan." In: FARLEY, Jennie, ed. *Women Workers in Fifteen Countries: Essays in Honor of Alice Hanson Cook.* Ithaca: ILR Press, New York School of Industrial and Labor Relations, Cornell University, pp. 57-67. (*Cornell International Industrial and Labor Relations Report*, no. 11.) Notes. LCCN:85-2375.

An overview of women's employment status, employment practices, legal status, government involvement and the change in emphasis from forest, agriculture, and family business to nonagricultural industries and some family business. A discussion by other professionals in the field follows the essay. [For a more in-depth view, see #734].

674. HEROLD, Renate. 1978. "Problems of women in the labor market (with special reference to Japan)." In: WHITE, Merry I. and Barbara MOLONY, eds. *Proceedings of the Tokyo Symposium on Women.* Tokyo: International Group for the Study of Women, pp. 36-49. (Tokyo Symposium on Women, [1st], 1978.) 5 notes.

Compares employment settings for women in Japan, Sweden, and West Germany. Discusses cultural context, education, occupational counseling, and support mechanisms.

675. HILL, M. Anne. Spring 1984. "Female labor force participation in Japan." *Journal of Human Resources* 19(2):279-287. 18 notes. ISSN:0022-166X.

Provides a technical analysis of female labor force participation in Japan taking into consideration the differences in working for others (e.g. companies) and working in family-run businesses or agriculture.

676. HILL, M. Anne. Winter 1989. "Female labor supply in Japan: Implications of the informal sector for labor force participation and hours of work." *Journal of Human Resources* 24(1):143-161. 32 refs. ISSN:0022-166X.

As a follow-up to her 1984 article [#675], HILL "examines labor supply decisions for married women" including employees, family workers and nonparticipants. In addition, annual hours and wage equations are estimated for the first two groups.

677. HOLDEN, Karen C. 1978. "Comparability of the measured labor force of older women in Japan and the United States." *Journal of Gerontology* 33(3):422-426. 24 refs. ISSN:0022-1422.

Discusses problems with definitions of "employment" and timing of data collection when comparing work force participation by older women in the United States and Japan.

678. HOLDEN, Karen C. 1983. "Changing employment patterns of women." In: PLATH, David W., ed. *Work and Lifecourse in Japan.* Albany: State University of New York Press, pp. 34-46. Bibl. LCCN:82-10481.

Asserts that, contrary to the popular belief that a Japanese woman "typically works for a few years after leaving school and that . . . she exits from the labor force at marriage," women have "increase[d] their participation in paid work and . . . continue to work during marriage and childbearing." Analyzes trends in labor force participation during the period 1960-1970 by examining a "succession of birth cohorts of women."

679. ISHIHARA, Kiyoko. Mar. 1938. "A glimpse of the working population of women." *Japanese Women* 1(2):2-3. No refs. ISSN:0388-1369.

ISHIHARA presents statistics on the numbers of women working in various industries in 1930. She is careful to point out that it was a time of depression and many more women are now at work in 1938.

680. Japan. Prime Minister's Office. May 1984. *Public Opinion Survey on Women's Employment.* [Tokyo]: Foreign Press Center. 14p. No refs.

During the fall of 1983, 3000 women from all areas of Japan were surveyed about their work. This report provides details on amount of employment, attitudes toward that work and later re-employment, problems of working women with children, and domestic responsibilities.

681. "Japanese married women are being actively wooed to return to work." Apr. 1970. *Labour Gazette* 70:259. No refs. ISSN:0023-6926.

Briefly notes the shortage of labor anticipated for the early 1970s and the expectation that middle aged women can fill the role. Problems expected: a need for retraining, technological innovation, and a "workday suitable to those with household commitments."

682. KASEY, Judy. 1979. "The working woman: Her role in Japan and in the United States." In: BELCHER, Jan and Katz TAKEDA, eds. *Essays on Comparative Culture between the U.S. and Japan.* Tokyo: Waseda University Press, pp. 1-15.

A paper from a collection of essays written by American undergraduates and designed to provide interesting reading in English for Japanese students. A general summary.

683. KAWASHIMA, Yōko. 1987. "Place and role of female workers in the Japanese labor market." *Women's Studies International Forum* 10(6):599-611. 6 refs. ISSN:0277-5395.

Describes the Japanese labor market of the 1980s with special emphasis on midpoint entry workers, part-timers, pieceworkers, and the feminization of the peripheral work force. Concludes that "the supplementary nature of female labor, a growth in size of the reserve army among women, and the total absence of united power among them, are three pillars which define female conditions in the Japanese labor market."

684. KOBAYASHI, Kazumasa. 1977. "Differential fertility by working status of women in Japan." In: KUPINSKY, Stanley, ed. *The Fertility of Working Women: A Synthesis of International Research.* New York: Praeger, pp. 317-341. Bibl. LCCN:76-12861.

Provides data on working women and birth rates from the 1930 and 1970 censuses. KOBAYASHI then analyzes the connections between type of work and family size, concluding that "differences in fertility have existed among wives of different working statuses or occupations."

685. KOBAYASHI, Shunji. Feb. 1978. "Japanese women's role in the 'economic miracle.'" [Translated by Fukuko KOBAYASHI.] *Feminist Japan* no. 4:9-11. [Also cited as 1(4).] No refs. ISSN:0386-197X.

In this essay, KOBAYASHI considers not only the visible role of women in the "economic miracle" via their low wages and part-time status, but also less-mentioned roles. He defines contributions women have made through their participation as indirect providers of capital by their massive household savings and as providers of social services the government chooses not to undertake in its emphasis on business and industry (e.g. care of the elderly). He calls for the consideration of women's views in economic policy to enable more humane and ecologically compatible decisions.

686. KOIKE, Kazuo. Winter 1980/1981. "A Japan-Europe comparison of female labor-force participation and male-female wage differentials." [Translated by Dennis M. SPACKMAN.] *Japanese Economic Studies* 9(2):3-27. 3 notes. ISSN:0021-4841.

A presentation attacking "the myths about female labor in Japan" by comparing Western and Japanese labor and wage statistics. KOIKE calls for skill development to make mothers reentering the labor market "eligible for the same course of career service as men."

687. KUWAHARA, Yasuo. 1 Oct. 1979. "Occupational structure by age and sex in Japan." *Japan Labor Bulletin* 18(10):4-8. 5 notes. ISSN:0021-4469.

Using figures from the years 1950-1975, KUWAHARA explains how women are "clustered" in certain occupations, primarily in the middle and lower occupational strata.

688. LEBRA, Joyce, Joy PAULSON, and Elizabeth POWERS, eds. 1976. *Women in Changing Japan.* Stanford: Stanford University Press/Westview Press. 322p. LCCN:75-33663.

A collection of essays concerning the various ways women make their living in Japan (e.g. women in factories, service industries, education). Each chapter provides a general overview, often including statistical data, and then profiles several women to illustrate various approaches to their lives and work. [For annotations of individual chapters, see title index under *Women in Changing Japan*.

689. LEE, David Kuo Chuen and Chin Lee GAN. Jan. 1989. "An economic analysis of fertility, market participation and marriage behaviour in recent Japan." *Applied Economics* 21(1):59-68. 17 refs. ISSN:0003-6846. [Note also the authors' "Corrigendum." Jun. 1989. *Applied Economics* 21(6):740. No refs.]

LEE and GAN describe this paper as the "first attempt to model fertility, participation rate and marriage rate as a simultaneous equation system for Japan," and as one which "examine[s] the relationships among fertility rates, wages, female labour participation and marriage rates." They conclude that a rise in men's wages has a positive effect on fertility, but the same may not be true for women "due to the dominance of substitution effect." The "corrigendum" corrects a phrase in a sentence.

690. LOSCOCCO, Karyn A. and Arne L. KALLEBERG. Dec. 1988. "Age and the meaning of work in the United States and Japan." *Social Forces* 67(2):337-356. 49 refs. ISSN:0037-7732.

A technical study of age-related work commitment and work values which concludes that although older male and female American workers and male Japanese workers have higher work commitment than younger workers, work commitment among Japanese females does not vary by age.

691. "Married women are growing as major force in job market." 7 Dec. 1982. *Japan Economic Journal* 20(1035):8. No refs. ISSN:0021-4388.

A brief report on the findings of a Ministry of Labor document, *Present State of Women's Labor—1982*. Major trends include higher rate of longevity in employed females and more 35-39-year-olds returning to the work force as part-timers.

692. MATSUSHITA, Keiichi. Oct./Dec. 1963. "Women at work." *Japan Quarterly* 10(4):512-522. No refs. ISSN:0021-4590.

A positive look at the labor status of women in the 1960s. Through statistics, MATSUSHITA documents the growth and diversification of women's employment.

693. "More women on the Japanese work scene: 45% consider employment 'a matter of course.'" 1 Feb. 1978. *Japan Report*, pp. 6-7. No refs. ISSN:0021-4604.

Summarizes recent statistics on number of working women and their reasons for seeking employment. Delineates problems of discrimination, childcare and protection vs. equality, and notes that as the female worker remains employed past marriage these problems must be addressed.

694. MOURDOUKOUTAS, Panos and S. N. SOHNG. Oct./Dec. 1988. "Japan's low unemployment: How do they do it?" *Business and Economic Review* 35:19-21. No refs. ISSN:0007-6465.

Includes a brief description of the "floating female labor force" as one factor at play in the low unemployment rate.

695. MURAMATSU, Yasuko and Yukiko ODA. 1980. "Women's employment in Japan." In: SHIPSTONE, Norah, ed. *Country Papers on Career Services for Women in Asia*. Lucknow: Asian Women's Institute, pp. 1-26. 10 notes. LCCN:81-903127.

In a volume of papers on the "problems of career counseling for the employment of different levels of women—college graduates, poor urban and rural," MURAMATSU and ODA present statistics on women's education, employment and training, counseling, and child care. Much of the data is from Japanese language sources.

696. MURAMATSU, Yasuko, ed. 1983. *Women and Work: Working Women and their Impact on Society*. Tokyo: International Group for the Study of Women. (Tokyo Symposium on Women, 2nd, 1983. *Proceedings*.) 236p. LCCN:84-187204.

Items annotated individually; see title index under *Women and Work: Working Women and their Impact on Society*.

697. NAOI, Michiko and Carmi SCHOOLER. Jun. 1990. "Psychological consequences of occupational conditions among Japanese wives." *Social Psychology Quarterly* 53(2):100-116. 28 refs. ISSN:0190-2725.

Compares social and psychological characteristics of women working for pay (and who are not self-employed) with those of women who are free to structure their own labors. Focuses particularly on psychological functioning, attitudes toward the elderly, intellectual flexibility and ability to self-direct activities. The authors conclude that women in the employ of others are socialized to accept traditional norms more than those who are self-employed or work in the home.

698. NISHIKAWA, Shunsaku and Yoshio HIGUCHI. Winter 1980/1981. "Determinants of female labor-force participation." [Translated by Mamoru ISHIKAWA.] *Japanese Economic Studies* 9(2):62-87. 5 refs. ISSN:0021-4841.

Provides a technical analysis of the sudden rise in participation in the labor force by women which occurred between 1976 and 1978. The authors are concerned that a continued increase in participation will have deleterious effects on wages and income of currently employed older men, given the excess in labor supply.

699. NISHIMURA, Namiko. 1986. "Women at work." *Journal of Japanese Trade and Industry* 5(3):46-49. No refs. ISSN:0285-9556.

Provides statistics on numbers of working women and discusses briefly changes in job categories and possible results of the Equal Employment Opportunity Law.

700. NODA, Machiko. Winter 1985. "What makes wives work?" *Japan Echo* 12(4):66-68. No refs. ISSN:0388-0435.

Explores the myth of "two-income affluence" and notes most women who work do so under pressure of housing and education costs. Also points out the rise in demand for convenience foods and household services which is creating a new market for women who wish to work. [For an introduction to the article, see #80.]

701. NUSS, Shirley A. Jan./Jun. 1980. "The position of women in socialist and capitalist countries." *International Journal of Sociology of the Family* 10(1):1-13. 16 refs. ISSN:0020-7667.

Japanese women are included in this study, which concludes that women in capitalist countries are more segregated in the labor force (particularly in clerical areas) than those in socialist countries. No specific data on Japanese women are given.

702. ŌHORI, Sueo. Apr./Jun. 1985. "The era of the working wife." *Japan Quarterly* 32(2):174-177. No refs. ISSN:0021-4590.

Documents changes in the number of working women and the opportunities available to women. Also provides statistical data on wage differentials for women and men.

703. OHTA, Ryūji. Jul./Aug. 1986. "The Japanese employment system in the 1990s." *Journal of the American Chamber of Commerce in Japan* 23:9-13. No refs. ISSN:0002-7847.

Although the section on women runs only three paragraphs, OHTA includes current statistics on numbers of employed women and also projections for the 1990s.

704. OKAMOTO, Hideo. 1985. "Corporations and social change." *Japan Echo* 12(2):64-67. No refs. ISSN:0388-0435.

A thoughtful analysis of the impending change in corporate structure and the role of corporations in society. Women's desire for professional careers and familial involvement of spouses have been effective catalysts toward this change.

705. OSAWA, Machiko. 1988. "Working mothers: Changing patterns of employment and fertility in Japan." *Economic Development and Cultural Change* 36(4):623-650. 30 refs. ISSN:0013-0079.

Explores the relationship between mother's time cost and number of desired children, focusing in particular on "differential fertility behavior between unpaid family workers and paid employees."

706. SANO, Yōko. 1983. "Women in the Japanese workforce." In: HANCOCK, Keith, *et al. Japanese and Australian Labour Markets: A Comparative Study.* Canberra: Australia-Japan Research Centre, pp. 435-457. 7 notes. LCCN:84-220557.

Discusses the internal labor market and the hiring of women, the probable impact of micro-electronics technology on the female job market, and possible policy implications for the above. An appendix lists the relevant government "measures" affecting women (e.g. Childcare Leave Act, Women's Workers' Week).

707. SANO, Yōko. 1987. "Women and the labour market in Japan." In: PEARSON, Gail and Lenore MANDERSON, eds. *Class, Ideology and Woman in Asian Societies.* Hong Kong: Asian Research Service, pp. 127-139. 8 refs.

Discusses opportunities in the labor market for women and differences in hiring practices for men and women. Suggests that the problem of wage differential cannot be solved until hiring practices are equalized.

708. SASO, Mary. 1990. *Women in the Japanese Workplace.* London: Hilary Shipman. 289p. Bibl. Index. LCCN:90-126866.

This lengthy, detailed study compares the position of working women in Japan with that of women working for Japanese companies in England, Wales and Ireland. After describing work roles historically, SASO discusses the contemporary work forces, employees' expectations of work and of their employers, wage differentials, legal structures controlling women's work, incentives and/or pressures leading to employment, mothers as workers and options for equalizing the burden on working parents, and the experiences of women working "on the shop floor." She concludes with an analysis of possible future scenarios for Japanese working women.

709. SHIBAYAMA, Emiko. Sep. 1990. "Women get on the job." *Look Japan* 36(414):8-10. No refs. ISSN:0456-5339.

A description of working women as of 1990, focusing on recent changes to employment trends, and part-time and temporary workers. Includes statistics.

710. SHIMADA, Haruo and Yoshio HIGUCHI. Jan. 1985. "An analysis of trends in female labor force participation in Japan." *Journal of Labor Economics* 3(1,part 2):S355-S374. 11 refs. ISSN:0734-306X.

Analyzes data on female labor force participation and household behavior, and estimates wage and income elasticities in order to provide international comparisons. Points out the problems inherent in Japanese female labor statistics (the "heterogeneous groups of the self-employed, unpaid family workers, and paid employees, whose behaviors are quite different").

711.   SHINOTSUKA, Eiko.   Sep. 1982.   "Women in the labor force."   *Economic Eye* 3(Sep.):22-26. No refs. ISSN:0389-0503. Reprinted in: *Economic Views from Japan:*

Selections from Economic Eye. 1986. Tokyo: Keizai Koho Center, pp. 157-165. LCCN:86-186491.

Reviews statistics on working women and calls for changes in the economy, especially in regard to pension and taxation systems. Expresses concern over the declining birth rate.

712. SHINOTSUKA, Eiko. 3 Dec. 1982. "Equality and care of the species." *Far Eastern Economic Review* 118(49):87-90. No refs. ISSN:0014-7591.

An essay exploring the effect of women working outside the home on Japanese societal structure. Calls for a careful examination of the possible future impact of current trends.

713. SHINOTSUKA, Eiko. Spring 1989. "Japanese women's limited job choices." *Economic Eye* 10(1):27-28,30. ISSN:0389-0503.

SHINOTSUKA briefly discusses the necessity for Japanese women to choose between career and raising children and calls for specialized training of women who enter the workforce after raising their children to enable better job opportunities.

714. TAKAHARA, Sumiko. 10 Feb. 1986. "Women at work." *Look Japan* (10 Feb. 1986):6-7. No refs. ISSN:0456-5339.

Presents a brief overview of statistics from the Ministry of Labor's 1985 *White Paper on Female Labor*. Topics include changes in the labor market, female control of family finances, and family saving patterns.

715. TAKAHASHI, Nabuko. Dec. 1968. "Women's employment in Japan in a period of rapid technological change." *International Labour Review* 98(6):493-510. 11 notes. ISSN:0020-7780.

Provides a detailed analysis of the changes in the structure of women's employment from 1955-1965. She also considers the impact of automation, wages, and effect of computerization on mental and physical health. Many statistics included.

716. UENO, Chizuko. Dec. 1989. "Women's labor under patriarchal captialism in the eighties." *Review of Japanese Culture and Society* 1989(Dec.):1-6. 12 notes. ISSN:0913-4700.

Using a Marxist-feminist perspective, UENO "analyze[s] women's dual burden of unpaid domestic work and paid labor," and discusses reasons for the sharp rise in employment for middle-aged women over the last twenty years as well as the possible effects of a growing visibility of class, race and ethnicity issues on gender issues.

717. UMETANI, Shun'ichirō. 1 Jan. 1975. "The Japanese women in the labor market." *Japan Labor Bulletin* 14(1):5-8. 6 notes. ISSN:0021-4469.

Analyzes statistics on women's labor force participation from 1973, touching on occupational choice, educational attainment, wages, and the effects of protective legislation on numbers of women employed in certain sectors.

718. United States. Department of Labor. Women's Bureau; and Japan. Ministry of Labor. Women's and Minors' Bureau. 1976. *Role and Status of Women Workers in the United States and Japan: A Joint United States-Japan Study.* Washington, D.C.: Government Printing Office. 247p. No refs. LCCN:76-601961. SuDocs: L36.102:J27.

Summarizes status of women in the labor force (including female labor force characteristics and wages), measures for women workers (legislation, employment assistance, benefits, daycare centers), and current problems of working women (vocational training, dual responsibility of family and job). The study provides a list of professional women's organizations. A combined United States/Japan section discusses future concerns such as re-entry into the work force and passage of laws prohibiting discrimination. The appendices contain many statistical tables (including employment, daycare centers, earnings, reasons for leaving work force) as well as translations of pertinent Japanese legislation (e.g. portions of the Constitution, Labor Standards Law, Working Women's Welfare Law).

719. USUI, Naoaki. Winter 1991. "Between war cry of career and whisper of sweet home." *Japan Update* no. 18:12-18. No refs. ISSN:0912-3474.

While listing a number of unusual jobs women have taken on (physicist, heavy dump truck driver, packaging designer), USUI states the "whisper of sweet home" is very strong and causes internal conflicts for working women.

720. WALSH, Doris L. Jun. 1987. "A familiar story." *American Demographics* 9:64. No refs. ISSN:0163-4089.

Briefly notes the greater numbers of women in the Japanese job market and changing attitudes toward divorce and housework.

721. "White paper on women at work." 1985. *Journal of Japanese Trade and Industry* 1985(1):75. No refs. ISSN:0285-9556.

Announces the publication of a "white paper" on working women for 1984 by the Ministry of Labor. Provides a few statistics from the report.

722. "The working girl." 1979. *Japan Pictorial* 2(3):1-7. No refs. ISSN:0388-6115.

This brief profile of two young working women describes their carefree lifestyle and desire to quit when they marry. It also notes that "management frowns at such early 'retirement,'" and considers it a "waste of the accumulated experience and training the girls have received."

723. "'Working women' in the mainstream." Dec. 1986. *Focus Japan* 13(12):3. No refs. ISSN:0388-0311.

A brief but noteworthy report points out the "M-curve" in women's employment by age is leveling out and that as of 1985 the percentage of women leaving jobs for marriage, childbirth and child rearing has dropped to 16.1%. Also notes several companies which are opening up management career paths to women.

724. YAMADA, Tadashi and Tetsuji YAMADA. Summer 1986. "Fertility and labor force participation of married women: Empirical evidence from the 1980 population census of Japan." *Quarterly Review of Economics and Business* 26(2):35-46. 31 notes. ISSN:0033-5797.

The authors show an "interdependency between the fertility and labor force participation of married women who spend most of their time in the labor market." The econometric model used to describe this is explained in full. Public policy implications discussed include the suggestion that "more-and-better fringe benefits and improved working conditions for working married women should be required by the Japanese government . . . to help maintain the job skills of married women and alleviate the burden of household experience."

725. YAMADA, Tadashi and Tetsuji YAMADA. Spring 1987. "Part-time work of married women in urban Japan." *Quarterly Review of Economics and Business* 27(1):41-50. 31 notes. ISSN:0033-5797.

The authors distinguish between part-time and full-time women workers in their model and find that, for part-time workers, "wage elasticity . . . is positive (about 0.98)" and observe "no simultaneous interdependency . . . between the fertility of married women and their decisions to work part-time."

726. YAMADA, Tadashi and Tetsuji YAMADA. Fall 1987. "Using aggregate data to estimate the part-time and full-time work behavior of Japanese women." *Journal of Human Resources* 22(4):574-583. 24 refs. ISSN:0020-166X.

The focus of this study is "the interdependency among labor force participation decisions of Japanese married women, particularly between the decisions to work part-time and full-time." The authors also examine the own-wage elasticities of this group.

727. YAMADA, Tadashi and Tetsuji YAMADA. Jan./Apr. 1987. "Labor employment of married women in Japan: Part-time work vs. full-time work." *Eastern Economic Journal* 13(1):41-48. 30 refs. ISSN:0094-5056.

YAMADA and YAMADA conclude that part-time and full-time workers who are married women cannot be treated as one group when analyzing labor force participation, especially when considering own-wage elasticity, the effect of men's wages, and vulnerability to business cycles.

728. YOSHIKAWA, Hiroshi and Fumio OHTAKE. May 1989. "An analysis of female labor supply, housing demand, and the saving rate in Japan." [With comments by Robert DEKLE and Jacques MAIRESSE.] *European Economic Review* 33(5):997-1030. 14 refs. ISSN:0014-2921.

In this technical analysis of housing demand and savings rates, YOSHIKAWA and OHTAKE suggest that female labor rates began to rise in the mid 1970s due to "the declaration of the economy's real growth beginning [in] the early 1970s" which resulted in "a sharp decline in the husband's permanent income."

Sex Role Differentiation and Discrimination

729. AKAMATSU, Tadashi Hanami. May 1969. "Women workers and retirement after marriage." *Japan Labor Bulletin* 8(5):6-8. No refs. ISSN:0021-4469.

Provides statistics on numbers of female married workers as of the late 1960s. Notes that compulsory retirement at marriage is being challenged by women and suggests that more women will continue to work even with the added problems of housework and child rearing.

730. ANDERSON, Kathryn H. and M. Anne HILL. Apr. 1983. "Marriage and labor market discrimination in Japan." *Southern Economic Journal* 49(4):941-953. 28 notes. ISSN:0038-4038.

A statistical analysis of age-at-marriage decisions of Japanese women and how employment practices affect this rate. Based on a 1975 survey of women living in the Tokyo metropolitan area. Technical.

731. ATSUMI, Reiko. 1988. "Dilemmas and accommodations of married Japanese women in white-collar employment." *Bulletin of Concerned Asian Scholars* 20(3):54-62. 32 notes. ISSN:0007-4810.

ATSUMI argues that gender role segregation is the result both of Japanese industrialists' exploitation of male employees (possible only with a wife at home for support) to achieve and maintain a high economic growth rate, and the government's desire to shift away responsibility for social needs (e.g. child care, elder care). The full-time women workers in her study had an additional adult family member at home and few had husbands who were company employees.

732. "The better half." 9 Jul. 1983. *Economist* 288(7297):survey, p.25. No refs. ISSN:0013-0613.

A very brief comment on Japan's discrimination against female 2labor.

733. BRINTON, Mary C. Sep. 1988. "The social-institutional bases of gender stratification: Japan as an illustrative case." *American Journal of Sociology* 94(2):300-334. 96 refs. ISSN:0002-9602.

A technical article analyzing "how the development and evaluation of human capital varies across cultural settings" and detailing "the implications this has for the degree of gender stratification in the economy." Provides a theoretical framework for gender studies in the Japanese context.

734. COOK, Alice H. and Hiroko HAYASHI. 1980. *Working Women in Japan: Discrimination, Resistance, and Reform.* Ithaca: New York State School of Industrial and Labor Relations, Cornell University. 124p. (*Cornell International Industrial and Labor Relations Report*, no. 10.) Bibl. Index. LCCN:80-17706.

Beginning with the information that "Japan's labor force has a higher percentage of women working than any other noncommunist country," by the end of the second paragraph the authors state the "Japanese employment system probably exploits women more extensively than is the case in any other industrialized country." After an overview of the employment status of women, the authors discuss court cases concerning equal pay, retirement, transfer, and maternity and menstrual leave, and then look to the future to discuss whether the resulting court decisions "will in fact change the status and role of women in the Japan[ese] employment system." A 17-page statistical appendix is included.

735. CREIGHTON, Millie R. Apr. 1989. "Women in the Japanese department store industry: Capturing the momentum of the Equal Employment Opportunity Law." *Working Paper* [*on Women in International Development*] no. 185. 25p. 34 notes and 25 refs. ISSN:0888-5354.

CREIGHTON reviews employment conditions of women prior to the Equal Employment Opportunity Law (1986) and discusses the current "women-oriented" nature of the department store industry including its predilection to both hire and promote women. She notes liberal maternity and child-care leave policies, reinstatment programs for those who quit to raise children, and in-store daycare facilities. She concludes with comments from female employees concerning themselves and their colleagues.

736. "Feminism: Thirty and out in Japan." [Title page title: "Japan's irate career women."] 27 Nov. 1972. *Newsweek* 80(22):87,89. No refs. ISSN:0028-9604.

A brief comment on the understood, if not openly stated, policy of Japanese companies that women retire at 25 or 30. Includes a few brief but choice quotations from management.

737. HAITANI, Kenji. 1976. *The Japanese Economic System: An Institutional Overview.* Lexington, MA: Lexington Books. 190p. Notes. Index. LCCN:76-11972.

Pages 104-105 briefly describe the status of the woman worker. The only unique information presented is a reference to a survey by Nikkei Business in 1975 which found that "only 3% of the women believe there is no difference in abilities and aptitudes between men and women."

738. HALLIDAY, Jon. 1975 [rep. 1978]. *A Political History of Japanese Capitalism.* New York: Monthly Review Press. 466p. Notes. Index. LCCN:78-18882.

A history of Japanese capitalism from a Marxist point of view. Includes comments (pp. 224-225) on the exploitation of women by business, and notes how the Japanese ideology promoting motherhood "make[s] women *prefer* grossly underpaid jobs as temporary workers."

739. HELM, Leslie, Kyōko TAKAHASHI, and Bob ARNOLD. 4 Mar. 1985. "Japan's secret economic weapon: Exploited women." *Business Week* no. 2883:54-55. No refs. ISSN:0007-7135.

A brief but pithy overview outlining the situation of women who work outside the home.

740. HUBER, Edna L. Spring 1982. "Sex inequality in Japanese employment." *Towson State Journal of International Affairs* 16(2):75-79. 14 notes. ISSN:0041-0063.

A brief summary covering sex-role differentiation in the work place and the response of the government, unions, and women (prior to the Equal Employment Opportunity Law of 1986).

741. JONES, H.J. Winter 1976/1977. "Japanese women and the dual-track employment system." *Pacific Affairs* 49(4):589-606. 63 notes. ISSN:0030-851X.

One of the earliest in-depth English language studies identifying and explaining the dual tract employment system based on the premise that "men live by work, women live by marriage." Discusses possible social ramifications of a continuance of this attitude and points to possibilities for change.

742. KAJI, Etsuko. Autumn 1973. "The invisible proletariat—Working women in Japan." *Ampo: Japan-Asia Quarterly Review* no. 18:48-58. No refs. LCCN:77-612830. [Also published in *Social Praxis* 1(4):375-387, 1974, ISSN:0304-2405, and *Japanese Women Speak Out* (#1180), pp. 26-40.]

Substantiating her argument with government and business statistics, KAJI argues that the exploitation of women as cheap labor made the growth of Japanese industry possible and that the exploitation continues into the 1970s through the dual employment structure for women and their use as a cheap, temporary labor force, as well as through the promulgation of the idea that child care is a private responsibility rather than a social issue.

743. KAWAKAMI, Yoshirō and Atsuko MUTO. 1983. "A survey of male presidents of small and medium-size companies in Tokyo." In: MURAMATSU, Yasuko, ed. *Women and Work: Working Women and their Impact on Society.* Tokyo: International Group for the Study of Women, pp. 155-168. (Tokyo Symposium on Women, 2nd, 1983. *Proceedings*.) No refs. LCCN:84-187204.

Presents results of a survey given to 139 male presidents in October 1982 concerning "their attitudes towards their female workers and female managers, and their opinion about working women in small and medium size companies." [Survey is included as an appendix to #848.]

744. KITAMURA, Setsuko. 1983. "The situation of single women employed in corporations." In: MURAMATSU, Yasuko, ed. *Women and Work: Working Women and their Impact on Society.* Tokyo: International Group for the Study of Women, pp. 217-220. (Tokyo Symposium on Women, 2nd., 1983. *Proceedings*.) No refs. LCCN:84-187204.

After interviewing personnel officers in five major corporations, KITAMURA found that the longer female employees worked, the more important personality became as a factor in the evaluation of their performance.

745. MANASIAN, David. 19 Mar. 1985. "Office flowers are coming out." *Management Today* (19 Mar. 1985):19. No refs. ISSN:0025-1925.

MANASIAN provides a rather overstated summary of the status of employed women (e.g. that few have management positions and that a few token "firsts" have been publicized heavily). Concludes by describing the Japanese feminist movement as one which "focuses on abstractions such as an alleged government plot to increase the birth rate and populate Asia with Japanese, rather than on concrete problems faced by women at work."

746. MASUDA, Reiko. Sep. 1990. "Nice try, but . . . ." *Look Japan* 36(414):4-7. No refs. ISSN:0456-5339.

Discusses the overall ineffectiveness of the Equal Employment Opportunity Law showing how the law allows "indirect discrimination" through its weak wording. Also describes some companies which are accommodating women, and women who break the mold. Outlines possible measures to enable women "to achieve a balance between job and family." A brief but useful summary.

747. MATSUMOTO, Nancy. Aug. 1989. "A question of goals." *[PHP] Intersect* (Aug. 1989):8-12. No refs. ISSN:0910-4607.

Explores attitudes toward the equality of women in the work place and the importance of family versus work. Includes comments of two university career counselors as well as other more regularly quoted sources.

748. MITSUI, Mariko. Dec. 1984. "Who pays for Japan's economic miracle?" *Ms.* 13(6):23. No refs. ISSN:0047-8318.

A brief description of economic discrimination against female employees with a few excerpts from the Sumitomo Shoji company's *Glossary of Common Sense for Considerate Office Ladies*.

749. MOUER, Ross and Yoshio SUGIMOTO. 1986. *Images of Japanese Society: A Study in the Social Construction of Reality.* London: KPI Limited. 552p. Bibl. Index.

In a work designed to reconstruct views of Japanese society, MOUER briefly points out the pitfalls of cross-cultural comparison of male-female wage differentials by noting that fringe benefits differ greatly, and that other "stratification variables affect the size of wage differential."

750. MOUER, Ross E. 1987. "Working women in Japan and male-female wage differentials." In: PEARSON, Gail and Lenore MANDERSON, eds. *Class, Ideology and Woman in Asian Societies.* Hong Kong: Asian Research Service, pp. 141-176. 62 refs.

Establishes a definition of wage differentials based on eight measures to enable analysis of dependent and independent variables affecting wage rates. Technical and detailed.

751. ŌHASHI, Terue. 1980. "The reality of female labor." [Translated by Rose CARTER.] *Feminist International* no.2:17-22. No refs. ISSN:0388-371X.

A detailed overview of sexual discrimination in the Japanese work place. ŌHASHI justifies her conclusions with statistics from a variety of sources.

752. OKUBAYASHI, Kōji. Jan. 1986. "Recent problems of Japanese personnel management." *Labour and Society: Journal of the International Institute for Labour Studies* 11(1):17-37. 29 notes. ISSN:0378-5408.

In a general discussion of various management topics, OKUBAYASHI suggests that the Equal Employment Opportunity Law will in fact cause changes in "conventional personnel management strategies which confine women to peripheral jobs."

753. OMORI, Maki. 1987. "Women workers and the Japanese industrial relations system." In: BERGMANN, Joachim and Shigeyoshi TOKUNAGA, eds. *Economic and Social Aspects of Industrial Relations: A Comparison of the German and the Japanese Systems.* Frankfurt: Campus Verlag, pp. 117-128. 8 refs.

Discusses several major features of the Japanese industrial sector (e.g. lifetime employment, trade unions, governmental policy) and shows how women are essential for sustaining the system but do not benefit from it.

754. PHARR, Susan J. 1982. "Tea and power: The anatomy of a conflict." In: O'BARR, Jean F., ed. *Perspectives on Power: Women in Africa, Asia and Latin America.* Durham: Duke University, pp. 37-49. 6 refs. LCCN:82-050929.

Reports on the attempts of working women to separate themselves from tea-making duties (assigned solely due to their gender).

755. PHARR, Susan J. 1984. "Status conflict: The rebellion of the tea pourers." In: KRAUSS, Ellis S., Thomas P. ROHLEN, and Patricia G. STEINHOFF, eds. *Conflict in Japan.* Honolulu: University of Hawaii Press, pp. 214-240. 35 notes. LCCN:84-108.

Analyzes the stages of status conflict, using as a case study the experience of women workers in the Kyoto City Office during the early 1960s, who organized to protest their responsibilities as tea makers and servers in addition to their regular clerical duties.

756. "Recession lay-offs in Japan—'Ladies first.'" Jun. 1975. In: *Japanese Women Speak Out.* Tokyo: White Paper on Sexism—Japan Task Force, pp. 40-41. No refs.

A release from *New Asia News* of 11 April 1975, documenting Toshiba's proposal to lay off 3,000 married women and 560 males past age 57 because of recession pressures.

757. SATŌ, Kinko. 1984. "Working women pose no threat." *Japan Echo* 11(4):50-54. No refs. ISSN:0388-0435.

A highly critical look at #1026. SATŌ counters by insisting that "the housewife culture" has already broken down and the concept of "equality in employment" does not threaten Japanese cultural equality. [Introduced by #1032.]

758. SENDER, Henny. 1 Jan. 1989. "The gaijin's secret weapon: Unappreciated Japanese women." *Institutional Investor* 23(1):267. No refs. ISSN:0020-3580.

SENDER briefly describes the pitfalls Japanese women can encounter even when working for Western firms.

759. SHINOTSUKA, Eiko. Spring 1984. "Female workers as described in a help-wanted information magazine." [Translated by Yōko Yamamoto PARKS.] *Japanese Economic Studies* 12(3):3-20. No refs. ISSN:0021-4841.

Describes the advertisements contained in *Travail*, a help-wanted magazine aimed at young women. Analyzes the types of jobs available and qualifications desired by prospective employers.

760. SUGAHARA, Mariko and Hiroshi TAKEUCHI. Oct./Dec. 1982. "Japanese style of management and women's entry into the job market." *Wheel Extended* 12(4):27-32. No refs. ISSN:0049-755X.

In an interview aimed at a non-Japanese audience, SUGAHARA and TAKEUCHI discuss possibilities for employed women to receive equal treatment and the "strength of the professional housewife."

761. SUZUKI, Kazue. Jun. 1987. "Welcome to the corporate world." *PHP Intersect* (Jun. 1987):42-43. No refs. ISSN:0910-4607.

Describes the varied training women and men receive when entering companies, and provides brief excerpts from a few manuals illustrating discriminatory attitudes toward women.

762. TAIRA, Kōji. 1970. *Economic Development and the Labor Market in Japan.* New York: Columbia University Press. 280p. Bibl. Index. LCCN:78-111459.

Although women are not discussed as a group, TAIRA includes two tables on wage differentials from 1880-1939 which may be of use.

763. TAKAHASHI, Nobuko. Jan. 1975. "Women's wages in Japan and the question of equal pay." *International Labour Review* 111(1):51-68. 26 notes. ISSN:0020-7780.

TAKAHASHI provides a thorough discussion of the equal pay question (prior to the passage of the Equal Employment Opportunity Law), covering the employment structure in Japan, wage structures, and attitudes toward women's work. Outlines changes in the education and employment sectors which would allow movement toward a goal of equal pay.

764. TAKEUCHI, Hiroshi. Jul. 1982. "Working women in business corporations—The management viewpoint." *Japan Quarterly* 29(3):319-323. No refs. ISSN:0021-4590.

Presents a traditional interpretation of the problems associated with hiring "girls." Although TAKEUCHI does acknowledge that a few "gifted girls" could make a contribution to a company, he lauds the "truly worthwhile life" of mother and housewife. He stresses the benefits to the company of hiring women returning to the workforce: low wages for part-time work, no benefits, and the ease of layoffs in times of recession.

765. TANAKA, Hiroshi. 1986. "Working women in Japan." *Equal Opportunities International* 5(1):1-7. 27 refs. ISSN:0261-0159.

Provides a tightly-written overview of the status of Japanese female laborers including employment status, legislation, extent of discrimination, management justification for same, and social attitudes towards working women.

766. THURLEY, E. and K. THURLEY. 1977. "The equal pay question in Japan." In: PETTMAN, Barrie O., ed. *Equal Pay for Women: Progress and Problems in Seven Countries.* Washington, D.C.: Hemisphere, pp. 147-173. 23 notes. LCCN:77-7335.

The authors assert that Japan is an example of "a classic case of conflict between the traditional cultural norms of discrimination, and economic necessity, in terms of labour shortages [1966-1967]." They address both the complexities underlying this assertion ("demographic structure, migration patterns, educational changes, and government intervention"), and their effect on the labour market. Many statistics on women's participation in the work force and wages are included. An excellent overview.

767. VALERY, Nicholas. 9 Jul. 1983. "What makes Yoshio run? Japan: A survey." *Economist* 288(7297):25p. insert between pp. 50 and 51; p. 25 on women. No refs. ISSN:0013-0613.

VALERY briefly notes the pool of educated housewives that Japan's business and industrial community under-utilize.

768. "The 'woman power' fraud: C. Itoh and Co., a case in point." Jun. 1975. In: *Japanese Women Speak Out.* Tokyo: White Paper on Sexism—Japan Task Force, pp. 11-13. No refs.

An abstract of a report detailing differences in the way men and women employees are treated by C. Itoh, a large Japanese trading company. Examples include the requirements that women's mothers be interviewed and that women live at home, and the lack of a promotion system for women. The material was compiled by the Women's Committee of the labor union at the company.

769. "Women creating a new wave in distribution. Part I. Working women describe their experience." Oct./Dec. 1982. *Wheel Extended* 12(4):16-26. No refs. ISSN:0049-755X.

A discussion based on the experiences of four women: KURODA Setsuko (marketing consultant), MIZUNO Junko (Seibu Department Store), MAEOKA Sakiko (Odakyu

Department Store), and MAKIYA Yōko (Keio Department Store). Touches on sex discrimination, advancement of women, social and industrial changes the authors expect to be initiated by women, and the problem of reinstatement after child rearing.

770. WORONOFF, Jon. Mar. 1980. "There's a lot of catching up to be done." *Asian Business* 16:38-39,42,45. No refs. ISSN:0254-3729.

WORONOFF summarizes the attitudes of many personnel managers about the problems associated with hiring women in general (low skills, short employment period) and especially 4-year college graduates (generally no skills but higher expectations given their degree: a "spoiled and self-satisfied elite"). WORONOFF expresses sympathy for the serious career woman who must fight these images.

771. WORONOFF, Jon. Nov. 1980. "Wasting Japan's women workers." *Oriental Economist* 48(841):22-24. No refs. ISSN:0030-5294.

WORONOFF briefly describes gender-based stratification in the Japanese labor market and points out that "if Japan keeps on neglecting more than a third of its workers while other countries offer women a more useful role, it is going to be the loser."

772. WORONOFF, Jon. Jun. 1981. "Career escalators: In Japan, women need not apply." *Asian Business* 17:59-60. No refs. ISSN:0254-3729.

In this brief summary of women's occupational status, WORONOFF describes women's career ladders as a "moving pavement" with nowhere to go.

773. WORONOFF, Jon. 1983. *Japan's Wasted Workers*. [Translated by Maki HAMADA-WORONOFF.] Totowa, NJ: Allanheld, Osmun and Co. 296p. Bibl. Index. LCCN:82-13785. [*Maboroshi no han'ei, Nippon*. English.]

Writing for a Japanese audience increasingly disenchanted with its employment system, WORONOFF summarizes many of the complaints and analyzes the routes Japan might choose. In a chapter called "What to do with Women'" he again states: "If Japan keeps on neglecting more than a third of its labor force while other countries offer women a more useful role, it is going to be the loser [see also #771]." While pushing the responsible employment of women, WORONOFF bluntly outlines the attitudes of both men and women which are impediments to this philosophy.

774. YASHIRO, Naohiro. Winter 1980/1981. "Male-female wage differentials in Japan: A rational explanation." [Translated by Jun Uramatsu SMITH.] *Japanese Economic Studies* 9(2):28-61. 23 refs. ISSN:0021-4841.

YASHIRO provides a thorough analysis and discussion concerning male-female wage differentials and discrimination in employment. Although he details many of the same points as seen elsewhere in the literature, both his conclusions about the origins of the discrimination and his recommendations for public policy changes are solidly supported by his scholarly analysis. He recommends making discrimination financially unattractive to businesses, reducing the separation rate among females, expanding daycare centers and their hours, regulating overtime equally for men and women, and, if a woman must leave the workforce for child rearing, certifying her attainment of skills to facilitate her reentry in later years.

Unions

775. CARTER, Aiko. 3 May 1974. "On being a woman in Japan. Part 4: Working women." *Japan Christian Activity News*, no. 453:3-4. No refs. ISSN:0021-4353. [Reprinted in CARTER, Aiko. 1975. *On Being a Woman in Japan*. Tokyo: Femintern Press.]

A brief and critical appraisal of the low status of women's labor and women's acceptance of that status. Also comments on the efforts of SHIOZAWA Miyoko, a union organizer among textile and food processing workers.

776. DEHARENG, Marcelle. Dec. 1971. "Japanese women at work." *Free Labour World* 258:8-10. 4 notes. ISSN:0770-1470.

After a description of working conditions for women, DEHARENG notes "claims" trade unions are making on behalf of their women members. DEHARENG is the Secretary of the Committee on Women Workers' Questions of the International Confederation of Free Trade Unions.

777. HANAMI, Tadashi. 1984. "Japan." In: COOK, Alice, Val R. LORWIN, and Arlene K. DANIELS, eds. *Women and Trade Unions in Eleven Industrialized Countries.* Philadelphia: Temple University Press, pp. 215-238. 20 refs. LCCN:83-17946.

A detailed survey of women in the labor force and their representation by, and participation in, trade unions. HANAMI begins with the first Japanese trade union, the Yūaikai [Friendship Society], but spends the bulk of his essay discussing the situation in the 1970s and 1980s.

778. SEO, Akwi [sic]. Sep. 1990. "One for all, all for one." *Look Japan* 36(414):10. No refs. ISSN:0456-5339.

Briefly describes the community-based Edogawa Union which serves part-time (and therefore primarily female) workers. Women involved in union management is an unusually high 50 percent.

779. TAKAGI, Sumiko. 1986. "Women on the labor front." *Ampo: Japan-Asia Quarterly Review* 18(2/3):48-54. No refs. LCCN:77-612830.

TAKAGI, active in both labor unions and the women's movement, severely criticizes labor unions' lack of efforts on behalf of women. Describes unions' priorities and contrasts them with those of the women's movement, notes several court cases challenging interpretations of labor law, discusses problems with the situation of "part-time" workers, outlines efforts to protest the Equal Employment Opportunity Law, and calls for a "genuine" Equal Employment Opportunity Law.

Women in Agriculture and Mining

780. ABE, Hatsumi. Jul. 1938. "Working women in agricultural districts." *Japanese Women* 1(4):2-3. No refs. ISSN:0388-1369.

A short report on the status of farm women using data from the 1930 census. Interprets average length of work day and other statistics, and further details financial and health problems in rural areas. Author is a member of the Labour Section, National Committee of the Young Women's Christian Association [YWCA].

781. BERNSTEIN, Gail Lee. 1976. "Women in rural Japan." In: LEBRA, Joyce, *et al. Women in Changing Japan.* Stanford: Stanford University Press, pp. 25-49. 21 notes. LCCN:75-33663.

Provides an oral history of KAWABATA Misao Sakai (age 66), a farm woman who worked as a young girl in a silk factory. Bernstein then discusses the transformation of rural Japan and the roles of its women, commenting specifically on their work, social life, and family relationships.

782. BERNSTEIN, Gail Lee. 1983. *Haruko's World: A Japanese Farm Woman and her Community.* Stanford: Stanford University Press. 199p. No refs. LCCN:82-61783.

A very readable and in-depth ethnographic study of farm women from western Shikoku in the mid-1970s which focuses on UTSUNOMIYA Haruko and her family. This is both a personal account of BERNSTEIN's time with the family, and a detailed report on family and community roles of rural women. Reviewed by BOOCOCK in #2305.

783. KADA, Reiko and Yukiko KADA. 1985. "The changing role of women in Japanese agriculture: The impact of new rice technology on women's employment." In: *Women in Rice Farming.* 1985. Brookfield, VT: Gower Publishing Co., pp. 37-53. (Women in Rice Farming Systems [Conference], Manila, Philippines, 26-30 September 1983.) 9 refs. LCCN:85-24939.

A study of women's agricultural labor which concludes that increased mechanization has assisted women in their primary agricultural roles but has led to increased off-farm employment rather than a lessening of duties. KADA includes statistics on female labor force participation in agriculture, farm production and farm mechanization trends, and women's participation in rice cultivation.

784. KAWAHARA, Yukiko. Apr. 1990. "Women left behind: Wives of seasonal migrant workers in Japan." *Asian Profile* 18(2):127-135. 46 notes and 31 refs. ISSN:0304-8675.

Describes the process of *dekasegi* [temporary labor migration] which is especially widespread in agricultural areas, and focuses in particular on the experiences of wives. Duties include farm upkeep and decision-making, winter tasks (*e.g.*, snow fences and shoveling) and village responsibilities (*e.g.*, fire station duty), additional social responsibilities, and single-parenting. . . . Concludes that "*dekasegi* did not lead to any radical changes in women's status."

785. MATSUBARA, Hiroshi. Oct. 1976. "Women of the fields." *East* 12(9/10):20-24. No refs. ISSN:0012-8295.

Translates portions of rice planting songs to describe the work of women farmers.

786. MATSUBARA, Hiroshi. Feb. 1978. "Women of the markets." *East* 14(3/4):69-77. No refs. ISSN:0012-8295.

Explores the traditional role of women in product distribution by focusing on *ichime* [women who "bring the products of the mountain or fishing villages for sale in open markets"]. For the general reader.

787. MOON, Okpyo. 1989. *From Paddy Field to Ski Slope: The Revitalisation of Tradition in Japanese Village Life.* Manchester: Manchester University Press. 191p. Bibl. Index. LCCN:89-12679.

Although focused primarily "political, economic and social implications" of change in a Japanese mountain hamlet as it transitions from a traditional agricultural village to a tourist area, MOON does include some material on the effect of technological change in agriculture on women's roles and relationships within the village.

788. NAKAGAWA, Etsuko. Jun. 1975. "Farming women—Loneliness and bills." In: *Japanese Women Speak Out.* Tokyo: White Paper on Sexism—Japan Task Force, pp. 44-46. No refs.

At the Asian Women's Congress to Fight Discrimination and Aggression, a farm woman from Akita Prefecture presents several cases of tragedy due to *dekasegi* [farm family members needing to leave farms for outside jobs to supplement incomes]. She also shows her own financial balance sheet for the 1971 harvest year.

789. NISHIZAWA, Emiko. 1987. "Rural women bear the yoke of a modern economy." *Ampo: Japan-Asia Quarterly Review* 19(2):22-24. No refs. LCCN:77-612830.

Describes the problems facing farm women through the lives of three: one who works part-time leaving home at 3 am, one who is elderly and caring for a grandchild while her daughter-in-law works, and a widow with a bachelor son.

790. OHKI, Reiko. 1985. "Women's labor and the technological development of rice cultivation in Japan." In: *Women in Rice Farming*. 1985. Brookfield, VT: Gower Publishing Co., pp. 55-64. (Women in Rice Farming Systems [Conference], Manila, Philippines, 26-30 September 1983.) No refs. LCCN:85-24939.

Focuses on the position of contemporary farm women, noting that involvement in three traditional jobs handled by women (weeding, planting and harvesting) has decreased with the advent of mechanized rice cultivation. However, with the increasing off-farm employment of men and the amount of manual labor still required on farms, women continue to be heavily involved in crop production. OHKI briefly notes problems yet to be addressed: ownership of land; health problems (especially stress); and the need for advanced training, guaranteed leisure time and old-age security.

791. SEGAWA, Kiyoko. 1978. "Japanese women in the last century." IN: WHITE, Merry I. and Barbara MOLONY, eds. *Proceedings of the Tokyo Symposium on Women.* Tokyo: International Group for the Study of Women, pp. 1-9. (Tokyo Symposium on Women, [1st], 1978.) No refs.

SEGAWA focuses on farm women during the Meiji era; their role as workers and their status as food distributors. She lists various regional terms for wives and analyzes the way in which power was transferred from one woman to another.

792. "A visit with a country wife." Aug./Sep. 1967. *East* 3(5):32-35. No refs. ISSN:0012-8295.

An interview with TAKATSUKA Mikiko, wife of a farmer who raises tea. It briefly relates her daily responsibilities.

793. "Women working underground again." Sep. 1939. *Japanese Women* 2(5):3. No refs. ISSN:0388-1369.

Due to a shortage of metal and coal miners, the protective standards prohibiting the employment of women and children in most mines have been temporarily relaxed. Notes conditions of employment and the split reaction of the women's movement.

Ama [Women Divers]

794. BIRUKAWA, Shōhei. 1965. "Geographic distribution of ama in Japan." In: RAHN, Hermann and Tetsurō YOKOYAMA, eds. *Physiology of Breath-hold Diving and the Ama of Japan.* Washington, D.C.: National Academy of Sciences, National Research Council. *Publication* 1341, pp. 57-70. 30 refs. LCCN:65-62909. [Also published separately as: *Geographical Research Paper* no. 1.) Tokyo: Tokyo Kyōiku University, Department of Geography, Institute of Human Geography, 1965. LCCN:71-570613.]

A scientific overview of *ama* [women divers], classifying them according to materials harvested and harvesting techniques, and then exploring geographical distribution and trends in numbers of women employed. The two texts are identical. In addition, the symposium paper (contained in RAHN) includes tables outlining diving patterns, work schedules, and age distribution; the separate paper includes more census data and several Japanese language citations.

795. HONG, Suk Ki and Hermann RAHN. May 1967. "The diving women of Korea and Japan." *Scientific American* 216(5):34-43. 3 refs. ISSN:0036-8733.

HONG and RAHN explain the physiological mechanisms which allow *ama* [women divers] to dive to depths of 80 feet and to hold their breath up to two minutes as they earn their living foraging for shellfish and edible seaweeds from the ocean floor.

796. KITA, Hiromasa. 1965. "Review of activities: Harvest, seasons, and diving patterns." In: RAHN, Hermann and Tetsurō YOKOYAMA, eds. *Physiology of Breath-hold Diving and the Ama of Japan.* Washington, D.C.: National Academy of Sciences, National Research Council. *Publication* 1341, pp. 41-55. 18 refs. LCCN:65-2909.

Provides details on flora and fauna harvested, suitable seasons for diving, and equipment used for diving.

797. LINHART, Ruth. 1988. "Modern times for ama-divers." In: NISH, Ian, ed. 1988. *Contemporary European Writing on Japan: Scholarly Views from Eastern and Western Europe.* Kent, England: Paul Norbury Publications, pp. 114-119. 11 notes. LCCN:88-193026.

LINHART debunks the myth of a woman-centered society among ama villages, at least for contemporary times, and casts doubts on the theory for the past. Also describes briefly changes technology and organization have brought to the profession.

798. MARAINI, Fosco. 1962. *The Island of the Fisherwomen.* New York: Harcourt, Brace and World. 95p. [Alternate title: *Hekura: The Diving Girls' Island.*] Bibl. LCCN:62-10498. [*L'Isola delle Pescatrici.* English.]

An Italian filmmaker's travelogue about his search for the "true" *ama*, women who dive for *awabi* [a type of shellfish]. He filmed on the island of Hekura on the Sea of Japan. Although basically a relating of his experiences, this work contains pictures and a general description of the *ama* and their lives.

799. MARTINEZ, D.P. 1990. "Tourism and the *ama*: The search for the real Japan." In: BEN-ARI, Eyal, Brian MOERAN, and James VALENTINE, eds. *Unwrapping Japan: Society and Culture in Anthropological Perspective.* Honolulu: University of Hawaii Press, pp. 97-116. 37 refs. LCCN:89-35666.

MARTINEZ discusses the adaptability of a host population within the tourism industry, focusing here on *ama* [diving women]. He analyzes the extent to which they manipulate their image to their own ends [encouraging tourism] while maintaining a village identity separate from the contrived tourist image.

800. MATSUBARA, Hiroshi. Jun. 1978. "Women who dive." *East* 14(7/8):14-20. No refs. ISSN:0012-8295.

This discussion of diving women is intended for the general reader but includes information on the operation of the fishing cooperative to which they belong.

801. NUKADA, Minoru. 1965. "Historical development of the ama's diving activities." In: RAHN, Hermann and Tetsurō YOKOYAMA, eds. *Physiology of Breath-hold Diving and the Ama of Japan.* Washington, D.C.: National Academy of Sciences, National Research Council. *Publication* 1341, pp. 25-40. 7 refs. LCCN:65-62909.

A brief overview of *ama* [women divers] and their techniques, with comments on the historical evidence for their existence for up to 2,000 years.

802. SEGAWA, Kiyoko. 1957. "A study on female divers (Ama)." *Bungaku tetsugaku shigaku gakkai rengo henshū kenkyū rombunshū. Japan Science Review: Literature, Philosophy, and History* [Annual] 8:44-45. No refs. LCCN:86-35705.

A very brief description of diving women.

Computers and the Computer Industry

803. AHL, David H. Aug. 1984. "Women's rights? Not in Japan." *Creative Computing* 10(8):62,64. No refs. ISSN:0097-8140.

Primarily a general (and typical) description of working women's problems. However, the author suggests that the computer industry "appears to be . . . welcoming women" and that the role of office ladies will expand to include computer work, thus raising their status. Although others [#804] may disagree, it's an interesting thesis [but not developed in this article].

804. Committee for the Protection of Women in the Computer World. 1983. "Computerization and women in Japan." *Ampo: Japan-Asia Quarterly Review* 15(2):16-27. No refs. LCCN:77-612830.

Examines the status of women "under computerization and OA [Office Automation]" by presenting four case studies. Delineates problems involved (e.g. health, status, production requirements, work environment) and sets an agenda for the effort to protect workers from exploitation.

805. NAKAJIMA, Keiko. 1983. "Women organize to tackle the world of new technology." *Ampo: Japan-Asia Quarterly Review* 15(2):28-29. No refs. LCCN:77-12830.

Reports on the formation of the "Committee for the Protection of Women in the Computer World" in 1982 and outlines the goals of the Committee. [See also #804.]

806. "Programming: New field for women." 1967. *Japan* 1967(1):18-22. No refs. LCCN:86-648185.

Profiles MIYATA Umeko, a computer programmer for the Fuji Bank.

807. UMESHIMA, Miyo. 1983. "Women's role in the computer industry." *Japan Echo* 10(4):51-56. No refs. ISSN:0388-0435.

Discusses ways in which women are employed in the computer industry, especially in software development, and notes the availability of equal pay, flexible working hours for married women, and challenging work.

808. "Women are rising force in program development jobs." 14 Aug. 1984. *Japan Economic Journal* 22(1121):7. No refs. ISSN:0021-4388.

Describes the work of YOSHIMURA Mitsuyo of NEC and SAWAI Kyōko of Tōshiba, both with high-level software development responsibilities within their respective companies.

Industrial Workers

809. BERNSTEIN, Gail Lee. 1988. "Women in the silk-reeling industry in nineteenth-century Japan." In: BERNSTEIN, Gail Lee and Haruhiro FUKUI, eds. *Japan and the World: Essays on Japanese History and Politics in Honour of Ishida Takeshi.* New York: St. Martin's Press, pp. 54-77. 104 notes. LCCN:87-23583.

Examines in detail the silk-reeling industry and its transition from a cottage industry run by women to a factory-based enterprise where young single women provided the work force. Notes both the benefits to the women and their families and the negative aspects. Discusses labor actions organized by women workers—the first recorded strikes in Japan.

810. "Better care for women workers." Jan. 1940. *Japanese Women* 3(1):2-3. No refs. ISSN:0388-1369.

Describes the Ministry of Public Welfare guidelines for employers of women. Includes statistics on numbers of women employed in various industries for 1938.

811. FISHER, Galen. 1915. "Women factory labourers." *Christian Movement in the Japanese Empire* 13:313-323. [Also cited as *Japan Christian Yearbook*.] No refs. LCCN:16-23733.

Reports on the physical condition of factory girls/women and working conditions which lead to disease. Calls for implementation of the 1911 Factory Law.

812. FUJITA, Kuniko. 1988. "Women workers, state policy, and the international division of labor: The case of Silicon Island in Japan." *Bulletin of Concerned Asian Scholars* 20(3):42-53. 57 notes. ISSN:0007-4810.

FUJITA broadens her thesis on gender inequality in industrial policy [#983] to include the effects of the global economic system and provides details on the integrated circuit industry in Kyushu, Japan. Includes many statistics, both on the industry and on its employment of women.

813. HARA, Kimi. Nov. 1980. "Industrialization and women workers in textile and electronics and electric machinery industries in Japan." *Asian Cultural Studies* 13:1-17. [Also cited as *Ajia bunka kenkyū*.] 10 refs. ISSN:0454-2150.

HARA provides statistics on employment of women in the textile and electronics industries and notes the major difficulties faced (e.g. part-time labor, repetitive work, environmental conditions, "invisibility of effort").

814. HIROKI, Michiko. 1986. *In the Shadow of Affluence: Stories of Japanese Women Workers.* Kowloon, Hong Kong: Committee for Asian Women. 54p. No refs.

Presents the situations of seven women to illustrate the major problems Japanese women face in the "so-called" land of lifetime employment and quality circles. The women profiled work in the electronics, textiles and insurance industries; several are involved heavily in union activities. Problems include night shifts, overtime, part-time employment, repetitious assembly line work, and productivity levels.

815. KIDD, Yasue Aoki. 1978. *Women Workers in the Japanese Cotton Mills, 1880-1920.* Ithaca: China-Japan Program, Cornell University 69p. (*Cornell East Asia Papers*, no. 20.) Bibl. and notes. LCCN:79-108068.

According to the preface, this is the first English analysis of Japanese cotton mill employment. In this master's thesis, KIDD examines working conditions within the context of Japanese culture and outlines ways in which both factory owners and the Japanese government exploited young rural women. KIDD relies heavily on HOSOI's *Jokō Aishi* [*The Pitiful History of Women Mill Workers*] and other Japanese language sources. The introduction by ISHIDA Takeshi of the University of Tokyo is very useful for context. Critiqued by TSURUMI in #2310.

816. KOIKE, Kazuo. 1983. "Workers in small firms and women in industry." In: SHIRAI, Taishirō. *Contemporary Industrial Relations in Japan.* Madison: University of Wisconsin Press, pp. 89-115. 2 notes. LCCN:83-47770.

Compares female labor force participation rates with those of Europe and the United States, pointing out that they do not appear to be dissimilar until one looks at type of position, especially for professional and technical and administrative employees. Explains the level nature of age wage profiles by noting that Japan has more older women workers and fewer women with ten or more years of service than other EC countries. Concludes by stressing that wage differentials by sex are not as large for Japanese women when job experience (length of service or age) is considered.

817. LENZ, Ilse. 1987. "The gender factor in industrial employment and the impact of microelectronic technology: Preliminary remarks on the case of Japan." In: BERGMANN, Joachim and Shigeyoshi TOKUNAGA, eds. *Economic and Social Aspects of Industrial Relations: A Comparison of the German and the Japanese Systems.* Frankfurt: Campus Verlag, pp. 129-151. 43 refs.

Provides a preliminary look at the growing impact of microelectronic technology on women's employment, using three industries as examples: semiconductor manufacturing, consumer electronics, and the software industry.

818. LO, Jeannie, 1 Jun. 1989. "Women of the lines." *Look Japan* 35(399):38-40. No refs. ISSN:0456-5339.

A description of a "typical day" for women on a typewriter assembly line and a brief discussion of difficulties women face if they prefer careers or become too old to marry. For a full treatment, see #853.

819. MATSUMOTO, Sheila. 1976. "Women in factories." In: LEBRA, Joyce, *et al. Women in Changing Japan.* Stanford: Stanford University Press, pp. 51-74. 37 notes. LCCN:75-33663.

Summarizes the role of women in factories historically and discusses the contemporary situation. Profiles two women, an unmarried 18-year-old and a 36-year-old mother of three children.

820. MATSUOKA, Asa. 1931. *Labor Conditions of Women and Children in Japan.* U.S. Department of Labor, Bureau of Labor Statistics. 102p. (U.S. Department of Labor, Bureau of Labor Statistics. *Bulletin* no. 558.) Bibl. [Also published as *Protective Labor Legislation for Women & Children in Japan*, Columbia University, 1931. LCCN:32-12418.]

A thorough discussion of the textile industry and the labor legislation regulating it. Includes a comparison of the Factory Acts of 1911 and 1923, requirements for an application for license as a recruiting agent, and descriptions of factory dormitories and welfare work in factories. Appendices provide the text of the Amended Factory Act (1911 original with 1923 and 1929 changes) and other associated laws and ordinances.

821. MORITANI, Masanori. 1982. "Silicon Island—Tomorrow's world leader?" *Japan Quarterly* 29(4):445-447. No refs. ISSN:0021-4590.

In this discussion of the conversion of Kyushu to a "Silicon Island," MORITANI describes the advantage of an "abundance of women laborers" and briefly relates the life of women on the job and in the company dormitories after working hours.

822. NAKAJIMA, Keiko. 1986. "Micro-electronics: For women the technology of oppression." *Ampo: Japan-Asia Quarterly Review* 18(2/3):42-47. No refs. LCCN:77-612830.

NAKAJIMA details the deleterious effects for women caused by the introduction of computers into the work place: reduction of numbers and varieties of jobs, and deterioration of workers' health.

823. Organisation for Economic Cooperation and Development. 1973. *Manpower Policy in Japan.* Paris: OECD. 169p. (*OECD Reviews of Manpower and Social Policy*, vol. 11.) No refs. LCCN:73-167816.

A brief statement on employment measures for women. Notes that the number of women employed since 1955 has increased, that women are employed in all fields of industry, and that they "are playing an important role in the industrial development of Japan." The role itself is not defined.

824. PODPALOVA, G.I. 1976. "Women's labour in Japan." In: *Japon*, Vol. 2. Paris: L'Asiatheque, pp. 96-102. (International Congress of Orientalists, 29th, Paris, 1973.) 17 Notes. LCCN:77-569259.

Briefly describes women's employment in the manufacturing sector: number of women involved, categories of employment, and wage differentials.

825. SAXONHOUSE, Gary. 1976. "Country girls and communication among competitors in the Japanese cotton-spinning industry." In: PATRICK, Hugh and Larry MEISSNER, eds. *Japanese Industrialization and its Social Consequences.* Berkeley: University of California Press, pp. 97-125. (Conference on Japanese Industrialization and its Social Consequences, 20-24 August 1973, University of Washington.) Bibl. LCCN:75-7199.

A technical article analyzing the high turnover rate of the female labor force in the cotton mills which occurred even though it would have benefited the mill owners to retain a more experienced work force. SAXONHOUSE includes statistics and comparisons with cotton industries elsewhere. Critiqued by TSURUMI in #2310.

826. SHIOZAWA, Miyoko. Winter 1977. "View from the bottom: Problems of Japan's women factory workers." *Japan Christian Quarterly* 43(1):31-37. No refs. ISSN:0021-4361.

SHIOZAWA (a labor organizer in the textile industry) discusses problems faced by women in the textile, electronic appliance, and food processing industries, especially low pay, poor working conditions, duration of the work day, and rotating shifts.

827. SHODA, Yoshi. 1928. "Japanese women in industry." In: *Women of the Pacific.* Honolulu: Pan Pacific Union, pp. 78-83. (Pan-Pacific Women's Conference, 1st, Honolulu, 9-19 August 1928.) Refs.

Discusses working and living conditions of women in the textile and mining industries, and the improvements which have begun to be implemented.

828. TANINO, Setsu. May 1938. "Present status of women workers in factories." *Japanese Women* 1(3):2,4 No refs. ISSN:0388-1369.

TANINO (a factory inspectress with the Metropolitan Police Board and Municipal Social Work Bureau of Tokyo) provides statistics on women factory workers in 1923 and 1937 and a very brief evaluation of their status.

829. TSURUMI, E. Patricia. Autumn 1984. "Female textile workers and the failure of early trade unionism in Japan." *History Workshop* no.18:3-27. 75 notes. ISSN:0309-2984.

After a description of living and working conditions for textile mill workers from the 1880s onward, TSURUMI critiques four commonly accepted reasons for the perceived lack of protest. She asserts that individual protest by running away was rampant, but organized protest was extremely difficult due to inaccessibility of women to organizers and the workers' very low educational backgrounds. Many quotations from Japanese primary and secondary sources, including song lyrics, are included as well as a discussion of those sources; see her 1986 paper [#2310] for a detailed review.

830. TSURUMI, E. Patricia. 1990. *Factory Girls: Women in the Thread Mills of Meiji Japan.* Princeton: Princeton University Press. 215p. Bibl. Index. LCCN:89-24325.

A thorough and detailed study of *kōjo* [factory girls] in the cotton and silk industries focusing primarily on the years 1872-1912. TSURUMI incorporates the voices of the women from diaries and songs and describes their lives in detail. She also sets context by describing the work of women during the end of the feudal period and by comparing the lives of *kōjo* with the women who remained home to work or those who chose weaving or prostitution to earn money for their families.

Journalists

831. "First woman of TV news." 12 Mar. 1984. *Advertising Age* 55(12 Mar. 1984, section 2):M11. No refs. ISSN:0001-8899.

A short but pithy description of SAKURAI Yoshiko, Nippon Television's first major woman newscaster.

832. HANI, Motoko. Summer 1979. "Stories of my life." *Japan Interpreter* 12(3/4):330-354. 9 notes. ISSN:0021-4450.

This excerpt from the 1928 autobiography of HANI Motoko (1873-1957), Japan's first newspaperwoman, covers her high school years in Tokyo and her part-time job with *Jogaku Zasshi* [see #1088], a short marriage, the establishment of her career in newspapers, a second marriage, and the founding of a women's magazine and a school. [See also #833 and #835.]

833. HANI, Motoko. 1981. "Memoirs of a successful woman." [Translated by Chieko MULHERN.] In: AOKI, Michiko Y. and Margaret B. DARDESS, eds. *As the Japanese See it: Past and Present.* Honolulu: University Press of Hawaii, pp. 137-146. No refs. LCCN:81-11526.

A brief excerpt from the autobiography of HANI Motoko, Japan's first newspaperwoman. [See also #832 and #835.]

834. KIMURA, Komako. 11 May 1918. "Shin Shin Fujin." *Woman Citizen* (11 May 1918):473. No refs.

KIMURA, editor of the *Shin Shin Fujin* [*New True Woman*] in Japan and woman's suffrage activist, discusses the severe political and editorial restrictions placed on Japanese women. She announces her intention to publish a bilingual journal, the *Japanese Suffragist*, in the United States to be disseminated in Japan.

835. MULHERN, Chieko Irie. Summer 1979. "Japan's first newspaper woman: Hani Motoko." *Japan Interpreter* 12(3/4):310-329. 31 notes. ISSN:0021-4450.

MULHERN details the life of HANI Motoko (1873-1957), newspaper reporter, magazine editor, and educator, by comparing her life with those of many of her contemporaries, including members of the Seitō [Bluestockings] group. [See also #832 and #833.]

836. MURRAY, Geoffrey. Apr. 1977. "Kaoru Kanetaka: TV documentary directress." *PHP* 8(4):39-47. No refs. ISSN:0030-798X.

Profiles KANETAKA Kaoru, who has produced travel documentaries since 1959 with the aim of internationalizing the outlook of the Japanese people.

837. PAULSON, Joy. 1976. "Women in media." In: LEBRA, Joyce, *et al. Women in Changing Japan.* Stanford: Stanford University Press, pp. 209-232. 15 notes. LCCN:75-33663.

PAULSON interviewed 12 women involved in television and print media about their upbringing, education, and current family situations. Includes a profile of a woman with a career in television.

838. SUZUKI, Kazue. Nov. 1987. "Atsuko Chiba: A tribute." *PHP Intersect* (Nov. 1987):42-43. No refs. ISSN:0910-4607.

Profiles CHIBA Atsuko, journalist for the *Asahi Shimbun*, who died of breast cancer in New York in July, 1987.

839. TAKENAKA, Shige. Nov. 1938. "On the status of women journalists." *Japanese Women* 1(6):1-2. No refs. ISSN:0388-1369.

TAKENAKA (Woman Journalists' Club of Japan and 27-year veteran of the *Tokyo Asahi*) briefly evaluates the status and numbers of female journalists in Japan.

840. WEATHERHEAD, Marc. May 1988. "A career in the media." *PHP Intersect* (May 1988):32-34. No refs. ISSN:0030-798X.

A profile of NAKAGAWA Yumiko, journalist at Asahi Television.

Managers and Executives

841. ADACHI, Kazuhiko. 1989. "Problems and prospects of management development of female employees in Japan." *Journal of Management Development* 8(4):32-40. 9 notes. ISSN:0262-1711.

Describes the lack of training for women in companies, notes the lack of effect of the Equal Employment Opportunity Law, reviews the typical management attitude toward women employees, and suggests that the coming lack of skilled workers will increase opportunities for women.

842. CARNEY, Larry S. and Charlotte G. O'KELLY. Summer 1987. "Barriers and constraints to the recruitment and mobility of female managers in the Japanese labor force." *Human Resource Management* 26(2):193-216. 52 refs. ISSN:0090-4848.

CARNEY and O'KELLY provide an analysis of "attitudinal and organizational barriers" career women face and include many quotations from interviews with such women. They go beyond, however, by speculating on possibilities for change, due in part to the internationalization of the Japanese economy, and also suggest that the Equal Employment Opportunity Law may be having a more positive effect than initially suggested.

843. IWAO, Sumiko. 1986. "Skills and life strategies of Japanese business women." In: WHITE, Merry I. and Susan POLLAK, ed. *The Cultural Transition: Human Experience and Social Transformation in the Third World and Japan.* Boston: Routledge and Kegan Paul, pp. 240-260. No refs. LCCN:85-2182.

IWAO uses the stories of Mrs. EDO (owner of a high-class, fifth-generation, family-owned restaurant in Asakusa, Tokyo) and Mrs. TANAKA (owner of a veterinary pharmaceutical firm) to illustrate her perspective on the successes of female managers in small and medium sized businesses. Qualities of these managers include attention to minute detail, placing service to the customer over profit, and being conservative in savings and expansions of the business. IWAO also provides context by describing how these same skills have been used by women historically since Japan was an agrarian society.

844.   "Japanese women join the lib movement."   10 Apr. 1971.   *Business Week* no.2171:70,72. No refs. ISSN:0007-7135.

Acknowledges the effect of "woman power" on the employment scene and notes that, slowly, women are beginning to move to the lower rungs of middle management.

845. KAMINSKI, Marguerite and Judith PAIZ. Fall 1984. "Japanese women in management: Where are they?" *Human Resource Management* 23(3):277-292. 21 refs. ISSN:0090-4848.

Using a cost-benefit analysis approach, KAMINSKI and PAIZ explore the choices of the United States and Japan to admit or not admit career women into the work place. Stressing the resultant tradeoffs, they provide data for readers to reach their own conclusions as to the wisdom of past practices and the probable future course for each business community. The authors add their own predictions for the Japanese sector.

846. KANDA, Michiko, *et al.* 1983. "Career advancement of women in Japan: Managers in large companies." In: MURAMATSU, Yasuko, ed. *Women and Work: Working Women and their Impact on Society.* Tokyo: International Group for the Study of Women, pp. 128-138. (Tokyo Symposium on Women, 2nd, 1983. *Proceedings*.) No refs. LCCN:84-187204.

Based on a survey of women employed as university professors, corporate managers, medical doctors, and "top-class" government officials, the authors conclude that most top-level women are single, have stayed with the same company since beginning employment, and can progress more easily in fields traditionally available to women. Questionnaire data provided.

847. LANSING, Paul and Kathryn READY. Spring 1988. "Hiring women managers in Japan: An alternative for foreign employers." *California Management Review* 30:112-127. 30 notes. ISSN:0008-1256.

After a review of the current state of women's employment in Japanese firms (with statistical documentation), LANSING and READY suggest that foreign concerns can gain highly qualified Japanese management personnel by hiring women.

848. MINAMI, Chie and Nao MOROTA. 1983. "Case studies of female presidents in small and medium-size companies." In: MURAMATSU, Yasuko, ed. *Women and Work: Working Women and their Impact on Society.* Tokyo: International Group for the Study of Women, pp. 139-154. (Tokyo Symposium on Women, 2nd, 1983. *Proceedings*.) 5 notes. LCCN:84-187204.

Presents the results of a survey given to 18 female company presidents, and discusses in depth the careers of three: one who inherited a family business, one who founded a company in the manufacturing sector, and one who began a company in the area of information services. [See also #743.]

849. SCHREFFLER, Roger. Jul. 1987. "Moving to management: Japanese women challenge the male bastion of automotive management." *Automotive Industries* 167:54-56. No refs.

Interviews three women in Nissan's international public relations department (HAGIWARA Hisayo, TSUJI Toshiko, and TOBA Masumi) concerning their work and family concerns.

850. STEINHOFF, Patricia G. and Kazuko TANAKA. Fall/Winter 1986/1987. "Women managers in Japan." *International Studies of Management and Organization* 16:108-132. 16 notes. ISSN:0020-8825.

STEINHOFF and TANAKA identify small and medium-sized enterprises as those most likely to have women in management positions, describe background and characteristics of such women, and discuss available career paths.

Office Ladies

851. CARTER, Rose and Lois DILATUSH. 1976. "Office ladies." In: LEBRA, Joyce, *et al.* *Women in Changing Japan.* Stanford: Stanford University Press, pp. 75-87. 19 notes. LCCN:75-33663.

A thorough look at the status of office ladies and societal attitudes toward their role. Includes two biographical profiles.

852. "Girls like Daddy." May 1990. *Focus Japan* 17(5):4. No refs. ISSN:0388-0311. Reprinted in: Autumn 1990. *Japan Update* no. 17:28. No refs. ISSN:0912-3474.

Describes young women who are increasingly attracted to leisure activities associated with middle-aged men such as horseback races, golf, and *karaoke* bars and are therefore termed "*oyaji gals*" ["middle-aged daddy" gals]. Questions whether this group is a temporary reaction to the *body-con, one-length girl* [women with hair of a uniform length who wear "figure-hugging" clothing] or if they are the next step in working women's evolution from office ladies in the 1960s, to feminists in the 1970s, and to *body-con* women in the 1980s.

853. LO, Jeannie. 1990. *Office Ladies/Factory Women: Life and Work at a Japanese Company.* Armonk, NY: M.E. Sharpe. 135p. Bibl. Index. LCCN:89-70365.

LO spent time working both as an office lady [OL] and as a factory line worker for Brother Industries. She describes in detail the work and social lives of her fellow female workers, including their attitudes toward work, marriage, dormitory life, and sports. Profiles of specific women are also included.

854. McLENDON, James. 1983. "The office: Way station or blind alley." In: PLATH, David W., ed. *Work and Lifecourse in Japan.* Albany: State University of New York Press, pp. 156-182. Bibl. LCCN:82-10481.

McLENDON studies the role of a general trading company (GTC) as a "marriage mart," initially as a "way station" until a suitable partner is found, but sometimes changing to a "blind alley" if a woman is unsuccessful in her search. He also includes a translation of the lyrics to one of Japan's top-selling records in 1979, "The Lordly Marriage Declaration," which describes the "perfect marital relationship" from a male perspective. A well-drawn and detailed portrait.

855. MIYA, Yoshiko. 1983. "The questionable promise of office automation for women." *Japan Echo* 10(4):57-60. No refs. ISSN:0388-0435.

Examines the introduction of computers into offices and concludes that job reduction and ill health for remaining workers is likely to result—that women's goal of being involved in decision-making processes will not be realized through office automation.

856. MOFFAT, Susan. 2 Jul. 1990. "Japan's new battle of the sexes." *Fortune* 122(1):14,16. ISSN:0015-8259.

Briefly describes a new generation of "office ladies" known as *oyaji-gayru* ["loosely translated as 'good-ol'-boy gals'"] as typified by Non-chan, "the heroine of a comic strip in *Spa!*" magazine.

857. TOMISHIGE, Keiko. Summer 1983. "Pour tea or kick the boss." *Journal of Popular Culture* 17:159-160. No refs. ISSN:0022-3840.

A brief article translated from the 1 June 1981 *Mainichi Shimbun* reporting data from two surveys of secretaries concerning their aspirations to management positions and describing a training program for women at the Executive Training School.

858. "A visit with an office girl." May/Jun. 1967. *East* 3(4):6-11. No refs. ISSN:0012-8295.

A pictorial "interview" with NAGAKUBO Natsuko, a typical "Office Lady," who has worked for her company for six years and who will retire when she marries in the coming fall.

Part-time Workers

859. BANDŌ SUGAHARA, Mariko. Apr./Jun. 1986. "When women change jobs." *Japan Quarterly* 33(2):177-182. No refs. ISSN:0021-4590.

Although it contains statistics on reasons for changing jobs, the article focuses more generally on the effect of lifetime employment and seniority systems on women workers. The author, an official in the Prime Minister's Office specializing in women's affairs, foresees "far-reaching economic and social consequences" as the result of the entry into the job market of "large numbers of educated, career-minded women."

860. "Japan: The female fiddle." 24 Apr. 1976. *Economist* 259(6922):57. No refs. ISSN:0013-0613.

Notes the "retirement" of over a million women due to their part-time status during the current recession.

861. MOLONY, Kathleen. 13 Feb. 1982. "Selective paternalism." *Nation* 234(6):184-185. No refs. ISSN:0027-8378.

A rebuttal to recent accounts of the Japanese miracle which focus on the "harmonious relationship between labor and management." MOLONY provides statistics on numbers of workers without lifetime employment and details the high number of women in this category.

Professional and Career Women

862. BORRUS, Amy. 25 Aug. 1986. "Look whose sun is rising now: Career women." *Business Week* (25 Aug. 1986):50. No refs. ISSN:0007-7135.

A brief view of women's prospects as professionals in the Japanese business world. Notes the preponderance of jobs available in the financial services industry and in high-tech companies.

863. BRINTON, Mary C. Aug. 1989. "Gender stratification in contemporary urban Japan." *American Sociological Review* 54(4):549-564. 33 refs. ISSN:0003-1224.

Presents data showing gender stratification in employment, and notes the importance of an initial entry to a career ladder in Japan. Explores the importance of ability and education on gaining career track employment, and points out that as women age they tend to move to family businesses or small firms.

864. CHERRY, Kittredge. Feb. 1984. "Breaking new ground." *PHP* 15(2):8-16. No refs. ISSN:0030-798X.

Describes the work of SAHASHI Kei, a female entrepreneur (and Buddhist nun), who established: the Idea Bank, a consumer research firm run by women and aimed at the women's market; the Bank of Consarun, a training center for housewives preparing to reenter the job market; and the School of Traditions, aimed at educating women to be better housewives.

865. "A creative career woman." 1980. *Japan Pictorial* 3(4):1-4. No refs. ISSN:0388-6115.

A brief profile of KONNO Yuri, a businesswoman who introduced telephone answering services and telephone counseling to Japan. The counseling service focuses on children and parents. She has since expanded to other women-oriented businesses such as maternity clothes shops. Her companies employ only women.

866. DILATUSH, Lois. 1976. "Women in the professions." In: LEBRA, Joyce, *et al. Women in Changing Japan.* Stanford: Stanford University Press, pp. 191-208. 16 notes. LCCN:75-33663.

Provides statistics on professional women (i.e. those with careers in medicine, education, and law) and the results of interviews with such women. Dividing them into women who followed "the woman's track" and those who pursued "the equal opportunity track," DILATUSH provides details on career choice, problems, and attitudes on women's roles.

867. D'ORAZIO, Nancy J. 1980. "Executive bilingual secretaries in foreign firms." *Bulletin of the Sophia University Socio-Economic Institute* no. 76. 24p. 16 notes. LCCN:82-204754.

D'ORAZIO interviewed bilingual secretaries who work for foreign managers from American computer and accounting firms, oil, chemical, manufacturing companies, and banks to determine job duties, salary, interaction with other company personnel, relationship with the foreign manager, and career prospects.

868. HAGIO, Fumiko. 1983. "Single women and work—The way was paved by the 'war singles.'" In: MURAMATSU, Yasuko, ed. *Women and Work: Working Women and their Impact on Society.* Tokyo: International Group for the Study of Women, pp. 221-224. (Tokyo Symposium on Women, 2nd, 1983. *Proceedings.*) No refs. LCCN:84-187204.

A short description of women widowed during World War II and "post-war baby boomer" single women and their working status. The author is a member of the Single Women's Association of Japan which was started by "war singles."

869. "Japanese ladies are still in the back seat." Oct. 1970. *Atlas* 19(10):47. No refs.

A brief rendering of the problems faced by young Japanese women wishing to pursue a career. Translated from *Shukan Asahi*, a weekly published by a major newspaper.

870. KAJIMA, Ume. 1963. *Michi Haruka: Milestones on my Pathway.* Tokyo: Kajima Institute. 206p. No refs. LCCN:75-462433. [*Michi haruka.* English.]

Selections from the diary of KAJIMA Ume, president of Kajima Construction Company, a family-owned civil engineering firm. Reports primarily on site visits for opening ceremonies during the late 1950s (i.e. no insights on day-to-day operations). Also discusses the activities of her father and her husband (a Japanese diplomat and Chairman of the Board of the Company). Briefly describes the Kajima Women's Association, a wives' support group, and the Seibi-kai, the women employee's support group.

871. LEBRA, Takie Sugiyama. Oct. 1981. "Japanese women in male dominant careers: Cultural barriers and accommodations for sex-role transcendence." *Ethnology* 20(4):291-306. 17 notes & 31 refs. ISSN:0014-1828.

LEBRA provides sociological profiles of the lives of ten career women and analyzes ways in which each benefits from, or overcomes obstacles associated with, "a set of Japanese cultural values and norms which are clearly biased for 'career men': socialization for domestic succession, examination rites of transition, bureaucratic rigidity, patronage, and asymmetry in sphere segregation."

872. MAXSON, Mary Lou. 1976. "Women in family businesses." In: LEBRA, Joyce, *et al. Women in Changing Japan.* Stanford: Stanford University Press, pp. 89-105. 2 notes. LCCN:75-33663.

Unlike the wives of *salariiman* [white collar employees], women in family businesses hold "keystone" status both in the business and in the household. Profiles three women involved in the Kano Small Motor Company (the wife of the owner, the head housekeeper, and the wife of a young employee) and provides statistical data on female family workers.

873. MURRAY, Geoffrey. Jun. 1977. "Madame Ohya—Japan's first female entrepreneur." *PHP* 8(6):38-45. No refs. ISSN:0030-798X.

Profiles Madame OHYA, a dynamic and unusual businesswoman with international holdings in restaurants, golf courses, and parking lots among others.

874. OSAKO, Masako Murakami. Oct. 1978. "Dilemmas of Japanese professional women." *Social Problems* 26(1):15-25. 48 refs. ISSN:0037-7732. [Later published in KAHN-HUT, Rachel, Arlene K. DANIELS, and Richard COLVARD, eds. *Women and Work: Problems and Perspectives*. New York: Oxford University Press, 1982, pp. 123-135, without the bibliography. LCCN:81-14025.]

OSAKO covers impediments to development of professional careers, including societal expectations, reward structures, and a lack of daycare and household help. She explores the question of whether "sexual inequality . . . exists despite recent [institutional and cultural] changes or because of them."

875. PEPPER, Anne G. Aug. 1988. "High level networking for Japanese women." *Journal of the American Chamber of Commerce in Japan* 25(8):43-46. No refs. ISSN:0002-7847.

Profiles the Japan Association of Female Executives [JAFE] and its founder, NAKAMURA Noriko. The Association provides networking opportunities, professional meetings and seminars, and, to enable professional women to continue working after childbirth, a high-quality nanny service.

876. PORTER, Doune. Jan./Feb. 1985. "Japan diary: Executive women in Japan." *Journal of Japanese Trade and Industry* 1985(1):71. No refs. ISSN:0285-9556.

Lists the problems facing women who desire professional careers and concludes that women cannot have both a family life and a professional life.

877. "Professionals' view of international communication." Oct./Dec. 1982. *Wheel Extended* 12(4):9-15. No refs. ISSN:0049-755X.

Four simultaneous interpreters, SATŌ Keiko, HARA Fujiko, MATSUOKA Yūko, and MORI Misako discuss their profession and its unique suitability for women.

878. SAISHO, Yuriko. 1981. *Women Executives in Japan: How I Succeeded in Business in a Male-Dominated Society*. Tokyo: YURI International, Inc. 214p. No refs. [Variant title: *Career Woman: My Way*.] [*Kyaria Ūman Watakushi no Michi*. English.]

An interesting combination of memoir and "how to" guide for Japanese women, and in English translation, for women seeking to do business with the Japanese. SAISHO, who founded and ran a successful marketing company and now heads YURI International, relates, cajoles, urges, and teaches at top speed via lists of points to remember, statistics, and stories of her own experience. Unique.

879. "The simultaneous interpreter: New profession for women." 1971. *Japan* 1971(2):20-22. No refs. LCCN:86-648185.

Describes the position of simultaneous interpreter, and notes women's suitability for the role given "Japanese female virtues—perseverance, sensitivity, and delicacy." Also points out the inability of men to spend three to five years in training with little remuneration.

880. SOLO, Sally. 19 Jun. 1989. "Japan discovers woman power." *Fortune* 119(13):153-154,156-158. No refs. ISSN:0015-8259.

SOLO describes the new ability of women to break into career positions given Japan's labor shortage and the Equal Employment Opportunity Law. Includes quotations from many such women and gives examples of their successes.

881. TAKAGI, Haruo. Winter 1988/1989. "Aspirations of women executives : A U.S.-Japan comparison." [Translated by Yōko Yamamoto PARKS.] *Japanese Economic Studies* 17:23-47. 8 notes. ISSN:0021-4841.

TAKAGI determines that both American and Japanese women have "a strong sense of career, exhibiting professional ability while seeking satisfaction through work and financial rewards, despite feelings of discrimination or being held back in promotions." In addition, three major factors affecting women's abilities to maintain a successful career are outlined: knowledge and skills, cooperative relationships (in the work place), and appropriate motivators in the overall organizational climate. TAKAGI then prescribes steps for management "to best utilize women executives."

882. TAKAI, Yuriko. 1983. "A portrait of women in the pre-war period reflected on my mother, and the working women in the post-war period." In: MURAMATSU, Yasuko, ed. *Women and Work: Working Women and their Impact on Society.* Tokyo: International Group for the Study of Women, pp. 7-12. (Tokyo Symposium on Women, 2nd, 1983. *Proceedings.*) No refs. LCCN:84-187204.

Discusses her mother's life as a Japanese merchant's wife in pre-World War II Korea, and her own career as an importer of veterinary medicines and head of the Kyōritsu Shōji Co.

883. TAZAWA, Y. 1974. "Female library staffs—an opinion from the opposite sex." *Librarians for Social Change* 5:9. No refs. ISSN:0305-165X.

A male librarian reacts to the rising number of women librarians, discussing both positive and negative aspects as he sees them.

884. THORNBRUGH, David. Dec. 1987. "At home in the construction industry." *PHP Intersect* (Dec. 1987):40-41. No refs. ISSN:0910-4607.

Describes the work of SUZUKA Noriko, creator of the Communications Research Center, an all-female firm specializing in home design. The firm's designs are based on in-depth surveys of housewives.

885. TONO, Haruhi. 1989. "Women workers and multinationals: The Shin-Shirasuna Case." *Ampo: Japan-Asia Quarterly Review* 20(4)/21(1):72-79. No refs. LCCN:77-612830.

Details the history of labor management strategies of the Shin-Shirasuna Electric Company which employs women as part-time workers in its head office and in smaller branch factories throughout rural Japan and in other Asian sites.

886. "Woman lawyers appear at last." Jan. 1939. *Japanese Women* 2(1):3. No refs. ISSN:0388-1369.

Three Japanese women have passed their bar examinations and begun their probationary practices; the laws allowing women to become lawyers were passed in 1933 and became effective in 1936. A footnote mentions the one female patent attorney in practice since 1935.

887. "Women librarians in Japan: A survey." 1974. *Librarians for Social Change* 5:10-12. No refs. ISSN:0305-165X.

Presents survey data collected in 1973 from female librarians, including type of library work, positive and negative aspects of their jobs, and types of discrimination suffered.

888. YORKE, Karen. Sep. 1982. "Fortunately, I was a woman." *PHP* 13(9):21-27. No refs. ISSN:0030-798X.

Describes the accomplishments and life philosophies of SAISHO Yuriko, founder of Nippo Marketing and Advertising Agency and Yuri International. [See also #878.]

Women in Science and Medicine

889. LONG, Susan Orpett. 1984. "The sociocultural context of nursing in Japan." *Culture, Medicine and Psychiatry* 8:141-163. 49 refs. ISSN:0165-005X.

Analyzes the status of Japanese hospital-based nurses, detailing the low professional status on one hand and the essential role of nurturing the patient and mediating between doctor and patient on the other. Draws parallels between housewife and nursing roles.

890. LONG, Susan Orpett. 1986. "Roles, careers and femininity in biomedicine—Women physicians and nurses in Japan." *Social Science and Medicine* 22(1):81-90. 43 refs. ISSN:0277-9536.

Provides a detailed review of the status of female physicians and nurses in Japan, focusing on their socioeconomic background, education levels, career patterns, and on patient perceptions of these women. Also discusses the secondary role employment takes in relation to responsibilities of home and family for both physicians and nurses.

891. NAKAMURA, Keiko. 10 Aug. 1985. "Clara Ako Yoshida: Blueprints for success." *Look Japan* (10 Aug. 1985):22. No refs. ISSN:0456-5339.

Interviews YOSHIDA Clara Ako, an architect and engineer, about her professional and family life.

892. NAKAMURA, Keiko. 10 Oct. 1985. "Yohko Awaya: 'I want to know more.'" *Look Japan* (10 Oct. 1985):22. No refs. ISSN:0456-5339.

An interview with AWAYA Yohko, an atomic physicist, concerning her work and home life.

893. NAKAMURA, Keiko. 10 Dec. 1985. "Kyōko Saio: Combating the food problem." *Look Japan* (10 Dec. 1985):23. No refs. ISSN:0456-5339.

Interviews SAIO Kyōko, Director of the Food Services Division at the National Food Research Institute of the Ministry of Agriculture, Forestry and Fisheries, about her work with soybeans.

894. NAKAMURA, Keiko. 10 Feb. 1986. "Tsuneko Okazaki: Studying the basic units of life." *Look Japan* (10 Feb. 1986):21. No refs. ISSN:0456-5339.

Interviews OKAZAKI Tsuneko, a molecular biologist widely recognized for her work on DNA replication.

895. NAKAMURA, Keiko. 10 Apr. 1986. "Motoko Ishii: Fascination with light." *Look Japan* (10 Apr. 1986): 21. No refs. ISSN:0456-5339.

Interviews ISHII Motoko, a lighting designer/engineer who has received worldwide recognition for her work.

896. NAKAMURA, Keiko. 10 Aug. 1986. "Minako Nagao: Detecting food carcinogens." *Look Japan* (10 Aug. 1986): 22. No refs. ISSN:0456-5339.

Interviews NAGAO Minako, head of the Carcinogenesis Division of the National Cancer Center, concerning her work and outside life.

897. NAKAMURA, Keiko. 10 Oct. 1986. "Mariko Yasugi: Seeking nature's principles." *Look Japan* (10 Oct. 1986):14. No refs. ISSN:0456-5339.

Interviews YASUGI Mariko, a mathematician at Kyoto Sangyō University who specializes in proof theory.

898. NAKAMURA, Keiko. 10 Dec. 1986. "Growing up with Japan's computer industry." *Look Japan* (10 Dec. 1986):18. No refs. ISSN:0456-5339.

Interviews YAMAMOTO Kinko, Managing Director of the Japan Information Processing Development Center, who works on "computer security and networks, computer graphics and systems evaluations."

899. NAKAMURA, Keiko. Jan. 1987. "Big discoveries in pollution research." *Look Japan* 32(370):28. No refs. ISSN:0456-5339.

Briefly profiles SŌMA Yoshie, a chemist working on pollution research.

900. NAKAMURA, Keiko. Jan. 1988. "In quest of the unknown." *Look Japan* 33(382):26-27. No refs. ISSN:0456-5339.

Profiles the late SUZUKI Hiroko, an astronomer, and describes both her work at the Nobeyama Radio Observatory and her discovery of three molecules nonexistent on earth.

901. RASMINSKY, Judy. May 1983. "She never looked back." *Working Woman* 8:118-122. No refs. ISSN:0145-5761.

Profiles SAIDA Kyōko, neurologist and researcher at Utano National Hospital in Kyoto and wife and mother of two children. More information provided here than in most profiles, both in terms of her professional accomplishments and her philosophy of life.

902. YAMAMOTO, Sugi. Sep. 1938. "Present status of women physicians." *Japanese Women* 1(5):1,4. No refs. ISSN:0388-1369.

YAMAMOTO (a physician and mother) reports on the status of, and opportunities for, the 4400 women physicians in Japan as of 1938. Notes the activities of Dr. YOSHIOKA Yayoi, president of Tokyo Women's Medical College and describes the professional associations for female physicians.

903. YAMAMOTO, Susumu. 1988. ["Interview with Mukai Chiaki."] *Japan Pictorial* 11(3):8. No refs. ISSN:0388-6115.

An extremely brief interview with MUKAI Chiaki, Japan's first female astronaut, researching space medicine in Houston while undergoing training for space flight.

904. YAMASHITA, Aiko. 1975. "Women chemists in Japan." *International Congress on the History of Science, 14th, 1975. Proceedings* 2:445-449. No refs.

Briefly describes the history of science education for women and women's early participation in the sciences. Notes the accomplishments of YASUI Sono, KURODA Chika, TSUJIMURA Michiyo, TANGE Ume, SUZUKI Hideru, KATŌ Sechi, and MAKITA Raku.

University Graduates in the Work Force

905. ARAI, Masao. Dec. 1979. "Women university graduates face glum employment outlook." *Business Japan* 24:44-45. No refs. ISSN:0300-4341.

Focuses primarily on the decision of the Bank of Tokyo not to hire women university graduates in 1980. The Bank is a preferred employer because it typically employs an average of 100 new women each year, and "women, if they are eager and able, are treated equally." The Bank's position is that because women are staying in their jobs longer, the turnover rate is lower; 1980 is an "adjustment" year.

906. FUJITANI, Atsuko. Sep. 1980. "Work and the female university graduate." *Economic Eye* (Sep.1980):6-11. No refs. ISSN:0389-0503.

Presents the results of a survey conducted by the Women's Studies Society of Japan. Surveying women who had graduated from universities in the years 1955-1960 and 1965-1970, this article provides data on work experience and attitudes. In addition, it calls for reappraisal of the seniority wage system and for continuing education opportunities at the university level for women wishing to re-enter the job market.

907. GOODMAN, Matthew. May 1986. "Japanese women in finance." *Tokyo Business Today* (May 1988):19-23. No refs. ISSN:0911-7008.

Explores the increasing opportunities for bright female graduates of prestigious Japanese universities or American MBA programs. Although openings are more prevalent in securities firms or international companies, even Japanese banks and governmental agencies are slowly hiring career women.

908. HARA, Kimi. Mar. 1975. "Status of Japanese women: Career-mindedness of university graduates—Problems in the compatibility of profession and home." *International Christian University Publications. II-B. The Journal of Social Science* no. 13:209-220. [Also cited as Kokusai Kirisutokyō Daigaku, Tokyo. *Kokusai Kirisutokyō Daigaku Gakuhō II-B. Shakai Kagaku Jānaru.*] 6 refs. ISSN:0454-2134.

After a short review of women's social status before and after World War II, HARA summarizes conclusions from four different studies on professional women and how they cope with their dual roles. Two studies deal with professional women in general, one with women students, and one with women physicians.

909. ISHIKAWA, Yōji. Apr./Jun. 1988. "The 1988 job market for recent graduates." *Japan Quarterly* 35(2):196-200. No refs. ISSN:0021-4590.

Includes statistics on numbers of female university graduates hired after enactment of the Equal Employment Opportunity Law in 1986.

910. "Japanese coeds pray for jobs." Summer 1983. *Journal of Popular Culture* 17:154. No refs. ISSN:0022-3840.

Discusses the increase of *ema* [votive tablet] offerings in the autumn of 1982 at Tokyo's Yushima Shrine, a shrine for the patron of learning. Female seniors of four-year institutions are at a severe disadvantage in the job market unless they have inside connections with companies, and many have turned to this traditional method of supplication.

911. KILBURN, David. Aug. 1988. "Foreign firms show promise for Japan's women graduates." *Journal of the American Chamber of Commerce in Japan* 25(8):33-42. No refs. ISSN:0002-7847.

A two-year update on the effect of the 1986 Equal Employment Opportunity Law and a report on opportunities for women with Western firms (e.g. IBM and Avon). Profiles women from two advertising agencies: J. Walter Thompson Japan (KOIKE Yoshiko) and McCann-Erickson Hakuhōdō (HOSHIAI Mie, NAGAYAMA Sayuri, AIHARA Sonoko, and ŌSAWA Ikuko).

912. MORIYAMA, Mayumi. Dec. 1979. "Women must consider future in choosing jobs." *Business Japan* 24:45-46. No refs. ISSN:0300-4341.

A brief request by the head of the Women's and Minors' Bureau of the Ministry of Labor that female college students plan to work at least ten years instead of three before quitting to raise families.

913. MOUER, Elizabeth Knipe. 1987. "Sibling order and occupational choice among university educated Japanese women." In: PEARSON, Gail and Lenore MANDERSON, eds. *Class, Ideology and Woman in Asian Societies.* Hong Kong: Asian Research Service, pp. 99-126. 65 refs.

MOUER surveys career professionals (teachers, public servants, and lawyers) and career housewives to determine the effect birth order and sexes of siblings has on the respondents and their spouses in regards to the woman's career choice.

914. MOUER-BORNER, E. 1988. "Gender-rôle socialisation, achievement motivation and occupational choice among professional women and housewives in Japan." In: NISH, Ian, ed. 1988. *Contemporary European Writing on Japan: Scholarly Views from Eastern and Western Europe.* Kent, England: Paul Norbury Publications, pp. 119-120. No refs. LCCN:88-193026.

Briefly summarizes her research on factors affecting decisions toward careers or full-time homemaking among university graduates: parental attitudes, marriage, and "life crises."

915. NOGUCHI, Sharon. Feb. 1984. "Career-minded coeds don't have it easy." *PHP* (Feb. 1984):28-35. No refs. ISSN:0030-798X.

Reports on the gap between expectation and reality concerning the job market on the part of graduating college women.

916. "Women university graduates need not apply." Jan./Mar. 1981. *Japan Quarterly* 28(1):18-22. No refs. ISSN:0021-4590.

Presents statistics on employment available for persons entering the job market in 1980 (for men, up 21% in office jobs and 26% in technical fields; for women, down 4.5% in both). Discusses the possible factors responsible for the decline: a surge in the number of female graduates seeking jobs, an increase in the amount of education they have obtained, and the track record of women's length of service. The article concludes that "the higher the educational level of a woman, the earlier the likelihood of her quitting her job."

917. WRIGHT, Louisa, Neil GROSS, and Yurinori ISHIKAWA. 12 Dec. 1983. "Goodbye kimono: Opportunities in foreign firms." *Time* 122(25):46. No refs. ISSN:0040-781X.

Describes the choice of many female college graduates to apply for work in foreign firms where opportunities for advancement and meaningful work may be greater.

Water Trade: Geisha, Hostesses and Prostitutes

918. AKIYAMA, Aisaburō. 1926. *Geisha Girl.* [Kyoto: Igyokn-do]. 28p. No refs. LCCN:42-43829.

A description of "this knotty problem" of "geisha girls." Discusses the history of the geisha and the profession as of the 1920s.

919. CHANDLER, Billie T. 1963. *Geisha Story: With Doll-and-Flower Arrangements.* Rutland, VT: Tuttle. 56p. No refs. LCCN:63-8718.

Written by a woman who is an accredited artist in flower arrangement and miniature landscape design, this work focuses on photographs of *hakata* [clay figures] of geisha in various settings, all with floral arrangements. CHANDLER provides a short history of the geisha and stories of particular individuals.

920.   CRIHFIELD, Liza. 1978. "If liberation is to come to Japan, all women must become geisha." In: WHITE, Merry I. and Barbara MOLONY, eds. *Proceedings of the Tokyo Symposium on Women*. Tokyo: International Group for the Study of Women, pp. 50-55. (Tokyo Symposium on Women, [1st], 1978.) No refs.

CRIHFIELD compares the roles of geisha and housewife, and discusses the complimentarity of these roles given the distinct spheres of public and private life for most Japanese. With a softening of the demarcation between these roles, she suggests geisha may become extinct. "However," says CRIHFIELD, "the geisha do not seem to be an endangered species yet."

921.   CRIHFIELD, Liza. 1979. *Ko-Uta: "Little Songs" of the Geisha World*. Rutland, VT: Tuttle. 106p. No refs. LCCN:78-66085.

Ko-uta are "little songs" sung by geisha to the accompaniment of *shamisen* [a stringed instrument], and whose lyrics stem from the traditions of the "hardworking, hard-playing merchant class of the late Edo period (mainly 19th century)." CRIHFIELD, an anthropologist who trained as a geisha, includes 25 songs for translation and interpretation.

922.   DALBY, Liza Crihfield. 1983. *Geisha*. Berkeley: University of California Press. 347p. Bibl. Index. LCCN:82-21934.

Combines an anthropological study of contemporary geisha with the personal experiences of the author as she became a geisha-in-training while undertaking her dissertation research. A thorough and readable work. Reviewed by BOOCOCK in #2305.

923.   DALBY, Liza Crihfield. Feb. 1983. "The art of the geisha." *Natural History* 92(2):46-55. No refs. ISSN:0028-0712.

DALBY summarizes the geisha world of the 1980s and its historical roots, and discusses the reasons Japanese women may choose a career as a geisha today. Although described as an excerpt of her book [#922], this article serves as a useful introduction to the topic.

924.   DALBY, Liza. 27 Jul. 1989. "Tempest in a teahouse: Geisha and old-style politicians go hand in hand." *Far Eastern Economic Review* 145(30):36-37. No refs. ISSN:0014-7591.

DALBY cuts through the brouhaha over Prime Minister UNO Sōsuke's relationship with a geisha by noting that public indignation over such relationships has in the past focused on the secrecy involved, i.e. that "shady deal-making" occurs in the presence of geisha. What is new this time is that the focus is on the sexual relationship.

925.   De BECKER, J.E. 1905 [rep. 1971]. *The Nightless City or, The History of Yoshiwara Yūkwaku*. [With a new forward by Terence BARROW.] Rutland, VT: Tuttle. 386p. No refs. LCCN:79-142767.

A thorough study of Tokyo's "entertainment quarter" originally done in 1899 and updated in 1905. DE BECKER gives a historical perspective and a contemporary (1905) report including statistics, maps, sample contracts and other documents, and descriptions of dress, food, charms, social rules, and individual geisha.

926.   De MENTE, Boye. 1966. *Some Prefer Geisha: The Lively Art of Mistress-Keeping in Japan*. Rutland, VT: Tuttle. 167p. No refs. LCCN:67-11428.

An anecdotal account of "mistress keeping" in the Occupation and post-Occupation years.

927. "Dog sitters." Apr. 1989. *PHP Intersect* (Apr. 1989):4-5. No refs. ISSN:0910-4607.

Briefly notes a new service for Ginza night club hostesses: a poodle-sitting service for their pets.

928. FUJIMOTO, T. [1917.] *The Story of the Geisha Girl.* London: Laurie. 157p. No refs. LCCN:a17-1496.

Written to present "the true features of our geisha girls," this work details the history of the geisha and describes the various ranks and the inner workings of the profession. It includes stories of contemporary geisha and describes women engaged in that profession in all the major cities. It is an uneven account—one page discusses income and comments on "what a profitable and interesting business for females" while the next page bemoans expenditures and states how "expensive is the life of a geisha girl and how hard it is to earn such a big sum by a young weak woman." Written by a Japanese man who seems to have had much first-hand experience.

929. "Geisha Sadayakko." Jul. 1980. *East* 16(7/8):5-14. No refs. ISSN:0012-8295.

A biographical sketch of a talented geisha, favorite of Prime Minister ITŌ Hirobumi in the late 1880s. She married an actor in 1891 at the age of 21 and then went on to a career in theater, doing traditional Japanese dance and acting in Shakespearean productions in Japan and on world tours. An unusual woman in the Meiji era. (For the general audience but more informative than most of this genre.)

930. "The geisha who knew too much." 19 June 1989. *U.S. News and World Report* 106(24):15-16. No refs. ISSN:0041-5537.

Notes briefly that the Japanese reaction to reports of Prime Minister UNO Sōsuke's alleged affair with a geisha three years earlier was not about the relationship itself, but rather to the break in confidence of the geisha and the intrusion into the private life of a politician by the press.

931. HARRIS, Sara. 1962. *House of 10,000 Pleasures: A Modern Study of the Geisha and of the Streetwalker of Japan.* New York: Dutton. 222p. No refs. LCCN:61-6018.

Although the title promises a "modern study," this work presents in novelized form two accounts—one of a traditional geisha and one of a former *pan-pan* girl [prostitute] married to an American serviceman.

932. ILLING, Richard. 1978. *Japanese Erotic Art and the Life of a Courtesan.* London: Thames and Hudson. 88p. No refs. LCCN:79-311410.

A collection of *shunga* [spring pictures], or pictures "of sexual life . . . expressly intended to give pleasure to the viewer," and *bijin-e* ["pictures of pretty girls"], i.e. portraits of geisha painted by famous artists of the day. Several of the full color prints are of geisha in their daily routines—tending to their hair, their wardrobes, and playing *shamisen* [a stringed instrument]; others are explicitly sexual.

933. JACKSON, Laura. 1976. "Bar hostesses." In: LEBRA, Joyce, *et al. Women in Changing Japan.* Stanford: Stanford University Press, pp. 133-156. 18 notes. LCCN:75-33663.

A detailed explanation of the hostess system in bars, nightclubs and other places of entertainment. Includes profiles of two women, a current hostess and a former hostess who now owns her own bar.

934. JONES, H.J. Dec. 1975. "Good wives—wise mothers and pan pan: Notes on the position of Japanese women." *Asian Profile* 3(6):617-629. 48 notes. ISSN:0304-8675.

JONES provides an insightful analysis of the historical process which has resulted in two main roles for Japanese women in the early 1970s: "good wife-wise mother" and "*pan-pan*" [prostitute]. First outlines changes in women's status over the centuries and then focuses on the postwar period. Shows that a failure to receive economic franchise has resulted in defeatist attitudes, nonparticipation in society, or the modification of the good wife-wise mother role into a role of "survival through control of dependents."

935. KAJITA, Ichirō and Marvin MEYER. Jun. 1958. "The moral status of the geisha." *Today's Japan* 3:23-25. [Also cited as *Orient/West*.] No refs. ISSN:0474-6465.

Explores the question of geisha as artist or geisha as prostitute as part of the debate over continuance of the geisha tradition after the banning of prostitution. Not particularly illuminating, but does include a few lists of multiple wives of historical luminaries.

936. KANEMATSU, Sachiko. Jan./Mar. 1988. "Women of Kabukichō." *Japan Quarterly* 35(1):84-89. No refs. ISSN:0021-4590.

A current report on prostitution in the Kabukichō area of Shinjuku by a guidance counselor for prostitutes, employed since 1956 to assist the implementation of the Anti-Prostitution Law. She profiles several women and pinpoints the ultimate cause of prostitution: women perceiving themselves as inferior, resulting in low self-esteem.

937. Kikuya. 1969. *I, a Geisha.* [Tokyo]: Tokyo News Service. 50p. No refs. LCCN:72-560863.

A proud, traditional geisha writes to introduce her profession to foreigners. She presents a history of geisha, her weekly schedule, a description of her geisha house, an outline of the cost of clothing, a description of the make-up and dressing process, a discussion of traditional restaurants, a summary of omens, and an explanation of games played with guests.

938. KINJO, Kiyoko. Jun. 1975. "Women in Okinawa." In: *Japanese Women Speak Out.* Tokyo: White Paper on Sexism—Japan Task Force, pp. 129-133.

A discussion of the prostitution problem in Okinawa resulting from the presence of American bases.

939. LAMOUR, Frank. 1989. "The green house district." *The Manipulator* no. 18:unpaged. No refs. ISSN:0178-3556.

Reprints photographs and portraits of young prostitutes taken around 1880 by Felix BEATO, Baron STILLFRIED, or KUSAKABE Kimbei in the Yokohama area. Includes one photograph of women in a cage. A brief article accompanies the photographs.

940. LONGSTREET, Stephen and Ethel LONGSTREET. 1970. *Yoshiwara: City of the Senses.* New York: McKay. 225p. No refs. LCCN:76-120170.

A book for the general reader designed to be an "attempt to look behind the legends . . . to discover the history, identify the founders, habits, rituals and beauties of the place." The result is a rather rambling discussion of geisha, prostitutes, eroticism and the Yoshiwara in general.

941. MACKIE, Vera. 1988. "Division of labour: Multinational sex in Asia." In: McCORMACK, Gavan and Yoshio SUGIMOTO, eds. *The Japanese Trajectory: Modernization and Beyond.* New York: Cambridge University Press, pp. 218-232. 49 notes. LCCN:88-1722.

Although focusing on contemporary prostitution of which Japanese males take advantage while abroad, MACKIE includes historical context for prostitution in Japan.

942. MATSUBARA, Hiroshi. 1965. "Maiko: A teenage career on the wane." *East* 1(5):22-25. No refs. ISSN:0012-8295.

Profiles OGAWA Kayoko, a 17-year-old *maiko* [apprentice geisha] from Kyoto, and describes her training in a general way.

943. MORI, Arinori. 1976. "On wives and concubines." [Parts 1-5.] In: *Meiroku Zasshi; Journal of the Japanese Enlightenment.* [Translated and introduced by William BRAISTED.] Cambridge: Harvard University Press, pp. 104-105,143-145,189-191,252-253,331-333. Notes. LCCN:76-27134.

A call for reform of the marital relationship and the abolishment of the concubine system by the founder of the Meirokusha, "a select group of pioneer Japanese scholars in western studies." Writing during the period 1874-1875, MORI (Minister of Education) calls marriage "the fundamental of human morals . . . [in which] . . . rights and obligations emerge between them . . . [the husband and wife] . . . so neither can take advantage of the other." A very radical position for the times.

944. PERKINS, P.D. 1954. *Geisha of Pontochō.* Tokyo: Tokyo News Service. 195p. No refs. Index. LCCN:54-14749.

With photographs and text, PERKINS describes the early-1950s lifestyle of the inhabitants of Pontochō, the geisha quarter in Kyoto. Includes descriptions of individual women.

945. "The premier and the geisha." 19 Jun. 1989. *Newsweek* 113(25):46. No refs. ISSN:0028-9604.

An early report on Prime Minister UNO Sōsuke's alleged interactions with a geisha points out that the relationship is not unusual but that the exposé of the affair is.

946. SAKATANI, Shiroshi. 1976. "On concubines." In: *Meiroku Zasshi, Journal of the Japanese Enlightenment.* [Translated and introduced by William BRAISTED.] Cambridge: Harvard University Press, pp. 392-400. Notes. LCCN:76-27134.

A discussion of equal rights for husbands and wives, condemning excesses in either direction, and calling for an end to the concubinage system (1875).

947. SASAKI, Tamio. Apr. 1971. "Yukaku—the gay quarter: Some detailed and documented observations on the bawdy in Edo." *East* 7(4):38-46. No refs. ISSN:0012-8295.

A general description of the Yoshiwara in Tokyo and other "play quarters."

948. SCOTT, A.C. 1960. *The Flower and Willow World; the Story of the Geisha.* [New York]: Orion Press. 208p. No refs. Index. LCCN:60-8359.

A description of the geisha world, basically sympathetic, which sets historical context, explains the organizational mechanics, and relates stories of several famous geisha. Intended for the general reader.

949. SEAMAN, Lee. Summer 1976. "Mizu shōbai—The water trades and the position of women in Japan." *Japan Christian Quarterly* 42(3):148-153. 2 notes. ISSN:0021-4361.

Relates the stories of four women, and describes the exploitative nature of the "hostess trade."

950. SMITH, Charles. 28 Dec. 1989. "Tax, foreign pressure and the power of women." *Far Eastern Economic Review* 146(52):26-27. No refs. ISSN:0014-7591.

In a brief discussion of issues presented in the December 1889 *Japan Weekly Mail*, SMITH relates the controversy over the possible banning of prostitution.

951. STEVENS, John. Feb. 1989. "Where have all the geisha gone?" *PHP Intersect* (Feb. 1989):6. No refs. ISSN:0910-4607.

A brief essay noting geisha's role historically and a current "waning of the public interest."

952. TAKASATO, Suzuyo. 1982. "Women on base." *Ampo: Japan-Asia Quarterly Review* 14(4):24-29. No refs. LCCN:77-612830.

Discusses prostitution on Okinawa, the problems of mixed-blood children, the poor mental health of many former prostitutes, and the importation of Filipina women as entertainers.

953. TAKEYASU, M. 1954. "Prostitution in Japan." *International Review of Criminal Policy* 5:59-61. 32 notes. ISSN:0074-7688.

Provides a thorough review of the status of, and the attempts to re-establish and to eliminate, prostitution following World War II. Includes relevant statistics through 1953 and translations of the legal code pertaining to prostitution.

954. TSUDA, Mamichi. 1976. "On destroying prostitution." In: *Meiroku Zasshi, Journal of the Japanese Enlightenment.* [Translated and introduced by William BRAISTED.] Cambridge: Harvard University Press, pp. 517-518. Notes. LCCN:76-27134.

A call in 1875 for the end to prostitution which, "exhausts the people's wealth and weakens their physical strength." Written by an Enlightenment scholar who also worked to "forbid traffic in human beings."

955. WILLIS, W. 26 Nov. 1867. "Prostitution in Japan." In: CORTAZZI, Hugh. 1985. *Dr. Willis in Japan: 1862-1877, British Medical Pioneer.* Dover, NH: Athlone Press, pp. 241-246. LCCN:85-1334.

As an appendix to this biography of Dr. W. WILLIS, CORTAZZI includes a report on prostitution written by WILLIS in 1867 describing the practice of and expenses associated with prostitution and mistress-keeping. It is (apparently) directed to British officials, as WILLIS ends by recommending that "Diplomatic or Consular agents" push for establishment of Lock Hospitals and regular examinations of prostitutes living in open ports.

956. YAMATA, Kiku. 1956. *Three Geishas.* New York: John Day Co. 253p. No refs. LCCN:56-10841. [*Trois Geishas.* English.]

After a general description of the history of geisha, YAMATA presents the stories of three geisha: Okichi, the geisha (supposedly) assigned to Townsend Harris, and two other more modern geisha whose Japanese memoirs were consulted in the creation of their tales. For the general reader.

Miscellaneous "Firsts" and Worker Profiles

957. CHERRY, Kittredge. Apr. 1985. "Women break the sushi barrier." *PHP Intersect* (Apr. 1985):45. No refs. ISSN:0910-4607.

Notes the employment of 15 women as professional sushi chefs and very briefly describes the training available.

958. "The feminine 'touch' in the camera industry." 1967. *Japan* 1967(2):27-31. No refs. LCCN:86-648185.

Briefly profiles MORI Michiko, a technical section assistant with Canon Camera Co., sketching out her work duties and her leisure activities.

959. "Fire fighting goes feminine." 1970. *Japan* 1970(1):21-24. No refs. LCCN:86-648185.

In 1969, women were employed as fire fighters in Yokohama and Kawasaki for the first time, but they have responsibilities only for public education and equipment maintenance.

960. "Housewives' choice." 13 Jun. 1987. *Economist* 303(7502):86. No refs. ISSN:0013-0613.

An interesting, although very brief, account of the use of housewives as part-time bank clerks who travel door-to-door to provide banking services.

961. "Japan's Mr. International Finance and Mrs. National Property." 1 Jul. 1989. *Economist* 312(7609):64. No refs. ISSN:0013-0613.

Briefly profiles NAKAYAMA Kyōko, the first *kachō* [section manager] in the Japanese Finance Ministry.

962. KAWAHARA, Chizuko. Jul. 1963. "Women at work." *Asia Scene* 8:48-51. No refs. ISSN:0004-4504.

An early 1960s (and therefore optimistic) look at career opportunities for women. Profiles KAGEYAMA Hiroko, a section head in the Nippon Telegraph and Telephone Corporation, TAJI Shinako, a middle school teacher, and ADACHI Emiko, a lecturer with the Association for Business Efficiency.

963. LEBRA, Joyce. 1976. "Women in service industries." In: LEBRA, Joyce, *et al. Women in Changing Japan.* Stanford: Stanford University Press, pp. 107-131. 7 notes. LCCN:75-33663.

An in-depth look at women in service industries (beauticians, seamstresses, stewardesses) providing information on types of employment, rationale for working, and future aspirations of workers. Provides a detailed profile on a seamstress.

964. "Me and my soothsayer." Sep. 1985. *PHP Intersect* Sep. 1985:18-19. No refs. ISSN:0910-4607.

Profiles Reika O. and OKUMA Chiyo, "soothsayers."

965. "She'll tell you about the U.N." 1970. *Japan* 1970(3):28-30. No refs. LCCN:86-648185.

A "Japanese woman of the traditional view" serves as a guide to the United Nations Pavilion at the Expo '70 Fair in Kobe.

966. SUGAWARA, Nobuo. Jul./Sep. 1989. "Takano Etsuko: Protector of fine cinema." *Japan Quarterly* 36(3):306-310. No refs. ISSN:0021-4590.

Profiles TAKANO Etsuko, an advocate for literary films, especially those from countries with fledgling film industries and those written and produced by women. TAKANO runs Iwanami Hall in Tokyo where these films are shown.

967. TSUJI, Ko. 1964. "My housekeeper Mrs. Shima." *East* 1(4):70-72. No refs. ISSN:0012-8295.

Describes the "ultimate" in a Japanese housekeeper, one Mrs. SHIMA.

968. WHIPPLE, Charles. Jul. 1989. "She delivers: A woman takes to the road." *[PHP] Intersect* (Jul. 1989):19-20. No refs. ISSN:0910-4607.

Profiles GOTŌ Yōko, of Gōto Delivery Service, who contracts to deliver items in Chiba Prefecture. She is "one of a few Japanese women with a license to drive heavy vehicles."

969. WHIPPLE, Charles. Jul. 1990. "Driver's seat: A young woman who moves the earth." *Intersect* 6(7):17-18. ISSN:0910-4607.

Profiles a former golf caddy now driving a 45 ton Caterpillar 773 vehicle for a living.

970. "Women customs inspectors." 1969. *Japan* 1969(3):29-31. No refs. LCCN:86-648185.

Notes the new occupation of "lady inspectors" for the Customs Office at Tokyo International Airport.

971. "Yuriko Uchimura—EXPO escort guide . . . diplomat in feminine guise." 1969. *Japan* 1969(4):29-30. No refs. LCCN:86-648185.

Briefly profiles a woman working for Expo '70.

8

Legal Status of Women

Overviews

972. BROWN, Catherine W. 1979. "Japanese approaches to equal rights for women: The legal framework." *Law in Japan: An Annual* 12:29-56. 115 notes. ISSN:0458-8584.

BROWN introduces the Article 90 doctrine, the legal basis for sexual discrimination cases beginning in 1966, reviews cases connected with its implementation, and analyzes its effectiveness. (Note: written prior to the Equal Employment Opportunity Law of 1986.)

973. BUCKLEY, Sandra and Vera MACKIE. 1986. "Women in the new Japanese state." In: McCORMACK, Gavan and Yoshio SUGIMOTO, eds. *Democracy in Contemporary Japan.* Armonk, NY: M.E. Sharpe, pp. 173-185. 67 notes. LCCN:86-17744.

BUCKLEY and MACKIE cut through government rhetoric to expose what they consider to be nationalistic and militaristic stances of the Nakasone government which are leading to the restriction of women's roles to those within the home. Using the Nationality Law, the proposed Equal Employment Opportunity Law, and the Eugenic Protection Law as examples, they describe the reactions and priorities of the Japanese women's movement as the groups within it struggle to meet these challenges.

974. BUCKLEY, Sandra. 1988. "Body politics: Abortion law reform." In: McCORMACK, Gavan and Yoshio SUGIMOTO, eds. *The Japanese Trajectory: Modernization and Beyond.* New York: Cambridge University Press, pp. 205-217. 33 notes. LCCN:88-1722.

Provides a history of legalized abortion in Japan and a description of the efforts of the Japanese Anti-Abortion Law Coalition to retain rights to the same.

975. CARTER, Aiko. 5 Apr. 1974. "On being a woman in Japan. Part 3: Legal status." *Japan Christian Activity News*, no. 451:1-3. No refs. ISSN:0021-4353. [Reprinted in CARTER, Aiko. 1975. *On being a woman in Japan.* Tokyo: Femintern Press.]

To outline women's legal status (as of 1974) CARTER relates the "first protest" in 1878 by a woman requesting her voting right as head of household, discusses divorce, and then focuses on "male chauvinist media." Brief comments only but with specific illustrations.

976. CHINO, Keiko. Jun. 1975. "Japanese women and government." In: *Japanese Women Speak Out.* Tokyo: White Paper on Sexism—Japan Task Force, pp. 66-67. No refs.

A critical description of a court case wherein state secrets concerning the reversion of Okinawa to Japan were released. ITASUMI Kikuko, the woman who passed the secrets, was condemned by the public for "yielding to sexual temptation;" the male reporter who received the secrets was heralded as "a champion of freedom of the press." CHINO uses this case as an example of how "power uses sex as a tool to maintain its control of the people and their basic rights."

977. CLIFFORD, William. 1976. *Crime Control in Japan.* Lexington, MA: Lexington Books. 200p. Notes. Index. LCCN:75-22883.

CLIFFORD provides comparative statistics for male and female offenders (1946-1972) within a chapter discussing female crime (pp. 125-132). He concludes that numbers of offenders have remained steady since the pre-World War II era with most crimes involving "infanticide, murder, theft, negligence causing death or injury, and . . . suicide." Also included in the work are a brief description of Women's Guidance Homes, prison population statistics, information on the Big Brothers and Sisters program for work with delinquents, and suicide statistics for women.

978. Committee to Support K-san. Jun. 1975. "'Give me back my child'—An unmarried working mother in the courts." In: *Japanese Women Speak Out.* Tokyo: White Paper on Sexism—Japan Task Force, pp. 47-50. No refs.

Recounts the case of an unmarried teacher who chose to have a child and raise it herself. The father's family abducted the child and placed it with foster parents. The courts allowed registration of the child in the mother's family register, but would not allow return of the child.

979. "Crimes and punishments of women." Jun. 1982. *East* 18(5/6):6-10. No refs. ISSN:0012-8295.

Rather sensationalist profiles of ITŌ Motoko, a bank clerk who swindled 50 million yen, and ENOMOTO Mieko, the wife of former Prime Minister TANAKA's [male] secretary, who testified during the Lockheed Scandal trials.

980. DAN, Alice. 1986. "The law and women's bodies: The case of menstruation leave in Japan." In: OLESEN, Virginia L. and Nancy Fugate WOODS, eds. *Culture, Society and Menstruation.* Washington, D.C.: Hemisphere Publishing Corporation, pp. 1-14. 15 refs. LCCN:86-3066.

Menstrual leave is permitted by law in Japan if a woman suffers heavily or if her work is injurious during menstruation. DAN discusses "the history, rationale and use of menstruation leave, as well as the opinions on the controversy about abolishing it."

981. "Discomfort women." 25 Nov. 1989. *Economist* 313(7630):36. No refs. ISSN:0013-0613.

A very brief but detailed comment on the growing recognition of sexual harassment as an issue in Japan, and on the growing number of court cases.

982. FUJIEDA, Mioko and Rebecca JENNISON. 1985. "The UN Decade for Women and Japan: Tools for change." *Women's Studies International Forum* 8(2):121-123. 6 refs. ISSN:0277-5395.

An introduction to the major concerns facing women in the 1980s, including employment, education, and reproductive rights, and a discussion of the possible effects of the United Nations Decade for Women on those issues.

983. FUJITA, Kuniko. 1987. "Gender, state and industrial policy in Japan." *Women's Studies International Forum* 10(6):589-597. 39 refs. ISSN:0277-5395.

In this scholarly examination of Japanese industrial policy, FUJITA notes the lack of a policy on women and calls for the inclusion of policies on gender role equality in training and education and for day care support systems to enable men and women to compete for jobs equally.

984. FUJITA, Kuniko. Oct. 1987. "Industrial policy and women in Japan." *Working Paper* [*on Women in International Development*] no. 143. 20p. 76 refs. ISSN:0888-5354.

Reviews theories on the bases for gender-related differences in income and occupations status and points out that most attempts toward gender role equality at a national level have been fragmented, and have neglected parallel policy needs for equal educational and training opportunities, day care support structures, etc. Calls for governmental leadership in developing and implementing an industrial policy, for "only industrial policy would be able to integrate all policies for women and incorporate them into the main national policy effectively."

985. FUJITA, Taki. 1956. "The Prostitution Prevention Law." *Contemporary Japan* 14(7/9):484-497. No refs. ISSN:0388-0214.

FUJITA (first chairwoman of the Women's and Minors' Problems Council, founded in 1948) traces the history of anti-prostitution efforts and discusses aspects of the new law.

986. HANAMI, Tadashi. 1 Dec. 1979. "Protection or equality?" *Japan Labor Bulletin* 18:7-10. No refs. ISSN:0021-4469.

In 1978 the Labor Standards Law Committee issued a report on women's labor. HANAMI provides background on the legal struggle for equality, explains the provisions of the report (which were later implemented in the Equal Employment Opportunity Law of 1986), and then discusses the reactions of various women's groups to the proposals.

987. HAYASHI, Yōko. 1986. "Myth and reality: Institutional reform for women." *Ampo: Japan-Asia Quarterly Review* 18(2/3):18-23. No refs. LCCN:77-12830.

Equating "government" with the Liberal Democratic Party [LDP] (conservatives) and the LDP with the business world, HAYASHI analyzes the "reforms" taken by the Japanese government during the United Nations Decade for Women. Specifically addresses the laws concerning resumption of maiden name after divorce, a wife's share of inheritance, the Nationality Law, the Equal Employment Opportunity Law, and then discusses implications for women of the policy for "perfecting the foundation of the family," under development since 1975.

988. HIRAO, Ayako. Mar. 1989. "What's in a name?" *PHP Intersect* (Mar. 1989):44-45. No refs. ISSN:0910-4607.

Describes the efforts of FUKUSHIMA Mizuho and others to change legislation requiring one member of a married couple to surrender their name so that both may retain their original names if desired. Describes the implications of the current law for women.

989. HOSHINO, Sumiko. Dec. 1989. "Married couples, separate surnames: A step toward more pluralistic lifestyles." [Translated by Minako HARA.] *Review of Japanese Culture and Society* 3(1):53-59. 8 notes. ISSN:0913-4700.

Details the *koseki* [family register] system and discusses the current movement toward legalization of separate surnames for married couples.

990. IDA, Keiko. 1986. "Revision of the prostitution law: A menace to human rights." *Ampo: Japan-Asia Quarterly Review* 18(2/3):77-80. No refs. LCCN:77-12830.

Traces the history of the law banning prostitution (enacted in 1956) and the subsequent widening of loopholes and development of regulation of the "Suds Lands" (i.e. Turkish baths) industry. Equates the current situation with the pre-World War II system of licensed brothels.

991.   IDE, Kikue.   1928.   "Legal and political relationships of women of Japan today—An interpretation."   In: *Women of the Pacific.*   Honolulu: Pan Pacific Union, pp. 191-200. (Pan-Pacific Women's Conference, 1st, Honolulu, 9-19 Aug. 1928.)   No refs.

A thorough, non-technical review of the public and private (i.e. family) legal status of women as of 1928 and an explanation of ways in which the women's suffrage movement might be able to affect change.

992.   ISHII, Ryosuke.   1986.   "The status of women in traditional Japanese society."   *Japanese Annual of International Law* no. 29:10-22.   ISSN:0448-8806.

An overview of laws and common practice with regards to marriage, divorce and inheritance from ancient times to the Early Modern Period.

993.   Japan.   Fujin Mondai Kikaku Suishin Honbu.   Jan. 1977.   *National Plan of Action.* [Tokyo]:   Headquarters for the Planning and Promoting of Policies Relating to Women.   15p. No refs.   LCCN:82-107072.   [Reprinted in its entirety in #994.]

Outlines five tasks to be the focus for government policy changes during the United Nations Women's Decade: improvement of legal status of women, acceleration of women's participation in every field on an equal footing with men, respect for maternity and protection of maternal health, securing stability of life in old age, and promotion of international cooperation.   Details steps for implementation of the above.

994.   Japan.   Fujin Mondai Kikaku Suishin Honbu.   Apr. 1985.   *United Nations Decade for Women and the Women of Japan.*   [Tokyo]:   Prime Minister's Office.   80p.   No refs. LCCN:86-126631.

A report for participants in the Nairobi Conference on the United Nations Women's Decade (July 1985) describing progress on the National Plan of Action during the Decade for Women.   Focuses on legal status, women's participation "in every field on an equal footing with men," respect for motherhood and protection of maternal health, greater security for the aged and others, promotion of international cooperation, and the process by which the National Plan of Action was implemented.   The Plan (Jan. 1977) and its related "Priority Targets for the Second Half of the Period Covered by the National Plan of Action for the Promotion of Measures Relating to Women" (May 1981) are included in their entirety.   [See also #993.]

995.   KAMIYA, Masako.   1986.   "Women in Japan."   *University of British Columbia Law Review* 20(2):447-469.   14 refs.   ISSN:0068-1849.

A detailed analysis of the legal status of Japanese women which carefully differentiates between *de jure* equality (via sexually neutral legislation) and *de facto* equality.   Focuses on the Constitution and Civil Code and the National Pension Law.   Also discusses the impact of the United Nations Women's Decade and the role of the feminist movement.

996.   "Kitchen cabinet."   16 Jun. 1975.   *Newsweek* 85(24):36.   No refs.   ISSN:0028-9604.

Briefly reports on the formation of an hypothetical government "Cabinet" by the women's magazine, *Women's Discussion.*   Discusses the proposed policies of its members who include KAMISAKA Fuyuko, TAWARA Moeko, ICHIKAWA Fusae, ENCHI Fumiko, and ISHIGAKI Ayako.

997. KŌNO, Yoshisuke Augustinus. 1970. *The Evolution of the Concept of Matrimonial Consent in Japanese Law.* Tokyo: Monumenta Nipponica. 103p. Bibl. LCCN:71-865038.

Covers the legal history of the concept of matrimonial consent and discusses how this history reflects the "way in which man progressively understands the natural law." Reviews marriage law from pre-Meiji times through the various drafts and revisions of the Civil Code of 1947. Quite technical, but useful for detailed study.

998. KUSANO, Izumi and Keiko KAWASAKI. 1983. "Japanese women challenge anti-abortion law." *Ampo: Japan-Asia Quarterly Review* 15(1):10-15. No refs. LCCN:77-12830.

Discusses the "1982 Coalition to Stop the Revision of the Eugenic Protection Law," formed to protest the proposed deletion of economic hardship as a condition for legal abortion. Sets this governmental attempt in the larger context of relegating all welfare tasks (e.g. care of the elderly) to the shoulders of women as (unpaid) family duty.

999. MacDONALD, A. Caroline. 1915. "The legal status of the Japanese wife." *Christian Movement in the Japanese Empire* 13:324-329. [Also cited as *Japan Christian Yearbook.*] No refs. LCCN:16-23723.

A brief report considering the position of a wife within the family system and her rights in marriage and divorce: in sum, a woman has equal rights with men as long as she is single; when she marries she becomes an "incapacitated person" so that "the rights of the [husband] are protected in order to maintain the peace of the household."

1000. MASS, Jeffrey P. Winter 1983. "Patterns of provincial inheritance in late Heian Japan." *Journal of Japanese Studies* 9(1):67-95. 99 notes. ISSN:0095-6848.

MASS provides a detailed study of inheritance patterns in Heian Japan with examples from four provincial *samurai* families. Laws regarding inheritance prior to the Heian period are also considered. MASS discusses women's ability to inherit and "alienate property" throughout his article.

1001. NAFTULIN, Lois J. 1980. "Women's status under Japanese laws." *Feminist International* no.2:13-16. No refs. ISSN:0388-371X.

Discusses the progressive legal status of women in Japan, points out the few legal discriminations which do exist, and sets the social context which determines implementation or non-implementation of the legal code.

1002. NAKAGAWA, Zennosuke. Apr./Jun. 1963. "A century of marriage law." *Japan Quarterly* 10(2):182-192. No refs. ISSN:0021-4590.

Reviews the changes in marriage laws from the Meiji era through the "New Code" established after World War II, discussing especially changes in women's legal rights.

1003. Nihon Rōdō Kyōkai. 1981 and 1986. *Problems of Working Women.* Tokyo: Japan Institute of Labor. 24p. and 26p. (*Japanese Industrial Relations Series*, v. series 8.) No refs. LCCN:81-188876 and 86-172834.

The 1981 version of this report concentrates primarily on basic statistics on working women and new legislation (as a result of the United Nations Women's Decade) focusing on equality of opportunity, maternal health care, childcare leaves, and vocational training available to women. A third section explains the administrative structure of the governmental agencies which deal with women. The 1986 report provides statistics documenting changing employment patterns for women, gives updates on the measures undertaken for the United Nations Women's Decade, and repeats the administrative structure section.

1004. NOLTE, Sharon. Sept. 1983. "Women, the State, and Repression in Imperial Japan." *Working Paper* [*on Women in International Development*] no. 33. 11p. 15 notes. LCCN:83-623537. Series ISSN:0888-5354.

NOLTE begins her exploration of a rationale for the restrictive legislation on women's political activities during the Meiji era by first defining "what the Meiji government expected of women" and then by showing how the government expected these restrictions to lead to a dedicated labor force, educated mothers, and social workers.

1005. ŌHASHI, Yukako. 1986. "My body belongs to me: Women fight against a retrogressive revision of the Eugenic Protection Law." *Ampo: Japan-Asia Quarterly Review* 18(2/3):94-99. No refs. LCCN:77-12830.

With a feminist perspective, ŌHASHI reviews the history of the Eugenic Protection Law and various attempts to modify it.

1006. "Personal Affairs Arbitration Law now one month old." Sep. 1939. *Japanese Women* 2(5):3. No refs. ISSN:0388-1369.

A brief report on the number and type of cases submitted to the Tokyo district commissioners during the first month in force.

1007. "Protective law for mothers and children in need becomes effective." Jan. 1938. *Japanese Women* 1(1):4. No refs. ISSN:0388-1369.

Describes the provisions of the legislation and notes the active role of the League for Protection of Motherhood in its passage.

1008. SMITH, Robert J. Spring 1983. "Making village women into 'good wives and wise mothers' in prewar Japan." *Journal of Family History* 8(1):70-84. 15 refs. ISSN:0363-1990.

Analyzes Ella Embree WISWELL's 1935-1936 field notes on Suye-mura for evidence of the transition in governmental policies on the position of women. Includes many excerpts of interviews. [See #50.]

1009. SUZUKI, Kazue. Mar. 1988. "Grounds for divorce." *PHP Intersect* (Mar. 1988):44-45. No refs. ISSN:0910-4607.

Reports briefly on new interpretations of divorce laws and their effect on women.

1010. TARR-WHELAN, Linda. Aug. 1988. "Japan's future edge: Women workers, family policies." *Journal of the American Chamber of Commerce in Japan* 25(8):19-24. No refs. ISSN:0002-7847.

TARR-WHELAN spent two months as a United States-Japan Leadership Fellow and speaks positively of Japan's governmental policies in support of families ("protection of the health of mothers and children, day-care, and early childhood education"). She terms them "a hidden and increasingly critical component of Japan's competitive edge" which will enable women workers to participate more fully in the economy.

1011. TONOMURA, Hitomi. Jul. 1990. "Women and inheritance in Japan's early warrior society." *Comparative Studies in Society and History* 32(3):592-623. 137 notes. ISSN:0010-4175.

Analyzes changes in inheritance patterns from the Heian and early Kamakura periods when elite women had undisputed rights to inherit or acquire property to the late Kamakura period when primogeniture was the rule. Details types of inheritances allotted to wives and daughters in the earlier periods and discusses productive roles allowed women. Documents later inheritance strategies for maintaining property within male family lines.

1012. UPHAM, Frank K. 1987. *Law and Social Change in Postwar Japan.* Cambridge: Harvard University Press. 269p. Notes. Index. LCCN:86-19472.

In his examination of "how law affects the course of social conflict and change in Japan," UPHAM includes a chapter on "civil rights litigation and the search for equal opportunity employment." He details employment discrimination cases brought prior to the passage of the Equal Employment Opportunity Act in 1986: SUZUKI vs. Sumitomo Cement (mandatory retirement at marriage), NAWATAYA vs. Akita Cooperative Bank (wage inequality) and YAMAMOTO vs. Suzuka City (promotion). He analyzes ways in which these cases affected both the composition of the new law and their impact (or lack thereof) on social consciousness and social change, foreseeing a possible "capture" of the women's movement by government bureaucracy.

1013. WOJTAN, Linda S. Fall 1981. "Women and the law: The tug of war between law and custom." *Update on Law-Related Education* 5(3):14-17,60-63. No refs. ISSN:0147-8648.

In a brief examination of how "codified law has been transferred into actual practice" in Japan, Egypt, the Soviet Union, and Israel, WOJTAN describes gaps between educational attainment and job status, and the traditional focus of the wife and mother role in Japan.

Constitution and Civil Code of 1948

1014. KAJI, Chizuko. Jan./Mar. 1984. "The post-war wife—no longer incompetent: Civil Code revisions and equality for women." *Japan Quarterly* 31(1):11-18. No refs. ISSN:0021-4590.

Although writing for a non-technical journal, KAJI provides a detailed discussion of the changes in women's legal status since World War II and closes with areas for further action. "Incompetent" in this context means "without legal capacity."

1015. PHARR, Susan J. 1977. "A radical U.S. experiment: Women's rights laws and the occupation of Japan." In: REDFORD, L.H., ed. *The Occupation of Japan: Impact of Legal Reform.* Norfolk: MacArthur Memorial Foundation, pp. 124-151. 23 notes. LCCN:81-151726.

Details the drafting of the women's rights sections of the Japanese constitution by Beate SIROTA (b. 1923), a then 22-year-old woman and lower-level member of the Occupation staff. Also briefly explores the questions of whether Douglas MACARTHUR was a radical feminist and why such far-reaching reform was implemented.

1016. PHARR, Susan. 1978. "Soldiers as feminists: Debate within U.S. Occupation ranks over women's rights policy in Japan." In: WHITE, Merry I. and Barbara MOLONY, eds. *Proceedings of the Tokyo Symposium on Women.* Tokyo: International Group for the Study of Women, pp. 25-35. (Tokyo Symposium on Women, [1st], 1978.) 17 notes.

Discusses both the interaction between high-level males and lower-level women in the Occupation organizational structure concerning the extent of reform appropriate in the area of women's rights and the "alliance for liberation" between United States female officers and Japanese women "in a common effort to press for women's rights policies."

1017. PHARR, Susan J. 1982. "Bureaucratic politics and social reform: The Women's and Minors' Bureau in occupied Japan." In: BURKMAN, Thomas W., ed. *The Occupation of Japan: Educational and Social Reform.* Norfolk: MacArthur Memorial Foundation, pp. 401-423. 43 notes.

Discusses the establishment of women's rights on the agenda of the Occupation Forces and the process by which lower-ranking (American) female personnel and Japanese women activists worked together to ensure acceptance of the radical changes. Focuses specifically on the creation of the Women's and Minors' Bureau and the pivotal role played by Lt. Ethel B. WEED in its establishment and staffing.

1018. PHARR, Susan J. 1987. "The politics of women's rights." In: WARD, Robert E. and Yoshikazu SAKAMOTO. *Democratizing Japan: The Allied Occupation.* Honolulu: University of Hawaii Press, pp. 221-252. 65 notes. LCCN:86-25023.

PHARR combines material from two earlier efforts [#1015 and #1017] in a revealing analysis of "how and why a United States occupying force chose to make Japan a laboratory for one of the world's most radical experiments with women's rights" by creating "legal guarantees for women's equality and rights" which are more progressive than those in the United States currently. The two case studies focus on Japan's version of an Equal Rights Amendment and the establishment of the Women's and Minors' Bureau in the Japan Ministry of Labor to ensure continuation of the reforms. The efforts of Beate SIROTA and Ethel B. WEED, among others, are detailed.

1019. SANO, Chiye. 1958 [rep. 1973.] *Changing Values of the Japanese Family.* Westport, CT: Greenwood. 142p. (Catholic University. *Anthropological Series*, no. 18) Bibl. LCCN:73-8257.

Explores the effect of the Constitution and "newly" revised Civil Code on family structure. Includes an examination of roles for working mothers and the possibility of professional careers for daughters. An appendix includes data on "occupations mentioned by parents as desirable jobs for daughters" divided by urban and rural respondents.

1020. STEINER, Kurt. Feb. 1950. "The revision of the civil code of Japan: Provisions affecting the family." *Far Eastern Quarterly* 9(2):169-184. 19 notes. ISSN:0363-6917.

Reviews post-World War II changes to the Japanese Civil Code which affected women, including divorce, inheritance rights, and location of domicile.

1021. YAMAKAWA, Kikue. Apr./Jun. 1948. "Japanese women under the new constitution." *Contemporary Japan* 17(4/6):141-144. No refs. ISSN:0388-0214.

A general description of the positive effects of the 1948 Constitution for women including enfranchisement, equal opportunity for education, creation of the Women and Children's Bureau within the Ministry of Labor, the Labor Standards Law, and the raising of women's status within the family.

Equal Employment Opportunity Law

1022. BERGESON, Jan M. and Kaoru Yamamoto OBA. 1986. "Japan's new Equal Employment Opportunity Law: Real weapon or heirloom sword?" *Brigham Young University Law Review* 1986:865-883. 102 notes. ISSN:0360-151X.

Summarizes Japanese attitudes toward law, surveys legislation affecting working women prior to the Equal Employment Opportunity Law [EEOL], and discusses in detail the provisions of the EEOL. Concludes that the EEOL will not effect significant change alone, but it will play a role along with "the passage of time and the evolution of sociological values" in a "process of gradual change in Japan."

1023. CRAFT, Lucille. Jun. 1986. "Salari-woman." *Tokyo Business Today* (Jun. 1986):60-63. No refs. ISSN:0911-7008.

An essay on working women and the possible effects of the Equal Employment Opportunity Law.

1024. EDWARDS, Linda N. Jan. 1988. "Equal employment opportunity in Japan: A view from the West." *Industrial and Labor Relations Review* 41(2):240-250. 26 refs. ISSN:0019-7939.

A thorough discussion of the Equal Employment Opportunity Law of 1986 and its proposed and probable effects on women. EDWARDS predicts little change without concurrent changes in personnel practices and the female labor supply, i.e. "jobs will have to be made compatible with family life" and "division of labor within the household will have to change to permit women . . . to pursue careers outside the home without . . . neglecting their children."

1025. "The equal employment opportunity bill." 1984. *Japan Quarterly* 31(3):255-258. No refs. ISSN:0021-4590.

Discusses the status of the bill as of May 1984, noting causes of feminist opposition and probable reasons for pushing the bill through the legislature by the Nakasone government. The resultant loss of protective legislation for women is also analyzed.

1026. HASEGAWA, Michiko. 1984. "Equal opportunity legislation is unnecessary." *Japan Echo* 11(4):55-58. No refs. ISSN:0388-0435.

Provides a critique of SATŌ [#757] and disagrees with her conclusion that the Equal Employment Opportunity Law should be passed. Asserts that Japan's strength comes from its family system and that division of labor between the sexes keeps the family strong. [Introduced by #1032.]

1027. KAJI, Etsuko. 1986. "Herded into the labor market." *Ampo: Japan-Asia Quarterly Review* 18(2/3):35-41. No refs. LCCN:77-12830.

An editor of *Ampo* provides a critical appraisal of the Equal Employment Opportunity Law, tracing its formation and implementation. KAJI stresses the amount of additional discrimination enabled by the law and the inadequacy of the law in assuring "substantial equality." Makes use of quotations from government and business officials, and from working women to substantiate her points.

1028. NAKAJIMA, Michiko. Winter 1985. "Women at work." *Japan Echo* 12(4):58-65. No refs. ISSN:0388-0435.

Articulates problems of the Equal Employment Opportunity Law and the Temporary Staff Business Law (dealing with temporary help agencies). Includes round table discussions of these laws and their implications for the future. [For an introduction to the article, see #80.]

1029. NAKANISHI, Tamako. Sep./Oct. 1983. "Equality or protection? Protective legislation for women in Japan." *International Labour Review* 122(5):609-621. 6 notes. ISSN:0020-7780.

A detailed summary of the debate concerning equal opportunity for employment and protective legislation prior to the enactment of the Equal Employment Opportunity Law. Provides historical background on labor laws affecting women, plus details on the reports of the Labour Standards Law Study Group and the Ministry of Labour's Committee of Experts on Sexuality in Employment, giving public reaction to both reports.

1030. PARKINSON, Loraine. Apr. 1989. "Japan's Equal Employment Opportunity Law: An alternative approach to social change." *Columbia Law Review* 89(3):604-661. 197 notes. ISSN:0010-1958.

An in-depth study of the Equal Employment Opportunity Law which details reasons for creation of the law and the provisions of the law itself, analyzes the choice of voluntary compliance as a means of enforcement rather than coercion and the choice of gradual "evolutionary" social change rather "revolutionary" change, evaluates the success of the law to date, and considers prospects for "continued change." Based entirely on (extensive) Japanese language sources.

1031. Saitama Women Against War. 1984. "Japan's unequal 'equal' employment opportunity bill." *Ampo: Japan-Asia Quarterly* Review 16(3):10-17. No refs. LCCN:77-12830.

Reviews current problems (wage differential, proliferation of "part-timers"), analyzes the proposed law and details its shortcomings, and outlines provisions to be incorporated in an alternative law.

1032. SEKI, Yoshihiko. 1984. "The equal employment opportunity bill." *Japan Echo* 11(4):48-49. 4 refs. ISSN:0388-0435.

Introduces articles by SATŌ [#757] and HASEGAWA [#1026], two strong voices in the debate concerning the Equal Employment Opportunity Law, and then briefly discusses contributions of others to the discussion.

1033. TSURUNO, M. 1986. "Equal employment opportunity law comes into force." *Wheel Extended* [Tokyo] 16(2):35-36. No refs. ISSN:0049-755X.

A brief, positive note on several implications of the Equal Employment Opportunity Law (enacted 1 Apr. 1986): growth of temporary personnel agencies, growth in the number of women presidents (of businesses), and the possible broadening of types of work done by women.

9

Status of Women as Reflected in the Spoken Language

1034. "Basic Japanese. Lesson 4: Feminine speech." Oct. 1990. *Mangajin* 1(4):8-13. 1 note. ISSN:1051-8177.

A simple presentation of several of the main elements of Japanese female speech, followed by examples drawn from popular cartoon strips showing speech (and facial expression and gestures) of several stereotypes of women in a variety of situations.

1035. BEFU, Harumi and Edward NORBECK. 1958. "Japanese usages of terms of relationships." *Southwestern Journal of Anthropology* 14:66-86. 5 notes. ISSN:0038-4801.

A clear presentation of kinship terms of reference and address. The sex of both speaker and referent is consistently taken into account.

1036. CHERRY, Kittredge. 1987. *Womansword: What Japanese Words Say About Women*. Tokyo: Kodansha International. 151p. No refs. Index. LCCN:86-40441.

CHERRY's title can be read in two ways: "woman's word" and "woman sword." The work contains casual, far-ranging, brief feminist essays on words and some Chinese characters in common Japanese usage that illustrate or reinforce (negative) social attitudes toward women. Full of fascinating detail. No macrons. Entries are grouped according to women's life cycle and arranged as in a dictionary.

1037. EKUSA, Ato. 1 Nov. 1990. "Mind-set of young working women." *Journal of Japanese Trade and Industry* 9(6):18. No refs. ISSN:0285-9556.

Describes the slang terms that young elite Tokyo-raised working women use to describe their male friends and women who come to Tokyo in search of mates.

1038. GARDNER, Elizabeth and Samuel E. MARTIN. 1952. *Honorific and Familiar Speech in Japanese*. New Haven: Yale University Press. 44p. LCCN:53-24177.

A general survey of the subject of speech registers; one brief selection is devoted explicitly to women's and men's speech.

1039. HERLOFSKY, William J. 1985. "Gaze as a regulator in Japanese conversation." *Papers in Japanese Linguistics* 10:16-33. 2 notes. Refs. ISSN:0197-3150.

Gaze is seen as related to turn-taking in Japanese conversation, as the speaker often looks directly at the listener in order to signal the end of a speaking turn. The sex of speaker and listener is one factor taken into account in this preliminary study, which notes that women gaze more than men in conversation.

1040. HINDS, J. 1971. "Personal pronouns in Japanese." *Glossa* 5(2):146-155. 3 notes. refs. ISSN:0017-1271.

A technical article arguing that Japanese has a class of personal pronouns, which the author analyzes.

1041. HINDS, John. 1976. *Aspects of Japanese Discourse Structure.* Tokyo: Kaitakusha. 152p. Index. Bibl. LCCN:76-375356.

A technical study with occasional specific reference to differences between female and male speech and speech behavior.

1042. IDE, Sachiko. Jun./Aug. 1982. "Japanese sociolinguistics: Politeness and women's language." *Lingua: International Review of General Linguistics* 57(2/4):357-385. ISSN:0024-3841.

A somewhat technical but general article presenting a grammar of honorifics, social rules for formality and politeness, and an investigation of the polite features of Japanese women's speech in particular.

1043. IKUTA, Shoko. Apr. 1983. "Speech level shift and conversational strategy in Japanese discourse." *Language Sciences* 5(1):37-53. ISSN:0388-0001.

An attempt to investigate "the mechanisms involved in speech level shift in Japanese conversational discourse that contain the *desi-mas* forms" (p. 37), using gender as one category of analysis. IKUTA concludes that "formal" or "polite" endings actually show distance of various sorts, and that men and women behave similarly in terms of speech level shifting in a smooth flow of conversation.

1044. JORDEN, Eleanor Hartz. 1974. "Female speech: Persisting myth and persisting reality." *Report of the Second U.S. Japan Joint Sociolinguistic Conference.* Tokyo: Japan Society for the Promotion of Science, pp.103-118.

JORDEN provides a sensible and standard presentation of features (other than syntactic) commonly asserted to be characteristic of women's speech.

1045. KAMEI, Takashi. Nov. 1978. "Covering and covered forms of women's language in Japanese—With special reference to the ornamental prefix *o-.*" *Hitotsubashi Journal of Arts and Sciences* 19(1):1-7. ISSN:0073-2788.

Traces characteristics of feminine lexicon to medieval women's language (*nyōbō-kotoba* and *jochū-kotoba*) in which "covering forms" (his term for alternate words) were substituted for "covered forms" (words that were taboo for women). Substitution was accomplished by replacement (with a new word), by adding a prefix (*o-*) or by attaching a suffix (*moji*). KAMEI focuses on the prefix *o-*, which is viable in modern speech, and distinguishes between the fixed "ornamental *o-*" and the "variable *o-*," which he sees as one "linguistic symbol of femininity" (p. 5).

1046. KINDAICHI, Haruhiko. 1978/1988. *The Japanese Language.* [Translated by Umeyo HIRANO.] Rutland, VT: Tuttle. 295p. Notes. LCCN:77-93226. [*Nippongo.* 1957.]

The classic postwar defense of the Japanese language by an eminent scholar. A general work that touches occasionally on gendered speech.

1047. KITAGAWA, Chisato. Fall/Winter 1977. "A source of femininity in Japanese: In defense of Robin Lakoff's 'Language and women's place.'" *Papers in Linguistics* 10(3/4):275-298. ISSN:0031-1251.

KITAGAWA applies LAKOFF's theories [as presented in her article on English published in *Language in Society* 2(1973):45] to the Japanese language. Argues that the sentence-final particle *wa*, like LAKOFF's tag question, is a way of giving options to the addressee, as a "linguistic device that can be utilized to meet the standard of 'femininity' . . . in a male-dominated society" (p. 276). The particle *wa* itself conveys strong insistence, or softened by a high sustained intonation is associated with gentle questions.

1048. LEE, Motoko Y. Summer 1976. "The married woman's status and role as reflected in Japanese: An exploratory sociolinguistic study." *Signs* 1(4):991-999. 17 notes. ISSN:0097-9740.

Investigates terms of address and references for spouses. Based on questionable data from self-report in interviews of Japanese couples living in the United States.

1049. LOVEDAY, Leo. 1981. "Pitch, politeness and sexual role: An exploratory investigation into pitch correlates of English and Japanese politeness formulae." *Language and Speech* 24(1):71-89. ISSN:0023-8309.

A fascinating attempt to "demonstrate how international differences occurring in the expression of politeness in [British] English and Japanese can be related to language communities' socio-cultural expectations of and attitudes towards male and female pitch" (p. 71), concluding that "pitch level in Japanese serves to highlight sexual differences. . . in a much more marked fashion than pitch level in the same circumstances does so in English" (p. 85).

1050. MAKINO, Seiichi and Michio TSUTSUI. 1986. *A Dictionary of Basic Japanese Grammar*. Tokyo: The Japan Times. 1986. 634p. Index. Bibl.

A grammar reference book arranged in dictionary form. Discussion of usage is included in many entries, appropriateness to men's and women's speech being an occasional consideration. The long introduction to the volume contains significant information relevant to women's speech, expecially as it relates to honorifics and sentence-final particles.

1051. MARTIN, Samuel E. 1964. "Speech levels in Japan and Korea." In: Dell HYMES, ed. 1964. *Language, Culture, and Society: A Reader in Linguistics and Anthropology*. New York: Harper and Row, pp. 407-415. LCCN:64-15151.

A brief, scholarly but clear preliminary comparison of speech levels in Japanese and Korean, with some consideration given to Ryukyuan. Sex differences are one factor considered. Includes bibliography. No notes.

1052. MAYNARD, Senko Kumiya. 1989. *Japanese Conversation: Self-Contextualization through Structure and Interactional Management*. Norwood, NJ: ABLEX Publishing Corporation. (*Advances in Discourse Processes*, vol. 35.) 250p. Notes and Bibl. Index. LCCN:89-6627.

An investigation of "casual conversation in Japanese with an interest in finding out which aspects of conversational structure and interaction are more or less Japanese-specific" (p.3), creating a "view of conversation as a many-faceted, structured activity with a strong indication for transactional coordination. This interactional coordination is realized by the participant's self-contextualization, with its level of sensitivity being socioculturally determined" (pp. 229-230). The study includes a contrastive analysis with American English casual conversation suggesting that social conceptualization is an undercurrent that prompts different conversation management in Japan and the United States. The sex of the participants is one factor taken into account in such transactions, and in the study.

1053. McGLOIN, Naomi Hanaoka. 1980. "Some observations concerning *no desu* expressions." *Journal of the Association of Teachers of Japanese* 15(2):117-149. ISSN:0885-9884. [A revised version appears in MIYAGAWA (#1058).]

Argues that "the function of *no desu* [a characteristic of women's speech] is to present information which is known only to the speaker or the hearer as if it were shared information, . . . creating rapport or involving the hearer in the conversation or the speaker's point of view" (p. 132).

1054. McGLOIN, Naomi Hanaoka.   Apr. 1986.   "Feminine *wa* and *no*: Why do women use them?" *Journal of the Association of Teachers of Japanese* 20(1):7-28. ISSN:0885-9884.

Explores the semantic/pragmatic function of sentence-final particles *wa* and *no* in an effort to explicate their femininity. Challenges the assertions of KITAGAWA [#1047] that the feminine *wa* always occurs in sustained high intonation, and that the sustained high intonation of *wa* is an option-giving device showing deference. Argues instead that *wa* and *no* contribute to a "rapport/empathy-creating strategy," *wa* by engendering "an emotional common ground with the addressee," *no* by creating "a feeling of shared knowledge" (p. 21).

1055. MILLER, Roy Andrew. 1967. *The Japanese Language*. Chicago: University of Chicago Press. 428p. LCCN:67-16777.

A general introduction to the history and structure of Japanese, set in a cultural and geographic context. Differences between men's and women's speech, especially as reflected in pronoun usage and honorifics, receive significant, if not primary, treatment.

1056. MILLER, Roy Andrew. 1971. "Levels of speech (keigo) and the Japanese linguistics response to modernization." In: SHIVELY, Donald H., ed. 1971. *Tradition and Modernization in Japanese Culture*. Princeton: Princeton University Press, pp. 601-667. 44 notes. LCCN:69-18071.

Beginning with an extended historical and critical treatment of both Japanese and Western scholarship on *keigo*, MILLER goes on to present interesting evidence of features of Japanese polite language that are undergoing change in what he sees as a trend toward increased complexity. Female speech is one minor element of the discussion.

1057. MIURA, Akira. 1983. *Japanese Words and Their Uses*. Rutland, VT: Tuttle. 240p. Bibl. Index. LCCN:82-51099.

Three hundred important Japanese words arranged in dictionary order, discussed in some detail with examples provided. The emphasis is on (sociolinguistic) differences from English usage; one aspect treated here and there is how women are referred to and how they are expected to speak.

1058. MIYAGAWA, Shigeru and Chisato KITAGAWA, eds. 1984. *Studies in Japanese Language Use*. Carbondale, IL: Linguistic Research, Inc. 370p. Bibl.

A collection of ten papers of varying quality, the preponderance relevant to Japanese women's use of language. McGLOIN on politeness strategies and SHIBAMOTO on subject ellipsis focus explicitly on women's language. Provides general introduction to politeness levels. [See #1053 for an earlier version of McGLOIN's paper.]

1059. MIZUTANI, Osamu and Nobuko MIZUTANI. 1987. *How to be Polite in Japanese*. Tokyo: Japan Times. 160p. Index.

A valuable overview of Japanese "politeness," with parts devoted to Politeness in Attitude, Verbal Politeness (including a brief section on differences between men's and women's speech), and Concern for Others, plus a general introduction discussing Factors Deciding the Level of Politeness, including gender. Women's speech is mentioned explicitly throughout.

1060. MOCHIZUKI, Michiko. 1980. "Male and female variants for 'I' in Japanese: Concurrence rules." *Papers in Linguistics* 13(3):453-474. Bibl. ISSN:0031-1251.

This technical linguistic article finds similarity on the axis of formality, and difference on the axis of politeness, between male and female first-person pronoun usage.

1061. OKADA, Miyo. 1963. *Keigo: Honorific Speech in Japanese.* [Revised ed.] New Haven: Far Eastern Publications, Yale University. 97p. (Mirror series J, no.5.) LCCN:62-24504.

An introductory survey of honorific speech intended originally for students completing elementary Japanese courses who plan to spend time in Japan. Includes "Sample Conversations," "Social Notes," and "Polite Letters," illustrating variations assumed to exist between male and female speech.

1062. PENG, Fred C.C., ed. 1975. *Language in Japanese Society: Current Issues in Sociolinguistics.* Tokyo: University of Tokyo Press. 246p. (ICU Symposium on Sociolinguistics [1st, 1974, Tokyo].) LCCN:73-331632.

A collection of articles of general relevance to questions on women's language. Including HINDS on third-person pronouns, SHIBATA touching on honorifics, and LA FORGE on community language learning.

1063. PRINDLE, Tamae K. May 1972. "Japanese consanguineal kin terms." *Anthropological Linguistics* 14(5):182-195. 11 refs. 4 notes. ISSN:0003-5483.

A detailed, technical "structural and historical study of Japanese kin terms" (p. 182), offering considerable information on gender divisions.

1064. RAMSEY, Shiela J. Apr. 1981. "The kinesics of femininity." *Language Sciences* 3(1):104-123. ISSN:0388-0001.

An analysis of the variations, intents, and effects of "cut off" gestures common among Japanese women, *i.e.,* covering or hiding all or part of the face with the hands. From surveying reactions of American and Japanese women college students shown slides of women's "cut off" gestures, RAMSEY concludes that though the gestures themselves may be universal, cultural attitudes toward them vary.

1065. SANDNESS, Karen. Mar. 1975. "The use of *kare* and *kanozyo. Journal of the Association of Teachers of Japanese* 10(1):75-86. ISSN:0885-9884.

Though conclusions are founded on written evidence (articles appearing in popular weekly magazines), this article is relevant to the spoken language. On the basis of a statistical study of the third-person pronoun usage versus the occurrence of proper names and descriptive noun phrases, SANDNESS repeats the conventional wisdom that both third-person pronouns are rarely used, and suggests that 1) "foreigners are much more apt to be referred to as *kare* or *kanazyo* than Japanese are" (p. 81); 2) and that in the materials she surveyed "females of all nationalities were more likely to be referred to as *kanazyo* . . . than males were to be referred to as *kare* . . ." (p. 82); that articles translated from English used only slightly more third-person pronouns than articles originally written in Japanese; and 4) that articles in the women's magazine used the greatest proportion of pronouns.

1066. SEWARD, Jack. 1983. *Japanese in Action: An Unorthodox Approach to the Spoken Language and the People who Speak it.* [Revised edition.] Tokyo: Weatherhill. 217p. Index. LCCN:68-55570.

An irreverant classic by a longtime resident foreigner. Chapter Fourteen deals specifically with male and female speech.

1067. SHIBAMOTO, Janet S. 1981. "Sex-related variation in the production of predicate types in Japanese." *Language Sciences* 3(2):257-282. ISSN:0388-0001.

SHIBAMOTO tests the common claim that men use more verbs, and women more adjectives, as predicates because of the "'emotional' and 'subjective' nature of female speech" (p. 257). Early treatment of data obtained from interviews of "middle class" Japanese divided into groups by sex and age. Analysis of data shows as much variation by age as by sex, showing little support for common assumptions.

1068. SHIBAMOTO, Janet S. 1985. *Japanese Women's Language*. Orlando, FL: Academic Press. 190p. Bibl. Index. LCCN:84-24320.

A ground-breaking sociolinguistic study, based on actual speech samples, of gender-related syntactic differences in the "informal" speech of Japanese men and women. SHIBAMOTO finds that women more often than men omit grammatical subjects and delete case markers; they also deviate more often from "canonical" word order, especially by right allocation. Problematic interview design (such as presence of foreign woman observer) has raised serious questions about data and analysis, but this study suggests tantalizing possibilities for further exploration. Includes a useful survey of the literature on Japanese women's language in the context of general sociolinguistic theory.

1069. SHIBAMOTO, Janet S. 1987. "Japanese sociolinguistics." *Annual Review of Anthropology* 16:261-278. ISSN:0084-6570.

A general introduction to traditional Japanese approaches to the relationship between language and society, and a brief presentation of current issues in sociolinguistic research in Japan, including "Honorification" and "Language and Sex." Useful bibliography.

1070. SHIBAMOTO, Janet S. 1987. "The womanly woman: Manipulation of stereotypical and nonstereotypical features of Japanese female speech." In: PHILIPS, Susan U., Susan STEELE, and Christine TANZ, eds. *Language, Gender, and Sex in Comparative Perspective*. London: Cambridge University Press, pp. 26-49. Bibl. LCCN:86-17086.

Compares data from interviews of small friendship groups of women (female groups from #1067, #1068, and #1069), with similar data from transcriptions of television "home dramas" to show how established characteristics of female speech vary when speakers do or do not "emphasize their femininity." SHIBAMOTO concludes that phonological, morphological and lexical behavior are more or less consciously controlled and are "accessible to stereotyping" (p. 48), whereas syntactic features are sex-related but are not consciously manipulated or stereotyped. A clear survey of research on sex-related features of the Japanese language. References included in bibliography for entire volume.

1071. SHIBATANI, Masayoshi. 1990. *The Languages of Japan*. Cambridge: Cambridge University Press. 411p. Bibl. Index. LCCN:89-993.

Descriptive grammars of Ainu and Japanese. Two brief sections are devoted, respectively, to men's and women's speech and to honorics in Japanese; honorific expressions in Ainu come under discussion, but they are not related to sex or gender.

1072. SUZUKI, Kazue. May 1988. "Fit to print?" *PHP Intersect* (May 1988):41. No refs. ISSN:0910-4607.

A brief overview of anti-female bias in the Japanese language as seen in dictionaries and newspapers. Also notes the attempts to eliminate sexist language from official reports by the Kanagawa Prefectural government and the Koganei City government.

1073. SUZUKI, Takao. 1976. "Language and behavior in Japan: The conceptualization of personal relations." *Japan Quarterly* 23(3):255-266. ISSN:0021-4590. Reprinted in: LEBRA, Takie Sugiyama and William P. LEBRA. 1986. *Japanese Culture and Behavior:*

Selected Readings. [Revised edition.] Honolulu: University of Hawaii Press, pp. 142-157. LCCN:86-4367.

An introductory article treating personal pronouns and kinship term usages and showing how these and other semantic elements change according to the social context. Most of the discussion is male-centered.

1074. SUZUKI, Takao. 1977. "Language and culture." In: MURAKAMI, Hyôe and Edward G. SEIDENSTICKER. 1977. *Guides to Japanese Culture*. Tokyo: Japan Culture Institute, pp. 24-28. LCCN:77-373003.

Synopsis of *Kotoba to Bunka* (#1075) and commentary focusing on pronoun usage.

1075. SUZUKI, Takao. 1978. *Japanese and the Japanese: Words in Culture*. Tokyo: Kodansha International. 152p. Notes. LCCN:77-15296. [*Kotoba to bunka.* 1973.]

An interesting, light comparison of Japanese with some Western languages, emphasizing cultural perspective. Chapter Five, "Words for Self and Others," is relevant here.

1076. TANAKA, Keiko. 1990. "Intelligent excellence: Women in Japanese advertising." In: BEN-ARI, Eyal, Brian MOERAN, and James VALENTINE, eds. *Unwrapping Japan: Society and Culture in Anthropological Perspective*. Honolulu: University of Hawaii Press, pp. 78-96. 12 refs. LCCN:89-35666.

Using examples of advertisements from women's magazines (*J.J.*, *Can Can*, *More*, *With*, and *Cosmopolitan*) TANAKA focuses on the use of the words "feminist," "intelligence" and "individualism" to illustrate societal attitudes toward women.

1077. TANAKA, Masako. 1977. "Kinship terminologies: The Okinawan case." In: McCORMICK, William C. and Stephen A. WURM, eds. 1977. *Language and Thought: Anthropological Issues*. Hague: Mouton Publishers, pp. 211-226. 6 notes. LCCN:78-319604.

A technical terminological analysis of kinship in Okinawa, where "morphologically identical relationship terms are applied to nonkin," finding three separate terminological systems. Gender is one factor in the study.

1078. WETZEL, Patricia J. Dec. 1988. "Are 'powerless' communication strategies the Japanese norm?" *Language in Society* 17(4):555-564. ISSN:0047-4045.

WETZEL calls attention to parallels between Japanese communication strategies and "female communication strategies in the West," suggesting that miscommunication between Japanese and American "business*men*" may resemble miscommunication between the sexes "in the West." WETZEL's redefinition of characteristic male and female language as "powerful" and "powerless" causes further problems of interpretation because the term "power" is culturally bound. She suggests that understanding different notions of power is "one key to understanding miscommunication between Japan and the West" (p. 555). An interesting introductory essay based on broad categorical cultural assumptions.

10

Education

1079. BENNETT, John W., Herbert PASSIN, and Robert K. McKNIGHT. 1958. *In Search of Identity: The Japanese Overseas Scholar in America and Japan.* Minneapolis: University of Minnesota Press, pp. 154-176. LCCN:58-10879.

In a chapter titled "Changing Social Roles of Japanese Women," BENNET, *et al.*, summarize the feelings of Japanese women educated in the United States who return to Japan and those of women educated in mission schools in Japan staffed by Westerners or by Japanese educated in the West. Although problems are thoroughly discussed, the authors reflect the optimism generated by legal changes made during the Occupation in their consideration of possible role changes. Includes statistics on women who studied in the United States.

1080. CLARKE, Elizabeth J. Spring 1974. "Women's education in Japan: A contemporary assessment." *Japan Christian Quarterly* 40(2):79-87. 12 notes. ISSN:0021-4361.

CLARKE provides an overview of women's education from Meiji times through the 1970s, concentrating primarily on historical context (the writings of KAIBARA Ekken and FUKUZAWA Yukichi) and delineating the contributions of Christian schools. Ends with a challenge to these schools by asking why more women educated there are not involved in the 91 Protestant schools currently operating in Japan. [See also #1092 and #1119.]

1081. Daigaku Fujin Kyokai. 1974. *Japanese University Women: Issues and Views. Volume One: Vocation and Education.* Tokyo: Daigaku Fujin Kyōkai. 43p. [Author also cited as Japanese Association of University Women.

Results of a survey of the members of the Japanese Association of University of Women in the fall of 1973 to detail "the prevailing patterns of social, economic and cultural life" of their members. Includes an introduction by OSHIMA Kiyoko, chapters on "Gainful employment" by SANO Chie, "Education" by ISHIZAWA Fusa, and "Method and Procedure" by EJIRI Mihoko. An appendix including the questionnaire, "Attitudes of Japanese University Women on Family and Vocational Life," is included.

1082. KODAMA, Miiko and Tomoko HIRANO. 1983. "Learning in the life course of Japanese women." In: MURAMATSU, Yasuko, ed. *Women and Work: Working Women and their Impact on Society.* Tokyo: International Group for the Study of Women, pp. 186-198. (Tokyo Symposium on Women, 2nd, 1983. *Proceedings*.) No refs. LCCN:84-187204.

Surveys the variety of nonformal learning undertaken by women from 1900 to date. Concludes by calling for the addition of occupational training to the standard culture and sports opportunities already available.

1083. KOYOMO, Teruko. 1957. "Service and sacrifice: Tokyo Women's Christian College." In: STEVENS, Dorothy A., ed. *Voices from Japan: Christians Speak.* Philadelphia: Judson Press, pp. 42-50. No refs. LCCN:57-8339.

A description of the college from 1918 through this (1957) writing. Founded by international and interdenominational efforts, this liberal arts college went against the prevailing concepts of the woman's three obediences (to parents, husbands, and sons) and trained women "to become individuals with minds of their own."

1084. PASSIN, Herbert and John W. BENNETT. Sep. 1954. "The America-educated Japanese, II." *Annals of the American Academy of Political and Social Science* 295:97-107. [Also cited as American Academy of Political and Social Science. *Annals.*] No refs. ISSN:0002-7162.

PASSIN and BENNET briefly summarize the difficulties of women returning to Japan after study in the United States (both pre-World War II and during the Occupation) [pp. 99-101].

1085. SENJU, Katsumi. 1971. "The development of female education in private school." *Education in Japan* 6:37-46. No refs. ISSN:0070-9220.

Provides a general history of women's private schools, especially at the post-secondary level.

1086. SHIBUKAWA, Hisako. 1971. "An education for making good wives and wise mothers (Ryōsai kenbo no kyōiku)." *Education in Japan* 6:47-57. No refs. ISSN:0070-9220.

SHIBUKAWA reviews the historical transitions in the definition of the policy of *ryōsai kenbo no kyōiku* ["education for making good wives and wise mothers"] from the Meiji period to the post-World War II era. Especially mentioned are the views of SHIMODA Utako, NITOBE Inazō and HANI Motoko.

Education Prior to World War II

1087. ARAKI, Noriko and Louise Ward DEMAKIS. Winter 1987. "The scholarship for Japanese women: 'A free gift from American women'." *Japan Christian Quarterly* 53(1):15-32. 46 notes. ISSN:0021-4361.

Discusses a scholarship established in the 1890s by the efforts of TSUDA Umeko in Japan and a group of prominent Philadelphia women, primarily Quakers, to educate Japanese women in the United States with the ultimate goal of improving the condition of Japanese women. Provides details on several of the recipients (including KAWAI Michi, HOSHINO Ai, HITOTSUYANAGI Maki, UCHIDA Fumi, FUJITA Taki, and MATSUOKA Yōko). Contains material on the workings of the scholarship committee as well as materials on higher education for women in Japan from the 1890s through World War II. The scholarship, which provided education primarily at Bryn Mawr, was terminated in 1976. A detailed report.

1088. BROWNSTEIN, Michael C. Autumn 1980. "*Jogaku Zasshi* and the founding of *Bungakukai.*" *Monumenta Nipponica* 35(3):319-336. 71 notes. ISSN:0027-0741.

Provides a detailed look at *Jogaku Zasshi* and the related *Bungakukai*, both magazines of the Meiji era aimed at women. Founded by IWAMOTO Yoshiharu, a Meiji educator, Christian, and proponent of women's education, *Jogaku Zasshi*'s purposes were to educate women and to provide a forum for progressive men interested in social and educational reform. The journal ran from 1885-1904; the literary spinoff *Bungakukai*, was shorter-lived. BROWNSTEIN provides details on the content and politics of the journals.

1089. BURTON, Margaret E. 1914. *The Education of Women in Japan.* New York: Fleming H. Revell. 268p. Bibl. Index. LCCN:14-11289.

Describes education for girls, beginning with the Meiji era, covering both Christian and government schools. Made interesting by her liberal use of quotations from letters and reports, and by references to particular schools and persons. Also describes several working women, businesswomen and physicians especially, and women's organizations active at the time. An appendix lists all Protestant mission schools for girls.

1090. CHAMBERLAIN, Basil Hall. Jul. 1878. "Educational literature for Japanese women." *Journal of the Royal Asiatic Society of Great Britain and Ireland* 10(3):325-343. [Also cited as Royal Asiatic Society of Great Britain and Ireland. *Journal.*] No refs. ISSN:0035-869X.

Comments on "moral treatises on the peculiar duties of females" which were standard reading for women in the 1870s, and provides translations of the *Imagawa for Women* and the *Greater Learning for Women* [#126].

1091. CHAPMAN, Christine. Jul./Sep. 1987. "The Meiji letters of Tsuda Ume, pioneer educator of women." *Japan Quarterly* 34(3):263-270. No refs. ISSN:0021-4590.

A biography of TSUDA Ume [later TSUDA Umeko, 184?-1929], who was sent to the United States by the Meiji Government at age six to be educated, and who returned to become a renowned educator of women. Includes many comments taken from her letters.

1092. CLARKE, Elizabeth J. Winter 1980. "The origin of women's higher education in Japan." *Japan Christian Quarterly* 46(1):26-33. 21 notes. ISSN:0021-4361.

A history of women's higher education, concentrating primarily on the 1920s and 1930s. Notes that schools were private and established either by Japanese women or by Christian missionaries. Of particular use may be the discussion of the term "*semmon gakkō*," the category in which women's institutions of higher education were placed. [See also #1080 & #1119.]

1093. DeFOREST, Charlotte B. Jan. 1961. "Masuko Ōtake, an outstanding woman of Japan." *Japan Christian Quarterly* 27(1):55-58. No refs. ISSN:0021-4361.

A tribute to ŌTAKE Masuko (d. 1955), a Christian Japanese woman educated in the United States. After receiving a doctorate from Yale University, ŌTAKE taught for many years at Kyushu University.

1094. DORE, R.P. 1965. *Education in Tokugawa Japan.* Berkeley: University of California Press. 346p. Bibl. Index. LCCN:65-1744.

In this thorough study of education in the Tokugawa period, DORE devotes only four pages to women, citing the dearth of Japanese language source materials. He emphasizes that women's education was vocational, "for a woman's profession was her womanliness and her vocation was marriage." The stakes were high for a woman: if a woman did not succeed she was subject to dismissal by means of divorce, while a male "samurai, by contrast, had to be very incompetent indeed to be deprived of his hereditary stipend."

1095. FUJITA, Taki. Jan. 1938. "The higher education of women in Japan." *Japanese Women* 1(1):2,4-5. No refs. ISSN:0388-1369.

Provides an overview of women's educational institutions and the employment of their graduates as of the late 1930s. Discusses the problems inherent in a national educational policy which disallows the foundation of a women's university, and concludes that "we, women of Japan, have a great work before us."

1096. HOSHINO, Ai. 1931. "The education of women." In: NITOBE, Inazō, *et al. Western Influences in Modern Japan: A Series of Papers on Cultural Relations.* Chicago: University of Chicago Press, pp. 215-230. No refs. LCCN:32-2471. [Originally published separately in the series *Western Influences in Modern Japan: A Series of Papers on Cultural Relations*, no. 11 [1929]. LCCN:30-24365.]

The president of Tsuda College provides an overview of the history of women's education (through 1929). Although basically a positive view, she does point out the lack of government support at the university level.

1097. HULL, Eleanor. 1957. *Suddenly, the Sun: A Biography of Shizuko Takahashi.* New York: Friendship Press. 130p. No refs. LCCN:57-11363.

As a girl, TAKAHASHI Shizuko Higuchi (b. 1876) studied at Joseph Cosand's School. She remained as a graduate to work off her tuition as a translator for the teachers. The first several chapters sketch out her life at the school.

1098. INOUE, Hisao. 1971. "A historical sketch of the development of the modern educational system for women in Japan." *Education in Japan* no. 6:15-35. No refs. ISSN:0070-9220.

Documents the growth of women's education during the 19th and early 20th centuries. Emphasizes the role of the government, and provides detail on Tokyo Girls' Normal School. Includes a list of women's institutions established from 1904-1927.

1099. JAHAN, Mehraj and Habibul Haque KHONDKER. Aug. 1986. "Women's education in a men's world: A comparison between Japan and Bengal in the 19th century." *Asian Profile* 14(5):419-425. 14 notes. ISSN:0304-8675.

Reviews the development of women's education in Meiji Japan, and compares it with attempts to promote women's education in Bengal. Describes Japan as more successful because the goals of the local elites and Western missionaries coincided, which was not the case in Bengal.

1100. KASUYA, Yoshi. 1933. *A Comparative Study of the Secondary Education of Girls in England, Germany, and the United States, with a Consideration of the Secondary Education of Girls in Japan.* New York: Columbia University Teachers College. 211p. (Columbia University. Teachers College. *Contributions to Education*, no. 566.) [Variant Title: *The Secondary Education of Girls . . .*] Bibl. LCCN:33-20414.

Although focusing primarily on European and American women, KASUYA includes a chapter on Japanese women's status, the nature of secondary education for girls, and a thorough discussion concerning reforms needed and possible implementation strategies.

1101. KAWAHARA, Chizuko. Jan. 1962. "Awakening of the Meiji women." *Asia Scene* 7:45-47. No refs. ISSN:0004-4504.

A brief description of changes for women during the Meiji era, especially in regard to education.

1102. KAWAI, Michi. 1940. *My Lantern.* Tokyo: Kyo Bun Kwan. 230p. No refs. LCCN:41-1960.

KAWAI Michi was, by all accounts, a remarkable woman. She was a graduate of Bryn Mawr, served as general secretary of the Japanese National YWCA [Young Women's Christian Association] for 20 years, and then founded Keisen Girls' School. This memoir covers her childhood, schooling, her experiences abroad, and the accomplishments outlined above. [Continued by #1103.]

1103. KAWAI, Michi. 1950. *Sliding Doors*. Tokyo: Keisen jō-gaku-en. 201p. No refs. LCCN:56-33410.

A sequel to *My Lantern* [#1102]; relates the experiences of the author and the Keisen Girls' High School from 1938-1949. The work focuses on KAWAI's "girls" throughout the war years and the struggles and growth of the school during the post-war years.

1104. KUROYANAGI, Tetsuko. 1982. *Totto-chan, the Little Girl at the Window*. [Translated by Dorothy BRITTON.] Tokyo: Kodansha, 195p. No refs. LCCN:82-80735. [*Madogiwa no Totto-chan*. English.]

The author was expelled from first grade but then attended Tomoe Gakuen, an unusual elementary school based in retired railway cars and run by KOBAYASHI Sosaku. The story is of her experiences at this unique school until it was destroyed in 1945 during the bombing raids of World War II. Several chapters of the Japanese edition of this book were used as education texts during the 1960s according to the author, who is now a television personality. [See also #1105.]

1105. KUROYANAGI, Tetsuko. Apr./Jun. 1983. "On Totto-chan." *Japan Quarterly* 30(2):153-155. No refs. ISSN:0021-4590.

KUROYANAGI (television personality and author of *Totto-chan: The Little Girl at the Window* [#1104]) talks about her reasons for writing the book and critiques the current education system in Japan.

1106. MENSENDIEK, C. William. 1986. *A Dream Incarnate: The Beginnings of Miyagi Gakuin for Women*. Sendai [Japan]: Miyagi Gakuin. 135p. Bibl. Index.

A history of the Miyagi Gakuin for Women, "the first higher school for girls above the elementary level in Sendai," which was begun in 1886 by the Board of Foreign Missions of the Reformed Church of the United States with Elizabeth POORBAUGH as its principal.

1107. MISHIMA, Sumie Seo. Sep. 1941. "Good-by to foreign friends." *Asia* 41:473-476. No refs.

MISHIMA deplores a state of international relations which forces American teachers to leave Japan and goes on to discuss women's education and an appropriate curriculum.

1108. NARUSE, Jinzō. 1910. "The education of Japanese women." In: ŌKUMA, Shigenobu, ed. *Fifty Years of New Japan*, Vol. 2. [Translated and edited by Marcus B. HUISH.] London: Smith, Elder and Co., pp. 192-225. 1 note. LCCN:10-35331. [*Kaikoku Gojūnen shi*. English.]

An overview of women's education by the President of Nippon Women's University. He takes an historical perspective on attitudes concerning women to provide the context for educational opportunities (or lack thereof), focusing on the Tokugawa period to date. The essay ends with a discussion on educational philosophy (criticizing Christian missionaries for trying to Westernize Japanese women) and a description of the Nippon Women's University.

1109. NORTHROP, B.G. 30 Jan. 1896. "The three first Japanese girls educated in America: Their influence in Japan." *Independent* 48:139-140. [Pages also labeled 3-4.] No refs.

Briefly describes the lives and accomplishments of three women (TSUDA Ume, Miss NAGAI, and Miss YAMAKAWA) who, in 1872, were sent by the Meiji government to the United States to study. NORTHROP was responsible for their placement with American families.

1110. SHIGA, Tadashi. 1971. "Historical view of the education of women before the time of Meiji." *Education in Japan* 6:1-14. No refs. ISSN:0070-9220.

SHIGA surveys the education of women from prehistoric times to the Meiji era, illustrating his points with examples from *The Tale of Genji* (by MURASAKI Shikibu) [#1760], from unidentified texts from the Kamakura period, and from *Onna Daigaku* [#126].

1111. SHŌJI, Masako. 1971. "Women educators who contributed to the education of women. I." *Education in Japan* 6:69-83. No refs. ISSN:0070-9220.

Discusses the contributions of ATOMI Kakei (Atomi Girls' School), SHIMODA Utako (Girls' School for Noble Families), HATOYAMA Haruko (Kyōritsu Women's College) and YOSHIOKA Yayoi (Tokyo Women's Medical School).

1112. TOYODA, Masako. [1938.] *"The Composition Class:" Japanese Life by a Schoolgirl.* [Compiled by Z. Tomatsu IWADO.] Tokyo: Herald of Asia. 146p. No refs.

A collection of essays written by a nine year old tin-man's daughter, TOYODA Masako, describing her life and schooling in 1930s Tokyo.

1113. "University education planned for girls." Mar. 1940. *Japanese Women* 3(2):2. No refs. ISSN:0388-1369.

Announcement of the decision to establish a government sponsored women's university and to admit women to existing universities.

1114. YAMAMOTO, Kazuyo. 1980. "Women's life-long education: Present condition and related themes." *Feminist International* no.2:9-12. No refs. ISSN:0388-371X.

YAMAMOTO describes the status of continuing education ("further education") for women, types of courses desired, current categories of class locations and sponsorships, and the possibilities of establishing university-sponsored adult education.

1115. YAMASAKI, Takako. 1971. "Women educators who contributed to the education of women. II." *Education in Japan* 6:85-89. No refs. ISSN:0070-9220.

A short biography of TSUDA Umeko [1864-1929], a prominent women's educator, containing a description of her educational philosophy.

1116. YAMAZAKI, Takako. 1989. "Tsuda Ume." In: DUKE, Benjamin C. 1989. *Ten Great Educators of Modern Japan.* Tokyo: University of Tokyo Press, pp. 124-147. No refs. Index. LCCN:90-164957.

Provides a biography of Tsuda Ume[ko] [1864-1929], the founder of Tsuda College for Women and one of the primary educators of women in turn-of-the-century Japan. Provides details on her father, her adolescence in the United States, and her teaching career.

Education Since World War II

1117. ADAMS, Robert Martin. 13 Feb. 1986. "Jane Austen in Japan." *New York Review of Books* 33(2):26-27. No refs. ISSN:0028-7504.

A description of a class at a four-year women's college in Kyoto as seen through the eyes of a frustrated American male English literature professor with no previous experience in Japan.

1118. ALBERY, Nobuko. 1978. *Balloon Top.* New York: Pantheon. 255p. No refs. LCCN:77-17652.

A coming-of-age novel (written in English) of a young girl in post-war Japan who, as a Waseda student, joins a drama club with ties to Zengakuren, a national student revolutionary group. The story tells of her experiences with the club and of her participation in the student demonstrations against ANPO [AMPO], the United States— Japan Security Treaty in the early 1960s.

1119. CLARKE, Elizabeth J. Spring 1990. "Higher education for women in Japan since 1945." *Japan Christian Quarterly* 56:84-92. 15 notes. ISSN:0021-4361.

CLARKE continues her history of women's higher education begun in her 1980 article on its origins [see #1092]. She discusses the effects of the Occupation, the development of the junior college, the period in the mid-1960s when educators questioned the appropriateness of post-secondary education for women and only 1.2 percent of college-age women attended, the effect of the United Nations Decade for Women, and the situation in the late 1980s and 1990 when 25 percent of college-age women enrolled (a 1989 figure).

1120. FUJIEDA, Mioko. Spring 1983. "The Women's Studies movement in Japan." *Japan Christian Quarterly* 49(2):74-79. 5 notes. ISSN:0021-4361.

Describes the purposes of the Women's Studies Movement, founded in 1980 with the aims of eliminating discrimination against women, establishing women's studies programs, and promoting research on women's studies topics. FUJIEDA (Kyoto Seika College) discusses the outgrowth of this movement from earlier, more radical, women's liberation activities and discusses the status of women in higher education. [Introduced by #390.]

1121. FUJII, Harue. 1982. "Education for women: The personal and social damage of an anachronistic policy." *Japan Quarterly* 29(3):301-310. No refs. ISSN:0021-4590.

FUJII gives an insightful summary of the transition from an educational policy promoting equal education for women in the late 1940s to the "education for separate roles" system encouraged in the early 1950s. Discusses the current consequences of the latter policy, especially as it affects the type of work available to women, and the lack of financial independence/security of housewives.

1122. FUJIMURA-FANSELOW, Kumiko. Nov. 1985. "Women's participation in higher education in Japan." *Comparative Education Review* 29(4):471-489. 50 notes. ISSN:0010-4086.

Investigates causes of "sex differentials in Japanese educational opportunities." Explores the problems of institutional structure in higher education and of the limited opportunities available to women after graduation. These effectively limit women's educational options within a society in which equal access to education officially exists.

1123. HEISEY, D. Ray. 1983. "The role of Asian women in national development efforts." *Women's Studies International Forum* 6(1):85-96. 24 refs. ISSN:0277-5395.

HEISEY outlines the projects of the institutional members of the Asian Women's Institute, including Tokyo Women's Christian University.

1124. HOLMES, Lulu. Spring 1948. "Women in the new Japan." *Journal of the American Association of University Women* 41(3):137-141. No refs. [Also cited as the *AAUW Journal*.] ISSN:0001-0278.

HOLMES writes in her capacity as the Adviser on Women's Education to the Supreme Commander of the Allied Powers in Tokyo. She discusses the changes instigated in women's education and describes the establishment of the Daigaku Fujin Kyōkai, a group similar to the American Association of University Women.

1125. ICHIBANGASE, Yasuko. 1971. "Women's status and task of education." *Education in Japan* 6:59-68. No refs. ISSN:0070-9220.

Contrasts the surface equality between Japanese men and women in voting rights and education with the practical reality of the "tracking system" in Japanese education, which leads to neither women as informed participants in the political process nor women educated to cope with a rapidly changing society.

1126. Japan. Shakai Kyōikukyoku. 1972-. *Women and Education in Japan.* Tokyo: Ministry of Education. No refs. LCCN:85-642647 (series).

An annual report (1972 earliest found, 1986 latest examined) describing the state of women's education, both formal and "nonformal." A source of hard to find data/material on various opportunities for women: e.g. leadership training courses, adult education classes, parent education courses, and the facilities which make them available. Also provides descriptions of traditional educational opportunities.

1127. KAKINUMA, Miyuki. 1980. "Women's Studies in Japan." *Feminist International* no.2:100-101. No refs. ISSN:0388-371X.

Assesses the state of women's studies in Japan, lists titles of courses being taught in Japanese universities, and notes the more prominent activists. Expresses a desire for coordination of efforts via the newly formed Women's Studies Association of Japan.

1128. MITSUI, Mariko. Winter 1985. "A package for sexism: Education in Japanese senior high schools." *Japan Christian Quarterly* 51(1):6-18. 30 notes. ISSN:0021-4361.

A critique of contemporary secondary schools which focuses on their role in the subjugation of Japanese women through compulsory home economics for women, textbooks with a heavy male bias, and a predominance of male teachers. MITSUI also provides descriptions of purpose from three admissions brochures to reinforce her points.

1129. MONK-TURNER, Elizabeth and Yōko BABA. Summer 1987. "Gender and college opportunities: Changes over time in the United States and Japan." *Sociological Inquiry* 57(3):292-303. 30 refs. ISSN:0038-0245.

MONK-TURNER and BABA discuss the increasing numbers of women attending two-year colleges in the United States and Japan, and examine the phenomenon in light of the number of "college-level occupations" available.

1130. MOUER, Elizabeth Knipe. 1976. "Women in teaching." In: LEBRA, Joyce, *et al. Women in Changing Japan.* Stanford: Stanford University Press, pp. 157-190. 52 notes. LCCN:75-33663.

Covers the history of women teachers in contemporary Japan and problems female teachers face. Profiles three women: a day care center director, a public high school teacher, and a public elementary school teacher.

1131. NAKANO, Akira. Apr./Jun. 1983. "What ever happened to progressive education?" *Japan Quarterly* 30(2):149-152. No refs. ISSN:0021-4590.

Discusses the appeal of KUROYANAGI Tetsuko's *Totto-chan: The Little Girl at the Window* [#1104] and provides comments from the author concerning the probable reasons for its success.

1132. NARUMIYA, Chie. 1986. "Opportunities for girls and women in Japanese education." *Comparative Education* 22(1):47-52. 38 notes. ISSN:0305-0068.

An overview of higher education for women since World War II. Notes the decline in opportunities for women to study once the outside pressure from the Occupation Forces was removed.

1133. NUITA, Yōko. Winter 1972. "Continuing education of women in Japan." *Improving College and University Teaching* 20(1):66-68. No refs. ISSN:0019-3089.

Briefly describes adult education provided by state and local government, private organizations, and the mass media, and makes suggestions for content changes and an increase in opportunities for taking classes.

1134. "The peculiar dress codes of Japanese schools." Nov./Dec. 1988. *East* 24(4):48-51. No refs. ISSN:0012-8295.

Discusses school dress codes and reprints the list of regulations concerning a junior high school girl's uniform (from Fukui prefecture). Includes sketch.

1135. PERITZ, Rene. 1982. "The young college woman in Japan: The traditions continue." In: *Proceedings of the Fourth International Symposium on Asian Studies, 1982. Vol. 2. Japan and Korea.* Hong Kong: Asian Research Service, pp. 329-345. 14 notes. LCCN:85-141732.

Working from a survey of women students from Hiroshima Jogakuin Daigaku completed in 1979, PERITZ draws broad conclusions concerning "the position of women as contributors and agents of change."

1136. REGUR, Nana Mizushima. 19 Dec. 1990. "A first in Japan: More women than men admitted to universitites, 2-year colleges." *Chronicle of Higher Education* 37(16):A29-A30. ISSN:0009-5982.

Briefly describes the increase in numbers of women enrolled in higher education and quotes HIGUCHI Keiko concerning reasons for the change and AMANO Masako on new majors for women and the possibility for enrollment of older women in Japanese universities.

1137. RODEN, Donald. Winter 1983. "From 'old miss' [old maid] to new professional: A portrait of women educators under the American occupation of Japan, 1945-52." *History of Education Quarterly* 23(4):469-489. 77 notes. ISSN:0018-2680.

Describes the training course for Deans of Women run during the Occupation by Helen HOSP for 17 Japanese women educators. Provides historical background on women's education and the profession of teaching before World War II, details the seminar itself, and through excerpts from autobiographical letters to HOSP, provides insight into the personal lives of these women.

1138. ROHLEN, Thomas P. 1983. *Japan's High Schools.* Berkeley: University of California Press. 363p. Refs. Index. LCCN:82-16118.

ROHLEN includes information on girls and women throughout this anthropological study of Japanese high schools. Material is scattered but accessible through the index.

1139. SPAE, Joseph J. Dec. 1966. "Women students in a Christian milieu." *Japan Missionary Bulletin* 20(11):699-708. 3 Refs. ISSN:0021-4531.

Reports on the work of MIZOGUCHI Yasuo to determine the changes in religious consciousness of women who have spent four years at a Christian women's university.

1140. SUTHERLAND, Margaret. 1988. "Women in higher education: Effects of crises and change." *Higher Education* 17(5):479-490. 24 refs. ISSN:0018-1560.

A comparative study of Australia, Europe, Japan and the United States to determine the effects of social and economic pressures on the progress of women in higher education including enrollment, disciplines of study, employment possibilities for graduates, and numbers of female teachers. Little Japan-specific data provided.

1141. WHEELER, Helen Rippier. Summer 1985. "Women's studies, higher education, and feminist educators in Japan today." *Journal of the National Association for Women Deans, Administrators and Counselors* (Summer 1985):31-36. 7 notes. ISSN:0094-3460.

WHEELER very briefly describes the history of feminism and the women's movement in modern Japan as context for her report on the definition and status of women's studies in Japan and on activities of feminist educators.

11

Political and Social Activism

Feminism and the Women's Movement
Overviews

1142. JAYAWARDENA, Kumari. 1986. *Feminism and Nationalism in the Third World.* Totowa, NJ: Zed Books. 275p. Bibl. Index. LCCN:86-7871.

In a chapter titled "The Challenge of Feminism in Japan," JAYAWARDENA presents a history of feminism in Japan. She draws heavily on standard sources [especially #1146 and #1167] to support her thesis that "Japan . . . presents an interesting study of how certain demands for women's emancipation can be granted by governments concerned with capitalistic growth, while undesired changes which would have raised the real issues of women's liberation are blocked."

1143. KUNINOBU, Junko Wada. Fall 1984. "The development of feminism in modern Japan." *Feminist Issues* 4(2):3-21. 39 notes. Bibl. ISSN:0270-6679.

Delineates four "waves" of feminism since the Meiji Restoration of 1868: "The Civil Rights Awakening (Meiji Period)," "Taishō Democracy and the New Woman," "Feminism in Postwar Japan," and "Women's Studies and the International Decade for Women." Discusses the major events and voices of each, including KISHIDA Toshiko, KAGEYAMA Hideko, HIRATSUKA Raichō and the Seitō group, and YAMAKAWA Kikue.

1144. MACKIE, Vera. Jan./Feb. 1988. "Feminist politics in Japan." *New Left Review*, no. 167:53-76. 92 notes. ISSN:0028-6060.

A thorough synopsis of feminist activities in Japan, beginning with an historical overview covering the "imperial legacy" up through the mid-1980s. Focuses on areas of activity (e.g. antimilitarism, birth control, equal employment opportunities) and political action techniques (e.g. alternative media, grassroots movements).

1145. TANAKA, Kazuko. 1977. *A Short History of the Women's Movement in Modern Japan.* [Third edition.] Tokyo: Femintern Press. 56p. 25 refs.

Beginning in early Meiji Japan with activists in the Social Democratic Rights Movement and with Enlightenment scholars, TANAKA (an activist in the Japanese women's movement) traces the history of women's rights. She begins with the impact of Christianity on female education and the efforts toward the abolishment of prostitution in the late 19th century, and continues into the early 20th century with the Seitō group, and labor and socialist movements. She completes her survey with the post-World War II women's movement, including the Japan Women's Convention and Mother's Convention, and the contemporary (i.e. 1970s) movement. Detailed.

1146. VAVICH, Dee Ann. 1967. "The Japanese woman's movement: Ichikawa Fusae—a pioneer in woman's suffrage." *Monumenta Nipponica* 22(3/4):402-436.   262 notes. ISSN:0027-0741.

In this tightly written and extensively documented study, VAVICH provides a detailed history of the Japanese women's movement as seen through the activities and programs of ICHIKAWA Fusae, an ardent fighter for women's suffrage and other political rights. Based on interviews, and Japanese and English sources, VAVICH first provides context with a description of "the development of the position of women . . . from the early myths through the Meiji period," and then discusses ICHIKAWA's efforts beginning with the Shin Fujin Kyōkai [New Women's Organization] and continuing through her service in the Diet.

Feminism and the Women's Movement
Pre-World War II

1147. ANDREW, Nancy. 1972. "The Seitōsha: An early Japanese women's organization, 1911-1916." *Papers on Japan* 6:45-69. [Also cited as *Harvard University. East Asian Research Center. Papers on Japan*.] 62 notes. LCCN:87-21221.

A solid look at the Seitōsha [The Bluestockings], a group founded to publish a women's literary magazine. The journal, *Seitō* [*Bluestocking*], quickly became a forum for discussion of women's issues and frequently was censored by the government. ANDREW describes the effect of the Society as "the awakening of educated young women to social consciousness and fuller awareness of their own dilemma," and profiles many of the group's members.

1148. BETHEL, Diana. 1980. "Visions of a humane society: Feminist thought in Taishō Japan." *Feminist International* no.2:92-94. 2 notes. ISSN:0388-371X.

Focuses on the debates of the early Japanese feminists HIRATSUKA Raichō and YOSANO Aikiko, that dealt primarily with "the problem of how to extricate women from the role obligations imposed by the traditional family against the background of the changing economic realities of Taishō Japan."

1149. CHABOT, Jeanette Taudin. 1985. "Takamure Itsue: The first historian of Japanese women." *Women's Studies International Forum* 8(4):287-290. 9 notes; 1 ref. ISSN:0277-5395.

A biography of TAKAMURE Itsue (1894-1964) who published the first complete history of women in Japan and proved, with "solid academic documentation," that Japan had been a matriarchal society and had a "female-male double chief ruling system" in earlier times.

1150. GAUNTLETT, Mrs. C. Tsune. Jul. 1940. "Fodder for thought." *Japanese Women* 3(4):1,3. No refs. ISSN:0388-1369.

GAUNTLETT, of the Women's Christian Temperance Union [WCTU], remembers her attendance at the 1920 Congress of Women in Geneva where she was struck by the necessity of the women's vote. She urges readers to work for their countries in the current situation but to continue their quest for enfranchisement.

1151. HIRATSUKA, Raichō. 1974. "Restoring women's talents, 1911." In: LU, David John, compiler. *Sources of Japanese History*. New York: McGraw-Hill, pp. 118-119. Notes. LCCN:73-6890.

Selections from the call for the liberation of women published in the inaugural issue of *Seitō* [*Bluestocking*]. It begins "In the beginning, woman was truly the sun . . ." and has been widely quoted.

1152. ICHIKAWA, Fusaye. 1928. "Woman suffrage movement in Japan." In: *Women of the Pacific.* Honolulu: Pan-Pacific Union, pp. 201-204. (Pan-Pacific Women's Conference, 1st, Honolulu, 9-19 Aug. 1928.) No Refs.

A history of the women's suffrage movement, beginning in 1907 with the founding of the New Women's Association and a fight for the right of assembly. Continues with the development of the Women's Suffrage League of Japan [WSLJ] and its activities promoting the granting of franchise to women. ICHIKAWA is the organizations's president.

1153. KANŌ, Masanao. 1980. "Takamure Itsue: Pioneer in the study of women's history." [Translated by Tomi NAGAI.] *Feminist International* no.2:67-69. No refs. ISSN:0388-371X.

Provides a short but detailed biographical sketch of TAKAMURE Itsue, poet, anarchist, feminist, and historian. TAKAMURE is recognized especially for her contributions to women's history and to the history of marriage.

1154. KATAYAMA, Tetsu. Apr. 1938. *Women's Movement in Japan.* [Tokyo]: Foreign Affairs Association of Japan. 38p. No refs. LCCN:39-11014. [Excerpted as "Legislation regarding domestic relations," "An outline of the women's movement," and "The political position of women" in *Japanese Women* 2(1):1-3, Jan. 1939; 2(5):1-3, Sep. 1939; and 2(6):1-3, Nov. 1939. ISSN:0388-1369.]

A history of the women's movement and a detailed analysis of women's political, economic, legal and social status by a member of the Central Executive Committee of the Mass Social Party.

1155. LIPPIT, Noriko Mizuta. 1979. "Seitō and the literary roots of Japanese feminism." *International Journal of Women's Studies* [Canada] 2(2):155-163. 13 notes. ISSN:0703-8240.

Discusses in detail the literary basis for *Seitō* [*Bluestocking*], its producers, its growth to a journal of social and political debate on the roles of women, and its historical significance.

1156. MACKIE, Vera. 1988. "Motherhood and pacifism in Japan, 1900-1937." *Hecate* 14(2):29-49. 90 notes. ISSN:0311-4198.

A detailed, scholarly article dealing with the publishing industry and the early women's movement in Japan. Discusses the role of the Seitō group, and the controversy over "motherhood protection" involving YOSANO Akiko and HIRATSUKA Raichō.

1157. McMAHILL, Cheiron Sariko. Mar. 1982. "Japan's first feminists: The life of Hideko Fukuda." *Off Our Backs* 12(3):6. No refs. ISSN:0030-0071.

A brief description of the activities of FUKUDA Hideko, educator, political activist, and founder and editor of *Sekai Fujin* (*Women of the World*) in the late nineteenth and early twentieth centuries.

1158. MIYAMOTO, Ken. Autumn 1975. "Itō Noe and the Bluestockings." *Japan Interpreter* 10(2):190-204. 6 refs & 13 notes. ISSN:0021-4450.

MIYAMOTO (a playwright) provides a history of *Seitō* [*Bluestocking*], a "publication [from the early 20th century which] stood for women's unconditional freedom from the confines of the traditional female roles," and provides biographical details on ITŌ Noe, one of the principal participants.

1159. MOLONY, Kathleen S. 1978. "Feminist ideology in prewar Japan." In: WHITE, Merry I. and Barbara MOLONY, eds. *Proceedings of the Tokyo Symposium on Women.* Tokyo: International Group for the Study of Women, pp. 13-24. (Tokyo Symposium on Women, [1st], 1978.) 11 notes.

MOLONY begins by defining feminism as an "ideology which views women as a distinct group of people suffering irrationally imposed restrictions." She then goes on to discuss the lives of HIRATSUKA Raichō, YAMAKAWA Kikue, and ICHIKAWA Fusae in this more comprehensive context.

1160. NAKAMURA, Toshiko. 1982. "Ibsen in Japan: Tsubouchi Shoyo and his lecture on new women." *Edda: Nordisk Tidsskrift for Litteraturforskning* 1982(5):261-272. [Title also cited as *Edda: Scandinavian Journal of Literary Research*.] 12 notes. ISSN:0013-0818.

Presents the views on women of TSUBOUCHI Shōyo, a Waseda University professor and a specialist on Western and Japanese drama, as revealed through his lecture series in 1910 on the plays of Henrik IBSEN.

1161. NOLTE, Sharon H. Oct. 1986. "Women's rights and society's needs: Japan's 1931 suffrage bill." *Comparative Studies in Society and History* 28(4):690-714. 92 notes. ISSN:0010-4175.

Provides a detailed political history of the women's suffrage movement in Japan (1919-1931), focusing on the demands of feminists and the government's responses (via the Hamaguchi and Suematsu bills).

1162. REICH, Pauline. Autumn 1976. "Japan's literary feminists: The Seitō group." [Excerpts translated by Pauline C. REICH and Atsuko FUKUDA.] *Signs* 2(1):280-291. 11 notes. ISSN:0097-9740.

REICH and FUKUDA provide translations of HIRATSUKA Raichō's "Yo no Fujintachi ni" ["To the women of the world"] and an excerpt of her "Manifesto," both published in *Seitō* [*Bluestocking*]. They then discuss the journal's history and provide information on the principal participants.

1163. SATŌ, Toshihiko. 1964. "Ibsen and emancipation of women in Japan." *Orient/West* 9:73-77. No refs. ISSN:0474-6465.

SATŌ reviews the founding of the feminist movement and discusses the impact of IBSEN's plays on the Seitōsha [The Bluestockings]. For the general audience.

1164. SATŌ, Toshihiko. 1967. "Ibsen in the Japanese feminist movement." *Arbok* (*Ibsenforbundet*) 1967:48-60. No refs. LCCN:a55-460.

In its early days, the Japanese feminist movement identified closely with the literary works of IBSEN. SATŌ shows how HIRAZUKA Raichō, founder of the journal *Seitō* [*Bluestocking*], was influenced by "Hedda Gabler."

1165. SATŌ, Toshihiko. 1981. "Ibsen's drama and the Japanese Bluestockings." *Edda: Nordisk Tidsskrift for Litteraturforskning* 1981(5):265-293. [Title also cited as *Edda: Scandinavian Journal of Literary Research*.] 76 notes. ISSN:0013-0818.

SATŌ discusses in detail the changes in Japan which made possible the founding of the Keishū Bungakkai [Lady Writer's Society] and Seitōsha [Bluestockings]. He then discusses the impact of IBSEN's works on the Japanese feminist movement in the early twentieth century.

1166. SIEVERS, Sharon L. Summer 1981. "Feminist criticism in Japanese politics in the 1880s: The experience of Kishida Toshiko." *Signs* 6(4):602-616. 48 notes. ISSN:0097-9740.

Details the activities of KISHIDA Toshiko, a well-received (female) public speaker for the Liberal Party from 1882-1884, whose goal was "equality, independence [and] respect [for women] and a monogamous relationship."

1167. SIEVERS, Sharon L. 1983. *Flowers in Salt: The Beginnings of Feminist Consciousness in Modern Japan.* Stanford: Stanford University Press. 240p. Notes. Index. LCCN:82-60104.

A study of women in the Meiji period with an emphasis on "the development of feminist consciousness" during that time. This is the basic text for information on women in the Popular-Rights Movement, the Japan Women's Patriotic Association, the Women's Reform Society and the Bluestockings. Also covers textile workers, women socialists, and includes a chapter on KANNO Suga, an anarchist and "the first woman to be executed as a political prisoner in Japan's modern history." Reviewed by BOOCOCK in #2305, BUCKLEY in #2306 and TSURUMI in #2310 and #2311.

1168. TSURUMI, E. Patricia. Apr./Jun. 1985. "Feminism and anarchism in Japan: Takamure Itsue, 1894-1964." *Bulletin of Concerned Asian Scholars* 17(2):2-19. 104 notes. ISSN:0007-4810.

TSURUMI provides a lengthy and detailed biography of TAKAMURE Itsue (1894-1964), poet, anarchist, essayist, feminist, and historian, who sought evidence of a "self-governing community where reproduction and childcare is organized by women for women with the support of the whole community" and who wrote the first scholarly history of Japanese women. TSURUMI points out that TAKAMURE, unlike her contemporaries, was able to live her feminist ideals in her private life as well as public life.

1169. YAMAZAKI, Tomoko. 1986. *The Story of Yamada Waka: From Prostitute to Feminist Pioneer.* [Translated by Ann Siller KOSTANT and Wakako HIRONAKA.] Tokyo: Kodansha. 159p. No refs. LCCN:85-40042.

Rather than a scholarly biography, this is YAMAZAKI's account of her search for information concerning YAMADA Waka's early years. As with many other young Japanese women, YAMADA was lured to the United States with promises of a good job and sold to a brothel. She escaped and eventually made her way back to Japan to become a prominent feminist, social critic, and author. YAMAZAKI bases her work primarily on interviews and on YAMADA's works.

Feminism and the Women's Movement
After World War II

1170. ANDREW, Nancy, Catherine BRODERICK, Chizuko IKEGAMI, and Yayori MATSUI. Feb. 1978. "Change in Japan: What are we up against?" *Feminist Japan* no. 4:52-54. [Also cited as 1(4).] No refs. ISSN:0386-197X.

A short but wide-ranging discussion of women's liberation in Japan as of the late 1970s. Focuses on problems of the women's movement—identity, definition of issues, and finances.

1171. ATSUMI, Ikuko. 1980. "Goals of feminism in modern Japan." *Feminist International* no.2:96. No refs. ISSN:0388-371X.

A concise summary of the different directions schools of feminism have taken: the Socialists who link women's rights to class struggle, ICHIKAWA Fusae's group who work to change women's status "within the prevailing social system," and a cultural movement which seeks to change the vertical nature of Japanese society without taking on a Marxist class struggle. The unifying principle is that "feminism should be defined as human liberation from a woman's point of view." A brief but very useful summary.

1172. BALDWIN, Frank. 1973. "The idioms of contemporary Japan, V: Ūman Ribu [Women's Lib.]." *Japan Interpreter* 8(2):237-244. 1 note. ISSN:0021-4450.

A sympathetic overview of the Japanese women's liberation movement by a male American Fulbright scholar. Focuses on organizational structure, types of *ribu* ["lib"] members, and major issues: equal employment opportunity and pay, right to abortion, and the underlying social and economic causes for infanticide. Relatively short, but a useful summary.

1173. "A brief history of *Feminist*." 1980. *Feminist International* no.2:104-105. No refs. ISSN:0388-371X.

A brief survey of *Feminist* (and its subsequent publications *Feminist Japan* and *Feminist International*), 1978-1980. The journal was begun "to raise women's consciousness by showing them a point of view based on the intelligence and sensibility of independent women" and to provide a Japanese women's magazine written and published by women. [See also #1179.]

1174. "From Mexico to Nairobi—How far?" 1986. *Ampo: Japan-Asia Quarterly Review* 18(2/3):30-33. No refs. LCCN:77-12830.

An interview with MATSUI Yayori during which she discusses her impressions of the Women's Conference in Nairobi and Japanese women in general, touches on the self-orientation of the Japanese women's movement, prostitution, and the lack of social or political awareness on the part of Japanese women.

1175. FUJIEDA, Mioko. Jun. 1975. "Discussion on liberation." In: *Japanese Women Speak Out.* Tokyo: White Paper on Sexism—Japan Task Force, pp. 5-10. No refs. [Excerpted in *Quest: A Feminist Quarterly* 4(2):74-92, Winter 1978, ISSN 0098-955X.]

Summarizes a discussion which focused on two questions: "Is the removal of sexism the only concern of the Women's Liberation Movement?" and "Why do Japanese women put up with oppression?" Participants conclude that the movement must focus more broadly on "socio-political problems" and that, in general, Japanese women do not feel sufficiently "sexually humiliated" to trigger protest and change.

1176. FUJIEDA, Mioko. Jul./Sep. 1975. "Where are we headed? Discussion on women's liberation." *Ampo: Japan-Asia Quarterly Review* 7(3):84-92. No refs. LCCN:77-12830.

A wide-ranging discussion on the women's movement/women's liberation movement in Japan. Topics include definition of purpose, women's acceptance of discrimination and oppression, and the different types of feminism extant in the Japan of the early 1970s.

1177. FUJIOKA, Wake A., compiler. 1968. *Women's Movements in Postwar Japan.* [Translated by Wake A. FUJIOKA.] Honolulu: University of Hawaii, East-West Center. 87p. (University of Hawaii, Honolulu. East-West Center. Institute of Advanced Projects. *Occasional Papers of Research Publications & Translations. Translation Series*, no. 29). No refs. LCCN:68-66352.

A selection of documents from *Shiryō: Sengo Nijū-nen shi* [*Sourcebook on Twenty Postwar Years in Japan*], containing primary materials on women's organizations, including Fujin Minshu Kurabu [The Women's Democratic Club], Shufuren [Housewives Federation], Hahaoya Taikai [Mother's Rally], Women in the Communist Party, and others.

1178. INOUE, Reiko. 1986. "15 years of Japanese women's activism." *Ampo: Japan-Asia Quarterly Review* 18(2/3):12-17. No refs. [Article title also cited as: "Strengthening the web: 15 years of Japanese women's activism."] LCCN:77-12830.

Traces the transition of the "women's movement" from the radical days of the early 1970s, when the aim was a complete transformation of society, to the 1980s when specific projects are attempted through political activism.

1179. "Interview with Atsumi Ikuko." 1980. *Feminist International* no.2:88-91. No refs. ISSN:0388-371X.

IKUKO Atsumi took the leadership in founding *Feminist* [see #1173]. She discusses here her definitions of feminism in general, Japanese feminism, and prospects for the future.

1180. *Japanese Women Speak Out.* Jun. 1975. Tokyo: White Paper on Sexism—Japan Task Force. 179p. No refs.

With the expressed purpose of "establish[ing] and deepen[ing] relationships with women in other countries" a group identified as White Paper on Sexism—Japan Task Force has written or reprinted a series of articles dealing with "the situation of women in Japan." Articles are annotated individually; they focus on four major issues: sexism, women's protest movements, women who experience double discrimination (minority group women), and views of the women's movement on topics of Asia-wide concern. [For individual entries, see title index under *Japanese Women Speak Out.*]

1181. KAJI, Etsuko. 1989. "Confronting the four Ps: Poverty, prostitution, patriarchy and pollution—Asian feminism." *Ampo: Japan-Asia Quarterly Review* 21(2/3):64-67. No refs. LCCN:77-12830.

Reports on the Asian Women's Forum including a workshop on the importation of women workers from Asia to Japan.

1182. KAKINUMA, Miyuki. 1980. "Interview—Yagi Akiko: Japanese anarchist." [Translated by Janet ASHBY.] *Feminist International* no.2:34-37. No refs. ISSN:0388-371X.

In earlier times, YAGI was a well-known feminist and anarchist. Currently living in an old-age home at the age of 84, she touches briefly on the events of her life and her life philosophy.

1183. LEBRA, Takie Sugiyama. Winter 1976. "Sex equality for Japanese women." *Japan Interpreter* 10(3/4):284-295. 24 notes. ISSN:0021-4450.

Identifies three paths toward equality that the women's movement in Japan has taken: dimorphism (two distinct spheres—husband provides income and wife provides domestic care); bimorphism (two roles shared equally); and amorphism (freedom of choice for both sexes to assume appropriate and desired roles). Notes that currently the bimorphism path is asymmetrical—the wife works and provides domestic care while the husband only works.

1184. MATSUZAWA, Kazuko. Spring 1974. "Japanese social structure and the status of women." *Japan Christian Quarterly* 40(2):71-78. 7 notes. ISSN:0021-4361.

Disputes the common assumption that Japanese attitudes toward women are a remnant of feudal society. Outlines a three-point agenda for an endemic Japanese women's liberation movement based on her analysis of the sources of attitudes toward women's roles.

1185. PP21 Women's Forum Organizing Committee. 1989. "Asian feminism as a basis for social change." *Ampo: Japan-Asia Quarterly Review* 21(2/3):74-79. No refs. LCCN:77-12830.

The opening address of the Asian Women's Forum sponsored by the People's Plan for the 21st Century [PP21].   Touches on themes including the status of the contemporary Japanese women's movement, exploitation of women to enable Japan's economic growth, reproductive technology and "commoditization" of sex.   Also notes exploitation of other Asian women through development strategies.   Concludes with a call to action for Asian feminism.

1186.   STROMAN, John.   May 1983.   "An outsider's look at Japanese women."   *PHP* 14(5):36-46.   No refs.   ISSN:0030-798X.

Interviews Anne BLASING, founder of the International Feminists of Japan, concerning her views on feminism in general, and the women's movement in Japan.

1187.   TAMGHINSKY, I.   1982.   "The women's movement in Japan."   *Far Eastern Affairs* [Moscow] no.4:55-66.   15 notes.   LCCN:75-642937.

An evaluation of women's status and the women's movement from the Soviet perspective. Details the efforts of the Japan Communist Party to better the condition of women.

1188.   UENO, Chizuko.   1988.   "The Japanese women's movement: The counter-values to industrialism."   In: McCORMACK, Gavan and Yoshio SUGIMOTO, eds.   *The Japanese Trajectory: Modernization and Beyond*.   New York: Cambridge University Press, pp. 167-185.   31 notes.   LCCN:88-1722.

Discusses the changes in the housewife role since the 1960s and the resulting discrimination in both the workplace and the home.   Articulates the position of the current women's movement on these challenges.

1189.   Women's Group of the Conference of Asians.   Jun. 1975.   "Women at the Conference of Asians."   In: *Japanese Women Speak Out*.   Tokyo: White Paper on Sexism—Japan Task Force, pp. 149-155.   No refs.

During a conference focusing on Japan's economic invasion of Asia, the women met in an attempt to discuss a rising and "powerful anti-Japanese movement," and to "find out how we can alter the current of past history, so that . . . [we] . . . will not stand on the side of the aggressors in the future."   The discussion provides an example of the involvement of the Japanese women's movement in world affairs.

Women's Organizations

1190.   ASADORI, Sumie.   1986.   "Guide to Japanese women's organizations."   *Ampo: Japan-Asia Quarterly Review* 18(2/3):106-107.   No refs.   LCCN:77-12830.

Provides addresses for 48 women's organizations as of 1986, from "general" to groups oriented toward issues such as labor, health, peace, and the arts.

1191.   BOULDING, Elise.   Jan. 1966.   "Japanese women look at society."   *Japan Christian Quarterly* 32(1):19-29.   1 ref.   ISSN:0021-4361.

BOULDING interviewed 280 women belonging to 32 different women's organizations and provides statistical profiles of members include the type of organization to which they belong, their education, and their religious preference.   Also includes summaries of the members' attitudes toward society and social change and their comments on the roles of women's organizations in the future.

1192.   CECCHINI, Rose Marie.   [1988/1990].   "From coffee shop to women's movement: Shambara Sisters, Kyoto."   In: CECCHINI, Rose Marie.   [1988/1990].   *Women's Actions for*

Peace and Justice: Christian, Buddhist and Muslim Women Tell their Stories. Maryknoll, NY: Maryknoll Sisters, pp. 173-183. 3 notes. LCCN:88-175808/89-63181.

Describes the history, membership and structure, and activities of the Shambara Sisters, a "self-initiated, autonomous Kyoto women's group" which began in the Shambara coffee shop.

1193. CECCHINI, Rose Marie. [1988/1990]. "Japanese women in action: International Women's Year Action Group, Tokyo." In: CECCHINI, Rose Marie. [1988/1990]. *Women's Actions for Peace and Justice: Christian, Buddhist and Muslim Women Tell their Stories.* Maryknoll, NY: Maryknoll Sisters, pp. 143-172. 31 notes. LCCN:88-175808/89-63181.

Provides a detailed description of the founding, mission and inner-workings of the International Women's Year Action Group, as well as the activities of its Education Group (reviews textbooks for gender role stereotypes), Mass Media Group (identifies discrimination and stereotyping in the media), Housewives Group (organizes programs for housewives), and Labor Group (varied activities including publication of *A Handbook for Part-Time Workers*), and the peace activities of the complete group.

1194. CECCHINI, Rose Marie. [1988/1990]. "New frontiers in feminine consciousness: Hiroshima Feminist Library." In: CECCHINI, Rose Marie. [1988/1990]. *Women's Actions for Peace and Justice: Christian, Buddhist and Muslim Women Tell their Stories.* Maryknoll, NY: Maryknoll Sisters, pp. 185-197. 8 notes. LCCN:88-175808/89-63181.

Details the history of the Hiroshima Feminist Library which began as a study/support group of 4 female psychology students and grew into a library/center supported by four independent groups focusing on women's work, feminist psychotherapy, women's liberation history, and sex politics. Provides a summary of the total group's critique of "Social Welfare on the Family Basis," an 1980 government proposal with militaristic overtones and policies restrictive to women.

1195. CECCHINI, Rose Marie. [1988/1990]. "On the future edge of history: Japan YWCA." In: CECCHINI, Rose Marie. [1988/1990]. *Women's Actions for Peace and Justice: Christian, Buddhist and Muslim Women Tell their Stories.* Maryknoll, NY: Maryknoll Sisters, pp. 199-231. 15 notes. LCCN:88-175808/89-63181.

Provides a history and details the structure of the Young Women's Christian Association [YWCA] movement in Japan, beginning in the late 1890s when the groundwork was laid, continuing with its establishment in 1905, the experiences of the World War II years, and its reestablishment following the War. Also describes the focus of specific city organizations including those in Tokyo, Kyoto, Hiroshima and Nagasaki, and discusses their role in peace education efforts. Includes first-hand accounts of the Hiroshima and Nagasaki bombings during World War II.

1196. "Chronicle," "Chronicle of 1937," and "News in Brief." Mar. 1938-Jul. 1940. *Japanese Women* vol. 1-3. No refs. ISSN:0388-1369.

A short "chronicle" or almanac section appearing in the following issues of *Japanese Women*: 1(2,3,4,5,6), 2(1,2,3,4,5,6), 3(1,2,3,4). Notes activities of prominent women (i.e. YAMADA Waka on tour in the United States) as well as events (i.e. establishment of the League of Japanese Women's Organizations).

1197. Federation of Young Women's Associations of Japan. [ca. 1938-1941.] *Outline of the Federation of Young Women's Associations of Japan.* Tokyo: The Federation. 21p. No refs. LCCN:42-9885.

Documents the structure and activities of the government-sponsored Young Women's Association of Japan founded in 1927 (not to be confused with the Young Women's Christian Association [YWCA], also active at this time). It was organized "for the culture of young women in their native places" and all unmarried women under 25 who had completed their compulsory education were expected to join.

1198. HAVENS, Thomas R.H. Summer 1974. "Women and the state in Japan, 1887-1945." *Japan Christian Quarterly* 40(3):154-159. 21 notes. ISSN:0021-4361.

Discusses the government-sponsored women's organizations in existence from 1887-1945. More conservative politically and socially, and with more appeal for rural women, these groups included the Japan Red Cross, Shojokai (an organization for young unmarried women), the Patriotic Women's Association, and the Greater Japan Women's Association. Includes a discussion of the roles the organizations played in preparing for World War II.

1199. HIGUCHI, Keiko. Autumn 1975. "The PTA—A channel for political activism." [Translated by Roy NAKAMURA.] *Japan Interpreter* 10(2):133-140. No refs. ISSN:0021-4450.

HIGUCHI evaluates the role of the PTA in regards to educational reform and as a training area for women who then influence "many aspects of community life."

1200. ICHIKAWA, Fusaye. Jan. 1938. "An introductory note." *Japanese Women* 1(1):1-2. No refs. ISSN:0388-1369.

In the introductory essay of the Women's Suffrage League [WSL] newsletter for foreign "co-workers," ICHIKAWA (president of the WSL) notes her desire to "furnish you the facts concerning women and the women's movement in Japan . . . ." Brief articles by women active in education, social service, and the women's movement are included, as are notes on the activities of women's organizations.

1201. ICHIKAWA, Fusaye. May 1940. ["Japanese women's organizations: A response."] *Japanese Women* 3(3):3-4. No refs. ISSN:0388-1369.

Differentiates between women's groups in pre-World War II Japan: those organized by the government and run by men; and those organized "by the free, independent will of the women themselves." ICHIKAWA was, at the time, president of the Women's Suffrage League of Japan.

1202. ICHIKAWA, Fusaye. May 1940. "On my return from China." *Japanese Women* 3(3):1,4. No refs. ISSN:0388-1369.

A brief report from the president of the Women's Suffrage League of Japan on her trip to China to meet with Chinese women in hopes of fostering cooperation and working toward peace between the two countries.

1203. INUKAI, Michiko. Aug./Sep. 1975. "Japanese women raise the rice spoon of revolt." *UNESCO Courier* 1975(8):12-15. No refs. ISSN:0041-5278.

Profiles the Shu-Fu-Ren [Union of Women], founded in 1948 by OKU Mumeo, and its considerable activities in environmental, consumer, educational, and political activism.

1204. JOHNSON, Linda L. Spring 1989. "Transforming lives: Women's study circles in historical and cross-cultural perspective." *Feminist Teacher* 4(1):13-15,35. 9 refs. ISSN:0882-4843.

JOHNSON briefly reports on women's writing circles after World War II as described by TSURUMI [#54].

1205. KAKINUMA, Miyuki. Feb. 1978. "Japanese feminism: A handbook." *Feminist Japan* no. 4:59-64. [Also cited as 1(4).] No refs. ISSN:0388-197X.

KAKINUMA (an editor of *Feminist*) has compiled a guide to women's organizations of Japan. She begins with a brief history of the post-war women's movement, details women's groups with their addresses and publications, lists women's buildings, and ends with a bibliography of materials on women's studies in Japan published in the 1960s and 1970s both in Japanese and in English.

1206. KASZA, Gregory J. Oct. 1990. "The state and the organization of women in prewar Japan." *Japan Foundation Newsletter* 18(2):9-13. 19 notes. ISSN:0385-2318.

KASZA describes four women's "administered mass organization[s] [AMOs]" active in pre-World War II Japan: the Dai Nihon Rengō Fujinkai [Great Japan Federated Women's Organization], the Dai Nihon Kokubō Fujinkai [Great Japan National Defense Women's Association], the Aikoku Fujinkai [Patriotic Women's Association], and the Dai Nihon Fujinkai [Great Japan Women's Association], and lists the traits common to both AMOs and the mass conscript army.

1207. MACKIE, Vera, Diana BETHEL, and Anne L. BLASING. 1980. "Women's groups in Japan: An overview of major groups." *Feminist International* no.2:106-110. No refs. ISSN:0388-371X.

For the Kantō region, nine groups are listed and their activites and publications discussed. A briefer summary of groups in the Kansai area is provided, followed by a discussion of the activities of the International Feminists of Japan.

1208. "Recent activities of L. J. W. O. [League of Japanese Women's Organizations]." Mar. 1938. *Japanese Women* 1(2):3. No refs. ISSN:0388-1369.

During the six months after its founding in September 1937, committees of the League of Japanese Women's Organizations took up discussions of day nurseries, replacement of hulled rice with more nutritious rice, and venereal disease.

1209. TOTTEN, George. 1966. *The Social Democratic Movement in Prewar Japan.* New Haven: Yale University Press. 455p. Notes. Index. LCCN:66-12515.

On pages 359-364, TOTTEN includes a description of women's organizations affiliated with the Social Democratic Movement from the 1890s to the late 1930s. Discussed are the New Women's Society, Red Wave Society, Social Democratic Women's Federation, and others. Material on women is also scattered throughout the text.

1210. "W.S.L. news." Jan.-Nov. 1938. *Japanese Women* 1(1):5-6, 1(2):3-4, 1(3):4, 1(4):3-4, 1(5):3, 1(6):3. No refs. ISSN:0388-1369.

An ongoing column in a newsletter published by the Women's Suffrage League [WSL] lists events of various women's organizations and activities of their individual members.

Lesbians

1211. BLASING, Anne. Mar. 1982. "The lavender kimono." *Off Our Backs* 12(3):6. No refs. ISSN:0030-0071.

Briefly reports on the status of lesbian groups in Japan and notes newsletters published by them.

1212. LEMESHEWSKY, A. Kaweah. 1987. "Facing both ways: Japanese lesbians in Japan and in the U.S." In: CHUNG, C., A. KIM, and A.K. LEMESHEWSKY, eds. *Between the Lines: An Anthology by Pacific/Asian Lesbians of Santa Cruz, California.* Santa Cruz, CA: Dancing Bird Press, pp. 37-41. No refs.

Reports on a interview with five Japanese lesbians, and includes comments on support networks, working as a single woman, and coming out.

1213. "Regumi: A new spelling of our name." 1989. *Connexions* 29:24-25. ISSN:0886-7062.

A lesbian identified as "Y" discusses goals and activities of the lesbian organization, *Regumi*, which is based in Tokyo and has branches nationwide, and the International Lesbian Group, also based in Tokyo. Also briefly excerpts an interview from *Gay Community News* with Mayumi TOMIHARA on the origin of the name *Regumi* and on the climate for lesbians in Japan.

Political Protest and Reform

1214. ADACHI, Kinnosuke. Nov. 1926. "The new women of Nippon." *Woman Citizen* 11:14-16,41-42,44. No refs.

A description of the Shin Fujin [New Women of Japan] and the political activities of its members. The article is very optimistic, discussing changes in political participation and employment and the push for change in marital agreements. It also notes the desire of women for a decrease in military strength.

1215. APTER, David E. and Nagayo SAWA. 1984. *Against the State: Politics and Social Protest in Japan.* Cambridge: Harvard University Press. 271p. Notes. Index. LCCN:83-15338.

A scholarly study of the Sanrizuka protest movement against the building of the New Tokyo (Narita) International Airport. What began as a group of farmers struggling to keep their land in the 1960s expanded to include various radical sects and anti-pollution, peace, and antinuclear groups. During this time women's traditional agricultural roles changed to that of militant demonstrators. APTER profiles several women and briefly describes how their organizations were a part of the whole. Material on women is scattered but accessible through the index.

1216. CALDECOTT, Leonie. 21 Jan. 1983. "Peace women of Shibokusa." *New Statesman* 105(2705):17-18. No refs. ISSN:0190-745X.

An account of the author's visit with farm women protesting military use of the Mt. Fuji foothills. A brief history of the area and the protest movement is included.

1217. CARTER, Aiko. 22 Mar. 1974. "On being a woman in Japan. Part 2: Front lines of the ongoing struggle." *Japan Christian Activity News* no.450:1-3. No refs. ISSN:0021-4353. Reprinted in CARTER, Aiko. 1975. *On being a Woman in Japan.* Tokyo: Femintern Press.]

In this section, CARTER focuses on several current protest movements: the Shibokusa Mothers' Movement, women whose farms at the foot of Mt. Fuji were displaced for combat training areas; and "Women in Battle," a group that works "to create the possibility for individuality . . ." and that centers itself on the theories of TAKAMURE Itsue. She also mentions people working against prostitution in other Asian countries and one woman who fought mandatory retirement.

1218. ESTERLINE, Mae Handy, ed. 1987. *They Changed Their Worlds: Nine Women of Asia.* Lanham: University Press of America. 170p. Bibl. LCCN:87-8208.

Includes biographical essays on two Japanese women, ISHIMURE Michiko, the "shy environmentalist" who was instrumental in the campaign against water pollution and mercury poisonings resulting in Minamata Disease (pp. 1-14), and ICHIKAWA Fusaye, "suffragette and politician," a leader in the Japanese women's movement, and a long-time member of the Diet. Although ICHIKAWA has contributed to, and is discussed extensively in, the literature [see indexes], this summary (pp. 16-32) may be useful. The information on ISHIMURE is not readily available elsewhere in English.

1219. "Feminist Kamichika Ichiko." Jul./Aug. 1989. *East* 25(2):17-23. No refs. ISSN:0012-8295.

A biographical sketch of KAMICHIKA Ichiko, a writer for *Seitō*, newspaper reporter, socialist, member of the Diet, and anti-prostitution crusader. The article provides more depth than is usually found in this magazine.

1220. HANE, Mikiso, ed. 1988. *Reflections on the Way to the Gallows: Rebel Women in Pre-War Japan.* [Translated by Mikiso HANE.] Berkeley: University of California Press. 274p. Notes. Index. LCCN:87-36469.

Continuing his service in providing first-hand accounts of early modern Japanese life [see also #17], HANE presents excerpts of the writings of FUKUDA Hideko, KANNO Sugako, KANEKO Fumiko of the Sekirankai [Red Wave Society], SAKAI Magara, HASHIURA Haruko, KUTSUMI Fusako, YAMAKAWA Kikue, TANNO Ketsu, TAKIZAWA Mii, IKEDA Seki, SATŌ Tsugi, and YAMASHIRO Tomoe. Contains a wealth of primary material concerning politically active Japanese women working on human rights and on social and economic justice.

1221. INGLIS, Jean. 1981. "What made me like this? The prison memories of Kaneko Fumiko." *Ampo: Japan-Asia Quarterly Review* 13(2):34-39. No refs. LCCN:77-12830.

Within this review of KANEKO Fumiko's Japanese language autobiography, *Nani ga watakushi o ko saseta ka*, INGLIS outlines KANEKO's life and explores reasons for her nihilistic philosophy. KANEKO (1905-1926) was convicted of conspiring to assassinate the Emperor and hanged herself in prison while awaiting execution.

1222. ISHIMURA, Chiaki and Kunio NISHIMURA. Jul. 1987. "Worrying about water." *Look Japan* 33(37):28. No refs. ISSN:0456-5339.

Describes the efforts of ŌYAMA Nobuyo, a film actress, to promote water conservation.

1223. "Japanese women take on the U.S. Army: Interview with Okubo Rakue." 1986. *Ampo: Japan-Asia Quarterly Review* 18(2-3):102-104. No refs. LCCN:77-12830.

OKUBO is active in the "Association to Oppose the Construction of U.S. Army Barracks and to Protect Nature and Children" in Zushi City, Kanagawa. Provides insight on the motivation of housewives active in consumer movements.

1224. LEWIS, Catherine. 1978. "Women in the consumer movement." In: WHITE, Merry I. and Barbara MOLONY, eds. *Proceedings of the Tokyo Symposium on Women.* Tokyo: International Group for the Study of Women, pp. 80-87. (Tokyo Symposium on Women, [1st], 1978.) No refs.

LEWIS provides background on the rise of the consumer movement and discusses ways in which housewives have come to broaden their activities into the political and consumer protection arenas as a logical extension of the "good wife-wise mother" role.

1225. LIN, John and Reginald RAJAPAKSE. 1984. "Workers, peasants, and women in Taishō Japan: Legacy of the Meiji mind." In: CONROY, Hilary, Sandra T.W. DAVIS, and Wayne PATTERSON, eds. *Japan in Transition: Thought and Action in the Meiji Era, 1868-1912.* Rutherford, NJ: Fairleigh Dickinson University Press, pp. 261-275. 53 notes. LCCN:82-48577.

At the end of the article, LIN briefly relates labor and political protests of women in Taishō Japan (1912-1926).

1226. MAKI, Shōhei. 1976. "The postwar consumer movement: Its emergence from a movement of women." *Japan Quarterly* 23(2):135-139. No refs. ISSN:0021-4590.

Describes the consumer movement from its beginnings in 1945, and discusses its strengths and weaknesses (resulting from its identification as a women's movement).

1227. MATSUI, Yayori. Jan./Mar. 1975. "Protest and the Japanese woman." *Japan Quarterly* 22(1):32-39. No refs. ISSN:0021-4590.

Provides details on the environmental protection and consumer movements initiated and carried out by women.

1228. MATSUI, Yayori. Jun. 1975. "Women in the anti-pollution movements." In: *Japanese Women Speak Out.* Tokyo: White Paper on Sexism—Japan Task Force, pp. 118-126.

A report by a journalist outlining the roles women have played in both the antipollution movements (especially the Minamata poisonings) and the consumer movements (especially in the determination of "proper prices for commodities" and in the "safety of consumer goods and foods.")

1229. ŌSHIMA, Kōichi. Winter 1980. "Kim Maria and Japan: Korean women students in Japan and the March First independence movement." *Japan Christian Quarterly* 46(1):40-45. 13 refs. ISSN:0021-4361.

A brief biographical sketch of KIM Maria (1893-1944) who was educated in Japan at Joshi Gakuin, and went on to be active in the March First Independence Movement (for Korean independence from Japan, 1 March 1919).

1230. SUZUKI, Sunao.   1982.   "Ukita Hisako." *Japan Quarterly* 29(1):93-95.   No refs. ISSN:0021-4590.

A biographical sketch of UKITA Hisako, who organized the Japan Peace Research Group in 1964.

1231. SWAIN, David L. Fall 1987. "Portrait of a peacemaker (10): Sekiya Ayako." *Japan Christian Quarterly* 53(4):244-246. No refs. ISSN:0021-4361.

Profiles SEKIYA Ayako, Christian, president of the Japan Young Women's Christian Association [YWCA], and anti-nuclear and peace educator.

1232. TONO, Haruhi. 1981. "Women do not allow war!" *Ampo: Japan-Asia Quarterly Review* 13(4):17-20. No refs. LCCN:77-12830.

Details signs of remilitarization by the Japanese government and describes the activities to protest this and other aggressive actions by Japanese (e.g. economic exploitation of Southeast Asia and the "sex tour" industry) by the Women Do Not Allow War! groups.

1233. USHIODA, Sharlie C. 1984. "Fukuda Hideko and the woman's world of Meiji Japan." In: CONROY, Hilary, Sandra T.W. DAVIS, and Wayne PATTERSON, eds. *Japan in Transition: Thought and Action in the Meiji Era, 1868-1912.* Rutherford, NJ: Fairleigh Dickinson University Press, pp. 276-293. 47 notes. LCCN:82-48577. [An earlier version of this paper appeared in *Peace and Change* 4(3):9-12, 1977. ISSN:0149-0508.]

USHIODA provides both historical context on women in Meiji Japan and a detailed biographical sketch of FUKUDA Hideko (1865-1927), "a political activist and writer" and a feminist. FUKUDA was jailed for participation in the Osaka Incident, was active in a pacifist group called the Heiminsha, and worked on the publication of its newspaper. She later founded a women's journal, *Sekai Fujin* [*Women of the World*], a "vehicle to inspire women to participate in activities of national and international importance." Includes excerpts translated from her autobiography and a discussion of the sources.

1234. UTSUMI, Aiko. 1986. "Korean women refuse fingerprinting." *Ampo: Japan-Asia Quarterly Review* 18(2/3):88-93. No refs. LCCN:77-12830.

Profiles YANG Yong-ja (a singer and songwriter) and SHI I-na (a 14-year-old), and reports on their refusal to be fingerprinted as part of the Alien Registration they are required to complete as "Koreans." Discusses the role of women in the society of Koreans-in-Japan and the greater issue of human rights in Japan.

1235. "A woman in the anti-nuke and anti-U.S. base movement: Interview with Toyama Noriko." 1986. *Ampo: Japan-Asia Quarterly Review* 18(2/3):104-105. No refs. LCCN:77-12830.

TOYAMA compares activist movements in Japan with unions where organization occurs at the top and then is passed down to the activists. She encourages women to organize themselves and to "take responsibility." She had just organized a protest against the American bases in Seya, a district of Yokohama, at the time of this writing.

1236. "Women opposing authoritarianism: Interview with Yanagiya Akiko . . . ." 1986. *Ampo: Japan-Asia Quarterly Review* 18(2/3):100-102. No refs. LCCN:77-12830.

YANAGIYA Akiko has a history of political activity, beginning in the 1960s as a student, continuing with the consumer movement, and currently as a member of the Municipal Assembly of Fujisawa City. She speaks of her campaign (unique because she is a divorcée with two children) and how she views the participation of women in local politics.

1237. YAMAYA, Shinko. 1976. "Women and the peace movement." *Peace Research in Japan* 1976:72-77. No refs. LCCN:78-644999.

The chairperson of the Peace Division of the Women's Christian Temperance Union [WCTU] describes their peace activities historically and outlines three foci for the current year: "1. Prohibition of nuclear weapons and relief of A-bomb survivors; 2. Japan-Korea relations; 3. Respect for human rights through participation in the anti-nationalization of the Yasukuni shrine movement."

Social Activism

1238. BEARD, Mary. 12 Jan. 1924. "The new Japanese women." *Woman Citizen* 9:10,28-30. No refs.

A report on the response of Japanese women to the 1923 earthquake—a response which made possible a Japanese women's movement. BEARD enthusiastically describes the organized strides toward overall social reconstruction as well as immediate relief work, and calls on American women to donate books for the Tokyo Women's Federation.

1239. GAUNTLETT, Mrs. Tsune. 1928. "Anti-vice movement in Japan." In: *Women of the Pacific.* Honolulu: Pan-Pacific Union, pp. 241-244. (Pan-Pacific Women's Conference, 1st, Honolulu, 9-19 Aug. 1928.) No refs.

Explains the system of licensed prostitution in Japan and the efforts of the Women's Christian Temperance Union [WCTU] and the Purity League to end it. Closes with a rationale for prostitution's abolishment.

1240. HASTINGS, Sally A. Nov. 1985. "From heroine to patriotic volunteer: Women and social work in Japan, 1900-1945." *Working Paper* [*on Women in International Development*] no. 106. 23p. 78 notes. ISSN:0888-5354.

Surveys the role of women in social work outside the home, an activity adopted from the West in Meiji times. Also discusses the opportunities made available to women and the ties between social work and political activity.

1241. HEMPHILL, Elizabeth Anne. 1980. *The Least of These: Miki Sawada and her Children.* New York: Weatherhill. 161p. Notes. Index. LCCN:80-15816.

SAWADA Miki, granddaughter of the founder of Mitsubishi, was raised as part of a wealthy family in the early 1900s. She married a diplomat and traveled throughout Europe and South America. During the Occupation she became concerned over the fate of mixed-blood children, abandoned by their American soldier fathers and Japanese mothers. She founded an orphanage, and by 1980 over 1600 children had been cared for there.

1242. ISHIMOTO, Shidzue. 1935. *East Way, West Way: A Modern Japanese Girlhood.* New York: Farrar and Rinehart. 194p. No refs. LCCN:36-33962. [Author also cited as KATŌ, Shidzue.]

An autobiography describing the author's happy childhood in a family in transition from feudal samurai to upper-class aristocrats, her attendance at the Peeress's School, her upbringing designed to transform her into a "good wife and wise mother," and her marriage to Baron ISHIMOTO, a young Christian humanist. She includes much discussion on women in society, especially from the view of a wealthy girl of a traditional family, and on the transition from young girl to daughter-in-law. [ISHIMOTO was later active in the family planning movement and in politics; for the full autobiography, see #1243.]

1243. ISHIMOTO, Shidzue. 1984. *Facing Two Ways: The Story of My Life.* [With an introduction and afterword by Barbara MOLONY.] Stanford: Stanford University Press. 418p. No refs. LCCN:83-40621. [Author also cited as KATŌ, Shidzue.]

The autobiography to age 37 of ISHIMOTO Shidzue, now KATŌ Shidzue, a woman described in the introduction as "one of the two or three most influential women in Japan's twentieth century history . . . a leader in Japan's feminist and birth control movements and a Socialist member of the Diet." MOLONY provides contextual materials and continues KATŌ's story to age 87 (1984). A personal analysis of the status of Japanese women during the last century. Reviewed by TSURUMI in #2311. [See also #1242.]

1244. KAJI, Etsuko and Jean INGLIS. Spring 1974. "Sisters against slavery: A look at anti-prostitution movements in Japan." *Ampo: Japan-Asia Quarterly Review* 6(2):19-23. [Also cited as series no. 20:19-23.] No refs. LCCN:77-12830.

A brief survey of antiprostitution movements in Japan; focuses primarily on the Kyofukai Movement begun in 1886 and the anti-prostitution protests of the 1970s against the Japanese male "tourist" trade to Korea.

1245. KATŌ, Shidzue. 1983. "My story as a witness of Japan from feudalism to economic power." In: MURAMATSU, Yasuko, ed. *Women and Work: Working Women and their Impact on Society.* Tokyo: International Group for the Study of Women, pp. 1-6. (Tokyo Symposium on Women, 2nd, 1983. *Proceedings*.) No refs. [Author also cited as ISHIMOTO Shidzue.] LCCN:84-187204.

An autobiographical talk given by the author at age 86. KATŌ started the birth control movement in Japan and was active as a politician for many years.

1246. "Living for the birds." 1989. *Japan Pictorial* 12(3):14-16. No refs. ISSN:0388-6115.

A very brief profile of WATANABE Tome, a grassroots conservationist working to feed and protect Japanese cranes.

1247. MADDEN, Maude Whitmore. 1919. *Women of the Meiji Era*. New York: Revell. 63p. No refs. LCCN:19-7811. (*History of Women* [Woodbridge, CT: Research Publications], Reel 907, No. 7557.)

Written by a missionary with 20 years experience in Japan, this is a collection of brief biographical sketches of women active in social reform and Christianity: Her Majesty Haruko, TSUDA Ume, YAJIMA Kajiko, HAYASHI Uta, IWAMOTO Kashi, HIROOKA Asa, KAWAI Michi, and SUTO Roku.

1248. MURRAY, Geoffrey. Sep. 1974. "Smile! You're not *really* handicapped." *PHP* 5(9):34-43. No refs. ISSN:0030-798X.

Profiles MIYAGI Mariko, actress and singer who founded Nemunoki Gakuen, a school/home for 47 handicapped children.

1249. MURRAY, Geoffrey. Aug. 1977. "Sachiko Hashimoto— Godmother of the Red Mafia." *PHP* 8(8):38-46. No refs. ISSN:0030-798X.

Profiles HASHIMOTO Sachiko, whose life-long service to the International and Japanese Red Cross Societies earned her the Henri Durant medal.

1250. MURRAY, Geoffrey. May 1979. "Miki Sawada—'Mama' to orphans." *PHP* 10(5):38-47. No refs. ISSN:0030-798X.

A detailed look at the Elizabeth Saunders Home established by SAWADA Miki for children of mixed parentage born during and after the Occupation. Includes the comments of several of its "graduates."

1251. NAKANO, Ann. Aug. 1984. "Shizue (Ishimoto) Katō: Woman warrior." *PHP* (Feb. 1984):68-72. No refs. ISSN:0030-798X.

A biographical sketch of KATŌ Shizue [ISHIMOTO Shizue] Diet member and birth control pioneer, with selections of her thoughts regarding women. [See also her autobiographical works: #1242, #1243, and #1245.]

1252. SHIMADA, Noriko, *et al.* 1975. "Ume Tsuda and Motoko Hani: Echoes of American cultural feminism in Japan." In: GEORGE, Carol V.R., ed. *Remember the Ladies: New Perspectives on Women in American History*. Syracuse: Syracuse University Press, pp. 161-178. 26 notes. LCCN:75-12295.

Discusses the social and educational reformers TSUDA Ume and HANI Motoko (both active from 1900-1930), and compares their work to that of 19th century Americans, Mary LYON and Catharine BEECHER.

1253. "Step by step." 1989. *Japan Pictorial* 12(2):26-33. No refs. ISSN:0388-6115.

Briefly profiles MIYAGI Mariko, an "actress, a singer and a film director" who also directs the Nemunoki School for Exceptional Children, "a facility for the care of physically and mentally disabled children who do not have parents or guardians." The bulk of the article is art work by the children.

1254. TAKENAKA, Chiharu. 1987. "Peace, democracy and women in postwar Japan." *Peace and Change* 12(3/4):69-77. 29 notes. ISSN:0149-0508.

Surveys the participation and leadership of women in the social change movement in Japan from the post-World War II period to the present. Includes activites in areas such as consumer and environmental protection, local political protest, and international public consciousness raising.

Party Politics and Government

1255. "All aboard the Doi express." 22 July 1989. *Economist* 312(7612):30. No refs. ISSN:0013-0613.

A very brief description of DOI Takako's campaign appearances as head of the Japan Socialist Party.

1256. ARIMA, Sumisato. Jan./Mar. 1987. "Can a 'resolute woman' save the Socialist Party?" *Japan Quarterly* 34(1):24-29. No refs. ISSN:0021-4590.

Presents an analysis of the Japan Socialist Party and its chances of image enhancement given the decision to install DOI Takako, a woman and constitutional law scholar, as its head. DOI is described as knowledgeable of international affairs and as a "supporter of ordinary people." In comparing her with Britain's THATCHER, ARIMA notes the latter rose to power through her political qualifications, while DOI was chosen because of her sex in order to broaden the Party's appeal.

1257. CARLBERG, Eileen. 1976. "Women in the political system." In: LEBRA, Joyce, *et al. Women in Changing Japan.* Stanford: Stanford University Press, pp. 233-253. 10 notes. LCCN:75-33663.

CARLBERG outlines women's political involvement during the 20th century and then discusses the state of women's position in political life in the early 1970s. Her comments are based on interviews with women in the Diet, central and local administrative jobs, and women in the judiciary. She then provides a composite biography of a female administrator based on her interviews. A very thorough study.

1258. "Find the lady." 16 Dec. 1989. *Economist* 313(7633):32. No refs. ISSN:0013-0613.

Notes the inability of the Socialist party to recruit women candidates, and points out that the current voting structure may line up male Socialist contenders against female colleagues.

1259. FUJITA, Taki. 1968. "Women and politics in Japan." *Annals of the American Academy of Political & Social Science* 375:91-95. [Also cited as American Academy of Political and Social Science. *Annals.*] 4 notes. ISSN:0002-7162.

In 1968, FUJITA was President of Tsuda College, active in government and women's issues, and a former Japanese representative to the United Nations. She surveys women's political involvement beginning in 1945 when women gained the right to vote and addresses voting records, female elected officials, and women's political power.

1260. FUKATSU, Masumi. Jan./Mar. 1990. "Doi Takako tackles the obstacles to power." *Japan Quarterly* 37(1):24-30. 3 notes. ISSN:0021-4590.

FUKATSU outlines DOI's proposals to be followed by a possible coalition government in the areas of politics, economics, international economic relations, and diplomacy. He then discusses the "obstacles" to the realization of these goals, namely, political opposition from other parties, the business community, the press, and the United States.

1261. GOTŌ, Masako. Jun. 1975. "Political participation of Japanese women." In: *Japanese Women Speak Out.* Tokyo: White Paper on Sexism—Japan Task Force, pp. 64-65. No refs.

A brief discussion of the political process which results in few women candidates or electees and little political clout for women despite the fact that many more women than men vote in elections. The author is a secretary to a Diet member representing the Japan Socialist Party.

1262. HARGADINE, Eileen. 1981. "Japan." In: LOVENDUSKI, Joni and Jill HILLS, ed. *The Politics of the Second Electorate: Women and Public Participation.* London: Routledge and Kegan Paul, pp. 299-319. Bibl. LCCN:81-199239.

In this comprehensive study of political behavior patterns of women in 20 countries, HARGADINE gives a brief history of women's political rights in Japan, women's socio-economic position and the political system in general, and then elaborates on women in national and local politics, voting habits, and attitudes toward women in politics. A succinct and detailed report which concludes that "women's contemporary social roles are not compatible with professional politics [in Japan]."

1263. HOPPER, Helen M. 1982. "Katō Shidzue, Socialist Party MP, and Occupation reforms affecting women, 1945-1948: A case study of the formal vs. informal political influence of Japanese women." In: BURKMAN, Thomas W., ed. *The Occupation of Japan: Educational and Social Reform.* Norfolk: MacArthur Memorial, pp. 375-399. 50 notes.

Details the role KATŌ Shidzue played in the democratization of women's status during the Occupation. Provides biographical material, details KATŌ's close relationship with SCAP during the Occupation, and outlines her efforts to encourage family planning in Japan.

1264. ICHIKAWA, Fusaye. 1928. "The political status of women in Japan." In: *Women of the Pacific.* Honolulu: Pan-Pacific Union, pp. 205-208. (Pan-Pacific Women's Conference, 1st, Honolulu, 9-19 Aug. 1928.) No refs.

Beginning with the statement that "women of Japan, even today, have no franchise and are not considered as citizens," the president of the Women's Suffrage League of Japan outlines precisely the lack of possibilities for political participation of women and then discusses each category. She notes a few exceptions in her conclusions.

1265. IMPOCO, Jim and Kevin SULLIVAN. 7 Aug. 1989. "Sex, taxes and 'the Madonna factor.'" *U.S. News and World Report* 107(6):36. No refs. ISSN:0041-5537.

Briefly discusses DOI Takako's appeal to voters.

1266. "Japan: Vote sisterhood." 9 Apr. 1977. *Economist* 263(9 Apr. 1977):54. No refs. ISSN:0013-0613.

Notes the efforts of the Chupiren to form a Japan Women's Party which will run at least ten candidates in the summer national election. Briefly contrasts the Women's Party platform with the newly published White Paper on Women (issued by the Japanese government).

1267. JONES, H.J. Aug. 1975. "Japanese women in the politics of the seventies." *Asian Survey* 15(8):708-723. 19 notes. ISSN:0004-4687.

A quantitative look at political views of Japanese women [see also #1268] providing data for interpretation of attitudes concerning Diet members, policy, political parties, female candidates, and political awareness. The second half of the article places the results of the surveys in their socio-political context.

1268. JONES, H.J. Summer 1976. "Japanese women and party politics." *Pacific Affairs* 49(2):213-234. 43 notes. ISSN:0030-851X.

Discusses the attitudes of political party leaders toward women's enfranchisement and provides information on the few women running for Diet office in the 1974 elections. Concludes with a discussion of women's participation in "supra-party politics," especially under the leadership of ICHIKAWA Fusae via the Women's Suffrage Hall, and via the Citizen's Movement. [See also #1267].

1269. "Kaifu's surprises." 21 Aug. 1989. *Time* 134(8):38. No refs. ISSN:0040-781X.

Notes the appointment of two women to Prime Minister KAIFU Toshiki's cabinet: TAKAHARA Sumiko as Economic Planning Agency director and MORIYAMA Mayumi as head of the Environmental Protection Agency.

1270. KAMICHIKA, Ichiko. 1956. "Japanese women enfranchised." *Contemporary Japan* 24(1/3):101-111. No refs. ISSN:0388-0214.

KAMICHIKA (member of the Diet and president of the *Fujin Times*) provides a history of the women's suffrage movement in Japan and a summary of women's voting records and election rates for the period 1946-1955.

1271. "Ladies' Day." 1 Jul. 1989. *Economist* 312(7609):28. No refs. ISSN:0013-0613.

Points out women's negative reaction to the consumption tax and the illicit liaisons of Prime Minister UNO Sōsuke, and notes how the Japan Socialist Party is capitalizing on this disapproval of Liberal Democratic Party policies and personnel.

1272. M.O. Mar. 1962. "Problems of the women's movement and the policy of the Communist Party of Japan." *World Marxist Review* 5(3):47-48. No refs. ISSN:0043-8642.

Provides a brief overview of activities in the women's movement of the early 1960s and calls for a joint effort on the part of the Communist Party of Japan and the women's movement to create "a single national organ that would unite all women and all democratic women's organs."

1273. "Mrs. Oku on Labour Advisory Committee." Jan. 1940. *Japanese Women* 3(1):3. No refs. ISSN:0388-1369.

Announces the appointment of OKU Mumeo to the Labour Supervising Committee of the Ministry of Welfare. Notes her involvement in the women's movement, in establishing co-operative stores, and in settlement house work.

1274. MURRAY, Geoffrey. Jan. 1975. "Fusae Ichikawa—Choice of the young in Japan." *PHP* 6(1):35-41. No refs. ISSN:0030-798X.

Describes briefly the election of 1974 and the political comeback of 81-year-old ICHIKAWA Fusae, made possible by a coalition of young people. Also provides a biographical sketch and a summary of her observations on democracy in Japan.

1275. MURRAY, Patricia. Autumn 1975. "Ichikawa Fusae and the lonely red carpet." *Japan Interpreter* 10(2):171-189. 42 notes. ISSN:0021-4450.

A detailed delineation of the political campaigns of ICHIKAWA Fusae with an emphasis on the 1974 elections. Biographical data also provided.

1276. "The new doienne." 30 Aug. 1986. *Economist* 300(7461):35. No refs. ISSN:0013-0613.

Briefly notes changes in the Socialist Party which are leading to the acceptance of a woman, DOI Takako, as its head.

1277. "Officeless ladies: Few women selected for coming polls." 15 Feb. 1990. *Far Eastern Economic Review* 147(7):12-13. No refs. ISSN:0014-7591.

Explores reasons for a drop in the number of women running for election to the lower house of the Japanese parliament as compared with the number of female candidates for the upper house in the 1989 election.

1278. PHARR, Susan J. 1981. *Political Women in Japan: The Search for a Place in Political Life.* Berkeley: University of California Press. 239p. Bibl. Index. LCCN:80-12984.

For this in-depth study, PHARR interviewed 100 young women involved in more than 50 voluntary political groups to determine "the political goals of young Japanese women and [the extent of] their struggle to attain them." Reviews women's political roles (or lack thereof) since 1868, and focuses on both the gender-role socialization process and political socialization. Discusses ways in which politically active women deal with "role-strain." An appendix provides details on PHARR's methods and a copy of her interview questionnaire.

1279. SAWACHI, Hisae. Oct./Dec. 1989. "The political awakening of women." *Japan Quarterly* 36(4):381-385. No refs. ISSN:0021-4590.

An essay detailing women's "new-found political clout" and the reactions of a male-dominated society.

1280. SAYLE, Murray. 11 Sep. 1989. "Sex, lies and Japanese politics: Women rewrite the rules." *New Republic* 201(11):18-22. No refs. ISSN:0028-6583.

Despite the subtitle, refers only briefly to DOI Takako, head of the Japan Socialist Party.

1281. SMITH, Charles. 20 Jul. 1989. "Women win out." *Far East Economic Review* 145(29):11-12. No refs. ISSN:0014-7591.

Suggests that July's upper house election could mark "a victory for women and intellectuals over organisation men" given the inclusion of women among the top candidates in the Liberal Democratic Party and the Japan Socialist Party.

1282. SUGAWARA, Mariko. 1983. "My career in modern society in Japan." In: MURAMATSU, Yasuko, ed. *Women and Work: Working Women and their Impact on Society.* Tokyo: International Group for the Study of Women, pp. 13-15. (Tokyo Symposium on Women, 2nd, 1983. *Proceedings*.) No refs. LCCN:84-187204.

SUGAWARA, from the Policy Office for the Aged of the Prime Minister's Secretariat, traces her career path and briefly discusses her personal life.

1283. SUZUKI, Kazue. Oct. 1987. "She's a politician first." *PHP Intersect* (Oct. 1987):42-43. No refs. ISSN:0910-4607.

Profiles DOI Takako, leader of Japan's Socialist Party.

1284. TAKEDA, Kiyoko. Oct./Dec. 1984. "Ichikawa Fusae: Pioneer for women's rights in Japan." *Japan Quarterly* 31(4):410-415. No refs. ISSN:0021-4590.

In this short biography of ICHIKAWA Fusae, women's suffrage leader and long-time member of the Diet, TAKEDA focuses on the intellectual influences on the development of ICHIKAWA's philosophy and details the many people with whom she interacted.

1285. TANAKA, Sumiko. Aug. 1980. "For abolition of discrimination against women, for solidarity for world peace." *Japan Socialist Review* no.381:3-27. No refs. ISSN:0021-4655.

TANAKA (of the Women's Policy Committee of the Japan Socialist Party) outlines her Party's 85-point program for women which has a goal of guaranteeing "women's participation in all areas of society . . . and to emancipate women and improve their social position, and calls on women throughout the country to arise in solidarity."

1286. TSUBOI, Yoshiharu. Winter 1986. "Can Chairwoman Doi save the Socialists?" *Japan Echo* 13(4):23-25. No refs. ISSN:0388-0435.

Analyzes the status of the Japan Socialist Party and suggests reforms which DOI (the first woman to head a major party) needs to implement. Although material on DOI herself is not the focus, the article does identify problems related to her gender.

1287. UTTING, Gerry. Nov. 1986. "Japan's Socialists turn to a woman." *World Press Review* 33(11):45. No refs. ISSN:0195-8895.

A report on the appointment of DOI Takako as head of the Japan Socialist party and on the troubles she has inherited.

1288. WEINSTEIN, Martin E. 1989. *The Human Face of Japan's Leadership: Twelve Portraits.* New York: Praeger. 410p. No refs. Index. LCCN:88-38360.

Included among the 12 profiles in this volume is an interview with KAWAGUCHI Yoriko, at the time Director of the International Business Affairs Division in the Ministry of Trade and Industry (MITI). She describes her upbringing, education, family life and role at MITI.

1289. "Woman power." 22 Jul. 1989. *Economist* 312(7612):30-31. No refs. ISSN:0013-0613.

Notes the appeal of DOI Takako of the Japan Socialist Party given the party's strategy of female candidates and opposition to the consumption tax.

Rulers and Ruling Family Members

1290. BUTLER, Kenneth D. 1978. "Woman of power behind the Kamakura Bakufu: Hōjō Masako." In: MURAKAMI, Hyōe and Thomas HARPER, eds. *Great Historical Figures of Japan.* Tokyo: Japan Culture Institute, pp. 91-101. LCCN:81-670213.

A biography of HŌJŌ Masako (1157-1225), also known as the Nun Shogun. She was "wife of the first Kamakura Shogun . . ., mother of the second and third shoguns, . . . daughter of . . . the first HŌJŌ Regent [and] one of the most powerful and influential women the male-dominated society of pre-modern Japan ever produced."

1291. "Gods, cavemen and a mysterious queen—from the history of Japan." 1965. *East* 2(3):11-16. No refs. ISSN:0012-8295.

Includes a brief account of Queen Himiko as described in Chinese chronicles around the year 247 C.E.

1292. HAMAGUCHI, Tan. 1904. "Some striking personalities in Japanese history." *Transactions and Proceedings of the Japan Society of London* 6(1904):235-269. [Also cited as Japan Society, London. *Transactions and Proceedings*.] No refs. LCCN:08-16048.

Describes the accomplishments of six women: Empress Jingō (d. 269 C.E.), conqueror of Korea; Empress Kōmyō (700-760), patroness of religion; MURASAKI Shikibu (971-1031?), author of *The Tale of Genji*; HŌJŌ Masako (1156-1225), regent; HOSOKAWA Tadaoki, "epitome of a samurai wife;" and KASUGANO Tsubone (d. 1643), foster mother to TOKUGAWA Iemitsu. Provides historical context for their activities.

1293. HIGUCHI, Chiyoko. Jun. 1971. "Something stronger than a mother's love: Lady Kasuga, nurturer of shoguns." *East* 7(6):38-42. No refs. ISSN:0012-8295.

A brief biography of SAITŌ Ofuku, later INABA Ofuku and Lady Kasuga. Originally hired as a wet nurse to TOKUGAWA Takechiyo, Ofuku became extremely powerful as TOKUGAWA fulfilled his duties as Shogun. For the general reader.

1294. HIGUCHI, Chiyoko. Oct. 1971. "When the lady wants power: She ruled with a mailed fist." *East* 7(9):25-30. No refs. ISSN:0012-8295.

A biography of HINO Tomiko (d. 1496), wife of ASHIKAGA Yoshimasa. HIGUCHI details the various political machinations carried out by HINO as wife and mother of shoguns. For the general reader.

1295. HIGUCHI, Chiyoko. Nov./Dec. 1971. "What befalls the fair: A Sengoku tragedy." *East* 7(10):32-37. No refs. ISSN:0012-8295.

The story of ODA Oichi (1564-1583), fifth daughter of ODA Nobuhide, who was of "real beauty" and was used as a political pawn by her brother. For the general reader.

1296. HIGUCHI, Chiyoko. Jan. 1972. "Fortune fair and fortune cruel." *East* 8(1):32-39. No refs. ISSN:0012-8295.

A brief sketch of "Chacha," later Yodogimi (1567-1615). She was the daughter of ODA Oichi [#1295], mistress to Hideyoshi, and mother of his heir. For the general reader.

1297. HIGUCHI, Chiyoko. Apr. 1972. "A princess for a cause: The story of Kazu no Miya." *East* 8(4):40-47. No refs. ISSN:0012-8295.

A rather maudlin rendition of the life of Kazu no Miya (d. 1877), half-sister to Emperor Kōmei and wife of the last TOKUGAWA Shogun, Iemochi.

1298. HIGUCHI, Chiyoko. 1973. "The petticoat Shōgun: Hōjō Masako." *East* 9(5):19-29. No refs. ISSN:0012-8295.

A fictionalized account of the life of HŌJŌ Masako [1157-1225], the "Nun General" and power behind Yoritomo, the Shōgun who established the Kamakura shogunate. HIGUCHI describes her as an "untamed and vigorous lioness."

1299. KILEY, Cornelius J. 1976. "The role of the queen in the archaic Japanese dynasty." In: *Japon*, Vol. 1. Paris: L'Asiatheque, pp. 45-49. (International Congress of Orientalists, 29th, Paris, 1973.) 11 notes. LCCN:77-569259.

In his brief discussion of the multilineal dynastic groups who have ruled Japan, KILEY notes that women (as well as men) inherited the rule.

1300. KOYAMA, Itoko. 1958. *Nagako, Empress of Japan*. [Translated by Atsuo TSURUOKA.] New York: John Day Co. 189p. No refs. LCCN:58-6350. [*Kōgōsama*. English.]

A biography of the wife of Emporor Hirohito. Not designed as a scholarly work, but the author did have access to some members of the Imperial Household for interviews, as well as to "certain [but undefined] documents." Written by a novelist in the form of fiction, it would be difficult to separate "poetic license" from fact using this source, but it does present a story of a woman and her family struggling to fill the dual roles of public personality and private individual. [See also #1449 for background on KOYAMA Itoko.]

1301. MIURA, Shumon. Winter 1989. "Of monarchy and matrimony." *Japan Echo* 14(4):83-84. No refs. ISSN:0388-0435.

A brief essay summarizing qualities sought in a wife for the emperor historically and discussing the changes which have made "love matches" possible for two sons of emperors in the twentieth century.

1302. SIMON, Charlie May. 1960. *The Sun and the Birch; the Story of Crown Prince Akihito and Crown Princess Michiko.* New York: Dutton. 192p. No refs. LCCN:60-6014.

A biography for the general reader; much of the material is suppositional. (Akihito became Emperor in 1989.)

1303. TSURUMI, E. Patricia. Oct./Dec. 1982. "The male present versus the female past: Historians and Japan's ancient female emperors." *Bulletin of Concerned Asian Scholars* 14(4):71-75. 21 notes. ISSN:0007-4810.

TSURUMI takes on both Japanese and Western historians of early Japan in this sharp critique of their determination that female emperors held the throne only to ensure succession. Using the *Kojiki* [#5] and *Nihongi* [#7] in a comparable manner, she pulls forth evidence to show that women ruled in their own right, and scolds her colleagues for the amount of "cultural baggage" they carry to their scholarly inquiry.

1304. UEMURA, Seiji. 1977. "The Empress Jingū and her conquest of Silla." *Memoirs of the Research Department of Tōyō Bunko* no.35:75-83. [Also cited as Tōyō Bunko, Tokyo. Kenkyūbu. *Memoirs of . . .*] 13 notes. ISSN:0082-562X.

Examines the evidence for a factual basis to the legend of the Empress Jingu and her expedition to Korea.

1305. WADA, Yashiko. Feb. 1978. "Woman and her power in the Japanese emperor system." *Feminist Japan* no. 4:15-18. [Also cited as 1(4).] 1 note; 1 ref. ISSN:0386-197X.

Based on ancient chronicles, the *Kojiki* [#5] and the *San Kuo Chih* (a Chinese work with a section on Japan), WADA instructs readers about the powerful political and religious roles played by women, especially that of the spiritual medium (shaman).

1306. YONEKURA, Isamu. Jun. 1974. "Himiko, Queen of the Wa: Japan around the middle of the third century." *East* 10(5):43-51. No refs. ISSN:0012-8295.

Describes the reign of Himiko [mid-3rd century C.E.] as portrayed in contemporary Chinese accounts. Notes the scholarly debate as to the location of her government and as to whether she ruled, or supported the rule of her brother, by shamanism. For the general reader.

12

Women During War

1307. BARKER, Rodney. 1985. *The Hiroshima Maidens.* New York: Viking. 240p. Bibl. LCCN:84-29925.

In the mid-1950s, 25 young women from Hiroshima were brought to the United States for plastic surgery. The author was nine, and a host brother to two of them. Now an editor and writer, he presents an account of these women focusing on TASAKA Hiroko, NIIMOTO Shigeko, and MORITA Tohoko.

1308. BRUIN, Janet and Stephen SALAFF. Oct./Dec. 1980. "'Never again!' Women *Hibakusha* in Osaka." *Bulletin of Concerned Asian Scholars* 12(4):20-25. 7 notes. ISSN:0007-4810. [Also published as "Never again: The organization of women atomic bomb victims in Osaka" in *Feminist Studies* 7(1):5-18, Spring 1981. ISSN:0046-3663.]

Describes the formation and work of the Women's Section, Osaka Association of A-bomb Victims. Includes four brief first-person accounts.

1309. *Children of Hiroshima.* 1980. [Tokyo]: Publication Committee for "Children of Hiroshima." 335p. No refs. Index. LCCN:81-173591. [*Gembaku no ko.* English.] [Selections previously published under the title *Children of the A-bomb: Testament of the Boys and Girls of Hiroshima.* Compiled by Arata OSADA. 1959. Tokyo: Uchida Rokakuho Publishing House. LCCN:59-16843.]

A collection of first-hand accounts of the Hiroshima bombing on 6 August 1945 by 105 students (primary school through college-age). Compiled by OSADA Arata, an educator and resident of Hiroshima, six years after the bombing.

1310. CHISOLM, Anne. 1985. *Faces of Hiroshima: A Report.* London: Cape. 182p. Bibl. LCCN:85-21936.

A report on the Hiroshima Maidens, 25 young women who were burned and scarred during the atomic blast, and later brought to the United States for plastic surgery. Based on extensive interviews with the Maidens, their host families, and their doctors in the United States, this book focuses primarily "on what it was like to live on as an involuntary symbol of the world's first experience of nuclear war" and secondarily on the events of the bombing.

1311. COHEN, Jerome B. 1949 [rep. 1973]. *Japan's Economy in War and Reconstruction.* Westport, CT: Greenwood. 504p. Notes. Index. LCCN:73-11851.

COHEN has compiled a thorough description of the economic development of Japan from 1937 to 1949. In his chapter on "Mobilizing Manpower," he provides a brief but detailed account of female labor during World War II (pp. 319-322). Useful statistics.

1312. COUSINS, Norman. 15 Dec. 1956. "Report on a homecoming." *Saturday Review [of Literature]* 39(50):9-12,40-41. No refs. ISSN:0036-4983.

COUSINS reports on the return of the Hiroshima Maidens and on plans to assist other survivors with medical treatment at home.

1313. DAY, Ida. 9 Nov. 1957. "The Maidens at home." *Saturday Review [of Literature]* 40(45):24-25. No refs. ISSN:0036-4983.

Provides a "person-by-person thumbnail account of the Maidens" one year after their return to Hiroshima.

1314. DAY, Ida. 2 Jan. 1960. "Triumph in Tokyo." *Saturday Review [of Literature]* 43(1):24-25. No refs. ISSN:0036-4983.

DAY reports on the status of the Maidens four years after their visit to the United States. She includes coverage of the first Tokyo showing of fashion designer MINOWA Toyoko, one of the "returnees."

1315. HASHIMOTO, Toyomi. 1988. "Hellish years after hellish days." In: GIOSEFFI, Daniela, ed. 1988. *Women on War: Essential Voices for the Nuclear Age*. New York: Simon and Schuster, pp. 211-216. No refs. LCCN:88-2391.

A survivor of the bombing of Nagasaki relates her family's experiences that day and details the medical problems she and her family have had since that time.

1316. HATANO, Isoko. 1962. *Mother and Son: The War Time Correspondence of Isoko and Ichiro Hatano*. Boston: Houghton-Mifflin. 195p. No refs. LCCN:62-8141. [*L'Enfant d'Hiroshima*. English.]

The letters of a mother and son beginning 10 May 1944 when the son was in junior high school in Tokyo and continuing through 20 February 1948. The letters reflect the wartime experiences of a family who suffer deprivations but not disasters, and provide a view of a mother's attitudes toward raising her eldest son.

1317. HAVENS, Thomas R.H. 1975. "Women and war in Japan, 1937-45." *American Historical Review* 80(4):913-934. 78 refs. ISSN:0002-8762.

In this detailed portrayal of women's lives during World War II, HAVENS both describes their day-to-day experiences and considers the long-term effects of the war on their traditional roles.

1318. HAVENS, Thomas R.H. 1978. *Valley of Darkness: The Japanese People and World War II*. New York: Norton. 280p. Notes and bibl. Index. LCCN:77-11115.

Discusses life on the home front during World War II, describing living conditions, the social and political organization of society, working women, marriage and fertility, and evacuation to the countryside.

1319. HERSEY, John. 1985. *Hiroshima: A New Edition with a Final Chapter Written Forty Years After the Explosion*. New York: Knopf. 196p. No refs. LCCN:85-40346.

HERSEY wrote his account of the Hiroshima bombing in 1946. His new chapter, "Aftermath," updates the stories of several survivors, including two women.

1320. *Hibakusha: Survivors of Hiroshima and Nagasaki.* 1986. [Translated by Gaynor SEKIMORI; foreword by George MARSHALL and introduced by Naomi SHOHNO.] Tokyo: Kōsei Publishing Co. 206p. No refs. LCCN:87-173433.

Includes first-hand accounts of the atomic bombings by survivors, medical personnel and other relief workers, both male and female.

1321. ICHIKAWA, Fusaye. Jan. 1940. "Problems confronting the women's movement today." *Japanese Women* 3(1):1. No refs. ISSN:0388-1369.

Summarizes the state of the women's movement in war-time Japan, and decries the lack of female leadership in women's organizations.

1322. *Japan at War.* 1980. Alexandria, VA: Time-Life Books. 208p. Bibl. Index. LCCN:80-24612.

Pages 112-121 contain a photographic essay, "Women's Work," with photographs of welders, schoolgirl seamstresses, and other female laborers. The very brief text comments on the changes in attitudes towards length of day and safety regulations. Other pictures of women scattered throughout the work.

1323. KANDA, Mikio, ed. 1989. *Widows of Hiroshima: The Life Stories of 19 Peasant Wives.* [Translated by Taeko MIDORIKAWA.] New York: St. Martin's Press. 183p. LCCN:88-18832. [*Genbaku ni otto o ubawarete.* English.]

Presents first-hand accounts of 19 women from Kawauchi Nukui, near Hiroshima. All lost spouses and children during the atomic bomb attack and they relate their life stories prior to, during, and after 6 August 1945.

1324. KANEKO, Shigeri. Jul. 1939. "Advisers for the soldiers' families." *Japanese Women* 2(4):3. No refs. ISSN:0388-1369.

Reports on the appointment of women to the Consultation Bureau for the Soldiers' Families to visit "families of soldiers at the front, listening to their complaints . . . [as well as] . . . giving guidance in their daily life." Notes that this is one case "in which women were appointed for responsible posts as a result of the current Sino-Japanese conflict."

1325. LIFTON, Betty Jean. 1985. *A Place Called Hiroshima.* Tokyo: Kodansha. 151p. No refs. LCCN:84-48127.

A photo-essay of Hiroshima including brief biographical sketches of women survivors. Thought-provoking, but probably more useful as a supplement to in-depth reports.

1326. MARTIN, Jo Nobuko. 1984. *A Princess Lily of the Ryukyus.* Tokyo: Shin Nippon Kyōiku Tōsho Co. 382p. No refs. LCCN:89-105595.

An autobiographical novel of the American invasion of Okinawa. Princess Lilies were students of the Himeyuri School who were organized as a volunteer nursing corps. MARTIN was a member of the corps; her novel is interspersed with flashbacks to her prewar childhood in Okinawa.

1327. MIYAO, Tsuyoshi. Jul. 1939. "Our women in the emergency." *Contemporary Japan* 8(5):643-650. No refs. ISSN:0388-0214.

Describes "activities on the home front" undertaken by various women's groups during the war in China.

1328. MOLONY, Barbara. 1980. "Women and wartime employment: A cross-cultural analysis of public policy in time of crisis." *Feminist International* no.2:79-82. 20 notes. ISSN:0388-371X.

Compares the extent to which Great Britain and the United States, and Germany and Japan, made use of their respective female labor forces during World War II.

1329. NAEVE, Virginia, ed. 1964. *Friends of the Hibakusha.* Denver: A. Swallow [for the World Peace Mission]. 318p. No refs. LCCN:64-18749.

A collection of primary materials relating to the *hibakusha* [survivors of atomic bombings] and to peace efforts stemming from the bombing's aftermath.

1330. "On the wrong side." Winter 1984. *Connexion* (Winter 1984):22-23. No refs. ISSN:0886-7062.

A compact but pithy article on women during World War II. Discusses the women's movement, the use of women in the labor force, and the involvement of women in political associations by the government. The article ends by stating that the changes were "neither progress [n]or liberation," and the same women who believed them so, also considered themselves as victims of the war rather than both victims and aggressors.

1331. SANO, Noriko. 1980. "Japanese women's movements during World War II." [Translated by Nancy ANDREW.] *Feminist International* no.2:77-78. 3 notes. ISSN:0388-371X.

SANO briefly describes the transition of women's rights leaders to supporters of the war effort during the late 1930s in their desire to forward their cause. She reminds women that "as long as they cannot check aggression on the part of their own nation, as long as they give tacit approval, women are as guilty as men."

1332. SELDEN, Kyoko. Jul./Sep. 1986. "Children of Nagasaki." *Bulletin of Concerned Asian Scholars* 18(3):32-38. 1 note. ISSN:0007-4810.

Includes first-accounts by four girls, ages four, five, six and eleven at the time of the bombing.

1333. "The Sino-Japanese Incident and the activities of Japanese women." Jan. 1938. *Japanese Women* 1(1):3. No refs. ISSN:0388-1369.

Comments on the efforts of the League of Japanese Women's Organizations during the war in China. Areas of interest include "spiritual mobilization," women and labor, child welfare, and health.

1334. SMETHURST, Richard J. 1978. "The army, youth, and women." In: BEAUCHAMP, Edward R., ed. *Learning to be Japanese: Selected Readings on Japanese Society and Education.* Hamden, CT: Linnet Books, pp. 137-166. Notes. LCCN:77-25119. [Item also appears in SMETHURST, Richard J. 1974. *A Social Basis for Prewar Japanese Militarism.* Berkeley: University of California Press, p. 22-49. LCCN:73-84385.]

Describes the army's efforts to "educate [women] in military values" through creation of a women's organization, the Greater Japan National Defense Association, in 1932. The politics of its survival and competition with the Patriotic Women's Association is also outlined.

1335. SWAIN, David L. Winter 1988. "Portrait of a peacemaker (11): Akizuki Sugako." *Japan Christian Quarterly* 54(1):48-50. No refs. ISSN:0021-4361.

AKIZUKI Sugako, a nurse working during the Nagasaki bombing, describes her experiences from 9 August 1945 through September of that year.

1336. WATANABE, Tadao. 14 Jul. 1956. "The Maidens come home." *Saturday Review [of Literature]* 39(28):20. No refs. ISSN:0036-4983.

The mayor of Hiroshima briefly reports on the homecoming ceremonies for the Hiroshima Maidens.

1337. WIEGAND, Karl L. 1982. "Japan: Cautious utilization." In: GOLDMAN, Nancy Loring, ed. *Female Soldiers—Combatants or Non-Combatants?* Westport, CT: Greenwood, pp. 179-188. Notes. LCCN:81-13318. (*Contributions in Women's Studies*, no. 33; ISSN 0147-104X.)

WIEGAND (former United States Air Force attaché to the American Embassy in Tokyo) first discusses women's gains in equality since 1946 and provides an overview of Japan's defense forces during World War II. He then presents statistics and examples to support the view that "women have achieved equality of opportunity for training, for pay, and for advancement (to the grade of lieutenant colonel or commander)." A useful look at a seldom discussed topic.

1338. *Women Against War: Personal Accounts of 40 Japanese Women.* [Compiled by the Women's Division of Sōka Gakkai; introduced by Richard MINEAR; translated by Richard L. GAGE.] 1986. Tokyo: Kodansha International. 247p. No refs. LCCN:86-45068.

With the aim of clarifying and underlining the absolute horror of war for those too young to remember, these 40 women provide firsthand accounts of their war and post-war experiences, ranging from the bombing of Hiroshima and deprivation in the countryside to the desperation involved in becoming a prostitute to survive as an individual (and often to enable a family's survival). Many of the women have become converts to Sōka Gakkai (a "new" Buddhist sect) and some refer to it in their accounts. However, this volume does not contain proselytizing, but simply eloquent appeals for peace.

1339. "The Women's Conference on Current Problems." May 1938. *Japanese Women* 1(3):3. No refs. ISSN:0388-1369.

Lists the seven resolutions passed at the 14 March 1938 Conference on Current Problems (topics include consumption, education, families of soldiers at the front, etc.)

1340. YAVENDITTI, Michael J. Apr./Jul. 1982. "The Hiroshima Maidens and American benevolence in the 1950s." *Mid-America* 64(2):21-39. 80 notes. ISSN:0026-2927.

Analyzes American intentions behind the project initiated by Norman COUSINS to bring 25 female survivors from Hiroshima to the United States for plastic surgery. Includes information on the women's reactions and experiences on their return, and on attitudes toward the project in Japan. While BARKER [#1307] provides a more personal account, YAVENDITTI is useful for his scholarly approach and portrayal of the negative aspects. His bibliography includes additional items on the experiences of the women in the United States (beyond the scope of this bibliography).

1341. YUKIHIRO, Fusako. Nov. 1962. "Mother's memoirs of an atomic bomb victim." [Translated by Miyo OIWA.] *Contemporary Japan* 27:298-310. No refs. ISSN:0388-0214.

From 1951-1954, a young girl suffered from "atomic bomb disease." This is a mother's recounting of the disease and of her daughter's hopes to continue her schooling. The daughter had been four years old when she accompanied her mother through Hiroshima as her mother searched for her second son.

WOMEN AS ARTISTS, PERFORMERS AND WRITERS

13

Women as Artists
and Performers

Women in the Visual Arts

1342. ADDISS, Stephen. 1990. "The three women of Gion." In: WEIDNER, Marsha, ed. 1990. *Flowering in the Shadows: Women in the History of Chinese and Japanese Painting*. Honolulu: University of Hawaii Press, pp. 241-263. 26 notes. LCCN:90-11001.

Describes the artistic careers of three women from the Gion district of Kyoto: Kaji (dates unknown), her daughter Yuri (1694-1764) and her granddaughter IKE Gyokuran (1727/28-1784), and of Gyokuran's husband, IKE Taiga. While operating a teahouse to maintain a livelihood, these women became famous for their *waka* poetry and their calligraphy; Gyokuran was also an accomplished *nanga* artist. Samples of their poetry, calligraphy and paintings are included.

1343. AKIYAMA, Terakazu. 1990. "Women painters in the Heian Court." [Translated and adapted by Maribeth GRAYBILL.] In: WEIDNER, Marsha, ed. 1990. *Flowering in the Shadows: Women in the History of Chinese and Japanese Painting*. Honolulu: University of Hawaii Press, pp. 159-184. 52 notes. LCCN:90-11001.

Argues that women were actively involved in painting in the "public arena" by the Insei period, discusses in detail works of Tosa no Tsubone and of Kii no Tsubone, and provides evidence of possible female "authorship" of the *Hokekyō sasshi* underdrawings and the illustrated *Tale of Genji*, both from the first half of the twelfth century.

1344. ANTON, Karen Hill. Feb. 1988. "Portrait of an artist." *PHP Intersect* (Feb. 1988):28-30. No refs. ISSN:0910-4607.

A biographical sketch of YANAGISAWA Noriko, a printmaker and wife of a Diet member.

1345. BROCK, Karen L. 1990. "Chinese maiden, Silla monk: Zenmyō and her thirteenth-century audience." In: WEIDNER, Marsha, ed. 1990. *Flowering in the Shadows: Women in the History of Chinese and Japanese Painting*. Honolulu: University of Hawaii Press, pp. 185-218. 60 notes. LCCN:90-11001.

Discusses the picture scrolls, *Tales of Gishō and Gangyō* [*Legends of the Kegon Sect* or *Lives of the Founders of the Kegon Sect*] and their possible use as instruction materials for the nuns of Zenmyōji.

1346. "Career girl: An expert on pottery." 1964. *East* 1(4):59. No refs. ISSN:0012-8295.

A very brief profile of ŌZEKI Noriko, a 21-year-old expert on pottery with Wakō Department Store, who "surprised her father by taking a job . . ." after graduating from the Bunka Dressmaking College.

1347. "Daughter, disciple . . . successor?" 1982. *Japan Pictorial* 5(1):14-16. No refs. ISSN:0388-6115.

YAMAGUCHI Setsuko, the only child of master potter Jotetsu of Akatsu, is studying the creation of tea ceremony utensils with her father in hopes of continuing the family tradition.

1348. *An Exhibition of Women Artists from Japan.* [Introduction by Michiko MIYAMOTO, guest curator.] 1978. New York: Publishing Center for Cultural Resources, A.I.R. Gallery. 24p. No refs.

A catalogue of works by six contemporary women artists: HORIUCHI Toshiko (fiber), YAMADA Momoko (rice paper), NIMURA Yūko (silk screen), KOMOTO Masa (silk screen), TADA Etsuko (canvas), and MISHIMA Kimiyo (ceramics and silk screen).

1349. FISTER, Pat. 1988. *Japanese Women Artists, 1600-1900.* [With a guest essay by Fumiko YAMAMOTO.] Lawrence: Spencer Museum of Art, University of Kansas. 197p. Bibl. Index. LCCN:87-63129.

An exhibition catalogue documenting a collection of Japanese women artists' work. Provides biographical data on the artists and provides contexts for, and interpretations of, their work. Probably the most complete English-language treatment of this group.

1350. FISTER, Patricia. 1990. "The life and art of Chō Kōran." In: WEIDNER, Marsha, ed. 1990. *Flowering in the Shadows: Women in the History of Chinese and Japanese Painting.* Honolulu: University of Hawaii Press, pp. 265-293. 55 notes. LCCN:90-11001.

In this biography of CHŌ Kōran (1804-1879), FISTER focuses on her poetry and painting as well as on her life with her poet husband, YANAGAWA Seigan. Also describes her relationships with other poets of the times and her political activities.

1351. FISTER, Patricia. 1990. "Women artists in traditional Japan." In: WEIDNER, Marsha, ed. 1990. *Flowering in the Shadows: Women in the History of Chinese and Japanese Painting.* Honolulu: University of Hawaii Press, pp. 219-240. 34 notes. LCCN:90-11001.

Focuses on the Edo and early Meiji periods, discussing "social backgrounds, artistic activities, and patronage of women artists." Includes materials on many individual women.

1352. "Interview with Eiko Ishioka, illustrator." Feb. 1978. *Feminist Japan* no. 4:30-33 [falls between pp. 58 & 59.] [Also cited as 1(4).] No refs. ISSN:0386-197X.

ISHIOKA Eiko is a designer who made her mark with a poster for a cosmetics firm in the 1960s which presented a new image of the Japanese woman. She discusses that advertisement campaign and her various pursuits since.

1353. MATSUBARA, Hiroshi. Dec. 1976. "Women of gold." *East* 13(1/2):13-18. No refs. ISSN:0012-8295.

Describes the production of gold leaf by the "traditionally calm women" of Kanazawa. More emphasis is placed on the technique than on the women.

1354. MATSUBARA, Hiroshi. Aug. 1977. "Women of the braided hats." *East* 13(9/10):75-82. No refs. ISSN:0012-8295.

Profiles FUSA Kaneko, a braider of hats called *botchi-gasa*.

1355. MATSUBARA, Hiroshi. Apr. 1977. "Women who make pottery." *East* 13(5/6):75-81. No refs. ISSN:0012-8295.

Briefly introduces MANO Shunkō who "incises" her pottery by carving designs on the clay before firing.

1356. MATSUBARA, Hiroshi. Jun. 1977. "Women tie-dyers." *East* 13(7/8):73-78. No refs. ISSN:0012-8295.

Explains the techniques of the female tie-dyers of Arimatsu.

1357. MATSUBARA, Hiroshi. Dec. 1977. "Women who weave." *East* 14(1/2):69-75. No refs. ISSN:0012-8295.

Focuses on the production of *ramie* cloth on traditional *izari-bata* looms. Brief and for the general reader.

1358. MATSUBARA, Hiroshi. Aug. 1978. "Women who reel silk." *East* 14(9/10):77-82. No refs. ISSN:0012-8295.

FURUYA Sadano briefly explains her techniques for reeling silk.

1359. MATSUBARA, Hiroshi. Oct. 1978. "Women who mold clay." *East* 14(11/12):7-10. No refs. ISSN:0012-8295.

In his description of pottery from the town of Shigaraki, MATSUBARA introduces YAMAMOTO Fumi, a 73-year-old woman who has had a lifelong involvement in pottery production.

1360. MURRAY, Geoffrey. Mar. 1978. "Akiko Taniguchi—Carving out a niche for herself." *PHP* 9(3):37-44. No refs. ISSN:0030-798X.

Profiles TANIGUCHI Akiko, one of ten professional *noh* mask-carvers and the only woman.

1361. O'BRIEN, Rodney. Jul. 1985. "Dream weaver: Kei Tsuji." *PHP Intersect* (Jul. 1985):22-23. No refs. ISSN:0910-4607.

Describes the work of TSUJI Kei, a weaver of rayon, who expresses her dream sequences through her weaving.

1362. O'BRIEN, Rodney. Sep. 1985. "Art soft: Yuki Katsura." *PHP Intersect* (Sep. 1985):38-39. No refs. ISSN:0910-4607.

Briefly describes the soft sculpture art of KATSURA Yuki (age 72).

1363. O'BRIEN, Rodney. Feb. 1987. "Rite of spring: Yayoi Kusama." *PHP Intersect* (Feb. 1987):22-23. No refs. ISSN:0910-4607.

Describes the wrapping art of KUSAMA Yayoi, contrasting her with Christo, an American who also practices the art of wrapping.

1364. O'BRIEN, Rodney. May 1987. "In character: Kaoru Hirabayashi." *PHP Intersect* (May 1987):22-23. No refs. ISSN:0910-4607.

Describes the work of HIRABAYASHI Kaoru, who uses *kanji* [Chinese characters] and *kana* [the Japanese syllabary] within her brush pictures and relief sculptures.

1365. O'BRIEN, Rodney. Jun. 1987. "A woman on women: Takeko Suzuki." *PHP Intersect* (Jun. 1987):30-31. No refs. ISSN:0910-4607.

Describes the work of SUZUKI Takeko, an artist who focuses on "punishingly frank" portrayals of femininity.

1366. O'BRIEN, Rodney. Aug. 1987. "Art in the TV age: Naoko Yasuda." *PHP Intersect* (Aug. 1987):38-39. No refs. ISSN:0910-4607.

A brief profile of YASUDA Naoko, a contemporary painter and illustrator.

1367. O'BRIEN, Rodney. Jan. 1988. "Kimono collage: Keiko Matsumoto." *PHP Intersect* (Jan. 1988):18-19. No refs. ISSN:0910-4607.

Notes from an exhibition by MATSUMOTO Keiko who combines paint and fabric to create representations of kimono.

1368. O'BRIEN, Rodney. Feb. 1988. "Seeing the light: Yumiko Shiozaki." *PHP Intersect* (Feb. 1988):18-19. No refs. ISSN:0910-4607.

Reports on an exhibition of three dimensional works by SHIOZAKI Yumiko which incorporate color, video, and light.

1369. SMOULER, Alfred. Sep. 1978. "Keiko Hida—Originator of 'grass pictures.'" *PHP* 9(9):37-44. No refs. ISSN:0030-798X.

Explains the art of *kusae* [collage/paper paintings] originated by HIDA Keiko and interviews the artist about her work.

1370. TOKUSHIGE, Emiko. 1990. "Emiko Tokushige." In: FOX, Howard N. 1990. *A Primal Spirit: Ten Contemporary Japanese Sculptors.* Los Angeles: Los Angeles County Museum of Art, pp. 88-95, 132. Bibl. LCCN:90-5521.

An autobiographical sketch in an exhibition catalog detailing TOKUSHIGE's introduction to weaving and fiber art and describing her work for this exhibition. Includes photographs of her pieces, and on p. 132, a chronology of her exhibits and a bibliography.

1371. WEIDNER, Marsha. 1990. "Introduction: Images and realities." In: WEIDNER, Marsha, ed. 1990. *Flowering in the Shadows: Women in the History of Chinese and Japanese Painting.* Honolulu: University of Hawaii Press, pp. 1-24. 49 notes. LCCN:90-11001.

A general discussion of women artists in China and Japan. For entry numbers of items introduced see title index under *Flowering in the Shadows*.

Dancers

1372. BASS, Susan. Dec. 1983. "Dance of life." *PHP* 14(12):68-74. No refs. ISSN:0030-798X.

Profiles HATANO Emi, a modern dancer and an associate professor of Modern Dance at Nihon University. Describes three of her compositions and her life philosophy.

1373. BOOTH, Alan. Aug. 1981. "Yasuko Nagamine—¡Flamenco!" *PHP* 12(8):38-47. No refs. ISSN:0030-798X.

Describes the life and work of NAGAMINE Yasuko, a trained flamenco dancer, who has combined flamenco, modern ballet, and *kabuki* dance in a "fiery" performance of "Dōjōji."

1374. BOOTH, Alan. Feb. 1984. "Mamako the mime." *PHP* 15(2):50-60. No refs. ISSN:0030-798X.

Describes the life and work of YONEYAMA Mamako, "Japan's leading mime artist," including her piece, "The Search for a Bull."

1375. KEENE, Donald. 1971. "Hanako." In: KEENE, Donald. *Landscapes and Portraits: Appreciations of Japanese Culture.* Tokyo: Kodansha, pp. 250-258. Bibl. LCCN:75-135144.

In a section titled "Some Japanese Eccentrics," KEENE profiles the career of ŌTA Hisa, a young entertainer "discovered" by L. Fuller, an American dancer who became her backer and patron. Under her stage name, Hanako, she performed from 1901-1916 to rave reviews in Europe and New York but to more cautious critiques in Des Moines.

1376. O'BRIEN, Rodney. Aug. 1988. "Soul movement: Hisako Horikawa." *PHP Intersect* (Aug. 1988):26-27. No refs. ISSN:0910-4607.

A review of a dance performance by HORIKAWA Hisako in which she dances "in the language of the spirit more than of the body," with only high-heeled shoes and chopsticks for a costume and by restricting her movements to a very small ramp.

1377. ŌYAMA, Shigeo. Jan./Mar. 1986. "Kanzaki En, classical dancer." *Japan Quarterly* 33(1):59-62. No refs. ISSN:0021-4590.

Discusses the traditional dance style of *jiuta mai*, and KANZAKI En, a younger dancer (b. 1953) who is carrying on the tradition.

1378. "Yōko Morishita: Born to the ballet." 1982. *Japan Pictorial* 5(1):38-39. No refs. ISSN:0388-6115.

A brief profile of Japan's "principal prima."

1379. "A young girl who devotes herself to traditional Japanese dancing." Dec. 1974. *East* 10(10):22-26. No refs. ISSN:0012-8295.

A profile of KOITO Kayoko (stage name YOSHIMURA Kakō), a young woman who is a student in the Yoshimura school of traditional dance.

Musicians

1380. COLE, Wendy. Sep. 1990. "Sultry Seiko: A Japanese star is repackaged for America." *Intersect* 6(9):14-16. ISSN:0910-4607.

Describes the attempt of the former pop icon with "wholesome good looks, fetching smile, and perky singing style" to transition into a vocalist with a "sexy whisper" in her voice for the United States music video market.

1381. "Japan's prizewinning percussionist: Sumie Yoshihara." 1981. *Japan Pictorial* 4(4):38-39. No refs. ISSN:0388-6115.

A brief profile of an often honored female percussionist who focuses on "contemporary" music.

1382. "Life with the tsuzumi." Aug./Sept. 1967. *East* 3(5):6-12. No refs. ISSN:0012-8295.

Breaking with a 300-year tradition, TANAKA Denzaemon, master of the *tsuzumi* [hand drum], has chosen his daughter to succeed him both as "master" of his school and also as his replacement in the orchestra at the Kabuki theater, traditionally closed to women.

1383. "Miss Keiko Kuyama: A first in symphonic conducting." 1970. *Japan* 1970(4):21-24. No refs. LCCN:86-648185.

A brief profile; describes KUYAMA's background, training, and personal life.

1384. MURRAY, Geoffrey. Mar. 1975. "Meiko Miyazawa—Rebel Japanese pianist." *PHP* 6(3):35-42. No refs. ISSN:0030-798X.

Interviews MIYAZAWA Meiko a young, outspoken, and thoughtful pianist about her career and outlook on life.

1385. "The passing of a queen." Sep./Oct. 1989. *East* 25(3):57. No refs. ISSN:0012-8295.

An obituary for MISORA Hibari, "queen of Japanese pop music."

1386. SAITŌ, Shinji. Oct./Dec. 1984. "Hayashi Yasuko." *Japan Quarterly* 31(4):416-417. No refs. ISSN:0021-4590.

Briefly profiles HAYASHI Yasuko, an operatic "prima donna."

1387. "Young lady and her piano." 1968. *Japan* 1968(2):20-23. No refs. LCCN:86-648185.

Profiles SAITŌ Fumie, a worker at Nippon Gakki Co., Ltd., who installs piano keyboards.

Takarazuka Performers

1388. BERLIN, Zeke. 10 May 1981. "Takarazuka: A romantic world." *Look Japan* 27(302):8-9. No refs. ISSN:0456-5339.

BERLIN provides a general description of Takarazuka Kageki [Takarazuka Revue Company]. This all-female troupe performs both classical *kabuki*-style plays and modern musical extravaganzas to sellout crowds worldwide.

1389. BRAU, Lorie. Winter 1990. "The women's theatre of Takarazuka." *TDR: The Drama Review* 34(4):79-95. 20 refs. ISSN:0012-5962.

A detailed description of the history, workings and appeal of the all-female theater company.

1390. CHERRY, Kittredge. Sep. 1984. "Reflections of a showgirl." *PHP* 15(9):48-58. No refs. ISSN:0030-798X.

Interviews KITAGAWA Emiko (stage name KIYOKAWA Hayami), a retired Takarazuka dancer, and discusses the history and appeal of the all-female revue company.

1391. "Fifty years of glory." Apr./May 1964. *East* 1(1):64-67. No refs. ISSN:0012-8295.

A brief history of the All Girls' Operetta Troupe, Takarazuka, begun in 1913 by a railroad company to attract visitors to a spa using their railway line. Now world renowned, it is described as a "treasure-box of women talents."

1392. MOCHIZUKI, Mamoru. 1959 [rep. 1973]. "Cultural aspects of Japanese girls' opera." In: Shiso no Kagaku Kenkyūkai. *Japanese Popular Culture.* [Translated and edited by Hidetoshi KATŌ.] Westport, CT: Greenwood, pp. 165-174. No refs. LCCN:73-1434.

An introduction to, and brief history of, the Takarazuka. MOCHIZUKI describes it as "escapist entertainment . . . performed by girls for girls." Notes the homosexual nature of the infatuation of high school fans for women stars but describes it as "safe and innocuous" and "something like the measles . . . which will soon pass away."

1393. MURRAY, Geoffrey. Feb. 1977. "Offstage with Jun Anna: Takarazuka star." *PHP* 8(2):37-45. No refs. ISSN:0030-798X.

Describes the regimen of the Takarazuka all-girl revue school and company and profiles ANNA Jun (stage name Nimaime), who plays male roles in the extravaganzas performed.

1394. ROBERTSON, Jennifer. 1989. "Butch and femme on and off the Takarazuka stage: Gender, sexuality and social organization in Japan." *Working Paper* [*on Women in International Development*] no. 181. 13p. Bibl. ISSN:0888-5354.

ROBERTSON explores concepts of sex, gender and sexuality within the context of the all-female Takarazuka Revue, focusing especially on its earlier years (1920-1940). Also explores the company's influence on the lesbian subculture in Japan. Includes detailed discussion of various Japanese terms for males, females and lesbians.

1395. ROBERTSON, Jennifer. Summer 1989. "Gender-bending in paradise: Doing "female" and "male" in Japan." *Genders* no. 5:50-69. 73 notes. ISSN:0894-9832.

A scholarly analysis of gender using the Takarazuka Revue (an all-female theater company founded in 1914) as a "focal context." ROBERTSON explores the "nature of the relationship between sex, gender, and sexuality on and off the Takarazuka stage."

1396. "Viva the Takarazuka!" Sep./Oct. 1988. *East* 24(3):24-25. No refs. ISSN:0012-8295.

A brief introduction to the Takarazuka Revue Company, composed entirely of women. The company was founded in 1914 and performs musical versions of classic works.

Women in Theater

1397. BRODERICK, Catherine. 1980. "Kabuki by foreigners: In the spirit of the feminine kabuki tradition." *Feminist International* no.2:73-76. No refs. ISSN:0388-371X.

BRODERICK briefly relates the origins of *kabuki* theater (created and performed by women in its early years) and tells of the work of UNNO Mitsuko who directs *kabuki* productions by male and female non-Japanese high school students.

1398. BUNCH, Ralph and Mutsuko MOTOYAMA. Jan./Apr. 1987. "Women, tradition and politics in Japanese classical theatre." *Journal of Asian and African Studies* 22(1/2):80-86. 23 notes. ISSN:0021-9096.

BUNCH provides an overview of the historical tradition of males only in *kabuki* and *nō* theater. Notes that while *kabuki* was developed by women, female participation was banned later to protect public morality. Calls for the reinstatement of women in classical theater to "enable its survival as living theater . . . rather than as a theater of artifact."

1399. HIGUCHI, Chiyoko. Jul./Aug. 1971. "My stage before family, love, death: Kabuki is born on the banks of the Kamo." *East* 7(7):18-23. No refs. ISSN:0012-8295.

A profile of Okuni (b. 1571), the woman who reputedly created and starred in *kabuki* theater.

1400. JOHNSON, Irmgard. Spring 1977. "Women in the man's world of Noh." *Journal of Asian Affairs* 2(1):1-8. 4 refs. ISSN:0364-877X.

A detailed account of women's contribution to, and participation in, the *nō* theater. JOHNSON makes the point that "the contribution of women to the maintenance, stability, and potential growth of the total Nō world is all-pervasive . . . ."

1401. JOHNSON, Irmgard. Apr. 1977. "Woman shokubun in the man's world of Nō." *East* 13(5/6):86-90. 1 note. ISSN:0012-8295.

An introduction to the role of women in *nō* theater for a general audience.

1402. POWELL, Brian. 1975. "Matsui Sumako: Actress and woman." In: BEASLEY, William G., ed. *Modern Japan: Aspects of History, Literature and Society.* Berkeley: University of California Press, pp. 135-146. Notes. LCCN:74-29802.

MATSUI Sumako (stage name of KOBAYASHI Masako) was one of Japan's first modern professional actresses and played the lead in both "A Doll's House" (1911) and "Die Heimat" (1912). Both plays provoked discussions of women's rights in Japan. POWELL describes her as one who "set a positive standard by which to measure [one's own] views on women, and she is therefore not without importance in the shaping of popular attitudes in modern Japan."

Women in Television and Film

1403. BIRNBAUM, Phyllis. 5 Nov. 1990. "The odor of pickled radishes." *New Yorker* 66(38):53-56,60-61,63-66,95-112. No refs. ISSN:0028-792X.

A lengthy and detailed profile of TAKAHIME Hideko, an accomplished acctress whose first role was in 1929 at the age of five. Includes excerpts of an interview and of her writings, and details about her films.

1404. "The girl next-door." 1979. *Japan Pictorial* 2(1):21-25. No refs. ISSN:0388-6115.

A profile of ŌTAKE Shinobu who has popular appeal as "the girl-next-door actress." At the time of the article she was 21 and newly famous.

1405. KATŌ, Kōichi. Jan-Mar 1987. "Prime time for schoolgirl amateurs." *Japan Quarterly* 34(1):89-92. No refs. ISSN:0021-4590.

Discusses the phenomenon of *o-nyanko* [kitties], high school girls chosen for their "ordinariness" to appear as "singers, dancers, hosts or heroines in dramas" on the immensely popular television entertainment show, "Yūyake Nyannyan" ("Sunset Kitties").

1406. MELLEN, Joan. [1975.] *Voices from the Japanese Cinema.* New York: Liverright. 295p. No refs. Index. LCCN:74-28197.

In a collection of interviews with persons in Japanese cinema, MELLEN (a film critic) includes discussions with Mme. KAWAKITA Kashiko ("the grand persona" of Japanese film), ASAKAWA Setsu (a set designer), and HIDARI Sachiko (an actress).

1407. "A visit with a young actress." Oct./Nov. 1967. East 3(6):22-25. No refs. ISSN:0012-8295.

A cursory introduction to IDE Mizue, a 20-year-old actress.

1408. YAMASHITA, Katsutoshi. Apr./Jun. 1983. "Pure, sweet and slightly dangerous—Japanese actresses." *Japan Quarterly* 30(2):169-172. No refs. ISSN:0021-4590.

YAMASHITA asserts that to be an actress in Japan, one must be "clean, pure, unsophisticated" in appearance and have "some sort of failure in her private life." He goes on to provide brief profiles of TOAKA Yukiyo, MATSUZATA Keiko, TAICHI Kiwako, and ŌTANI Naoko.

14

Modern Prose Writers: Fiction, Drama, Essays

Anthologies of Modern Prose

1409. ARKIN, Marian and Barbara SHOLLAR. 1989. *Longman Anthology of World Literature by Women, 1875-1975*. White Plains, NY: Longman, Inc. 1274p. Bibl. Index. LCCN:88-8274.

Contains both fiction and poetry, including short stories by HIGUCHI Ichiyō, MIYAMOTO Yuriko and TSUSHIMA Yūko. [Poetry listings are in the poetry chapter.]

1410. APOSTOLOU, John L. and Martin H. GREENBERG, eds. 1987. *Murder in Japan: Japanese Stories of Crime and Detection*. New York: Dembner Books, 224p. LCCN:86-29121.

Fourteen stories about murder, mostly from the modern (male) Japanese literature canon but including a few by professional mystery writers (only one a woman, NATSUKI Shizuko). Introduction by APOSTOLOU and brief biographical notes.

1411. BIRNBAUM, Phyllis, compiler and translator. 1982. *Rabbits, Crabs, etc.—Stories by Japanese Women*. Honolulu: University of Hawaii Press. 147p. LCCN:82-8365.

Six important stories written between 1937 and 1976 (three from the 1970s) by six women, with a short preface and brief literary biographical introductions. A miscellaneous selection of fiction by women who convey in common, says BIRNBAUM, "a sense of the world's unfairness by speaking for themselves rather than for the general condition of their sisters." (p. ix) [See ENCHI Fumiko, KANAI Mieko, KŌNO Taeko, OKAMOTO Kanoko, SONO Ayako and UNO Chiyo.]

1412. DUNLOP, Lane, compiler and translator. 1986. *A Late Chrysanthemum: Twenty-one Stories from the Japanese*. San Francisco: North Point. 178p. LCCN:85-72979.

Includes only one story by a woman, HAYASHI Fumiko's "A Late Chrysanthemum."

1413. GENKAWA, Tomoyoshi and Bernard SUSSER. 1989. *The Kyoto Collection: Stories from the Japanese*. Osaka: Nihei-sha. 197p. LCCN:90-167473.

Called the Kyoto collection because the translators worked there, this small anthology of seven stories includes two by women: ŌBA Minako and NIKI Etsuko, who is not otherwise represented below.

1414. GESSEL, Van C. and Tomone MATSUMOTO, eds. 1985. *The Shōwa Anthology: Modern Japanese Short Stories, Vol. 2.* Tokyo: Kodansha. 210p. Bibl. LCCN:86-175482.

A splendid anthology whose second volume includes six difficult but rewarding stories written between 1961 and 1982 by some of the best women writing fiction in Japan today. Translations range from quite good to superb. Brief literary-biographical introductions with a bibliography of works available in English translation included for each of the authors. [See KANAI Mieko, KŌNO Taeko, KURAHASHI Yumiko, ŌBA Minako, SHIBAKI Yoshiko and TSUSHIMA Yūko.]

1415. GLUCK, Jay, ed. 1965. *Ukiyo: Stories of "The Floating World" of Postwar Japan.* New York: Vanguard Press. 255p. LCCN:63-21851.

An early anthology of writings from the "drifting decade after the end of the war," beginning with the Imperial Rescript announcing Japan's surrender and including entries by military and civilian "amateur diarists" (one a woman) and some pieces written orginally in English. Long, personal introduction by GLUCK provides cultural and historical background for the uninitiated, starting with *The Tale of Genji.* GLUCK is concerned mainly with what is "unwestern" in Japanese literature. Intriguing selection, including otherwise untranslated authors. Five stories and one poetic diary are by women. [See KOYAMA Itoko, MIYAMOTO Yuriko, MIZUKI Yōko, NAKAMOTO Takako, SETO Nanako and SHIBAKI Yoshiko.]

1416. HIBBETT, Howard, ed. 1977. *Contemporary Japanese Literature: An Anthology of Fiction, Film, and Other Writings Since 1945.* New York: Knopf. 468p. LCCN:77-74982.

Includes two brilliant stories and one poem by Japanese women, all from 1971. Eminently readable translations. Brief literary-biographical introductions. [See KŌNO Taeko and KURAHASHI Yumiko.]

1417. Japan Quarterly Editorial Board, compiler. 1960. *Modern Japanese Short Stories.* [Translated by E.G. SEIDENSTICKER, John BESTER, and Ivan MORRIS.] 286p. LCCN:60-53544.

An early anthology of stories that first appeared in translation in the *Japan Quarterly* [volumes 2(1) through 6(3)]. Contains three important stories by women, written between 1948 and 1956, including a brilliant story by KŌDA Aya who is seriously underrepresented in English translation. Literary-biographical notes follow the stories. [See ENCHI Fumiko, HAYASHI Fumiko and KŌDA Aya.]

1418. KEENE, Donald, compiler. 1956. *Modern Japanese Literature: An Anthology.* New York: Grove Press. 440p. LCCN:56-8439.

The seminal anthology of modern Japanese literature in English. Includes two stories by women. [See HIGUCHI Ichiyō and HAYASHI Fumiko.]

1419. LIPPIT, Noriko Mizuta and Kyoko Iriye SELDEN, translators and eds. 1982. *Stories by Contemporary Japanese Women Writers.* Armonk, NY: M.E. Sharpe. 221p. LCCN:82-10270.

An outstanding selection of twelve stories arranged in chronological order from 1938 to 1977. Useful introduction giving historical overview of literature by Japanese women. Includes short literary-biographies with bibliographical information. The translations do not do the stories justice. [See ENCHI Fumiko, HAYASHI Fumiko, HAYASHI Kyōko, HIRABAYASHI Taiko, KŌNO Taeko, MIYAMOTO Yuriko, NOGAMI Yaeko, ŌBA Minako, SATA Ineko, TAKAHASHI Takako, TOMIOKA Taeko and UNO Chiyo.]

1420. MORRIS, Ivan, ed. 1961. *Modern Japanese Stories: An Anthology with Translations by E.G. Seidensticker and Others.* Rutland: Tuttle. 512p. LCCN:61-11971.

Another early anthology, including two stories (1948 and 1950) by women, briefly introduced. Translations pleasant but free. [See HAYASHI Fumiko and HIRABAYASHI Taiko.]

1421. ŌE, Kenzaburō, ed. 1985. *The Crazy Iris and Other Stories of the Atomic Aftermath*. New York: Grove Press. 204p. LCCN:85-71162. [Published in Great Britain as: ŌE, Kenzaburō, ed. 1985. *Fire from the Ashes: Short Stories about Hiroshima and Nagasaki*. London: Readers International. 204p.] [*Nan to mo shirenai mirai ni*. Selections.]

A compelling thematic anthology compiled and introduced by an eminent novelist and critic (literary, social, political). Includes four stories (1953-1977) by women. Brief biographical notes appended. [See HAYASHI Kyōko, ŌTA Yōko, SATA Ineko and TAKANISHI Hiroko.]

1422. QUEEN, Ellery, ed. 1978. *Ellery Queen's Japanese Golden Dozen: The Detective Story World in Japan*. Rutland, VT: C.E. Tuttle. 288p. LCCN:77-83615.

Two of the twelve are by women, both of whose mystery novels have been liberally translated into English. Includes a pleasant introduction to the mystery genre in Japan. [See NATSUKI Shizuko and TOGAWA Masako.]

1423. SAEKI, Shoichi, compiler. 1966. *The Shadow of Sunrise: Selected Stories of Japan and the War, selected and introduced by Shoichi Saeki*. Tokyo: Kodansha. 187p. LCCN:66-25757. [Republished as *The Catch and Other War Stories*. 1981. Rutland, VT: Tuttle. 187p. LCCN:80-84420.

A topical anthology of stories written soon after World War II including one two-page story (1949) by HAYASHI Fumiko.

1424. TANAKA, Yukiko and Elizabeth HANSON, eds. 1982. *This Kind of Woman: Ten Stories by Japanese Women Writers, 1960-1976*. Stanford: Stanford University Press. 287p. LCCN:81-51332.

Important and varied stories in chronological order by ten representative writers. Includes historical introduction and biographical sketches. Translations generally quite readable. [See ENCHI Fumiko, KŌNO Taeko, KURAHASHI Yumiko, ŌBA Minako, SETOUCHI Harumi, TAKAHASHI Takako, TOMIOKA Taeko, TSUMURA Setsuko, TSUSHIMA Yūko and YAMAMOTO Michiko.]

1425. TANAKA, Yukiko. 1987. *To Live and to Write: Selections by Japanese Women Writers, 1913-1938*. Seattle: Seal Press. 225p. LCCN:87-4595.

Works by nine women writing between the two world wars, a time of intellectual excitement, self-confidence, and growing political and feminist consciousness among Japanese women. Includes ten pieces, not all of them fiction and several of them in excerpt, chosen to "reveal important aspects of the authors' lives and focus on the themes of women's creativity and autonomy." (p. xi) Contains short but useful historical introduction and biography and photograph of each writer. [See HAYASHI Fumiko, HIRABAYASHI Taiko, MIYAMOTO Yuriko, NAKAMOTO Takako, NOGAMI Yaeko, OKAMOTO Kanoko, SATA Ineko, TAMURA Toshiko and UNO Chiyo.]

1426. UEDA, Makoto, ed. 1986. *The Mother of Dreams and Other Short Stories: Portrayals of Women in Modern Japanese Fiction*. Tokyo: Kodansha. 279p. LCCN:86-45069.

An interesting anthology of very short fiction organized thematically around common images of women in Japanese fiction: the maiden, the wife, the mistress, the mother, and the working woman. Eight (written between 1953 and 1985) are by women, several of them writers of "popular" fiction not anthologized elsewhere. Literary-biographical introductions include useful bibliographical information. [See ARIYOSHI Sawako, ENCHI

Fumiko, HARADA Yasuko, HIRABAYASHI Taiko, HIRAIWA Yumie, MORI Yōko, SETOUCHI Harumi and TSUBOI Sakae.]

1427. VERNON, Victoria V. 1988. *Daughters of the Moon: Wish, Will, and Social Constraint in Fiction by Modern Japanese Women.* Berkeley: Institute of East Asian Studies, University of California. 245p. Bibl. Index. LCCN: 86-45977.

The first book-length feminist analysis of Japanese fiction published in the United States, and the first devoted to fiction by Japanese women. Using contemporary American and European feminist theory, VERNON focuses on writers of three generations: HIGUCHI Ichiyō, SATA Ineko, and KURAHASHI Yumiko. VERNON asserts that the contemporary Japanese woman writer's task is "to free herself from the images that cling, to form her own image, and to end the long centuries of silenced metaphor." (p. 214) Includes translations of two stories; see SATA Ineko and KURAHASHI Yumiko.

Writers of Modern Prose

1428. ABE Mitsuko (1912-)

Fiction writer. Born in Tokyo; entered Japan Women's University in 1930, but had to leave two years later apparently because she had started a student reading group on *Das Kapital*. Her first connection with the literary world came through studying *tanka* in the school of SASAKI Nobutsuna. Married the son of an officer in the Japanese Salvation Army and had six children. Studied from 1964 to 1967 at the Japan Bible School and became active in Christian mission work. In 1941 her first story ("Pussywillow" [Nekoyanagi]) was nominated for the Akutagawa Prize, but her real literary debut came in 1964, when she won the Tamura Toshiko Prize for Women's Literature.

"The gleaner." 1972. [Translated by Peter W. SCHUMACHER.] *Japan Christian Quarterly* 38(4):216-224. ISSN:0021-4361. [*Ochibabiroi.*]

1429. AKIMOTO Matsuyo (1911-)

Playwright. Born in Tokyo. Begain writing one-act plays after World War II, focusing on the underclasses and their traditional culture. Also wrote television scenarios.

"An investigation on Lady Scab—a play in three acts." Synopsis in: Kokusai Bunka Shinkōkai (#1520), pp. 8-12. [Kasabuta Shikibu kō. 1969.]

1430. AMINO Kiku (1900-1978)

Fiction writer. Born in Tokyo. Was graduated in English literature from the newly-established Japan Women's University. Best-known for her unpretentious, sometimes daring autobiographical fiction. A comparatively uncelebrated writer despite her acknowledged skill.

"Once in a lifetime." Synopsis in: Kokusai Bunka Shinkōkai (#1520), pp. 12-16. [*Ichigo ichie.* Synopsis. 1966.]

1431. ARAI Motoko (1960-)

Writer of science fiction. Born in Tokyo. Graduated in German literature from Rikkyō University in 1983. Won a newcomer's award in science fiction for a story she wrote during high school. The youngest, and one of a very few women among science fiction writers today. Extremely popular, especially with high school students. Has won many prestigious science fiction awards.

Green Requiem. 1984. [Translated by Naomi ANDERSON.] (*Kodansha English Library*, vol. 4.) 151p. [*Guriin rekuiemu.* 1983.]

A Ship to the Stars. 1984. [Translated by Naomi ANDERSON.] (*Kodansha English Library*, vol. 6.) 150p. [*Hoshi e iku fune*. 1981.]

1432. ARIYOSHI Sawako (1931-1984)

Fiction writer, playwright. Born in Wakayama City, spent part of her early life in Indonesia, like Hanako in *The River Ki*, a novel based partly on her own family history. Was baptised a Catholic during high school. ("The Village of Eguchi" [Eguchi no sato] is about Christianity in Japan). Majored in English at a Tokyo junior college. As a student, was interested in drama, especially kabuki and *bunraku*, but also participated in study groups on Proletarian writers. Gained early recognition (at age 25) as a writer of serious fiction in 1956 with "Jiuta," which was nominated for the Akutagawa Prize. This and other works of her "early period" deal with clashes between the traditional world of the Japanese arts and contemporary culture. ARIYOSHI then went on to write a series of multi-generational historical novels, beginning in 1959 with *The River Ki* and including *The Doctor's Wife* in 1966. From the mid-1960s she also wrote novels treating specific contemporary social problems: racial prejudice, pollution, and in *The Twilight Years*, the difficulties of caring for a rapidly aging population. She is a good story-teller; her novels (sometimes referred to as *chūkan shōsetsu*, halfway between serious and popular fiction) are well-constructed, readable and insightful. They are concerned with women's history, and with women's place in the family and society during an age of confusing transition; their heroines derive their special strength from (feminine) nature as opposed to (masculine) culture.

The Doctor's Wife. 1978. [Translated by Wakako HIRONAKA and Ann Siller KOSTANT.] New York: Kodansha. 174p. LCCN:79-301318. Synopsis titled "The Wife of Hanaoka Seishū" in: Kokusai Bunka Shinkōkai (#1520), pp. 16-20. [*Hanaoka seishū no tsuma*. 1966.]

The River Ki. 1980. [Translated by Mildred TAHARA.] Tokyo: Kodansha. 243p. [*Ki no kawa*. 1959.] LCCN:79-66240.

The Twilight Years. 1984. [Translated by Mildred TAHARA.] Tokyo: Kodansha. 216p. [*Kōkotsu no jidai*. 1972.] LCCN:84-47687.

"Danchi life as seen by Ariyoshi Sawako." 1972. [Translated by F. UYTTENDAELE.] *Japan Missionary Bulletin* 26(5):321-327. ISSN:0021-4531. [Yūhigaoka sangōkan. Excerpt. 1970.]

"Her Highness Princess Kazu." 1986. [Translated by Mildred TAHARA.] *Translation* 17:164-182. [Also cited as *Journal of Literary Translation*.] ISSN:0093-9307. [Kōjo Kazunomiya. Excerpt. 1978.]

"Incense and flowers." Synopsis in: HOSHO, Masao. Aug. 1963. "Ariyoshi Sawako, 'Incense and Flowers.'" *Japan P.E.N. News* no. 11:15-17. ISSN:0075-3300. [Kōge. Synopsis. 1961.]

"The ink stick." 1975. [Translated by Mildred TAHARA.] *Japan Quarterly* 22(4):348-369. ISSN:0021-4590. [Sumi. 1961.]

"Jiuta." 1975. [Translated by Mildred TAHARA.] *Japan Quarterly* 22(1):40-58. ISSN:0021-4590. [Jiuta. 1956.]

"Prayer." 1960. [Translated by John BESTER.] *Japan Quarterly* 7(4):448-481. ISSN:0021-4590. [Kitō. 1959.]

"The tomoshibi." 1986. [Translated by Keiko NAKAMURA.] In: UEDA (#1426), pp. 241-257. [Tomoshibi. 1961.]

"The village of Eguchi." 1971. [Translated by Yukio SAWA and Herbert GLAZER.] *Japan Quarterly* 18(4):427-442. ISSN:0021-4590. [Eguchi no sato. 1959.]

CHŪJŌ Yuriko see MIYAMOTO Yuriko [#1453]

1433. ENCHI Fumiko (1905-1986) [Also cited as ENJI Fumiko.]

Fiction writer, playwright, scholar, translator, critic. Born in Tokyo, the daughter of the eminent scholar of Japanese language UEDA Kazutoshi (Mannen), raised in a literary environment, surrounded by Edo fiction, frequenting the kabuki and *shingeki* theater, and reading *The Tale of Genji* from the age of ten. Educated mostly at home. Began her literary career in 1926 as a playwright. Married a journalist at age 25 and had one daughter. Published her first novel in 1936, but struggled to gain a reputation as a novelist. After a period of extreme personal hardship during and following World War II when her house was burned in an air raid and she underwent a difficult operation for uterine cancer, she began to write novels one after another, beginning with *The Waiting Years* (1949-1957). The works won important prizes, gained popular notice, and earned her a prominent place in the literary establishment. Many of them, including *The Waiting Years* and *Masks*, explore women's sexuality. ENCHI also translated into modern Japanese the greatest classics by women, including *The Tale of Genji* (10 volumes, completed in 1973) and the *Izumi Shikibu Diary*. *The Waiting Years* and *Masks* foreground the spiritual, even supernatural, powers of women who suppress their own sexual and social desires under the cruel oppression of men. "A Boxcar of Chrysanthemums," in contrast, looks at the purity and quiet strength of a woman who accepts a lowly role and performs her "duty" with sincere devotion. It frames this story with that of a novelist confronting the image of this pure woman and preparing to write a story about her.

> *Masks.* 1983. [Translated by Juliet Winters CARPENTER.] New York: Knopf. 141p. [*Onna men.* 1958.] LCCN:82-48726.
> *The Waiting Years.* 1971. [Translated by John BESTER.] Tokyo: Kodansha. 203p. LCCN:72-158644. Synopsis titled "Slope for womenfolk" in: Kokusai Bunka Shinkōkai (#1519), pp. 211-214. [*Onnazaka.* 1921-1931.]
> "Blind man's buff." 1986. [Translated by Beth CARY.] In: UEDA (#1426), pp. 165-177. [Mekura oni. 1962.]
> "A bond for two lifetimes—gleanings." 1982. [Translated by Phyllis BIRNBAUM.] In: BIRNBAUM (#1411), pp. 25-47. Also translated as: "Love in two lives: the remnant." 1982. [Translated by Noriko Mizuta LIPPIT and Kyoko Iriye SELDEN.] In: LIPPIT (#1419), pp. 76-91. [Nisei no en shūi. 1957.]
> "Boxcar of chrysanthemums." 1982. [Translated by Yukiko TANAKA and Elizabeth HANSON.] In: TANAKA (#1424), pp. 69-86. [Kikuguruma. 1967.]
> "Enchantress." 1960. [Translated by John BESTER.] In: Japan Quarterly Editorial Board (#1417), pp. 72-93. [Yō. 1956.]
> "Skeletons of men." Oct./Dec. 1988. [Translated by Susan MATISOFF.] *Japan Quarterly* 35(4):417-426. ISSN:0021-4590. [Otoko no hone. 1956.]
> "Tale of an enchantress." 1972. Synopsis in: Kokusai Bunka Shinkōkai (#1520), pp. 24-28. [Namamiko monogatari. Synopsis. 1959-1961.]

1434. GŌ Shizuko (1929-)

Fiction writer. Born in Yokohama. Was graduated from high school, then mobilized for factory work during World War II. Contracted tuberculosis. Later continued her education in Japanese literature, influenced by the "postwar" novelist NOMA Hiroshi. Known for *Requiem*, a brutal novel about young girl's experiences during World War II to which she lost her youth and ultimately her life; it explores issues of ideology and truth. GŌ won the prestigious Akutagawa Prize for *Requiem* in 1972.

> *Requiem.* [Translated by Geraldine HARCOURT.] New York: Kodansha. 122p. [*Rekuiemu.* 1972.] LCCN:84-48698.

1435. HARADA Yasuko (1928-)

Fiction writer. Born in Tokyo but grew up on Hokkaido, where most of her stories are set. Began her career as a newspaper reporter in Hokkaido, attracted attention while still in her twenties with *Banka* [*Elegy*], a hair-raising novel about a young woman growing up without spiritual guidance who learns slowly to accept responsibility for the effect she has on the people she deals with. *Banka* became the number one best seller in 1957, and a popular movie was based on it. HARADA writes unromantic love stories with a social focus portraying a new generation of women disillusioned with traditional morality, striving to "confirm and lay hold of [their] own existence" and to decide what to "use [their] tomorrow for" ("Evening Bells," p. 64).

> "Evening bells." [Translated by Chia-ning CHANG and Sara DILLON.] In: UEDA (#1426), pp. 47-69. [Banshō. 1960.]

1436. HAYASHI Fumiko (1903-1951)

Prolific writer of novels, short stories and poetry. TANAKA (#1425) describes her as the first Japanese woman to enjoy both popular success and critical recognition (p. 99) and as unusual for her day in dealing aggressively with the male-dominated publishing world, using her popularity to her advantage (p. 103). Born in Shimonoseki, she spent her early childhood moving around Kyushu with her parents. (She was one of several illegitimate children; her mother eventually married a stepfather.) Was graduated in 1922 from Onomichi Women's High School, in which she had enrolled herself with the encouragement of an elementary school teacher. After high school, ambitions for a better life drove her to Tokyo, where she worked as a maid, factory worker, waitress, barmaid, and a check-clerk for footgear at a public bath as she struggled to make a living. She earned early literary fame with a long autobiographical novel in diary form, *Hōrōki* [*Vagabond's Song*], which was serialized in 1928 and 1929 in *Nyonin Geijutsu* [*Women and the Arts*], a new literary magazine by and for women that was influential in the careers of many women writers. *Vagabond's Song* was later published as a book, which became a best seller (inspiring three films), established HAYASHI's reputation and delivered her from poverty. HAYASHI associated with anarchist and leftist writers but was not a revolutionary and never identified herself as a "proletarian writer." In a down-to-earth style she wrote for a wide audience with sympathy, hope and intimate knowledge of the poor and the uprooted living on the fringes of society, especially women. HAYASHI read and traveled widely, making extended trips to Europe, China and Southeast Asia as a journalist during World War II. Her 1945 work, *Ukigumo* [*Floating Clouds*], is a non-autobiographical social novel drawing on her experience in Southeast Asia; it portrays the general moral disillusion of the Japanese people immediately after the War. A short masterpiece, "Bangiku" [Late Chrysanthemum], is an unemotional depiction of an aging geisha who takes the measure of her past life and present self when she meets a former lover.

> *The Floating Clouds*. 1965. [Translated by Yoshiyuki KOITABASHI and Martin COLCUTT.] Tokyo: Hara Shobō. 219p. [*Ukigumo*. 1945.]
> "Bones." 1966. [Translated by Ted TAKAYA.] In: SAEKI (#1423), pp. 133-154. [Hone. 1949.]
> "Downtown." 1961. [Translated by Ivan MORRIS.] In: MORRIS (#1420), pp. 349-364. Also translated as "Tokyo." 1956. [Translated by Ivan MORRIS.] In: KEENE (#1418), pp. 415-428. [Shitamachi. 1948.]
> "Late Chrysanthemum." 1960. [Translated by John BESTER.] In: Japan Quarterly Editorial Board (#1417), pp. 188-208. Also translated as: "A Late Chrysanthemum." 1986. [Translated by Lane DUNLOP.] In: DUNLOP (#1412), pp. 95-112. Synopsis appeared in: Kokusai Bunka Shinkōkai (#1519), pp. 150-152. [Bangiku. 1948.]
> "Narcissus." 1982. [Translated by Kyoko Iriye SELDEN.] In: LIPPIT (#1419), pp. 49-61. [Suisen. 1949.]
> "Roving record." 1939. In: Kokusai Bunka Shinkōkai (#1518), pp. 192-200. [*Hōrōki*. Synopsis. 1922-1927.]
> "Splendid carrion." 1952. [Translated by Sakae SHIOYA.] *Western Humanities Review* 4:219-228. ISSN:0043-3845. [Uruwashiki sekizui.]
> "Vagabond's Song." 1987. [Translated by Elizabeth HANSON.] In: TANAKA (#1425), pp. 105-125. [*Hōrōki*. Excerpts. 1930.]

1437. HAYASHI Kyōko (1930-)

Fiction writer. Born in Nagasaki, lived in Shanghai from 1931 to 1945, returning to Nagasaki as a high school student five months before the atomic bomb. Battled radiation sickness and continual poor health. Began her writing career in 1962, earning critical recognition in 1975 with "Matsuri no ba" [Ritual of Death], a story about the immediate aftermath of the bomb awarded the coveted Akutagawa Prize. She has come to be known as the *gembaku sakka* [atomic bomb writer] of Nagasaki, but the scope of her antiwar writings is broad. "Kōsa" [Yellow Sand] for example, is one of a number of stories set in China based on her childhood wartime experiences.

> *As if it Never Happened.* Synopsis in: "On Hayashi Kyōko's *As If It Never Happened (Naki ga gotoki*). Mar. 1982. *Japanese Literature Today* no. 7:24-26. LCCN:76-648281. [*Naki ga gotoki.* Synopsis. 1980.]
>
> "The empty can." 1985. [Translated by Margaret MITSUTANI.] In: ŌE (#1421), pp. 127-143. [Akikan. 1978.]
>
> "Ritual of death." 1978. [Translated by Kyoko SELDEN.] *Japan Interpreter* 12(1):54-93. ISSN:0021-4450. [Matsuri no ba. 1975.]
>
> "Two grave markers." 1986. [Translated by Kyoko SELDEN.] *Bulletin of Concerned Asian Scholars* 18(1):23-35. ISSN:0007-4810. Also published in: TSURUMI, E. Patricia, ed. 1988. *The Other Japan: Postwar Realities.* Armonk, NY: M.E. Sharpe, pp. 46-59. LCCN:87-2335/89-4834. [Futari no bohyō. 1975.]
>
> "Yellow sand." 1982. [Translated by Kyoko Iriye SELDEN.] In: LIPPIT (#1419), pp. 197-207. [Kōsa. 1977.]

1438. HIGUCHI Ichiyō (1872-1896)

Writer of short fiction, diarist. Born in Tokyo into a wealthy and intellectual family. HIGUCHI was interested in literature from a very early age and at fifteen entered the Haginoya School of traditional Japanese poetry, where she studied *waka* composition under a leading female poet, NAKAJIMA Utako. Two years later, when her father and elder brother died leaving the family in financial straits, the job of supporting the family fell to Ichiyō. She resolved to earn a living by writing popular fiction and sought guidance from NAKARAI Tōsui, a popular novelist who served as her mentor until a suggestion of scandal forced their separation. For a while she operated a small notions and confectionery store near the Yoshiwara pleasure district. She is known for her brilliant, unromantic short stories set in or near the Yoshiwara pleasure quarters (the most famous are "Nigorie" and "Takekurabe") and for her lyrical twelve-volume diary, which begins with her days in the Haginoya School. Her style combines the elegant sensibility of Heian poetry and prose with the wit and common sense of Saikaku, mixing archaic language with colloquial. Despite the extreme brevity of her writing career (some four years) because of her early death, Ichiyō was certainly the foremost woman writer of her time, and her reputation has not diminished since. Most accounts of modern Japanese fiction by women begin with her.

> DANLY, Robert Lyons. 1981. *In the Shade of Spring Leaves: The Life and Writings of Higuchi Ichiyō, a Woman of Letters of Meiji Japan.* New Haven: Yale University Press. 355p. Bibl. Index. LCCN:81-50434. Includes the following stories, all translated by Robert Lyons DANLY:
>
> > "Child's play." Pp. 254-287. Also translated as "They compare heights." 1930. [Translated by W.M. BICKERTON.] *Transactions of the Asiatic Society of Japan* 2nd series 7:131-137. LCCN:39-23, and as "Growing up." 1956. [Translated by E.G. SEIDENSTICKER.] In: KEENE (#1418), pp. 70-110. [Takekurabe. 1894/1895.]
> >
> > "Encounters on a dark night." Pp. 182-204. [Yamiyo. 1894.]
> >
> > "Flowers at dusk." Pp. 167-173. [Yamizakura. 1891.]
> >
> > "On the last day of the year." Pp. 205-217. [Ōtsugomori. 1894.]
> >
> > "Separate ways." Pp. 288-295. Also translated as "The parting of the ways." 1930. [Translated by W.M. BICKERTON.] *Transactions of the Asiatic Society of Japan* 2nd series 7:120-130. LCCN:39-23. Also translated in: ARKIN (#1409), pp. 139-143. [Translated by Robert Lyons DANLY.] [Wakaremichi. 1896.]
> >
> > "The sound of the koto." Pp. 178-181. [Koto no ne. 1893.]

"A snowy day." Pp. 174-177. [Yuki no hi. 1893.]
"The thirteenth night." Pp. 241-253. Also translated in *Monumenta Nipponica* 14(3-4):157-174. 1960-1961. [Translated by Hisako TANAKA.] ISSN:0027-0741. Synopsis in: SUGIMORI, Hisahide. Jan. 1962. "Higuchi Ichiyō, 'The Thirteenth Night.'" [Translated by Kenneth STRONG.] *Japan P.E.N. News* no. 8:1-2. ISSN:0075-3300. [Jūsan'ya. 1895.]
"Troubled waters." Pp. 216-240. [Nigorie. 1895.] Also translated as "Muddy Bay." 1958. [Translated by Hisako TANAKA.] *Monumenta Nipponica* 14(1-2):173-204. [Nigorie. 1895.] ISSN:0027-0741.

1439. HIRABAYASHI Taiko (1905-1972)

Writer of fiction. Born in Nagano Prefecture. Interested in Russian literature from childhood; went to Tokyo with the ambition of becoming a socialist writer and became friendly with a group of anarchists. Formed a close friendship with HAYASHI Fumiko, who gave her practical advice on getting published; soon became known as a serious writer of proletarian fiction. A vital and independent woman who "represented the radical spirit that became an important voice in modern Japanese literature." (TANAKA (#1425), p. 73.)

Secret. Synopsis in: "Hirabayashi Taiko, 'Secret.'" 1971. *Japan P.E.N. News* no. 24:7-10. No refs. ISSN:0075-3300. [Himitsu. Synopsis. 1968.]
"The black age." Oct./Dec. 193. [Translated by Edward G. SEIDENSTICKER.] *Japan Quarterly* 10(4):479-493. ISSN:0021-4590. [Kuro no jidai. 1950.]
"Blind Chinese soldiers." 1982. [Translated by Noriko Mizuta LIPPIT.] In: LIPPIT (#1419), pp. 44-48. [Mō chūgokuhei. 1946.]
"The goddess of children." 1952. [Translated by Ken MURAYAMA.] *Pacific Spectator* (4):451-457. ISSN:0735-0252. [Kishimojin. 1946.]
"I mean to live." 1963. [Translated by Edward G. SEIDENSTICKER.] *Japan Quarterly* 10(4):49-479. ISSN:0021-4590. [Watashi wa ikiru. 1947.]
"A man's life." 1961. [Translated by George SAITO.] In: MORRIS (#1420), pp. 365-382. [Hito no inochi. 1950.]
"Self-mockery." 1987. [Translated by Yukiko TANAKA.] In: TANAKA (#1425), pp. 75-96. [Azakeru. 1927.]
"This kind of woman." 1959. Synopsis in: Kokusai Bunka Shinkōkai (#1519), pp. 103-105. [Kō iū onna. 1946.]
"A woman to call mother." 1986. [Translated by Richard DASHER.] In: UEDA (#1426), pp. 211-223. [Haha to iū onna. 1966.]

1440. HIRAIWA Yumie (1932-)

Prolific popular novelist. Born in Tokyo, was graduated from Tokyo Women's College with a major in Japanese literature. Began her literary career writing historical novels, which quickly won high acclaim. Went on to write novels and short stories in modern settings, including romances and detective fiction, and became famous for her fiction serialized in newspapers and for her overwhelmingly popular scenarios for television. As the titles of her best-known works suggest, she is particularly concerned with what it means to live as a Japanese woman. "Yūgao no onna" [Lady of the Evening Faces] (also a television drama) is from a collection of sketches serialized in 1978 and 1979 called "Nippon no onna" (Women of Japan). The title of the story is an allusion to a character in *The Tale of Genji*, but the story is set in the present day.

"Lady of the evening faces." 1986. [Translated by Patricia LYONS.] In: UEDA (#1426), pp. 259-277. [Yūgao no onna. 1979.]

1441. ISHIMURE Michiko

Poet, fiction writer, essayist, activist. Lived in Minamata, Kyushu. At the forefront of the Minamata movement against chemical pollution, demanding reparations to the hundreds of

Minamata residents stricken in the mid-1950s with mercury poisoning as a result of chemicals discharged by local industry. She has written extensively on the subject, creating "a new literary genre, a mixture of authentic autobiography, fiction and journalism." (p. v, *Paradise in the Sea of Sorrow: Our Minamata Disease.*)

> *Paradise in the Sea of Sorrow: Our Minamata Disease.* 1990. [Translated by Livia MONNET.] Kyoto: Yamaguchi Publishing House. 379p. Bibl. LCCN:90-160558. [*Kugai jōdo: Waga Minamata-byō.* 1972.]
>
> *Story of the Sea of Camellias.* 1983. [Translated by Livia MONNET.] Kyoto: Yamaguchi Publishing House. 350p. LCCN:84-145658. Published earlier as: "Story of the sea of camellias. I." Jan./Mar. 1982. [Translated by Livia MONNET.] *Japan Quarterly* 29(1):53-87. 30 notes. ISSN:0021-4590. "Story of the sea of camellias. II." Apr./Jun. 1982. [Translated by Livia MONNET.] *Japan Quarterly* 29(2):222-243. 21 notes. ISSN:0021-4590. [*Tsubaki no umi no ki.*]
>
> "The Boy Yamanaka Kuhei." 1988. [Translated by Christopher STEVENS.] In: TSURUMI, E. Patricia, ed. 1988. *The Other Japan: Postwar Realities.* Armonk, NY: M.E. Sharpe, pp. 139-148. LCCN:87-23365/89-4834. [First chapter of *Kugai jōdo.* 1969.]
>
> "Pure land poisoned sea." Jul./Sep. 1971. [Translated by James KIRKUP and Michio NAKANO.] *Japan Quarterly* 18(3):299-306. No notes. ISSN:0021-4590. [*Kugai jōdo.* Exerpt. 1969.]
>
> "Quo Vadis Homo Nipponicus." Autumn 1973. [Translated by Yasuko TASHIRO and Frank BALDWIN.] *Japan Interpreter* 8(3):392-395. No refs. ISSN:0021-4450. [*Jimetsu kōshinkyoku.* 1972.]

1442. KANAI Mieko (1947-)

Poet, fiction writer, critic. Born in Takasaki, Gumma Prefecture. Was graduated from Gumma Prefecture Women's Higher School. Had achieved important critical recognition as both fiction writer and poet by the age of twenty. KANAI is a difficult, self-consciously intellectual writer who deals (as in "Puratonteki ren'ai" [Platonic Love], the title story of her 1979 prize-winning anthology), with the powers and limitations of words, the process of writing, and the reader's participation in the creation of a text. Her imagination is highly visual, her images often grotesque (as in "Usagi" [Rabbits]). [See also #1656.]

> "Platonic love." 1985. [Translated by Amy Vladeck HEINRICH.] In: GESSEL (#1414), pp. 361-368. [Puratonteki ren'ai. 1979.]
>
> "Rabbits." 1982. [Translated by Phyllis BIRNBAUM.] In: BIRNBAUM (#1411), pp. 1-16. [Usagi. 1976.]
>
> "Tama." 1989. [Translated by Mark JEWEL.] *Japanese Literature Today* 11:5-11. ISSN:0385-1044. [Tama ya. 1988.]

1443. KASHIWABA Sachiko (1953-)

Writer of fiction for young adults; pharmacist. Born in Iwate Prefecture, was graduated from Tōhoku School of Pharmacy. Beginning in 1974, won a series of awards for fiction aimed at young people. *Kiri no mukō no fushigi na machi* [*The Marvelous Village Veiled in Mist*] is one such work.

> *The Marvelous Village Veiled in Mist.* 1987. [Translated by Christopher HOLMES.] Tokyo: Kodansha. (Kodansha English Library.) 164p. [*Kiri no mukō no fushigi na machi.* 1975.]

1444. KATAYAMA Hiroko (1878-1957)

Tanka poet. Translator of Irish literature and of the Indian poet Tagore. Essayist. Born in Azabu, Tokyo. KATAYAMA's father was a diplomat and she was educated in both Japanese and English. From 1954, she studied *tanka* under SASAKI Nobutsuna, becoming one of the initial members of his *tanka* coterie Kokoro no Hana [Flowers of the Heart]. After the death of her husband (a prominent banker), she moved to Karuizawa, where she continued to frequent literary circles. In 1929 she was one of the founders of *Hi no Tori* [*Firebird*] with WATANABE Tomeko. In her later years of illness and solitude she turned to writing essays in addition to *tanka*; excerpts of two essays are cited below.

"From Candlemas." Jan./Mar. 1955. [Translated by Shio SAKANISHI.] *Japan Quarterly* 2(1):70-75. No refs. ISSN:0021-4590. [Includes excerpts of her essays: "An eggplant patch," pp. 70-72 and "Bride's trousseau," pp. 72-75.] [*Tōkasetsu*. 1964.]

1445. KIZAKI Satoko (1939-)

Fiction writer. Born in Manchuria. After her father was appointed to teach applied sciences at Toyama University, Satoko attended primary and secondary school in Toyama. Graduated in English literature from Tokyo Women's Junior College. In 1962 she married HARADA Hiroshi, a plant physiologist, with whom she spent 15 years off and on in France and the United States. Returning to Japan in 1979, she began to write fiction—much of it inspired by her experiences abroad. In 1980 she won the Bungaku-kai newcomer's prize for "Rasoku" ["Bare feet"], about a young woman who has recently returned from a difficult life in Paris. "Aogiri" ["Phoenix tree"], the self-reflection of a young woman caring for an aunt who is dying of breast cancer, won her the Akutagawa Prize. She was baptised a Catholic in 1982.

The Phoenix Tree and Other Stories. 1990. [Translated by Carol A. FLATH.] Tokyo: Kodansha. 242p. LCCN:90-31399. Includes the following stories:
"Barefoot." Pp. 7-46. [Rasoku. 1980.]
"Flame trees." Pp. 47-121. [Kaenboku. 1981.]
"Mei Hua Lu." Pp. 123-142. [Mei Howa Ruu.1987.]
"The phoenix tree." Pp. 143-242. [Aogiri. 1984.]

1446. KŌDA Aya (1904-1990)

Essayist, fiction writer. Born in Tokyo, daughter of the eminent novelist and critic KŌDA Rohan, who gave her a strict Confucian upbringing. Grew up near the Sumida River and the pleasure quarters although not as a part of that world. Lost her mother and elder sister in early childhood and her younger brother at age 22, and, except for the ten-year period of her marriage, lived with her father from the beginning of her life to the end of his in 1947. Began her writing career immediately after her father's death, with reminiscences of him. Then, surprisingly, worked for four months as a maid in a geisha establishment, apparently in an effort to escape her publisher's persistent demands for manuscripts about her famous father. Drew on that experience to write her first full-scale novel, *Nagareru* [*Drifting*] (not yet translated), published in 1955. "Kuroi suso" [The Black Kimono], published the same year, is the title story in a prize-winning collection of semi-autobiographical stories. Her works deal not so much with social issues as with personal memory and the passage of time, with the transformation and survival of traditional culture and esthetics in the postwar world, and with the hardships of ordinary women living in a changing world.

"The black kimono." 1960. [Translated by Edward G. SEIDENSTICKER.] In: Japan Quarterly Editorial Board (#1417), pp. 94-111. [Kuroi suso. 1955.]
"Floating." 1959. Synopsis in: Kokusai Bunka Shinkōkai (#1519), pp. 234-237. [*Nagareru*. 1955.]
"The pincushion." 1975. [Translated by Lane DUNLOP.] *Prairie Schooner* 49(2):129-133. ISSN:0032-6682. [Kami. 1951.]
"Rain." 1985. [Translated by Lane DUNLOP.] *Prairie Schooner* 59(3):67-72. ISSN:0032-6682.

1447. KOMETANI Foumiko/Fumiko

Fiction writer, essayist, social and literary critic. Born in Osaka, graduated with a major in Japanese literature from Osaka Women's University. Began her career as a painter; in 1960 she won a scholarship to participate in a workshop for artists in New Hampshire, where she met her husband, Josh GREENFIELD, an American writer. They have lived in New York,

Japan and Los Angeles. Many of her essays have to do with racial discrimination, and with cultural differences between Japan and the United States. Her fiction is largely autobiographical; the main character (as in both stories listed below) often being a Japanese housewife married to a Jewish writer in Los Angeles and caring for a mentally handicapped young son.

> *Passover.* 1989. [Translated by KOMETANI Foumiko.] New York: Carroll and Graf Publishers. 148p. LCCN:89-30472. Includes the following stories:
> "Passover." Pp. 1-88. [Sugikoshi no matsuri. 1985.]
> "A guest from afar." Pp. 89-144. [Enrai no kyaku. 1985.]

1448. KŌNO Taeko (1926-)

Fiction writer, critic, playwright. Born to an Osaka merchant family, attended a women's high school, and read widely including TANIZAKI Jun'ichirō and Emily BRONTË. (KŌNO later wrote a play based on *Wuthering Heights* and (with TOMIOKA Taeko) a travel record of a journey to the heaths where the novel is set.) Her education was interrupted by World War II. She was expected to follow the family merchant tradition, and worked in a bank for a while, but she ultimately overcame her parents' objections and moved to Tokyo determined to become a writer. Beginning in 1962, her short stories won critical acclaim, including the Akutagawa Prize for "Kani" [Crabs] in 1963. Her explicit treatment of sexual fantasies and violence, motifs in her early stories (such as "Ari takaru" [Ants Swarm]), shocked readers, and her narrative experimentation has occasionally baffled the critics, but today KŌNO is a leading presence in the literary establishment. She describes extraordinary occurences as though they were perfectly natural, creating a mental world nearly independent of surrounding physical reality. Attaining that independence at the expense of the physical world, mainly in order to be able to speak or write her own story, in her own words, is a recurrent theme in her work.

> *A Pastoral Year.* Synopsis in: "On Kōno Taeko's *A Pastoral Year (Ichinen no bokka)*." Mar. 1981. *Japanese Literature Today* no. 6:25-27. LCCN:76-648281. [*Ichinen no bokka.* Synopsis. 1979.]
> "Ants swarm." 1982. [Translated by Noriko Mizuta LIPPIT.] In: LIPPIT (#1419), pp. 105-119. [Ari takaru. 1964.]
> "Bone Meat." 1977. [Translated by Lucy LOWER.] In: HIBBETT (#1416), pp. 42-52. [Hone no niku. 1969.]
> "Boy-hunt." 1972. Synopsis in: Kokusai Bunka Shinkōkai (#1520), pp. 115-119. [Yōji-gari. Synopsis. 1961.]
> "Crabs." 1982. [Translated by Phyllis BIRNBAUM.] In: BIRNBAUM (#1411), pp. 99-131. [Kani. 1963.]
> "Crimson markings." Winter 1987. [Translated by Yukiko TANAKA.] *Literary Review* 30(2):184-193. ISSN:0024-4589. [Shuken. 1980.]
> "Iron fish." 1985. [Translated by Yukiko TANAKA.] In: GESSEL (#1414), pp. 348-360. [Tetsu no uo. 1976.]
> "The last time." 1982. [Translated by Yukiko TANAKA and Elizabeth HANSON.] In: TANAKA (#1424), pp. 43-67. [Saigo no toki. 1966.]

1449. KOYAMA Itoko (1910-1989)

Fiction writer. Born in Kōchi on the island of Shikoku. Was graduated from women's higher school and married the head of a paper factory; they were later divorced. Began writing under a masculine pen name. Worked on the staff of the women's magazine, *Hi no Tori* [Firebird]. Wrote popular romantic stories (e.g. "Teiden" [Black Out]) and novels after World War II; won the coveted Naoki Prize for popular fiction in 1954. KOYAMA is probably best known for *Kōgosama* [Nagako, Empress of Japan] which appeared in 1955.

> *Nagako, Empress of Japan.* 1958. [Translated by Atsuo TSURUOKA.] New York: John Day. 1958. 189p. [*Kōgosama.* 1955.]

"Black-out." 1963. [Translated by Grace SUZUKI and Jay GLUCK.] In: GLUCK (#1415), pp. 110-119. [Teiden.]

1450. KURAHASHI Yumiko (1935-)

Fiction writer; critic. Born in rural Kōchi Prefecture on the island of Shikoku. Was encouraged by her family to be a doctor, but failed the entrance exam for medical school twice. Studied and was licensed to be a dental hygienist, but enrolled in the French Department of Meiji University against her family's wishes instead of practicing. She was graduated in 1960, having written a thesis on SARTRE's *L'Être et le Néant*, and continued her studies in graduate school. Wrote fiction as an undergraduate, during a period of great student unrest. Just before graduation (she was by then 25), her story, "Parutai" [Partei], won a Meiji University literary prize, was published in a major literary journal and was nominated for the Akutagawa Prize a few months later. After her brilliant, early debut, she created stories with an aggressive intellectualism (what she called "anti-realism") new to the Japanese reading public. She continued to gain recognition, winning the Tamura Toshiko Prize for women's writing in 1963. Her immediate success was followed by severe criticism for taking too much from fiction by Western authors she avowedly imitated (SARTRE, CAMUS and KAFKA), and the originality of her work was challenged by a major literary critic. At age 29, she married by arranged marriage and the following year went to the University of Iowa on a Fulbright to study creative writing. After a ten-year period of silence, her work changed both stylistically and thematically, and traditional myth became an important motif.

"Parutai" [Partei] (her first story)—the "personal history" of a woman who wanted to become a member of the Community Party but could not allow her own life to be interpreted in impersonal terms as "inevitable"—seems to reflect KURAHASHI's detached attitude toward the political passion of student dissidents who were generally younger than she. A very different sort of work, "Kakō ni shisu" [To Die at Estuary], one of a series of "anti-tragedies" by KURAHASHI, is based on Sophocles' *Œdipus at Colonus*.

The Adventures of Sumiyakist Q. 1979. [Translated by Dennis KEENE.] St. Lucia [Australia]: University of Queensland Press. 369p. LCCN:80-451138. [*Sumiyakisuto Q no bōken*. 1969.]

"The boy who became an eagle." 1974. [Translated by Samuel GROLMES and Yumiko TSUMURA.] *New Directions* 29:116-133. LCCN:37-1751.

"The end of summer." 1988. [Translated by Victoria V. VERNON.] In: VERNON (#1427), pp. 229-240. [Natsu no owari. 1960.]

"The monastery." 1985. [Translated by Carolyn HAYNES.] In: GESSEL (#1414), pp. 218-231. [Kyosatsu. 1961.]

"Partei." 1982. [Translated by Yukiko TANAKA and Elizabeth HANSON.] In: TANAKA (#1424), pp. 1-16. Also published as: "Partei." 1973. [Translated by Samuel GROLMES and Yumiko TSUMURA.] *New Directions* 26:8-22. LCCN:37-1751; and as "Partei." 1961. [Translated by Saburō HANEDA.] *The Reeds* 7:87-108. ISSN:0484-2081. Synopsis titled "Communist Party" in: Kokusai Bunka Shinkōkai (#1520), pp. 120-122. [Parutai. 1960.]

"To die at the estuary." 1977. [Translated by Dennis KEENE.] In: HIBBETT (#1416), pp. 247-281. [Kakō ni shisu. 1970.]

"The ugly devils." 1972. [Translated by Samuel GROLMES and Yumiko TSUMURA.] *New Directions* 24:55-67. LCCN:37-1751.

"The week for the extermination of the mongrels." 1983. [Translated by Samuel GROLMES and Yumiko TSUMURA.] *Mundus Artium* 14(1):103-113. ISSN:0027-3406.

1451. MASUDA Mizuko

Fiction writer, literary critic. Born in Tokyo, graduated from Tokyo University of Agriculture and Industry with a degree in plant immunology. Her fiction is characterized by meticulously logical prose and scientific metaphor. She earned notice in literary circles in the late 1970s and has continued to write prolifically and to win greater acclaim. A common theme in her work, including the story listed below, is the difficulty of personal relationships and the necessity for individual people to maintain personal independence and discrete personalities, like "single cells" that combine, separate, and recombine in constantly changing configurations.

"Living alone." Dec. 1988. [Translated by Seiji M. LIPPIT.] *Review of Japanese Culture and Society* 2(1):77-91. ISSN:0913-4700. [Hitorigurashi. 1982.]
"Single cell." Synopsis in: "On Masuda Mizuko's 'Single Cell' (Shinguru seru)." Mar. 1988. [Translated by Mark JEWEL.] *Japanese Literature Today* no. 13:14-15. LCCN:76-648281. [Shinguru seru. Synopsis. 1987.]

1452. MIURA Ayako (1922-)

Fiction writer. Born in Hokkaido; was graduated from women's higher school there. Became an elementary school teacher, but soon took ill and spent the next 13 years in a sanitorium fighting tuberculosis (age 24 to 36). After a long period of near desperation, she turned to religion and in 1952 was baptised a Catholic, partly under the influence of a close male friend who, however, died of tuberculosis. In 1959, at the age of 37, she married another devout Christian, MIURA Mitsuyo. Together they operated a variety store, apparently with the intention of converting the customers to Christianity. The stories she heard daily from those customers contributed to her understanding of human nature, and some of them became inspiration for her extremely popular novels. *Hyōten* [*Freezing Point*], serialized in the *Asahi Shimbun* from December 1964 through November 1965, began a "Hyōten boom." A movie was based on it, as well as radio and TV dramas.

Freezing Point. 1986. [Translated by Hiromu SHIMIDZU and John TERRY.] Wilmington: Dawn Press. 496p. [*Hyōten.* 1964-1965.]
Shiokari Pass. 1987. [Translated by Bill FEARNEBOUGH and Sheila FEARNEBOUGH.] Rutland, VT: Tuttle. 272p. LCCN:87-50161. [*Shiokari Tōge.* 1968.]
The Wind is Howling. 1977. [Translated and abridged by Valerie GRIFFITHS.] Downers Grove, IL: Intervarsity Press, 190p. No refs. LCCN:77-74845. Excepted as: "The Church of Christ." 1972. [Translated by David REID.] *Japan Christian Quarterly* 38(4):225-231. ISSN:0021-4361. [*Michi ariki.* 1970.]

1453. MIYAMOTO Yuriko (1899-1951)

Fiction writer, social critic. Best known for her autobiographical fiction, which follows her personal and intellectual development throughout her life. Born in Tokyo to an upper-class intellectual family. Started writing fiction in elementary school; began reading Russian literature, especially TOLSTOY, at the age of fifteen. When she was seventeen, a story she had written about the poor and exploited farmers in Tōhoku (based on her experience at her grandfather's estate) was published in a prestigious journal and she attracted attention as a young literary genius. She entered the English department of the newly-established Japan Women's College (women were not admitted to the Imperial Universities until after World War II) but withdrew the same year to become a professional writer. In 1918, at the age of nineteen (perhaps to escape overprotective middle-class parents, TANAKA (#1425), p. 42) she suddenly went to New York City where she enrolled as an auditor at Columbia University; in a matter of months she met an older Japanese graduate student of classical Persian and married him against her parents' wishes, then returned to Japan some two months later in 1919. This unsatisfactory marriage lasted five years. *Nobuko* is based on their marriage, their clashes in ideology and lifestyle, and their separation. NOGAMI Yaeko (see #1463) introduced MIYAMOTO to YUASA Yoshiko, a scholar of Russian literature, a woman of independent lifestyle, and a declared lesbian, who was to be an important influence on MIYAMOTO's life. The two women lived together for a number of years, including three traveling in the Soviet Union and Europe. Yuriko returned to Japan a committed Socialist. Not long afterwards she joined the All-Japan Proletarian Artists' Association [NAPF] (coordinating the Women's Committee) and the Communist Party. In 1932 she married MIYAMOTO Kenji, an important Marxist critic and NAPF leader, but two months later government repression forced him underground, and he was soon arrested and imprisoned for his political beliefs until the end of World War II. Their correspondence while he was in prison was later published as *Jūninen no tegami* [Twelve Years of Letters]. MIYAMOTO Yuriko herself was interrogated, arrested and even tortured during the War, but she managed to continue writing throughout by focusing on literary topics (such as women writers). After the War, she was accorded great respect as one of the few writers who had not recanted their Communist beliefs; she lectured throughout the country and wrote social commentary and some of her best-known autobiographical fiction, including "Banshū heiya" [Banshū Plain] and "Fūchisō" [The Weathervane Plant].

"Banshū Plain." 1984. [Translated by Brett De BARY.] *Bulletin of Concerned Asian Scholars* 16(2):40-45. ISSN:0007-4810. Also translated by Yukiko SAKAGUCHI and Jay GLUCK. In: GLUCK (#1415), pp. 73-80. Synopsis in: Kokusai Bunka Shinkōkai (#1519), pp. 88-91. [*Banshū heiya*. Excerpts. 1947.]

"The family of Koiwai." 1982. [Translated by Noriko Mizuta LIPPIT.] In: LIPPIT (#1419), pp. 3-21. [Koiwai no ikka. 1938.]

"Nobuko." [Excerpts.] 1987. [Translated by Yukiko TANAKA.] In: TANAKA (#1425), pp. 47-64. Also translated by Brett DE BARY. Oct./Dec. 1975. *Bulletin of Concerned Asian Scholars* 7(4):44-52. ISSN:0007-4810; in: ARKIN (#1409), pp. 368-373; and in: Kokusai Bunka Shinkōkai (#1518), pp. 222-229. [*Nobuko*. Excerpts/Synopsis. 1924-1927.]

"The weathervane plant." 1984. [Translated by Brett DE BARY.] *Bulletin of Concerned Asian Scholars* 16(2):46-47. ISSN:0007-4810. Reprinted in the *Journal of the Association of Teachers of Japanese* 19(1):29-33. April 1984/1985. ISSN:0885-9884. [Fūchisō. 1946.]

1454. MIZUKI Yōko (1913-)

Known primarily as a television scenario writer who often focuses on controversial social problems. She has also written for movies and the theater and for radio. Born in Tokyo; studied Japanese literature at the new Japan Women's College, and went on to study drama. She has written television versions of many Japanese classics, including HAYASHI Fumiko's *Ukigumo* [*Floating Clouds*] and HIGUCHI Ichiyō's "Nigorie" [Troubled Waters]. "Please Not a Word to Anybody" is a very short story ironically conveying the essence of the long life of a misunderstood and mostly solitary woman.

"Please not a word to anybody." 1963. [Translated by Grace SUZUKI and Jay GLUCK.] In: GLUCK (#1415), pp. 149-151.

1455. MORI Mari

Fiction writer. Born in Tokyo, the daughter of MORI Ōgai and his second wife. Sickly and talented, she led a pampered childhood. She received an excellent modern education, studied French literature, and married a professor of French literature. Had two children, divorced, then remarried, divorced again, after which she remained independent, earning a reputation as a writer. She began her writing career—after the age of forty—with reminiscences of her extremely famous father.

"The forest of lovers." 1972. Synopsis in: Kokusai Bunka Shinkōkai (#1520), pp. 145-148. [Koibitotachi no mori. 1961.]

1456. MORI Reiko (1928-)

Fiction writer. Essayist. Playwright. Critic. Writer of children's stories. Born in Fukuoka, daughter of an architectural engineer. In 1947 was baptised a Baptist. Began her varied literary career writing free verse. "Mokkingubaado no iru machi [Desert Song—literally, the town where mockingbirds sing] is a story about life in the United States and international marriage. It won the prestigious Akutagawa Prize.

"Desert song." 1985-1986. [Translated by Noah BRANNEN.] *Japan Christian Quarterly* 51(4):232-244, 52(1):25-44. ISSN:0021-4361. [Mockingbird no iru machi. 1979.]

"A twilight place." 1973. [Translated by Miriam L. OLSEN.] *Japan Christian Quarterly* 38(4):232-240. ISSN:0021-4361. [Usugurai basho. Essay. 1971.]

1457. MORI Yōko (1940-)

Popular ficiton writer. Received a modern Western education; read French literature and studied Western classical music. Like the heroine of her 1978 prize-winning first work *Jōji* [The Affair], she married an Englishman living in Japan. The two "bedtime stories" translated are from a longer collection and feature mature women who struggle to maintain their independent identities and self-respect in a world that expects from them weakness and compliance.

"Two bedtime stories: 'Be it ever so humble' [Sasayakana kōfuku] and 'Spring storm' [Haru no arashi]." 1986. [Translated by Makoto UEDA.] In: UEDA (#1426), pp. 117-132. [Beddo no otogibanashi. 1984/1985.]

1458. MUKŌDA Kuniko (1929-1981)

Radio and television script writer. Essayist, short story writer. One of the most popular and prolific television scenario writers of the 1970s, known for many classics of the serialized "home drama" genre. Shortly before her untimely death in a plane crash in 1981, she began writing autobiographical essays, and a collection of short stories, *Omoide torampu* [Playing Card Memories] in which "Inugoya" [Doghouse], "Dauto" [Doubt] and "Kawauso" [River Otter] appeared. As these stories demonstrate, Mukōda's prose is spare, her stories economically told with gentle wit and an occasional sharp detail that betrays the psychological workings of her characters.

"The doghouse." Oct. 1984. *East* 20(5):64-68. [Inugoya. 1980.]

"Doubt." 1984. [Translated by Dan SEMOUR.] *Japan Quarterly* 31(3):281-287. ISSN:0021-4590. [Dauto. 1980.]

"The river otter." 1986. [Translated by Marian E. CHAMBERS.] *Japan Quarterly* 33(3):320-327. ISSN:0021-4590. [Kawauso. 1980.]

1459. NAKAMOTO Takako (1903-)

Fiction writer. Born in Yamaguchi Prefecture into a poor family that valued education. Graduated from Yamaguchi Girls' High School. Went to Tokyo with ambitions toward a literary career. Her success came while she was writing for HASEGAWA Shigure's literary magazine for women, *Nyonin geijutsu* [*Women in the Arts*], which was associated with the Proletarian literary movement and in which "Suzumushi no mesu" [The Female Bell-Cricket] appeared. She soon gravitated toward social activism, organizing female textile workers and working with the Communist Party. She was interrogated and tortured by the police, and spent several years in a prison for women. She apparently recanted her political beliefs and was criticized by contemporaries for cooperating with the government in writing fiction to encourage productivity among the people. During World War II she stopped writing altogether, not to resume until the mid-1950s, when she serialized social protest fiction in the Communist paper *Akahata* [*Red Flag*] and elsewhere. "Kichi no onna" [The Only One] is about a woman with a *burakumin* [outcaste] background who makes her living as a prostitute for the American Occupation forces after the War.

"The female bell-cricket." 1987. [Translated by Yukiko TANAKA.] In: TANAKA (#1425), pp. 135-144. [Suzumushi no mesu. 1929.]

"The only one." 1965. [Translated by Grace SUZUKI.] In: GLUCK (#1415), pp. 159-173. [Kichi no onna. 1954.]

1460. NAKAYAMA Chinatsu (1948-)

Actress, essayist, fiction writer. Born in Kumamoto, Kyushu. Raised in Osaka, where she attended a children's theater school, appearing for the first time on stage at the age of ten. From 1959 until 1968, she was with the Tōei Theatre in Tokyo, quickly becoming famous as a child actress. (One of the stories below, "Star Time," is written from that experience). In 1968 she broke her stage contract to become a television "talent." She began writing in 1970, and became an early activist in the women's movement, then in local politics. In 1980 she was elected a member of the lower house of the Diet, but lost her seat six years later. She has continued to write prolifically, both fiction and essays focusing on women's issues.

Behind the Waterfall. 1990. [Translated by Geraldine HARCOURT.] New York: Atheneum. 213p. LCCN:89-18437. Includes the following stories:
"Good afternoon ladies." (pp. 111-213) [Misesu no afutanuun.]
"The sound of wings." (pp. 47-110) [Haoto.]
"Star time." (pp. 1-45) [Koyaku no jikan. 1980.]

1461. NATSUKI Shizuko (1938-)

Mystery writer. Born in Tokyo, graduated in English literature from Keiō University. One of her stories was nominated for the Edogawa Rampo Mystery Award while she was still a student. She went on to win the award in 1973. NATSUKI is a prolific writer of television scripts and mystery novels of suspense exploring the psychology of women and focusing on real social problems. She has traveled widely, and many of her novels are set abroad. She seems particularly interested in gender roles and sexual identity, as seen, for example, in *Kokubyaku no tabiji* [*Innocent Journey*]. She has been referred to as the "Agatha Christie of Japan," a reflection of her preeminence in the field.

Innocent Journey. 1989. [Translated by Robert B. ROHMER.] New York: Ballantine Books. 281p. LCCN:88-92834. [*Kokubyaku no tabiji.* 1976.]
Murder at Mount Fuji. 1984. [Translated by Robert B. ROHMER.] New York: St. Martin's Press, 199p. LCCN:83-24458. [*W no higeki.* 1982.]
The Obituary Arrives at Two O'Clock. 1988. New York: Ballantine Books. 298p. LCCN:88-91978. [*Fuhō wa gogo niji ni todoku.* 1983.]
Portal of the Wind. 1990. [Translated by Robert ROHMER.] New York: Ballantine Books. 217p. [*Kaze no tobira.* 1980.]
The Third Lady. 1987. [Translated by Robert B. ROHMER.] New York: Ballantine Books, 249p. LCCN:86-91663. [*Daisan no onna.* 1973.]
"Cry from the cliff." 1978. In: QUEEN (#1422), pp. 123-146. [Dangai kara no koe. 1976.]
"I can't help loving him." 1982. [Translated by Robert B. ROHMER.] *Ellery Queen's Mystery Magazine* 80(1):115-131. ISSN:0013-6328. [Aisazu ni wa irarenai. 1971.]
"It's best not to listen." 1988. In: *Ellery Queen's Prime Crimes.* Secaucus, NJ: Castle, pp. 87-97.
"The love motel." Jul. 1989. [Translated by Robert B. ROHMER.] *Ellery Queen Mystery Magazine* (Jul. 1989):116-135. ISSN:1054-8122. [1989.]
"The pawnshop murder." May 1980. *Ellery Queen Mystery Magazine* 75(5):75-90. ISSN:0013-6328. Reprinted in: APOSTOLOU (#1410), pp. 184-202. [Shichiya no tobira. 1978.]
"The sole of the foot." 1981. *Ellery Queen Mystery Magazine* 78(3):85-103. ISSN:0013-6328. Reprinted In: APOSTOLOU (#1410), pp. 203-224. [Ashi no ura. 1979.]
"The stairs." Jun. 1985. *Ellery Queen's Mystery Magazine* 85(6):22-30. ISSN:0013-6328. [Kaidan. 1976.]
"The taste of cocoa." Mar. 1988. *Ellery Queen's Mystery Magazine* 91(3):65-74. ISSN:1054-8122.
"A very careful man." 1987. *Ellery Queen's Mystery Magazine* 89(1):44-60. ISSN:0013-6328. [1986.]

"The woman on the phone." May 1990. [Translated by Robert B. ROHMER.] *Ellery Queen's Mystery Magazine* 95(5):62-86. ISSN:1054-8122.

1462. NIKI Etsuko

A popular mystery writer; writer of children's stories. Born in Tokyo, raised in Toyama Prefecture. Lost the use of her legs in early childhood; was educated at home by her older brother from the death of their father until until the brother was conscripted into the military. Began writing children's stories at 26 and soon became a regular contributor to children's and women's magazines. In 1957 she won the Edogawa Rampo Prize in mystery writing for *Neko wa shitte ita* [*The Cat Knew*]. Eventually came to be known as the preeminent female mystery writer of her day. Married a translator.

"The distant drawing." In: GENKAWA (#1413), pp. 177-197. [Tōi ezu. 1969.]

1463. NOGAMI Yaeko (1885-1985)

Fiction writer and playwright. Born in Oita Prefecture in Kyushu, raised in a progressive intellectual atmosphere. Graduated in 1906 from the famous early Christian girl's school Meiji Jogakkō and immediately married NOGAMI Toyoichirō, scholar of Nō drama and student of NATSUME Sōseki, arguably the most influential novelist of his day. Under her husband's encouragement, she began to write fiction, and with Sōseki's help she published her first work, a piece of the *shasei-bun* ["realistic description"] in literary vogue at the time, in the haiku journal *Hototogisu*. Her husband was apparently extraordinarily supportive, and freedom from financial worry fostered her literary career. Without ever emerging as a brilliant light on the literary scene, she gradually earned a reputation as an intellectual, humanist writer concerned with fundamental moral issues in works like *Kaijin-maru* [*The Neptune*], about a shipwrecked crew reduced to eating human flesh for survival—a work especially surprising in an age when it was assumed that women wrote about the home. In fact, her work (spanning three quarters of a century) shows considerable variety and breadth and includes both social and historical novels.

The Neptune, the Foxes. 1957. [Translated by Ryōzō MATSUMOTO.] Tokyo: Kenkyusha. 226p. [*Kaijin-maru.* 1922. *Kitsune.* 1946.]
"A certain Socialist." 1939. In: Kokusai Bunka Shinkōkai (#1518), pp. 274-279. [Aru Soshiarisuto. Synopsis. 1928.]
"The full moon." 1982. [Translated by Kyoko Iriye SELDEN.] In: LIPPIT (#1419), pp. 22-43. [Meigetsu. 1942.]
"Hideyoshi and Rikyū." [Synopsis.] Jul. 1965. *Japan P.E.N. News* no. 15:12-14. LCCN:76-648281. Synopsis also in: Kokusai Bunka Shinkōkai (#1520), pp. 177-181. [*Hideyoshi to Rikyū*. Synopsis. 1962-1963.]
"The labyrinth." 1959. Synopsis in: Kokusai Bunka Shinkōkai (#1519), pp. 25-28. [*Meiro*. Synopsis. 1936-1956.]
"Story of a missing leg." 1987. [Translated by Yukiko TANAKA.] In: TANAKA (#1425), pp. 153-158. [Kataashi no mondai. 1931.]
"Windows and an out-of-tune instrument." Winter 1987. [Translated by Juliet Winters CARPENTER.] *Literary Review* 30(2):224-231. ISSN:0024-4589. [Mado to onboro gakki. 1977.]

1464. ŌBA Minako (1930-)

Fiction writer, playwright, essayist, critic. Born in Tokyo, moved around frequently as a child (her father was a doctor with the navy), so has no home town in the traditional sense. She saw the mushroom cloud over Hiroshima and was conscripted in 1945 to help atomic bomb victims. Graduated an English major from Tsuda College. She began writing poetry in college, under the influence of T.S. ELIOT, and became actively involved in student theater. Married on the condition that she could continue to write fiction; in 1959 she moved with her husband (an engineer) to Sitka, Alaska, where they remained for eleven years. In 1968 her story

"Sambiki no kani" [Three Crabs] won the prestigious Akutagawa Prize. Her literary career has continued to flourish ever since this late but brilliant debut.

"Sambiki no kani" [Three Crabs] is a difficult story presenting the experience of a Japanese wife and mother living among a strange group of intellectual cosmopolitan types in Sitka. It develops not according to logical progression but largely through penetrating dialogue and the poetic juxtaposition of images. ŌBA's works in general are concerned with the independent, yet engaged existence of a (Japanese) woman in society. "Yamauba no bishō" [Smile of a Mountain Witch] explores the special mental capacities of women, and the power and liability inherent in those capacities—what it means to see into other people's minds and to need to appease them or make them happy. In her essays, ŌBA has been an interpreter of American ways, especially popular feminism, to the Japanese public.

"Double suicide: A Japanese phenonmenon." 1975. [Translated by Manabu TAKECHI and Wayne ROOT.] *Japan Interpreter* 9(3):344-350. ISSN:0021-4450. [Taidanaru gōgan—gendai no shinjū-kō. 1974.]

"Fireweed." Jul./Sep. 1981. [Translated by Marian CHAMBERS.] *Japan Quarterly* 28(3):403-427. ISSN:0021-4590. [Higusa. 1968.]

"The pale fox." 1985. [Translated by Stephen W. KOHL.] In: GESSEL (#1414), pp. 337-347. [Aoi kitsune. 1973.]

"The repairman's wife." In: GENKAWA (#1413), pp. 87-132. [Yorozu shūzen'ya no tsuma. Excerpt from *Garakuta hakubutsukan* [*The Junk Museum*]. 1975.]

"Sea-change." Mar. 1980. [Translated by John BESTER.] *Japanese Literature Today* no.5:12-19. LCCN:76-648281. [Tankō. 1979.]

"The smile of a mountain witch." 1982. [Translated by Noriko Mizuta LIPPIT.] In: LIPPIT (#1419), pp. 182-196. [Yamauba no bishō. 1976.]

"Three crabs." 1982. [Translated by Yukiko TANAKA and Elizabeth HANSON.] In: TANAKA (#1424), pp. 87-113. Also translated by Stephen KOHL and Ryōko TOYAMA in *Japan Quarterly* 25(3):323-340. ISSN:0021-4590. [Sambiki no kani. 1968.]

1465. *OCHIAI Keiko (1945-)*

Feminist fiction writer, essayist, critic. Born in Tochigi Prefecture. Graduated in English and American literature from Meiji University. Became a popular disc jockey. In 1971 she published privately a reedited collection of poetry she had been composing since she was in junior high school. In 1974 she left her disc jockey job to concentrate on her writing; in 1976 she opened the Crayon House, a feminist bookstore in Tokyo devoted to selling (and later to publishing) books for children and for women. From the following year she began to focus on writing fiction, essays, and feminist criticism centering on women's issues and issues in education. She has won numerous prestigious awards.

"Behind the screen." Dec. 1987. [Translated by Ralph F. McCARTHY.] *Look Japan* p.30. ISSN:0456-5339. [Tsuitate no mukō.]

1466. *ŌHARA Tomie (1912-)*

Writer of fiction. Born in Kōchi on Shikoku. Her father was an elementary school principal; she lost her mother at age eleven. Left Kōchi Teacher's College for Women because she contracted tuberculosis. Began to read and write fiction and poetry during her long period of convalescence; joined a literary coterie, fell in love with another member who asked her to marry him but suddenly rejected her. (She learned much later that he had acquiesced to his family's wishes and married a healthy woman of property.) ŌHARA went to Tokyo hoping to concentrate her energies on a literary career. She spent the World War II years and the immediate postwar years in illness and poverty, supporting herself by teaching the tea ceremony, and always continuing to write. Returning for a month to Kōchi in 1944, she came across the letters of NONAKA En, a Tosa woman who had spent forty years from early childhood under house arrest with her family after her father fell into political disgrace. This woman became the heroine of *En to iū onna* [*A Woman Called En*], Ōhara's best-known work.

Critics have seen a self-portrait in Ōhara's portrayal of En, a strong woman, denied by fate a normal life, who turned to scholarship and writing for personal fulfillment.

> *A Woman Called En.* 1986. [Translated by Kazuko FURUHATA and Janet SMITH.] London: Pandora Press. 121p. LCCN:85-19430. Synopsis in: YAMAMOTO, Kenkichi. Jul. 1960. "Ōhara Tomie, 'A Woman called En.'" *Japan P.E.N. News* no. 5:10-11. ISSN:0075-3300, and in: Kokusai Bunka Shinkōkai (#1520), pp. 189-192. [*En to iū onna.* 1960.]

1467. OKAMOTO Kanoko (1889-1939)

Fiction writer, *tanka* poet, scholar. Born to a large family in Tokyo. While still in girl's higher school, developed an interest in *tanka* and visited YOSANO Akiko, the preeminent woman *tanka* poet. Became a member of Akiko's new poetry group and published her own *tanka* (most of it love poetry) in the romantic poetry journal *Myōjō*, whose direct personal expression and affirmation of love and the self seemed to reflect her own personal and artistic temperment. In 1910 she married OKAMOTO Ippei, who later became a famous illustrator/cartoonist. Her son Tarō, the subject of Kanoko's stirring and extremely sensual piece "Boshi jojō" [A Mother's Love], was born the following year. In 1912 she published her first poetry anthology. She also joined the feminist Seitōsha group. In a long period of family discord, bankruptcy at home, and personal tragedy including a tumultuous love affair, a mental breakdown, and the death of two children, she sought solace in Mahayana Buddhism, and she wrote some important works of Buddhist scholarship. In 1929 she traveled with her husband and son and two young men to Europe, where she spent three years nurturing her literary talents. On her return to Japan, she plunged feverishly into writing. She made her debut in the fiction world in 1936, publishing all the works listed below and several others, until her death four years later from a cerebral hemmorhage. Her works are so varied that they strike most critics as incongruous but always they have "a passion that seems to teeter uncomfortably close to madness." (BIRNBAUM (#1411), p. 49.)

> *The Tale of an Old Geisha and Other Stories.* 1985. [Translated and introduced by Kazuko SUGISAKI.] In: *The White Blackbird and other Writings by Anaïs Nin. The Tale of an Old Geisha and Other Stories by Kanoko Okamoto.* 1985. Santa Barbara: Capra Press. 46,78p. LCCN:84-21465. Includes:
> > "North country." Pp. 65-78. [Michioku. 1938.]
> > "Sushi." Pp. 14-37. [Sushi. 1939.]
> > "The tale of an old geisha." Pp. 38-64. Synopsis in: "Rōgishō." Oct. 1964. *Japan P.E.N. News* no. 13:12-14. LCCN:76-648281. [Rōgishō. 1928-1929.]
> "A floral pageant." 1987. [Translated by Hiroko Morita MALATESTA.] In: TANAKA (#1425), pp. 205-225. Also translated as: "Scarlet flower." 1963. [Translated by Edward G. SEIDENSTICKER.] *Japan Quarterly* 10(3):331-348. ISSN:0021-4590. [Hana wa tsuyoshi. 1937.]
> "Ivy gates." 1989. [Translated by Lane DUNLOP.] *Literary Review* 32(2):153-160. ISSN:0024-4589.
> "A mother's love." 1982. [Translated by Phyllis BIRNBAUM.] In: BIRNBAUM (#1411), pp. 49-97. [Boshi jojō. Excerpt. 1937.]
> "Shining river." 1959. Synopsis in: Kokusai Bunka Shinkōkai (#1519), pp. 60-61. [*Kawa akari.* 1939.]

1468. ŌTA Yōko (1903-1963)

Fiction writer. Born in Hiroshima. From an early age, read widely in Japanese and Western literature, including GOETHE and TOLSTOY. Went to Tokyo to participate in the literary scene, became associated with several small magazines. Began publishing fiction about marriage and divorce, based on her own family history. Was exposed to the atomic bomb in Hiroshima, and from that experience turned to writing stories about the atomic bomb and the imminence of death. Both of the following stories are of this genre.

"City of corpses." 1990. In: MINEAR, Richard. 1990. *Hiroshima: Three Witnesses*. Princeton: Princeton University Press, pp. 117-273. LCCN:89-10460. Synopsis in: Kokusai Bunka Shinkōkai (#1519), pp. 195-197. [Shikabane no machi. 1958.]

"Fireflies." 1985. [Translated by Koichi NAKAGAWA.] In: ŌE (#1421), pp. 85-111. [Hotaru. 1953.]

1469. SATA Ineko (1904-)

Fiction writer. Essayist. Born in Nagasaki. Her mother was only fourteen, her father eighteen. She lost her mother in infancy, and she was raised by her father's mother. Since her father was often unemployed, Ineko worked at all sorts of jobs from childhood to help support the family: at a caramel factory, a restaurant, and the Maruzen bookstore. Married a wealthy Keiō student at the age of twenty, but left, pregnant, months later and supported herself as a waitress. During this time she got to know members of a literary coterie who opened her eyes to the wonders of literature. She married one of them, the Leftist critic KUBOKAWA Tsurujirō. Under his influence and that of NAKANO Shigeharu, she joined the Proletarian literature movement, publishing first essays, then Proletarian-style stories like "Karameru kōjō kara" [From a Caramel Factory] in 1928. With MIYAMOTO Yuriko (#1453), she served on the women's committee of the Nihon Puroretaria Sakka Dōmei [Proletarian Authors' Committee], and she edited *Hataraku Fujin* [*Working Women*] for a time. In 1932 she joined the Communist Party, was arrested and forced to renounce her political convictions (as was her husband). "Kurenai" [Crimson] is based on this critical period in her life and begins a series of autobiographical stories about a woman desperately seeking a way to live her own life in her own way. During World War II she visited soldiers at the front in Manchuria and Korea and wrote stories in cooperation with the war effort, for which she suffered severe criticism and self-reproach afterwards. She divorced her husband just before the end of the war. She then became active in the socialist group Fujin Minshu Kurabu (Women's Democratic Club) and was then expelled from the Communist Party for criticizing the Party's proclamation about the Club in 1950. "Yoru no kioku" [Memory of a Night] tells the story of a woman expelled by the Party and rejected, although reluctantly, by her former friends. SATA rejoined the Party in 1955, but was expelled once more in 1964. "Toki ni tatsu" [Standing in Time], from which there are two separate excerpts listed below, is a full-length work consisting of twelve stories apparently based on the reflections of the mature author on her varied past, beginning in the 1920s with her first marriage which ended in attempted suicide, through her arrest and political "conversion" during the war, and after.

"Camellia blossoms on the little mountain." Mar. 1987. [Translated by Mark JEWEL.] *Japanese Literature Today* no.12:5-14. ISSN:0385-1044. [Chiisai yama to tsubaki no hana. 1986.]

"Clay doll." Jul. 1962. [Translated by John BESTER.] *Japan P.E.N. News* no.9:1-9. ISSN:0075-3300. [Doro ningyō. 1960.]

"The colorless paintings." 1985. [Translated by Ann Shiloh SHIMURA.] in: ŌE (#1421), pp. 113-125. [Iro no nai e. 1961.]

"Crimson." 1987. [Translated by Yukiko TANAKA.] In: TANAKA (#1425), pp. 167-180. Synopsis titled "Scarlet" in: Kokusai Bunka Shinkōkai (#1519), pp. 1-3. [*Kurenai*. Excerpt/Synopsis. 1936.]

"The Inn of the Dancing Snow." 1988. [Translated by Victoria V. VERNON.] In: VERNON (#1427), pp. 217-228. [Yuki no mau yado. 1972.]

"Memory of a night." 1982. [Translated by Kyoko Iriye SELDEN.] In: LIPPIT (#1419), pp. 62-75. [Yoru no kioku. 1955.]

"Re-encounter." 1980. [Translated by Mack HORTON.] *Feminist International* 2:83-87. ISSN:0388-371X. Also translated as: "Standing still in time." Mar. 1977. [Translated by Charles TERRY.] *Japanese Literature Today* no.2:5-11. ISSN:0385-1044. [Toki ni tatsu. Excerpt. 1975.]

"Water." Synopsis in: Kokusai Bunka Shinkōkai (#1520), pp. 200-204. [Mizu. Synopsis. 1962.]

1470. SETO Nanako (1932-1957)

Writer of the following poetic diary, a modern example of a Heian genre, kept during a long terminal illness apparently related to radiation from the bombing of Hiroshima when she was thirteen.

"A crane that cannot come back." In: GLUCK (#1415), pp. 203-220.

1471. SETOUCHI Harumi/Jakuchō (1922-)

Fiction writer. Born in Tokushima, on Shikoku. Graduated from Tokyo Women's University. Married in 1943 and followed her husband to Beijing. Left three years later and returned to her family in Tokushima, where two years after that, she had an affair with one of her husband's students and fled to Kyoto, finding work there in a hospital. She returned to Tokyo in 1951 hoping to become a novelist. She published her first story in 1956, but the following year another story, "Kashin" [Stamen] was criticized as being pornographic, and SETOUCHI had trouble getting her work in print for several years afterwards. *Natsu no owari* [*The End of Summer*] and "Miren" [Lingering Affection] are autobiographical stories about women trying to understand their own sexuality and to liberate themselves from the constraints of sexual bonds with men. In 1960 she wrote a prize-winning biographical novel about another woman author, TAMURA Toshiko (#1478), who led an equally provocative life. In 1971-1972 she serialized in *Asahi shimbun*, *Chūsei enshō* [*Medieval Conflagration*], her own version of the Kamakura tale *Towazugatari*, a work about a woman who leaves a life of sexual love and dependency on men to become a Buddhist nun traveling independently around the country. In 1973 SETOUCHI herself took Buddhist vows at Chūsonji in Hiraizumi, taking the Buddhist name Jakuchō. The following year she went into "retirement" in Sagano, west of Kyoto, but she has continued to write as prolifically as ever.

> *The End of Summer*. 1989. [Translated by Janine BEICHMAN in collaboration with Alan BRENDER.] New York: Kodansha. 151p. LCCN:88-81918. Synopsis in: Kokusai Bunka Shinkōkai (#1520), pp. 212-215. [*Natsu no owari*. 1962.]
> "The autumn colors again." 1976. [Translated by Patricia MARTON and Teruko KACHI.] *Asian and Pacific Quarterly of Cultural and Social Affairs* 8(2):69-70. No refs. ISSN:0251-3110. [Mata mo kōyō ga. 1974.]
> "The burnet plant: An old couple's garden." 1985. [Translated by Nancy ANDREW.] *Japanese Literature Today* 10:6-11. ISSN:0385-1044. [Waremokō. 1984.]
> "Lingering affection." 1982. [Translated by Mona NAGAI and Akiko WILLING.] In: TANAKA (#1424), pp. 17-42. [Miren. 1963.]
> "Pheasant." 1986. [Translated by Robert HUEY.] In: UEDA (#1426), pp. 189-209. [Kiji. 1963.]

1472. SHIBAKI Yoshiko (1914-)

Fiction writer. Essayist. Born in Tokyo, graduated from girls' high school, but left college to work and support her family after the death of her father. At the same time she began to write stories and to participate in literary circles. Won the prestigious Akutagawa Prize in 1941. After World War II she wrote a series of works depicting in detail the way of life of the the urban lower class, especially bar hostesses and prostitutes. Beginning in 1960, she wrote a trilogy of historical novels telling the story of one family, showing how different generations, especially the women, have lived through dramatic social change from the beginning of the Meiji period to the present.

> "Garden in twilight." 1981. [Translated by K. NINOMIYA and S. GOLDSTEIN.] *Western Humanities Review* 35(3):219-239. [1980.] ISSN:0043-3845. [Tasogare no niwa. 1980.]
> "Ripples." 1985. [Translated by Michael C. BROWNSTEIN.] In: GESSEL (#1414), pp. 317-336. [Hamon. 1970.]
> "Snow flurry." Mar. 1986. [Translated by Mark JEWEL.] *Japanese Literature Today* no.11:6-16. ISSN:0385-1044. [Kazahana. 1985.]

"The turning." 1984. [Translated by Kazuji NINOMIYA and Sanford GOLDSTEIN.] *Western Humanities Review* 38(1):21-42. ISSN:0043-3845.

"Ups and downs." 1965. [Translated by Grace SUZUKI.] In: GLUCK (#1415), pp. 100-111. [Fuchin.]

"Winter roses." 1982. [Translated by Kazuji NINOMIYA and Sanford GOLDSTEIN.] *Western Humanities Review* 36(3):229-246. ISSN:0043-3845. [Fuyu bara. 1981.]

1473. SONO Ayako (1931-)

Fiction writer, essayist, journalist. Born in Tokyo. Received a Catholic education from early childhood, was baptised at seventeen. She studied English literature at Sacred Heart Women's College. Participated in literary circles while still a student. Became a member of the influential literary coterie Shinchōsha, and married another member, MIURA Shumon, before graduating in 1954. The same year, her short story about the Occupation Army, "Enrai no kyakutachi" [Visitors from Afar], was nominated for the Akutagawa Prize and launched her prolific writing career. Her cultural focus is international. Her broad-ranging travels in Asia, Central America, and Europe (including the Vatican) are reflected in her work; some of her fiction is set abroad. From large-scale social novels to short stories exploring her personal Christian belief, SONO Ayako's works focus on role, mission and life purpose, especially for women. In general they offer an affirmative view of humanity. She wrote an intriguing novel based on the life of Marilyn MONROE, called *When Candy is Crushed*.

Watcher from the Shore: A Novel. 1990. [Translated by Edward PUTZAR.] Tokyo: Kodansha International. 376p. [*Kami no yogoreta te*. 1979.]

"Age of fools." 1980. *Japan Echo* 7(2):118-121. ISSN:0388-0435. [Baka no jidai. 1979.]

"Drifting in outer space." 1972. [Translated by Robert EPP.] *Japan Christian Quarterly* 38(4):206-215. ISSN:0021-4361. [Uchū ni fuyū suru. 1970.]

"The environs of Seiganji Temple." 1960. [Translated by Kazue KUMA.] *Today's Japan* 5:33-40. LCCN:87-21388. Reprinted in: SCHNEPS, Maurice and Alvin D. COX. 1966. *The Japanese Image, Vol. II*. Philadelphia: Orient/West, pp. 145-154. [*Orient/West* 10(1). Winter/Spring 1966. Special Issue. ISSN:0474-6465.] [Seiganji fūkei. 1957.]

"Fuji." 1982. [Translated by Phyllis BIRNBAUM.] In: BIRNBAUM (#1411), pp. 17-23. [Fuji. 1975.]

"Snow light." Synopsis in: Kokusai Bunka Shinkōkai (#1520), pp. 227-230. [Yukiakari. Synopsis. 1957.]

"Village embarcation." Fall 1984. [Translated by Charles M. DeWOLF.] *Japan Christian Quarterly* 50(4):225-227. [1983.]

"Visitors from across the sea." Synopsis in: KOMATSU, Shinroku. Dec. 1960. "Sono Ayako, 'Visitors from Across the Sea.'" *Japan P.E.N. News* no. 6:8-9. ISSN:0075-3300. [Enrai no kyakutachi. Synopsis. 1954.]

1474. SUMII Sue (1902-)

Fiction writer. Feminist, activist. Born in 1902 in Nara Prefecture; went to Tokyo at 17 to work in the publishing world. Married writer INUTA Shigeru, who was active in the leftist Nōmin Bungei Kai (Farmer's Literary Association); she wrote fiction in that vein, and then children's fiction to support the family through her husband's long illness. (He died in 1957.) SUMII is best known for her prodigious *Hashi no nai kawa* [*The River with No Bridge*], a six-volume novel, based on childhood experiences, about the *burakumin* underclass. The first volume [translation cited below] "traces the questioning of the system by an individual child" (xi).

The River with No Bridge. 1989. [Translated by Susan WILKINSON.] Rutland, VT: Tuttle. 359p. Notes. LCCN:89-51715. [*Hashi no nai kawa*. 1961-1973.]

1475. TAKAGI Kiyoko (1923-)

Writer of fiction and essays for young readers. Born in Tokyo. Lost her mother and two younger sisters during the bombing of Tokyo when she was 12; her father was killed a few months later, leaving her a war orphan. Her father had operated a glass factory. In 1977, to commemorate the 33rd anniversary of the death of her family, she published what was later rewritten as *Garasu no usagi* [*The Glass Rabbit*], which became a million seller; it was made into a movie, and was adapted for television.

> *The Glass Rabbit*. 1986. [Translated by James M. VARDAMAN.] Tokyo: Kodansha. 167p. (Kodansha English Library, v. 21.) [*Garasu no usagi.*]

1476. TAKAHASHI Takako (1932-)

Born in Kyoto Prefecture. Graduated in French literature from Kyoto University, where she met TAKAHASHI Kazumi (he later had a brief but brilliant career as a novelist), and they were married shortly after graduation. She went on to get a Master's degree, writing her thesis on François MAURIAC. Published a translation of MAURIAC's *Thérèse Desquéroux*. Shortly after the death from cancer of her famous novelist husband in 1971, she published her first collection of short stories, followed in quick succession by novels and other short story collections.

TAKAHASHI was baptised into the Catholic Church in 1975. In 1980 she went to Paris for spiritual training; she now lives in a convent, following a routine similar to that of a nun, except that she has continued to write. "Kou" [Longing], a story from the 1970s, creates a woman aware of both spiritual and physical drives who gradually chooses Christ over her male human lover and a convent over her own room. "Sōjikei" [Congruent Figures] (published the month her husband died) is a penetrating story about a mother who has rejected her own daughter for being exactly like herself. "Ningyō ai" [Doll Love] is typical of TAKAHASHI Takako's fictional world, full of psychological symbols, seemingly independent of outward reality.

> *Child of Wrath*. Synopsis in: "On Takahashi Takako's *Child of Wrath* (*Ikari no ko*)." Mar. 1986. [Translated by Charles M. DeWOLF.] *Japanese Literature Today* no. 11:16-18. LCCN:76-648281. [*Ikari no ko*. Synopsis. 1985.]
> "Congruent figures." 1982. [Translated by Noriko Mizuta LIPPIT.] In: LIPPIT (#1419), pp. 153-181. [Sōjikei. 1971.]
> "Doll love." 1982. [Translated by Mona NAGAI and Yukiko TANAKA.] In: TANAKA (#1424), pp. 197-223. [Ningyō ai. 1976.]
> "The oracle." Dec. 1989. [Translated by Nina BLAKE.] *Review of Japanese Culture and Society* 3(1):97-110. ISSN:0913-4700. [Otsuge. 1977.]

1477. TAKENISHI Hiroko (1929-)

Social critic and fiction writer. Born in Hiroshima. Graduated from Waseda University, where she studied Japanese literature. Began as an editor, then published social criticism and essays, which attracted critical attention, as did the 1963 story "The Rite," [Gishiki] about the survivors and mourners of the victims of the atomic bomb. She has also published extensively on classical Japanese literature, including *The Tale of Genji* and classical poetry written by women. Strongly influenced in style and approach by these early women writers.

> "The rite." 1985. [Translated by Eileen KATO.] In: ŌE (#1421), pp. 169-200. [Gishiki. 1963.]
> "Speaking of love. [An essay.]" 1985. [Translated by John BESTER.] In: *Japan Echo* 12(Special Issue):74-76. ISSN:0388-0435. [Aisuru to iū kotoba. 1979.]

1478. TAMURA Toshiko (1884-1945)

Fiction writer; essayist. Born in Tokyo. Her father deserted the family when she was a small child. After the death of her younger sister, she lived alone with her mother. Studied

Japanese literature briefly at the newly-founded Japan's Women's University. Began writing fiction in her early teens and at eighteen became a "protegé" of the preeminent KŌDA Rohan, who apparently offered her little help, but whose ornate, classical style she for a while imitated. She married one of his other students, who turned out to be a much less successful writer than she—a source of difficulty in their marriage. She also wrote plays, even appeared in a starring role on the stage. Her fiction was sensual and emotional, most of it autobiographical in inspiration. *Akirame* [*Resignation*, 1911] depicts an unconventional young woman forced to leave school because she insists on writing for the theater, but who eventually adopts, on her own initiative, a traditional woman's role. This novel, which won a literary competition sponsored by *Asahi shimbun*, is unusual in its sensual, if never sexual, protrayal of the main character's love relationships with two other women. The surprisingly equivocal ending, apparently disappointing to her feminist contemporaries, suggests an ambivalence common to her other works. The desire for liberation from male domination is evident in her work, but though she published in *Seitō*, TAMURA was not a member of the Seitōsha.

Her life occasionally aroused public scandal. In 1918, she left her husband and went with her married lover, a journalist, to Vancouver where they worked for a Japanese language newspaper for the next fourteen years, and both became respected community leaders, although she stopped writing fiction almost completely. After his sudden death, TAMURA lived for a time in Los Angeles, then returned to Japan in 1936 and began to write fiction set in Japanese communities in North America, but with little outward success. After a period of debt and more romantic scandal, she went to China under the auspices of the Japanese military; she eventually took a job in Shanghai editing a Japanese language magazine for Chinese women under the sponsorship of the Japanese occupation government. She died in China without equalling her former reputation. Twenty years later her friends established the annual Tamura Toshiko Prize for literature written by women, of which SETOUCHI Harumi (#1471) was the first recipient (for her fictional biography of TAMURA Toshiko).

"Glory." 1987. [Translated by Yukiko TANAKA.] In: TANAKA (#1425), pp. 19-38. [Eiga. 1916.]

"A woman writer." 1987. [Translated by Yukiko TANAKA.] In: TANAKA (#1425), pp. 11-18. [Onna sakusha. 1913.]

1479. TOGAWA Masako (1933-)

Mystery writer. Born in Tokyo. Made a name for herself as a cabaret-style vocalist. Best known as a prolific writer of detective fiction characterized by careful construction and erotic tenor. She has also written many other erotic popular novels.

A Kiss of Fire. 1987. [Translated by Simon GROVE.] New York: Dodd, Mead & Co. 245p. LCCN:87-19962. [*Hi no seppun.* 1985.]

The Lady Killer. 1985. [Translated by Simon GROVE.] New York: Dodd, Mead & Co. 151p. [*Ryōjin nikki.* 1963.]

The Master Key. 1984. [Translated by Simon GROVE.] New York: Dodd, Mead & Co. 198p. LCCN:85-1523. [*Ōinaru gen'ei.* 1962.]

"The vampire." 1978. In: QUEEN (#1422), pp. 233-257. [Kiiroi kyūketsuki. 1970.]

1480. TOMIOKA Taeko (1935-)

Poet, fiction writer, playwright, critic. Born in Osaka in a working-class neighborhood. Her father abandoned the family when she was a child. Graduated from Osaka Women's University in English literature. Published her first poetry collection (which won an important prize) when she was still a student, and quickly made a name as a poet (see #1718). In 1965-1966 she spent a traumatic ten months in New York City, where she was abandoned by the man with whom she had gone there, an artist. After that she gave up poetry "as an elitist art." (TOMIOKA quoted in TANAKA (#1424, p. 142.)

Since 1971, she has shifted her focus to fiction, at which she has been equally successful. "Oka ni mukatte hito wa narabu" [Facing the Hills They Stand] was her first work of fiction. A grim, matter-of-fact story about several generations of a poor, unproductive, amoral, uncommunicative village family whose matriarch sits by herself and mumbles, "All you do is make [me have] babies . . . as if it were somebody else's affair." (p. 129.) The characterization of gender roles is particularly interesting. She has written many stories more clearly related to her own experiences, such as "Meido no kazoku" [Family in Hell] (one of a group of four stories whose titles place them in different Buddhist realms of existence), creating, for example, a woman living with a man who leaves her for another woman, and a grown daughter's relationship with a dying father who had refused to have anything to do with the family since her childhood. She creates a non-elitist world that is both bizarre and familiar, sometimes funny but never bitter. A woman of many interests and talents, she has translated Gertrude STEIN, written a book of literary criticism on IHARA Saikaku, and published a book on (her own) experiences learning English conversation. She also writes for radio, television and the stage.

> *Tale of Snow Buddhas.* Synopsis in: "On Tomioka Taeko's *A Tale of Snow Buddhas (Yuki no hotoke no monogatari).* Mar. 1988. [Translated by Mark JEWEL.] *Japanese Literature Today* no. 13:12-13. LCCN:76-648281. [*Yuki no hotoke no monogatari.* Synopsis. 1987.]
>
> "Central Park and Inokashira Park. [An essay.]" 1985. [Translated by Geraldine HARCOURT.] *Japan Echo* 12(Special Issue):77-80. ISSN:0388-0435. [Sentoraru Paaku to Inokashira Kōen. 1967.]
>
> "Children's painting." 1982. [Translated by William LEET.] *Journal of Asian Culture* 6:137-161. ISSN:0162-6795. [Kodomo no e, from *Tōsei bonjin-den* (*Modern Tales of Ordinary People).* 1976-1977.]
>
> "Facing the hills they stand." 1982. [Translated by Kyoko Iriye SELDEN.] In: LIPPIT (#1419), pp. 120-152. [Oka ni mukatte hito wa narabu. 1971.]
>
> "Family in hell." 1982. [Translated by Susan Downing VIDEEN.] In: TANAKA (#1424), pp. 141-177. [Meido no kazoku. 1974.]
>
> "Happii basudei." 1980. [Translated by Kyoko SELDEN.] *St. Andrew's Review* 5(4):89-101. ISSN:0036-2751. [Happii basudei. 1974.]
>
> "Scenery viewed by a dog." 1981. [Translated and discussed by Noriko M. LIPPIT.] *Japan Quarterly* 28(2):271-284. ISSN:0021-4590. [Inu ga miru fūkei. 1974.]
>
> "Time table." Oct. 1986. [Translated by Kyoko Irie SELDEN.] *Review of Japanese Culture and Society* 1(1):110-123. ISSN:0913-4700. [Jikanwari. 1975.]

1481. TSUBOI Sakae (1899-1967)

Writer of adult and juvenile fiction. Born on a small island in the Inland Sea, grew up in a large, happy but poor family whom she helped support by physical labor from childhood, receiving only an eighth grade education. In 1925 she went to Tokyo to marry a man from her home town, the young anarchist (later Marxist) poet, TSUBOI Shigeji, through whom she became acquainted with the Proletarian literary movement. She assisted him in his career as editor-in-chief of the NAPF publication, and met several important Leftist writers including HAYASHI Fumiko [#1436], HIRABAYASHI Taiko [#1439], and later, when her husband was imprisoned for his political beliefs, MIYAMOTO Yuriko [#1453] and SATA Ineko [#1469], who were in a similar situation, and she joined them on the editorial staff of *Hataraku Fujin* [*Working Woman*]. These women encouraged her to begin writing fiction at the age of 36 with no literary training or practice, and in 1940 helped finance her first collection of stories in 1940, which won an important literary prize. During World War II, she concentrated on juvenile fiction in order to avoid censorship. "Jūgoya no tsuki" [Moon of the Fifteenth Night] and "Kaki no ki no aru ie" [Under the Persimmon Tree] are essentially juvenile fiction). After the War, from 1947 to 1949, she serialized *Tsuma no za* [*The Wife's Seat*], a novel quietly questioning the partriarchal structure of the "modern" Japanese family. "Tsukiyo no kasa" [Umbrella on a Moonlight Night] is a story in this vein. TSUBOI is best known today for *Nijūshi no hitomi* [*Twenty-Four Eyes*], a novel for children and adults about a young teacher at a rural island elementary school and the tragic fates of her twelve beloved pupils during the War. The book was the basis of a spectacularly popular movie starring the leading film actress TAKAMINE Hideko.

> *Twenty-four Eyes*. 1983. [Translated by Akira MIURA.] Rutland, VT: C.E. Tuttle. 244p. LCCN:82-51098. Synopsis in: Kokusai Bunka Shinkōkai (#1519), pp. 215-218. [*Nijūshi no hitomi*. 1952.]
> "Moon of the fifteenth night." 1980. [Translated by William B. GIESECKE.] *Japan Quarterly* 27(3):390-397. ISSN:0021-4590. [Jūgoya no tsuki. 1940.]
> "Summer oranges." 1980. [Translated by William B. GIESECKE.] *Japan Quarterly* 27(3):387-390. ISSN:0021-4590. [Natsumikan. 1947.]
> "Umbrella on a moonlit night." 1986. [Translated by Chris HEFTEL.] In: UEDA (#1426), pp. 83-96. [Tsukiyo no kasa. 1953.]
> "Under the persimmon tree." 1965. [Translated by Kiyonobu UNO.] *The Reeds* 10:49-63. ISSN:0484-2081. [Kaki no ki no aru ie. 1944.]

1482. TSUMURA Setsuko (1928-)

Fiction writer. Born in Fukui Prefecture, the daughter of a silk merchant. She lost both her parents at a young age. Her education was interrupted by World War II. She learned dressmaking to support herself, but went back to school a few years after the War and graduated from Shūgakuin Junior College with a major in Japanese literature. Determined to become a novelist, she followed the conventional path of joining several literary coteries and regularly submitting manuscripts to the small magazines they published. She married the aspiring novelist YOSHIMURA Akira, a fellow member of one of the groups. In the meantime she wrote popular fiction for young women's magazines for financial support. She and her husband labored under difficult circumstances to establish their literary reputations, until, after several near misses, "Gangu" [Playthings] finally won for her the Akutagawa Prize in 1965. An untranslated novel, *Omoi saigetsu* [*Heavy the Months and Years*], recounts the trials of a wife and mother of two who is trying to keep the family going and at the same time establish herself as a novelist (with a struggling novelist husband). "Yakōdokei" [Luminous Watch] is about a woman, deserted by her husband, who earns a scant living for herself and her daughter by washing other people's *tabi* [socks].

> "Luminous watch." 1982. [Translated by Elizabeth HANSON and Yukiko TANAKA.] In: TANAKA (#1424), pp. 115-140. [Yakōdokei. 1969.]
> "Playthings." 1980. [Translated by Kyoko EVANHOE and Robert N. LAWSON.] *Japan Quarterly* 27(1):87-107. ISSN:0021-4590. [Gangu. 1965.]

1483. TSUSHIMA Yūko (1947-)

Fiction writer; essayist; critic. Born in Tokyo, the daughter of novelist DAZAI Osamu, who died a controversial death with another woman when TSUSHIMA was a little over a year old. Graduated an English major from Shirayuri Women's College and went on briefly to graduate study at Meiji University during the time of student unrest. She began to write—and to publish—fiction as a student, winning several important literary prizes in quick succession (including the Tamura Toshiko Prize for Women's Literature in 1975) and with dazzling speed earning a name as a novelist in an intellectual, anti-realistic style totally different from her father's. For TSUSHIMA "reality" is what is truly her own: products of the individual unconscious. She claims influence by James JOYCE and Virginia WOOLF. A strong theme in her work is the individual psychic development of a female character. "Shateki" [Shooting Gallery] creates a woman struggling to be both a mother and a person. The heroine of "Chōji [Child of Fortune] needs to learn to live actively in society without necessarily accepting its norms; she is caught between the need to become a responsible mother to her adolescent daughter (in a stage of development not unlike her own) and the stong pull to regress to an infantile autistic world like that of her brother, who died in childhood.

Child of Fortune. 1983. [Translated by Geraldine HARCOURT.] Tokyo: Kodansha International. 161p. LCCN:82-48168. [*Chōji*. 1978.]

The Shooting Gallery and Other Stories. 1988. [Translated and compiled by Geraldine HARCOURT.] New York: Pantheon Books. 138p. LCCN:87-22171. Includes the following stories, all translated by Geraldine HARCOURT:

"The chrysanthemum beetle." Pp. 45-79. [Kikumushi. 1983.]

"Clearing the thickets." Pp. 107-121. [Kusamura. 1976.]

"An embrace." Pp. 122-138. [Hōyō. 1984.]

"Missing." Pp. 80-90. [Yukue fumei. 1973.]

"A sensitive season." Pp. 1-21. [Hatsujōki. 1974.]

"The shooting gallery." Pp. 91-106. [Shateki. 1975.]

"The silent traders." Pp. 33-44. Reprinted in: GESSEL (#1414), pp. 400-411. Also published in *Japanese Literature Today* no. 9:6-10. Mar. 1984. LCCN:76-648281. [Danmari ichi. 1982.]

"South wind." Pp. 22-34. Published earlier in: *Japan Quarterly* 33(1):72-80. Jan./Mar. 1986. [Minami kaze. 1978.]

"A bed of grass." 1982. [Translated by Yukiko TANAKA and Elizabeth HANSON.] In: TANAKA (#1424), pp. 225-287. [Kusa no fushido. 1976.]

"Island of joy." 1980. [Translated by Lora SHARNOFF.] *Japan Quarterly* 27(2):263-269. (Introduced on p. 249.) ISSN:0021-4590. [Yorokobi no shima. 1978.]

"The mother in the house of grass." Winter 1987. [Translated by Sara DILLON.] *Literary Review* 30(2):265-296. ISSN:0024-4589. [Mugura no haha. 1976.]

"To scatter flower petals." 1980. [Translated by Lora SHARNOFF.] *Japan Quarterly* 27(2):250-262. (Introduced on p. 249.) ISSN:0021-4590. Also translated as: "Scattering flowers." [Translated by Phyllis LYONS.] In: ARKIN (#1409), pp. 368-373. [Hana o maku.]

1484. UNO Chiyo (1897-)

Writer of fiction. Born in Yamaguchi Prefecture, the daughter of a sake brewer. Her mother died two years later; UNO was raised by a (benevolent) stepmother she assumed to be her real mother until well into her teens. When she was fourteen, her father forced her to marry a seventeen year old cousin, but she returned after only ten days. She finished girls' high school and became an elementary school teacher, but soon fell in love with a colleague, was rejected, and then spent a year in Korea and China. This was the beginning of a long series of marriages and love affairs, and of moving from place to place—like the characters in her fiction. In 1921, with no training or help, she wrote her first short story, which won an important literary contest and launched her on a long and brilliant career.

Iro zange [*Confessions of Love*] is her first important full-length work, ostensibly the retelling of the personal confessions of the bohemian painter TŌGŌ Seiji, with whom UNO lived for five years after hearing his story. "Ohan," her most critically acclaimed work, is based on a story she heard from another man, and creates a weak character caught between his passive but clinging wife and an aggressive, domineering geisha. She wrote many other stories from her own experiences (e.g. "Kōfuku" [Happiness]). UNO's life was the subject of scandal, but in her introduction to "Mohō no tensai" [A Genius of Imitation] TANAKA comments that "her spectacular financial success in publishing certainly contributed to a more positive image of women writers in pre-war Japan." (TANAKA (#1425), p. 183.) In 1936, UNO began publishing an enormously popular fashion magazine for women (a characteristically outlandish act, given that the country was gearing up for war and authorities frowned on extravagence and frivolity). The following year she began the literary journal, *Buntai* (*Literary Style*).

Confessions of Love. 1989. [Translated by Phyllis BIRNBAUM.] Honolulu: University of Hawaii Press, 157p. LCCN:88-39612. Summarized as: *An Amatory Confession* in: Kokusai Bunka Shinkōkai (#1518), pp. 468-472. [*Iro zange*. 1933.]

"A genius of imitation." 1982. [Translated by Yukiko TANAKA.] In: TANAKA (#1425), pp. 189-196. [Mohō no tensai. 1936.]

"Happiness." 1982. [Translated by Phyllis BIRNBAUM.] In: BIRNBAUM (#1411), pp. 133-147. [Kōfuku. 1970.]

"Ohan." 1961. [Translated by Donald KEENE.] In: KEENE, Donald. 1961. *The Old Woman, the Wife, and the Archer; Three Modern Japanese Short Novels*. New York: Viking Press, pp. 51-118. LCCN:61-16603. Synopsis in: Kokusai Bunka Shinkōkai (#1520), pp. 260-263. [Ohan. 1947.]

"Shopgirl." 1941. [Translated by Mitsugi TESHIGAWARA.] In: Japan Writer's Society. 1941. *Young Forever, and Five Other Novelettes by Contemporary Japanese Authors*. Tokyo: Hokuseido, pp. 122-139. LCCN:42-566. [Garasu no naka no musume.]

"To stab." 1982. [Translated by Kyoko Iriye SELDEN.] In: LIPPIT (#1419), pp. 92-104. Synopsis in: "Uno Chiyo, 'Sting.'" Jun. 1966. *Japan P.E.N. News* no. 19:7-10. ISSN:0075-3300. [Sasu. 1963-1966.]

1485. YAMADA Eimi (1959-)

Popular contemporary fiction writer. Born in Tokyo, studied Japanese literature at Meiji University. Also reads widely in French and American literature. *Bedtime Eyes*, summarized below, was her first novel, for which she was awarded the annual prize of the major literary magazine *Bungei* in 1985.

Bedtime eyes. Synopsis in: "On Yamada Eimi's *Bedtime Eyes*." Mar. 1986. [Translated by Charles M. DeWOLF.] *Japanese Literature Today* no. 11:20-21. LCCN:76-648281.

1486. YAMAMOTO Michiko (1936-)

Poet and fiction writer. Born in Tokyo to a wealthy family. Began writing (and publishing) poetry at an early age. Graduated in Japanese literature from junior college. In 1969 went with her husband to Darwin, Australia, where she lived for more than three years. She wrote very little there but the experience provided material for some of her best-known stories, including several listed below. Won the Akutagawa Prize for "Betei-san no niwa" [Betty-san], a long short story about a Japanese war bride who lives with her husband and two sons, transplanted (the original title means Betty-san's garden), in the inhospitable climate of central Australia—a work about sexual, social, and national identity and (the illusion of) bondage and free choice. Recently YAMAMOTO has been living with her family in Seattle, and she has continued to write.

Betty-san: Stories. 1983. [Translated by Geraldine HARCOURT.] Tokyo: Kodansha. 152p. LCCN:82-48786. Includes the following stories, all translated by Geraldine HARCOURT:
   "Betty-san." Pp. 7-67. [Betei-san no niwa. 1972.]
   "Chair in the rain." Pp. 115-152. [Ame no isu. 1972.]
   "Father Goose." Pp. 69-82. [Rōjin no kamo. 1972.]
   "Powers." Pp. 83-114. [Mahō. 1972.]
"The man who cut the grass." 1982. [Translated by Yukiko TANAKA and Elizabeth HANSON.] In: TANAKA (#1424), pp. 179-195. [Kusa o karu otoko. 1975.]

1487. YAMAZAKI Toyoko (1924-)

Fiction writer. Born in Osaka. Graduated from a Kyoto women's higher school with a major in Japanese literature. Worked as a reporter for the *Mainichi News*. Began her writing career with several long popular novels about the special traditions of the old Osaka merchant families (*Bonchi* is the third in this series) and then went on to what might be called novels of manners, well-researched and provocative works set in the world of finance, medicine, and big business. Focusing on gender roles and female bonding, *Bonchi* follows the career of a son of a traditional merchant family that has operated for several generations as a matriarchy.

The Barren Zone: A Novel. 1985. [Translated by James T. ARAKI.] Honolulu: University of Hawaii Press. 381p. LCCN:84-52221. [*Fumō chitai*. 1976.]

Bonchi: A Novel. 1982. [Author also cited as Toyoko YAMASAKI. Translated by Harue SUMMERGILL and Travis SUMMERGILL.] Honolulu: University of Hawaii Press. 404p. LCCN:81-23071. [*Bonchi.* 1960.]

Proprietress. Synopsis in: TOGAERI, Hajime. Jul. 1959. "Yamazaki Toyoko, 'Proprietress.'" *Japan P.E.N. News* no. 3:10-11. ISSN:0075-3300. [*Hana noren.* Synopsis. 1958.]

1488. YOSHIDA Tomoko (1934-)

Fiction writer and playwright. Born in Hamamatsu in Shizuoka Prefecture. Graduated from Nagoya Women's Junior College. Worked in a girls' high school until 1960. In 1970, she won the Akutagawa Prize for "Mumyō chōya" [The Long Night of Illusion] which is about insanity. YOSHIDA focuses on the inner life of people in the modern world.

"The long night of illusion." 1977. [Translated by James KIRKUP and Harvey EIKO.] *Japan Quarterly* 24(1):57-95. ISSN:0021-4590. [Mumyō chōya. 1970.]

1489. YOSHIYA Nobuko

Prominent writer of fiction for girls and young women. Essayist. Born in Niigata into a family of provincial nobility (from Hagi in Yamaguchi Prefecture). She was the fifth of eight children and the only daughter. Her father was a government official who served in local governments in various parts of Japan. Nobuko spent her formative years in Tochigi Prefecture, where her father occupied a post at the time. She later learned that her father had played a significant role in oppressing local farmers who were protesting against water pollution related to the local mines. While attending Tochigi Higher School for Women, she wrote and published a prize-winning children's story. Upon graduation, she went to Tokyo, where she studied English and the Bible with the help of Christian organizations committed to the education of women. It is said that reading Louisa May ALCOTT inspired her to become a novelist. From her early twenties she wrote prolifically and soon estabilished a reputation as a writer of juvenile fiction. Before the Second World War she traveled widely in Asia; during the War she evacuated to Kamakura, where she studied haiku with TAKAHAMA Kyoshi. Afterwards, she turned to serious adult fiction, including the work listed below, winning the Women's Literature Prize in 1951. She also wrote an autobiographical history of women in the Japanese literary establishment.

"The Adaka Family." Synopsis in: Kokusai Bunka Shinkōkai (#1519), pp. 208-210. [*Adakake no hitobito.* 1951-1952.]

1490. YOSHIYUKI Rie (1939-)

Poet; fiction writer. Born in Tokyo, the daughter of poet and novelist YOSHIYUKI Eisuke and younger sister of the novelist YOSHIYUKI Junnosuke. Graduated from Waseda University with a Japanese literature major. Plays with the relationship between fantasy and reality.

"The little lady." 1982. [Translated by Geraldine HARCOURT.] *Japanese Literature Today* 7:5-18. ISSN:0385-1044. [Chiisana kifujin. 1981.]

Critical Studies of Modern Prose

1491. ACASO, F. Jun. 1969. "Ayako Miura, A Christian novelist." *Japan Missionary Bulletin* 23(5):318-319. No refs. ISSN:0021-4531.

A very brief introduction to MIURA Ayako, "a Protestant lady living with her husband in Asahigawa, Hokkaido," focusing on her 1968 novel *Shiogari Tōge* [*Shiogari (Shiokari) Pass*] as a "Christian novel, with Christian characters, Christian problems, and a Christian thread through its pages: the story of a conversion." (p. 318)

1492. AMANO, Michie. Oct./Dec. 1980. "The stage as I see it." *Japan Quarterly* 27(4):503-512. ISSN:0021-4590.

Includes an extended review, entitled "The Cry of a Woman," of the play *Still Wanting the Mountain Cuckoo* by the woman playwright AKIMOTO Matsuyo (1911-).

1493. BIRNBAUM, Phyllis. 31 Oct. 1988. "Profiles: Modern girl." *New Yorker* 64(39):39-59. No refs. ISSN:0028-792X.

A charming and revealing visit with UNO Chiyo by the translator of *Confessions of Love*. Interwoven with amusing sketches from UNO's varied and eccentric career.

1494. BUCKLEY, Sandra. 1988. "Reading women's texts: *Stories by Contemporary Japanese Women* and *This Kind of Woman: Ten Stories by Japanese Women Writers, 1960-1976*." *Bulletin of Concerned Asian Scholars* 20(3):63-8. 24 notes. ISSN:0007-4810.

A feminist review of LIPPIT and SELDEN's *Stories by Contemporary Japanese Women Writers* (#1419), and TANAKA and HANSON's *This Kind of Woman* (#1424), praising their selection of authors and stories but offering the strong objection that, "while acknowledging that many of the stories are attempts to redefine the lives of women in a male-dominated society, the introductions proceed to read the lives of the protagonists back into the androcentric tradition their authors are working to deconstruct." (p. 65)

1495. CARPENTER, Juliet Winters. Jul./Sep. 1990. "Enchi Fumiko: 'A Writer of Tales.'" *Japan Quarterly* 37(3):343-356. 2 notes. ISSN:0021-4590.

An overview of ENCHI's life and works, told in interesting concrete detail.

1496. COPELAND, Rebecca L. 1988. "Uno Chiyo: Not just 'a writer of illicit love.'" *Japan Quarterly* 35(2):176-182. No refs. ISSN:0021-4590.

An amusing introduction to the life and works of UNO Chiyo, "a writer of illicit love" (p. 177) whose fiction displayed a "self-revealing passion" (p. 177) even when based on stories told to her by men, as in *Confessions of Love* and "Ohan."

1497. DANLY, Robert Lyons. 1981. *In the Shade of Spring Leaves: The Life and Writings of Higuchi Ichiyō*. New Haven: Yale University Press. 355p. Bibl. Index. LCCN:81-50434.

A supremely elegant literary biography with a traditional life-and-works approach, including eloquent translations of all major works.

1498. DeBARY, Brett. Apr. 1984/1985. "Wind and leaves: Miyamoto Yuriko's 'The Weathervane Plant.'" *Journal of the Association of the Teachers of Japanese* 19(1):7-28. ISSN:0085-9884.

An introduction to the late autobiographical work *Fūchisō*, placing it in the context of MIYAMOTO Yuriko's career, including an analysis of the work using Elaine SHOWALTER's characterization of writing by women as "'double-voiced discourse' containing both 'dominant' and 'muted' themes." (p. 13)

1499. ENOMOTO, Yoshiko. 1987. "Breaking out of despair: Higuchi Ichiyō and Charlotte Brontë." *Comparative Literature Studies* 24(3):251-263. 16 notes. ISSN:0010-4132.

ENOMOTO makes a brief presentation of external similarities in the two women's circumstances and in their personalities and attitudes toward life, especially the difficulties of being a writer and a woman, showing how their sense of "powerlessness and loneliness" (p. 255) is reflected in their works.

1500. "Feminist fiction in Japan." Oct. 1931. *Living Age* 341:177. No notes.

An early survey, alluding to "several prominent lady novelists [who] have suddenly been converted to the theories of Karl MARX . . . [t]hanks in part to the official suppression of radicalism," and concluding with a very brief plot summary of NOGAMI Yaeko's novel *Machiko*, the ambivalence of whose central conception the writer of this article takes to be representative of "the state of mind of modern Japan." (p. 177)

1501. FUJIMOTO, Kazuko. 1973. "Discrimination and the perception of difference." *Concerned Theatre Japan* 2(3):112-151. 41 notes. ISSN:0010-518X.

A long, political article drawing from ISHIMURE Michiko's work on the Minamata disease and essays by MORISAKI Kazue on Japanese racial discrimination, especially toward people of Korean descent. Essays by MORISAKI are included in the same issue.

1502. GESSEL, Van C. Summer 1988. "The 'medium' of fiction: Enchi Fumiko as narrator." *World Literature Today* 62(3):380-385. 9 notes. ISSN:0196-3570.

GESSEL provides an insightful investigation focusing on "falseness" of the narrative structure of ENCHI Fumiko's *Namamiko monogatari [A Tale of False Oracles]*, which he considers to be "most impressively shaped" (p. 380).

1503. GESSEL, Van C. Oct./Dec. 1988. "Echoes of feminine sensibility in literature." *Japan Quarterly* 35(4):410-416. No refs. ISSN:0021-4590.

A brief thematic overview of works (mostly available in English translation) by ENCHI Fumiko, KŌNO Taeko, TAKAHASHI Takako and TSUSHIMA Yūko. GESSEL links the current flowering of literature by Japanese women to a persistent strain of "feminine" sensibility in Japanese literature, whose poetry is dominated by the lyric ("feminine") rather than the epic ("masculine") despite the lack of women writers for centuries at a time.

1504. GESSEL, Van C. 1989. "Due time: Modern Japanese women writers." *Journal of Japanese Studies* 15(2):439-447. No notes. ISSN:0095-6848.

A sound comparative review of *Daughters of the Moon* by Victoria VERNON (#1427/1575), *To Live and to Write* by TANAKA Yukiko (#1425) *A Woman Called En* by ŌHARA Tomie (#1466), *Masks* by ENCHI Fumiko (#1433), and *The Shooting Gallery and Other Stories* by TSUSHIMA Yūko (#1483).

1505. GÖSSMANN, Hilaria. 1988. "The emancipation of women as shown in the novels of Sata Ineko." In: NISH, Ian, ed. 1988. *Contemporary European Writing on Japan: Scholarly Views from Eastern and Western Europe*. Kent, England: Paul Norbury Publications, pp. 231-244. 2 notes. LCCN:88-193026.

A glance at the principle female characters in several novels chosen to demonstrate SATA Ineko's position "that self-sacrifice is a destructive and self-limiting goal, which in the end brings only unhappiness and dissatisfaction." (p. 235)

1506. HEINRICH, Amy Vladeck. 1985. "Startling resonances: Some comparative feminist issues." In: BALAKIAN, Anna and James J. WILHELM, eds. *Proceedings of the Xth Congress of the International Comparative Literature Association* 2:606-613. New York: Garland. (International Comparative Literature Association Congress, 10th, 1982, New York.) 17 notes. LCCN:85-7081.

An interesting article quoting from an essay by SETOUCHI Harumi listing "[Necessary] Conditions for [Becoming] a Woman Writer." (p. 608). Offering a look at contemporary Japanese women writers from the vantage point of feminist criticism on American women writers, HEINRICH focuses on "how women writers view themselves as artists . . . and the nature of the texts they produce" and on resonances between the Japanese and the

American traditions of women writers, keeping in mind important differences in "culture, literary heritage, means of expression." (p. 60)

1507. HEINRICH, Amy Vladeck. Summer 1988. "Double Weave: The Fabric of Japanese Women's Writing." *World Literature Today* 62(3):404-414. 19 notes. ISSN:0196-3570.

Arguing that there are "separate sets of threads for the male tradition and the female tradition in Japanese literature," HEINRICH looks for patterns in the "weave" of the female tradition and finds commonalitites—in the search for a "field of action" and "forms of self-assertion" (p. 413)—between contemporary Japanese women's fiction and both women's literature of past centuries in Japan and women's writing in the West.

1508. "Hirabayashi Taiko, 'Secret.'" 1971. *Japan P.E.N. News* no. 24:7-10. No refs. ISSN:0075-3300. [*Himitsu*. Synopsis. 1968.]

Introduces HIRABAYASHI Taiko and provides a synopsis of "Secret."

1509. HOSHO, Masao. Aug. 1963. "Ariyoshi Sawako, 'Incense and Flowers.'" *Japan P.E.N. News* no. 11:15-17. ISSN:0075-3300. [Kōge. Synopsis. 1961.]

A synopsis of "Kōge" (1961) and a biographical sketch of the author.

1510. INOUE, Yōji, Jun'ichirō SAKO, and Shigeru SEKI. Spring 1985. "Miura Ayako and her world." *Japan Christian Quarterly* 51(2):96-102. No refs. ISSN:0021-4361.

A roundtable discussion among three Japanese clergymen, all of whom have published widely on Christianity, two of them (SAKO and SEKI) on Japanese Christian literature. The focus is on MIURA Ayako's Christian faith and her writing as a means of evangelism.

1511. Japan PEN Club, comp. 1990. *Japanese Literature in Foreign Languages, 1945-1990*. [Tokyo]: Japan Book Publishers Association. 383p. LCCN:91-156838.

A somewhat idiosyncratic but extremely valuable resource on Japanese prose and poetry translated into Western languages, plus relevant books, articles, and doctoral dissertations in those languages.

1512. JOHNSON, Eric. 1974. "Modern Japanese women writers." *Literature East and West* 18(1):90-102. No refs. ISSN:0024-4767.

An early introductory survey, briefly tracing the history of literature by Japanese women from Heian times, and then discussing NOGAMI Yaeko, OKAMOTO Kanoko, MIYAMOTO Yuriko, UNO Chiyo, HAYASHI Fumiko, and KŌDA Aya.

1513. KATO, Shuichi. 1979/1981. *A History of Japanese Literature. Volume Three: The Modern Years*. [Translated by Don SANDERSON.] London: MacMillan/Tokyo: Kodansha. Vol. 3 of a 3 vol. set. Notes. Index. LCCN:77-75967(set). [*Nihon bungakushi*.]

An interesting, somewhat idiosyncratic history by an eminent literary scholar (of German, French, and English as well as Japanese literature) and critic-at-large. Originally written for a Japanese audience and serialized in the *Asahi Journal*. This is the final volume, covering the period from the Bakumatsu to the post World War II years. Surprisingly little space is given to women, but the following writers are mentioned or discussed briefly: HIGUCHI Ichiyō, ISHIMURE Michiko, NOGAMI Yaeko and YOSANO Akiko.

1514. KEENE, Donald. 1978. *Some Japanese Portraits*. New York: Kodansha International. 228p. No refs. LCCN:76-39679.

A pleasant miscellany including a "portrait" of only one woman, HIGUCHI Ichiyō.

1515. KEENE, Donald. 1984. *Dawn to the West: Japanese Literature in the Modern Era.* New York: Holt, Reinhart and Winston, 1984. 2 vols. Bibl. LCCN:82-15445.

Part of a monumental history of Japanese literature prepared over many years by one of the most prominent and wide-ranging American scholars in the field. Partly because of KEENE's decision not to discuss living authors, women do not occupy an important place in this work. However, one chapter in the first volume (on fiction), is devoted to HIGUCHI Ichiyō, and another to "The Revival of Writing by Women," in which he treats NOGAMI Yaeko, OKAMOTO Kanoko, UNO Chiyo, HAYASHI Fumiko, MIYAMOTO Yuriko, SATA Ineko, and HIRABAYASHI Taiko. HIGUCHI Ichiyō is further discussed in the criticism section of volume two.

1516. KEENE, Donald. Apr./Jun. 1989. "The diary of Higuchi Ichiyō." *Japan Quarterly* 36(2):167-178. No refs. ISSN:0021-4590.

A brief speculative essay considering Ichiyō's reasons for keeping this diary, which is today valued as one of her greatest literary products. KEENE offers a charming and poignant portrait.

1517. Kokusai Bunka Kaikan, Tokyo. Toshoshitsu. 1979. *Modern Japanese Literature in Translation: A Bibliography.* Tokyo: Kodansha International. 311p. [Author also cited as: International House of Japan Library.] LCCN:78-66395.

An invaluable listing, by author, of fiction, drama, poetry, and essays published since 1868 that have been translated into English and many European and Asian languages. Original Japanese titles included.

1518. Kokusai Bunka Shinkōkai, ed. 1939. *Introduction to Contemporary Japanese Literature.* Tokyo: Kokusai Bunka Shinkōkai. 485p. Notes. Index.

A large compendium of synopses and brief (2-3p.) comments by preeminent Japanese scholars (no women) on individual major works of fiction by prominent writers from 1902 to 1935. Not appropriate as an introduction to the field, but convenient as a source of basic information on novels one might want to read in Japanese.

1519. Kokusai Bunka Shinkōkai, ed. 1959. *Introduction to Contemporary Japanese Literature: Part II, 1936-1955.* Tokyo: Kokusai Bunka Shinkōkai. 296p. Notes. Index.

A continuation of the series, this volume containing synopses and brief reviews of 71 works from this period plus ten omitted from volume I. Of the 81 total, 10 are women. Includes photographs of authors and index of literary prizes.

1520. Kokusai Bunka Shinkōkai, ed. 1972. *Introduction to Contemporary Japanese Literature: Synopses of Major Works, 1956-1970.* Tokyo: University of Tokyo Press. 313p. Bibl. Index.

The third volume in this series, containing a substantial introduction and biographical sketches of 72 authors published between 1956 and 1970, with synopses of works by 57 authors, 13 of them women.

1521. KOMATSU, Shinroku. Dec. 1960. "Sono Ayako, 'Visitors from Across the Sea.'" *Japan P.E.N. News* no. 6:8-9. ISSN:0075-3300.

A brief synopsis of *Enrai no kyakutachi* (1954) and a biographical sketch of the author.

1522. KONAKA, Yōtarō. Summer 1988. "Japanese atomic bomb literature." [Translated by Winifred OLSEN.] *World Literature Today* 62(3):420-424. 8 notes. ISSN:019-3570.

Focuses on the circumstances and work of a few luminaries, including ŌTA Yōko, and discusses (in passing) women "atomic bomb writers" as a group.

1523. LIPPIT, Noriko Mizuta. 1978. "Literature, ideology, and women's happiness: The autobiographical novels of Miyamoto Yuriko." *Bulletin of Concerned Asian Scholars* 10(2):2-9. 16 notes. ISSN:0007-4810. Reprinted as "Literature and ideology: The feminist autobiography of Miyamoto Yuriko." In: LIPPIT, Noriko Mizuta. 1980. *Reality and Fiction in Modern Japanese Literature.* White Plains, NY: M.E. Sharpe, pp. 146-162. LCCN:79-67859.

Believing that "for [MIYAMOTO] Yuriko, being a humanist meant being a feminist and a communist revolutionary, and the humanist, feminist, and revolutionary struggles were necessary truly to liberate human beings" (p. 2), LIPPIT treats three central problems in Yuriko's life: "consciousness and practice, women's happiness and creativity, and politics and literature" as they "shaped and are reflected in" her autobiographical works. (p. 2) She outlines the author's life and focuses briefly on *Nobuko* and its sequel *Futatsu no niwa* [*The Two Gardens*, 1947], *Koiwai no ikka* ["The Family of Kowai"], *Banshū heiya* ["Banshū Plain"], and *Fūchisō* ["The Weathervane Plant"].

1524. LIPPIT, Noriko Mizuta. 1979. "Beyond madness: Female protagonists' experience of nothingness and freedom in modern Western and Japanese literature." In: WHITE, Merry I. and Barbara MOLONY, eds. *Proceedings of the Tokyo Symposium on Women.* Tokyo: International Group for the Study of Women, pp. 56-66. (Tokyo Symposium on Women, [1st], 1978.)

Beginning from the premise that traditionally a "unity" between "social roles" and "sex roles—as mothers, wives, widows, spinsters, childless women, and so forth" is "characteristic of women's identification in novels" (p. 56), LIPPIT goes on to look at female characters created by modern women writers, claiming that " . . . Joan DIDION, Doris LESSING, ŌBA Minako, TSUSHIMA Yūko and TOMIOKA Taeko have created female characters who, naked, deprived of any social role, challenged the meaning of life, fully confronting the possibility of self-destruction." (p. 62)

1525. LIPPIT, Noriko Mizuta. 1980. "'I' in the novel: Self-revelation and self-concealment in the novels of Tomioka Taeko." In: LIPPIT, Noriko Mizuta. 1980. *Reality and Fiction in Modern Japanese Literature.* White Plains, NY: M.E. Sharpe, pp. 191-200. 3 Notes. LCCN:79-67859.

LIPPIT sees TOMIOKA Taeko's fictional works as "autobiographical" but not as "I-novels of self-search," (p. 191), and concludes that, "Underlying her treatment of 'I' is her criticism of elite intellectual artists who egotistically insisted that their personal failure or agony was the license for the greatness of art, a criticism which . . . reflects . . . fundamental changes in the identity of artists and [other] intellectuals in the age of mass culture." (p. 200)

1526. LIPPIT, Noriko Mizuta. 1988. "Affirming the other's madness: Feminism in translation." *Bulletin of Concerned Asian Scholars* 20(3):68-69. No refs. ISSN:0007-4810.

In response to BUCKLEY (#1494), LIPPIT argues that "the acts of translation and interpretation must always negotiate between the demands to preserve and to transform," and "only in resisting the phallocentric force of either demand . . . can a subversive and authentic 'feminine' voice emerge." (p. 69)

1527. MAMOLA, Claire Zebroski. 1989. *Japanese Women Writers in English Translation: An Annotated Bibliography.* New York: Garland. 469p. 971 refs. Index. LCCN:89-1319.

A listing of 971 items, 583 of them with summaries. MAMOLA dedicates her bibliography to materials (both fiction and nonfiction) written by Japanese women.

1528. MARKS, Alfred H. and Barry D. BORT. 1975. *Guide to Japanese Prose.* Boston: G.K. Hall. 150p. (*The Asian Literature Bibliography Series.*) Index. LCCN:74-20608.

A selective annotated bibliography of prose works from earliest times through the early 1970s that have been translated into English. Does not include secondary scholarship. Contains reviews of several volumes of modern fiction listed here.

1529. McCLAIN, Yōko. 1980. "Eroticism and the writings of Enchi Fumiko." *Journal of the Association of Teachers of Japanese* 15(1):32-46. 21 notes. ISSN:0885-9884.

A brief look at "A Bond for Two Lifetimes—Gleanings" and two stories not yet translated ("Yūkon" [The Excursion of One's Spirit] and "Saimu" [Glowing Fog]), listing literary and personal (medical) influences on ENCHI's writing, and concluding that in ENCHI's "erotic" works ". . . [s]exual love is often in the fantasy world of the heroine who can partly be identified with the author" (p.35), and that ". . . Enchi is interested in the eroticism of a middle-aged or older woman, in narratives that combine realism and fantasy, and in aesthetically pleasing writing." (p. 36)

1530. McCLAIN, Yōko. Nov. 1982. "Nogami Yaeko: A writer steady as a cow?" *Journal of the Association of Teachers of Japanese* 17(2):153-172. 24 notes. ISSN:0885-9884.

An overview of NOGAMI Yaeko's literary career. The title comes from NATSUME Sōseki's admonition to his students to be like a cow instead of a horse and to "pace yourself steadily until you die" (p. 53)—advice which those students (and Sōseki himself) ignored. McCLAIN notes that the only one of Sōseki's many "students" who fits the description is NOGAMI Yaeko, "who probably has had the longest writing career of any author in Japan . . . ." (p. 153)

1531. MITSUTANI, Margaret. Spring 1985. "Higuchi Ichiyō: A literature of her own." *Comparative Literature Studies* 22(1):53-79. 52 notes. ISSN:0010-4132.

A scholarly presentation of HIGUCHI Ichiyō as a woman artist who (as opposed to her predecessor TANABE Kaho) did not adopt a man's voice in a man's world, and yet who was "that rarity of rarities—an artist recognized in her own time." (p. 55) MITSUTANI sees in the portrayal of Ichiyō's later heroines a "sense of self" and "a note of modernity that can still be heard today." (p. 65)

1532. MITSUTANI, Margaret. 1986. "Renaissance in women's literature." *Japan Quarterly* 33(3):313-319. No refs. ISSN:0021-4590.

Introduces three writers: KOMETANI Fumiko (Foumiko), YAMADA Eimi, and the prolific popular translator of *The Tale of Genji* into modern Japanese, TANABE Seiko. MITSUTANI also ranges widely among the works of contemporary women like TOMIOKA Taeko, TSUSHIMA Yūko, KURAHASHI Yumiko, GŌ Shizuko, HAYASHI Kyōko, ŌBA Minako, and KŌNO Taeko. She pauses to discuss the origins and implications of the unfortunate term *joryū sakka*, usually translated as "woman writer."

1533. MIURA, Shumon. 1985. "Literature in postwar Japan." *Japan Echo* 12(Special Issue):3-8. ISSN:0388-0435.

A general overview and personal assessment focusing on the six (male) authors whose short stories are printed in this issue, and on the authors of four essays also included, two of whom (TAKENISHI Hiroko and TOMIOKA Taeko) are women.

1534. MONNET, Livia. 1988. "Not only Minamata: An Approach to Ishimure Michiko's work." In: NISH, Ian, ed. 1988. *Contemporary European Writing on Japan: Scholarly Views from Eastern and Western Europe*. Kent, England: Paul Norbury Publications, pp. 225-231. 17 notes. LCCN:88-193026.

A general (but scholarly) overview of ISHIMURE Michiko's works. In particular, *Kugai jōdo* [*Paradise in the Sea of Sorrow*] is described as revealing "the modern artist's distrust of human consciousness, history, and language" and as presenting implicitly, "the breakdown of the contemporary industrial civilisation and, implicitly, the approaching end of the human race." (p. 229)

1535. MONNET, Livia. Apr. 1989. "'In the beginning woman was the sun': Autobiographies of modern Japanese women writers, 1." *Japan Forum* 1(1):55-81. 106 refs. "'In the beginning woman was the sun': Autobiographies of modern Japanese women writers, 2." Oct. 1989. *Japan Forum* 1(2):197-233. 248 refs. ISSN:0955-5803.

Assuming, "in contradiction to practitioners of poststructuralist theory," that "both Author and Literature are very much alive, vibrant, contradictory, and as challenging as ever, . . . that literary texts are indelibly gender-marked, and autobiography [is] one of the most telling instances of sexual difference in the *écriture*," MONNET focuses on three autobiographies: those of HIRATSUKA Raichō, TAKAMURE Itsue and ISHIMURE Michiko.

1536. MORI, Jōji. 1974. "Drag the doctors into the area of metaphysics: An introduction to Kurahashi Yumiko." *Literature East and West* 18(1):76-89. No refs. ISSN:0024-4767.

Beginning with the speculation that in Japan, where "the tradition of treating women as persons to be listened to more attentively than men has been stronger—perhaps more than anywhere else" (p. 76) and women writers are placed in a special category because they are valued so highly, MORI introduces KURAHASHI as a woman writer who "does not write like an *onna* [woman]" (p. 77), whose style has "a disciplined austerity rarely seen except in formal reasoning." (p. 77) There follows an interesting overview of her major images and themes.

1537. MULHERN, Chieko. 1989. "Literary traditions: Regional essays—Japan." In: ARKIN, Marian and Barbara SHOLLAR, eds. *Longman Anthology of World Literature by Women, 1875-1975*. New York: Longman, pp. 1152-1162. Bibl. LCCN:88-8274.

A concise, readable chronological history full of information not available elsewhere in English, concluding that Japanese women writers today "are undeniably serving as the most articulate and influential leaders not only in updating female cosmology but also in awakening men to reassess the male paradigm as they have never done before. In this sense, contemporary Japanese women are fulfilling their sacerdotal role as effectively as their shamanistic ancestors." (p. 1161)

1538. MULHERN, Chieko Irie. Feb. 1989. "Japanese Harlequin romances as transcultural women's fiction." *Journal of Asian Studies* 48(1):50-70. 3 notes and bibl. ISSN:0021-9118.

A fascinating genre analysis of Japanese popular romances commissioned since 1983 by Sanrio Company in response to the popularity of translated Harlequin romances in Japan. MULHERN discusses motifs in works by thirteen Sanrio authors.

1539. MUTA, Orie. 1990. "Aspects of love in contemporary novels by Japanese women." *Hecate* 16(1/2):151-163. 24 notes. ISSN:0311-4198.

A sweeping survey focusing on novels from the 1950s onward and discussing them in terms of patterns related to gender perception: Abomination of Femaleness and the Communal Life, the Motif of Incest, Masochistic Sexuality, the Vision of Androgeny, Murderous Intentions, the Devouring Mother, Male Eroticism, the Search for the Self in Sex, Rejection of Relations. Generally deals with the tension between the need for love and the need for self.

1540. NAKAJIMA, Kawatarō. Jan./Mar. 1962. "Detective fiction in Japan." *Japan Quarterly* 9(1):50-56. No refs. ISSN:0021-4590.

A general survey discussing one work by NIKI Etsuko and mentioning several other women.

1541. NAKAMURA, Mitsuo. 1966/1968 [revised ed.] *Modern Japanese Fiction, 1868-1926.* Tokyo: Kokusai Bunka Shinkōkai. (*Japanese Life and Culture Series.*) 180p. Index. LCCN:68-58248.

An overview, not really appropriate for the uninitiated non-Japanese reader, by a prominent Japanese scholar, novelist, and literary critic. The first of two volumes, covering the Meiji and Taishō periods. No special attention is given to women writers, but HIGUCHI Ichiyō and YOSANO Akiko are treated at relative length, and some of their female contemporaries are mentioned.

1542. NAKAMURA, Mitsuo. 1969. *Contemporary Japanese Fiction, 1926-1968.* Tokyo: Kokusai Bunka Shinkōkai. 185p. Index. LCCN:70-80077.

A continuation of *Modern Japanese Fiction* [#1541], by the same author and sharing basic characteristics. NOGAMI Yaeko is the only woman writer given prominence, twelve others are listed in the index.

1543. NOGUCHI, Yone. May 1904. "Modern Japanese women writers." *Critic* 44:429-432. No notes.

NOGUCHI (a male poet) begins with "the eternally lamentable" HIGUCHI Ichiyō as "interpreter of Japanese women's sacrifice and passion" (p. 429) and introduces her prominent female literary colleagues and survivors, the *waka* poet NAKAJIMA Utako, WAKAMATSU Shizuko and TANABE Kaho. An interesting view of the scene by a male contemporary of the people he describes.

1544. NOGUCHI, Yone. Jul. 1904. "Japanese women in literature." *Poet Lore* 15(3):88-89. ISSN:0032-1966. No refs.

A very brief, emotional account of the history of women writers in Japan, written seven years after the death of HIGUCHI Ichiyō. NOGUCHI (a Japanese-born poet who writes in both Japanese and English) sees this history as culminating in the Meiji period, when "the sudden invasion of European civilization and especially that of America purified our shut-up atmosphere," "prejudice was destroyed," and "women stepped to the front straightaway" (p. 91), and concluding with the remark that the literary achievements of Japanese women are not recognized in the United States.

1545. OKAZAKI, Yoshie. 1955. *Japanese Literature in the Meiji Period.* Tokyo: Toyo Bunko. 673p. (*Japanese Culture in the Meiji Period*, vol. 1.)

A detailed history of Meiji fiction, drama, poetry, essays, and literary criticism, intended for the Japanese reader and therefore not easily accessible as an introductory overview. HIGUCHI Ichiyō and YOSANO Akiko are the only women given prominent treatment.

1546. "On Hayashi Kyōko's *As If It Never Happened* (*Naki ga gotoki*). Mar. 1982. *Japanese Literature Today* no. 7:24-26. LCCN:76-648281.

Contains a synopsis of the novel (published in 1980), a summary of the critical reception, and a biographical sketch of HAYASHI Kyōko.

1547. "On Kōno Taeko's *A Pastoral Year* (*Ichinen no bokka*)." Mar. 1981. *Japanese Literature Today* no. 6:25-27. LCCN:76-648281.

Contains a synopsis of the prize-winning novel published in 1979, a summary of critical reaction, and a biographical note on the author.

1548. "On Masuda Mizuko's 'Single Cell' (*Shinguru seru*)." Mar. 1988. [Translated by Mark JEWEL.] *Japanese Literature Today* no. 13:14-15. LCCN:76-648281.

An introduction to the story (published in 1987) and the critical reaction to it, plus a brief profile of this newly acclaimed author whose works are marked by "the recurring motif of a solitary life." (p. 15)

1549. "On Takahashi Takako's *Child of Wrath* (*Ikari no ko*)." Mar. 1986. [Translated by Charles M. DeWOLF.] *Japanese Literature Today* no. 11:16-18. LCCN:76-648281.

A plot summary of the novel published in 1985, a sampling of critical reaction in Japan, and a profile of TAKAHASHI.

1550. "On Tomioka Taeko's *A Tale of Snow Buddhas* (*Yuki no hotoke no monogatari*). Mar. 1988. [Translated by Mark JEWEL.] *Japanese Literature Today* no. 13:12-13. LCCN:76-648281.

A plot summary of the novel published in 1987, followed by a brief overview of critical reaction to the work, and a profile of TOMIOKA Taeko.

1551. "On Yamada Eimi's *Bedtime Eyes*." Mar. 1986. [Translated by Charles M. DeWOLF.] *Japanese Literature Today* no. 11:20-21. LCCN:76-648281.

A brief plot summary of this first novel by a young feminist writer and numerous relevant quotations from (anonymous) Japanese critics. Includes a brief introduction to YAMADA Eimi.

1552. PHILLIPS, Susan. 1988. "Beyond borders: Class struggle and feminist humanism in *Banshū Heiya*." *Bulletin of Concerned Asian Scholars* 19(1):56-65. 37 notes. ISSN:0007-4810. Reprinted in: TSURUMI, E. Patricia, ed. *The Other Japan: Postwar Realities*. Armonk, NY: M.E. Sharpe, pp. 5-13. 37 refs. LCCN:87-23365.

An overview of MIYAMOTO Yuriko's personal development and career, regarding her first postwar literary effort, *The Banshū Plain*, as an optimistic, humanist work expressing the belief that "not just those committed to a specific political ideology but all humanity [is] capable of effecting significant social transition through collective effort." (p.12)

1553. POUNDS, Wayne. Nov. 1990. "Enchi Fumiko and the Hidden Energy of the Supernatural." *Journal of the Association of Teachers of Japanese* 24(2):167-183. 38 notes. ISSN:0885-9884.

An examination of *Masks* in the context of shamanism and the supernatural tradition.

1554. PUTZAR, Edward. 1973. *Japanese Literature: A Historical Outline*. [Adapted from the work by Sen'ichi HISAMATSU.] Tucson: University of Arizona Press. 246p. LCCN:70-189229. [*Nihon bungaku*. Adaptation. 1960.]

A chronological history of Japanese literature, originally intended for a Japanese audience, from 400 to 1945. Women, especially poets, are mentioned throughout, and the discussion of the Heian Period includes sections on Imperial Anthologies, *The Tale of Genji*, and the *Pillow Book*. The modern chapter is organized by groups and movements and focuses on literary ideology and on fiction. Women are mentioned, sometimes discussed, in passing.

1555. REEDY, Jitsuko. Fall 1980. "Shizuko Wakamatsu." *Japan Christian Quarterly* 46(4):215-220. 19 notes. ISSN:0021-4361.

A personal introduction to the life and views of this early translator, based on a biography by YAMAGUCHI Reiko.

1556. REICH, Pauline C. Autumn 1976. "Japan's literary feminists: The Seitō group." [Excerpts translated by Pauline C. REICH and Atsuko FUKUDA.] *Signs* 2(1):280-291. 11 notes. ISSN:0097-9740.

Introduces early literary figures including HIGUCHI Ichiyō, YOSANO Akiko, OKAMOTO Kanoko, and HAYASHI Fumiko, and provides translations of HIRATSUKA Raichō's "Manifesto" from the first issue of *Seitō* in 1911, and "To the Women of the World" [*Yo no fujintachi ni*. 1913.].

1557. RIEGER, Naoko Alisa. 1986. *Enchi Fumiko's Literature: The Portrait of Women in Enchi Fumiko's Selected Works*. Hamburg, Germany: Roland Schneider, Hans Stumpfeldt, Klaus Wenk. (*MOAG Mitteilungen der Gesellschaft für Natur- und Völkerkunde Ostasiens*, 103). 218p. Notes. Bibl. Index. LCCN:87-128793.

A study by a student of Osar BENL (translator of *Genji monogatari* into German), influenced by contemporary feminist literary criticism and heavily grounded in Japanese scholarship. The stated main purpose is to follow "Enchi's investigation into the suffering of Japanese women caused by thier dependence on men and male-dominated social norms and values" by looking at "the moral and psychological development of female protagonists in eight novels and short stories . . . selected from the different periods of Enchi's literary career." (p. 4) Contains an extended bibliography, mainly of Japanese primary and secondary sources.

1558. RIMER, J. Thomas. 1988. *A Reader's Guide to Japanese Literature*. New York: Kodansha International. 208p. Bibl. LCCN:88-45080.

An eloquent but necessarily superficial introduction to Japanese literature readily available in English, aimed at helping those new to Japanese literature decide what to read first. Of thirty entries on modern literature, two deal with works by women: HIGUCHI Ichiyō's "Comparing Heights" and ARIYOSHI Sawako's *The Doctor's Wife*.

1559. SAKANISHI, Shio. Oct./Dec. 1955. "Women writers of today." *Japan Quarterly* 2(4):489-495. No refs. ISSN:0021-4590.

A sober article focusing first on KŌDA Aya, ENCHI Fumiko and KOBORI Anne, all of whom had the career advantage of famous literary fathers (KŌDA Rohan, UEDA Kazutoshi and MORI Ōgai, respectively); going on to cast a critical eye on the works of SATA Ineko, YUKI Shigeko, and SONO Ayako, and to describe current women's organizations for amateur writers.

1560. SCHIERBECK, Sachiko Shibata. 1989. *Postwar Japanese Women Writers: An Up-to-Date Bibliography with Biographical Sketches*. [Edited by Søren EGEROD.] Copenhagen: University of Copenhagen Press. 196p. (*Occasional Papers of the East Asian Institute, University of Copenhagen*, vol. 5. ISSN:0903-6822.) Bibl. LCCN:90-134286.

A general historical introduction followed by brief portraits (with photographs) of 53 women who have written fiction since World War II, including a short list of "selected" works in Japanese, and in English, French and German translation. Summaries of major, untranslated works are also provided. A number of the writers SCHIERBECK includes are not listed in this bibliography, since they are not yet represented in English translation.

1561. SCHREIBER, Mark. 1987. "The Agatha Christie of Japan: An interview with Shizuko Natsuki, who defied Japanese tradition to become an award-winning mystery writer." *Armchair Dectective* 20(1):54-57. ISSN:0004-217X.

An interesting interview, focusing on why and under what conditions NATSUKI Shizuko writes, emphasizing her cosmopolitanism, and repudiating any similarity to Agatha CHRISTIE.

1562. SHEA, George Tyson. 1964. *Leftwing Literature in Japan: A Brief History of the Proletarian Literary Movement.* Tokyo: Hōsei University Press. 478p. Bibl. Index. LCCN:65-84606.

A detailed history of "the first socialist literature of the early 1900's to the democratic literary movement which arose after World War II" (p. i), focusing on the proletarian literary movement from 1921 to 1934. Several women are mentioned in passing, and a very few, in particular MIYAMOTO Yuriko and SATA Ineko, are treated in detail.

1563. SUGIMORI, Hisahide. Jan. 1962. "Higuchi Ichiyō, 'The Thirteenth Night.'" [Translated by Kenneth STRONG.] *Japan P.E.N. News* no. 8:1-2. ISSN:0075-3300.

A brief synopsis of *Jūsan'ya* and a biographical sketch of the author.

1564. SWANN, Thomas E. and Kinya TSURUTA. 1982. *Approaches to the Japanese Short Story.* Tokyo: Waseda University Press. 341p. Notes.

A collection of brief essays, an early "attempt to introduce Western readers to the excellence of some of Japan's best short story writers and their works." (p. x) Of the 34 stories by fifteen authors discussed, only two are relevant here: HAYASHI Fumiko's "Late Chrysanthemum," presented by Janice BROWN, and HIGUCHI Ichiyō's "Growing Up," by Makoto UEDA.

1565. TAKADŌ, Kaname. Fall 1978. "Postwar Japanese playwrights and Christianity." [Translated by David L. SWAIN.] *Japan Christian Quarterly* 44(4):230-235. ISSN:0021-4361.

Introduces TANAKA Sumie (1908-) a rare woman playwright and her playwright husband TANAKA Chikao.

1566. TAKAGI, Kiyoko. 1983. "Religion in the life of Higuchi Ichiyō." *Japanese Journal of Religious Studies* 10(2):123-147. 9 refs. ISSN:0304-1042.

A look at the religious consciousness of a transitional figure in the Japanese tradition, detailing Buddhist, Shinto and Christian elements in her life and concluding that "even though she had a fairly good intellectual understanding of religion, she never got to the point of embracing religion in her heart and living her life as a religious person. The empty space in her she filled . . . by carrying out customary religious practices." (p. 146)

1567. TAKAHASHI, Aguri. 27 Aug. 1931. "Feminist literature progresses in Japan: Group of modern authoresses prefer simple settings." *The Trans-Pacific* 1931(27 Aug.):5,12. LCCN:72-620605.

Interesting as a contemporary account of Marxist proletarian women writers, concluding that "literary women are increasing daily, but in truth there are a very few who can bear comparison with male authors in their technique." (p. 12)

1568. TAKITA, Yoshiko. Spring 1985. "Wakamatsu Shizuko and *Little Lord Fauntleroy.*" *Comparative Literature Studies* 22(1):1-8. 15 notes. ISSN:0010-4132.

TAKITA provides an overview of the ideals and work of Meiji Christian writer and translator WAKAMATSU Shizuko, focusing on why and how she chose to translate Frances Hodgeson BURNETT's juvenile novel, *Little Lord Fauntleroy.* The work became an early example of juvenile literature in Japan, where it was read by adults as well as children and helped to foster the value of "home" (p. 8) and a "romantic idea of the child" (p. 7).

1569. TANAKA, Hisako. 1956. "Higuchi Ichiyō." *Monumenta Nipponica* 12:171-194. 34 notes. ISSN:0027-0741.

An early, introductory article on Ichiyō, intended "to sketch her life adhering closely to her diary and briefly to touch upon her literary products, which are delicately interwoven with the mosaic of her own strenuous life." (p. 172)

1570. TANAKA, Hisako. 1956. "Women writers of Meiji and Western literature." *Transactions of the International Conference of Orientalists in Japan* 1956:57-92. 57 notes and bibl. ISSN:0538-6012. [Title also cited as *Kokusai Tōhō Gakusha Kaigi Kiyō.*]

In this early article (written long before it was the feminist academic fashion to shed light on women left out of the canon), TANAKA introduces five Meiji period women writers (novelists MIYAKE Kaho and HIGUCHI Ichiyō, poet YOSANO Akiko, and two translators of Western literature, WAKAMATSU Shizuko and KOGANEI Kimiko) "with special emphasis on the bearing of Western literature upon their literary activities." (p. 51). The extended bibliography consists primarily of Japanese sources.

1571. TANAKA, Yukiko. 1988. "Feminist reading(s) and reading into feminist theory." *Bulletin of Concerned Asian Scholars* 20(3):69-72. ISSN:0007-4810.

In this response to BUCKLEY (#1494), TANAKA argues that the writers included in *To Live and to Write* (#1425) are not "primarily concerned" with "gender equality," that in fact, "although their gender seems to go against them as social beings, they managed to maintain confidence in their female voices as authors." (p. 70)

1572. TOGAERI, Hajime. Jul. 1959. "Yamazaki Toyoko, *Proprietress.*" *Japan P.E.N. News* no. 3:10-11. ISSN:0075-3300.

A brief synopsis of *Hana noren* (1958) and a biographical sketch of the author.

1573. "Uno Chiyo, 'Sting.'" Jun. 1966. *Japan P.E.N. News* no. 19:7-10. ISSN:0075-3300.

A brief synopsis of "Sasu" (1963-1966) and a brief biographical sketch of the author.

1574. USUI, Yoshimi. Oct./Dec. 1957. "The young woman novelist today." *Japan Quarterly* 4(4):519-522. No refs. ISSN:0021-4590.

A revealing personal reading of women's fiction by a prominent (male) critic. USUI claims that until recently major women writers were all divorcées, since "For women, the only part of their experience worth revealing is that obtained outside the narrow confines of the home," (p. 520), but that the current lessening of emphasis on personal experience in the writing of fiction has given rise to new writers, like HARADA Yasuko and ARIYOSHI Sawako, who are "women of talent rather than experience." (p. 522)

1575. VERNON, Victoria V. 1988. *Daughters of the Moon: Wish, Will, and Social Constraint in Fiction by Modern Japanese Women*. Berkeley: Institute of East Asian Studies, University of California. (Japan Research Monograph, vol. 9.) 245p. Bibl. Index. LCCN:86-45977.

The first book-length feminist analysis of Japanese fiction published in the United States, and the first devoted to fiction by Japanese women. Using contemporary American and European feminist theory, VERNON focuses on writers of three generations: HIGUCHI Ichiyō, SATA Ineko, and KURAHASHI Yumiko. VERNON asserts that the contemporary Japanese woman writer's task is "to free herself from the images that cling, to form her own image, and to end the long centuries of silenced metaphor." (p. 214) Includes translations of two stories SATA's "Inn of the Dancing Snow" and KURAHASHI's "End of Summer."

1576. WALKER, Janet A., Laurel Rasplica RODD, and Lynne MIYAKE. 1989. "Women and literature: A forum." *Journal of the Association of Teachers of Japanese* 23(1):79-92. No refs. ISSN:0885-9884.

Includes reviews of three important contributions to our understanding of Japanese women writers and their works: UEDA Makoto's *Mother of Dreams and Other Short Stories* (#1426), Victoria VERNON's *Daughters of the Moon* (#1427/1575) and TANAKA Yukiko's *To Live and to Write* (#1425).

1577. YAMAGIWA, Joseph K. 1959. *Japanese Literature of the Showa Period: A Guide to Japanese Reference and Research Materials.* Ann Arbor: University of Michigan Press. 212p. (*University of Michigan Center for Japanese Studies Bibliographical Series* no. 8.) LCCN:59-62962.

Aimed at an audience reasonably familiar with Japanese literature, this volume contains a wealth of information on almost all recognized twentieth-century groups of writers or poets, with considerable attention to their membership and their publications (journals). Also a valuable, though outdated, bibliographic source for Japanese materials.

1578. YAMAMOTO, Fumiko. 1984. "Kurahashi Yumiko: A dream of the Present? A bridge to the past?" *Modern Asian Studies* 18(1):137-152. 43 notes. ISSN:0026-749X.

YAMAMOTO discusses KURAHASHI's 1970 novel, *Yume no ukihashi* [A Floating Bridge of Dreams], pointing out resonances with the Heian tradition and *The Tale of Genji* in particular.

1579. YAMAMOTO, Kenkichi. Jul. 1960. "Ōhara Tomie, 'A Woman called En.'" *Japan P.E.N. News* no. 5:10-11. ISSN:0075-3300.

A brief synopsis of *En to iū onna* (1960) and a brief biographical sketch of the author.

15

Modern Poets

1580. ARKIN, Marian and Barbara SHOLLAR, eds. 1989. *Longman Anthology of World Literature by Women, 1875-1975.* White Plains, NY: Longman. 1274p. Index. LCCN:88-8274.

Includes poetry by YOSANO Akiko, ISHIGAKI Rin, IBARAGI Noriko, SHIRAISHI Kazuko, KŌRA Rumiko and TOMIOKA Taeko. Helpful biographical introductions by Phyllis LYONS.

1581. BENNETT, Jean, ed. 1976. *Japanese Love Poems.* Garden City, NY: Doubleday. 104p. LCCN:76-2753.

An anthology of poetry from both the aristocratic and the folk traditions, culled from various other anthologies of Japanese poetry in many different translation styles, arranged topically without original text. Brief introductory note for the general reader. Includes 16 women, in addition to "anonymous"; YOSANO Akiko is the only modern poet represented.

1582. BLYTH, Reginald Horace. 1949-1952/1963-1964. *Haiku.* Tokyo: Hokuseido Press. 4 vols. Bibl. Indexes. LCCN:53-20278.

A prodigious wealth of information about haiku, and a splendid collection of poems, arranged seasonally and topically. Volumes contain historical and generic essays, genealogical and other tables, and romanized texts for all poems. Fifteen women poets are represented, of whom HONDA Aoi and HASEGAWA Kanajo are modern.

1583. BLYTH, Reginald Horace. 1963/1964. *A History of Haiku in Two Volumes.* Tokyo: Hokuseido Press. 2 vols. LCCN:63-23741.

A thorough and fascinating classic of Western Orientalism. A critical formal introduction to the haiku, and a history of that genre from its origins in linked verse, considering Chinese influence, to the modern day. Studded with translations, including Japanese and romanized texts.

1584. BOWNAS, Geoffrey, ed. 1964. *The Penguin Book of Japanese Verse.* [Translations by Geoffrey BOWNAS and Anthony THWAITE.] Baltimore: Penguin Books. 242p. LCCN:64-6583.

A sampling of Japanese poetry from all ages in pleasing, interesting translation. YOSANO Akiko [#1729] is the only modern woman poet included. Useful introduction for the general reader. Occasional notes. Index of poets.

1585. CLACK, Robert Wood. 1977. *The Soul of Yamato.* (edited for publication by R.W. Douglas CLACK.) New York: Gordon Press. 2 vol. LCCN:76-789.

An anthology collected over many years and apparently prepared in 1953, published posthumously. Introduction to the Japanese language and "The Nature of Japanese Poetry," followed by translations, in chronological order, of a wide variety of poems from prehistoric times to the early 20th century. Translations are in original syllable count. No Japanese or romanized text. Each chronological period is preceded by its own historical introduction; most authors are introduced, and many poems are accompanied by brief commentary. Includes the poems of: CHINO Masako, HOSHINO Tatsuko, IMAI Kuniko, Imozeni, INAGAKI Etsuko, ITAMI Kimiko, KUJŌ Takeko, MATSUO Shizuko, NAKAHARA Ayako, NAKAMURA Teijo, Naojo, NISHIGORI Kurako, OKAMOTO Kanoko, SAISHO Atsuko, Empress Shoken, SUGIURA Suiko, WAKAYAMA Kishiko, YAMAKAWA Tomiko, YANAGIWARA Akiko and YOSANO Akiko.

1586. COSMAN, Carol, Joan KEEFE, and Kathleen WEAVER, eds. 1978. *The Penguin Book of Women Poets.* New York: Viking. 399p. LCCN:78-15342.

Contains an excellent selection of classical and modern poetry by women, with biographical and stylistic information. A substantial portion is Japanese poetry; modern poets are represented by ISHIGAKI Rin and YOSANO Akiko.

1587. DAVIS, Albert R., ed. 1978. *Modern Japanese Poetry.* [Translated by James KIRKUP.] St. Lucia, Queensland: University of Queensland Press. (*Asian and Pacific Writing,* vol. 9.) 323p. Bibl. LCCN:79-300530.

Excellent translations of an impressive number of women free verse poets. Many of the poems are not available elsewhere in English. Includes the poetry of: AOTA Mitsuko, IBARAGI Noriko, IKEDA Some, ISHIGAKI Rin, ITŌ Mariko, KŌRA Rumiko, MATSUSHIMA Mami, MITSUI Futabako, MORI Michiyo, NAGASE Kiyoko, NISHIO Katsuko, NOMA Fumiyo, SHINKAWA Kazue, SHIRAISHI Kazuko, SUYAMA Hisayo, TADA Chimako, TOMIOKA Taeko, YOSANO Akiko, YOSHIWARA Sachiko and YOSHIYUKI Rie.

1588. *The Eastern Sun is So Inviting: Ocarina's Anthology of International Poetry—Stress on Japan.* Jun./Jul. 1980. *Ocarina: A Journal of Poetry and Aesthetics* [Madras, India: Tagore Institute of Creative Writing] vol. 3 (special issue). [Guest editors Tsutomu FUKUDA and Naoshi KORIYAMA].

Includes the work of both pominent and unknown contemporary free verse poets: ATSUMI Ikuko, IBARAGI Noriko, ISHIKAWA Itsuko, ŌHARA Shōko, SADAMATSU Keiko, TAKADA Toshiko, TAKIGUCHI Masako, TEZUKA Hisako and YOSHIWARA Sachiko. No original Japanese or romanized text, or biographical information on poets.

1589. ERICKSON, Lois J. 1968. *Songs from the Land of Dawn by Toyohiko Kagawa and other Japanese Poets.* Freeport, NY: Books for Libraries Press. 80p. LCCN:68-58828.

An anthology of wartime Christian poetry. KAGAWA is a man, but several of the Christian contemporaries whose poems are included are women. They are all people associated with a government hospital for victims of leprosy on the island of Ōshima in the Inland Sea. Individual poems are not listed below.

1590. FITZSIMMONS, Thomas. 1972. *Japanese Poetry Now.* [Translated by Thomas FITZSIMMONS.] New York: Schocken Books. 134p. LCCN:70-181882.

A good selection of modern free verse by men, plus one woman: SHIRAISHI Kazuko. Interesting translations, by a poet. No original or romanized text.

1591. GUEST, Harry, Lynn GUEST and Shōzō KOJIMA, comp. and eds. 1972. *Post-war Japanese Poetry.* [Translated by Harry GUEST, Lynn GUEST and Shōzō KOJIMA.] Harmondsworth: Penguin Books. 167p. LCCN:73-158152.

Includes poems by IBARAGI Noriko and TOMIOKA Taeko in an otherwise male-dominated selection.

1592. HIGGINSON, William J. with Penny HARTER. 1989. *The Haiku Handbook: How to Write, Share, and Teach Haiku.* Tokyo: Kodansha International. 331p. Reprint of 1985 edition: New York: McGraw-Hill, 331p. LCCN:84-17174.

An excellent resource, for all the purposes listed in the subtitle. Offers an interesting mix of well-known Japanese haiku and haiku composed in English and other languages (some by Americans of Japanese descent)—all considered together. Also provides substantial literary-historical information on haiku (including contemporary haiku) and related genres. Biographical information on most poets, and romanized original texts for Japanese haiku are included. Contains the work of: EBISUYA Kiyoko, HASHIMOTO Takako, IZUMI Sumie, KAMIKO Yoshiko, OGAWA Yoshino, TAKEDA Chie and YOSANO Akiko.

1593. HOFFMANN, Yoel, compiler. 1986. *Japanese Death Poems Written by Zen Monks and Haiku Poets on the Verge of Death.* Rutland, VT: Tuttle. 366p. 44 notes. LCCN:85-52347.

An anthology of haiku with brief biographical and stylistic commentary, preceded by a substantial general introduction to Japanese poetry and "death and its poetry in the cultural history of Japan" (p. 27). Ten of the haiku poets included are identifiable as women; TOKUGAWA Kasenjo is the only modern poet.

1594. HUGHES, Glenn and Yozan T. IWASAKI. 1927. *Three Women Poets of Modern Japan: A Book of Translations.* Seattle: University of Washington Book Store. (*University of Washington Chapbooks*, no. 9.) 43p. LCCN:27-25447.

An early anthology of poetry by women—YOSANO Akiko, YANAGIWARA Akiko and KUJŌ Takeko—beginning with the observation that, "Of the millions of little poems written in Japan, few are excellent, and few survive, but in this survival the poems by women have an even chance with those by men." (p. 11) Introduction and biographical notes on poets.

1595. HUGHES, Glenn and Yozan T. IWASAKI. 1928. *Fifteen Poets of Modern Japan: A Book of Translations.* Seattle: University of Washington Book Store. (*University of Washington Chapbooks*, no. 17.) 34p. LCCN:28-23393.

A small anthology with an extremely brief introduction. Includes poems of varied form by HARA Asao [cited as HARU Asao], KUJŌ Takeko, YANAGIWARA Akiko, and YOSANO Akiko. No original or romanized text.

1596. KEENE, Donald, ed. 1956. *Modern Japanese Literature: An Anthology.* New York: Grove Press. 440p. LCCN:56-8439.

The seminal anthology of modern Japanese literature in English. Includes two poems by YOSANO Akiko.

1597. KIJIMA, Hajime, ed. 1975. *The Poetry of Postwar Japan.* Iowa City: University of Iowa Press. 267p. LCCN:75-17718.

A useful anthology of readable translations including seven women free verse poets: FUKUI Hisako, IBARAGI Noriko, ISHIGAKI Rin, KŌRA Rumiko, SHIRAISHI Kazuko, TAKIGUCHI Masako and TOMIOKA Taeko.

1598. KIRKUP, James. 1976. "Thirteen modern Japanese poets." *Mundus Artium* 9(1):8-33. No notes. ISSN:0027-3406.

A mini-anthology including four women: KŌRA Rumiko, SUYAMA Hisayo, TADA Chimako and YOSHIWARA Sachiko. Illustrated, with several photographs of sculpture by SHIMADA Tadae (a woman). No introduction or Japanese text for the poems.

1599. KŌNO, Ichirō and Rikutarō FUKUDA. 1957. *An Anthology of Modern Japanese Poetry.* Tokyo: Kenkyusha. 173p. LCCN:80-509353.

An anthology useful for its inclusion of five women poorly represented elsewhere in English: FUKAO Sumako, HAYASHI Fumiko, NAGASE Kiyoko, SAWAKI Takako and UEDA Shizue.

1600. MISHIMA, Yukio and Geoffrey BOWNAS, eds. 1972. *New Writing in Japan.* [Translated by Yukio MISHIMA and Geoffrey BOWNAS.] Harmondsworth: Penguin Books. 249p. LCCN:73-157181.

Includes poetry by two women—SHIRAISHI Kazuko and MIZUSHIMA Hatsu, a modern haiku poet not otherwise represented here.

1601. MIYAMORI, Asatarō. 1932. *An Anthology of Haiku Ancient and Modern.* Tokyo: Maruzen. 841p. Index. LCCN:33-19317.

A vast collection of haiku, including a literary-historical survey, plus biographical information and commentary on individual poems. Includes both Japanese and romanized text. An invaluable resource despite the occasionally bizarre translations. Poems are titled. Many poems by women are included.

1602. MIYAMORI, Asatarō. 1936[1970]. *Masterpieces of Japanese Poetry Ancient and Modern.* Westport, CT: Greenwood Press. 2 vol. LCCN:88-194141.

A prodigious two-volume anthology of *tanka/waka* in four-line rhyming stanzas with attributed titles. Includes Japanese text, romanization, biographical headnotes for all poets, and occasional commentary on poems. IMAI Kuniko, KUJŌ Takeko, NAKAHARA Ayako, NISHIGORI Kurako, SAISHO Atsuko, SHIGA Mitsuko, Empress Shoken, WAKAYAMA Kishiko, YAMAKAWA Tomiko and YOSANO Akiko are represented.

1603. MIYAMORI, Asatarō. 1938. *An Anthology of Japanese Poems.* Tokyo: Maruzen. 289p. Index. LCCN:39-961.

An "abridged and revised edition" of the 1936 *Masterpieces of Japanese Poetry Ancient and Modern* [#1602]. Shorter, but similar in character and presentation. Includes poems of IMAI Kuniko, SHIGA Mitsuko, Empress Shoken, WAKAYAMA Kishiko and YOSANO Akiko.

1604. NINOMIYA, Takamichi and D.J. ENRIGHT, eds. 1957. *The Poetry of Living Japan.* New York: Grove Press. 104p. LCCN:58-12186.

Contains poems by 30 prominent poets, only one of them a woman: FUKAO Sumako. NINOMIYA describes her as "the only [woman poet] (outside the traditionalists) to establish herself as a major figure." (p. 103).

1605. OMORI, Miyao. [1955.] *The Songs of Hiroshima: An Anthology.* Hiroshima: YMCA Service Center. 78p.

A collection of poems by *hibakusha* [atomic bomb survivors], including three women (HARADA Setsuko, NAGASE Kiyoko and YAMADA Kazuko).

1606. ŌOKA, Makoto and Thomas FITZSIMMONS, eds. 1987. *A Play of Mirrors.* Rochester, MI: Katydid Books. (*Asian Poetry in Translation: Japan #7.*) LCCN:86-21130.

Contains a good selection of free verse by SHIRAISHI Kazuko and TADA Chimako.

1607. REXROTH, Kenneth and Ikuko ATSUMI, eds. 1977. *The Burning Heart: Women Poets of Japan*. [Translated by Kenneth REXROTH and Ikuko ATSUMI.] New York: Seabury Press. 184p. LCCN:77-1833. Republished in 1982 as *Women Poets of Japan*. New York: New Directions. 184p. LCCN:81-18693.

An excellent selection of poems from the sixth century to the present day, including those of 38 modern women poets. No romanized text. Includes expansive biographical sketches of poets, a survey of women poets, and a table of historical periods.

1608. SATO, Hiroaki. 1973. *Ten Japanese Poets*. [Translated by Hiroaki SATO.] Hanover, NH: Granite Publications. 136p. LCCN:73-86247.

An excellent anthology including free verse by SHIRAISHI Kazuko and TOMIOKA Taeko among the ten.

1609. SATO, Hiroaki and Burton WATSON, eds. 1981. *From the Country of Eight Islands: An Anthology of Japanese Poetry*. [Translations by Hiroaki SATO and Burton WATSON; introduced by J. Thomas RIMER.] Garden City, NY: Doubleday Anchor Books. 652p. Bibl. Index. LCCN:80-1077.

A pleasant anthology of poetry from the earliest times to the present day, translated (in different styles) by the two compilers, both of them prolific translators and independent scholars. Three modern women are represented: ISHIGAKI Rin, TOMIOKA Taeko and YOSANO Akiko. Includes a brief introduction by J. Thomas RIMER, a glossary, and short biographies of the poets.

1610. SATO, Hiroaki. 1983. *One Hundred Frogs: From Renga to Haiku to English*. Tokyo: Weatherhill. 241p. Index. Bibl. LCCN:82-17505.

A delightful poetry collection/study of *renga* and the haiku that arose from it. Explores problems of translation and cross-cultural interpretation and offers a wealth of varied translations. A few women are included among the haiku poets (KATSURA Nobuko, MITSUHASHI Takejo and SUGITA Hisajo); none in the *renga* section.

1611. SATŌ, Kiyoshi, *et al*. 1953. *Green Hill Poems*. Tokyo: Hokuseido Press. 182p. LCCN:55-42250.

An anthology of poems mostly original poems written in English but including some translations from the Japanese, by a group of poets associated with Aoyama ("Green Hill") Gakuen, a school known for its excellent English department. Only one modern woman poet is represented, YOSANO Akiko.

1612. SHIFFERT, Edith Marcombe and Yūki SAWA, eds. 1972. *Anthology of Modern Japanese Poetry*. Rutland, VT: Tuttle. 195p. Notes and bibl. Index. LCCN:78-167936.

A brief but useful introduction to modern free verse, haiku, and *tanka/waka*, sketching the historical development and citing major poets and journals associated with each. The author provides a sampling of poems (without original or romanized text). Only 5 women are included (HASHIMOTO Takako, NAKAGAWA Mikiko, SAITŌ Fumi, TAKAORI Taeko and TSUDA Kiyoko), but 3 of them are not represented elsewhere.

1613. WILSON, Graeme, comp. 1972. *Three Contemporary Japanese Poets: Anzai Hitoshi, Shiraishi Kazuko, Tanikawa Shuntarō*. [Translated by Graeme WILSON and Ikuko ATSUMI.] London: London Magazine Editions. 80p. LCCN:73-169670.

Includes a selection of SHIRAISHI Kazuko's poetry.

1614. WILSON, Graeme. Nov. 1980. "The poetry of Japanese women. [Part I.]" *Oriental Economist* 48(841):32-33. ISSN:0030-5294.

1615. WILSON, Graeme. Dec. 1980. "The poetry of Japanese women. [Part II.]" *Oriental Economist* 48(842):52-53. ISSN:0030-5294.

A sampling of poems throughout the ages, apparently gathered to demonstrate the translator's contention in Part I that in contrast to "the Western tradition," it is extremely difficult to distinguish the poetry written by Japanese men from that written by Japanese women, because "the Japanese sensibility, not just in poetry but in all cultural fields, is, by Western criteria, essentially feminine," (p. 33) and going on in Part II to point out some distinguishing elements after all. Includes poems of KUJŌ Takeko, SAITŌ Fumi, SHIRAISHI Kazuko and YOSANO Akiko.

1616. WILSON, Graeme. Spring 1981. "Fifteen poems by Japanese women." *Asian and Pacific Quarterly* 13(1):75-80. ISSN:0251-3110.

A mini-anthology of poetry from the earliest times to the present. Does not include commentary, or romanized or original text. Three modern women, SHIRAISHI Kazuko, SUGI Mayumi and YOSANO Akiko, are represented.

1617. WILSON, Graeme M., compiler and translator. 1984. "Small anthology of modern Japanese poetry." *Asian and Pacific Quarterly of Cultural and Social Affairs* 16(3):4-81. ISSN:0251-3110.

A pleasant, varied anthology of poems in different forms. Includes poems by five women: ANRYŪ Suharu, IBARAGI Noriko, KUJŌ Takeko, SHIRAISHI Kazuko and YOSANO Akiko.

1618. WILSON, Graeme. Autumn 1986. "Poems by Japanese women." *Asian and Pacific Quarterly of Social and Cultural Affairs* 18(2):59-64. ISSN:0251-3110.

Translations (without original texts) of 31 poems, all but two premodern, some anonymous. No commentary or biographical information on poets. Modern selections include poetry of IBARAGI Noriko and YOSANO Akiko.

1619. WRIGHT, Harold P. Autumn 1969. "The poetry of Japan." *Asia* [Asia Society, NY] 16:61-90. 11 notes.

A historical essay for the general reader, with a mini-anthology embedded in the prose. No romanized texts. A few women (FURUTA Miyuki, Empress Shoken and UBUKATA Tatsue) are included in his selection.

1620. YASUDA, Kenneth. 1947[1976]. *A Pepper-pod: A Haiku Sampler.* Rutland, VT: Tuttle. LCCN:76-351622. [Author also cited as Shōson.]

An introduction to the qualities of haiku, which YASUDA calls "versegrams," citing and discussing many examples followed by a sampling of Japanese haiku in English translation with romanized originals (to which he gives titles). Includes haiku of HONDA Aoi, HOSHINO Tatsuko, ITAMI Kimiko, MATSUO Shizuko, NAKAMURA Teijo and TANAKA Kayo.

1621. YASUDA, Kenneth. 1957. *The Japanese Haiku: Its Essential Nature, History, and Possibilities in English with Selected Examples.* Rutland, VT: Tuttle. 232p. Bibl. Index. LCCN:57-8795.

A useful manual of haiku, presenting many rules and elements of composition. Among the "selected" examples are 6 haiku by prominent women, of whom only HOSHINO Tatsuko is of the modern period.

Modern Poets

1622. ABE Midorijo (1886-1980)

Haiku poet. Born in Sapporo; lived in Sendai. Began writing haiku after marriage during convalescence from illness. Studied under TAKAHAMA Kyoshi, became a member of his Hototogisu group. Edited her own haiku journal.

[Untitled (2 poems)]. In: BLYTH (#1583), vol. 2, pp. 235-236.

Akiko see *UENO Akiko [#1722]*
Akiko see *YOSANO Akiko [#1729]*

1623. ANRYŪ Suharu (1923-)

A *tanka/waka* poet belonging to MIYA Shūji's Tama group. Bedridden.

"Tree." In: WILSON (#1617), p. 76.
[Untitled.] In: REXROTH (#1607), p. 73.

Aoi see *HONDA Aoi [#1641]*

1624. AOTA Mitsuko (1907-)

Free verse poet. Born in Nara.

"Under the tree." In: DAVIS (#1587), p. 141. [Ki no shita.]

ASAO Haru see *HARA Asao [#1635]*

1625. ATSUMI Ikuko (1940-)

Poet, scholar, teacher of American literature who writes both in Japanese and English. Translator of poetry from Japanese to English and vice versa.

"At Manila Airport in summer." Aug. 1971. *Solidarity* [Manilla, Philippines], p. 20. ISSN:0038-1160.
"Different dimensions." In: REXROTH (#1607), p. 128. Also translated in: *Iowa Review* 7(2/3):25. ISSN:0021-065X.
"Double bed." Also translated in: *Iowa Review* 7(2/3):26. ISSN:0021-065X.
"False creek: Willing a murder." [Translated by Ikuko ATSUMI and Graeme WILSON.] Nov./Dec. 1970. *Quadrant* P. 61. ISSN:0033-5002.
"Heart burial." In: "Nine Japanese poets." 1973. *Chelsea* 32:7-30. ISSN:0009-2185.
"Inside the bell." 1980. *Feminist International* 2:32-33. ISSN:0388-371X.
"Interchange." Winter 1965. *Prism International* p. 11. ISSN:0032-8790.
"Lesson." In: "Nine Japanese poets." 1973. *Chelsea* 32:7-30. ISSN:0009-2185.
"Platform." Winter 1965. *Prism International* p. 12. ISSN:0032-8790.
"Restaurant Kentricon." In: "Nine Japanese poets." 1973. *Chelsea* 32:7-30. ISSN:0009-2185.
"The ring." In: REXROTH: (#1607), p. 127.
"What parachute soldiers don't see." Feb. 1978. *Feminist International* 1(4):29. ISSN:0388-371X. Also published in: *The Eastern Sun...* (#1588), p. 31.

1626. Awajijo

Haiku poet.

[Untitled.] In: BLYTH (#1583) vol. 2, pp. 302-303.

1627. BABA Akiko (1928-1975)

Tanka/waka poet and scholar of classical Japanese literature, expecially poetry and Nō.

[Untitled.] In: *Japanese Literature Today* no. 12:15. Mar. 1987. LCCN:76-648281.
[Untitled (3 poems).] In: REXROTH (#1607). p. 74.

1628. CHINO Masako (1880-1946)

Tanka/waka poet, short story writer, essayist.   Born in Osaka; her father was a pharmaceutical wholesaler. Began her career early in *tanka/waka*, publishing her poetry regularly in YOSANO Akiko's *Myōjō* from the age of 21. Graduated from Nihon Women's University in Tokyo at 28 (and later taught there), having published a collection of poems composed with YOSANO Akiko and YAMAKAWA Tomiko that attracted critical attention. Married another *Myōjō* poet, CHINO Shōshō, who was a professor of German. They spent considerable time in Europe.

"I feel joyful." [Kokoroyoshi.] In: MIYAMORI (#1602), vol. 2, p. 773.
"The spring moon." [Haru no tsuki.] In: MIYAMORI (#1602), vol. 2, pp. 772-773.
[Untitled (2 poems).] In: CLACK (#1585), vol. 2, p. 559.
[Untitled.] In: REXROTH (#1607), p. 68.

1629. EBISUYA Kiyoko

Contemporary haiku poet belonging to a Matsuyama haiku club that publishes its work in a monthly called *Itadori*.

[Untitled.] In: HIGGINSON (#1591), p. 45.

Empress Shoken see **Shoken, Empress [#1700]**

1630. FUKAO Sumako (1888-1974)

Free verse poet. Born in Hyōgo Prefecture. Biographer of YOSANO Akiko, her mentor and friend. Began as a romantic poet, with 54 poems on the death of her husband in 1920. Strongly influenced by World War II, she participated in the peace movement and the women's movement, and wrote poetry imbued with social criticism. With NAKAMURA Chio she founded Zen-Nihon Onna Shijin Kyōkai [Association of Japanese Women Poets].

"Bright house." In: REXROTH (#1607), p. 88.
"Dante's scourge." In: NINOMIYA (#1604), p. 85.
"Human talks." In: KŌNO (#1599), p. 12.
"Presentiment." In: KŌNO (#1599), p. 12.
"Will-o'-the-wisp." In: NINOMIYA (#1604), pp. 84-85.

1631. FUKUI Hisako (1929-)

Free verse poet. College teacher from Kōbe.

"A boat." In: KIJIMA (#1597), p. 156.
"Fruit and knife." In: KIJIMA (#1597), p. 155-156.
"If the time to die comes to me." In: KIJIMA (#1597), p. 154-155.
"Now is the time." In: REXROTH (#1607), p. 104.
"Two tableaus." In: KIJIMA (#1597), pp. 157-158.
"Your words." In: KIJIMA (#1597), p. 157.

1632. FUKUNAKA Tomoko (1928-)

"The Japanese Rod McKuen" [p. 156 in REXROTH (#1607)] Popular poet influenced by contemporary popular Japanese and American music. Close to the media.

"It's not the same." In: REXROTH (#1607), pp. 102-103.

1633. FURUTA Miyuki (1951-)

An eleven-year-old fifth-grade student whose mother died suddenly of a cerebral hemorrage. The title poem of the book below first appeared in a column for poetry by children in the *Asahi Shimbun* [*Asahi Newspaper*].

Why, Mother, Why? 1965. [Translated by Harold P. WRIGHT.] Tokyo: Kodansha International. 63p. LCCN:65-25101.
"Why, Mother, why?" In: WRIGHT (#1619), p. 89.

1634. GOTŌ Miyoko (1898-1978)

Tanka/waka poet. Born in Tokyo. Studied under *tanka/waka* poet SASAKI Nobutsuna, through whose guidance she began publishing. Married *tanka/waka* poet GOTŌ Shigeru; they often published together. She was one of the founders of *Nyonin Tanka* [*Women's Tanka*], a journal that supported women poets. Her best-acclaimed poems are on the subject of mothering and mother's love, many of them inspired by the death of her own elder daughter. She combines traditional values and a social conscience—helping to recreate *tanka/waka* for her generation.

I am Alive: The Tanka Poems of Gotō Miyoko, 1898-1978. 1988. [Translated and introduced by Reiko TSUKIMURA.] Michigan: Oakland University, Katydid Press. 189p. Index. Extensive commentary by TSUKIMURA. 112 notes. LCCN:88-8378.
"Becoming a mother." 1980. [Translated by Lora SHARNOFF.] *Feminist International* 2:63. ISSN:0388-371X.
"Becoming a mother again." 1980. [Translated by Lora SHARNOFF.] *Feminist International* 2:63. ISSN:0388-371X.
"Fetal movement." 1980. [Translated by Lora SHARNOFF.] *Feminist International* 2:63. ISSN:0388-371X.
"A little girl and a fetus." 1980. [Translated by Lora SHARNOFF.] *Feminist International* 2:63. ISSN:0388-371X.
[Untitled.] In: REXROTH (#1607), p. 71.

Hagijo see SAWADA Hagijo [#1692]

Hakuyōjo see SHIBATA Hakuyōjo [#1694]

1635. HARA Asao (1888-1969)

Tanka/waka poet. Born in Miyagi Prefecture. Studied under YOSANO Akiko and SAITŌ Mokichi.

"My child is asleep." In: MIYAMORI (#1602), vol. 2, pp. 760-761.
"My complaint." In: MIYAMORI (#1602), vol. 2, pp. 760-761.
[Untitled (poems 1-4).] In: HUGHES (#1595), pp. 11-12.

1636. HARADA Setsuko

A nurse who lived through the Hiroshima bombing in 1945.

"Square rain is tapping." In: OMORI (#1605), p. 27.

Haruko see TAKAGI Haruko [#1708]

1637. HASEGAWA Kanajo (1887-1969)

Haiku poet. Born in Tokyo to a Nihombashi merchant family. Lost her father early, worked her way through school, where she studied English. Married a haiku poet and colleague of TAKAHAMA Kyoshi. Kanajo was active in women's haiku circles and promoted "kitchen haiku" that focused on unpretentious description of everyday life. She has been criticized for relegating women's haiku to the kitchen, but was an important poet who helped lay the foundation for the flourishing women's haiku movement today.

[Untitled.] In: BLYTH (#1583) vol. 2, p. 328.
"Battledore." In: MIYAMORI (#1601), p. 816.

1638. *HASHIMOTO Takako (1899-1963)*

Haiku poet, born in Tokyo. Studied with SUGITA Hisajo and later YAMAGUCHI Seishi.

[Untitled.] In: BLYTH (#1583) vol. 2, pp. 236 and 239.
[Untitled.] In: HIGGINSON (#1591), p. 36.
[Untitled.] In: REXROTH (#1607), p. 81.
[Untitled (2 poems).] In: SHIFFERT (#1612), p. 169.

Hatsu see *MIZUSHIMA Hatsu [#1669]*

1639. *HATSUI Shizue (1900-)*

Tanka/waka poet. Critic. Born in Hyōgo Prefecture. Studied pharmacy. Received guidance from the eminent and versatile poet KITAHARA Hakushū. Belonged to Cosmos and contributed regularly to *Nyonin Tanka [Women's Tanka]*.

[Untitled (2 poems).] In: REXROTH (#1607), p. 72.

1640. *HAYASHI Fumiko (1903-1951)*

Prolific novelist, short story writer, writer of free verse. [See #1436 for a full biographical sketch.]

"Home-coming." [Translated by Hisakazu KANEKO.] Oct. 1967. *London Magazine* 7:34. ISSN:0024-6085.
"The Lord Buddha." In: REXROTH (#1607), p. 89.
"Song in despair." In: KŌNO (#1599), pp.23-24.

Hisajo see *SUGITA Hisajo [#1702]*

1641. *HONDA Aoi (1875-1939)*

Haiku poet. Born in Kanda, Tokyo, to an aristocratic family. Graduated from the Gakushūin (The Peers' School). Married a member of the Upper House of the Diet. Studied under TAKAHAMA Kyoshi; became a member of Hototogisu. Active in amateur haiku circles.

[Untitled.] In: BLYTH (#1582), vol. 2, p. 325
[Untitled.] In: YASUDA (#1620), p. 104.

1642. *HOSHINO Tatsuko (1903-1984)*

Haiku poet. Second daughter of the preeminent haiku poet, critic and leader of the Hototogisu school, TAKAHAMA Kyoshi. In 1930 she founded *Tamamo [Jeweled Seaweed]*, a literary journal that supported women poets of the Hototogisu style.

[Untitled.] [Translated by George SAITO.] In: *Japanese Literature Today* no. 4:10-11. Mar. 1979. LCCN:76-648281.
[Untitled.] In: BLYTH (#1583), vol. 2, pp. 237-238, 328 & 330.
[Untitled.] In: CLACK (#1595), vol. 2, p. 571.
[Untitled.] In: REXROTH (#1607), p. 83.
[Untitled.] In: YASUDA (#1620), p. 104.
[Untitled.] In: YASUDA (#1621), p. 201.

1643. IBARAGI Noriko (1926-)

Major free verse poet. Born in Osaka. Originally wanted to be a playwright. Her poems are full of sharp social and political criticism. Expresses admiration for the *Man'yōshū* and KANEKO Mitsuharu.

"Children." In: GUEST (#1590), p. 103.
"Death by hanging." In: KIJIMA (#1597), pp. 111-112.
"Dialogue." In: REXROTH (#1607), p. 100.
"In camera." In: WILSON (#1618), p. 64.
"Invisible messengers." In: GUEST (#1590), pp. 104-105. Also translated as: "The invisible mailmen" by Hajime KIJIMA in: KIJIMA (#1597), pp. 108-110 and in: *Literary Review* 6(1):116-117. Autumn 1962. ISSN:0024-4589.
"The living, the dead." [Ikiteiru mono, shindeiru mono.] In: DAVIS (#1587), p. 205.
"My camera." In: KIJIMA (#1597), p. 110. Also translated in: ARKIN (#1580), p. 747.
"Never in my wildest dreams." [Yume yume utagau.] In DAVIS (#1587), pp. 208-209.
"Outrun." In: KIJIMA (#1597), p. 111. Also translated in: ARKIN (#1580), p. 748.
"Running." In: WILSON (#1617), p. 77.
"Soul." Translated by Hajime KIJIMA in: KIJIMA (#1597), pp. 107-108 and in: *Literary Review* 6(1):115. Autumn 1962. ISSN:0024-4589. Also published in: *The Eastern Sun...* (#1588), p. 29.
"What a little girl had on her mind." In: REXROTH (#1607), p. 101.
"When my beauty was at its best." [Ichiban kirei datta toki.] In: DAVIS (#1587), pp. 206-207. Also translated in: ARKIN (#1580), p. 747.

1644. IKEDA Some (b.c. 1875)

"A woman of ninety who wrote the poem [below] in memory of her experiences at the time of the A-bomb upon Hiroshima." [DAVIS (#1587), p. 288.]

"Umeboshi." In: DAVIS (#1587), p. 272.

1645. IMAI Kuniko (1880-1948)

Tanka/waka poet. Born in Tokushima, Shikoku, where her father was head of a women's teachers' college. When her father was transferred, she and her sister were left in Nagano Prefecture in the care of their grandmother, where they remained until Kuniko was 18. She began writing prose and poetry at an extremely early age, winning literary prizes and corresponding with leading women *tanka/waka* poets including OKAMOTO Kanako, SUGIURA Midoriko/Suiko, and WAKAYAMA Kishiko. She went to join the rest of her family in Hokkaido (her father was then mayor of Hakodate), but she seems to have had trouble fitting into the family she hardly knew, and she devoted her energies to poetry. Eventually she went to Tokyo to escape a marriage her mother had arranged for her and soon became a reporter for the prominent journal *Chūō kōron*. She married a colleague there and published her first collection of *tanka/waka* in 1912 and was launched on a brilliant career, which, however, was not well accommodated by her private life as wife and mother. (The clash between marriage and career became a subject of her writing.) Studied under SHIMAKI Akahiko and became a member of his prominent *tanka/waka* group, Araragi, but left after his death in 1926 to found and edit her own journal, *Asuka*, in times when women did not often do such things. The most important woman *tanka/waka* poet of the early Shōwa years.

"Images of Kwannon." [Kwannon no zō.] In: MIYAMORI (#1602), vol. 2, p. 768. Also published in MIYAMORI (#1603), pp. 282-283.
"My children in sleep." [Nemureru kora.] In: MIYAMORI (#1602), vol. 2, p. 769.
"My younger sister's tomb." [Imōto no haka.] In: MIYAMORI (#1602), vol. 2, p. 770. Also published in MIYAMORI (#1603), pp. 283-284.
"Waterbirds." [Mizutori.] In: MIYAMORI (#1602), vol. 2, p. 770.
[Untitled (3 poems).] In: CLACK (#1585), vol. 2, p. 558.

1646.   *Imozeni*

Haiku poet.

> [Untitled.]   In: BEILENSON, Peter.   1968.   *A Haiku Garland: A Collection of Seventeen-Syllable Classic Poems*.   Mount Vernon, NY: Peter Pauper Books.   Unpaginated.   No refs.   LCCN:70-16872.
>
> [Untitled.]   In: CLACK (#1585), vol. 2, p. 575.

1647.   *INAGAKI Etsuko (1873-1950)*

Haiku poet.   Historical novelist (writing in English); see author index.   Taught Japanese language at Columbia University.

> [Untitled (2 haiku).]   In: CLACK (#1585), vol. 2, p. 570.

1648.   *INAHATA Teiko (1931-)*

Haiku poet, editor of *Hototogisu*.   Granddaughter of TAKAHAMA Kyoshi.   Born in Yokohama, spent her childhood in Kamakura, and school years in Ashiya, near Kobe.   Studied haiku with her father, TAKAHAMA Toshio.   Writes in the *shasei* (objective description) style, based on imagery from nature, that has come to be associated with *Hototogisu*.

> [Unititled.]   In: *Japanese Literature Today* no. 14:22.   Mar. 1989.   LCCN:7-648281.

1649.   *INOUE Mitsuko (1919-)*

Free verse poet.   A member of the VOU group, KITASONE Katsue's small magazine for "modernist" poetry between World War I and World War II.   The group also includes SHIRAISHI Kazuko, to whom INOUE is compared.

> "Compass."   In: REXROTH (#1607), p. 106.
>
> "Get angry."   In: REXROTH (#1607), p. 106.
>
> "Minerva's whispering."   1956.   [Translated by K. KITASONO.]   *New World Writing* 6:62-63.   ISSN:0548-7099.

1650.   *ISHIGAKI Rin (1920-)*

Major free verse poet, social critic.   Born in the Asakusa district of Tokyo.   Her mother died when she was four.   Began writing (and publishing) in elementary school.   Led a difficult, independent life.   Worked in a bank for many years.   Her down-to-earth poems about real daily life contain serious social criticism.

> "Catching at a straw."   [Wara.]   In: DAVIS (#1587), pp. 166-167.
>
> "Clams."   In: SATO (#1609), p. 574.   Also translated in: *Chicago Review* 25(2):109.   1973.   ISSN:0009-3696; and in: COSMAN (#1586), p. 288.
>
> "Cliffs."   In: "Nine Japanese poets."   1973.   *Chelsea* 32:7-30.   ISSN:0009-2185.
>
> "Cocoon."   In: KIJIMA (#1597), p. 58.
>
> "Encouragement to leave home."   [Iede no susume.]   In: DAVIS (#1587), pp. 169-170.
>
> "Festival of the blind."   In: SATO (#1609), p. 576-577.   Also translated in: *Chicago Review* 25(2):116.   1973.   ISSN:0009-3696.
>
> "Island."   In: SATO (#1609), pp. 574-575.
>
> "Landscape."   In: SATO (#1609), p. 573.
>
> "Living."   In: "Nine Japanese poets."   1973.   *Chelsea* 32:7-30.   ISSN:0009-2185.
>
> "Nameplate."   In: KIJIMA (#1597), p. 59.
>
> "Nursery rhyme."   In: KIJIMA (#1597), p. 57.
>
> "The pan, the pot, the fire I have before me."   In: SATO (#1609), pp. 571-572.   Also translated in: ARKIN (#1580), p. 638; and in: *Chicago Review* 25(2):108.   1973.   ISSN:0009-3696.
>
> "Roof."   In: SATO (#1609), pp. 572-573.   Also translated in: ARKIN (#1580), p. 639; and in: *Chicago Review* 25(2):111.   1973.   ISSN:0009-3696.

"Shellfish." In: REXROTH (#1607), p. 96.
"That night." In: *Chicago Review* 25(2):113. 1973. ISSN:0009-3696.
"To live." [Kurashi.] In: DAVIS (#1587), p. 168.
"Tragedy." In: KIJIMA (#1597), pp. 56-57. Also translated in: ARKIN (#1580), p. 639.
"Tsuetsuki Pass." In: SATO (#1609), p. 575. Also translated in: *Chicago Review* 25(2):115. 1973. ISSN:0009-3696.
"View of the sea." In: *Chicago Review* 25(2):119. 1973. ISSN:0009-3696.
"Walking-With-A-Cane-Pass." In: REXROTH (#1607), pp. 97-98.

1651. *ISHIKAWA Itsuko (1933-)*

Contemporary free verse poet. Born in Tokyo. Graduate of Ochanomizu (Women's) University. Active in poetry circles; several anthologies of her poetry have been published.

"Forgotten children." In: *The Eastern Sun...* (#1588), p. 28.

1652. *ITAMI Kimiko (1925-)*

Haiku poet. Born in Kōchi, Shikoku. Married ITAMI Mikihiko, who was her haiku teacher. Also studied free verse under MURANO Shirō and ITŌ Shinkichi.

[Untitled.] In: CLACK (#1585), vol. 2, p. 571.
[Untitled.] In: YASUDA (#1620), p. 102.

1653. *ITŌ Mariko (1939-)*

Free verse poet. From Hiroshima.

"The ladder." [Kaidan.] In: DAVIS (#1587), p. 279.

1654. *IZUMI Sumie*

Contemporary haiku poet. Along with TAKEDA Chie [#1710], belongs to a Matsuyama haiku club that publishes its work in a monthly called *Itadori*.

[Untitled.] In: HIGGINSON (#1591), p. 45.

1655. *KAMIKO Yoshiko*

A school child, age 6 when she composed the following poem:

[Untitled.] In: HIGGINSON (#1591), p. 153.

1656. *KANAI Mieko (1947-)*

Well-known for her free verse poetry as well as fiction [see also #1442]. Won her first prize for poetry at the age of 20. REXROTH (#1607) describes her as a "poet . . . of eroticism and violence" (p. 159).

"The house of Madam Juju." 1977. [Translated by Christopher DRAKE.] In: HIBBETT, Howard, ed. 1977. *Contemporary Japanese Literature: An Anthology of Fiction, Film, and Other Writings Since 1945*. New York: Knopf, pp. 342-343. LCCN:77-74982.
"In the town with cat-shaped maze." In: REXROTH (#1607), p. 129-131.

Kanajo (1887-1969) see *HASEGAWA Kanajo [#1637]*

Kasenjo see *TOKUGAWA Kasenjo [#1717]*

1657. KATSURA Nobuko (1914-)

Prominent haiku poet and critic. Born in Osaka. Began writing haiku and frequenting haiku circles in the late 1930's. Married, but was widowed two years later, lost her family home in the Second World War. Since the War has been extremely active, writing experimental haiku (seasonless, joint, irregular) and criticism, and founding and editing a haiku journal.

> [Untitled.] [Translated by George SAITO.] In: *Japanese Literature Today* no. 4:10. Mar. 1979. LCCN:76-648281.
> [Untitled.] In: *Japanese Literature Today* no. 14:21. Mar. 1989. LCCN:76-648281.
> [Untitled.] In: SATO (#1610), p. 124.

> *Kayo* see *TANAKA Kayo [#1713]*

> *Kimiko* see *ITAMI Kimiko [#1652]*

> *Kiyoko* see *NAGASE Kiyoko [#1671]*

1658. KŌRA Rumiko (1932-)

Writer of poetry, criticism, fiction. Major free verse writer. Raised a strong voice against the renewal of the Japan-American Security Treaty and the Vietnam War.

> "Autumn." In: KIJIMA (#1597), pp. 200-201.
> "Awake." [Mezame.] In: DAVIS (#1587), p. 251. Also translated as: "Awakening" in: KIJIMA (#1597), pp. 199-200 and in: ARKIN (#1580), p. 848.
> "Contemplation." [Aru hansei.] In: DAVIS (#1587), p. 249.
> "Encounter." [Kaigo.] In: DAVIS (#1587), p. 248. Also translated in: KIRKUP (#1598), pp. 26-27.
> "The friend." In: KIJIMA (#1597), pp. 202-203.
> "In this country." [Translated by Thomas FITZSIMMONS and Rikutarō FUKUDA.] In: *Orient/West* 9:61. 1964. ISSN:0474-6465.
> "Jewelry counter." [Hoseki uriba.] In: DAVIS (#1587), p. 247.
> "The moon." In: KIJIMA (#1597), p. 202.
> "She." In: KIJIMA (#1597), p. 201.
> "A tree." [Ki.] In: DAVIS (#1587), p. 250. Also translated in: KIRKUP (#1598), p. 26; and as: "The tree" in: KIJIMA (#1597), p. 199 and in: ARKIN (#1580), p. 848.
> "Woman." In: REXROTH (#1607), p. 123.

1659. KUBO Yorie (1884-1941)

Haiku poet. Born in Matsuyama, Shikoku, home of MATSUOKA Shiki. As a child she attended Shiki's haiku sessions. Much later she studied with TAKAHAMA Kyoshi. She also wrote fiction and essays.

> [Untitled.] In: BLYTH (#1583), vol. 2, pp. 232 and 235.

1660. KUJŌ Takeko (1887-1928)

Extremely popular essayist and *tanka/waka* poet. Daughter of the Abbot of Nishi-Honganji Temple in Kyoto. Married an aristocratic diplomat and spent some time in Europe, then spent another ten years by herself in Japan. Studied *tanka/waka* under SASAKI Nobutsuna. A leader in Buddhist women's social and charitable organizations.

> "Evaluation." In: WILSON (#1615), p. 53. Also translated in: WILSON (#1617), p. 68.
> [Untitled. (6 poems).] In: CLACK (#1585), vol. 2, pp. 551-552.
> [Untitled (poems 1-27).] In: HUGHES (#1594), pp. 37-43.
> [Untitled (poems 1-7).] In: HUGHES (#1595), pp. 22-23.
> [Untitled.] In: REXROTH (#1607), p. 69.

The following poems are contained in MIYAMORI (#1602), vol. 2:
"The great earthquake and fire of 1923." [Taishō jūni-nen no dai shin kwa sai.] p. 753.
"Heaven and earth." [Ame-tsuchi.] p. 752.
"Joking." [Zaregoto.] p. 754.
"My footsteps." [Waga ashi-ato.] pp. 752-753.
"My mind." [Waga kokoro.] pp. 751-752.
"Parting." [Wakare.] pp. 750-751.
"Spring has come again." [Haru kaeru.] pp. 753-754.
"A visitor." [Raikyaku.] p. 751.

1661. KURE Miyo (1927-)

Free verse poet; essayist. Born in Tokyo. Was graduated from Kamakura Women's College. Active in literary circles; has published collections of her own poems and essays.

"As if for the first time." [Translated by William L. ELLIOTT and Kazuo KAWAMURA.] In: *Japanese Literature Today* no. 13:19. Mar. 1988. LCCN:76-648281.

1662. KURIHARA Sadako (1913-)

Free verse poet and activist. From Hiroshima. Wrote anti-war poetry during World War II; afterwards wrote against the bomb and the American occupation.

"Four poems (1941-45) by the Hiroshima poet Kurihara Sadako." Jan./Mar. 1989. [Translated by Richard H. MINEAR.] *Bulletin of Concerned Asian Scholars* 21(1):46-49. No notes. ISSN:0007-4810. Includes the following poems:
"Respect for humanity." P. 46.
"War close up." P. 47.
"Let us be midwives!" P. 47.
"The city ravaged by the flames." Pp. 48-49.

1663. KUSANO Hisao

An otherwise unknown writer of free verse.

"Village women cannot sleep." In: *Japanese Women Speak Out* Jun. 1975. Tokyo: White Paper on Sexism—Japan Task Force, pp. 42-43.

1664. MATSUO Shizuko (1890-)

Haiku poet. Born in Fushimi, south of Kyoto. Married another haiku poet, MATSUO Iwao, with whom she studied under TAKAHAMA Kyoshi leader of the Hototogisu group.

[Untitled.] In: CLACK (#1585), vol. 2, p. 572.
[Untitled.] In: YASUDA (#1620), p. 102.

1665. MATSUSHIMA Mami

According to DAVIS (#1587, p. 297), she was "a student in Kyoto" who wrote free verse.

"In a poor hamlet." [Sabishii mura de.] In: DAVIS (#1587), p. 282.

Midorijo see *ABE Midorijo [#1622]*

Mikajo see *YAGI Mikajo [#1724]*

1666. MITSUHASHI Takajo (1899-1972)

Haiku poet and critic. From Chiba Prefecture. Apparently studied haiku with the great *tanka/waka* poet YOSANO Akiko.

[Untitled (2 poems).] In: REXROTH (#1607), p. 80.
[Untitled.] In: SATO (#1610), p. 123.

1667. MITSUI Futabako (1918-)

Free verse poet, essayist. Daughter of eminent Symbolist poet SAIJŌ Yaso; at first wrote poetry in that vein. Continued to be influenced by Western poetry, especially French.

"Grazing." In: REXROTH (#1607), p. 95.
"Looking back." In: DAVIS (#1587), p. 161. [Poesie.]

1668. MIZUMACHI Kyōko (1891-1974)

Tanka/waka poet. Born in Takamatsu, Shikoku. Graduated in Japanese literature from what is now Ochanomizu University. Began writing *tanka/waka* seriously as an undergraduate. Taught at several high schools. With several other women, founded *Kusa no Mi* [*The Fruit of the Grasses*], a journal for women *tanka/waka* poets. She eventually left this group to start her own journal.

"A bird in the sun's ray." [Hikari no naka no tori.] In: MIYAMORI (#1602), vol. 2, pp. 781-782.

1669. MIZUSHIMA Hatsu (1896-?)

Haiku poet. Born in Niigata Prefecture. Spent World War II in Korea. First began writing haiku when she was in her 50's.

"Twenty-four haiku." In: MISHIMA (#1600), p. 243-246.

1670. MORI Michiyo (1901-1977)

Writer of poetry and fiction. From Mie Prefecture. Taught at Tokyo Women's College, married the eminent poet KANEKO Mitsuharu, with whom she traveled widely and sometimes published jointly.

"Cobra dancing." [Kobura no odori.] In: DAVIS (#1587), p. 113.

1671. NAGASE Kiyoko (1906-)

Free verse poet. Born in Okayama. After World War II, she edited an Okayama journal for women poets. Active in society.

"At the foot of the mountain." In: KŌNO (#1599), p. 96.
"Mother." [Haha.] In: DAVIS (#1587), p. 133. Also translated in: REXROTH (#1607), p. 90.
"My harvests." [Waga mugi.] In: Davis (#1645), p. 134.
"O you who come to me at dawn." [Translated by William L. ELLIOTT and Kazuo KAWAMURA.] In: *Japanese Literature Today* no. 13:23. Mar. 1988. LCCN:76-648281.
"The ruins have not yet grown cold." In: OMORI (#1605), pp. 17-18.

1672. NAKAGAWA Mikiko (1897-1980)

Tanka/waka poet, editor, essayist, teacher. Born in the Shinjuku district of Tokyo. Editor of the *tanka/waka* journal *Columbine*.

[Untitled (3 poems).] In: SHIFFERT (#1612), p. 149.

1673. NAKAHARA Ayako (1898-1969)

Tanka/waka poet, critic, editor. Born in Nagasaki. Studied under YOSANO Akiko.

[Untitled.] In: CLACK (#1585), vol. 2, p. 569.

The following poems are contained in MIYAMORI (#1602), vol. 2:
"Gentle women." [Taoyame.] p. 797.
"My heart." [Waga kokoro.] pp. 796-797.
"The rose." [Bara.] p. 798.
"Swords." [Tsurugi.] p. 798.

1674. NAKAMURA Chio (1913-)

Free verse poet. Contributed to the "modernist" poetry journal *VOU* from 1935. Founded the Zen-Nihon Onna Shijin Kyōkai [Association of Japanese Women Poets] with FUKAO Sumiko, edited the journal *Joseishi* [*Women's Poetry*], and published an anthology of poetry by women.

"A diary without dates." In: REXROTH (#1607), p. 91.

1675. NAKAMURA Teijo (1900-1988)

Haiku poet, editor. Born in Kumamoto, Kyushu. Began writing haiku naturally from the age of eighteen. Married, moved to Tokyo, and came to know SUGITA Hisajo of the Hototogisu group. Participated in HASEGAWA Kanajo's women's haiku circle. In 1932, moved to Yokohama to join SUGITA Hisajo's breakaway Hanagoromo (Flowered Kimono); but soon met TAKAHAMA Kyoshi and became his student and eventually a member of Hototogisu in 1934. Wrote elegant haiku about daily life that became quite popular. Was influential in encouraging women to write haiku.

[Untitled (4 poems).] In: BLYTH (#1583), vol. 2, pp. 237-239.
[Untitled.] In: CLACK (#1585), vol. 2, p. 572.
[Untitled.] [Translated by George SAITO.] In: *Japanese Literature Today* no. 4:10-11. Mar. 1979. LCCN:76-648281.
[Untitled.] In: REXROTH (#1607), p. 82.
[Untitled.] In: YASUDA (#1620), p. 104.

1676. Naojo

Haiku poet.

[Untitled.] In: CLACK (#1585), vol. 2, p. 575.

1677. NISHI Junko

According to REXROTH (#1607), p. 159, she "disappeared leaving two small mimeographed collections of her poems . . . published in Amagasaki, Hyōgo Prefecture, in 1970."

"Remorse came slowly." In: REXROTH (#1607), p. 133.
"Revolution." In: REXROTH (#1607), p. 132.

1678. NISHIGORI Kurako (1890-1945)

Tanka/waka poet. A Christian; attended divinity school.

"The doors of life." [Inochi no tobira.] In: MIYAMORI (#1602), vol. 2, p. 767.
"Voiceless voices." [Koe naki koe.] In: MIYAMORI (#1602), vol. 2, p. 767.
[Untitled (2 poems).] In: CLACK (#1585), vol. 2, p. 557.

1679. NISHINO Toshiko

Haiku poet.

[Untitled.] [Translated by George SAITO.] In: *Japanese Literature Today* no. 4:11. Mar. 1979. LCCN:76-648281.
[Untitled.] In: BLYTH (#1583), vol. 2, p. 328.

1680. NISHIO Katsuko (1923-)

Born in Ibaraki Prefecture. Began writing poems and stories for children. Now a prominent free verse writer.

"At a cannery." [Kanzume kōjō.] In: DAVIS (#1587), p. 278.

1681. NIWA Akiko (1890-)

Tanka/waka poet. Student of YOSANO Akiko.

"The great-tit." [Shijūgara.] In: MIYAMORI (#1602), vol. 2, p.774.
"The October sea." [Jūgatsu no umi.] In: MIYAMORI (#1602), vol. 2, pp. 774-775.

1682. NOMA Fumiyo (1945-)

Free verse poet born in Nagasaki. Barely escaped the bomb as an infant.

"The real meaning." [Makoto no imi.] In: DAVIS (#1587), p. 281.

1683. OGAWA Yoshino

HIGGINSON (#1591) describes her as a "woman of Hokkaido who makes a living selling her poems on towels, poem cards, and the like" (p. 142).

[Untitled.] In: HIGGINSON (#1591), p. 142.

1684. ŌHARA Shōko

Contemporary free verse poet.

"The sound of waves." In: The Eastern Sun... (#1588), p. 20.

1685. OKAMOTO Kanoko

A well-known tanka/waka poet also known for her fiction. Born to a large family in Tokyo. While still in girl's higher school, she developed an interest in tanka/waka and visited YOSANO Akiko. Became a member of Akiko's new poetry group and published her own tanka/waka (most of it love poetry) in the romantic poetry journal Myōjō, whose direct personal expression and affirmation of love and the self seemed to reflect her own personal and artistic temperament.   In 1910 she married OKAMOTO Ippei, who later became a famous illustrator/cartoonist.   Her son Tarō, the subject of Kanoko's stirring and extremely sensual piece "Boshi jojō" [A Mother's Love] was born the following year. In 1912 she published her first poetry anthology. She also joined the feminist Seitōsha group. In a long period of family discord, bankruptcy at home, and personal tragedy including a tumultuous love affair, a mental breakdown, and the death of two children, she sought solace in Mahayana Buddhism, and she wrote some important works of Buddhist scholarship. In 1929 she traveled with her husband and son and two young men to Europe, where she spent three years nurturing her literary talents. On her return to Japan, she plunged feverishly into writing. She made her debut in the fiction world in 1936 but died four years later from a cerebral hemorrhage.

"At the foot of Mount Fuji." [Fuji no fumoto nite.] In: MIYAMORI (#1602), vol. 2, p. 783.
"The golden bee." [Kogane no hachi.] In: MIYAMORI (#1602), vol. 2, pp. 783-784.
"The sound of waves." [Nami no oto.] In: MIYAMORI (#1602), vol. 2, p. 782.
[Untitled (2 poems).] In: CLACK (#1585), vol. 2, p. 562. [Cited as AKIMOTO Kanoko in CLACK.]
[Untitled.] In: REXROTH (#1607), p. 70.

1686. ŌNISHI Tamiko (1924-)

Tanka/waka poet. Born in Iwate Prefecture on the northern part of Honshū. Began writing *tanka/waka* together with ISHIKAWA Takuboku when she was in girls' higher school; studied *tanka/waka* formally (under MAEKAWA Samio) while she was a student at Nara Teacher's College. Taught school for a while, married, and moved to Ōmiya (near Tokyo) with her husband; both of them had literary ambitions. Became active in *tanka/waka* circles and make a name for herself, partly for *tanka/waka* on the subject of waiting home alone for an unfaithful husband.

[Untitled.] In: *Japanese Literature Today* no. 7:20. Mar. 1982. LCCN:76-648281.
[Untitled. (2 poems.)] In: *Japanese Literature Today* no. 12:16. Mar. 1987. LCCN:76-648281.

1687. Reihōjo

Haiku poet.

[Untitled.] In: BLYTH (#1583), vol. 2, p. 303.

1688. SADAMATSU Keiko

Contemporary free verse poet.

"In the wind flooding." In: *The Eastern Sun...* (#1588), p. 25.

1689. SAISHO Atsuko (1825-1900)

Tanka/waka poet. Born in Kyoto. Married a Satsuma samurai, was widowed young. Served the Meiji empress.

[Untitled.] In: CLACK (#1585), vol. 2, pp. 429-430.
The following poems are contained in MIYAMORI (#1602), vol. 2:
"Falling flowers." [Chiru hana.] p. 600-601.
"Fragrance of chrysanthemums." [Kiku no ka.] p. 600.
"Shadows of pine-trees." [Matsu no kage.] p. 601.
"Spring rain." [Harusame.] p. 599.
"Uguisu." [Uguisu.] pp. 598-599.
"Young green shoots." [Wakana.] p. 599-600.

1690. SAISHŌ Nobuko

Free verse and *tanka/waka* poet. Born in Tokyo. Graduated from Japan Women's College. Active in literary circles. Member of Araragi. Anthologies of her poems have been published.

"Waiting for the porridge." [Translated by William L. ELLIOTT and Kazuo KAWAMURA.] In: *Japanese Literature Today* no. 13:16. Mar. 1988. LCCN:76-648281.

1691. SAITŌ Fumi (1909-)

Tanka/waka poet. Editor. Born in Tokyo. Writes anti-realist, modernist-poetry. Participated in several poetry coteries, including Araragi and Tankajin, begun by her father, SAITŌ Ryū. Founded and edited the journal *Genkei* [*Original Form*].

"Hand." In: WILSON (#1615), p. 53.
"Six *tanka*." [Translated by Edith SHIFFERT.] In: *Literary Review* 6(1):104. Autumn 1962.
[Untitled (12 poems).] In: SHIFFERT (#1612), pp. 150-153.

1692. SAWADA Hagijo (1890-1982)

Haiku poet. Born in Toyama. Husband also a haiku poet. Began composing haiku in her teens, made a name for herself at the beginning of the 20th century. Suddenly stopped writing, which gave rise to the rumor that all her haiku were really written by her husband. There is a personal anthology of her poems.

> [Untitled.] In: BEILENSON, Peter. 1968. *A Haiku Garland: A Collection of Seventeen-Syllable Classic Poems.* Mount Vernon, NY: Peter Pauper Books. Unpaginated. No refs. LCCN:70-16872.

1693. SAWAKI Takako (1907-)

Major haiku poet. Lived in Kyushu. Studied haiku with Hisajo. Joined the Hototogisu group, which she left to join Ashibi. Later formed several other haiku groups.

> "Winter." In: KŌNO (#1599), p. 123.

1694. SHIBATA Hakuyōjo (1906-1984)

Haiku poet. Born in Kobe. Graduated from Tōhoku Imperial University. Began writing haiku in her 20's, met with success. Was one of the founders of *Josei Haiku* [*Women's Haiku*] in 1954; after that ceased publication in 1961, founded *Haiku Nyoen* [*Women's Garden of Haiku*], which she edited. Throughout her career encouraged and promoted haiku written by women.

> [Untitled.] [Translated by George SAITO.] In: *Japanese Literature Today* no. 4:11. Mar. 1979. LCCN:76-648281.
> [Untitled.] In: BLYTH (#1583), vol. 2, p. 301.

1695. SHIGA Mitsuko (1885-1976)

Tanka/waka poet. Born in Shinano Prefecture. The poet ŌTA Mizuho is her husband. Her father wrote both *tanka/waka* and Chinese poetry.

> "Domestic animals." [Kachiku.] In: MIYAMORI (#1602), vol. 2, p. 721. Also published in MIYAMORI (#1603), p. 270.
> "My old home." [Furusato.] In: MIYAMORI (#1602), vol. 2, pp. 721-722.

1696. SHINDŌ Chie (1920-)

Free verse poet influenced by modern French poetry. Born in Tokyo. Received a cosmopolitan education; studied poetry under MIYOSHI Tatsuji. Active in literary circles since World War II.

> "Space." In: REXROTH (#1607), p. 99.

1697. SHINDŌ Ryōko

Free verse poet. Born in Kagoshima, on the southern tip of Kyushu. Now lives in Atami. Active in poetry circles.

> "North hotel." [Translated by William L. ELLIOTT and Kazuo KAWAMURA.] In: *Japanese Literature Today* no. 13:18. Mar. 1988. LCCN:76-648281.

1698. SHINKAWA Kazue (1929-)

Acclaimed free verse poet and prose writer. Born in Ibaraki Prefecture. During World War II studied with the symbolist poet SAIJŌ Yaso, who had evacuated to her area.

> "An event that doesn't make news." [Kiji ni naranai jiken.] In: DAVIS (#1587), p. 217. Also translated as: "An event which makes no news." In: REXROTH (#1607), p. 105.
> "Never bind me." [Watashi o tabanenaide.] In: DAVIS (#1587), pp. 215-216.

"Ovum." 1980. [Translated by Lora SHARNOFF.] *Feminist International* 2:62. ISSN:0388-371X.

"Spermatozoan." 1980. [Translated by Lora SHARNOFF.] *Feminist International* 2:62. ISSN:0388-371X.

1699. SHIRAISHI Kazuko (1931-)

Free verse poet, among the best-known in Japan today, male or female. Born in Vancouver; went to Japan at age of seven. Graduated from Waseda. Published in KITASONO Katsue's modernist surrealist journal, *VOU*. Claims Dylan THOMAS as an influence, experiments with poetry and jazz. An independent, prolific, popular, and widely acclaimed poet.

Seasons of Sacred Lust: The Selected Poems of Shirashi Kazuko. 1978. [Edited by Kenneth REXROTH. Poems translated by Ikuko ATSUMI, John SOLT, Carol TINKER, Yasuyo MORITA, and Kenneth REXROTH.] New York: New Directions. 86p. [*Seinaru inja no kisetsu.* Selections.] LCCN:77-14936.

"All day long a tiger." In: WILSON (#1613), pp. 46-47.

"The anniversary of Samansa's death." In: REXROTH (#1607), pp. 108-109.

"Bird." In: DAVIS (#1587), pp. 229-230. Also translated in: ARKIN (#1580), pp. 841-842.

"The Chinese Ulysses." In: REXROTH (#1607), p. 112-114.

"Cold meat." In: WILSON (#1613), p. 44.

"Egg of fire." In: WILSON (#1613), p. 42. Also translated as: "Fire egg." In: WILSON (#1615), p. 53 and in: WILSON (#1617), p. 79.

"False creek: Willing a witness." [Translated by ATSUMI Ikuko and Graeme WILSON.] Nov./Dec. 1970. *Quadrant* pp. 60-61. ISSN:0033-5002.

"I fire at the face of the country where I was born." In: REXROTH (#1607), pp. 110-111.

"I wonder if you were tooting bec." In: ŌOKA (#1606), pp. 278-280.

"Lake." In: MISHIMA (#1600), p. 221.

"The lion's humming." In: KIJIMA (#1597), p. 192. Also translated as: "Lion's humming." In: WILSON (#1613), pp. 39-40.

"The man root: For Sumiko's birthday." In: REXROTH (#1607), p. 115-117.

"The man with the sky on." In: FITZSIMMONS (#1595), pp. 39-40.

"Memory of Joe." In: MISHIMA (#1600), pp. 221-224.

"My America." In: KIJIMA (#1597), pp. 193-198.

"My Tokyo." In: MISHIMA (#1600), pp. 225-229. Also translated in: KIJIMA (#1597), pp. 184-189 and "Nine Japanese poets." 1973. *Chelsea* 32:7-30. ISSN:0009-2185.

"My sand people." (From *Sand Tribe*.) In: ŌOKA (#1606), pp. 263-271.

"Non-stop." In: KIJIMA (#1597), p. 193. Also translated in: WILSON (#1613), pp. 45-46.

"Nick and Muriel." In: MISHIMA (#1600), pp. 220-221.

"Phallic root for Sumiko, on her birthday." In: FITZSIMMONS (#1595), pp. 37-39. Also translated as: "Phallus—For Sumiko's birthday." In: KIJIMA (#1597), pp. 189-192.

"Phallus." [Translated by ATSUMI Ikuko.] *Iowa Review* 7(2-3):35. ISSN:0021-065X.

"Pond." In: SATO (#1608), pp. 49-50. Also translated by ATSUMI Ikuko and Graeme WILSON in: Nov./Dec. 1970. *Quadrant* pp. 60-61. ISSN:0033-5002.

"The season of the secret lecher." [Excerpts.] In: SATO (#1608), pp. 30-39.

"Street." In: MISHIMA (#1600), p. 220. Also translated in: SATO (#1608), pp. 47-48; and in: WILSON (#1616), pp. 79-80.

"Tiger's play." In: WILSON (#1613), p. 43.

"Town under a rainfall of eggs." [Tamago no furu machi.] In: DAVIS (#1587), p. 228. Also translated in: ARKIN (#1580), p. 840. Also translated as: "The town where eggs are falling." In: WILSON (#1613), p. 41.

"Under the sand bridge." (From *Sand Tribe*.) In: ŌOKA (#1606), pp. 263-271.

Shizuko see *MATSUO Shizuko [#1664]*

Shizunojo see *TAKESHITA Shizunojo [#1711]*

1700. Shoken, Empress (Wife of Meiji) (1849-1913)

Consort of the Emperor Meiji. Well-known as a *tanka/waka* poet who wrote public, often didactic, verse.

[Untitled.] In: CLACK (#1585), vol. 2, pp. 450-452.
[Untitled. ("The skies have cleared...").] In: WRIGHT (#1619), p. 78.
The following poems are contained in MIYAMORI (#1602), vol. 2:
  "A boat in a lake." [Kojō no fune.] p. 582.
  "Fireflies." [Hotaru.] p. 579.
  "Fringed pinks." [Nadeshiko.] p. 583-584.
  "The grasses in full bloom." [Sōkwa sakari-nari.] p. 579.
  "Handwriting reveals the character." [Fude jinshin wo utsusu.] p. 581-582.
  "High waves roar." [Nami no sawagi.] pp. 584-585.
  "The imperial army." [Mi-ikusa.] p. 577.
  "Long life." [Chōmei.] p. 583.
  "Moon on a street fair." [Ichino tsuki.] p. 580.
  "Morning cicadas." [Asa-zemi.] p. 584.
  "The people's mind." [Tami no kororo.] pp. 574-575.
  "Plovers in the moonlight." [Getsuzen no chidori.] p. 580-581.
  "The road of right." [Michi.] p. 578-579. Also published in MIYAMORI (#1603), p. 225.
  "Silk and brocade." [Aya nishiki.] p. 576. Also published in MIYAMORI (#1603), pp. 224-225.
  "Skylarks in the blue sky." [Seiten no hibari.] p. 581.
  "Spring." [Haru.] pp. 577-578.
  "Spring dawn in a village on the stream." [Suikyō no shunsho.] p. 586.
  "Summer grasses on the path across a plain." [Yakei kasō.] pp. 586-587.
  "The summer moon in the country." [Denka no kagetsu.] p. 585.
  "The true treasure." [Makoto no takara.] p. 575. Also published in MIYAMORI (#1603), pp. 223-224.

1701. SUGI Mayumi (1941-)

Free verse poet.

  "Proposal." In: WILSON (#1616), p. 80.

1702. SUGITA Hisajo (1890-1946)

Haiku poet, fiction writer, essayist. Born in Kagoshima Prefecture, educated in Tokyo. Married an art teacher, who took her back to a small town in Kyushu, where Hisajo spent the rest of her life. Began writing haiku and contributing to both *Hototogisu* and *Kareno*. Came to know TAKAHAMA Kyoshi and HASHIMOTO Takako. Her marriage was difficult because the values of husband and wife were at odds. She stopped writing haiku and they both tried Christianity to improve their marriage, but eventually she gave up and went back to writing. She caused considerable scandal in literary circles and eventually was expelled from Hototogisu. One popular theory was that she was insane.

  [Untitled (7 poems).] In: BLYTH (#1583), vol. 2, pp. 232-234, 325-326.
  [Untitled (2 poems).] In: REXROTH (#1607), p. 79.
  [Untitled.] In: SATO (#1610), p. 122.

1703. SUGIURA Suiko (1885-1960) (also cited as SUGIURA Midoriko)

Tanka/waka poet. From Saitama Prefecture. Married unknown painter SUGIURA Tomotake. Studied under KITAHARA Hakushū, but left because they disagreed. Later studied under

SAITŌ Mokichi with the Araragi group, where she came to know IMAI Kuniko. Earned a reputation as a troublemaker.

"My soul." [Waga tamashii.] In: MIYAMORI (#1602), vol. 2, pp. 778-779.
"Plantains." [Ōbako.] In: MIYAMORI (#1602), vol. 2, p. 778.
[Untitled.] In: CLACK (#1585), vol. 2, p. 561.

1704. SUYAMA Hisayo (1882-1977)

Born in Hiroshima. Wrote haiku and free verse after World War II, especially in the 1960's.

"Arranging flowers." [Hana o ikeru.] In: DAVIS (#1587), p. 273. Also in: KIRKUP (#1598), pp. 273-274.
"Haiku." In: DAVIS (#1587), p. 274.
"My hands." [Te.] In: DAVIS (#1587), p. 275.
"The stream." [Nagare.] In: DAVIS (#1587), p. 276.
"Wind." [Kaze.] In: DAVIS (#1587), p. 277.

1705. SUZUKI Miyoko

Contemporary haiku poet.

[Untitled.] [Translated by George SAITO.] In: *Japanese Literature Today* no. 4:11. Mar. 1979. LCCN:76-648281.

1706. TADA Chimako (1930-)

Free verse poet and essayist, translator from the French. Born in Tokyo. Graduated from Keiō University in English literature. Known as an intellectual and philosophical poet on European models. Also interested in Buddhism.

Moonstone Woman: Selected Poems of Tada Chimako. 1990. [Introduction by Makoto ŌOKA; translated by Robert BRADLEY, Kazuko ODAGAWA and Kerstin VIDAEUS.] Rochester, MI: Katydid Books. (*Asian Poetry in Translation*, no. 11.) 63p. LCCN:89-71621.
"Dead sun." [Shinda taiyo.] In: DAVIS (#1587), p. 222. Also translated in: ŌOKA (#1606), p. 145 and in: KIRKUP (#1598), pp. 24-25.
"A dirge." [Banka.] In: DAVIS (#1587), p. 221. Also translated in: KIRKUP (#1598), p. 24.
"Fireworks." [Hanabi.] In: DAVIS (#1587), p. 218.
"I." [Watashi.] In: DAVIS (#1587), p. 220.
"Jungle gym." (From *The Territory of Children*.) In: ŌOKA (#1606), pp. 162-163.
"King's army." In: ŌOKA (#1606), pp. 150-152.
"Lost kingdom." In: ŌOKA (#1606), pp. 159-161.
"Me." In: ŌOKA (#1606), p. 146.
"Mirror." In: REXROTH (#1607), p. 107.
"Morning or sea." [Asa aruiwa umi.] In: DAVIS (#1587), p. 223.
"The odyssey or 'on absense.'" In: ŌOKA (#1606), p. 153-155.
"The poetry calendar." In: ŌOKA (#1606), p. 148.
"Song." In: ŌOKA (#1606), p. 149.
"Song of Kairos." [Kairosu no uta.] In: DAVIS (#1587), pp. 219-220.
"Universe of the Rose." In: ŌOKA (#1606), pp. 156-158.
"Wind invites wind." In: ŌOKA (#1606), p. 147.

1707. TAKADA Toshiko (1914-1989)

Free verse poet, editor, critic. Born in the Nihombashi district of Tokyo. Spent World War II in Harbin, Manchuria, with her husband. A popular poet and a leader in poetry circles.

"The seacoast at Mera." In: REXROTH (#1607), p. 92.
"The voice of the wind." In: *The Eastern Sun...* (#1588), p. 32.

1708. TAKAGI Haruko (1915-)

Haiku poet. Born in Kamakura, the fifth daughter of TAKAHAMA Kyoshi. Began learning haiku with her father in her late teens. Has published several collections of her haiku, but is less well-known than her sister HOSHINO Tatsuko.

> [Untitled.] [Translated by George SAITO.] In: *Japanese Literature Today* no. 4:10. Mar. 1979. LCCN:76-648281.

> *Takajo* see *MITSUHASHI Takajo [#1666]*

> *Takako* see *HASHIMOTO Takako [#1638]*

1709. TAKAORI Taeko (1912-)

Tanka/waka poet. Graduated from Sacred Heart Women's Academy in Tokyo. Travelled extensively in Europe. Active in Kansai *tanka/waka* circles.

> [Untitled (8 poems).] In: SHIFFERT (#1612), pp. 154-156.

1710. TAKEDA Chie

Contemporary haiku poet. Along with IZUMI Sumie [#1654], belongs to a Matsuyama haiku club that publishes its work in a monthly called *Itadori*.

> [Untitled.] In: HIGGINSON (#1591), p. 45.

1711. TAKESHITA Shizunojo (1887-1951)

Haiku poet. Born in Shizuoka Prefecture. Graduated from Shizuoka Women's Teachers' College. Studied haiku with the Hototogisu group, first under YOSHIOKA Zenjidō, later receiving guidance from TAKAHAMA Kyoshi. Supervised the production of a high school haiku journal. Characteristically uses an unusual number of Sino-Japanese words in her own haiku.

> [Untitled.] In: BLYTH (#1583), vol. 2, pp. 232 & 235.

1712. TAKIGUCHI Masako (1918-)

Free verse poet. Born in Seoul. Returned to Japan impoverished as a result of World War II. Writes strong feminist, social protest poetry.

> "About men." [Translated by Greg CAMPBELL.] 1970. *TransPacific* no. 5:20. LCCN:72-620605.
> "Blue horse." In: KIJIMA (#1597), p. 47. Also translated in: REXROTH (#1607), p. 94.
> "Flame." In: KIJIMA (#1597), p. 38.
> "Future." In: KIJIMA (#1597), p. 45.
> "Just one." In: KIJIMA (#1597), pp. 47-48.
> "On man." In: KIJIMA (#1597), p. 45.
> "Slaughterhouse." In: REXROTH (#1607), p. 93.
> "The steel leg." In: *The Eastern Sun...* (#1588), p. 22.

1713. TANAKA Kayo

Haiku poet. Born in Tokyo. Became a government bureaucrat. A member of KANAO Ume's Kisetsu [Seasons] since 1953.

> [Untitled.] In: YASUDA (#1620), p. 97.

Tatsuko see *HOSHINO Tatsuko [#1642]*

1714. TAWARA Machi (1962-)

Tanka/waka poet. Born in Osaka, moved to Fukui. Graduated in Japanese literature from Waseda University. Began writing *tanka/waka* seriously an an undergraduate, becoming a member of Kokoro no Hana [Flowers of the Heart]. Writes in modern Japanese about the everyday life of a young Japanese with an immediacy that has won extraordinary popularity for herself and a new enthusiasm for *tanka/waka* in general. Appears in magazine interviews and on television.

> *Salad Anniversary.* 1989. [Translated by Juliet Winters CARPENTER.] Tokyo: Kodansha. 203p. LCCN:88-46060. [*Sarada kinenbi.*] Also translated by Jack STAMM as: *Salad Anniversary.* 1988. Tokyo: Kawade Shobō Shinsha. 184p. LCCN:89-102378.

Teijo see *NAKAMURA Teijo [#1675]*

Teiko see *INAHATA Teiko [#1648]*

1715. Ten-Year-Old Korean Girl

> "I am a Korean." In: *Japanese Women Speak Out.* 1979. Tokyo: White Paper on Sexism—Japan Task Force, p. 142.

1716. TEZUKA Hisako

Contemporary free verse poet.

> "August." In: *The Eastern Sun...* (#1588), p. 18.

1717. TOKUGAWA Kasenjo (1906-1964)

Haiku poet. Born in Osaka. Graduated from Fukuoka Women's Higher School in Japanese literature. Studied under Tōyōjō. Her husband as also a haiku poet.

> Poem on p. 217 in: HOFFMANN (#1593).

1718. TOMIOKA Taeko (1935-)

Began her career as a free verse poet, publishing her first book of poetry while she was a student at Osaka University. Had a brilliant career as a young poet until the late 1960's, when she turned to prose and began another, equally brilliant, career as a novelist, essayist, and critic. [See also #1480.]

> *See You Soon.* 1979. [Translated by Hiroaki SATO. Introduced by Burton WATSON.] Chicago: Chicago Review Press. 101p.
> "Age." In: SATO (#1609), p. 606.
> "And then soon." In: SATO (#1608), p. 99.
> "Between." In: DAVIS (#1587), p. 266. Also translated in: KIJIMA (#1597), pp. 222-223; and in: SATO (#1609), p. 606.
> "Cat poet." In: *Chicago Review* 25(2):41-42. 1973. ISSN:0009-3696.
> "Chairs." In: KIJIMA (#1597), p. 231. Also translated as "Chair" in: "Nine Japanese poets." 1973. *Chelsea* 32:7-30. ISSN:0009-2185.
> "Don't explain." In: *Chicago Review* 25(2):45. 1973. ISSN:0009-3696.
> "The girlfriend." In: KIJIMA (#1597), pp. 232-233. Also translated in: SATO (#1608), p. 101; in: REXROTH (#1607), pp. 124-125; and in: ARKIN (#1580), p. 889.
> "Greetings." In: KIJIMA (#1597), p. 233. Also translated in: SATO (#1608), pp. 94.
> "How are you." In: KIJIMA (#1597), pp. 227-229. Also translated in: SATO (#1608), pp. 97-98.

"I plough the garden." [Niwa o tagayasu] [Translated by Tamae K. PRINDLE.] In: *Bulletin of Concerned Asian Scholars*. 14(4):66-70. Oct./Dec. 1982. ISSN:0007-4810.

"Just the two of us. (Living together?)" In: SATO (#1609, p. 609. Also translated as: "Living together." In: KIJIMA (#1597), p. 226.

"Life story." In: GUEST (#1590), pp. 146-148. Also translated as: "The story of myself." [Shinjogatari.] in: DAVIS (#1587), pp. 264-265; as: "Let me tell you about myself." in: KIJIMA (#1597), pp. 223-225; and in: SATO (#1609), pp. 607-608.

"Madrigal." In: *Chicago Review* 25(2):46. 1973. ISSN:0009-3696.

"Marry me please." In: KIJIMA (#1597), p. 230.

"Nude drawing." In: SATO (#1608), p. 95.

"Please say something." In: KIJIMA (#1597), pp. 229-230. Also translated in: SATO (#1609), pp. 609-610.

"See you soon." In: SATO (#1609), p. 610. Also translated as: "Well then see you tonight." In: SATO (#1608), p. 100.

"Still life." In: "Nine Japanese poets." 1973. *Chelsea* 32:7-30. ISSN:0009-2185. Also translated in: ARKIN (#1580), p. 888.

"There's nothing to do in New York." In: SATO (#1609), pp. 610-614.

"This time last autumn." In: *Chicago Review* 25(2):43. 1973. ISSN:0009-3696.

"Too much worry." In: "Nine Japanese poets." 1973. *Chelsea* 32:7-30. ISSN:0009-2185.

"What color was the sky." In: KIJIMA (#1597), pp. 226-227. Also translated in: *Chicago Review* 25(2):44. 1973. ISSN:0009-3696.

"What is your name?" In: SATO (#1608), p. 96.

"Who's afraid of T.S. Elliot?" In: ARKIN (#1580), p. 889.

1719. TSUDA Kiyoko (1920-)

Haiku poet. Born in Nara. Studied haiku under HASHIMOTO Takako and YAMAGUCHI Seishi.

[Untitled (2 poems).] In: SHIFFERT (#1612), p. 174.

1720. UBUKATA Tatsue (1905-)

Tanka/waka poet, essayist, critic. Born in Ise. Graduated in home economics from Nihon Women's University in 1926. Married into an old Gumma Prefecture family. Her first *tanka/waka* teacher was IMAI Kuniko, and she was a member of Asuka. With KITAMI Shihoko, she founded the women's *tanka/waka* journal *Nyonin Tanka*. Extremely active in *tanka/waka* circles.

[Untitled. ("A radiance...")] In: WRIGHT (#1619), p. 79.
[Untitled. ("Holding each other...")] In: WRIGHT (#1619), p. 79.

1721. UEDA Shizue

Contemporary free verse poet.

"Resistance." In: KŌNO (#1599), pp. 149-150.

1722. UENO Akiko (1919-)

Haiku poet. Born in Kamakura. Sixth daughter of TAKAHAMA Kyoshi. Married in 1942 (to another haiku poet) and went with her husband to Manchuria, returning to Japan before the end of World War II. Visited France and traveled through Europe with her father. Has edited *Shunchō [Spring Tide]* since the death of her husband, the former editor.

[Untitled.] [Translated by George SAITO.] In: *Japanese Literature Today* no. 4:10. Mar. 1979. LCCN:76-648281.

1723. *WAKAYAMA Kishiko (1888-1968)*

Tanka/waka poet. Married to the (more famous) poet WAKAYAMA Bokusui.

[Untitled (5 poems).] In: CLACK (#1585), vol. 2, pp. 553-554.
The following poems are contained in MIYAMORI (#1602), vol. 2:
  "A cooper." [Okeya.] p. 756. Also published in MIYAMORI (#1603), pp. 277-278.
  "The copse." [Zōki-bayashi.] p. 755.
  "The cosmos flower." [Kosumosu.] p. 755. Also published in MIYAMORI (#1603), p. 277.
  "A great moon." [Ōki tsuki.] pp. 756-757.
  "Lean crows." [Yase-garasu.] pp. 757-758.
  "A silver dragonfly." [Gin-yamma.] p. 757.

1724. *YAGI Mikajo (1924-)*

Haiku poet. Born in Osaka. REXROTH (#1607, p. 153) describes her as one who "writes typical modern haiku."

[Untitled (2 poems).] In: REXROTH (#1607), p. 84.

1725. *YAMADA Kazuko*

Free verse poet. OMORI (#1605) describes her as "a widow, who is also one among the A-bomb sufferers, [who] has been leading with her child a poverty-stricken life." (p. 38)

"The chilly wind." In: OMORI (#1605), pp. 25-26.
"To the dead." In: OMORI (#1605), p. 26.
"The wind." In: OMORI (#1605), p. 26.

1726. *YAMAKAWA Tomiko (1879-1909)*

Tanka/waka poet. Born in Fukui Prefecture. Part of the Myōjō group; a rival of YOSANO Akiko for YOSANO Tekkan's affections. Married briefly, then was widowed. Led a brief and complicated life. Published a book of poetry composed with YOSANO Akiko and CHINO Masako.

"Fever." [Netsubyō.] In: MIYAMORI (#1602), vol. 2, p. 687.
[Untitled.] In: CLACK (#1585), vol. 2, p. 531.
[Untitled (2 poems).] In: REXROTH (#1607), p. 67.

1727. *YAMATO Setsuko*

Free verse poet.

"Superwoman next door." 1986. *Ampo: Japan Asia Quarterly Review* 18(2/3):10-11. LCCN:77-612830.

1728. *YANAGIWARA Akiko / YANAGIWARA Byakuren / White Lotus (1885-1967)*

Tanka/waka poet, novelist, essayist, playwright. Studied with SASAKI Nobutsuna. Daughter of a Count, briefly married to a millionaire.

[Untitled (4 poems).] In: CLACK (#1585), vol. 2, p. 543.
[Untitled (poems 1-33).] In: HUGHES (#1594), pp. 27-34.
[Untitled (poems 1-10).] In: HUGHES (#1595), pp. 29-31.
The following poems are contained in MIYAMORI (#1602), vol. 2:
  "Flowers." [Hana.] pp. 723-724.
  "My soul." [Waga tamashii.] p. 724.
  "My verses." [Waga uta.] pp. 724-725.
  "A ship." [Fune.] p. 725.

"When I was lost in thought." [Mono-omou koro.] p. 723.
"Where are the gods?" [Kami wa izuko ni.] p. 722.

Yorie see *KUBO Yorie [#1659]*

1729. YOSANO Akiko (1878-1942)

The best-known modern Japanese woman poet. *Tanka/waka* and free verse poet, teacher, critic, essayist, children's literature writer. Born in the old merchant town of Sakai. Went to Tokyo to study with—and marry—the modern *tanka/waka* leader YOSANO Tekkan. Together they founded the Shinshisha [New Poetry Society] and edited the influential *Myōjō* [*Morning Star*]. Drawing for inspiration on classical poetry by women (ONO no Komachi, Izumi Shikibu), she worked toward modernizing the *tanka/waka* form; she also translated *Genji Monogatari* [*Tale of Genji*] into modern Japanese. Also a pacifist and a feminist.

"The poetry of Yosano Akiko." Apr./Jun. 1974. [Translated by Ikuko ATSUMI and Graeme WILSON.] *Japan Quarterly* 21(2):181-187. ISSN:0021-4590.

Tangled Hair: Selections from Midaregami *by Akiko Yosano.* 1971. [Translated by Sanford GOLDSTEIN and Seishi SHINODA.] Lafayette, IN: Purdue University Studies. 165p. [*Midare-gami.* Selections.] LCCN:70-128023. Also translated as: *Tangled Hair: Love Poems of Yosano Akiko* by Dennis MALONEY and Hide OSHIRO. 1987. Fredonia, NY: White Pine Press. 47p. [*Midare-gami.* Selections.] Selections are also translated in: ARKIN (#1580), p. 188; and in: "Hair in sweet disorder" by H.H. HONDA. 1956. *The Reeds* 2:3-31. ISSN:0484-2081.

"Yosano Akiko: Return to the female." Apr./Jun. 1990. *Japan Quarterly* 37(2):204-229. 2 notes. ISSN:0021-4590. [Contains many poems in translation as well as analysis by Janine BEICHMAN.]

"First labor pains." In: ARKIN (#1580), p. 190.

"The flesh." Translated by Graeme WILSON in: *Western Humanities Review* 31:214 1977. ISSN:0043-3845.

"Labor pains." In: REXROTH (#1607), p. 87.

"Love." In: BENNETT (#1581), p. 12.

"A mouse." In: KEENE (#1596), p. 203. Also published as: "The mouse." In: CLACK (#1585), vol. 2, p. 528.

"The mother-ofpearl shell [sic]" In: CLACK (#1585), vol. 2, p. 527

"My great grandmother's rosary." In: CLACK (#1585), vol. 2, p. 526.

"My mother soul." In: CLACK (#1585), vol. 2, p. 529.

"Never let them kill you, brother!" In: DAVIS (#1587), pp. 5-6. Also translated as: "My brother you must not die." In: ARKIN (#1580), p. 189, and as: "Heaven forbid that you shall die!" In: SATŌ (#1611), pp. 66-67. [Translated by NISHIMURA Shigeshi.] [Kimi shinitamou koto nakare.]

"No camellia." In: BOWNAS (#1584), p. 160. Also translated in: COSMAN (#1586), p. 289.

"Our love." [Koi.] In: DAVIS (#1587), p. 7.

"Prisoners." In: WILSON (#1616), p. 79. Also translated in: WILSON (#1614), p. 33.

"Spring is short." In: BOWNAS (#1584), p. 159. [A *tanka/waka.*] Also translated in: COSMAN (#1586), p. 289.

"The sutra is sour." In: BOWNAS (#1584), p. 159. [A *tanka/waka.*]

"Two poems." Jan. 1955. [Translated by the Kenneth REXROTH.] In: "Perspective of Japan: An Atlantic supplement." *Atlantic* 195(1):147. ISSN:0276-9077.

"White bird." In: WILSON (#1618), p. 63.

"Willows." Apr./June 1955. *Japan Quarterly* 2(2):223. ISSN:0021-4590. Also published in: CLACK (#1585), vol. 2, p. 526.

"Winter twilight." In: WILSON (#1617), p. 65.

"'You never touch.'" In: BOWNAS (#1584), p. 159. Also translated in: In: COSMAN (#1586), p. 289.

[Untitled ("Never even to have touched...")] In: BENNETT (#1581), pp. 51.

[Untitled (6 haiku).] In: CLACK (#1585), vol. 2, p. 530.

[Untitled (10 *tanka/waka*).] In: CLACK (#1585), vol. 2, pp. 516-525.

[Untitled.] In: HIGGINSON (#1591), p. 189.

[Untitled (poems 1-30).] In: HUGHES (#1594), pp. 15-22.

[Untitled (poems 1-4).] In: HUGHES (#1595), pp. 32-34.

[Untitled (2 *tanka/waka*).] In: KEENE (#1596), p. 207.

[Untitled (11 poems).] In: REXROTH (#1607), pp. 63-66.

[Untitled (39 *tanka/waka*).] In: SATO (#1609), pp. 431-435.

The following poems are contained in MIYAMORI (#1602), vol. 2:

"The Cherry flowers." [Sakura.] p. 680-81. Also published in MIYAMORI (#1603), pp. 256-257.

"Crimson butterfly." [Kurenai no chō.] p. 684-685.

"An eye." [Me.] pp. 681-682.

"The flowery field." [Hana-no.] p. 677.

"The *hanabishisō*." [Hanabishisō.] p. 685. Also published in MIYAMORI (#1603), p. 257.

"A little bird." [Kotori.] p. 681.

"Love." [Koi.] p. 682.

"A maiden-hair tree." [Ichō.] p. 679.

"A meteor." [Ryūsei.] p. 677-678.

"A pagoda." [To.] p. 686. Also published in MIYAMORI (#1603), p. 258.

"The rising sun." [Noboru hi.] p. 684.

"A rose." [Bara.] p. 680.

"Sky of early autumn." [Hatsu-aki no sora.] pp. 683-684.

"Spring." [Haru.] p. 683.

"The stable." [Umaya.] p. 678.

"White lotus-flowers." [Byaku-ren.] p. 679.

1730. YOSHIWARA/YOSHIHARA Sachiko (1932-)

Free verse poet. Born in Tokyo. Graduated in French literature from Tokyo University. Trained as an actress.

"Anaemia." [Hinketsu.] In: DAVIS (#1587), p. 255.

"Appetite." [Shokuyoku.] In: DAVIS (#1587), p. 258. Also translated in: KIRKUP (#1598), pp. 22-23.

"Blasphemy." In: REXROTH (#1607), p. 121.

"Candle." In: REXROTH (#1607), pp. 118-119.

"Fever." [Netsu.] In: DAVIS (#1587), p. 254.

"Flowers." [Hana.] In: DAVIS (#1587), p. 253.

"I forget." In: REXROTH (#1607), p. 122.

"Kitchen table." [Shokutaku.] In: DAVIS (#1587), p. 256.

"Madness." [Kyo.] In: DAVIS (#1587), p. 252.

"Name." [Namae.] In: DAVIS (#1587), p. 257. Also translated in: KIRKUP (#1598), p. 22.

"Noonface permutations." In: *The Eastern Sun...* (#1588), p. 23.

"Rainbow." [Niji.] In: DAVIS (#1587), p. 259.

"Resurrection." [Fukkatsu.] In: DAVIS (#1587), p. 260. Also translated in: REXROTH (#1607), p. 120.

"To a new life." 1980. [Translated by Lora Sharnoff.] *Feminist International* 2:62. ISSN:0388-371X.

1731. YOSHIYUKI, Rie (1939-)

Began as a free verse poet [see also #1490 for the biographical sketch in modern fiction section.] Published her first volume of poetry the year after graduating from Waseda University.

"Carrying." [Hakobu.] In: DAVIS (#1587), p. 280.
"Sacrificial victim." In: REXROTH (#1607), p. 126.

Critical Studies of Modern Poetry

1732. ATSUMI, Ikuko. 1974. "Five modern women poets on love." *Literature East and West* 18(1):58-75. No refs. ISSN:0024-4767.

An introductory article on ISHIGAKI Rin, TOMIOKA Taeko, YOSHIHARA Sachiko, TADA Chimako and SHIRAISHI Kazuko, with excerpts from poems liberally quoted in the text.

1733. ATSUMI, Ikuko. Spring/Summer 1976. "Modern Japanese women poets: After the Meiji Restoration." *Iowa Review* 7(2/3):227-237. 2 notes. ISSN:0021-065X.

ATSUMI introduces poetry by Japanese women since 1868, dividing "really good poets" into two categories: "an erotic type who bursts into flame, emphasizes love, and lets eros overflow the whole universe, and a mental type who hides passion in the enduring spirit, observes the inner self and treats objects in an intellectual way" (p. 231). Cites *tanka/waka*, haiku and free verse by YOSANO Akiko, CHINO Masako, KUJŌ Takeko, BABA Akiko, SUGITA Hisajo, NAKAMURA Teijo, HOSHINO Tatsuko, YAGI Mikajo, MITSUHASHI Takajo, ISHIGAKI Rin, TAKIGUCHI Masako and TOMIOKA Taeko, and mentions many others.

1734. ATSUMI, Ikuko and Graeme WILSON. Apr./Jun. 1984. "The poetry of Yosano Akiko." *Japan Quarterly* 21(2):181-187. No notes. ISSN:0021-4590.

A three-page intellectual biographical sketch of Akiko placing her in the context of contemporary poetic movements, and stressing "her importance in the development in Japan of the modern 'long poem' in Western style" (p. 181). ATSUMI includes a mini-anthology (21 poems) varied in form in eloquent translation without original or romanized text.

1735. BEICHMAN, Janine. Jan./Mar. 1990. "Yosano Akiko: The early years." *Japan Quarterly* 37(1):37-54. 3 notes. ISSN:0021-4590.

A personal introduction followed by a pleasant account of Akiko's childhood and adolescence, emphasizing Akiko's unusually keen esthetic sense and "her fear of death and . . . joy of life" (p. 53) the author considers central to her poetry.

1736. BEICHMAN, Janine. Apr./Jun. 1990. "Yosano Akiko: Return to the female." *Japan Quarterly* 37(2):204-229. 2 notes. ISSN:0021-4590.

An examination of what the author sees as a gradual transition from the style of *Tangled Hair*, "deliberately" written "as if she were a man" (p. 218) to a more female consciousness, reflected by "distant, vague things, things that fade away" (p. 218) in natural imagery, and a recurrence of birth and labor imagery in poetry beginning with the collection *Spring Thaw* 1911. Contains numerous poems in translation, including 41 *tanka/waka* with romanized text.

1737. BOWEN, Helene. Spring 1988. "Women and treason in pre-war Japan: The prison poetry of Kanno Sugo [sic] and Kaneko Fumiko." *Lilith* [Australia] no. 5:9-25. 6 notes. ISSN:0813-8990.

A conversational biographical treatment of the *tanka/waka* poetry of the first two women in modern Japanese history to be sentenced to death for treason, KANNO Suga and KANEKO Fumiko. BOWEN looks at the poetry (as opposed to their trial testimony) for evidence of "their emotions [their feelings about] . . . their political commitment, being in prison and waiting for death." (p. 21).

1738. CARPENTER, Juliet Winters. Apr./Jun. 1989. "Tawara Machi: To create poetry is to live." *Japan Quarterly* 36(2):193-199. ISSN:0021-4590.

An appealing introduction to TAWARA Machi and her extraordinarily popular *tanka/waka*, and to the phenomenon of the "salad phenomenon." (p. 195) Includes liberal citation of poetry, with romanized Japanese text.

1739. CRANSTON, Edwin A. March 1977. "Young Akiko: The literary debut of Yosano Akiko." *Literature East and West* 18(1):19-43. 4 notes. ISSN:0024-4767.

A scholarly article of literary history focusing on the early biographical, social, and literary circumstances of Akiko's extraordinary career as a *tanka/waka* poet. Ends with *Midaregami*, published in 1908.

1740. HIGUCHI, Chiyoko. May 1972. "Poem child, love child: Yosano Akiko." *East* 8(5):14-21. No notes. ISSN:0012-8295.

A somewhat romanticized account with interesting details of Akiko's career as a poet and social critic.

1741. KEENE, Donald. 1984. *Dawn to the West: Japanese Literature in the Modern Era*. New York: Holt, Reinhart and Winston, 1984. 2 vol. Bibl. LCCN:82-15445.

Part of a monumental history of Japanese literature prepared over many years by one of the most prominent and wide-ranging American scholars in the field. Partly because of KEENE's decision not to discuss living authors, women do not occupy an important place in this work. However, one chapter in the first volume (on fiction), is devoted to HIGUCHI Ichiyō, and another to "The Revival of Writing by Women," in which he treats NOGAMI Yaeko, OKAMOTO Kanoko, UNO Chiyo, HAYASHI Fumiko, MIYAMOTO Yuriko, SATA Ineko, and HIRABAYASHI Taiko. The second volume (on poetry, drama and criticism) discusses or mentions in passing the following women: *tanka/waka*—GOTŌ Miyoko, SAITŌ Fumi, UBUKATA Tatsue, YAMAKAWA Tomiko, YOSANO Akiko; haiku—HASHIMOTO Takako, SUGITA Hisajo; free verse—IBARAGI Noriko. HIGUCHI Ichiyō is discussed further in the criticism section.

1742. Kokusai Bunka Shinkokai, ed. 1948/1970. *Introduction to Classic Japanese Literature*. Tokyo: Kokusai Bunka Shinkokai/Westport, CT: Greenwood Press. 443p. LCCN:50-31232/72-98847.

The first in a series of books written by committees of eminent Japanese literary scholars and translated into English, containing considerable valuable information but not accessible to the general reader. This volume beings with the earliest times and ends in the Meiji period. Women are not especially well represented, but there is a section on YOSANO Akiko's *Midaregami* [*Tangled Hair*].

1743. "Lesbian poets." Fall 1983. *Connexions: An International Women's Quarterly* 10:18. No refs. ISSN:0886-7062.

A very brief survey citing MIYAMOTO Yuriko, HIRATSUKA Raichō and YOSHI[Y]A Nobuko as Japanese women writing more or less directly about lesbian life styles.

1744. OKAZAKI, Yoshie. 1955. *Japanese Literature in the Meiji Era*. [Translated by V.H. VIGLIELMO.] Tokyo: Ōbunsha. 673p. Index. LCCN:56-22381.

A detailed history originally written for a Japanese audience and therefore difficult for the beginner, although full of information. Most of the work is devoted to literature by men, but space is given to some women, notably YOSANO Akiko (poetry) and HIGUCHI Ichiyō (prose), and poems by several women are quoted.

1745. ŌOKA, Makoto. Summer 1988. "Contemporary Japanese poetry." [Translated by James O'BRIEN.] *World Literature Today* 62(3):414-417. No notes. ISSN:0196-3570.

ŌOKA (a contemporary, avant-garde poet) discusses the "boom" (p. 416) of poetry by contemporary women who, he says, take as their subject "for the most part, . . . daily life in the home," (p. 417) and, apparently, are too rooted in "the middle class pleasures" (p. 416) to hear "at [their] back[s] the roar of a revolutionary storm which begins to rage in each country as our century comes to an end" (p. 416).

1746. RIMER, J. Thomas and Robert E. MORRELL. 1975. *Guide to Japanese Poetry*. Boston: G.K. Hall. 151p. (*Asian Literature Bibliography Series*.) LCCN:74-20610.

A useful handbook providing a historical overview of Japanese poetry from prehistory to the early 1970s, including a wide-ranging, extensively and helpfully annotated bibliography of Japanese poetry translated into English. Includes reviews of many of the items listed here.

1747. SHIRAISHI, Kazuko. Spring/Summer 1976. "The Orient in me." [Translated by Ikuko ATSUMI and Graeme WILSON.] *Iowa Review* 7(2/3):196-198. No notes. ISSN:0021-065X. Reprinted in: ARKIN, Marian and Barbara SHOLLAR, eds. 1989. *Longman Anthology of World Literature by Women, 1875-1975*. London: Longman, pp. 842-844. LCCN:88-8274.

A self-reflective musing on "what it means to write a poem in the Japanese language" (p. 196) and "to find herself, however proud of [her] outlandishness, to be traveling jazzwise in that main stream of Oriental thinking which leads either to Zen or to the sword" (p. 198). No poetry quoted.

1748. SWAIN, David L. Summer 1988. "Portrait of a peacemaker (13): Kurihara Sadako." *Japan Christian Quarterly* 54(3):181-184. No notes. ISSN:0021-4361.

Discusses the circumstances of KURIHARA Sadako and quotes some of her postwar and antiwar poetry. Includes an illuminating description of its strange fate in the hands of occupation censors.

1749. TASAKA, Seiki. Fall 1975. "Jukichi Yagi and his wife Tomoko: Their life and faith." [Translated by Satoko TASAKA.] *Japan Christian Quarterly* 41(4):215-221. 5 notes. ISSN:0021-4361.

TASAKA focuses primarily on YAGI Jukichi, but gives an interesting brief account of the fate of YAGI Tomiko who was married to two famous poets (YAGI and HOSHINO Hideo) in succession. None of her poems are quoted.

1750. TSUKIMURA, Reiko. *I am Alive: The Tanka Poems of Gotō Miyoko, 1898-1978*. 1988. Michigan: Oakland University, Katydid Press. 189p. Index. 112 notes. LCCN:88-8378.

TSUKIMURA provides an extensive commentary and scholarly introduction for the general reader to the life of GOTŌ Miyoko and her poetry, a collection of *tanka/waka* spanning more than sixty years. Although GOTŌ's literary background and the form she chose were traditional, she was "strongly independent" and a "woman of powerful passions" whose poems "reflect in microcosm Japan's struggle for identity as a modern nation" (p. 13). Her best known poems are about motherhood and helped to "revitalize the tanka tradition" (p. 14). GOTŌ founded *Nyonin tanka* (*Women's Tanka*) in 1949 with two other poets.

1751. YAMAGIWA, Joseph K. 1959. *Japanese Literature of the Showa Period: A Guide to Japanese Reference and Research Materials*. Ann Arbor: University of Michigan Press. 212p. (*University of Michigan Center for Japanese Studies Bibliographical Series* no. 8.) LCCN:59-62962.

Aimed at an audience reasonably familiar with Japanese literature, this volume contains a wealth of information on almost all recognized twentieth-century groups of writers or poets, with considerable attention to their membership and their publications (journals)—including the poetry groups and journals indicated but unexplicated in the present bibliography. Also a valuable, though outdated, bibliographic source for Japanese materials.

16

Premodern Prose Writers: Tales, Diaries, Miscellanies

Anthologies of Premodern Prose Including Material by, or Commonly Attributed to, Women

1752. KEENE, Donald, ed. 1955. *Anthology of Japanese Literature from the Earliest Era to the Mid-Nineteenth Century.* New York: Grove Press. 442p. Bibl. LCCN:55-5110.

Still the standard anthology of premodern Japanese literature, offering a fair sampling of prose and poetry (much of it in excerpt) from earliest times to the Meiji Restoration. Includes six prose selections by women, all from the Heian Period; see: *Murasaki Shikibu nikki, Kagerō nikki, Genji monogatari, Makura no sōshi, Sarashina nikki, Tsutsumi Chūnagon monogatari.*

1753. McCULLOUGH, Helen Craig. 1990. *Classical Japanese Prose: An Anthology.* Stanford: Stanford University Press. 578p. Bibl. LCCN:89-78331.

A general historical survey of genres precedes an anthology of prose introduced individually and translated in full or in excerpt. See: *Izayoi nikki, Kagerō nikki, Tsutsumi Chūnagon monogatari, Towazugatari, Makura no sōshi,* and *Eiga monogatari.*

1754. MINER, Earl, compiler and editor. 1969. *Japanese Poetic Diaries.* [Translated by Earl MINER.] Berkeley: University of California Press. 211p. Notes. LCCN:69-11846.

Translations of four diaries, the *Izumi Shikibu nikki* [*Izumi Shikibu Diary*] (pp. 93-153) and three by men. Begins with a long introduction describing general characteristics of the Japanese literary diary, especially as it differs from the diary tradition in English belles-lettres, and including a 9-page section about Izumi Shikibu, with interpretive comments on her diary. MINER's *Izumi Shikibu Diary* is more readable, if less scholarly, than the CRANSTON version of the same classic (see #1763). Includes maps and illustrations.

1755. OMORI, Annie Shepley and Kochi DOI. 1920 [1961, corrected reprint edition]. *Diaries of Court Ladies of Old Japan.* Tokyo: Kenkyusha. 209p. Notes.

Early, charming if inaccurate translations of *Sarashina nikki* [*The Sarashina Diary; As I Crossed a Bridge of Dreams*], *Murasaki Shikibu nikki* [*The Diary of Murasaki Shikibu*] and the *Izumi Shikibu nikki* [*The Diary of Izumi Shikibu*]. Enthusiastic, original introduction by Amy LOWELL.

1756. REISCHAUER, Edwin O. and Joseph K. YAMAGIWA. 1951. *Translations from Early Japanese Literature.* Cambridge: Harvard University Press. 467p. Notes. Index. LCCN:51-10360.

A scholarly translation, with prolific notes and brackets, of four major works of classical Japanese literature, including two traditionally ascribed totally or in part to women: a "minor classic" of the Kamakura Period (p. 3), *The Izayoi nikki* [*The Diary of the Waning Moon*] by the Nun Abutsu, translated and introduced by REISCHAUER (see #1762); and the *Tsutsumi Chūnagon monogatari* (see #1773), a collection of ten "short stories" of uncertain date and authorship, several of which are attributed to women, introduced and translated by YAMAGIWA and REISCHAUER. Ample annotation.

1757. WATANABE, Tōkichi. 1959. *A Treasury of Japanese Literature*. Tokyo: Nihon Gakujutsu Shuppansha. 361p. Bibl.

An anthology of highlights of classical Japanese fiction and poetry with original Japanese and English translation printed on opposite pages. Includes abundant footnotes in Japanese. See: *Genji monogatari, Murasaki Shikibu nikki, Makura no sōshi* and *Sarashina nikki*.

Individual Works of Premodern Prose by, or Commonly Attributed to, Women

1758. Ariake no wakare

Tale by an unknown, not unlikely female author, assumed to have been written in the last half of the twelfth century. It is a complex tale, and like *Torikaebaya* [*The Changelings*] (#1771), focuses on gender roles in the late Heian Period.

"Ariake no tsuki (Parting at Dawn)." 1980-1981. *Traditions* no. 12:7-33, no. 13:33-56, no. 14:59-71, no. 15:55-71. [Also cited as *Traditions* 3(4):7-33, 4(1):33-56, 4(2):59-71, 4(3):55-71.] LCCN:77-644976.

1759. Eiga monogatari

McCULLOUGH, William H. and Helen Craig McCULLOUGH. 1980. *A Tale of Flowering Fortunes: Annals of Japanese Aristocratic Life in the Heian Period*. Stanford: Stanford University Press. 2 vol. Notes. Bibl. Index. LCCN:78-66183.

"A chronicle of the great aristocratic family of Fujiwara at the peak of its power and affluence during the tenth and eleventh centuries . . . [w]ritten probably by one or more female contemporaries, or near contemporaries, of most of the events described" (p. vii). Focuses on the life of FUJIWARA Michinaga, the greatest of the Fujiwaras, whose ascendency corresponds to the time during which the *Genji monogatari* [*The Tale of Genji*] and *Makura no sōshi* [*Pillow Book*] were being written. An invaluable source of information amplifying or counterbalancing the fictional world of Genji. This heavily annotated scholarly translation of the first thirty chapters of the original work contains a detailed introduction and a wealth of genealogical background and information on court ranks and offices.

"A tale of flowering fortunes." In: McCULLOUGH (#1753), pp. 200-250. [*Eiga monogatari*. Excerpts.]

1760. Genji monogatari

A prose tale studded with *waka* poetry, the supreme example of the *monogatari* [tale] tradition, *the* Japanese classic. A long work of 54 chapters, all or most written around the year 1000 by Murasaki Shikibu, set mainly in Kyoto, depicting the life and many loves of the fictional character Hikaru Genji (Prince Genji/The Shining One) and two of his descendants, Prince Niou and Kaoru. The last ten chapters, set south of Kyoto in Uji, often treated separately in *Genji* scholarship, are known as the Uji chapters. This tale is the subject of voluminous scholarship; it has been translated numerous times into modern Japanese (by YOSANO Akiko, ENCHI Fumiko and TANABE Seiko among prominent women writers) and three times into English. It inspired many later *monogatari*, especially in the Kamakura Period (see #1761 and #1772), some of the best-known Nō plays, scroll and screen paintings, woodblock prints, modern fiction (including at least two murder mysteries). There are several contemporary comic book versions, of which one has been translated into English (below).

Murasaki Shikibu. 1882/1884. *Genji monogatari: The Most Celebrated of the Classical Japanese Romances*. [Translated by Kenchio SUYEMATZ.] London: Trubner/[Tokyo]: Z.P. Maruya and Co (Second edition, revised). 280p. Notes.

The first translation of *Genji monogatari* into English; actually an adaptation for a Victorian English audience by a Japanese translator. Includes the first 17 chapters, through "E-awase, A Picture Contest."

Murasaki Shikibu. 1926-1933. *The Tale of Genji*. [Translated by Arthur WALEY.]

Originally published in six separately titled volumes:
The Tale of Genji. 1926. Boston: Houghton Mifflin. 300p. ["Translation of nine chapters of *Genji monogatari*."] Later republished in 1955 by Anchor Books. 253p. LCCN:55-2413.
The Sacred Tree. 1926. Boston: Houghton Mifflin. 304p. LCCN:26-26576. [Part 2.]
A Wreath of Cloud. 1927. Boston: Houghton Mifflin. 312p. LCCN:27-26380. [Part 3.]
Blue Trousers. 1928. Boston: Houghton Mifflin. 333p. LCCN:28-26621. [Part 4.]
The Lady of the Boat. 1932. Boston: Houghton Mifflin. 309p. LCCN:32-26883. [Part 5, vol. 1.]
The Bridge of Dreams. 1933. Boston: Houghton Mifflin. 341p. LCCN:33-27192. [Part 5, vol. 2.]

Later published in one volume as:
Murasaki, Lady. 1960. *The Tale of Genji: A Novel in Six Parts*. [Translated by Arthur WALEY.] New York: Modern Library [Random House]. 1135p. LCCN:60-52014.

For decades the form in which *The Tale of Genji*—transformed and embellished in WALEY's charming prose—reached English-speaking readers. A complete translation except for Chapter 38: "Suzumushi [The Bell Cricket]."

Murasaki Shikibu. 1976. *The Tale of Genji*. [Translated by Edward SEIDENSTICKER.] New York: Knopf. 2 vol. [Available as a 1090p. paperback as of 1978.] LCCN:76-13680.

The most recent, the most accurate, and the only complete translation of *The Tale*. Contains woodcut illustrations by YAMAMOTO Shunshō from the 1650 *Eiri Genji monogatari* [*Illustrated Tale of Genji*], and a brief but useful introduction.

Murasaki Shikibu. 1989. *An Illustrated Tale of Genji: A Classic Japanese Romance*. [Adapted and illustrated by Koh TSUBOI, edited by Yoshiko SHIMIZU and Yōtarō KONAKA.] Tokyo: Shinjinbutsu Ōraisha, Inc. 300p.

A *manga* [comic] version of the entire tale.

Murasaki Shikibu. "Kiritsubo." [Translated by Arthur WALEY.] In: WATANABE (#1757), pp. 86-103. [*Genji monogatari*. Chapter 1.]

Murasaki Shikibu. 1922. "Parting." [Translated by Oswald WHITE.] *Transactions of the Asiatic Society of Japan* 50:79-95. LCCN:39-23.

A translation of part of the Sasaki (Broom-tree) chapter of the *Genji*, with an amusing introduction defending the tale against Western Orientalists who find it boring and excruciatingly long.

Murasaki Shikibu. "Yūgao." [Translated by Arthur WALEY.] In: KEENE (#1752), pp. 106-136. 18 notes. [*Genji monogatari.* Excerpt.]

1761. Hamamatsu Chūnagon monogatari

ROHLICH, Thomas H. 1983. *A Tale of Eleventh-Century Japan: Hamamatsu Chūnagon Monogatari.* Princeton: Princeton University Press. 247p. Bibl. Index. LCCN:82-61380. [*Hamamatsu Chūnagon monogatari.*]

An academic introduction and translation of *Hamamatsu Chūnagon monogatari*, a work probably from the second half of the eleventh century traditionally attributed to the Daughter of Takasue, undisputed author of the *Sarashina nikki* [*Sarashina Diary*, #1770]. A somewhat fantastic tale written in the style of the *Tale of Genji*, with which it has distinct parallels.

1762. Izayoi nikki

A mid-Kamakura diary, written by Abutsu-ni, also the author of *Utatane* (#1774). She was the second wife of FUJIWARA no Tameie, heir to the literary heritage of the great poet and critic FUJIWARA no Teika. She took vows as a Buddhist nun in 1275, after the death of her husband. *Izayoi nikki* is the poetic account of a journey she made to Kamakura in 1277 to plead before the shogunate the case of her son Tamesuke (eventual founder of the Reizei school of poetry), whose rights to an estate were being questioned by an older half-brother Tameuji. The suit was decided in favor of Tamesuke, but not until some thirty years after her death.

Abutsu ni. "The Journal of the Sixteenth-Night Moon." In: McCULLOUGH (#1753), pp. 340-376. [*Izayoi nikki.*]

Abutsu ni. "The Diary of the Waning Moon."   In: REISCHAUER (#1756), pp. 1-135.

1763. Izumi Shikibu nikki

CRANSTON, Edwin A. 1969. *The Izumi Shikibu Diary: A Romance of the Heian Court.* Cambridge: Harvard University Press. (Harvard-Yenching Institute. *Monograph Series*, vol. 19.) 332p. 717 notes. LCCN:69-13766. [*Izumi Shikibu nikki.*]

A densely annotated scholarly edition of the *Izumi Shikibu nikki* (*Izumi Shikibu Diary*) in English. CRANSTON includes a detailed introduction, a description of the author and the textual history of the work, plus a valuable literary history of the period and the development of prose fiction in Japan with an annotated catalog of important works of all related genres. The diary itself is a fictionalized account in prose and poetry of the ostensible author's (scandalous) love affair with an Imperial prince from 1003 to 1004. Known primarily as a great poet and as a woman of passion, Izumi Shikibu has been a source of inspiration to modern Japanese women writers, who have often looked to the Heian Period as the first glorious flowering of their art.

Izumi Shikibu. "Izumi Shikibu diary." In: MINER (#1754), pp. 93-153.

Izumi Shikibu. "The Izumi Shikibu diary." In: OMORI (#1755), pp. 149-196.

1764. Kagerō nikki

SEIDENSTICKER, Edward. 1964. *The Gossamer Years: The Diary of a Noblewoman of Heian Japan.* Rutland, VT: Tuttle. 201p. 552 notes. LCCN:64-22750. [*Kagerō nikki.*]

Generally considered to be the first of the poetic diary genre by a woman, "a combined autobiography-diary covering twenty-one years in the life of a mid-Heian FUJIWARA noblewoman known today as "the mother of Michitsuna," . . . "the record of her unhappy marriage to her kinsman, FUJIWARA Kaneie, beginning in 954 with his first love letters, and ending in 974 with their very nearly complete estrangement" (p. 7). This work is regarded as an important step in the flowering of Heian prose, and its influence can be seen in the *Tale of Genji*. SEIDENSTICKER includes an interesting introduction, with comments on the process of translation (and retranslation), prolific notes, and a valuable appendix of visual aids.

Mother of Michitsuna. "Kagerō nikki: Journal of a 10th Century Noblewoman." [Translated by Edward G. SEIDENSTICKER.] June 1955. *Transactions of the Asiatic Society of Japan* third series 4:1-243. Notes. Index. LCCN:39-23.

An earlier version of *The Gossamer Years*. Differences between the two translations are discussed in the later version.

Mother of Michitsuna. "Kagerō nikki." [Translated by Edward G. SEIDENSTICKER.] In: KEENE (#1752), pp. 97-105. 1 note. [*Kagerō nikki*. Excerpts.]

Mother of Michitsuna. "The gossamer journal." In: McCULLOUGH (#1753), pp. 102-155. [*Kagerō nikki*. First book.]

1765. Kenreimon-in Ukyō no Daibu shū

HARRIES, Phillip Tudor. 1980. *The Poetic Memoirs of Lady Daibu*. Stanford: Stanford University Press. 324p. Bibl. LCCN:79-65519. [*Kenreimon-in Ukyō no Daibu shū*.]

A heavily annotated scholarly translation of *Kenreimon-in Ukyō no Daibu shū*, a lyrical autobiographical work containing some 350 poems, by a woman who served an empress at court at the end of the twelfth and beginning of the thirteenth centuries, during the times of upheaval portrayed so differently in the *Tales of the Heike*. The volume begins with a substantial scholarly introduction to the "Life and Times" of the author, to questions of genre, and to the work itself. HARRIES includes appendixes, a bibliography of both English and Japanese language sources, notes on pages opposing the translation, a general index, and an index of first lines to the poetry.

1766. Makura no sōshi

The only rival for *Genji monogatari*'s place as the greatest Japanese classic. A prose *zuihitsu* [miscellany] including occasional *waka*, by a lady-in-waiting to Teishi/Sadako, a consort of the Emperor Ichijō (r. 986-1011). Contains personal recollections of her life at court, plus sketches of her contemporaries, musings on customs and etiquette, esthetics, the seasons, etc., and lists of her own likes and dislikes in various categories. Known for its lucid prose style, wit, and frankness.

WALEY, Arthur. 1928/1929. *The Pillow-Book of Sei Shōnagon*. London: Allen and Unwin/Boston: Houghton and Mifflin. 162p. LCCN:29-26343. [*Makura no sōshi*.]

WALEY's own version of this mid-Heian classic by SEI Shōnagon. Selected passages from the seemingly miscellaneous original are translated, rearranged and woven into a delightful account of the Heian Court, its world views, its intrigues and romances. WALEY characteristically omits the famous opening lines of the original *Makura no sōshi*.

SEI Shōnagon. 1930. *The Sketch Book of the Lady Sei Shōnagon*. [Translated by Nobuko KOBAYASHI; with a brief introduction by Adam BECK.] London: J. Murray. 139p. LCCN:30-14925. [*Makura no sōshi*.]

Excerpts from a complete (relatively free) translation made by the Japanese translator, edited to suit the tastes of a Western audience.

SEI Shōnagon. 1967. *The Pillow Book of Sei Shōnagon*. [Translated and edited by Ivan MORRIS.] New York: Columbia University Press. 2 vols. Bibl. Index. 1161 notes. LCCN:24962. Also published in: 1970. Baltimore: Penguin. LCCN:72-181073. [*Makura no sōshi*.]

An elegant, complete and richly annotated English translation and study of *Makura no sōshi*. The two-volume version in particular contains a wealth of background information on the period.

SEI Shōnagon. "The pillow book." [Translated by Arthur WALEY.] In: KEENE (#1752), pp. 137-144. 7 notes. [*Makura no sōshi*. Excerpts.]

SEI Shōnagon. "The pillow book of Sei Shōnagon." In: McCULLOUGH (#1753), pp. 156-199. [*Makura no sōshi*. 21 sections.]

SEI Shōnagon. "Pillow sketches." [Translated by Nobuko KOBAYASHI.] In: WATANABE (#1757), pp. 104-115. [*Makura no sōshi*. Excerpts.]

PURCELL, T. A. and William ASTON. 1888. "A literary lady of old Japan." *Transactions of the Asiatic Society of Japan* 16(3):215-224. LCCN:39-23.

A brief selection of entries from SEI Shōnagon's *Makura no sōshi* [*Pillow Book*], with an introduction describing "old Japanese literature" as being "essentially feminine" characterized by "gentleness and grace and a vein of playful humour" (p. 216).

1767. *Mumyōzōshi*

"Mumyōzōshi." 1984. [Translated and introduced by Michele MARRA.] *Monumenta Nipponica* 39(2):115-145, 39(3):281-305, 39(4):409-434. 355 notes. ISSN:0027-0741.

Introduction, translation, and scholarly explication of the 13th-century *Mumyōzōshi* [*Book Without a Name*], sometimes attributed to FUJIWARA no Shunzei but now acknowledged "beyond any reasonable doubt" (p. 115) to have been written by a woman. The *Mumyōzōshi* is "the earliest extant example of prose criticism in the history of Japanese literature" (p. 115); structured as "a lengthy dialogue between three or four highly educated ladies, narrated by an eighty-three-year-old nun" (p. 119). The women exchange their views in some detail on old tales; *Genji monogatari* [*The Tale of Genji*] figures prominently in their discussions. An invaluable source of information on tales that have not survived.

1768. *Murasaki Shikibu nikki*

BOWRING, Richard. 1982. *Murasaki Shikibu, her Diary and Poetic Memoirs: A Translation and Study*. Princeton: Princeton University Press. 290p. Bibl. LCCN:81-47908.

BOWRING provides the only reliable complete translation of the diary, plus the poetry, of the author of *The Tale of Genji*. The work is an invaluable source of information on Heian life and fiction in addition to the author herself. Commentary and text printed on opposite pages. Complete with biographical and bibliographical information (largely Japanese) and lists of textual variations.

Murasaki Shikibu. "Diary of Murasaki Shikibu." [Translated by Annie Shepley OMORI and Kochi DOI.] In: KEENE (#1752), pp. 145-155. 11 notes. [*Murasaki Shikibu nikki*.]

Murasaki Shikibu. "Diary of Murasaki Shikibu." In: OMORI (#1755), pp. 69-145. [*Murasaki Shikibu nikki*.]

Murasaki Shikibu. "Murasaki Shikibu nikki." [Translated by Annie Shepley OMORI and Kochi DOI.] In: WATANABE (#1757), pp. 116-125. [*Murasaki Shikibu nikki*. Excerpts.]

1769. *Sanuki no Suke nikki*

FUJIWARA no Nagako. 1977. *The Emperor Horikawa Diary*. [Translated by Jennifer BREWSTER.] Honolulu: University of Hawaii Press. 155p. LCCN:77-89194. [Author also cited as Sanuki no Suke.]

Annotated English translation of a short work by Fujiwara no Nagako, who for eight years served in the court of the Emperor Horikawa (r. 1086-1107). Written soon after his death from an extended illness in 1107 at the age of twenty-eight, this diary is an expression of grief, a fond portrait of an otherwise almost unknown emperor, and an intimate account of his final illness. It is counted as a minor classic of the literary diary genre, but it offers a surprisingly concrete and human look at life (and death) in the Heian court.

1770. Sarashina nikki

SUGAWARA no Takasue no Musume. 1971. *As I Crossed a Bridge of Dreams: Recollections of a Woman in Eleventh-Century Japan*. [Translated by Ivan MORRIS.] London: Oxford University Press. 159p. 234 notes. LCCN:79-144386. [*Sarashina nikki*.]

A translation of what has come to be called the *Sarashina nikki* [*Sarashina Diary*], a contemplative work of prose and poetry written by a woman of the lower Heian aristocracy, born in 1008 and known only as the daughter of SUGAWARA no Takasue. Typical of its genre, this "diary" is autobiographical in that it records her emotional, esthetic, and literary experience, and *The Tale of Genji* figures larger in it than her husband or children. MORRIS includes a substantial introduction, useful annotations, and illustrations, photographs and maps.

Takasue, Daughter of. "The Sarashina Diary." [Translated by Annie Shepley OMORI and Kochi DOI.] In: KEENE (#1752), pp. 156-161. 4 notes. [*Sarashina nikki*. Excerpts.]

Takasue, Daughter of. "The Sarashina Diary.: In: OMORI (#1755), pp. 1-68. [*Sarashina nikki*. Excerpts.]

Takasue, Daughter of. "Sarashina nikki." [Translated by Annie Shepley OMORI and Kochi DOI.] In: WATANABE (#1757), pp. 126-143. [*Sarashina nikki*. Excerpts.]

1771. Torikaebaya monogatari

WILLIG, Rosette F. 1983. *The Changelings: A Classical Court Tale*. Stanford: Stanford University Press. 248p. Bibl. LCCN:81-50789. [*Torikaebaya monogatari*.]

A translation of *Torikaebaya monogatari*, probably written sometime between 1080 and 1105, "the story of a brother and sister whose natural inclinations lead them to live as members of the opposite sex. Their difficulties in concealing certain physical attributes and the complications they face in their sexual encounters are fully chronicled. Eventually the hero and heroine take each other's place in society, and thus return to their true sexes" (p. 1). The name and sex of the author of the work are unknown, but WILLIG's speculation regarding the latter is interesting.

1772. Towazugatari

BRAZELL, Karen. 1973. *Confessions of Lady Nijō*. Garden City, NY: Anchor Books. 288p. 220 notes. LCCN:72-96272. [*Towazugatari*.]

A pleasantly readable translation of *Towazugatari*, a comparatively recently-discovered "autobiographical narrative . . .of thirty-six years (1271-1306) in the life of Lady Nijō, starting when she became the concubine of a retired emperor in Kyoto at the age of fourteen and ending, several love affairs later, with an account of her new life as a wandering Buddhist nun" (p. vii). A splendid late example of the poetic diary/tale looking back in content and in convention to the *Tale of Genji* while anticipating medieval literature in its broader scope and its Buddhist orientation. BRAZELL includes a useful introduction for the nonspecialist.

WHITEHOUSE, Wilfred and Eizo YANAGISAWA. 1974. *Lady Nijo's Own Story: The Candid Diary of a Thirteenth-Century Japanese Imperial Concubine*. Rutland, VT: Tuttle. 395p. Notes. LCCN:73-93503. [*Towazugatari*.]

Another pleasant translation of *Towazugatari,* offering an interesting comparison with the version by BRAZELL (above). Includes short appendices containing information on historical context.

Nijō, Lady. "The Confessions of Lady Nijō." In: McCULLOUGH (#1753), pp. 288-339. [*Towazugatari.* Book one.]

Nijo, Lady. "Towazu-gatari." *Traditions* 1(1):61-80, 1(2):49-67, 1(3):79-95, 1(4):71-95, 2(1):75-96, 2(2)/no.6:81-95, 2(3)/no.7:57-82, 2(4)/no.8:57-73, 3(1)/no.9:51-64, 3(2)/no.10:37-47, 3(3)/no.11:17-41, 3(4)/no.12:61-80, 4(1)/no.13:57-72, 4(2)/no.14:39-58, 4(3)/no.15:35-53. LCCN:77-644976.

1773. Tsutsumi Chūnagon monogatari

HIRANO, Umeyo. 1963. *The Tsutsumi Chūnagon Monogatari: A Collection of 11th Century Short Stories of Japan.* Tokyo: The Hokuseido Press. 105p. Bibl. LCCN:63-5054. [*Tsutsumi Chūnagon monogatari.*]

An early translation of these stories, since retranslated by BACKUS (below). HIRANO includes a short introduction for the general reader and a bibliography of Japanese sources.

BACKUS, Robert L. 1985. *The Riverside Counselor's Stories: Vernacular Fiction of Late Heian Japan.* Stanford: Stanford University Press. 234p. Notes. LCCN:84-40446. [*Tsutsumi Chūnagon monogatari.*]

The most recent translation of *Tsutsumi Chūnagon monogatari,* a collection of ten vernacular "short stories," some of which are attributed to women. BACKUS begins with an introduction placing the work in its (literary) historical context and presenting many textual problems associated with it.

"The lady who loved insects." [Translated by Arthur WALEY.] In: KEENE (#1752), pp. 170-176. 7 notes. ["Mushi mezuru himegimi" from: *Tsutsumi Chūnagon monogatari.*]

"The lady who admired vermin." [Translated by Robert L. BACKUS.] In: McCULLOUGH (#1753), pp. 256-263. [*Tsutsumi Chūnagon monogatari.* Excerpt.]

"Lampblack." [Translated by Robert L. BACKUS.] In: McCULLOUGH (#1753), pp. 264-270. [*Tsutsumi Chūnagon monogatari.* Excerpt.]

"The lesser captain picks a sprig of flowering cherry." [Translated by Robert L. BACKUS.] In: McCULLOUGH (#1753), pp. 251-256. [*Tsutsumi Chūnagon monogatari.* Excerpt.]

"Tsutsumi Chūnagon monogatari." In: REISCHAUER (#1756), pp. 137-267.

1774. Utatane

WALLACE, John R. Winter 1988. "Fitful slumbers: Nun Abutsu's *Utatane.*" *Monumenta Nipponica* 43(4):391-416. 88 notes. ISSN:0027-0741.

An introduction offering biographical and textual information precedes an annotated, scholarly translation of a short autobiographical work of prose and poetry from the early life of the woman who came to be known as the Nun Abutsu, author of *Izayoi nikki* [*Diary of the Waning Moon* (see #1762)]. *Utatane* contains reminiscences of an unhappy love affair with a man of superior status, and the accounts of two journeys to temples in a futile attempt to free herself from resultant psychological bonds.

1775. Yowa no nezame

HOCKSTEDLER, Carol. 1979. *The Tale of Nezame: Part Three of Yowa no Nezame Monogatari.* Ithaca: China-Japan Program, Cornell University. (*Cornell University East Asia Papers,* no. 22. ISSN:8756-5293.) 269p. Bibl. LCCN:79-130060. [*Yowa no nezame.* Part 3.]

A partial translation of the incomplete *Yowa no nezame*, "a romance written in the style of *The Tale of Genji* depicting the life and loves of a noblewoman of eleventh-century Japan" . . . "recount[ing] the experiences of a woman of nearly magical beauty and talent" . . . "doomed by tricks of fate and the weaknesses of men to a life of suffering and disappointment" (p. 1). An intensely personal fictional work of unknown authorship traditionally attributed to the Daughter of Takasue, author of the Sarashina diary (see #1770), this work has attracted the attention of modern women writers. Includes a brief introduction, a bibliography of both English and Japanese sources, and annotations.

Critical Studies of Premodern Prose

1776. ABE, Akio. 1964. "The contemporary studies of *Genji Monogatari*." *Acta Asiatica* 6:41-56. No refs. ISSN:0567-7254.

A survey of trends in Japanese scholars' approaches to *The Tale of Genji* (and classical literature in general) from the 19th-century Kokugaku (National Learning) commentaries to contemporary folklore studies.

1777. AKIYAMA, Ken. 1977. "The Tale of Genji (Genji monogatari)." In: MURAKAMI, Hyôe and Edward G. SEIDENSTICKER, eds. 1977. *Guides to Japanese Culture*. Tokyo: Japan Culture Institute, pp. 93-98. LCCN:77-373003.

Synopsis, with commentary, of part of an influential Japanese work of *Genji* criticism for the general (Japanese) reader.

1778. ASTON, W.G. 1899. *A History of Japanese Literature*. New York: D. Appleton and Co. 408p. Notes. Index.

A chronological account, from a Victorian point of view, of twelve centuries of Japanese literature, including highlights of Heian poetry and fiction written by women. ASTON writes, "It is a remarkable, and I believe, unexampled fact, that a very large and important part of the best literature which Japan has produced was written by women" (p. 55).

1779. BARGEN, Doris G. Summer 1986. "A case of spirit possession in *The Tale of Genji*." *Mosaic: A Journal for the Interdisciplinary Study of Literature* 19(3):15-24. 15 notes. ISSN:0027-1276.

Interpreting the spirit possession and death of Yūgao as "an oblique criticism of male behavior toward women in a polygynous society," BARGEN concludes that "[un]like subsequent possessed heroines," Yūgao has "no voice," and her spirit possession neither punishes the man nor soothes her own agitation; it ends in "self-destructive protest" (p. 23).

1780. BARGEN, Doris G. Jun. 1988. "Spirit possession in the context of dramatic expressions of gender conflict: the Aoi episode of the *Genji Monogatari*." *Harvard Journal of Asiatic Studies* 48(1):95-130. 8 notes. ISSN:0073-0548.

A provocative article arguing that in the case of Lady Rokujō's spirit possession of Lady Aoi, ". . . what begins as a physically violent women's quarrel is transformed into an esoteric spiritual rite in which the psychologically allied women vent their repressed anger at a third party—Genji—and at the polygynous society that allows men to neglect their women with near impunity" (p. 101).

1781. BERRY, Margaret. Dec. 1976. "The meeting of the twain: Japanese and Greek." *Asian Profile* 4(6):529-538. 1 note. ISSN:0304-8675.

A search for exemplification of Japanese and Greek literary ideals in *The Tale of Genji* and Walter PATER's *Marius the Epicurean*.

1782. BERRY, Margaret. May 1982. "*Genji*: Gate to Japan for the Undergrad." *CEA Critic* 44(4):18-25. Bibl. & 13 notes. ISSN:0007-8069.

A guide for undergraduate teachers attempting to teach Japanese esthetics and culture using the *Tale of Genji* as a basic resource. Includes cautionary comment by Terry KELLEHER.

1783. BOWRING, Richard. Jun. 1981. "Japanese diaries and the nature of literature." *Comparative Literature Studies* 18(2):167-174. 10 notes. ISSN:0010-4132.

A theoretical article refuting the hypothetical proposition that "in Heian Japan the deciding factor as to whether a work was literary or not was, in the ultimate analysis, the sex of the author" (p. 168), and pointing out that "the word that modern critics use to designate Heian women's diaries [*nikki bungaku*]. . . is a modern invention" (p. 172). BOWRING warns the reader of current "distortions being engendered by the anachronistic use of categories" (p. 173).

1784. BOWRING, Richard. 1984. "The female hand in Heian Japan: A first reading." In: STANTON, Donna and Jeanine P. PLOTTEL, eds. *The Female Autograph*. New York: Literary Forum, pp. 55-62. 6 notes. LCCN:84-14827 (*New York Literary Forum*, vol. 12/13. ISSN:0149-1040.)

BOWRING examines conventional wisdom about the lives of aristocratic women in the tenth and eleventh centuries to answer the question, "How did women textualize themselves during this period?" (p. 57).

1785. BOWRING, Richard. 1988. *Murasaki Shikibu*: The Tale of Genji. New York: Cambridge University Press. 111p. Bibl. LCCN:87-26553.

An extremely useful and interesting handbook offering both common sense and information not apparent from the English translations. Includes a guide to further reading on the period and an extensive bibliography of *Genji* scholarship in English.

1786. CRANSTON, Edwin A. 1971. "Murasaki's 'Art of Fiction.'" *Japan Quarterly* 18(2):207-213. 17 notes. ISSN:0021-4590.

A reassessment of Murasaki's "defense of fiction" from the *Hotaru* chapter [WALEY's "Glow-worm"; SEIDENSTICKER's "Fireflies"], retranslating the famous section to show that WALEY's version is extremely misleading. Pointing to the ironic context into which the "defense" is placed in the tale, CRANSTON argues, finally, that "Murasaki Shikibu shows herself . . . more sophisticated even than her polished and learned latter-day translator" (p. 213).

1787. CRANSTON, Edwin A. Winter 1972. "A bridge of dreams: Review article on *As I Crossed a Bridge of Dreams: Recollections of a Woman in Eleventh-Century Japan*, translated by Ivan Morris." *Monumenta Nipponica* 27(4):435-454. 54 notes. ISSN:0027-0741.

A highly technical article reviewing Ivan MORRIS's *As I Crossed a Bridge of Dreams* (#1770), pointing out numerous factual, translation, and copy errors.

1788. CRANSTON, Edwin A. May/Sep. 1976. "Aspects of *The Tale of Genji*." *Journal of the Association of Teachers of Japanese* 11(2/3):183-199. 2 notes. ISSN:0885-9884.

CRANSTON provides a readable overview of *The Tale of Genji*, seeing it "as a thematic novel and as a book of memorable scenes" (p. 191) and as a psychological drama, "largely a novel of inner action" (p. 195).

1789. CRANSTON, Edwin A. 1978. "The Seidensticker *Genji.*" *Journal of Japanese Studies* 4(1):1-25. 9 notes. ISSN:0095-6848.

A scholarly review offering a close look at Edward G. SEIDENSTICKER's translation of *The Tale of Genji* (#1760), comparing individual passages with equivalent passages in Arthur WALEY's version, and offering his own alternate translations for the same passages.

1790. DEMETILLO, Ricaredo. Jan. 1955. "The art of Lady Murasaki." *Diliman Review* (1):55-68. ISSN:0012-2858.

An overview, based on the WALEY translation, for the uninitiated. The focus is on psychological realism and on the often-analyzed conversation on the value of the tales, between Tamakatsura and Genji in the *Hotaru* ("Glow-Worm") chapter.

1791. EOYANG, Eugene. 1982. "The world of Genji: Perspectives on the *Genji Monogatari.*" *Yearbook of Comparative and General Literature* 31:44-75. No refs. ISSN:0084-3695.

EOYANG provides an account of the planning and mechanics of the Eighth Conference on Oriental-Western Literary and Cultural Relations, devoted to *The Tale of Genji.* Including the full program of papers, four of which were reprinted in the *Yearbook of Comparative and General Literature* (see #1824, #1884, #1892, and #1896).

1792. FIELD, Norma. 1987. *The Splendor of Longing in* The Tale of Genji. Princeton: Princeton University Press. 372p. Bibl. LCCN:86-21224.

A thoughtful, appealing, and difficult study of structural motifs in *The Tale of Genji,* informed both by current *Genji* scholarship in Japan and by contemporary Western critical theory, and organized around the female characters in the "novel." Ample notes and extensive bibliography.

1793. FUJII, Sadakazu. Jun./Sep. 1982. "The relationship between the romance and religious observances: *Genji Monogatari* as myth." *Japanese Journal of Religious Studies* 9(2/3):127-146. 16 notes. ISSN:0304-1042.

A catalog of religious observances associated with specific incidents in *The Tale of Genji,* reinterpreting the scenes as examples of spiritual communication between the living and the dead, and explicating the concept of *hitokata* or *katashiro* [ritual substitute] as it relates to the "rebirth" of the Ukifune lady.

1794. GATTEN, Aileen W. Spring 1977. "Wisp of smoke: Scent and character in *The Tale of Genji.*" *Monumenta Nipponica* 32(1):35-48. 49 notes. ISSN:0027-0741.

A discussion (complete with recipes) of the art of incense blending including its role in Heian aristocratic society and its function in defining character in *The Tale of Genji.*

1795. GATTEN, Aileen. Jun. 1981. "The order of the early chapters of the *Genji Monogatari.*" *Harvard Journal of Asiatic Studies* 41(1):5-46. 51 notes. ISSN:0073-0548.

A technical account of the textual history of *The Tale of Genji,* emphasizing that the chapters were not written in "chronological" order and that they were bound separately, and claiming that the individual chapter scrolls were unnumbered. GATTEN points out various textual incongruities in the currently-published order of the first seventeen chapters, summarizes various scholars' solutions to the textual problems, and finally proposes her own chapter order.

1796. GATTEN, Aileen. 1982. "Murasaki's literary roots." *Journal of the Association of Teachers of Japanese* 17(2):173-191. 6 notes. ISSN:0885-9884.

A long, detailed review of BOWRING's *Murasaki Shikibu: Her Diary and Poetic Memoirs* (#1768). GATTEN is critical, especially of the poetry translations.

1797. GATTEN, Aileen. 1982. "Three problems in the text of 'Ukifune.'" In: PEKARIK, Andrew, ed. *Ukifune: Love in* The Tale of Genji. New York: Columbia University Press, pp. 83-111. 38 notes. LCCN:82-1157.

An interesting presentation of the implications of apparent discrepancies in the text of the Ukifune chapter of *The Tale of Genji*: "a variant passage, a contradiction in the chronology, and the faulty introduction of a character [Ukifune's maid, Ukon]."

1798. GATTEN, Aileen. 1986. "Weird ladies: Narrative strategy in the *Genji Monogatari.*" *Journal of the Association of Teachers of Japanese* 20(1):29-48. 8 notes. ISSN:0885-9884.

Focuses on two "anomolous" female comic characters, the Safflower Princess and Gen no Naishi no Suke, and on their special functions in the narrative of *The Tale of Genji*.

1799. GOFF, Janet Emily. Jan. 1982. "*The Tale of Genji* as a source of the Nō: Yūgao and Hajitomi." *Harvard Journal of Asiatic Studies* 42(1):177-229. 120 notes. ISSN:0073-0548.

A somewhat technical article focusing on two Nō plays about the heroine Yūgao, elucidating patterns in the kinds of material drawn from the *Genji* and how it was rearranged "to conform to the structure of the Nō, and . . . to thematic considerations such as attachment to the world of the past and the search for salvation" (p. 178).

1800. HARPER, Thomas J. Spring 1976. "'The progress of fiction:' A twelfth-century critique of *The Tale of Genji*." *Criticism in Translation* 1(1):1-5. Bibl. LCCN:86-21354.

HARPER provides an introduction to, and a translation of, *Monogatari no yukue*, from the final chapter of the historical tale *Imakagami* [*The Mirror of the Present*]. In this famous piece, *The Tale of Genji* is defended against medieval accusations that it is morally reprehensible and a bad influence.

1801. HEINRICH, Amy. 1982. "Blown in flurries: The role of poetry in "Ukifune." In: PEKARIK, Andrew, ed. *Ukifune: Love in* The Tale of Genji. New York: Columbia University Press, pp. 153-171. 10 notes. LCCN:82-1157.

An investigation of the 22 poems in the "Ukifune" chapter of *The Tale of Genji* and their "three functions—to delineate character, to define relationships, and to advance the plot. . ." (p. 154).

1802. HENIG, Suzanne. Dec. 1967. "Virginia Woolf and Lady Murasaki." *Literature East and West* 11(4):421-423. 5 notes. LCCN:65-9986.

An introduction to Virgina WOOLF's celebrated review of *The Tale of Genji*, reprinted in #1907.

1803. HERRICK, Robert. 10 Oct. 1928. "The perfect lover: [A review of] *The Tale of Genji*. Translated by Arthur Waley." *New Republic* 56(723):214-216. ISSN:

A contemporary review of the WALEY translation of *The Tale of Genji*, comparing it in passing to a surprising list of Western classics and focusing on the commanalities between the "working of a licitly polygamous society" of the hero Genji and "an illicitly polygamous society such as ours" (p. 215).

1804. HIROSE, Isako. 1989. *Genji monogatari nyūmon / An Introduction to the Tale of Genji*. [Translated by Susan TYLER.] Tokyo: Hirose Isako. 221p. LCCN:89-188150.

A luxury bilingual introduction to *The Tale of Genji*, proceeding chapter by chapter, with illustrations from the 12th-century *Genji monogatari emaki*.

1805. HORTON, Mack H. 1984. "In the service of realism and rhetoric: The function and development of the lady-in-waiting character in *The Tale of Genji.*" *Phi Theta Papers* 16:102-136. 24 notes. ISSN:0553-9536.

An examination of the treatment of "subsidiary" female characters in *The Tale of Genji*, "both as characters in their own right and as rhetorical devices for the delineation of the principals" (p. 102), showing how the author handles them with progressive sophistication that culminates in the Uji chapters.

1806. IKEDA, Daisaku in association with Makoto NEMOTO. 1979. *On the Japanese Classics: Conversations and Appreciations.* [Translated by Burton WATSON.] New York: Weatherhill. 202p. Notes. Index. LCCN:78-26624. [*Koten o kataru.* 1974.]

"Discussions held between Honorary President Daisaku Ikeda of Sōka Gakkai [Buddhist sect] and Professor Makoto Nemoto . . . specialist in Chinese history [and] . . . professor of Sōka University." (Burton WATSON, Translator's Note, p. 13) Roughly one quarter of the book is devoted to *Genji monogatari* [*The Tale of Genji*].

1807. INOUE, Eimei. 1986. "The life of Prince Genji: Archetypal affinities between the ancient heroes of the world." In: MATSUMOTO, Natsubori, *et al.* 1986. *Voice of the Writer, 1984: Collected Papers of the 47th International P.E.N. Congress in Tokyo.* Tokyo: Japan P.E.N. Club, pp. 130-136. No notes. (International Congress of the P.E.N. Club, 47th, Tokyo.) LCCN:87-131906.

Looking to *The Tale of Genji* for "mythological functions" . . . "which can also hint at archetypal affinities concerning the pattern of the life of the hero in the ancient world" (p. 136).

1808. JANEIRA, Armando Martins. 1970. *Japanese and Western Literature: A Comparative Study.* Rutland, VT: Tuttle. 394p. Notes. Bibl. Index. [Author also cited as: MARTINS JANEIRA, Armando.] LCCN:73-123899.

An ambitious work in four parts: A Western Interpretation of Japanese Literary Culture, On the Nature of Japanese Culture, Confrontations [between Japanese Classical Drama and European Medieval Drama], and Two Western Writers Who Lived Within Eastern Civilization, Lafcadio Hearn, and Wenceslau de Moraes. Part One includes considerable discussion of *Genji monogatari* [*The Tale of Genji*] and the diaries of Izumi Shikibu, Murasaki Shikibu and SEI Shōnagon.

1809. KAHAN, Gail Capitol. 1969. "As a driven leaf: Love and psychological characterization in *The Tale of Genji.* In: FRENCH, Calvin L., ed. 1969. *Studies in Japanese Culture, II.* Ann Arbor: University of Michigan Press, pp. 155-173. (*Center for Japanese Studies Occasional Papers*, no. 11.)

An overview of love in *The Tale of Genji.* For the general reader.

1810. KAPLAN, Frederick L. 1974. "The imagery of the dilapidated house or untended garden in Heian literature." *Literature East and West* 18(2/4):314-320. 10 notes. ISSN:0024-4767.

A brief but specific presentation of "the dilapidated house or untended garden used as an imagistic device to indicate loss of social status, loss of love, or psychic disorientation" (p. 314). Examples are drawn from *The Gossamer Years* and *The Tale of Genji.*

1811. KATO, Shuichi. 1979/1981. *A History of Japanese Literature. Volumes One and Two.* [Translated by David CHIBBETT (vol. 1) and Don SANDERSON (vol. 2).] London: MacMillan/Tokyo: Kodansha. Vol. 1 & 2 of a 3 vol. set. Notes. Index. LCCN:77-75967(set). [*Nihon bungakushi.*]

An interesting, somewhat idiosyncratic history by an eminent literary scholar (of German, French, and English as well as Japanese literature) and critic-at-large. Originally written for a Japanese audience and serialized in the *Asahi Journal*. In vol. one ("The First Ten Thousand Years"), an introduction presenting "The Distinctive Features of Japanese Literature" precedes a chronological historical survey from the "seventh or eighth century AD" (p. 29) through the sixteenth century that ranges freely into most areas of Japanese culture. There is considerable treatment throughout of both prose and poetry genres associated with women; one section is devoted to the Aesthetics of the *Kokinshū*, one to Women's Diaries, and one to the *Genji monogatari*. Volume Two ("The Years of Isolation") deals with the Edo Period but lists no women writers in the index. See #1513 for coverage of volume three.

1812. KEENE, Donald. 1955. *Japanese Literature: An Introduction for Western Readers*. New York: Grove Press. 114p. Notes. Bibl. Index. LCCN:55-6276.

A delightful general introduction written when very little classical Japanese literature beyond *The Tale of Genji* and the *Pillowbook* had reached an English-speaking audience. Women writers surface occasionally in the discussion, and the *Genji* is treated in comparative detail.

1813. KEENE, Donald. 1959. "*The Tale of Genji*." In: De BARY, William Theodore. *Approaches to the Oriental Classics: Asian Literature and Thought in General Education*. New York: Columbia University Press, pp. 186-195. (Conference on Oriental Classics in General Education, 1958, Columbia University.) 1 note. LCCN:59-9905.

KEENE suggests some approaches to teaching *The Tale of Genji* [in the WALEY translation (see #1760)] to undergraduates in such a way that they will not find it "effete, immoral, or inconsequential" (p. 187), or feel after reading the work "like eating a raw steak to reestablish . . . contact with a cruder, more virile society" (p. 192).

1814. KEENE, Donald. 1971. "Feminine sensibility in the Heian era." In: KEENE, Donald. *Landscapes and Portraits: Appreciations of Japanese Culture.* Tokyo: Kodansha International, pp. 26-39. Notes & bibl. LCCN:75-135144.

In this impressionistic essay for the nonspecialist, KEENE considers "the reasons why women played so conspicuous a part in Heian literature and the peculiar significance for Japanese literature in general of the triumph of feminine sensibility" (p. 26), citing "masculine" and "feminine" "tone and imagery" (p. 27) and assuming that "the difference between masculine and feminine expression is obvious. . ." (p. 28).

1815. KEENE, Donald. Apr./Jun. 1985. "Diaries of the Heian Period." *Japan Quarterly* 32(2):152-158. No refs. ISSN:0021-4590.

After an introductory glance at the Tosa Diary, KEENE focuses on the *Kagerō nikki* [*The Gossamer Years*, #1764], considering the emotional life and the personality of the author.

1816. KEENE, Donald. Jul./Sep. 1985. "Diaries of the Kamakura Period." *Japan Quarterly* 32(3):281-289. No refs. ISSN:0021-4590.

Part of a series that was later published as *Travelers of a Hundred Ages* (#1817). Focuses on *Kaidōki* (*Account of the Seacoast Road*), of unknown authorship, and *Utatane* (#1774), by the Nun Abutsu.

1817. KEENE, Donald. 1989. *Travelers of a Hundred Ages: The Japanese as Revealed Throughout 1,000 Years of Diaries*. New York: Henry Holt. 468p. Bibl. LCCN:88-31585.

A pleasant and illuminating collection of brief individual accounts of diaries from the Heian Period through the late Tokugawa Period, including all the famous ones, and some less famous, by women: *The Gossamer Years*; *The Izumi Shikibu Diary*; *The Sarashina Diary*;

The Collection of the Mother of Jōjin the *Ajari*; *The Sanuki no Suke Diary*; *The Poetic Memoirs of Lady Daibu*; *Fitful Slumbers*; *The Diary of the Waning Moon*; *The Diary of Lady Ben*; *The Diary of Lady Nakatsukasa*; *The Confessions of Lady Nijō*; *Account of the Takemuki Palace*; "some [late Tokugawa] diaries by women," and *The Diary of Iseki Takako.*

1818. KONISHI, Jin'ichi. 1966. "*Fūryū*: An ideal of Japanese esthetic life." In: SCHNEPS, Maurice and Alvin D. COX, eds. 1965. *The Japanese Image: Essays, Stories, and Poems about Japan by Outstanding Japanese and Western Writers.* [Selections from *Orient/West* Magazine volume 1.] Tokyo and Philadelphia: Orient/West, Inc, pp. 271-278. 6 notes.

A look at an important esthetic term from the Heian Period to modern times, noting its origins in the Chinese poetic and painting traditions, showing its effect as a formative element of *The Tale of Genji* (focusing on the Taoist realm of everyday life), and following its very different development since the Kamakura Period.

1819. KONISHI, Jin'ichi. 1986. *A History of Japanese Literature Volume Two: The Early Middle Ages.* [Translated by Aileen GATTEN; edited by Earl MINER.] Princeton: Princeton University Press. 461p. Bibl. LCCN:83-43082. [*Nihon bungeishi.*]

A detailed history by an eminent Japanese scholar, including information and interpretations nowhere else in English, of the history of Japanese literature since the Heian Period. Chapter 8, "Prose in Japanese," offers an excellent articulation and analysis of tale and diary literature of the period, most of which was written by women.

1820. KRISTEVA, Isvetana. 1984. "Japanese lyrical diaries and the European autobiographical tradition." In: DANIELS, Gordon, ed. 1984. *Europe Interprets Japan.* Kent, England: Paul Norbury Publications, pp. 155-162.

A ". . . preliminary . . . step toward a . . . comparative study" (p. 155) of the Japanese diary tradition, beginning with the assumption that "feeling and emotion . . . constitute the mainstream of the Japanese lyrical diary, whereas in Europe the chief impulse comes from thought and ideas" (p. 157). KRISTEVA goes on to list five other significant differences between the two categories, relating them to historical development and world view.

1821. KRISTEVA, Isvetana. 1988. "The Genji-intext in Towazu-gatari." In: NISH, Ian, ed. 1988. *Contemporary European Writing on Japan: Scholarly Views from Eastern and Western Europe.* Kent, England: Paul Norbury Publications, pp. 251-257. 21 notes. LCCN:88-193026.

An investigation of implicit and explicit allusions to *The Tale of Genji* in *Towazugatari* [*The Confessions of Lady Nijō*], with emphasis on their varied functions in the latter work.

1822. "Lady Murasaki: *Genji monogatari (The Tale of Genji)* circa eleventh century." In: POUPARD, Dennis and Jelena O. KRSTOVIC, eds. 1988. *Classical and Medieval Literature Criticism* 1:413-476. ISSN:0896-0011.

A concise introduction to the work followed by extensive quotations from reviews and essays by a wide variety of scholars and literary critics, both specialists and generalists. A convenient source for contemporary reviews of the WALEY translation, most of which are not listed here, plus a bibliography for further reading. (Volume 6, published in 1991, offers a similar treatment of SEI Shōnagon.)

1823. LIN, Wen-yüeh. 1975. "*The Tale of Genji* and the Song of Enduring Woe." [Translated by Diana YU.] *Renditions* 5:38-49. 8 notes. ISSN:0377-3515. Summarized in: LIN, Wen-yüeh. 1976. "*The Tale of Genji* and the Song of Unending Sorrow," *Tamkang Review* 7:281-285. ISSN:0049-2949.

An interesting attempt by a Chinese *Genji* scholar and translator to show the importance of PO Chü-yi's famous poem about the tragic effects of the legendary beauty YANG Kwei-fei of the T'ang dynasty, as reflected in the first chapter of *The Tale of Genji*.

1824. LIN, Wen-yüeh. 1982. "*The Tale of Genji*: A Chinese translator's retrospective note." *Yearbook of Comparative and General Literature* 31:45-61. No refs. ISSN:0084-3695.

With quotations from both languages, this Chinese translator of *Genji* explains some of the difficulties encountered (including honorific language, specialized terminology related to Heian court life, the *waka* form) and the choices he made.

1825. LINDBERG-WADA, Gunilla. 1988. "The rôle of *Kokinshū* poetry as a source of allusion (*hikiuta*) in *Genji Monogatari*." In: NISH, Ian, ed. 1988. *Contemporary European Writing on Japan: Scholarly Views from Eastern and Western Europe*. Kent, England: Paul Norbury Publications, pp. 244-257. 1 note. LCCN:88-193026.

A general summary of poetic allusion as a mode of expression, based on an analysis of 128 *Kokinshū* poems in *The Tale of Genji*.

1826. LUBELL, B. and F.H. MARTINSON. Aug. 1973. "The Takayoshi Genji and Authur Waley's 'The Tale of Genji.'" *Asian Profile* 1(1):185-241. 15 notes. 0304-8675.

An explication of correspondences (or lack thereof) between the 12th-century handscroll paintings *Genji monogatari emaki* (also called the *Takayoshi Genji*) and the *Tale of Genji* as translated by Arthur WALEY.

1827. MAKI, J.M. Jul. 1940. "Lady Murasaki and the *Genji Monogatari*." *Monumenta Nipponica* 3(2):480-503. 48 notes. ISSN:0027-0741.

An introductory article for the Western reader, beginning with a biographical account of Murasaki Shikibu, placing her work briefly in the context of Heian literature and culture. MAKI then reflects on the tale itself as a work of "psychological realism" (p. 500), urging the modern reader not to hold against Lady Murasaki her "belief in possessions' power to kill, an undue deference to omens and portents and an uncritical acceptance of a necessary connection between human actions and natural calamities" (p. 143).

1828. MARKS, Alfred H. and Barry D. BORT. 1975. *Guide to Japanese Prose*. Boston: G.K. Hall. 150p. (*The Asian Literature Bibliography Series*.) Index. LCCN:74-20608.

A selective annotated bibliography of prose works from earliest times through the early 1970s that have been translated into English. Does not include secondary scholarship. Heian and Kamakura tales and diaries by women are listed and discussed briefly.

1829. MASON, Penelope. Spring 1980. "The house-bound heart: The prose-poetry genre of Japanese narrative illustration." *Monumenta Nipponica* 35(1):21-43. 30 notes. ISSN:0027-0741.

An early overview of narrative illustrations accompanying texts (tales and diaries) incorporating prose and poetry. MASON discusses illustrations for *The Tale of Genji* and the Izumi Shikibu diary.

1830. MATHY, Francis, S.J. 1969. "Mono no aware." In: FRENCH, Calvin L., ed. 1969. *Studies in Japanese Culture, II*. Ann Arbor: University of Michigan Press, pp. 139-153. (*Center for Japanese Studies Occasional Papers*, no. 11.) 10 notes.

A scholarly explication of the concept of *mono no aware*, with significant attention to MOTOORI Norinaga's use of the term in his work on *The Tale of Genji*.

1831. MATSUMOTO, Shigeru. 1970. *Motoori Norinaga, 1730-1801*. Cambridge: Harvard University Press. 261p. Notes. Bibl. Index. LCCN:77-95928.

A biography of the great scholar of the national revival (*Kokugaku*) movement, famous for his work justifying and explicating *Genji monogatari* as a Japanese classic. One chapter is devoted to *mono no aware*, a key esthetic and psychological or spiritual term at the center of MOTOORI's *Genji* (and other) scholarship, and the *Genji* figures prominently in the book.

1832. McCLEOD, Dan. 1974. "Some approaches to *The Tale of Genji*." *Literature East and West* 18(2/4):301-313. Bibl. ISSN:0024-4767.

An introduction for the nonspecialist, with suggestions for incorporating *The Tale of Genji* into a general literature curriculum. Includes "A selected bibliography on *The Tale of Genji*."

1833. McCULLOUGH, Helen C. Sep. 1977. "The Seidensticker *Genji*." *Monumenta Nipponica* 32(1):93-110. 19 notes. ISSN:0027-0741.

An review article full of valuable textual observations on the Seidensticker translation of *The Tale of Genji* (see #1760). McCULLOUGH admits to a twinge of relief that the wonder of the work is really Murasaki Shikibu's after all, and not simply WALEY's magic of translation. She concludes that "The real world of the shining prince is . . . a considerably more somber place than WALEY would have us believe, and the contradictions it embraces lend new poignance to the familiar atmosphere of melancholy beauty" (p. 110).

1834. MEECH-PEKARIK, Julia. 1982. "The artist's view of Ukifune." In: PEKARIK, Andrew, ed. *Ukifune: Love in* The Tale of Genji. New York: Columbia University Press, pp. 173-215. 43 notes. LCCN:82-1157.

A meticulous overview of painted illustrations to *The Tale of Genji*, focusing on portrayals of the Ukifune lady and speculating as to the participation of women in the tradition of *monogatari* illustrations.

1835. MELETINSKY, Elizar M. Fall 1984. "The typology of the medieval romance in the West and in the East." [Translated by R. Scott WALKER.] *Diogenes* no.127:1-22. ISSN:0392-1921.

A vast study including *The Tale of Genji* as the Japanese example of medieval romance, discussed in a global context.

1836. MILLER, Marilyn. 1985. *The Poetics of Nikki Bungaku: A Comparison of the Traditions, Conventions, and Structure of Heian Japan's Literary Diaries with Western Autobiographical Writings*. New York: Garland Press. 412p. Notes & bibl. LCCN:84-48371.

Based on a PhD dissertation, this theoretical volume attempts to "present a structural analysis and definition of . . . the *nikki* or poetic diary . . . and to suggest the structural similarities of such works to Western autobiographical writings as that term is now understood" (pp. 1-2), presenting several models and outlining transformational rules. Includes comparisons of the *Kagerō nikki* and ROUSSEAU's *Confessions*; *Murasaki Shikibu nikki* with SAINT-SIMON's *Memories*; and SEI Shōnagon's *Makura no sōshi* with MONTAIGNE's *Essais* and GIDE's *Journals*.

1837. MILLS, D.E. Mar. 1980. "Murasaki Shikibu—Saint or sinner?" *Bulletin of the Japan Society, London* no. 90:3-14. ISSN:0021-4701.

An examination of medieval critical debate on the morality, or lack thereof, of the *Tale of Genji* and its author.

1838. MINER, Earl. 1969. "Some thematic and structural features of the *Genji Monogatari*." *Monumenta Nipponica* 24(1/2):1-19. ISSN:0027-0741.

An important early article, reflecting Japanese *Genji* scholarship, pointing out unifying motifs and large structural divisions in the tale and attempting to sketch important elements in its world view.

1839. MINER, Earl. 1977. "Some features of the *Genji Monogatari*." In: TAKEDA, Katsuhiko, ed. 1977. *Essays on Japanese Literature*. Tokyo: Waseda University Press, pp. 16-40. LCCN:78-315676.

A general introductory essay focusing on unifying themes in *The Tale of Genji* and suggesting a variety of possible critical approaches.

1840. MINER, Earl. 1982. "The heroine: Identity, recurrence, destiny." In: PEKARIK, Andrew, ed. *Ukifune: Love in* The Tale of Genji. New York: Columbia University Press, pp. 63-81. 16 notes. LCCN:82-1157.

A look at ways of defining the "existence" of the Ukifune lady "in relation to thoughts of other characters or through things in the world" (p. 64), specifically by images (including those inherent in her "name," "The Boat on the Waters") and the part she plays in recurrent patterns in the Uji chapters and the work as a whole.

1841. MINER, Earl. 1982. "Narrative parts and conceptions." In: PEKARIK, Andrew, ed. *Ukifune: Love in* The Tale of Genji. New York: Columbia University Press, pp. 231-250. 15 notes. LCCN:82-1157.

An attempt to divide *The Tale of Genji* and specifically the "Ukifune" chapter into several kinds of narrative units signaled by consistent beginning and ending markers.

1842. MIYAKE, Lynne. 1988. "Women's voice in Japanese literature: Expanding the feminine." *Women's Studies* 17:87-100. 17 notes. ISSN:0049-7878.

In this general article, MIYAKE argues (mainly on the basis of Heian tales and diaries) that there is a women's voice in Japanese literature, that its existence has been beneficial to the Japanese literary tradition, and that "Japanese literature and culture . . . demonstrates the ethnocentricity of the cultural and psychoanalytic (especially of the Freudian and Lacanian orientation) modes of interpretations formulated by Western feminist criticism" (p. 99).

1843. MIYOSHI, Masao. 1978. "Translation as interpretation." *Journal of Asian Studies* 38(2):299-302. No refs. ISSN:0021-9118.

A review of Edward G. SEIDENSTICKER's translation of *The Tale of Genji* (#1760), emphasizing peculiar features of Heian Japanese language, punctuation, and literary imagination that make the original work extremely resistant to translation into English.

1844. MORRIS, Ivan. Jan./Feb. 1964. "Translating 'The Tale of Genji.'" *Orient/West* 9(1):1-24. 2 notes. ISSN:0474-6465.

A presentation of some of the *Tale of Genji*'s obstacles to translation, and an assessment of Arthur WALEY's approach to the task.

1845. MORRIS, Ivan. 1964. *The World of the Shining Prince: Court Life in Ancient Japan*. New York: Knopf. 348p. Notes & bibl. LCCN:64-12310.

For many years the standard companion to *The Tale of Genji* in undergraduate courses. Contains background information on Heian daily life, customs, beliefs, and institutions, with examples and quotations from the WALEY translation (see #1760).

1846. MORRIS, Ivan. 1965. "On translating the Japanese classics." In: SCHNEPS, Maurice and Alvin D. COX, eds. 1965. *The Japanese Image: Essays, Stories, and Poems about*

Japan by Outstanding Japanese and Western Writers. [Selections from *Orient/West* Magazine volume 1.] Tokyo and Philadelphia: Orient/West, Inc, pp. 327-335.

The second half of this little piece is devoted to an examination of a long passage from the *Genji monogatari*, citing WALEY's translation, raising difficulties, and proposing other solutions.

1847. MORRIS, Ivan. 1971. *The Tale of Genji Scroll*. Tokyo: Kodansha International. 154p. Bibl. LCCN:77-128695.

Large, splendid reproductions of all extant fragments, both calligraphy and paintings, of the early twelfth-century *Genji monogatari emaki* [*The Tale of Genji Scroll*], also known as the *Takayoshi Genji*.

1848. MORRIS, Ivan, ed. 1981. *Madly Singing in the Mountains: An Appreciation and Anthology of Arthur Waley*. Berkeley: Creative Arts Book Company. 403p. LCCN:68-28349.

Part I contains a variety of essays by WALEY's friends, readers, and successors offering glimpses into the personal, intellectual, esthetic, and scholarly life of Arthur WALEY, translator of *The Tale of Genji* and the *Pillow-book*, including many references to those translations. Part II is an anthology of WALEY's own writings and translations, including the introductions to individual volumes of his *Genji* in the original edition, excerpts from the *Pillow-book* and the *Genji*, and a reprint of "The Lady who Loved Insects."

1849. MORRIS, Ivan and Andrew PEKARIK. 1982. "Deception and self-deception." In: PEKARIK, Andrew, ed. *Ukifune: Love in* The Tale of Genji. New York: Columbia University Press, pp. 139-151. No refs. LCCN:82-1157.

An interesting preliminary essay "based on notes left by Ivan MORRIS" (p. 139) on the deceptions inherent in the triangular romantic relationships that pervade *The Tale of Genji* and recur in the "Ukifune" chapter in Ukifune's relationships with Kaoru and Niou; focuses briefly on communication impediments, secrets, lies, and (self-)denials of guilt.

1850. MORRIS, Ivan. 1987. "On translating *Genji*." In: *The World of Translation*. New York: P.E.N. America Center, pp. 267-279. (Conference on Literary Translations, New York City, May 1970.) No refs. LCCN:87-143272.

A paper delivered at a conference on translation held at Columbia University in 1969, including some simple comments on the process MORRIS (who translated the *Pillowbook* but not *The Tale of Genji*) followed in translating from classical Japanese—from understanding the text to producing (and annotating) a pleasing English version. Includes a consideration of the opening lines of the *The Tale of Genji*, reproduced in the original and in several translations. For a general audience.

1851. MORRIS, Mark. Jun. 1980. "Sei Shōnagon's poetic categories." *Harvard Journal of Asiatic Studies* 40(1):5-54. 90 notes. ISSN:0073-0548.

An extremely technical article in which MORRIS looks closely at the lists or catalogues that form an important part of the *Pillowbook* [*Makura no sōshi*] (see #1766). From the context of traditional Japanese poetics, MORRIS explores "what the catalogues are like, and looking at the . . . scholarly response to them, gauge[s] what sort of materials made their way into them or influenced their form and . . . what SEI Shōnagon achieved with this peculiar, almost subliterary genre" (p. 7).

1852. MORRIS, Mark. May 1990. "Desire and the Prince: New work on *Genji monogatari*—a review article." *Journal of Asian Studies* 49(2):291-304. 5 notes and 23 refs. ISSN:0021-9118.

A scholarly review of BOWRING's *Murasaki Shikibu: The Tale of Genji*, FIELD's *The Splendor of Longing in The Tale of Genji*, and SHIRANE's *The Bridge of Dreams: A Poetics of "The Tale of Genji"*, beginning with Virginia WOOLF's reception of the WALEY version of the tale, and WALEY's own views.

1853. MOTOORI, Norinaga. 1958. "Good and evil in the Tale of Genji." In: *Sources of Japanese Tradition*. 1958. [Compiled by Ryūsaku TSUNODA, William Theodore de BARY and Donald KEENE.] New York: Columbia University Press, pp. 532-535. *(Records of Civilizations: Sources and Studies*, vol. 54. *Introduction to Oriental Civilizations)*. LCCN:58-7167.

Selections from *Tama no Ogushi* [*Little Jeweled Comb*], MOTOORI's study of the *Genji monogatari*, with brief introduction.

1854. MUDRICK, Marvin. Autumn 1955. "*Genji* and the age of marvels." *The Hudson Review* 8(3):327-345. 2 notes. ISSN:0018-702X.

An interesting reading of *The Tale of Genji* by a prominent critic, who praises WALEY's "immense and heroic labor" while chiding the translator for his "petulance" and "peevishness" with respect to its great author (p. 327).

1855. Murasaki Shikibu. [1958.] "On the art of the novel." [Translated by Arthur WALEY.] In: *Sources of Japanese Tradition*. 1958. [Compiled by Ryūsaku TSUNODA, William Theodore de BARY and Donald KEENE.] New York: Columbia University Press, pp. 176-183. *(Records of Civilizations: Sources and Studies*, vol. 54. *Introduction to Oriental Civilizations)*. 3 notes. LCCN:58-7167.

The famous and controversial passage of literary criticism from the *Hotaru* ("Glow-worm") chapter of *The Tale of Genji*, quoted from the WALEY translation; preceded by a detailed introduction of the *Genji*.

1856. *Murasaki Shikibu: The Greatest Lady Writer in Japanese Literature*. 1970. Tokyo: [Mombushō], Japan[ese] National Commission for UNESCO. 424p. 1222 references. LCCN:70-561803.

A comprehensive guide to traditional *Tale of Genji* scholarship in Japan, by several noted Japanese *Genji* scholars. A good introduction to the approaches and special problems on which such scholarship focuses. Includes a history of *Genji* studies from the time of Murasaki Shikibu to the mid-twentieth century, and an annotated bibliography of major scholarly works. The English translation is problematic but not unreadable. Most useful to Western scholars of Japanese literature who are not *Genji* specialists.

1857. MURASE, Miyeko. 1983. *Iconography of* The Tale of Genji: Genji Monogatari Ekotoba. New York: Weatherhill. 351p. Notes & Bibl. LCCN:83-3452.

A catalogue of paintings (scrolls, albums, screens) related to *The Tale of Genji*, from the Heian through Edo periods, organized by the *Genji* chapters they were intended to illustrate or epitomize.

1858. MURAYAMA, Ryū. Jan./Feb. 1990. "Fujitsubo: Hers and Genji's love was forbidden." *East* 25(5):19-24. No refs. ISSN:0012-8295.
1859. MURAYAMA, Ryū. Mar./Apr. 1990. "Lady Aoi: The sadness of a loveless marriage." *East* 25(6):20-24. No refs. ISSN:0012-8295.
1860. MURAYAMA, Ryū. May/Jun. 1990. "Lady Rokujō: Flames of jealousy fed by self-respect." *East* 26(1):12-17. No refs. ISSN:0012-8295.
1861. MURAYAMA, Ryū. Jul./Aug. 1990. "Yūgao: The transiency of a burning love." *East* 26(2):20-24. No refs. ISSN:0012-8295.

1862. MURAYAMA, Ryū. Sep./Oct. 1990. "Genji women: Wakamurasaki "My Fair Lady." *East* 26(3):24-29. No refs. ISSN:0012-8295.

1863. MURAYAMA, Ryū. Nov./Dec. 1990. "Genji women: Utsusemi and Suetsumuhana: Middle-class women of marked individuality." *East* 26(4):41-45. No refs. ISSN:0012-8295.

A series for the general reader.

1864. MUSGRAVE, Leilani. 1965. "The Kagero Nikki: The diary of a 10th century Japanese noblewoman." *Horizontal* [Canberra] 1:32-37.

MUSGRAVE evaluates the personal character of the diary's author, and provides an account of the important "stresses" inherent in her situation.

1865. NICHOLS, James R. Apr./Jun. 1970. "*The Tale of Genji*: A novel of manners, 1020 AD." *Japan Quarterly* 17(2):178-182. 17 notes. ISSN:0021-4590.

An essay for the general reader, contending (on the basis of the WALEY translation—see #1760) that *The Tale of Genji* is "a novel of manners" like a Jane AUSTEN or Edith WHARTON novel, and that in fact, although "Jane Austen's characters are the English country gentry and Edith Wharton's the ruthlessly indifferent New York elite," "Murasaki's semi-feudal and frivolous aristocracy is only superficially different" (p. 179).

1866. NOGUCHI, Takehiko. 1985. "The substratum constituting monogatari: Prose structure and narrative in the *Genji Monogatari*." In: MINER, Earl, ed. *Principles of Classical Japanese Literature*. Princeton: Princeton University Press, pp. 130-150. LCCN:84-42895.

Examines *The Tale of Genji* on the basis of six structural principles: character pairing, plot foreshadowing, coherence of cause and outcome, correspondence or parallel developments, contrast, and ellipsis. These principles were originally outlined by HAGIWARA Hiromichi, a nineteenth-century scholar of Japanese studies.

1867. OGAWA, Nobuo. Nov. 1990. "Clues to Heian perception of action: The suffixes *-tsu* and *-nu* in *Genji Monogatari*." *Journal of the Association of Teachers of Japanese* 24(2):147-165. 21 notes. ISSN:0885-9884.

A technical article concluding that "the determining factors in the use of [tsu] are a confirming judgment on strong, usually emotional, involvement in the situation on the part of the speaker" (p. 163).

1868. OYAMA, Atsuko. 1961. "How was the Genji Monogatari written?" *Acta Asiatica* 1(2):59-67. 3 notes. ISSN:0567-7254.

A series of specific assertions about the order of composition and the identity of the author(s) of *The Tale of Genji*, listing irregularities in the text such assertions would explain.

1869. PEKARIK, Andrew. 1982. "Rivals in love." In: PEKARIK, Andrew, ed. *Ukifune: Love in* The Tale of Genji. New York: Columbia University Press, pp. 217-230. No refs. LCCN:82-1157.

This article cites detailed textual evidence in claiming that Murasaki Shikibu takes sides between competing suitors like Genji and Tō no Chūjō, or Kaoru and Niou, in the adjectives she uses to describe them and their behavior, many of which imply "judgments of right and wrong" (p. 217).

1870. PEKARIK, Andrew, ed. 1982. *Ukifune: Love in* The Tale of Genji. New York: Columbia University Press. 278p. (*Companions to Asian Studies*.) LCCN:82-1157.

A volume in memory of Ivan MORRIS including ten articles, some excellent, all of interest, on various aspects of the last ten chapters (the "Uji chapters") of *The Tale of Genji*. An early stage in the current proliferation of sophisticated *Genji* studies in English.

1871. POLLACK, David. Winter 1983. "The informing image: 'China' in *Genji Monogatari.*" *Monumenta Nipponica* 38(4):359-375.   39 notes.   ISSN:0027-0741.   Reprinted in: POLLACK, David. 1986. *The Fracture of Meaning: Japan's Synthesis of China from the Eighth through the Eighteenth Centuries.* Princeton: Princeton University Press, pp. 35-76. LCCN:85-43305.

A somewhat difficult article exploring "the dialectic" or "the process at work in selecting foreign cultural elements and synthesizing them into the native culture" (p. 361), focusing on Chinese materials that appear in *The Tale of Genji*, especially the importance of YANG Kwei-fei and WANG Chao-chün to the "Paulownia Court" chapter and the richness of the "Suma" chapter that derives from allusions to Chinese stories of exile.

1872. PUETTE, William J. 1983. *Guide to* The Tale of Genji. Rutland, VT: Tuttle. 196p. Bibl. LCCN:82-74088.

A chapter-by-chapter guide to character and incident, for the beginner. Includes charts and tables.

1873. PUTZAR, Edward D. Mar. 1967. "Japanese literature theoretically speaking." *Literature East and West* 11(1):23-35. No refs. ISSN:0024-4767.

PUTZAR provides a general essay considering Murasaki Shikibu's discussion of the art of the novel (from the *Hotaru* chapter ["Glow-worm" (WALEY); "Fireflies" (SEIDENSTICKER)]) of *The Tale of Genji* as "representative of the nominalist philosophy of aesthetics" (p. 38) to which the modern age in the West, as well as Japan, is especially receptive.

1874. PUTZAR, Edward. 1973. *Japanese Literature: A Historical Outline.* [Adapted from the work by Sen'ichi HISAMATSU.] Tucson: University of Arizona Press. 246p. LCCN:70-189229. [*Nihon bungaku.* Adaptation. 1960.]

A chronological history of Japanese literature from 400 to 1945, originally intended for a Japanese audience.   Women, especially poets, are mentioned throughout, and the discussion of the Heian Period includes sections on Imperial anthologies, *The Tale of Genji*, and the *Pillow Book*. The modern chapter is organized by groups and movements and focuses on literary ideology and on fiction. Women are mentioned, sometimes discussed, in passing.

1875. RAMIREZ-CHRISTENSEN, Esperanza. 1982. "The operation of the lyrical mode in the *Genji Monogatari.*" In: PEKARIK, Andrew, ed. *Ukifune: Love in* The Tale of Genji. New York: Columbia University Press, pp. 21-61. 17 notes. LCCN:82-1157.

A substantial article focusing on specific passages in the "Uji" chapters of *The Tale of Genji* to explicate the relationship of poems to their prose contexts and of descriptive passages to incident, showing that "the *Genji* is a hybrid genre in which narrative is being employed for lyrical or poetic ends" and ". . . [its] climaxes . . . are . . . those moments of heightened emotion in which outer and inner worlds are fused together in a transfiguring metaphor or pattern of images" (p. 21).

1876. RIMER, J. Thomas. 1978. *Modern Japanese Fiction and its Traditions: An Introduction.* Princeton: Princeton University Press. 313p. Notes. Bibl. Index. LCCN:78-51188.

A presentation of "certain structural principles important in the tradition of Japanese narrative fiction" (p. viii), focusing most often on classical texts that inform and provide the basis for allusion in modern Japanese fiction. It includes an overview of major Heian genres, discusses *The Tale of Genji* as a "source book," and devotes one chapter (pp. 200-244) to "*The Tale of Genji* as a Modern Novel."

1877. RIMER, J. Thomas. 1988. *A Reader's Guide to Japanese Literature.* Tokyo: Kodansha International. 208p. Bibl. Index. LCCN:88-45080.

A survey of major works in English translation, for the newcomer to Japanese literature. Each work is accorded a brief section including a thematic overview and a list of English translations of that work and others by the same author, or of the same genre, with occasional references to related scholarship in English. There are such sections devoted to *Genji monogatari* [*The Tale of Genji*], *Sarashina nikki* [*The Sarashina Diary; As I Crossed a Bridge of Dreams*], *Makura no sōshi* [*The Pillow Book*].

1878. ROSENFIELD, John M., Fumiko E. CRANSTON, and Edwin A. CRANSTON. 1973. *The Courtly Tradition in Japanese Art and Literature: Selections from the Hofer and Hyde Collections.* Cambridge: Fogg Art Museum, Harvard University. 316p. Notes. Index. LCCN:73-85473.

The catalog accompanying an exhibit of "calligraphy and painting of narrative and religious themes" (p. 6). Includes a wealth of information on the texts and illustrations of *The Tale of Genji* and other Heian prose and poetry by women. Abundant notes.

1879. SEIDENSTICKER, Edward. 1974. "Murasaki Shikibu and her diary and other writings." *Literature East and West* 18(1):1-7. No refs. ISSN:0024-4767.

A general essay on the Murasaki Shikibu nikki—"one of the classics, although maybe it does not really deserve to be" (p. 1)—contrasting the temperament of its author with those of other female diarists, and comparing changes in mood and attitude with similar changes in the course of the *Genji monogatari*, her "other writings."

1880. SEIDENSTICKER, Edward G. 1977. *Genji Days.* Tokyo: Kodansha International. 225p. Notes. LCCN:76-44157.

Excerpts from a personal diary kept while the author was translating *The Tale of Genji*. An unusual source of information on SEIDENSTICKER's reading of specific episodes and of *Genji* as a whole, as well as on particular translation problems.

1881. SEIDENSTICKER, Edward G. 1978. "Eminent women writers of the Court: Murasaki Shikibu and SEI Shōnagon." In: MURAKAMI, Hyoe and Thomas J. HARPER, eds. *Great Historical Figures in Japan.* Tokyo: Japan Culture Institute, pp. 60-71. LCCN:81-670213.

An introduction for the general audience to the authors of the two great Heian Period prose classics, *The Tale of Genji* (see #1760) and the *Pillowbook* (see #1766). SEIDENSTICKER also speculates as to why women should have dominated Heian prose: "That numbers of extrordinarily gifted women should appear as the literature was having one of its finest days is certainly a happening not common in the literary history of the world. Even in the literary history of Japan, however, it happened only once" (p. 61).

1882. SEIDENSTICKER, Edward. Winter 1980. "Chiefly on translating the *Genji*." *Journal of Japanese Studies* 6(1):15-47. No refs. ISSN:0095-6848.

Some general observations on literary translation (by a master of the art), an endeavour which "because it wishes to pass the scrutiny of commercial editors and to attract the "general" reader, hopes to have literary grace in some measure, whether or not it is commensurate with that of the original" (p. 15), reflecting on the character of some well-known English translations of classical Japanese poetry, and citing specific challenges encountered in translating *The Tale of Genji*.

1883. SEIDENSTICKER, Edward. 1982. "Rough business in 'Ukifune' and elsehere." In: PEKARIK, Andrew, ed. *Ukifune: Love in* the Tale of Genji. New York: Columbia University Press, pp. 1-19. 1 note. LCCN:82-1157.

SEIDENSTICKER provides a pleasant essay citing hints of "rough business" in *Genji*—politics, the lower rungs of the aristocracy, intimations of the triumph of the "world of the medieval warrior" (p. 18), concluding that there is more "rough business" in Ukifune than in the rest of the work, as "seems appropriate" (p. 19).

1884. SEIDENSTICKER, Edward. 1982. "*The Tale of Genji*: Here and there." *Yearbook of Comparative and General Literature* 31:47-53. ISSN:0084-3695.

A delightful short chronicle of the WALEY and SEIDENSTICKER translations of *The Tale of Genji* and their reception in England and America, followed by an assessment of the original *Genji*'s current status in Japan, concluding that "in its native land *Genji* belongs to the realm of folklore rather than that of literature" (p. 53) because everyone knows about it and no one has actually read it.

1885. SHIMIZU, Yoshiko. 1979. "Flavor and taste in *The Tale of Genji*." *Chanoyu Quarterly* 22:60-62. ISSN:0009-1537.

Pointing up Murasaki Shikibu's reticence on the subject of food in the *Tale of Genji* by highlighting the comparatively full descriptions of food and taste in the *Utsubo monogatari* [*Tale of a Hollow Tree*], probably written by a man, SHIMIZU concludes that polite Heian women did not talk about food.

1886. SHIRANE, Haruo. 1982. "The Uji chapters and the denial of romance." In: PEKARIK, Andrew, ed. *Ukifune: Love in* The Tale of Genji. New York: Columbia University Press, pp. 113-138. 30 notes. LCCN:82-1157.

A general examination of "romance" (as defined by Henry JAMES) in *The Tale of Genji* as a whole, seeing the Ukifune story as its denial: Echoing the characters Murasaki's and Oigimi's "distrust for marriage and romantic love," Ukifune rejects Kaoru directly, and "renunciation becomes a denial of this world as well as an assertion of the self" (p. 136).

1887. SHIRANE, Haruo. Summer 1985. "The aesthetics of power: Politics in *The Tale of Genji*." *Harvard Journal of Asiatic Studies* 45(2):615-647. Notes & bibl. ISSN:0073-0548.

A far-ranging article that anticipates SHIRANE's book (see #1888), interpreting images of kingship and motifs of transgression, exile, aesthetic performances and competitions, and rivalry in love (and progeny) as patterns reflecting political realities in the Heian period; and concluding with the assessment that "the *miyabi* [courtly elegance] ideal finds its most perfect embodiment in the form of Genji and . . . it is precisely such a man of arts, letters, and love, a hero of sensibility, who should ultimately assume power" (p. 647).

1888. SHIRANE, Haruo. 1987. *The Bridge of Dreams: Poetics in* The Tale of Genji. Stanford: Stanford University Press. 276p. Bibl. LCCN:86-30031.

A useful companion to *The Tale of Genji*, drawing on "textual, aesthetic, structural, socio-historical, folklore" among various fields of modern *Genji* scholarship (p. xiii) to explore multiple aspects of the entire text.

1889. STINCHECUM, Amanda Mayer. Winter 1980. "Who tells the tale? 'Ukifune': A study in Narrative voice." *Monumenta Nipponica* 35(4):375-403. Notes. ISSN:0027-0741.

An extremely valuable scholarly article presenting both thematic and linguistic evidence from the *Ukifune* chapter of *The Tale of Genji*, focusing on an explanation of some characteristics of Heian Japanese pertaining to point of view in order to show shifts and fragmentation in narrative point of view and the manipulation of esthetic distance.

1890. TAHARA, Mildred. May 1972. "Lady Murasaki and her sisters." *Orientations* 3(5):60-66. ISSN:0030-5448.

A very general historical introduction to women writers of the Heian period.

1891. TAUDIN-CHABOT, Jeanette. 1984. "The feminine tradition in Japanese literature." In: DANIELS, Gordon, ed. 1984. *Europe Interprets Japan*. Kent, England: Paul Norbury Publications, pp. 162-167. ISBN:0-904404-420.

A vigorous attempt to trace the strong feminine element in Japanese literature to a matriarchal society in which women were priestesses and transmitters of the "*kotodama*." TAUDIN-CHABOT remarks that "*Manyoshū* does reflect feminine qualities of [ancient] Japan. It is only that the position of women in the society changed, and consequently in later generations vitality was no longer considered 'feminine'" (p. 163).

1892. THOMAS, Roger. 1982. "A *Genji* bibliography: Non-Japanese sources." *Yearbook of Comparative and General Literature* 31:68-75. No refs. ISSN:0084-3695.

A useful annotated bibliography, including entries (in English as well as European langugages) not listed here.

1893. UEDA, Makoto. 1967. "Truth and falsehood in fiction: Lady Murasaki on the art of the novel." In: UEDA, Makoto. *Literary and Art Theories in Japan*. Cleveland, OH: The Press of Western Reserve Library, pp. 25-36. LCCN:67-14521.

A straightforward explication for the general reader of Murasaki Shikibu's famous and controversial "defense of fiction" from the *Hotaru* chapter of *The Tale of Genji* [SEIDENSTICKER translation as "Fireflies"; WALEY translation as "Glow-Worm"].

1894. URY, Marian. Summer 1976. "The imaginary kingdom and the translator's art: Notes on re-reading Waley's *Genji*." *Journal of Japanese Studies* 2(2):267-294. 75 notes. ISSN:0095-6848.

A personal reading of WALEY's version of *The Tale of Genji* (see #1760) showing in an interesting and general way how he "appropriat[ed]" (p. 294) the work and created his own "imaginary kingdom" (p. 294). URY speculates why and to what effects.

1895. URY, Marian. Jun. 1977. "The complete *Genji*." *Harvard Journal of Asiatic Studies* 37(1):183-201. 212 notes. ISSN:0073-0548.

Compares specific passages in the two major translations (with additional references to the 1966 German translation by Oscar BENL), and points out the advantages of SEIDENSTICKER's complete, plain, and clear translation of the *The Tale of Genji* over WALEY's "hybrid" (p. 189) product. URY observes that "If Waley specialized in charm, Seidensticker reveals dimensions of irony which readers of the earlier translation must scarcely have suspected . . ." (p. 189).

1896. URY, Marian. 1982. "*The Tale of Genji* in English." *Yearbook of Comparative and General Literture* 31:62-67. ISSN:0084-3695.

A general comparison of the WALEY and SEIDENSTICKER translations as they reflect the tastes and literary personalities of the two men.

1897. URY, Marian. Summer 1983. "The real Murasaki." *Monumenta Nipponica* 38(2):175-189. 24 notes. ISSN:0027-0741.

A review of BOWRING's *Murasaki Shikibu: Her Diary and Poetic Memoirs* (see #1768) finding some fault with style and accuracy, but welcoming it as "A highly useful, much-needed contribution to its field" (p. 189).

1898. WALKER, Janet A. Jun. 1977. "Poetic ideal and fictional reality in the *Izumi Shikibu nikki*." *Harvard Journal of Asiatic Studies* 37(1):135-182. 47 notes. ISSN:0073-0548.

A scholarly investigation of one of the most important poetic diaries of the Heian Period, finding that "In part, the author adhered to . . . an idealized view of love influenced by the poetic anthology . . . in which ritualized and stylized poetic exchanges play an important role," but that "the author's sense of loyalty to the facts of the affair as she knew them forced her to depart radically from the traditional poetic view . . ." (p. 136). WALKER examines the evidence of a resultant tension in the work.

1899. WATANABE, Minoru. Summer 1984. "Style and point of view in the *Kagerō nikki.*" [Introduced and translated by Richard BOWRING.] *Journal of Japanese Studies* 10(2):368-384. No refs. ISSN:0095-6848.

WATANABE provides a somewhat technical article citing textual examples to characterize the style of the author of *The Gossamer Years* as progressing from "the immediate voice"—"a presentation of the objective in terms of the meaning that it holds for the prime actor" (p. 372) to being on the verge of acquiring the "ability to stand outside herself as actor, to stand where she could begin to see herself . . . to describe herself in objective terms" (p. 383). Although she fails to "break away completely" from "her initial position of direct participant" (p. 384), she achieved "the first step that led to the birth of Heian women's literature" (p. 384), he concludes.

1900. WILSON, William R. 1972. "The Bell-Crickets Chapter of *The Tale of Genji*: An introduction and translation." *Literature East and West* 16:1196-1216. Notes. ISSN:0024-4767.

A translation of the "*Suzumushi*" chapter, which Arthur WALEY mysteriously did not include in his translation of *The Tale of Genji*, with a brief discussion of why WALEY might have omitted it, and why the chapter is in fact important thematically and in plot and character development. (The chapter is translated by SEIDENSTICKER, see #1760.)

1901. "The women who wrote classics: A dream-seeking life: The life of Sugawara-no-Takasue's daughter, the author of the Sarashina Nikki." Sep./Oct. 1989. *East* 25(3):62-70. No refs. ISSN:0012-8295.

A speculative account of the ancestry, life, and social, geographical and literary context of Takasue's daughter. Final article in series.

1902. "The women who wrote classics: Izumi Shikibu, a poet who devoted herself to love." Nov./Dec. 1988. *East* 24(4):12-17. No refs. ISSN:0012-8295.

A brief note introducing the *Izumi Shikibu nikki*, followed by an amusing profile of Izumi Shikibu, "a passionate woman" when "life" was a symbol for "love affair" (p. 13). Includes many poems, translated by Edwin A. CRANSTON.

1903. "The women who wrote classics: Murasaki Shikibu, the author of a picture-scroll romance." Aug. 1988. *East* 24(2):24-28. No refs. ISSN:0012-8295.

An interesting sketch for the general reader, beginning with a one-page summary of *The Tale of Genji*, then focusing on what is known, or rumored to be known, about its author Murasaki Shikibu's life and personality. First in a series.

1904. "The women who wrote classics: Sei Shōnagon." Sept./Oct. 1988. *East* 24(3):12-17. No refs. ISSN:0012-8295.

After a brief note introducing the *Pillowbook*, this general article speculates about SEI Shōnagon's personality and biography, with many quotations from the MORRIS translation of the *Pillowbook* (see #1766). Part of a series.

1905. "The women who wrote classics: The Kagerō Nikki, the diary of Michitsuna's Mother." Jan./Feb. 1989. *East* 24(5):54-58. No refs. ISSN:0012-8295.

An account of "Kagerō's" story as recorded in the *Diary* (#1764), and a few notes on the poetic diary genre. In the series for the general reader.

1906. "The women who wrote classics: The Sanukinosuke Nikki: Fujiwara no Nagako's memoir of a nominal emperor." May/Jun. 1989. *East* 25(1):48-52. No refs. ISSN:0012-8295.

An amusing summary of the work and portraits of the author and her subject.

1907. WOOLF, Virgina. Dec. 1967. "*The Tale of Genji*: The first volume of Mr. Arthur Waley's translation of a great Japanese novel by Lady Murasaki." *Literature East and West* 11(4):424-427. No refs. ISSN:0024-4767.

A reprint of the famous, originally anonymous, review in the July 1925 issue of *Vogue*, remarking that "something of [Lady Murasaki's] charm for us is doubtless accidental" (p. 426) and that *The Tale of Genji*, although beautiful, is not "a star of the first magnitude" (p. 427). The article is introduced by HENIG (see #1802).

1908. YOSHIDA, Sanroku. 1983. "Time and seasonal awareness in *The Tale of Genji*." *Journal of Intercultural Studies* no.10:111-121. ISSN:0388-0508.

YOSHIDA provides an analysis of time, seasonal observances, and seasonal imagery from nature, showing how such cycles pattern *The Tale of Genji* and inform its world view with winter tending to predominate as the world darkens in the final "Uji" chapters.

1909. ZOLBROD, Leon. 1980. "The four-part theoretical structure of *The Tale of Genji*." *Journal of the Association of Teachers of Japanese* 15(1):22-31. 12 notes. ISSN:0885-9884.

Divides *The Tale of Genji* into four parts: 1) Chapters 1-21, characterized by autumn; 2) Chapters 22-33, by spring; 3) Chapters 34-44 by summer; 4) Chapters 45-54 by winter, so that "the tale may be found to reveal a single, coherent story of epic proportions" (p. 30).

17

Premodern Poets

1910. BARON, Virginia Olsen. 1968. *The Seasons of Time: Tanka Poetry of Ancient Japan.* New York: Dial Press. 63p. Index. No refs. LCCN:68-15254.

A collection of poems, mainly from the *Man'yōshū* and the *Kokinshū*, translated by various translators and arranged by season, with a general introduction to the *tanka/waka*. No Japanese or romanized texts provided. Includes the poetry of Lady Fujiwara, Lady Ise, Lady Nakatsukasa, Princess Ōku, ONO no Komachi and Taniha Ōmé.

1911. BEHN, Harry. 1964. *Cricket Songs, Japanese Haiku Translated by Harry Behn.* New York: Harcourt, Brace and World. Unpaginated. Afternote. LCCN:64-11489.

A selection of famous haiku pleasantly translated into a 5-7-5 form. No Japanese or romanized text. Includes three poems by Chiyo(jo).

1912. BEHN, Harry. 1971. *More Cricket Songs.* New York: Harcourt, Brace and World. Unpaginated. LCCN:77-137755.

Poems as in BEHN (#1911), above. Includes one additional poem by Chiyo(jo).

1913. BEILENSON, Peter. 1968. *A Haiku Garland: A Collection of Seventeen-Syllable Classic Poems.* Mount Vernon, NY: Peter Pauper Books. Unpaginated. No refs. LCCN:70-16872.

A selection for the general reader with brief introduction. Both premodern and modern haiku are translated into three (5-7-5) lines and are arranged by season. Seven haiku by Chiyo-ni and one each by Sono-jo, Chine-jo, Seifu-jo, and Shisei-jo are included. No Japanese or romanized text provided.

1914. BENNETT, Jean, ed. 1976. *Japanese Love Poems.* Garden City, NY: Doubleday. 104p. LCCN:76-2753.

An anthology of poetry from both the aristocratic and the folk traditions, culled from various other anthologies of Japanese poetry in many different translation styles, arranged topically without original text. Brief introductory note for the general reader. Includes 16 women, in addition to "anonymous."

1915. BLYTH, Reginald Horace. 1949-1952/1963-1964. *Haiku.* Tokyo: Hokuseido Press. 4 vols. Bibl. Indexes. LCCN:53-20278.

A prodigious wealth of information about haiku, and a splendid collection of poems, arranged seasonally and topically. Volumes contain historical and generic essays, genealogical and other tables, and Japanese and romanized texts for all poems. Fifteen women poets are represented, including thirteen premodern poets.

1916. BLYTH, Reginald Horace. 1963/1964. *A History of Haiku in Two Volumes.* Tokyo: Hokuseido Press. 2 vols. LCCN:63-23741.

A thorough and fascinating classic of Western Orientalism. A critical formal introduction to the haiku, and a history of that genre from its origins in linked verse, considering Chinese influence, to the modern day. Studded with translations, with Japanese and romanized texts. Fifteen premodern women haiku poets are represented.

1917. BOSLEY, Keith, ed. 1979. *Poetry of Asia: Five Millenniums of Verse from 33 Languages.* Tokyo: Weatherhill. 315p.

An ambitious anthology of poetry from a vast area including East, South, and Southeast Asia and the Middle East. Poetry of Chiyo-ni, Lady Ise, ONO no Komachi and Princess Shikishi is quoted from other anthologies of poetry in translation.

1918. BOWNAS, Geoffrey, ed. 1964. *The Penguin Book of Japanese Verse.* [Translations by Geoffrey BOWNAS and Anthony THWAITE.] Baltimore: Penguin Books. 242p. LCCN:64-6583.

A sampling of Japanese poetry from all ages in pleasing, interesting translation. Twenty-two premodern women poets are included. Useful introduction for the general reader. Occasional notes. Index of poets.

1919. BROWER, Robert H. and Earl MINER. 1961. *Japanese Court Poetry.* Stanford: Stanford University Press. 527p. Bibl. Index. LCCN:61-10925.

A rich and comprehensive study (based on Western critical approaches) of classical Japanese poetry from 550 to 1350 C.E., studded with translations and analyses of individual poems, a certain proportion of which are by women. The standard general work in English on Japanese poetry. Translations tend to be elaborate and explanatory. Romanized original text of poems included with translations. Glossary. Poem finding list.

1920. BROWER, Robert H. and Earl MINER. 1965. "Translations from the Man'yōshū and Imperial Anthologies." In: SCHNEPS, Maurice and Alvin D. COX, eds. 1965. *The Japanese Image: Essays, Stories, and Poems about Japan by Outstanding Japanese and Western Writers.* [Selections from *Orient/West* Magazine volume 1.] Tokyo and Philadelphia: Orient/West, Inc, pp. 242-250.

A mini-anthology, arranged thematically, including poems by Princess Shokushi, Izumi Shikibu, and Lady Ise. Romanized Japanese text accompanies translations.

1921. BROWER, Robert H. and Earl MINER. 1967. *Fujiwara Teika's Superior Poems of Our Time: A Thirteenth-Century Poetic Treatise and Sequence.* Stanford: Stanford University Press. 148p. Index. LCCN:67-17300.

A translation with scholarly introduction, notes and commentary of an early 13th-century, 83-poem anthology of *tanka/waka* compiled by FUJIWARA Teika as a handbook for aspiring writers. Includes the poems of Lady Ise, Izumi Shikibu, Lady Kii and ONO no Komachi. Romanized Japanese text on opposing page.

1922. BUCHANAN, Daniel C., ed. and translator. 1973. *One Hundred Famous Haiku.* Tokyo and San Francisco: Japan Publications Trading Co. 120p. Index. LCCN:72-95667.

A good selection of Edo and early modern haiku, with original (calligraphic) Japanese and romanized texts. Includes haiku by four women (Chiyo-jo, Seifu(jo), Sogetsu(-ni) and Ukihashi; Chiyo-jo is well represented.

1923. CARTER, Steven D. 1989. *Waiting for the Wind: Thirty-Six Poets of Japan's Late Medieval Age*. New York: Columbia University Press. 345p. Index of first lines. Bibl. LCCN:89-30578.

A selection of major poetry from roughly 1250 to 1500 containing some 400 *tanka/waka* by 36 poets, including only four women (Abutsu-ni, Empress Eifuku, Lady Chikako Jusammi and KYŌGOKU Tameko). This unbalance CARTER sees as "a reflection of the social realities of the medieval period, especially of a shift . . . from the court as the center of literary activity to the cells of clerics and the halls of the warrior class" (p. xxv). Poets are chosen and organized to represent the two sides of a famous literary debate between the Nijō and the Kyōgoku-Reizei schools of poetry. Romanized Japanese texts included.

1924. CHAMBERLAIN, Basil Hall. 1902. "Basho and the Japanese poetical epigram." *Transactions of the Asiatic Society of Japan* 30:242-362. Bibl. LCCN:39-23.

An early introduction to the haiku by a great Victorian Japanologist and literary scholar. Proceeds historically and includes a number of poems by women: Mitsu-jo, Sono-jo, Chigetsu-ni, Shūshiki, Sute-jo, and, especially, Chiyo-jo.

1925. CLACK, Robert Wood. 1977. *The Soul of Yamato*. New York: Gordon Press. 2 vol. LCCN:76-789.

An anthology collected over many years and apparently prepared in 1953, published posthumously. Begins with an introduction to the Japanese language and "The Nature of Japanese Poetry," and follows with translations, in chronological order, of a wide variety of poems from prehistoric times to the early 20th century. Translations are in original syllable count. No Japanese or romanized text. Each chronological period is preceded by its own historical introduction; most authors are introduced, and many poems are accompanied by brief commentary.

1926. COSMAN, Carol, Joan KEEFE, and Kathleen WEAVER, eds. 1978. *The Penguin Book of Women Poets*. New York: Viking. 399p. LCCN:78-15342.

Contains an excellent selection of classical and modern poetry by women, with biographical and stylistic information. A substantial portion of the work is devoted to Japanese women.

1927. GALT, Tom, trans. 1982. *The Little Treasury of One Hundred People, One Poem Each*. [Translated by Tom GALT.] Princeton: Princeton University Press. 106p. Index. LCCN:81-48140. [*Ogura Hyakunin isshu*.]

Translations into an English form that approximates the Japanese *tanka/waka*, with both Japanese (calligraphic) and romanized texts accompanied by brief commentary. Introductory note to the entire volume, and an index and glossary of poets as an appendix. Authors of poems are not otherwise identified.

1928. HENDERSON, Harold Gould. 1934. *Bamboo Broom: An Introduction to Haiku*. New York: Houghton-Mifflin. 124p. LCCN:34-7430.

The classic introduction to haiku, including many translations in a simple style with romanized original text and word-for-word gloss. Discusses the work of one woman, Chiyo[jo].

1929. HENDERSON, Harold Gould. 1958. *An Introduction to Haiku: An Anthology of Poems and Poets from Bashō to Shiki*. Garden City, NY: Doubleday. 190p. LCCN:58-11314.

The classic introduction to haiku; includes many translations in simple style, with romanized Japanese text and word-for-word gloss. Chiyo[jo] and ENOMOTO Seifu[jo] are discussed. [This is an expanded version of #1928.]

1930. HIGGINSON, William J. with Penny HARTER. 1989. *The Haiku Handbook: How to Write, Share, and Teach Haiku*. Tokyo: Kodansha International. 331p. Reprint of 1985 edition: New York: McGraw-Hill, 331p. LCCN:84-17174.

An excellent resource, for all the purposes listed in the subtitle. Offers an interesting mix of well-known Japanese haiku and haiku composed in English and other languages (some by Americans of Japanese descent)—all considered together. Also provides substantial literary-historical information on haiku (including contemporary haiku) and related genres. Biographical information on most poets, and romanized original texts for Japanese haiku are included.

1931. HIRSHFIELD, Jane and Mariko ARATANI. 1988. *The Ink Dark Moon: Love Poems by Ono no Komachi and Izumi Shikibu*. New York: Scribners. 116p. LCCN:87-32934.

Poetic, if not scholarly, translations of *tanka/waka* (with headnotes) by two of the most brilliant and passionate Heian women poets, ONO no Komachi and Izumi Shikibu. Brief introduction for the beginner.

1932. HOFFMANN, Yoel. 1986. *Japanese Death Poems Written by Zen Monks and Haiku Poets on the Verge of Death*. Rutland, VT: Tuttle. 366p. 44 notes. LCCN:85-52347.

An anthology of haiku with brief biographical and stylistic commentary, preceded by a substantial general introduction to Japanese poetry and "death and its poetry in the cultural history of Japan" (p. 27). Ten of the haiku poets included are identifiable as women.

1933. HONDA, H.H. 1965. *Stray Leaves from the Manyoshu: Two Hundred Poems from the Manyoshu, Books 1-7*. Tokyo: Hokuseido Press. 88p. [*Man'yōshū*. Selections.]

A varied selection, translated, sometimes into rhymed verse. No original or romanized text. Includes 17 women.

1934. HONDA, H.H., trans. 1970. *The Kokin Waka-shū*. Tokyo: Hokuseido Press. 292p. Index. LCCN:77-475104. [*Kokin Wakashū*.]

Brief general introduction to the spirit of the Kokinshū poetry, followed by a complete translation of the twenty books of this first Imperial anthology, with occasional notes to explain wordplay or literary allusion. Poems are translated into various forms; the original text is not given.

1935. KEENE, Donald, ed. 1955. *Anthology of Japanese Literature from the Earliest Era to the Mid-Nineteenth Century*. New York: Grove Press. 442p. Bibl. LCCN:55-5110.

The standard general anthology of premodern Japanese literature. Includes poetry by women from *The Man'yōshū*, *The Kokinshū*, and *The Shinkokinshū*. Includes a brief introduction for the general reader (of 1955).

1936. LEVY, Howard S. 1977. *100 Selections from Lesser Known Japanese Poetry Classic[s]*. South Pasadena, CA: Langstaff Publications. 91p. (*East Asian Poetry in Translation Series*, vol. 7). LCCN:78-319414.

An informative introduction, including brief biographical notes on poets, many of whom are in fact quite well-known, notably Izumi Shikibu, who is liberally represented.

1937. LEVY, Howard S. and Junko OHSAWA. 1977. *Japanese Love Poems.* Seoul: Warm-Soft Village Branch; distributed by South Pasadena: Langstaff Publications. 4 vol. (*East Asian Poetry in Translation Series*). LCCN:78-670065.

Tanka/waka, many of them by women, in unusual translation. Includes a rather personal introduction and very brief biographical notes on poets. ONO no Komachi, Izumi Shikibu, and Princess Shikishi are well-represented.

1938. LEVY, Ian Hideo, trans. 1981. *The Ten Thousand Leaves: A Translation of the Man'yōshū, Japan's Premier Anthology of Classical Poetry. Vol. 1.* Princeton: Princeton University Press. 409p. (Princeton Library of Asian Translations.) 30 notes. Index. LCCN:80-8561.

The most recent retranslation of the first five (of twenty) books of the vast eighth-century anthology the *Man'yōshū*; an attempt at balance between accuracy and literary quality. LEVY includes an interesting introduction. (See also #1933, #1974 and #1977.)

1939. MacCAULEY, Clay. 1917. *Hyakunin-isshu, and Nori no hatsu-ne—Single Songs of a Hundred Poets and The Dominant Note of the Law: Literal Translations into English with Renderings According to the Original Metre.* [Also cited as *Hyakunin-isshu (Single Songs of a Hundred Poets) and Other Verse from old Japan.*] Yokohama: Kelly and Walsh, Ltd. 234p. Notes. Index. LCCN:80-457017. Originally published (1899) in: *Transactions of the Asiatic Society of Japan* 27(4):1-152. LCCN:39-23. MacCAULEY's translations included in: MORSE, Peter. 1989. *Hokusai, the One hundred poets.* New York: George Braziller. 222p. Index. LCCN:88-25175. [*Ogura Hyakunin isshu.*]

An 1899 translation of the *Ogura Hyakunin isshu* retaining the original syllable count, with romanized text (according to archaic writing style), literal gloss, and explanatory notes for each poem. Includes historical introduction to the text followed by general outline of the features of Japanese poetry and exploratory analysis of the work. MORSE edition includes appendix with comparisons of 36 translations of poem number 9 by ONO no Komachi.

1940. MATSUHARA, Iwao. 1958. *Flowers of the Heart: Being Inspirations from Ancient Japanese Poetry.* Tokyo: Hokuseido Press. 195p. LCCN:59-34920.

An attempt to convey "the truth of the heart" (p. vii) of Japanese culture to readers living in an age focusing on technological advances. The poems, mainly from the *Man'yōshū* and *Kokinshū*, accompanied by original Japanese and romanized text, are given titles, and are arranged into categories like "Pictures of the Dew-Drop World." The poems are presented not as direct translations, but as "short compositions suggested by [the original] poems " (p. viii), in a four-line rhymed form. Contains *tanka/waka* by Izumi Shikibu, ONO no Komachi, Shikishi and Sachiko.

1941. MAYHEW, Lenore. 1985. *The Monkey's Raincoat: Linked Poetry of the Basho School with Haiku Selections.* Rutland, VT: Tuttle. 151p. Notes and bibl. Index. LCCN:85-51629. [*Sarumino.* 1690.]

A translation of a 17th-century *haikai* [haiku linked-verse] classic (*Sarumino*) with brief historical and generic introduction and short biographical sketches of the five major contributors, none of them women. One poem by Chigetsu and two by Ukō are, however, included. (See also #1944).

1942. McCULLOUGH, Helen Craig. 1985. *Kokin Wakashū: The First Imperial Anthology of Japanese Poetry, with Tosa Nikki and Shinsen Waka.* [Translated and annotated by Helen Craig McCULLOUGH.] Stanford: Stanford University Press. 388p. Index. LCCN:84-50756. [Kokin wakashū. English.]

A complete annotated scholarly translation of three 10th-century poetry collections; the first and the third contain a significant proportion of *tanka/waka* by women. Translated poems (in 5-7-5 form) are accompanied by headnotes and romanized Japanese text. [See also #2178 for the companion study; #1934 and #1955 for other translations.]

1943. MINER, Earl Roy. 1968. *An Introduction to Japanese Court Poetry.* [Translations by Earl Roy MINER and Robert H. BROWER.] Stanford: Stanford University Press. 173p. Index. LCCN:68-17138.

A condensation and simplification of BROWER and MINER (#1919), with an emphasis on major poets (several of them women) and covering poetry from the seventh century to 1500. The philosophy of translation is similar to that in *Japanese Court Poetry*; many translations of poems appearing in both volumes are, in fact, identical. Romanized original text of poems cited. Poetry finding list. Glossary.

1944. MINER, Earl and Hiroko ODAGIRI. 1981. *The Monkey's Straw Raincoat and Other Poetry of the Bashō School.* Princeton: Princeton University Press. 394p. Notes & bibl. Indexes. LCCN:80-28811.

Historical and generic introduction followed by translation (with original text and commentary) of the famous 1693 linked *haikai* verse sequence "Sarumino" plus four other sequences. Though the principal participants are men, verses by six women are included (Chine(jo), Chigetsu, Ōshū, Sen, Tagami no Ama and Ukō). (See also #1941.)

1945. MIYAMORI, Asatarō. 1932. *An Anthology of Haiku Ancient and Modern.* Tokyo: Maruzen. 841p. Index. LCCN:33-19317. [Also published by Greenwood Press (Westport, CT), 1970, LCCN:76-98856.]

An extremely broad collection of haiku, including a historical survey plus biographical information and commentary on individual poems. Contains both Japanese and romanized text. An invaluable resource despite the occasionally bizarre translations. Poems are titled. Many poems by women are included.

1946. MIYAMORI, Asatarō. 1936[1970]. *Masterpieces of Japanese Poetry Ancient and Modern.* Westport, CT: Greenwood Press. 2 vol. LCCN:70-98857. [LCCN for 1936 edition:88-194141.]

A prodigious two-volume anthology of *tanka/waka* in four-line rhyming stanzas with attributed titles. Includes Japanese and romanized text, biographical headnotes for all poets, and occasional commentary on poems.

1947. MIYAMORI, Asatarō. 1938. *An Anthology of Japanese Poems.* Tokyo: Maruzen. 289p. Index. LCCN:39-961.

An "abridged and revised edition" of the 1936 *Masterpieces of Japanese Poetry Ancient and Modern* [#1946]. Shorter, but similar in character and presentation.

1948. Nippon Gakujutsu Shinkōkai. 1958. *Haikai and Haiku.* Tokyo: Kenkyusha. 191p. Index.

A general introduction to haiku and *haikai* [haiku linked-verse], followed by an excellent selection of haiku written between 1688 and 1912, arranged chronologically and by poet with a brief consideration of each poem, some of which are by women. Also includes biographical notes, glossaries of Japanese esthetic terms and season words, and prominent examples of a haikai sequence and a haiku dairy, but none by women. No original or romanized text.

1949. Nippon Gakujutsu Shinkōkai, trans. 1965. *The Manyōshū.* [Foreword by Donald KEENE.] 1965. New York: Columbia University Press. 502p. (*Records of Civilizations: Sources and Studies*, no.70.) Notes. Index. LCCN:65-15376.

A surprisingly pleasing translation by committee of one thousand poems (roughly a quarter of the whole) from the *Man'yōshū*, the earliest extant (eighth-century) anthology of Japanese poetry, including poems from more than a hundred years earlier. Useful general introduction. Maps. Romanized text of original poems. Brief biographical notes on poets.

1950. PAGE, Curtis Hidden. 1923. *Japanese Poetry: An Historical Essay with 230 Translations.* Boston: Houghton Mifflin. 181p. Index.

An overview of Japanese poetry from primitive times to the 19th century, by a "translator of Ronsard, Molière and Anatole France." A short chapter (XVI, pp. 134-138) is devoted to the Edo haiku poet (Kaga no) Chiyo.

1951. PORTER, William N. 1909[1979]. *A Hundred Verses from Old Japan, being a Translation of the* Hyakunin Isshu. Rutland, VT: Tuttle. 100p. Index. LCCN:77-83039.

The standard, earlier version of GALT (#1927). Poems, in iambic tetrameter, are well annotated.

1952. REXROTH, Kenneth, ed. 1955. *One Hundred Poems from the Japanese.* [Translations by Kenneth REXROTH.] New York: New Directions. 140p. LCCN:56-2557.

A sampling of Nara and Heian poetry, plus a few famous haiku. Thirteen women are represented. Romanized Japanese text accompanies translations. Includes an introduction, biographical notes, and a bibliography of very early sources on Japanese poetry in English and other Western languages.

1953. REXROTH, Kenneth, ed. 1976. *One Hundred More Poems from the Japanese.* New York: New Directions. 120p. LCCN:76-7486.

A sampling of poetry, by poet, several of them women, from the *Man'yōshū* and the *Kokinshū*, plus a few haiku. Romanized original text accompanies all translations. Biographical notes.

1954. REXROTH, Kenneth and Ikuko ATSUMI, eds. 1977. *The Burning Heart: Women Poets of Japan.* [Translated by Kenneth REXROTH and Ikuko ATSUMI.] New York: Seabury Press. 184p. LCCN:77-1833. Republished in 1982 as *Women Poets of Japan.* New York: New Directions. 184p. LCCN:81-18693.

An excellent selection of poems from the sixth century to the present day, including poems by 28 well-known poets from the classical period and ten haiku poets whose poems are translated into various forms. No romanized text. Contains expansive biographical sketches of poets, a survey of women poets, and a table of historical periods.

1955. RODD, Laurel Rasplica. 1984. *Kokinshū: A Collection of Poems Ancient and Modern.* [Translated and annotated by Laurel Rasplica RODD with Mary Catherine HENKENIUS.] Princeton: Princeton University Press. 442p. Notes. Bibl. Index. LCCN:83-43090.

A complete translation of the early 10th-century Imperial anthology (the first of 21) containing 1,111 poems, almost all of them the 31-syllable *tanka/waka.* For the women included see McCULLOUGH (#1942). Translations are accompanied by romanized Japanese text. Contains a scholarly introduction and an excellent article by J. Timothy WIXTED on Chinese models for the famous *Kokinshū* prefaces.

1956. SATŌ, Hiroaki and Burton WATSON, eds. 1981. *From the Country of Eight Islands: An Anthology of Japanese Poetry.* [Translations by Hiroaki SATŌ and Burton WATSON; introduced by J. Thomas RIMER.] Garden City, NY: Doubleday Anchor Books. 652p. Notes. Bibl. Index. LCCN:80-1077.

A pleasant anthology of poetry from the earliest times to the present day, translated (in different styles) by the two compilers. Twelve premodern women are represented. Includes a brief introduction by RIMER, a glossary, and short biographies of the poets.

1957. SATŌ, Hiroaki. 1983. *One Hundred Frogs: From Renga to Haiku to English*. Tokyo: Weatherhill. 241p. Index. Bibl. LCCN:82-17505.

A delightful collection/study of *renga* and the haiku that arose from it. Explores problems of translation and cross-cultural interpretation and offers a wealth of varied translations. Chiyo(jo) is included among the premodern haiku poets; no women are represented in the *renga* section.

1958. SATŌ, Kiyoshi, *et al*. 1953. *Green Hill Poems*. Tokyo: Hokuseido Press. 182p. LCCN:55-42250.

An anthology of poems, mostly original poems written in English but including some translations from the Japanese, by a group of poets associated with Aoyama ("Green Hill") Gakuen, a school known for its excellent English department. Izumi Shikibu is the only premodern woman poet represented.

1959. STEWART, Harold. 1960. *A Net of Fireflies: Japanese Haiku and Haika Paintings*. Rutland, VT: Tuttle. 180p. Notes & bibl. Index. LCCN:60-15603.

An attractive selection of haiku and paintings, arranged by seasons. No Japanese or romanized text. Includes a general essay on haiku and *haiga* [haiku painting].

1960. STEWART, Harold. 1969. *A Chime of Windbells: A Year of Japanese Haiku in English Verse*. Tokyo: Tuttle, 236p. Bibl. Index. LCCN:69-12084.

Another pleasant collection of haiku arranged by season, translated into couplets (no original or romanized texts). Ends with a long historical essay.

1961. TANAKA, F. Fukuzō, trans. 1938. *Songs of the Hyakunin-Isshu Anglicized*. [Los Angeles, CA: F.F. Tanaka.] 124p. LCCN:39-2889. [*Ogura hyakunin isshu*.]

Another translation of the *Hundred Poems by a Hundred Poets*.

1962. UNDERWOOD, Edna Worthley. 1919. *Moons of Nippon: Translations from Poets of Old Japan*. Chicago: Ralph Fletcher Seymour. 111p. 20 notes. LCCN:20-4080.

Brief introduction followed by a miscellaneous selection of poetry from the age of the *Man'yōshū* through the thirteenth century, translated into various formats. Brief headnotes for poems; no original or romanized text.

1963. WALEY, Arthur. 1919[1956]. *Japanese Poetry: The Uta*. London: Percy Lund, Humphries and Co. 110p. Bibl. LCCN:77-373293.

An early anthology of *tanka/waka* (*uta*), mostly from the *Man'yōshū* and the *Kokinshū*, with a very brief descriptive and historical introduction, a general guide to the grammar of classical Japanese and a small dictionary. Romanized texts accompany the translations. WALEY observes, "Since the classical language has an easy grammar and limited vocabulary a few months should suffice from the mastering of it" (p. 8).

1964. WATANABE, Tōkichi. 1959. *A Treasury of Japanese Literature*. Tokyo: Nihon Gakujutsu Shuppansha. 361p. Bibl.

An anthology of highlights of classical Japanese fiction and poetry with Japanese and English translation printed on opposite pages. Includes abundant footnotes in Japanese.

1965. WATSON, Burton. 1975. *Japanese Literature in Chinese. Volur
Prose in Chinese by Japanese Writers of the Early Period.* New York:
Press. 134p. Notes. LCCN:75-17896.

Excellent sensible and scholarly introduction to a neglected genre tr:
with men. Includes only one poem identified as being by a woman (Pr̶i̶n̶c̶e̶s̶s̶ ̶

1966. WATSON, Burton. 1976. *Japanese Literature in Chinese. Volume Two: Poetry and
Prose in Chinese by Japanese Writers of the Later Period.* New York: Columbia University
Press. 189p. Notes. Index. LCCN:75-15896.

This volume includes poems by two poets identified as women (EMA Saikō and ŌZAKI
Bunki). Provides a useful, brief historical introduction to Japanese literature written in
Chinese, a heretofore neglected topic in scholarship in English.

1967. WILSON, Graeme. Nov. 1980. "The poetry of Japanese women. [Part I.]" *Oriental
Economist* 48(841):32-33. ISSN:0030-5294.

1968. WILSON, Graeme. Dec. 1980. "The poetry of Japanese women. [Part II.]" *Oriental
Economist* 48(842):52-53. ISSN:0030-5294

A sampling of poems throughout the ages, apparently gathered to demonstrate the
translator's contention in Part I that in contrast to "the Western tradition," it is extremely
difficult to distinguish the poetry written by Japanese men from that written by Japanese
women, because, "the Japanese sensibility, not just in poetry but in all cultural fields, is,
by Western criteria, essentially feminine" (p. 33), and going on in Part II to point out some
distinguishing elements after all.

1969. WILSON, Graeme. Spring 1981. "Fifteen poems by Japanese women." *Asian and
Pacific Quarterly* 13(1):75-80. ISSN:0251-3110.

A mini-anthology of poetry from the earliest times to the present. Does not include
commentary, or romanized or original text. Nine women are represented.

1970. WILSON, Graeme. Fall 1983. "Kokinshu: The first imperial anthology of Japanese
poetry." *Asian Culture Quarterly* 1(3):75-83. No refs. ISSN:0378-8911.

Two pages of introductory remarks on the *Kokinshū* and earlier poetry, with emphasis on
Japanese writing systems, followed by elaborate translations of 33 *tanka/waka*.

1971. WILSON, Graeme. Spring 1986. "Selections from the Manyoshu." *Asian and Pacific
Quarterly of Cultural and Social Affairs* 18(1):55-65. ISSN:0251-3110.

A selection including poems by nine women in addition to "anonymous." No original or
romanized text, commentary, or biographical information.

1972. WILSON, Graeme. Autumn 1986. "Poems by Japanese women." *Asian and Pacific
Quarterly of Social and Cultural Affairs* 18(2):59-64. ISSN:0251-3110.

Translations (without original text) of 31 poems, all but two premodern, some anonymous.
No commentary or biographical information on poets.

1973. WRIGHT, Harold P. Autumn 1969. "The poetry of Japan." *Asia* [Asia Society, NY]
16:61-90. 11 notes.

A historical essay for the general reader, with a mini-anthology embedded in the prose. No
romanized texts. A few women are included in his selection.

1974. WRIGHT, Harold, trans. 1986. *Ten Thousand Leaves: Love Poems from the Manyōshū.*
Woodstock, NY: Overlook Press. 94p. 136 notes. LCCN:85-13681.

136 love poems in appealing translation into five lines and arranged by the translator into a thematic sequence, interspersed with an eclectic assortment of reproductions from Japanese art. The volume begins with a simple contextualizing introduction and concludes with biographical notes on the poets. No original or romanized text.

1975. YASUDA, Kenneth. 1947[1976]. *A Pepper-pod: A Haiku Sampler.* Rutland, VT: Tuttle. LCCN:76-351622. [Author also cited as Shōson.]

An introduction to the qualities of haiku (which YASUDA calls "versegrams") citing and discussing many examples followed by a sampling of Japanese haiku in English translation with romanized originals (to which he gives titles).

1976. YASUDA, Kenneth. 1957. *The Japanese Haiku: Its Essential Nature, History, and Possibilities in English with Selected Examples.* Rutland, VT: Tuttle. 232p. Bibl. Index. LCCN:57-8795.

A useful manual of haiku, presenting many rules and elements of composition. Among the "selected" examples are haiku by the prominent premodern women poets Chiyo(jo) and Ukō(ni).

1977. YASUDA, Kenneth. 1972. *Land of the Reed Plains: Ancient Japanese Lyrics from the Man'yōshū.* [Translated with comments by Kenneth YASUDA.] Rutland: Tuttle. [*Man'yōshū.* English and Japanese. Selections.] 124p. Index. LCCN:70-188015.

A brief sampling of short poetry from the 8th-century *Man'yōshū.* YASUDA includes an introduction for general readers. Biographical notes.

Premodern Poets

1978. Abe, Maiden/Lady / ABE no Iratsume (c. 740)

Man'yōshū poet, 8th century.

Poems on p. 87 in: CLACK (#1925), vol. 1.
Poems on pp. 32-33 in: HONDA (#1933).
Poems 269, 505, 506, 514 in: LEVY (#1938).
Poems on p. 145 in: MIYAMORI (#1946), vol. 1.
Poems on p. 115 in: Nippon Gakujutsu Shinkōkai (#1949).
Poem on p. 76 in: WILSON (#1969).

1979. Abutsu, Nun / Abutsu-ni (died c. 1283)

A lady-in-waiting to a princess who later became Ex-Empress Akamon'in; she was called Akamon'in no Shijō. In 1253 she became a wife of FUJIWARA no Tameie (son of FUJIWARA no Teika), then gave birth to Tamesuke, whose rights to Tameie's real and literary estate she vigorously defended. Known for *Izayoi nikki* [*Diary of the Waning Moon,* #1762], a poetic record of her journey from Kyoto to Kamakura in order to champion her son's rights to his father's legacy. She also wrote *Utatane* [#1774]. After Tameie's death in 1275 she took Buddhist vows as the Nun Abutsu.

Poems on pp. 78-83 in: CARTER (#1923).
Poems on p. 264 in: CLACK (#1925), vol. 1.
Poems on p. 78 in: COSMAN (#1926).
Poem on p. 45 in: REXROTH (#1954).

1980. Ae, Princess / Ae no Himemiko

Man'yōshū poet. Later became Empress Gemmyō [see #2010].

Poem 35 in: LEVY (#1938).

1981. Akai-ko (5th century)

According to MIYAMORI (#1946, p. 48), Akai-ko was observed as a beautiful young child by the Emperor Yūryaku (5th century), who told her to wait for him to send for her. She faithfully awaited the command, which never came, and as an old woman sought an audience with the Emperor. He was overcome by her faithfulness and recited two verses, to which she replied in kind.

Poem on p. 29 in: CLACK (#1925), vol. 1.
Poem on p. 49 in: MIYAMORI (#1946), vol. 1.

1982. Akazome Emon, Lady / Akazome no Emon (11th century)

An important court *tanka/waka* poet. Served Rinshi, daughter of FUJIWARA no Michinaga, the most powerful man of his day. Married a provincial official. Ninety-two of her poems are in Imperial anthologies. Known also for her personal poetry collection; traditionally regarded as one author of *Eiga monogatari* [*Tales of Flowering Fortunes*] [see #1759].

Poem on p. 55 in: BENNETT (#1914).
Poems on p. 204 in: CLACK (#1925), vol. 1.
Poem 59 in: GALT (#1927).
Poem on p. 94 in: KEENE (#1935).
Poem 44 in: LEVY (#1936).
Poem 180 in: LEVY (#1937).
Poem 59 in: MacCAULEY (#1939).
Poems on p. 324 in: MIYAMORI (#1946), vol. 1.
Poem 59 in: PORTER (#1951).
Poem on p. 9 in: REXROTH (#1952).
Poems on pp. 23-24 in: REXROTH (#1954).
Poem 59 in: TANAKA (#1961).

1983. Amaneiko / Assistant Handmaiden Amaneiko / HARUZUMI no Amaneiko (late 9th century)

Kokinshū tanka/waka poet. Daughter of HARUZUMI no Yoshinawa. Served as Palace Attendant [Naishi no suke].

Poem on p. 133 in: CLACK (#1925), vol. 1.
Poem 107 in: HONDA (#1934).
Poem 107 in: McCULLOUGH (#1942).
Poem on p. 230 in: MIYAMORI (#1946), vol. 1.
Poem 107 in: RODD (#1955).

1984. ANZAI Senchō-jo (d. 1802)

Haiku poet. From Kamakura. Her collected poems were published posthumously under the title of her death poem.

Poem on p. 282 in: HOFFMANN (#1932).

ARIWARA no Narihira, Mother of see *Itō, Princess [#2029]*

Asukabehime see *Kōmyō, Empress [#2057]*

1985. Ato Tobira, Maiden/Lady (8th century)

A young woman represented by one love poem in the *Man'yōshū*.

Poem 710 in: LEVY (#1938).

Poem on p. 238 in: Nippon Gakujutsu Shinkōkai (#1949).
Poem 16 in: WALEY (#1963).
Poem on p. 22 in: WRIGHT (#1974).

1986. Awata, Princess / Awata Joō (d. 764)

Represented in the *Man'yōshū* by one *tanka* composed at a banquet in 744.

Poem on p. 36 in: YASUDA (#1977).

1987. Awatame, Maiden / Awatame no Otome

Author of two love poems in the *Man'yōshū* addressed to Ōtomo no Yakamochi, poet and compiler of the *Man'yōshū*.

Poems 707 and 708 in: LEVY (#1938).

Chigetsu see **KAWAI Chigetsu [#2044]**

Chikami no Otome see **Sano no Chigami [#2110]**

1988. Chine/Chine-jo (1660?-1688)

Haiku poet. Sister of Bashō; disciple of MUKAI Kyorai.

Poem in: BEILENSON (#1913) [unpaginated].
Poem on p. 810 in: BLYTH (#1915), vol. 3.
Poems on pp. 217-218 in: BLYTH (#1916), vol. 1.
Poem on p. 149 in: HOFFMANN (#1932).
Poems on p. 175 in: MINER (#1944).
Poem on pp. 418-419 in: MIYAMORI (#1945).
Poem on p. 52 in: REXROTH (#1954).

1989. Chiyo/Chiyo-jo/Chiyo-ni / FUKUDA Chiyo-ni / Kaga no Chiyo/Chiyo-jo (1703?-1775)

Well-known haiku poet from Kaga Province. It is not clear where she studied haiku, but by age 16 or 17 she had already gained a reputation as a poet. Two anthologies of her poems were published during her lifetime. She became a Buddhist nun at age 52 (and her name was changed to Chiyo-ni).

"Dead child." Jul. 1982. [Translated by Graeme WILSON.] *Ariel* [Calgary, Alberta] 13(Jul. 1982):50. ISSN:0004-1372.
Poems in: BEHN (#1911) [unpaginated].
Poem in: BEHN (#1912) [unpaginated].
Poems in: BEILENSON (#1913) [unpaginated].
Poems on pp. 430, 468, 542, 582 in: BLYTH (#1915), vol. 2.
Poems on pp. 681, 796, 812, 934, 971 in: BLYTH (#1915), vol. 3.
Poems on pp. 1074, 1102, 1193 in: BLYTH (#1915), vol. 4.
Poems on pp. 218-225 in: BLYTH (#1916), vol. 1.
Poem on p. xli in: BLYTH (#1916), vol. 2.
Poem on p. 66 in: BOSLEY (#1917).
Poems on pp. 66-69, 95-96 in: BUCHANAN (#1922).
Poems on pp. 299-301 in: CHAMBERLAIN (#1924).
Poems on pp. 354-355 in: CLACK (#1925), vol. 2.
Poem on p. 152 in: COSMAN (#1926).
Poems on p. 63 in: HENDERSON (#1928).
Poem on pp. 82-85 in: HENDERSON (#1929).
Poem on p. 117 in: HIGGINSON (#1930).
Poem on p. 152 in: HOFFMANN (#1932).
Poem on p. 65 in: Nippon Gakujutsu Shinkōkai (#1948).

Poems on pp. 134-138 in: PAGE (#1950).
Poem on pp. 53-54 in: REXROTH (#1954).
Poem on p. 119 in: SATŌ (#1957).
Poems on pp. 14, 55, 65, 72 & 88 in: STEWART (#1959).
Poems on pp. 54, 86-87, 126 in: STEWART (#1960).
Poem on p. 53 in: WILSON (#1968).
Poem on p. 79 in: WILSON (#1969).
Poems on pp. 45-46 in: YASUDA (#1975).
Poems on p. 190 in: YASUDA (#1976).

1990. A Court Lady

A consort of the Emperor Tenji. Author of one poem in the *Man'yōshū*, on the death of Emperor Tenji in 671.

Poem on p. 12 in: BOWNAS (#1918).
Poem 150 in: LEVY (#1938).
Poem on p. 14 in: Nippon Gakujutsu Shinkōkai (#1949).

1991. Daibu, Lady / Kenrei Mon'in Ukyō no Daibu (fl. c. 1200)

A court lady; when she was young she served Empress Tokuko, who was later known as Kenrei Mon'in (1155-1213). Twenty-three of her *tanka/waka* are included in Imperial anthologies, but she is best known for her poetic memoirs, which depict the tumultuous period of the Gempei Wars at the end of the 12th century from the point of view of a woman.

The Poetic Memoirs of Lady Daibu. 1980. Phillip Tudor HARRIES. Stanford: Stanford University Press. 324p. Bibl. LCCN:79-65519. [*Kenreimon-in Ukyō no Daibu shū*.]
Poems on pp. 352-353 in: MIYAMORI (#1946), vol. 1.
Poems on p. 3 in: REXROTH (#1954).

Daihaku, Princess see **Ōku, Princess [#2090]**

1992. Daini [no] Sammi (fl. c. 1100)

FUJIWARA no Katako, daughter of Murasaki Shikibu [#2079]. A *tanka/waka* poet.

Poem on p. 75 in: BENNETT (#1914).
Poems on p. 406 in: BROWER (#1919).
Poem on p. 211 in: CLACK (#1925), vol. 1.
Poem 58 in: GALT (#1927).
Poem 58 in: MacCAULEY (#1939).
Poem 58 in: PORTER (#1951).
Poem on p. 27 in: REXROTH (#1954).
Poem 58 in: TANAKA (#1961).

1993. Daisaiin Senshi (964-1035)

Tanka/waka poet. Daughter of Emperor Murakami. Became the Priestess of the Imperial family at the Kamo Shrine at the age of 12 and served there until illness forced her to retire at age 68. In later years became a devout Buddhist; considered *tanka/waka* a form of Buddhist spiritual training.

The Buddhist Poetry of the Great Kamo Priestess Daisaiin Senshi and Hosshin Wakashū. By Edward KAMENS. 1990. Ann Arbor, MI: University of Michigan, Center for Japanese Studies. 170p. Notes. LCCN:89-71219.

1994. DEN Sute-jo (1634-1698)

Haiku poet, *tanka/waka* poet. From a wealthy merchant family in Hyōgo Prefecture. Married at 18 and bore six children. Became a Buddhist nun at age 41, after the death of her husband, and devoted herself to religion and to poetry. She studied haiku with KITAMURA Kigin (1624-1705). There is a personal collection of her poems.

Poem on p. 823 in: BLYTH (#1915), vol. 3.
Poems on pp. 210-211 in: BLYTH (#1916), vol. 1.
Poems on pp. 317-318 in: CHAMBERLAIN (#1924).
Poems on pp. 409-410 in: MIYAMORI (#1945).
Poems on p. 50 in: REXROTH (#1954).
Poem on p. 104 in: STEWART (#1959).
Poem on p. 53 in: STEWART (#1960).
Poem on p. 47 in: YASUDA (#1975).

Den-jo see *Taniguchi Den-jo [#2138]*

Eguchi, Lady see *Shirome [#2118]*

Eguchi Sarome see *Shirome [#2118]*

1995. Eifuku, Empress/Ex-Empress / Eifuku Mon'in (1271-1342)

Consort of Emperor Fushimi from 1388; both were outstanding poet-patrons of the Kyōgoku style during difficult political times when the Nijō style of poetry also tended to dominate.

Poems on pp. 32 (repeated on p. 402), 353, 357, 372-373, 377, 379, 381 (repeated on p. 448), 381 (repeated on p. 449), 386, 395 and 396 in: BROWER (#1919).
Poems on pp. 140-150 in: CARTER (#1923).
Poems on p. 263 in: CLACK (#1925), vol. 1.
Poem on p. 21 in: HOFFMANN (#1932).
Poems on pp. 127, 130-131 and 136 in: MINER (#1943).
Poems on pp. 433-434 in: MIYAMORI (#1946), vol. 1.
Poem on p. 187 in: MIYAMORI (#1947).
Poem on p. 21 in: REXROTH (#1953).
Poem on p. 78 in: WILSON (#1969).

1996. EMA SAIKŌ (1787-1861)

A student of RAI San'yō who wrote poetry in Chinese.

"To inscribe on my portrait," on p. 58 in: WATSON (#1966), vol. 2.

1997. ENOMOTO Seifu/Seifu-jo/Seifu-ni (1732-1814)

Haiku poet and compiler. From Musashi (Hachiōji) near Tokyo. At 39, after the death of her husband, she became active in *haikai* [haiku linked-verse] circles, studying under several masters.

Poem in: BEILENSON (#1913) [unpaginated].
Poem on p. 464 in: BLYTH (#1915), vol. 2.
Poem on p. 1263 in: BLYTH (#1915), vol. 4.
Poem on p. 13 in: BLYTH (#1916), vol. 2.
Poem on p. 48 in: BUCHANAN (#1922).
Poem p. 117 in: HENDERSON (#1929).
Poems on pp. 579-580 in: MIYAMORI (#1945).
Poem on p. 56 in: REXROTH (#1954).
Poems on p. 70 in: YASUDA (#1975).

1998. Ensei Mon'in Shindainagon (fl. ca. 1280)

Tanka/waka poet.

Poem on p. 383 in: BROWER (#1919).

1999. FUJIWARA, Lady / FUJIIWARA Family, Concubine from / FUJIWARA no Iratsume (late 7th century)

Man'yōshū poet. Daughter of FUJIWARA Kamatari, wife of Emperor Temmu, with whom she exchanged poems included in the *Man'yōshū*.

Poem on p. 48 in: BARON (#1910).
Poem on p. 11 in: HONDA (#1933).
Poems 104 and 766 in: LEVY (#1938).
Poem on p. 17 in: Nippon Gakujutsu Shinkōkai (#1949).

2000. FUJIWARA Kōshi/Takaiko (842-910)

Kokinshū tanka/waka poet. Grand Empress (Kōtaigō), called Nijō no Kisaki [Nijō Empress]. Daughter of Nagara; sister of Mototsune; consort of Emperor Seiwa, Mother of Emperor Yōzei.

Poem 4 in: HONDA (#1934).
Poem 4 in: McCULLOUGH (#1942).
Poem 4 in: RODD (#1955).

2001. FUJIWARA no Hyōe fl. ca. 900

Kokinshū tanka/waka poet. Wife of FUJIWARA no Tadafusa.

Poems 455 & 789 in: HONDA (#1934).
Poems 455 & 789 in: McCULLOUGH (#1942).
Poems 455 & 789 in: RODD (#1955).

2002. FUJIWARA no Katsumi (late 10th century)

Little known *tanka/waka* poet. The *tanka/waka* below is from the *Gosenshū Imperial Anthology*.

Poem 8 in: LEVY (#1936).
Poem 69 in: LEVY (#1937).

2003. FUJIWARA no Korechika, Mother of / Gidō Sanshi/Sanji, Mother of / Takako

Tanka/waka in *Hyakunin isshu* [*One Hundred Poems by One Hundred Poets*]. Mother of FUJIWARA Korechika / Gidō Sanshi, Minister of State.

Poem 54 in: GALT (#1927).
Poem on p. 195 in: KEENE (#1935).
Poem 148 in: LEVY (#1937).
Poem 54 in: MacCAULEY (#1939).
Poem 54 in: PORTER (#1951).
Poem 54 in: TANAKA (#1961).

2004. FUJIWARA no Michitsuna's Mother / Commander Michitsuna, Mother of (937?-995)

Poet and author of *Kagerō nikki* [*The Gossamer Years*]. Related to many of the greatest women of her day. Known as a beauty. Second wife of FUJIWARA no Kaneie, one of the most important men of his day.

The Gossamer Years: The Diary of a Noblewoman of Heian Japan. 1964. [Translated by Edward SEIDENSTICKER.] Rutland, VT: Tuttle. 201p. 552 notes. LCCN:64-22750. [Kagerō nikki.]
Poem 23 in: LEVY (#1937).
Poem on p. 50 in: REXROTH (#1952).
Poems on p. 26 in: REXROTH (#1954).

2005. FUJIWARA no Naoiko/Chokushi (fl. ca. 900)

Kokinshū tanka/waka poet.

Poem 807 in: HONDA (#1934).
Poem 807 in: MCCULLOUGH (#1942).
Poem 807 in: RODD (#1955).

2006. FUJIWARA no Nobunari, Daughter of / Sukeko, Lady-in-Waiting to Empress Inbu / Inbu Mon'in no Taifu Sukeko / Inbu-monin no taifu

Lady-in-waiting to Empress Inbu, daughter of FUJIWARA no Nobunari. Tanka/waka poet. Represented in Hyakunin isshu [One Hundred Poems by One Hundred Poets].

Poem 90 in: GALT (#1927).
Poems 47 & 125 in: LEVY (#1937).
Poem 90 in: MacCAULEY (#1939).
Poem 90 in: PORTER (#1951).
Poem 90 in: TANAKA (#1961).
Poem on p. 52 in: WILSON (#1968).

2007. FUJIWARA no Shunzei, (Adopted) Daughter of / FUJIWARA no Toshinari, (Adopted) Daughter of / Shunzei's (Adopted) Daughter (fl. ca. 1200)

Prominent Shinkokinshū tanka/waka poet; adopted daughter (actually granddaughter) of the great Shinkokinshū poet Shunzei.

Poem on p. 59 in: BENNETT (#1914).
Poems on pp. 274, 289, 315 in: BROWER (#1919).
Poems 100, 108, 111, 116, 225, 280, 283 in: LEVY (#1937).
Poems on pp. 119-120 in: MINER (#1943).
Poems on pp. 430-431 in: MIYAMORI (#1946), vol. 1.
Poems on pp. 43-44 in: REXROTH (#1954).
Poem on p. 63 in: WILSON (#1972).

FUJIWARA no Tameko see Junii, Lady Tameko [#2033]

2008. FUJIWARA no Yoruka, Lady (9th century)

Kokinshū tanka/waka poet. Probably served in Handmaid's Office at the Imperial Palace.

Poems 80, 364, 736, 738 in: HONDA (#1934).
Poems 80, 364, 736, 738 in: McCULLOUGH (#1942).
Poem on p. 226 in: MIYAMORI (#1946), vol. 1.
Poems 80, 364, 736, 738 in: RODD (#1955).
Poem on p. 80 in: WILSON (#1970).

2009. Fuki, Lady (7th century)

Early Man'yōshū poet. Served Princess Toochi, daughter of Emperor Temmu.

Poem on p. 66 in: Nippon Gakujutsu Shinkōkai (#1949).
Poem on p. 43 in: YASUDA (#1977).

FUKUDA Chiyo-ni see *Chiyo [#1989]*

2010. Gemmyō, Empress (661-721)

Daughter of Emperor Tenji, mother of Emperor Mommu, whom she succeeded as 43rd sovereign. Ordered compilation of early histories including the *Kojiki* [#5]. Composed two poems in the *Man'yōshū*, one under the name of Princess Ae [#1980].

Poem 76 in: LEVY (#1938).
Poem on p. 81 in: Nippon Gakujutsu Shinkōkai (#1949).
Poem on p. 28 in: YASUDA (#1977).

2011. Genshō, Empress (680-748)

Author of one poem in the *Man'yōshū*. Daughter of Empress Gemmyō [#2010]. Reigned for nine years as 44th sovereign.

Poem on p. 65 in: CLACK (#1925), vol. 1.
Poem on p. 81 in: Nippon Gakujutsu Shinkōkai (#1949).

Gidō Sanshi, Mother of see *FUJIWARA no Korechika, Mother of [#2003]*

2012. Giō (12th century)

Legendary consort of TAIRA no Kiyomori who turned nun and withdrew to Saga, west of Kyoto. Her story is told in the *Heike monogatari* [*Tales of Heike*], from which the poem cited below is quoted.

Poem on p. 38 in: REXROTH (#1954).

Girl in Harima Province see *Harima, Young woman of [#2015]*

2013. Go Dan'ochi, Wife of (7th century)

Author of one poem, to her husband, in the *Man'yōshū*. Nothing else is known about her.

Poem 500 in: LEVY (#1938).
Poem on p. 66 in: Nippon Gakujutsu Shinkōkai (#1949).

2014. Hakuni (1755?-1817)

Haiku poet.

Poem on p. 182 in: HOFFMANN (#1932).

2015. Harima, Young Woman of / Harima no Otome (early 8th century)

Author of two farewell love poems in the *Man'yōshū*. Nothing else is known about her.

Poem on p. 151 in: MIYAMORI (#1946), vol. 1.
Poem on p. 93 in: MIYAMORI (#1947).
Poem on p. 239 in: Nippon Gakujutsu Shinkōkai (#1949).
Poem on p. 58 in: WRIGHT (#1974).
Poem on p. 70 in: YASUDA (#1977).

Hashibito, Empress see *Nakatsu, Princess [#2081]*

2016. Heguri, Lady (9th century)

Two love poems by her in the *Man'yōshū* are addressed to poet ŌTOMO no Yakamochi, one compiler of the *Man'yōshū*.

Poem on p. 43 in: BENNETT (#1914).
Poem on p. 58 in: BOWNAS (#1918).
Poems on pp. 115-116 in: Nippon Gakujutsu Shinkōkai (#1949).
Poems on pp. 76-77 in: WILSON (#1969).
Poem on p. 60 in: WILSON (#1971).

2017. Hirokawa, Princess (9th century)

Author of two love poems in the *Man'yōshū*. Great granddaughter of Emperor Temmu.

Poem on p. 57 in: BOWNAS (#1918).
Poem on p. 40 in: KEENE (#1935).
Poems 694 and 695 in: LEVY (#1938).
Poem on p. 92 in: Nippon Gakujutsu Shinkōkai (#1949).
Poem on p. 32 in: WILSON (#1967).
Poem on p. 59 in: WILSON (#1971).
Poem on p. 695 in: WRIGHT (#1974).

2018. Hitachi, Maiden of/A Young Woman of / Hitachi no Otome

Author of one farewell love poem in the *Man'yōshū*.

Poem 521 in: LEVY (#1938).
Poem on p. 239 in: Nippon Gakujutsu Shinkōkai (#1949).

2019. Hitomaro, Wife of (7th century)

KAKINOMOTO Hitomaro is generally regarded as the greatest poet of the *Man'yōshū*. This woman is credited with one poem addressed to him in the *Man'yōshū*. Nothing else is known of her.

Poem 504 in: LEVY (#1938).

2020. Horikawa, Lady/Lady-in-Waiting (early 12th century)

Tanka/waka poet, represented in *Hyakunin isshu* [*One Hundred Poems by One Hundred Poets*]. Attendant to the retired Empress Taiken.

Poem on p. 74 in: BENNETT (#1914).
Poem on p. 216 in: CLACK (#1925), vol. 1.
Poem 80 in: GALT (#1927).
Poem 26 in: LEVY (#1937).
Poem 80 in: MacCAULEY (#1939).
Poem 80 in: PORTER (#1951).
Poem on p. 32 in: REXROTH (#1952).
Poem on p. 41 in: REXROTH (#1954).
Poem 80 in: TANAKA (#1961).
Poem on p. 77 in: UNDERWOOD (#1962).

2021. Ichi-jo (18th century)

Haiku poet, native of Ise Province.

Poem on p. 588 in: MIYAMORI (#1945).

ICHIHARA Tayo-jo   see   *Tayo-jo [#2141]*

2022. IMAIZUMI Sogetsu-ni (late 18th c.)

Haiku poet.

> Poem on p. 1030 in: BLYTH (#1915), vol. 4.
> Poems on pp. 14 in: BLYTH (#1916), vol. 2.
> Poem on p. 83 in: BUCHANAN (#1922).
> Poem on p. 378 in: CLACK (#1925), vol. 2.
> Poem on pp. 584-585 in: MIYAMORI (#1945).
> Poem on p. 58 in: REXROTH (#1954).
> Poem on p. 70 in: YASUDA (#1975).

2023. Inaba, Daughter of Prince Motoyo (fl. ca. 900)

Kokinshū tanka/waka poet; daughter of Prince Motoyo, who was appointed provincial governor of Inaba in 889; lady-in-waiting.

> Poem 808 in: HONDA (#1934).
> Poem 808 in: McCULLOUGH (#1942).
> Poem 808 in: RODD (#1955).

> **Inbu Mon'in no Taifu Sukeko** see *FUJIWARA no Nobunari, Daughter of [#2006]*

> **Inno Betto** see *Kōka, Stewardess of Empress [#2055]*

2024. Ise, Lady (c.877-939)

Kokinshū tanka/waka poet known for 22 poems; author of a personal poetry collection, the *Ise-shū*. Her father was provincial governor of Ise from 885 to 890, FUJIWARA Tsugukage. She was a lady-in-waiting to Empress Onshi, a consort to Emperor Uda, and mother of the poet Nakatsukasa.

> Poem on p. 21 in: BARON (#1910).
> Poems on pp. 43 & 72 in: BENNETT (#1914).
> Poems on p. 56 in: BOSLEY (#1917).
> Poem on p. 84 in: BOWNAS (#1918).
> Poems on pp. 202 and 211 in: BROWER (#1919).
> Poem on pp. 244-245 in: BROWER (#1920).
> Poem 47 on pp. 94-95, 49 on pp. 96-97 and 69 on pp. 116-117 in: BROWER (#1921).
> Poems on p. 134 in: CLACK (#1925), vol. 1.
> Poem on p. 183 in: HIGGINSON (#1930).
> Poems 31, 43, 44, 61, 68, 138, 459. 676, 681, 733, 741, 756, 780, 791, 810, 920, 926, 968, 990, 1000, 1006, 1051 in: HONDA (#1934).
> Poems on p. 79 in: KEENE (#1935).
> Poems 62, 77, 113, 120, 159 & 294 in: LEVY (#1937).
> Poems 31, 43, 44, 61, 68, 138, 459. 676, 681, 733, 741, 756, 780, 791, 810, 920, 926, 968, 990, 1000, 1006, 1051 in: McCULLOUGH (#1942).
> Poems on p. 95 in: MINER (#1943).
> Poems on pp. 703 in: MINER (#2180).
> Poems on pp. 224-225 in: MIYAMORI (#1946), vol. 1.
> Poem on p. 33 in: REXROTH (#1952).
> Poems on pp. 17-18 in: REXROTH (#1954).
> Poems 31, 43, 44, 61, 68, 138, 459. 676, 681, 733, 741, 756, 780, 791, 810, 920, 926, 968, 990, 1000, 1006, 1051 in: RODD (#1955).
> Poems on pp. 127-129 in: SATO (#1956).
> Poem on p. 51 in: UNDERWOOD (#1962).
> Poem on p. 94 in: WALEY (#1963).
> Poem on p. 64 in: WATANABE (#1964).
> Poem on p. 32 in: WILSON (#1967).

Poems on pp. 77 & 79 in: WILSON (#1970).
Poem on p. 61 in: WILSON (#1972).

2025. Ise, Shrine Princess (9th century)

Exchanged *tanka/waka* with the eminent poet and romantic hero ARIWARA no Narihira in the *Ise monogatari* [*Tales of Ise*]; also included in the *Kokinshū*.

Poem on p. 85 in: MINER (#1943).

2026. Ise Tayū / Ise no Taifu, Lady (987?-1063?)

Tanka/waka poet. Lady-in-waiting to Empress Jōtō Mon'in. Represented in the *Hyakunin isshu* [*One Hundred Poems from 100 Poets*].

Poem 61 in: GALT (#1927).
Poem 61 in: MacCAULEY (#1939).
Poems on pp. 315-317 in: MIYAMORI (#1946), vol. 1.
Poem on p. 145 in: MIYAMORI (#1947).
Poem 61 in: PORTER (#1951).
Poems on pp. 30-33 in: REXROTH (#1954).
Poem 61 in: TANAKA (#1961).

2027. ISHIKAWA, Lady / ISHIKAWA no Iratsume

One woman by this name was a prominent early *Manyōshū* poet, known for witty dialogue poems and exchanges of poems with men. She was a court lady during the time of Prince Ōtsu (663-686). It is not clear, however, that all the poems below are all by the same Lady Ishikawa.

Poem on p. 13 in: BOWNAS (#1918).
Poem on p. 3 in: CLACK (#1925), vol. 1.
Poem on p. 10 in: HONDA (#1933).
Poems 97-98, 108, 126, 128-129, 518 in: LEVY (#1938).
Poem on p. 116 in: MIYAMORI (#1946), vol. 1.
Poem on p. 81 in: MIYAMORI (#1947).
Poems on pp. 19 and 59 in: Nippon Gakujutsu Shinkōkai (#1949).
Poem on p. 27 in: UNDERWOOD (#1962).
Poem on p. 52 in: WILSON (#1968).
Poem on p. 62 in: WILSON (#1971).
Poem on p. 78 in: WRIGHT (#1974).
Poem on p. 51 in: YASUDA (#1977).

2028. ISHIKAWA Concubine / Ishikawa no Bunin / ISHIKAWA Family, Concubine from the (7th century)

Apparently a concubine of the Emperor Tenji (d. 671). Author of one *Man'yōshū* poem mourning his death.

Poem 154 in: LEVY (#1938).

2029. Itō, Princess / ARIWARA no Narihira, Mother of (d. 861)

Kokinshū tanka/waka poet. Represented by one poem in the *Kokinshū*, addressed to her son, Narihira, one of the most important poets of his day. Daughter of Emperor Kammu.

Poem 900 in: HONDA (#1934).
Poem 900 in: McCULLOUGH (#1942).
Poem 900 in: RODD (#1955).

2030. *Iwa no Hime, Empress (d. 347)*

Early love poems in the *Manyōshū* attributed to her. Empress-consort of Emperor Nintoku, to whom all the following poems are addressed.

Poem on p. 54 in: BENNETT (#1914).
Poems on pp. 6-7 in: BOWNAS (#1918).
Poems on pp. 8-9 in: HONDA (#1933).
Poems 85-89 in: LEVY (#1938).
Poems on pp. 6-7 in: Nippon Gakujutsu Shinkōkai (#1949).
Poem on p. 62 in: WILSON (#1971).
Poem on p. 66 in: WRIGHT (#1974).
Poem on p. 23 in: YASUDA (#1977).

2031. *Izumi Shikibu / Lady Izumi (born ca. 976)*

Major *tanka/waka* poet; lady-in-waiting in the salon of Akiko (Shōshi), daughter of Michinaga, consort of Emperor Ichijō. Rival of Murasaki Shikibu. Assumed to be the author of the *Izumi Shikibu nikki [Izumi Shikibu Diary]*. Known for her passionate style; with ONO no Komachi, an inspiration to women writing poetry (and fiction) in this century.

The *Izumi Shikibu Diary: A Romance of the Heian Court.* 1969. Edwin A. CRANSTON. Cambridge: Harvard University Press. (Harvard-Yenching Institute. *Monograph Series*, vol. 19.) 332p. 717 notes. LCCN:69-13766. Selections also translated in: *Japanese Poetic Diaries* by Earl MINER. 1969. Berkeley: University of California Press, pp. 93-153. LCCN:69-11846; and in: OMORI, Annie Shepley and Kochi DOI. 1920 [1961, corrected reprint edition]. *Diaries of Court Ladies of Old Japan*. Tokyo: Kenkyusha, pp. 149-196. [*Izumi Shikibu nikki*.]
Poem on p. 46 in: BENNETT (#1914).
Poems on pp. 218, 222, 227 in: BROWER (#1919).
Poems on pp. 244-245 in: BROWER (#1920).
Poem 32 on pp. 78-79 in: BROWER (#1921).
Poems on pp. 163-165 in: CLACK (#1925), vol. 1.
Poems on p. 76 in: COSMAN (#1926).
Poem on p. 6 In: CRANSTON, Edwin A. 1983. "Waka translations: Prismatics." *Stone Lion Review* 11:5-7. No refs. ISSN:0747-6744.
Poem 56 in: GALT (#1927).
Poems on pp. 41-116 in: HIRSHFIELD (#1931).
Poems on pp. 92 and 94 in: KEENE (#1935).
Poems 21, 30, 31, 34, 40, 54, 65 in: LEVY (#1936).
Poems 6, 38, 46, 54, 65, 72, 119, 128-134, 143, 173-177 in: LEVY (#1937).
Poem 56 in: MacCAULEY (#1939).
Poems on p. 29, 127 and 135 in: MATSUHARA (#1940).
Poems on pp. 23, 95-96 in: MINER (#1943).
Poems on pp. 298-301 in: MIYAMORI (#1946), vol. 1.
Poem on p. 138 in: MIYAMORI (#1947).
Poem 56 in: PORTER (#1951).
Poem on p. 34 in: REXROTH (#1952).
Poems on pp. 26–28 in: REXROTH (#1953).
Poems on pp. 28–29 in: REXROTH (#1954).
Poems on pp. 142-148 in: SATO (#1956).
Poems on pp. 102-103 in: SATŌ (#1958). [Translated by MATSUHARA Iwao.]
Poem 56 in: TANAKA (#1961).
Poem on pp. 69 and 71 in: UNDERWOOD (#1962).
Poems on pp. 86 and 89 in: WALEY (#1963).
Poem on p. 33 in: WILSON (#1967).
Poems on p. 62 in: WILSON (#1972).

2032. Jitō, Empress (645-702)

Early *Manyōshū* poet. Daughter of Emperor Tenji, Empress-Consort of Emperor Temmu, who founded the capital at Asuka in Yamato, and mother of Emperor Mommu. She was the reigning empress for ten years.

Poem on p. 14 in: BOWNAS (#1918).
Poem on p. 35 in: CLACK (#1925), vol. 1.
Poem on p. 73 in: COSMAN (#1926).
Poem 2 in: GALT (#1927).
Poem on p. 17 in: HONDA (#1933).
Poems 28, 236 (questionable attribution) in: LEVY (#1938).
Poem 2 in: MacCAULEY (#1939).
Poem on p. 107-109 in: MIYAMORI (#1946), vol. 1.
Poems on pp. 17 and 19 in: Nippon Gakujutsu Shinkōkai (#1949).
Poem 2 in: PORTER (#1951).
Poems on pp. 6-7 in: REXROTH (#1954).
Poems on p. 23 in: SATO (#1956).
Poem 2 in: TANAKA (#1961).
Poem on p. 40 in: YASUDA (#1977).

2033. Jūnii, Lady Tameko / FUJIWARA no Tameko (13th century)

Tanka/waka poet. Older sister of KYŌGOKU Tamekane. Served Eifuku Mon'in.

Poem on p. 218 in: CLACK (#1925), vol. 1.
Poem on p. 33 in: WILSON (#1967).

2034. Jūsammi Chikako, Lady / Chikako of the Third Rank (fl. ca. 1290-1310)

Tanka/waka poet of the Kyōgoku style. From a high aristocratic background and a family of poets. Served Emperor Fushimi, poet and patron of the Kyōgoku poets.

Poems on pp. 363, 380, 400, and 406 in: BROWER (#1919).
Poems on pp. 120-126 in: CARTER (#1923).
Poems on pp. 132-133 in: MINER (#1943).
Poem on p. 62 in: WILSON (#1972).

2035. Kaga, Lady-in-Waiting (fl. early 12th century)

Tanka/waka poet. Only one extant poem.

Poem 58 in: LEVY (#1937).

Kaga, Princess see **Kagami, Princess [#2036]**

Kaga no Chiyo / Kaga no Chiyo-jo see **Chiyo [#1989]**

2036. Kagami, Princess (fl. 650-700)

Early *Manyōshū* poet. Possibly the younger sister of Princess Nukada; wife of FUJIWARA Kamatari, who was the founder of the Fujiwara line.

Poem on p. 10 in: BOWNAS (#1918).
Poem on p. 30 in: HONDA (#1933).
Poems 92, 93 and 489 in: LEVY (#1938).
Poem on p. 12 in: Nippon Gakujutsu Shinkōkai (#1949).
Poem on p. 52 in: WRIGHT (#1974).

2037. Kamo, Princess

Man'yōshū poet. Daughter of the Chinese-style and *tanka* poet Prince Nagaya (676-729).

Poems 556 and 565 in: LEVY (#1938).
Poem on p. 55 in: WRIGHT (#1974).

2038. KAMUNAGIBE Maso, Maiden / KANNAGIBE Maso, Lady

Two love poems in the *Man'yōshū* attributed to her. No biographical data.

Poems 703-704 in: LEVY (#1938).
Poem on p. 67 in: WRIGHT (#1974).

Kana-jo see Mukai Kana-jo [#2078]

2039. Kan-in, Lady / Kan'in no Myōbu (fl. ca. 900s)

Tanka/waka poet. Represented in the *Kokinshū* by two poems.

Poem on p. 159 in: CLACK (#1925), vol. 1.
Poems 740 & 837 in: HONDA (#1934).
Poems 740 & 837 in: McCULLOUGH (#1942).
Poem on p. 307 in: MIYAMORI (#1946), vol. 1.
Poems 740 & 837 in: RODD (#1955).

2040. Kan'in Fifth Princess / Kan'in no Go no Miko

One *Kokinshū tanka/waka* attributed to her. Wife of Prince Atsunori (son of Emperor Uda), to whom the poem was addressed. Otherwise unknown.

Poem 857 in: HONDA (#1934).
Poem 857 in: McCULLOUGH (#1942).
Poem 857 in: RODD (#1955).

KANNAGIBE Maso, Lady see KAMUNAGIBE Maso, Maiden [#2038]

2041. KASA, Lady / KASA no Iratsume (8th century)

Poet of the *Man'yōshū*, which contains 29 *tanka* by her addressed to the preeminent poet ŌTOMO no Yakamochi, one of the compilers of the anthology.

Poems on p. 58 in: BOWNAS (#1918).
Poems on p. 69 in: CLACK (#1925), vol. 1.
Poem on p. 73 in: COSMAN (#1926).
Poems 395-397 and 587-610 in: LEVY (#1938).
Poem on pp. 97-98 in: MIYAMORI (#1946), vol. 1.
Poem on p. 72 in: MIYAMORI (#1947).
Poems on pp. 106-108 in: Nippon Gakujutsu Shinkōkai (#1949).
Poems on pp. 40-41 in: REXROTH (#1952).
Poem on p. 32 in: REXROTH (#1953).
Poems on p. 13 in: REXROTH (#1954).
Poems on pp. 65-68 in: SATO (#1956).
Poem on p. 27 in: WALEY (#1963).
Poems on p. 59 in: WILSON (#1971).
Poems on p. 59 in: WILSON (#1972).
Poems 18, 29, 36, 45, and 82 in: WRIGHT (#1974).
Poem on p. 67 in: YASUDA (#1977).

2042. Kasanui, Princess (7th or 8th century)

Unknown *Man'yōshū* poet.

Poem on p. 53 in: WRIGHT (#1974).

2043. Kasen-ni (d. 1729)

Haiku poet. A nun.

Poem on p. 218 in: HOFFMANN (#1932).

2044. KAWAI Chigetsu/Chigetsu-ni (1632-1706) / KAAI Chigetsu

Haiku poet. From Kyoto Prefecture; apparently served in the Imperial Palace. Married a merchant. When he died in 1656, she became a nun. She and her adopted son, the haiku poet Otokuni, were both students of Bashō.

Poem on p. 493 in: BLYTH (#1915), vol. 2.
Poem on p. 1036 in: BLYTH (#1915), vol. 4.
Poems on pp. 194 [questionable attribution], 207-210 in: BLYTH (#1916), vol. 1.
Poems on pp. 339-340 in: CHAMBERLAIN (#1924).
Poem on p. 309 in: CLACK (#1925), vol. 2.
Poem on p. 111 in: MAYHEW (#1941).
Poems on pp. 121, 135, 151, 223, & 323 in: MINER (#1944).
Poems on pp. 411-414 in: MIYAMORI (#1945).
Poem on pp. 38 in: Nippon Gakujutsu Shinkōkai (#1948).
Poems on p. 49 in: REXROTH (#1954).
Poems on pp. 323-324; poetic prose on p. 325 in: SATŌ (#1956).
Poem on p. 33 in: WILSON (#1967).
Poem on p. 48 in: YASUDA (#1975).

2045. Kaya no Otome / Kaya, Maiden / Kusa no Iratsume (Ukareme) (7th century)

Credited with one poem in the *Man'yōshū*. Possibly a consort of Emperor Jomei (reigned (629)-641).

Poem 512 in: LEVY (#1938).

Kenrei Mon'in Ukyō no Daibu see *Daibu, Lady [#1991]*

2046. KI, Lady / KI no Iratsume (8th century)

Man'yōshū poet (KI no Iratsume). Given name Ojika/Wojika. A consort of Prince Aki; exchanged poems with Ōtomo no Yakamochi.

Poem on p. 59 in: BOWNAS (#1918).
Poem on p. 89 in: CLACK (#1925), vol. 1.
Poems 643-645, 762-763, 782 in: LEVY (#1938).
Poem on p. 149 in: MIYAMORI (#1946), vol. 1.
Poem on p. 181 in: Nippon Gakujutsu Shinkōkai (#1949).
Poem on p. 12 in: REXROTH (#1954).
Poem on p. 61 in: WILSON (#1971).
Poems on pp. 17, 30, 75 in: WRIGHT (#1974).

2047. Ki, Princess

Man'yōshū poet. Daughter of Emperor Temmu; younger sister of Prince Hozumi.

Poem 390 in: LEVY (#1938).

Poem on p. 85 in: Nippon Gakujutsu Shinkōkai (#1949).
Poem on p. 30 in: WRIGHT (#1974).

2048. KI no Aritsune / Aritsune's Daughter

Wife of Ariwara no Narihira. One *tanka/waka* in the *Kokinshū*, addressed to him, is attributed
to her.

Poem 784 in: HONDA (#1934).
Poem 784 in: MCCULLOUGH (#1942).
Poem 784 in: RODD (#1955).

2049. KI no Menoto (fl. ca. 880s)

Kokinshū tanka/waka poet. Nurse of Emperor Yōzei.

Poems 454 & 1028 in: HONDA (#1934).
Poems 454 & 1028 in: McCULLOUGH (#1942).
Poems 454 & 1028 in: RODD (#1955).

2050. Ki no Tsurayuki, Daughter of / Tsurayuki, Lady (ca. 950)

Tanka/waka poet. Daughter of the great poet and compiler of the *Kokinshū*.

Poem on p. 157 in: CLACK (#1925), vol. 1.
Poem on p. 290 in: MIYAMORI (#1946), vol. 1.
Poem on p. 133 in: MIYAMORI (#1947).

2051. Kii, Lady (fl. ca. 1100)

Established poet. Served in the court of Emperor Horikawa. One of her poems is included in
the *Hyakunin isshu* [*One Hundred Poems by One Hundred Poets*].

Poem 54 on pp. 100-101 in: BROWER (#1921).
Poem 72 in: GALT (#1927).
Poem 43 in: LEVY (#1936).
Poem 109 in: LEVY (#1937).
Poem 72 in: MacCAULEY (#1939).
Poem 72 in: PORTER (#1951).
Poem 72 in: TANAKA (#1961).

Kikusha-ni see **TAGAMI Kikusha-ni [#2127]**

2052. Kōgyoku, Empress/ Saimei, Empress (594-661)

Early *Manyōshū* love poems are attributed to her. She was the Empress-consort of Emperor
Jomei and mother of Emperors Tenji and Temmu.

Poem on p. 11 in: BOWNAS (#1918).
Poems 485-487 in: LEVY (#1938). [Questionable attribution.]
Poem on p. 4 in: Nippon Gakujutsu Shinkōkai (#1949).
Poem on p. 32 in: WILSON (#1967).
Poem on p. 17 in: YASUDA (#1977).

2053. Kojijū, Lady (fl. ca. 1200)

Tanka/waka poet, represented in the *Shinkokinshū*.

Poem 158 & 259 in: LEVY (#1937).
Poem on p. 351 in: MIYAMORI (#1946), vol. 1.
Poem on p. 77 in: WILSON (#1969).

2054. Kojima, A young woman named / A Maiden of Tsukushi (8th century)

Unknown *Man'yōshū* poet, apparently from the ancient city Dazaifu in Kyushu, where ŌTOMO no Tabito was governor-general. Represented by a single poem.

Poems on p. 61 in: HONDA (#1933).
Poem 381 in: LEVY (#1938).
Poem on p. 238 in: Nippon Gakujutsu Shinkōkai (#1949).

2055. Kōka Mon'in no Bettō / Kōka, Stewardess of Empress / Inno Bettō / Lady-in-Waiting to Empress Seishi / MINAMOTO no Toshitaka, Daughter of (12th century)

Tanka/waka poet. Represented in the *Hyakunin isshu* [*Hundred Poems by Hundred Poets*].

Poem 88 in: GALT (#1927).
Poem 59 in: LEVY (#1937).
Poem 88 in: MacCAULEY (#1939).
Poem 88 in: PORTER (#1951).
Poem on p. 74 in: REXROTH (#1952).
Poem on p. 42 in: REXROTH (#1954).
Poem 88 in: TANAKA (#1961).
Poem on p. 75 in: UNDERWOOD (#1962).

2056. Kōken, Empress (718-770)

Poem attributed to her in the *Man'yōshū*. Forty-sixth sovereign (reigned 749-758). Daughter of Emperor Shōmu and Empress Kōmyō. Later reigned again as Empress Shōtoku. A devout Buddhist.

Poem on p. 162 in: KEENE (#1935).
Poem on p. 83 in: Nippon Gakujutsu Shinkōkai (#1949).

Komachi see **ONO no Komachi [#2093]**

2057. Kōmyō, Empress / Asukabehime (701-760)

Poems attributed to her in the *Man'yōshū*. Consort of Emperor Shōmu, mother of reigning Empress Kōken/Shōtoku. She and her husband were both devout Buddhists. Knew Chinese literature and was a calligrapher.

Poem on p. 84 in: Nippon Gakujutsu Shinkōkai (#1949).

2058. Kose, Lady / Kose no Iratsume (8th century)

Man'yōshū poet. Became the wife of ŌTOMO no Yasumaro (to whom the poem below is addressed). He was the father of Tabito and Lady ŌTOMO no Sakanoue.

Poem 54 in: GALT (#1927).
Poem 102 in: LEVY (#1938).
Poem 54 in: MacCAULEY (#1939).
Poem 54 in: PORTER (#1951).
Poem 54 in: TANAKA (#1961).

2059. Koshikibu no Naishi (Lady-in-Waiting)

Tanka/waka poet. Beloved daughter of the more famous poet Izumi Shikibu. Both have poems in the *Hyakunin isshu* [*One Hundred Poems from One Hundred Poets*].

Poem 60 in: GALT (#1927).
Poem 60 in: MacCAULEY (#1939).
Poem on p. 326-328 in: MIYAMORI (#1946), vol. 1.
Poem on p. 149 in: MIYAMORI (#1947).

Poem 60 in: PORTER (#1951).
Poem 60 in: TANAKA (#1961).

Koyū-ni see *MATSUMOTO Koyū-ni [#2069]*

2060. KUBOTA Seifu-jo (1783-1848)

Haiku poet.

Poem on p. 597 in: MIYAMORI (#1945).

2061. Kunaikyō, Lady (d. 1207)

Tanka/waka poet. Served Emperor Gotoba. Also known as a painter.

Poems on p. 104 in: BOWNAS (#1918).
Poem 102 in: LEVY (#1937).

2062. Kurahashibe Otome / Kurahashibe, Princess (8th century)

Author of one poem in the *Man'yōshū*, to her husband, a frontier guard.

Poem 441 in: LEVY (#1938).
Poem on p. 42 in: WRIGHT (#1974).

2063. Kuramochi, Wife of

Author of a poem with two envoys in the *Man'yōshū*, addressed to a husband who had deserted her, and supposedly composed on her death bed.

Poem on p. 110-111 in: Nippon Gakujutsu Shinkōkai (#1949).

2064. Kuso

Kokinshū tanka/waka poet represented by a single poem. Daughter of MINAMOTO no Tsukuru, or possibly of ABE no Kiyoyuki.

Poem 1054 in: HONDA (#1934).
Poem 1054 in: McCULLOUGH (#1942).
Poem 1054 in: RODD (#1955).

2065. KYŌGOKU Tameko / Jūnii Tameko (d. 1316?)

Tanka/waka poet, elder sister of KYŌGOKU Tamekane. Served first in the quarters of a consort of Emperor Go-Saga; later became lady-in-waiting to Emperor Fushimi's empress, later known as Eifuku Mon'in.

Poems on pp. 386-388 (repeated on p. 462) in: BROWER (#1919).
Poems on pp. 110-119 in: CARTER (#1923).
Poem on p. 127 in: MINER (#1943).
Poem on p. 53 in: WILSON (#1968).
Poem on p. 78 in: WILSON (#1969).

2066. Kyōshin

Kokinshū poet, represented by a single *tanka/waka*. Buddhist nun. Said to have been the mother of Yoruka. Kyōshin is her religious name.

Poem 885 in: HONDA (#1934).
Poem 885 in: McCULLOUGH (#1942).
Poem 885 in: RODD (#1955).

Lady of the Court see *A Court Lady [#1990]*

2067. Lady in Waiting, A Former

Author of one *tanka* in the *Man'yōshū,* a poem addressed to Prince Katsuraki (TACHIBANA Moroe, 684-757).

Poem on p. 31 in: YASUDA (#1977).

Lady-in-Waiting to Empress Seishi see *Kōka Mon'in no Bettō [#2055]*

2068. Lady-in-Waiting to Princess Takakura (early 12th century)

Tanka/waka poet represented in the *Shinkokinshū* Imperial Anthology. Served a princess in the court of Emperor Toba (reigned 1107-1123).

Poem 96 in: LEVY (#1937).

2069. MATSUMOTO Koyū-ni (?-1782)

Haiku poet from Edo.

Poem on p. 625 in: BLYTH (#1915), vol. 2.
Poems on pp. 13–14 in: BLYTH (#1916), vol. 2.
Poem on p. 382 in: CLACK (#1925), vol. 2.
Poems on pp. 581-584 in: MIYAMORI (#1945).
Poem on p. 57 in: REXROTH (#1954).
Poem on p. 69 in: YASUDA (#1975).

MATSUZAKI Tayo-jo see *Tayo-jo [#2141]*

2070. Michinoku

Kokinshū tanka/waka poet.

Poem 992 in: HONDA (#1934).
Poem 992 in: McCULLOUGH (#1942).
Poem 992 in: RODD (#1955).

Michitsuna, Mother of Commander see *FUJIWARA no Michitsuna's Mother [#2004]*

Mikata Shami, Wife of see *Sono no Omi Ikuha, Lady [#2122]*

Mikuni no Machi see *Sanjō no Machi Shizuko [#2109]*

2071. Minabe, Princess [early 8th century]

Man'yōshū poet. Daughter of Emperor Tenji, elder sister of Empress Gemmyō, to whom one poem is addressed.

Poem 77 in: LEVY (#1938).
Poem on p. 81 in: Nippon Gakujutsu Shinkōkai (#1949).
Poem 29 in: YASUDA (#1977).

MINAMOTO no Toshitaka, Daughter of see *Kōka Mon'in no Bettō [#2055]*

2072. Mitsu-jo (1572-1647)

Haiku poet.

Poem on p. 315 in: CHAMBERLAIN (#1924).

2073. MIWA Suiu-jo (1766-1846)

Haiku poet.

Poem on pp. 590-591 in: MIYAMORI (#1945).

2074. Momoe of Kawachi/Kōchi, Maiden

Her poems in the *Man'yōshū* are from an exchange with ŌTOMO no Yakamochi, who apparently paid her a visit. Otherwise unknown.

Poems 701-702 in: LEVY (#1938).

2075. MONONOBE Tojime, Lady

Poem in the *Man'yōshū* about her absent husband, a frontier guard.

Poem on p. 43 in: WRIGHT (#1974).

2076. Mother of a Mission Member (c. 680-)

Author of a *chōka* (long poem) in the *Man'yōshū* on being separated from her son.

Poem on p. 52 in: WILSON (#1968).
Poem on p. 63 in: WILSON (#1971).

2077. Moto-jo

Haiku poet. Wife of haiku poet Chora, who died in 1776.

Poem on p. 155 in: HOFFMANN (#1932).

2078. MUKAI Kana-jo (17th century)

Haiku poet. "Wife" of Basho disciple Kyorai.

"Wisteria flowers." In: MIYAMORI (#1945), p. 418.
Poem on pp. 216-217 in: BLYTH (#1916), vol. 1.

2079. Murasaki Shikibu (fl. ca. 1000)

Brilliant Heian prose writer and *tanka/waka* poet.· Best known for *Genji monogatari* [*The Tale of Genji*] [#1760] and the *Murasaki shikibu nikki* [*The Murasaki Shikibu Diary*] [#1768], both of which contain many poems. There is also a Murasaki Shikibu personal poetry collection. She was the daughter of FUJIWARA no Tametoki, who studied Confucianism and wrote Chinese and Japanese poetry. Married a man of the provincial class and bore a daughter (the poet Daini no Sammi [#1992]). After her husband's death, she served Shōshi/Akiko, consort to Emperor Ichijō, where she was at the center of an important literary salon.

Murasaki Shikibu, her Diary and Poetic Memoirs: A Translation and Study. 1982. Richard BOWRING. Princeton: Princeton University Press. 290p. Bibl. LCCN:81-47908.
Poem on p. 4 in: BENNETT (#1914).
Poems on pp. 174-203 in: CLACK (#1925), vol. 1.
Poem 57 in: GALT (#1927).
Poem on p. 60 in: HOFFMANN (#1932).
Poem 57 in: MacCAULEY (#1939).
Poems on p. 701 in: MINER (#2180).
Poems on pp. 321-323 in: MIYAMORI (#1946), vol. 1.
Poem on p. 148 in: MIYAMORI (#1947).
Poem 57 in: PORTER (#1951).
Poem on p. 56 in: REXROTH (#1952).
Poems on pp. 21-22 in: REXROTH (#1954).

Poem 57 in: TANAKA (#1961).
Poem on p. 52 in: WILSON (#1968).

2080. NAKATOMI, Lady (8th century)

Her poems written to ŌTOMO no Yakamochi included in the *Man'yōshū*.

Poems 675-679 in: LEVY (#1938).
Poem on p. 79 in: WRIGHT (#1974).

2081. Nakatsu, Princess (d. 665)

Famous early *Man'yōshū* poet. Daughter of Emperor Jomei, younger sister of Emperor Tenji, older sister of Emperor Temmu, consort of Emperor Kōtoku. Also called Empress Hashibito.

Poems 10-12 in: LEVY (#1938).

2082. Nakatsukasa, Lady (fl. late 10th century)

Tanka/waka poet. One of the Thirty-Six Poetic Geniuses. Daughter of Lady Ise and Crown Prince Atsuyoshi.

Poem on p. 15 in: BARON (#1910).
Poem on p. ii in: BROWER (#1919).
Poems on p. 171 in: CLACK (#1925), vol. 1.
Poem 4 in: LEVY (#1936).
Poem 33 in: LEVY (#1937).
Poem on p. 317 in: MIYAMORI (#1946), vol. 1.
Poem on p. 146 in: MIYAMORI (#1947).
Poem on p. 74 in: WALEY (#1963).

2083. Nijō

Kokinshū tanka/waka poet. Daughter of MINAMOTO Itaru.

Poems on pp. 25, & 57-58 in: BENNETT (#1914).
Poem 986 in: HONDA (#1934).
Poem 986 in: McCULLOUGH (#1942).
Poem 986 in: RODD (#1955).

2084. Nijō, Empress / Nijō no Kisaki / Kōshi/Takaiko (842-910)

Kokinshū tanka/waka poet. Consort of Emperor Seiwa; mother of Emperor Yōzei.

Poems on p. 121 in: CLACK (#1925), vol. 1.
Poem 4 in: HONDA (#1934).
Poem 4 in: McCULLOUGH (#1942).
Poem on p. 239-240 in: MIYAMORI (#1946), vol. 1.
Poem on p. 136 in: MIYAMORI (#1947).
Poem 4 in: RODD (#1955).

2085. Nijōin [no] Sanuki (d. 1165)

Well-known Kamakura *tanka/waka* poet. Daughter of Emperor Goshirakawa; consort of retired Emperor Nijō (reigned 1159-1165).

Poem on p. 215 in: CLACK (#1925), vol. 1.
Poem 92 in: GALT (#1927).
Poem 92 in: MacCAULEY (#1939).
Poem 92 in: PORTER (#1951).
Poem 92 in: TANAKA (#1961).

2086. Nintoku, Wife of Emperor

Wife of Emperor Nintoku or possibly of another emperor. Questionable attribution of an early *Man'yōshū* poem addressed to an emperor.

Poem 484 in: LEVY (#1938).

2087. Niu, Princess

Possibly Prince Niu. Author of lament on the death of Prince Iwata in the *Man'yōshū*.

Poem on pp. 15-16 in: BOWNAS (#1918).
Poems 420-422 and 553-554 in: LEVY (#1938).

2088. Nukada (Nukata), Princess (late 7th century)

Important poet of the *Man'yōshū*, which contains ten *tanka* (short poems) and three *chōka* (long poems) by her. Daughter of Prince Kagami, consort of Emperor Temmu; mother of Princess Toochi. Best known for her poem arguing that autumn is esthetically and emotionally more pleasing than spring.

"Nukada no Ōkimi: A profile with poems." by Takako AOKI. 1982. [Text translated by Lisa NAKATA; poems translated by Kimiko HIROTA.] *Chanoyu Quarterly* 30:7-30. No refs. ISSN:0009-1537.
Poem on p. 39 in: BENNETT (#1914).
Poems on pp. 9-10 in: BOWNAS (#1918).
Poem on p. 85 in: BROWER (#1919).
Poem on p. 72 in: COSMAN (#1926).
Poem on p. 182 in: HIGGINSON (#1930).
Poems on pp. 2, 4 & 30 in: HONDA (#1933).
Poems 7-9, 16-20, 112-113, 155, 448 in: LEVY (#1938).
Poem on p. 38 in: MINER (#1943).
Poem on pp. 112-113 in: MIYAMORI (#1946), vol. 1.
Poem on p. 78 in: MIYAMORI (#1947).
Poems on pp. 10-12 and 13 in: Nippon Gakujutsu Shinkōkai (#1949).
Poems on pp. 3-5 in: REXROTH (#1954).
Poem translated by Kenneth REXROTH in: *Paris Review* 18:120 Spring 1977. ISSN:0031-2037.
Poems on p. 20 in: SATO (#1956).
Poem on p. 25 in: UNDERWOOD (#1962).
Poem on p. 32 in: WILSON (#1967).
Poem on p. 60 in: WILSON (#1971).
Poem on p. 65 in: WRIGHT (#1974).
Poem on p. 34 in: YASUDA (#1977).

2089. OGAWA Shōfū-ni (1688-1758)

Haiku poet. Wife of a disciple of Bashō. Later became a Buddhist nun.

Poem on p. 934 in: BLYTH (#1915), vol. 3.
Poem on p. 225 in: BLYTH (#1916), vol. 1.
Poem on p. 419-420 in: MIYAMORI (#1945).

Ōgi-jo see *Sen [#2114]*

OGIMACHI Yasuko see *YANAGIWARA Yasuko [#2157]*

Okakeme, A Young Woman of Buzen see *Ōyakame, Maiden [#2102]*

2090. Ōku, Princess / Ōku no Himemiko / Daihaku, Princess (661-701)

Early *Man'yōshū* poet. Daughter of Emperor Temmu, sister of Prince Ōtsu (condemned to death at an early age), to whom her poems are addressed.

Poem on p. 44 in: BARON (#1910).
Poem on p. 96 in: BENNETT (#1914).
Poems on p. 13 in: BOWNAS (#1918).
Poem on p. 34 in: CLACK (#1925), vol. 1.
Poems on pp. 14-15 in: HONDA (#1933).
Poem on p. 34 in: KEENE (#1935).
Poems 105-106, 163-166 in: LEVY (#1938).
Poems on p. 21 in: Nippon Gakujutsu Shinkōkai (#1949).
Poem on p. 19 in: WALEY (#1963).
Poem on p. 59 in: WILSON (#1972).
Poem on p. 73 in: YASUDA (#1977).

  ŌME Shūshiki see **Shūshiki [#2121]**

2091. ŌMIWA, Lady / ŌMIWA no Iratsume (8th century)

Exchanged poems with ŌTOMO no Yakamochi in the *Man'yōshū*. Otherwise unidentified.

Poem 618 in: LEVY (#1938).

2092. ONO no Chifuru, Mother of (Daughter of ONO no Michikaze)

Kokinshū tanka/waka poet, represented by a single poem addressed to her son who was about to become Vice Governor of Michinoku, in the north.

Poem 368 in: HONDA (#1934).
Poem 368 in: MCCULLOUGH (#1942).
Poem 368 in: RODD (#1955).

2093. ONO no Komachi / Komachi (834-880)

Prominent *Kokinshū tanka/waka* poet, known for her passionate and technically elaborate love poetry, and for her great beauty. Subject of many legends; one of the Six Poetic Geniuses.

Poem on p. 57 in: BARON (#1910).
Poems on pp. 4, 24, 46, & 54 in: BENNETT (#1914).
Poems on p. 56 in: BOSLEY (#1917).
Poems on pp. 84-85 in: BOWNAS (#1918).
Poems on pp. 29, 188, 204-205, 217, 222, 274 in: BROWER (#1919).
Poem 6 on pp. 52-53 in: BROWER (#1921).
Poems on p. 120 in: CLACK (#1925), vol. 1.
Poems on pp. 74-75 in: COSMAN (#1926).
Poem 9 in: GALT (#1927).
Poems on pp. 3-38 in: HIRSHFIELD (#1931).
Poems 113, 552-554, 557, 623, 635, 656-658, 727, 782, 797, 822, 938-939, 1030, 1104 in: HONDA (#1934).
Poems on pp. 78-79, 81 in: KEENE (#1935).
Poems 1, 20, 34, 36, 37, 104, 161, 265-279 in: LEVY (#1937).
Poem 9 in: MacCAULEY (#1939).
Poems on pp. 67, 97, 99, 105, 111, 115, 121, 125, 139, 143, 145, 179, 183, 185 and 189 in: MATSUHARA (#1940).
Poems 113, 552-554, 557, 623, 635, 656-658, 727, 782, 797, 822, 938-939, 1030, 1104 in: McCULLOUGH (#1942).
Poems on pp. 82-84 in: MINER (#1943).
Poems on pp. 195-198 in: MIYAMORI (#1946), vol. 1.

Poems on pp. 106-107 in: MIYAMORI (#1947).
Poem 9 in: PORTER (#1951).
Poems on pp. 45-46 in: REXROTH (#1952).
Poems on pp. 33-34 in: REXROTH (#1953).
Poems on pp. 14-16 in: REXROTH (#1954).
Poems 113, 552-554, 557, 623, 635, 656-658, 727, 782, 797, 822, 938-939, 1030, 1104 in: RODD (#1955).
Poems on pp. 113-116 in: SATO (#1956).
Poem 9 in: TANAKA (#1961).
Poem on pp. 39 and 41 in: UNDERWOOD (#1962).
Poems on pp. 66 & 73 in: WALEY (#1963).
Poems on pp. 66 & 70 in: WATANABE (#1964).
Poem on p. 32 in: WILSON (#1967).
Poem on p. 52 in: WILSON (#1968).
Poem on p. 77 in: WILSON (#1969).
Poems on pp. 77-79, & 81-82 in: WILSON (#1970).
Poems on pp. 60-61 in: WILSON (#1972).
Poem [translated by Graeme WILSON] in: *Ariel* [Calgary, Alberta] 13(July 1982):51. ISSN:0004-1327.

2094. ONO no Komachi, Elder Sister of [ga Ane] / Komachi's Elder Sister (9th century)

Author of one *tanka/waka* in the *Kokinshū*.

Poem 790 in: HONDA (#1934).
Poem 171 in: LEVY (#1937).
Poem 790 in: McCULLOUGH (#1942).
Poem 790 in: RODD (#1955).
Poem on p. 61 in: WILSON (#1972).

ONO no Michikaze, Daughter of see *ONO no Chifuru, Mother of [#2092]*

2095. Ōshū (17th century)

Haiku poet; a courtesan.

Poem on p. 1008 in: BLYTH (#1915), vol. 4.
Poems on p. 137 in: MINER (#1944).
Poem on pp. 441-442 in: MIYAMORI (#1945).

2096. ŌTAGAKI Rengetsu / ŌTAGAKI Sei/Nobu (1790-1875)

Haiku poet. A Buddhist nun.

Poems on p. 419 in: CLACK (#1925), vol. 2.
Poems on pp. 587-589 in: MIYAMORI (#1946), vol. 2.
Poem on p. 63 in: WILSON (#1972).

2097. Oto (late 9th-10th century)

Kokinshū tanka/waka poet, represented by a single poem. Daughter of MIBU no Yoshinari, who became Assistant Governor of Tōtomi in 887.

Poem 413 in: HONDA (#1934).
Poem 413 in: McCULLOUGH (#1942).
Poems on pp. 234-235 in: MIYAMORI (#1946), vol. 1.
Poem 413 in: RODD (#1955).

ŌTOMO, Lady see *ŌTOMO no Sakanoue, Lady [#2099]*

2098.   ŌTOMO no Katami (ca. 750)

Man'yōshū poet.   Member of a prominent poetic family.

Poems 664, 697-699 in: LEVY (#1938).
Poem on p. 23 in: WALEY (#1963).

2099.   ŌTOMO no Sakanoue, Lady / ŌTOMO no Sakanoue no Iratsume / ŌTOMO no Iratsume ŌTOMO no Katami / Sakanoue no Iratsume (fl. ca. 728-746)

Major *Man'yōshū* poet.   A leader of the great poetic ŌTOMO family; daughter of poet ŌTOMO no Yasumaro, half-sister of ŌTOMO no Tabito, and mother-in-law and aunt of ŌTOMO no Yakamochi (poet and *Man'yōshū* compiler).   Composed *tanka*, *chōka* and *sedōka*.

Poem on p. 3 in: BENNETT (#1914).
Poems on pp. 60-62 in: BOWNAS (#1918).
Poem on pp. 102 in: BROWER (#1919).
Poems on pp. 82-83 in: CLACK (#1925), vol. 1.
Poems on pp. 74-75 in: COSMAN (#1926).
Poems on pp. 34-35, 40-41 & 65 in: HONDA (#1933).
Poems on pp. 42-43 in: KEENE (#1935).
Poems 379-380, 401, 410, 460-461, 519, 525-529, 563-564, 585-586, 619-620, 47, 49, 651-652, 656-661, 666-667, 673-674, 683-689, 721, 723-726, 760-761 in: LEVY (#1938).
Poem on p. 347 in: McCULLOUGH (#1942).
Poems on pp. 133-135 in: MIYAMORI (#1946), vol. 1.
Poems on pp. 88-89 in: MIYAMORI (#1947).
Poems on pp. 123-129 in: Nippon Gakujutsu Shinkōkai (#1949).
Poems on pp. 65-66 in: REXROTH (#1952).
Poems on pp. 8-9 in: REXROTH (#1954).
Poems on pp. 62-64 in: SATO (#1956).
Poems on pp. 28-29, 32 & 39 in: WALEY (#1963).
Poem on p. 52 in: WILSON (#1968).
Poems on pp. 58-59, 61 in: WILSON (#1971).
Poems on pp. 15, 64, 71, & 80 in: WRIGHT (#1974).

2100.   ŌTOMO no Sakanoue no Ōiratsume / ŌTOMO no Sakanoue, Lady, Elder Daughter of (8th century)

Man'yōshū poet, wife of ŌTOMO no Yakamochi.   Her mother, uncle/father-in-law and husband were among the major poets of the age.

Poems 581-584 and 729-731 in: LEVY (#1938).
Poem on p. 184 in: Nippon Gakujutsu Shinkōkai (#1949).
Poems on pp. 21, 24, 71 in: WRIGHT (#1974).

2101.   ŌTOMO of Tamura, Lady, Elder Daughter of (8th century)

Man'yōshū poet.   Daughter of Sukunamaro from the village of Tamura (husband of ŌTOMO no Sakanoue no Iratsume).   The poem below is addressed to her half-sister, ŌTOMO no Sakanoue no Ōiratsume, above.   Her name comes from the village of Tamura, where she lived.

Poems 756-759 in: LEVY (#1938).
Poem on p. 129 in: Nippon Gakujutsu Shinkōkai (#1949).
Poem on p. 47 in: YASUDA (#1977).

2102. Ōyakeme, Maiden / A Young Woman of Buzen (8th century)

Unknown *Man'yōshū* poet, apparently a young woman from what is now Fukuoka Prefecture on northern Kyushu. Represented by a single poem.

Poem 709 in: LEVY (#1938).
Poem on p. 168 in: MIYAMORI (#1946), vol. 1.
Poem on p. 238 in: Nippon Gakujutsu Shinkōkai (#1949).
Poem on p. 47 in: REXROTH (#1953).
Poem on p. 75 in: WILSON (#1969).
Poem on p. 85 in: YASUDA (#1977).

2103. ŌZAKI Bunki (19th c.)

A little-known writer of Chinese poetry; student of YAMAMOTO Hokuzen (1752-1812).

"Night thoughts." In: WATSON (#1966), p. 59.

2104. REIZEI, Lady

A medieval *tanka/waka* poet of the prominent Reizei school.

Poems on pp. 405 in: BROWER (#1919).

Rengetsu-ni see **ŌTAGAKI Rengetsu [#2096]**

2105. Sachiko

Tanka/waka poet.

Poem on pp. 172-173 in: MATSUHARA (#1940).

2106. SAEKI Azumabito, Wife of (8th century)

Known for a poem in the *Man'yōshū* addressed to her husband.

Poem 621 in: LEVY (#1938).

2107. Sagami, Lady (11th century)

Tanka/waka poet. Lady-in-waiting to Princess Yūshi, married ŌE no Kinyori, "Lord" of Sagami. Her husband divorced her when she had an affair, alluded to in the *tanka/waka* below.

Poems on p. 206 in: CLACK (#1925), vol. 1.
Poem 58 in: LEVY (#1936).
Poems 35, 52 & 189 in: LEVY (#1937).
Poems on pp. 334-335 in: MIYAMORI (#1946), vol. 1.
Poems on p. 34 in: REXROTH (#1954).
Poem on p. 95 in: WALEY (#1963).

Saimei, Empress see **Kōgyoku, Empress [#2052]**

Sakanoue no Iratsume see **ŌTOMO no Sakanoue, Lady [#2099]**

2108. Saki-jo (17th century)

Haiku poet. Gion geisha.

Poem on p. 443 in: MIYAMORI (#1945).

2109. Sanjō no Machi Shizuko/Seishi / Mikuni no Machi Shizuko

Kokinshū tanka/waka poet. Daughter of KI no Natora; sister of Aritsune; minor consort of Emperor Montoku. Mother of Prince Koretaka. She is the person described as Shizuko, Imperial Concubine of Emperor Montoku.

　　Poem 930 in: HONDA (#1934).
　　Poem 930 in: McCULLOUGH (#1942).
　　Poem 930 in: RODD (#1955).

2110. SANO no Chigami/Chikami no Otome / SANU Chigami / SANO, Lady (early 8th century)

Late *Man'yōshū* poet. Participated in a long exchange of poems lamenting her parting with NAKATOMI no Yakamori, who was apparently banished for having an affair with her while she was serving in the Bureau of the Ise Shrine (Saigūryō) and supposed to have no relations with men.

　　Poem on p. 41 in: BENNETT (#1914).
　　Poems on p. 122-123 in: MIYAMORI (#1946), vol. 1.
　　Poem on p. 32 in: WILSON (#1967).
　　Poem on p. 76 in: WRIGHT (#1974).

2111. Sanuki (late 9th/10th century)

Author of one *Kokinshū tanka/waka*. Daughter of Abe no Kiyoyuki.

　　Poem 1055 in: HONDA (#1934).
　　Poem 1055 in: McCULLOUGH (#1942).
　　Poem 1055 in: RODD (#1955).

2112. Sanuki, Lady (1141-1217?)

Important *tanka/waka* poet. Daughter of poet Gensammi Yorimasa.

　　Poem on p. 104 in: BOWNAS (#1918).
　　Poem on p. 210 in: CLACK (#1925), vol. 1.
　　Poems 211 and 239 in: LEVY (#1937).
　　Poem on p. 53 in: WILSON (#1968).

　　Sei see *ŌTAGAKI Rengetsu [#2096]*

2113. SEI Shōnagon (fl. ca. 1000)

Tanka/waka poet, brilliant prose writer, regarded as a great stylist. Best known for her *Makura no sōshi* [*The Pillow Book*, #1766] which contains many poems and much information about the circumstances and social context of poetry composition. Her father was the well-known poet KIYOHARA no Motosuke, a compiler of the Gosenshū. In 993(?) she entered the service of Teishi/Sadako, consort of Emperor Ichijō and rival to Shōshi (whom Murasaki Shikibu served). After Teishi's fortunes declined, SEI Shōnagon resigned from service and became the wife of a provincial governor.

　　Poem 62 in: GALT (#1927).
　　Poem on p. 95 in: KEENE (#1935).
　　Poem 62 in: MacCAULEY (#1939).
　　Poem 62 in: PORTER (#1951).
　　Poem on p. 71 in: REXROTH (#1952).
　　Poem on p. 25 in: REXROTH (#1954).
　　Poem 62 in: TANAKA (#1961).

　　Seifu/Seifu-jo see *ENOMOTO Seifu [#1997]*

2114. Sen / Ōgi-jo (?-1763)

According to MINER (#1944), Sen was born in Zeke, a "kept woman" named Ōgi-jo at the time the poem was written, and later a nun.

Poem on p. 323 in: MINER (#1944).

Senchō-jo see *ANZAI Senchō-jo [#1984]*

2115. SHIBA Sono-jo / Sonome (1664-1726)

Haiku poet from Ise. Married a doctor, who was also a major haiku poet of the Danrin school. They became students of Bashō. After the death of her husband she moved to Edo [Tokyo], where she frequented the Kikaku school of haiku.

Poem in: BEILENSON (#1913) [unpaginated].
Poems on pp. 22-23 in: BLYTH (#1915), vol. 1.
Poem on p. 633 in: BLYTH (#1915), vol. 2.
Poem on p. 655 in: BLYTH (#1915), vol. 3.
Poems on pp. 212-214 in: BLYTH (#1916), vol. 1.
Poem on pp. xxxii in: BLYTH (#1916), vol. 2.
Poems on p. 344 in: CHAMBERLAIN (#1924).
Poem on p. 312 in: HOFFMANN (#1932).
Poems on pp. 404-408 in: MIYAMORI (#1945).
Poem on p. 34 in: STEWART (#1960).
Poem on p. 48 in: YASUDA (#1975).

2116. Shihi, Lady / Shii, Old Lady (Late 7th century)

One early *Manyōshū* poem, an exchange with Empress Jitō, attributed to her; otherwise unknown.

Poem on p. 14 in: BOWNAS (#1918).
Poem on p. 18 in: HONDA (#1933).
Poem 237 in: LEVY (#1938).
Poem on p. 19 in: Nippon Gakujutsu Shinkōkai (#1949).
Poem on p. 23 in: SATO (#1956).
Poem on p. 41 in: YASUDA (#1977).

2117. Shikishi / Shokushi, Princess / Shikishi Naishinnō (d. 1201)

Prominent *Shinkokinshū tanka/waka* poet. Daughter of Emperor Goshirakawa. She later became a Buddhist nun.

Poems of Princess Shikishi [12 seasonal poems]. 1973. [Translated by Hiroaki SATO.] Hanover, NH: Granite Publications. 18pp. LCCN:73-86249.
"Poetry of Princess Shikishi [10 poems]." 1974. [Translated by Hiroaki SATO.] *Chanoyu Quarterly* no. 10:56-57. ISSN:0009-1537.
Poem on p. 58 in: BOSLEY (#1917).
Poem on p. 101 in: BOWNAS (#1918).
Poems on pp. 294, 301, & 307 in: BROWER (#1919).
Poem on p. 243 in: BROWER (#1920).
Poems on p. 256 in: CLACK (#1925), vol. 1.
Poems on p. 77 in: COSMAN (#1926).
Poem 89 in: GALT (#1927).
Poems on p. 193 in: KEENE (#1935).
Poem 82 in: LEVY (#1936).
Poems 4, 123, 149, 224, 225, 237, 243, 281, 299 in: LEVY (#1937).
Poem 89 in: MacCAULEY (#1939).
Poem on p. 57 in: MATSUHARA (#1940).

Poems on pp. 118-119 in: MINER (#1943).
Poems on p. 691 in: MINER (#2180).
Poems on pp. 360-361 in: MIYAMORI (#1946), vol. 1.
Poem on p. 158 in: MIYAMORI (#1947).
Poem 89 in: PORTER (#1951).
Poems on p. 36 in: REXROTH (#1954).
Poems on pp. 181-189 in: SATO (#1956).
Poem 89 in: TANAKA (#1961).
Poems on p. 62 in: WILSON (#1972).

2118. Shirome / Lady Eguchi / Eguchi Sarome (10th century)

Kokinshū tanka/waka poet. Said to have been the daughter of ŌE no Tamabuchi; an entertainer of the port of Eguchi, Settsu Province.

Poem on p. 135 in: CLACK (#1925), vol. 1.
Poem 387 in: HONDA (#1934).
Poem 387 in: McCULLOUGH (#1942).
Poem on p. 236-237 in: MIYAMORI (#1946), vol. 1.
Poem 387 in: RODD (#1955).
Poem on p. 19 in: REXROTH (#1954).
Poem on p. 55 in: WALEY (#1963).

2119. Shisei-jo (d. 1751)

Haiku poet. Wife of KIMURA Ranshū.

Poem in: BEILENSON (#1913) [unpaginated].
Poem on p. 242 in: BLYTH (#1915), vol. 1.
Poem on p. 1176 in: BLYTH (#1915), vol. 4.
Poem on p. 435 in: MIYAMORI (#1945).
Poem on p. 96 in: STEWART (#1959).

2120. Shizuka / Shidzuka/Shizuka Gozen (12th century)

A dancer, famous lover of MINAMOTO no Yoshitsune (brother of MINAMOTO no Yoritomo, the first Kamakura shogun), who turned against him and ultimately had Yoshitsune and their son killed. Her story is told in the *Heike monogatari* [*Tales of the Heike*] and in several Nō and kabuki plays.

Poem on p. 354-355 in: MIYAMORI (#1946), vol. 1.
Poem on p. 40 in: REXROTH (#1954).
Poem on p. 79 in: UNDERWOOD (#1962).

Shōfū / Shōfū-ni see *OGAWA Shōfū-ni [#2089]*

Shokyū-ni see *YAGI Shōkyū-ni [#2153]*

Shōtoku, Empress see *Kōken, Empress [#2056]*

Shūkushi see *Shūshiki [#2121]*

Shunzei's Daughter see *FUJIWARA no Shunzei, Daughter of [#2007]*

2121. Shūshiki / ŌME Shūshiki (1669-1725)

Well-known haiku poet from the Edo merchant class. Her husband was also a haiku poet. Both were students of Kikaku.

Poem in: BEILENSON (#1913) [unpaginated].

Poems on pp. 214-216 in: BLYTH (#1916), vol. 1.
Poem on p. 344 in: CHAMBERLAIN (#1924).
Poem on p. 352 in: CLACK (#1925), vol. 2.
Poem on p. 306 in: HOFFMANN (#1932).
Poems on pp. 415-416 in: MIYAMORI (#1945).
Poem on p. 51 in: REXROTH (#1954).
Poem on p. 36 in: STEWART (#1959).
Poem on p. 47 in: YASUDA (#1975).

Sogetsu-ni see *IMAIZUMI Sogetsu-ni [#2022]*

2122. SONO no Omi Ikuha, Lady / SONO Ikuha, Daughter of / Mikata Shami, Wife of

Unknown *Man'yōshū* poet. Wife of Mikata, with whom there is an exchange of poems.

Poem 124 in: LEVY (#1938).
Poem on p. 43 in: REXROTH (#1953).
Poem on p. 65 in: WRIGHT (#1973).
Poem on p. 57 in: WRIGHT (#1974).
Poem on p. 49 in: YASUDA (#1977).

Sono-jo see *SHIBA Sono-jo [#2115]*

Sonome see *SHIBA Sono-jo [#2115]*

2123. Sotoorihime

Kokinshū tanka/waka poet. Said to have been the beautiful younger sister of Ōnaka no Hime, consort of Emperor Ingyō (5th century), to whom her single *tanka/waka* in the *Kokinshū* is addressed. Lived in Fujiwara; later moved to Chinu in Kawachi.

Poem 1110 in: HONDA (#1934).
Poem 1110 in: McCULLOUGH (#1942).
Poem 1110 in: RODD (#1955).

Suiu-jo see *MIWA Suiu-jo [#2073]*

Sukeko, Lady-in-Waiting to Empress Inbu see *FUJIWARA no Nobunari, Daughter of [#2006]*

2124. Suminoe, Girl of/ Suminoe no Uneme

Unknown *Man'yōshū* poet.

Poem 69 in: LEVY (#1938).
Poem on p. 22 in: YASUDA (#1977).

2125. Suō, Lady/ Lady-in-Waiting / Suwō, Lady/Lady-in-waiting (11th century)

Daughter of the governor of Suwō Province. Served at the Court of Emperor Goreizei (reigned 1046-1068).

Poem on p. 24 in: BENNETT (#1914).
Poem 67 in: GALT (#1927).
Poem 48 in: LEVY (#1937).
Poem 67 in: MacCAULEY (#1939).
Poem 67 in: PORTER (#1951).
Poem on p. 75 in: REXROTH (#1952).
Poem on p. 35 in: REXROTH (#1954).
Poem 67 in: TANAKA (#1961).

2126.   Suruga / Courtmaiden of Suruga

Unknown *Man'yōshū* poet, presumably from Suruga.

    Poem 507, p. 252 in: LEVY (#1938).
    Poem on p. 31 in: HONDA (#1933).

   Sute-jo see *DEN Sute-jo [#1994]*

   Suwo, Lady see *Suō, Lady [#2125]*

2127.   TAGAMI Kikusha-ni (1753-1826)

Haiku poet. From a wealthy family in Himeji; well-trained in the leisure arts, especially painting, for which she was known in addition to haiku. There is a personal collection of her haiku.

    Poem on p. 480 in: BLYTH (#1915), vol. 2.
    Poem on p. 742 in: BLYTH (#1915), vol. 3.
    Poems on pp. 14-15 in: BLYTH (#1916), vol. 2.
    Poems on p. 586-587 in: MIYAMORI (#1945).
    Poem on p. 59 in: REXROTH (#1954).

2128.   Tagami no Ama

Buddhist nun from Nagasaki who composed poetry with Bashō and disciples in 1691.

    Poems on p. 155 in: MINER (#1944).

2129.   Tagima Maro, Wife of (late 7th century)

Author of one *Man'yōshū* poem addressed to her husband on a journey. Otherwise unknown.

    Poem on p. 26 in: Nippon Gakujutsu Shinkōkai (#1949).

2130.   Taifu, Lady

Kokinshū tanka/waka poet. Daughter of MINAMOTO no Tasuku.

    Poem 1056 in: HONDA (#1934).
    Poem 290 in: LEVY (#1937).
    Poem 1056 in: McCULLOUGH (#1942).
    Poem 1056 in: RODD (#1955).

2131.   Tajima, Princess / Tajima no Himemiko (d. 708)

Daughter of Emperor Temmu [reigned 673-686]. Author of four *Man'yōshū* poems, three of them dealing with her forbidden love for her half-brother, Prince Hozumi, who became prime minister in 705.

    Poem 114-116 in: LEVY (#1938).
    Poem on p. 22-23 in: Nippon Gakujutsu Shinkōkai (#1949).
    Poem on p. 26 in: SATO (#1956).
    Poem on p. 64 in: WRIGHT (#1973).
    Poem on p. 69 in: WRIGHT (#1974).

2132.   Takamatsuin Uemon no Suke (d. 1160)

Tanka/waka poet. Served in the Court during the reign of Emperor Toba.

    Poem 221 in: LEVY (#1937).

2133. Takata, Princess (8th century)

Man'yōshū poet. Great-great granddaughter of Emperor Temmu.

Poems 537-542 in: LEVY (#1938).
Poems on p. 92 in: Nippon Gakujutsu Shinkōkai (#1949).

2134. TAKECHI Kurohito, Wife of (fl. ca. 700)

Man'yōshū poet. Wife of another *Man'yōshū* poet, to whom her poem is addressed.

Poem 281 in: LEVY (#1938).

2135. Tama (17th Century)

Haiku poet. Courtesan.

Poem on pp. 442-443 in: MIYAMORI (#1945).

2136. Tamochi, Princess (7th century)

Author of *Man'yōshū* poems lamenting the death of Prince Kauchi, Governor-General of Dazaifu, in 689.

Poem on p. 26 in: Nippon Gakujutsu Shinkōkai (#1949).

2137. Tango, Lady (late 12th century)

Shinkokinshū tanka/waka poet.

Poem 147 in: LEVY (#1937).
Poem on p. 53 in: WILSON (#1968).
Poem on p. 78 in: WILSON (#1969).

2138. TANIGUCHI Den-jo

Haiku poet.

Poem on p. *li* in: BLYTH (#1916), vol. 2.

2139. Taniha Ōmé (8th century)

An unknown young woman to whom one *Man'yōshū* poem is attributed.

Poem on p. 35 in: BARON (#1910).
Poem on p. 238 in: Nippon Gakujutsu Shinkōkai (#1949).

2140. Tatsu-jo

Haiku poet.

"The cherry blossoms." In: MIYAMORI (#1945), p. 590.

2141. Tayo-jo/Tayo-ni (1772-1865) / ICHIHARA Tayo-jo / MATSUZAKI Tayo-jo

Haiku poet; studied under Otsuni.

Poems on pp. 15-16 in: vol. 2 of BLYTH (#1916).
Poem on p. 589 in: MIYAMORI (#1945).

Tayū see *Taifu, Lady [#2130]*

2142. Toneri no Ōtome (7th century) / Toneri Kine / Toneri, Attendant Maiden

Manyōshū poems attributed to her. A court lady during the reign of Emperor Tenji.

Poems 61, 118 & 152 in: LEVY (#1938).
Poems on pp. 14 & 67 in: Nippon Gakujutsu Shinkōkai (#1949).
Poem on p. 75 in: YASUDA (#1977).

Tsukushi, Maiden of see *Kojima, A young woman named [#2054]*

2143. *Tsune-jo (18th century)*

Haiku poet.

Poem on p. 591 in: MIYAMORI (#1945).

Tsurayuki, Lady see *KI no Tsurayuki, Daughter of [#2050]*

2144. *Uchiko, Princess (807-847)*

Kamo Shrine priestess who wrote poetry in Chinese. Daughter of Emperor Saga.

Poem on p. 164 in: KEENE (#1935).
"Spring day in a mountain lodge." in: WATSON (#1965), p. 46.

2145. *Ukihashi (Late 17th Century)*

Haiku poet; courtesan (early geisha).

Poem on p. 84 in: BUCHANAN (#1922).
Poem on pp. 439-441 in: MIYAMORI (#1945).
Poem on p. 55 in: REXROTH (#1954).
Poem on p. 72 in: STEWART (#1959).
Poem on p. 46 in: YASUDA (#1975).

2146. *Ukō / Ukō-ni (18th century)*

Haiku poet. Personal name Tome. Wife of more famous haiku poet Bonchō. Shaved her head and became a Buddhist nun (with a change of name to Ukō-ni) without entering a convent.

Poem in: BEILENSON (#1913) [unpaginated].
Poem on p. 1201 in: BLYTH (#1915), vol. 4.
Poems on p. 177 in: BLYTH (#1916), vol. 1.
Poem on p. 340 in: CLACK (#1925), vol. 2.
Poem on pp. 117 & 121 in: MAYHEW (#1941).
Poems on pp. 107, 125, 131, 137, 149, 161, 171, 181, 209, 215, 221, 305 & 323 in:
    MINER (#1944).
Poem on pp. 417 in: MIYAMORI (#1945).
Poem on p. 38 in: Nippon Gakujutsu Shinkōkai (#1948).
Poem on p. 121 in: STEWART (#1960).
Poem on p. 48 in: YASUDA (#1975).
Poem on p. 190 in: YASUDA (#1976).

2147. *Ukon, Lady (10th century)*

A court lady represented by one *tanka/waka* to a lover who had deserted her, in *Hyakunin isshu* [*One Hundred Poems by One Hundred Poets*]. She was active in 966.

Poem 38 in: GALT (#1927).
Poem on p. 93 in: KEENE (#1935).
Poems 27 & 300 in: LEVY (#1937).
Poem 38 in: MacCAULEY (#1939).
Poem 38 in: PORTER (#1951).
Poem on p. 89 in: REXROTH (#1952).

Poem on p. 20 in: REXROTH (#1954).
Poem 38 in: TANAKA (#1961).
Poem on p. 93 in: UNDERWOOD (#1962).
Poem on p. 52 in: WILSON (#1968).
Poem on p. 62 in: WILSON (#1972).

2148. Unakami, Princess (early 8th century)

An exchange of poems with Emperor Shōmu is found in the *Man'yōshū*. Daughter of Prince Shiki.

Poem 531 in: LEVY (#1938).
Poem on p. 36 in: HONDA (#1933).

2149. Uneme (from Ōmi)

Kokinshū tanka/waka poet. A serving woman from Ōmi.

Poem 1109 in: HONDA (#1934).
Poem 1109 in: McCULLOUGH (#1942).
Poem 1109 in: RODD (#1955).

2150. Utsuku

Kokinshū tanka/waka poet known for 3 poems.

Poems 376, 640 and 742 in: HONDA (#1934).
Poems 376, 640 and 742 in: McCULLOUGH (#1942).
Poems 376, 640 and 742 in: RODD (#1955).

2151. Wives of Guards

Unknown *Man'yōshū* poets. Wives of frontier guards to/about whom they wrote poems about separation.

Poems on pp. 56-57 in: BOWNAS (#1918).

Woman of Buzen see Ōyakeme, Maiden [#2102]

2152. YABE Masako (1745-1773)

Tanka/waka poet. Student of OZAWA Ro-an; a Buddhist nun.

Poem on p. 396 in: CLACK (#1925), vol. 2.
Poem on p. 481 in: MIYAMORI (#1946), vol. 2.

2153. YAGI Shokyū-ni (1713-1781)

Haiku poet from Chikuzen. Married YAGI Fufū, the secretary to the haiku poet, Yaha. After her husband's death, she made a poetic pilgrimage throughout Japan.

Poem on p. 360 in: CLACK (#1925), vol. 2.
Poems on pp. 436-439 in: MIYAMORI (#1945).
Poem on p. 47 in: YASUDA (#1975).

2154. Yamaguchi, Princess (8th century)

Unidentified *Man'yōshū* poet. Exchanged poems with ŌTOMO no Yakamochi.

Poems 613-617 in: LEVY (#1938).

2155. Yamato-hime, Empress (7th century)

Empress-consort of Emperor Tenji, granddaughter of Emperor Jomei. Early *Manyōshū* poems by her lament the death of her husband. She and Tenji are subjects of legend.

Poem on p. 13 in: HONDA (#1933).
Poems on p. 7-8 in: Nippon Gakujutsu Shinkōkai (#1949).
Poem on p. 101 in: REXROTH (#1952).

2156. YANAGAWA Kōran (1804-1879)

Wrote poetry in Chinese. Wife of poet YANAGAWA Seigan. According to WATSON (#1966) ". . . it was generally supposed that he rewrote her works for her. After his death, however, she surprised the world by producing poetry that was even superior to her previous works" (p. 57).

"Coming home at night in the snow." In: WATSON (#1966).

2157. YANAGIWARA Yasuko / ŌGIMACHI Yasuko (1783-1866)

Tanka/waka poet. Student of KAGAWA Kageki; daughter of Ōgimachi Sanjō Saneatsu; married YANAGIWARA Tadamitsu.

Poem on p. 417 in: CLACK (#1925), vol. 2.
Poems on pp. 509-510 in: MIYAMORI (#1946), vol. 2.

2158. Yokobue (12th Century)

Flute player. Subject of a well-known episode in the *Heike monogatari* [*Tales of Heike*] about a tragic love affair with Tokiyori that ended with both taking Buddhist orders.

Poem on p. 39 in: REXROTH (#1954).

2159. Yosa/Yoza, Lady/Princess

Unknown *Man'yōshū* poet.

Poem 59 in: LEVY (#1938).
Poem on p. 74 in: WRIGHT (#1974).

2160. Yosami no Iratsume / Yosami, Wife of Hitomaro / Yosami (8th century)

Probably a village woman in Iwami. Author of a well-known *Man'yōshū* lamenting the death of her husband (who survived the wife listed above as Hitomaro, Wife of [#2019]).

Poem on p. 29 in: BOWNAS (#1918).
Poem on p. 51 in: CLACK (#1925), vol. 1.
Poems 140, 224-225 in: LEVY (#1938).
Poem on p. 65 in: MIYAMORI (#1946), vol. 1.
Poems on p. 51-52 in: Nippon Gakujutsu Shinkōkai (#1949).
Poem on p. 38 in: SATO (#1956).
Poems on pp. 10-11 in: REXROTH (#1954).

Young Woman of Harima see *Harima, Young Woman of [#2015]*

Yoza, Princess see *Yosa, Princess [#2159]*

Critical Studies of Premodern Poetry

2161. AOKI, Takako. 1982. "Nukada no Ōkimi: A profile with poems." [Text translated by Lisa NAKATA; poems translated by Kimiko HIROTA.] *Chanoyu Quarterly* 30:7-30. No refs. ISSN:0009-1537.

An illuminating portrait of the *Man'yōshū* poet Princess Nukada, placing her in historical and literary context. Speculation based on scant historical record and her poems.

2162. ASTON, W.G. 1899. *A History of Japanese Literature.* New York: D. Appleton and Co. 408p. Notes. Index.

A chronological account, from a Victorian point of view, of twelve centuries of Japanese literature, including highlights of Heian poetry and fiction written by women. ASTON muses, "It is a remarkable, and I believe, unexampled fact, that a very large and important part of the best literature which Japan has produced was written by women" (p. 55).

2163. CHAMBERLAIN, Basil Hall. 1902. "Basho and the Japanese poetical epigram." *Transactions of the Asiatic Society of Japan* 30:242-362. Bibl. LCCN:39-23.

An early introduction to the haiku, by a great Victorian Japanologist and literary scholar. Proceeds historically and includes a number of poems by women: Mitsu-jo, Sono-jo, Chigetsu-ni, Shūshiki, Sute-jo, and, especially, Chiyo-jo.

2164. CRANSTON, Edwin A. 1970. "The poetry of Izumi Shikibu." *Monumenta Nipponica* 25(1/2):1-11. 41 notes. ISSN:0027-0741.

A general scholarly introduction to this "Heian poetess" with a "reputation for genius, passion, and piety" (p. 1), followed by a large selection of poems on Buddhism and on love, with some thematic discussion. Romanized text of poems included.

2165. CRANSTON, Edwin. 1975. "The dark path: Images of longing in Japanese love poetry." *Harvard Journal of Asiatic Studies* 35:60-100. 21 notes. ISSN:007-0548.

A catalog of common images (darkness, dreams, tears/water, fire, black hair, empty beds, the crying of deer) found in Japanese love poetry from the seventh through the thirteenth centuries, including, with a minimum of discussion, romanized original text and translation by CRANSTON of numerous poems, 34 by women: 17 by Izumi Shikibu, seven by Ono no Komachi and 10 others.

2166. CRANSTON, Edwin A. 1988. "A web in the air." *Monumenta Nipponica* 43(3):305-352. 55 notes. ISSN:0027-0741.

A long, scholarly review article on McCULLOUGH (#1942 and #2178), including an evaluation of the competing translation and study by RODD and HENKENIUS (#1955), commenting on other recent works in English on classical Japanese literature that deal with the age of the *Kokinshū*, and comparing various approaches to translating its poetry. In McCULLOUGH's translations, which CRANSTON calls "classical translations," CRANSTON sees "the wit, refinement, and conservatism" by which she epitomizes the 'mature Kokinshū style'" (p. 335). He cites numerous poems, many of them in multiple translation; eleven are by women, mainly ONO no Komachi, whose poetry is discussed in detail.

2167. HARRIES, Phillip T. 1980. "Personal poetry collections: Their origin and development through the Heian period." *Monumenta Nipponica* 35(3):299-317. 109 notes. ISSN:0027-0741.

A specialized article distinguishing the genre of the personal poetry collection (*shikashū*) from those of the Imperial anthology (*chokusenshū*) and the private anthology (*shisenshū*), and tracing its history through the Heian period. Women poets used this genre, and several personal collections by women are included in HARRIES' discussion, notably by Ise, Akazome Emon, and Izumi Shikibu. No poetry is quoted.

2168. HEINRICH, Amy. 1982. "Blown in flurries: The role of poetry in "Ukifune." In: PEKARIK, Andrew, ed. *Ukifune: Love in* The Tale of Genji. New York: Columbia University Press, pp. 153-171. 10 notes. LCCN:82-1157.

An investigation of the 22 poems in the "Ukifune" chapter of *The Tale of Genji* and their "three functions—to delineate character, to define relationships, and to advance the plot. . ." (p. 154).

2169. HEINRICH, Amy Vladeck. Apr. 1987. "On attempting the impossible: Translating the *Kokinshū*." *Journal of the Association of Teachers of Japanese* 21(1):59-76. 5 notes. ISSN:0085-9884.

A balanced article reviewing McCULLOUGH's *Kokinshū* (#1942) and *Brocade by Night* (#2178) and RODD's *Kokinshū* (#1955). Explores "untranslatable" effects of the original, comparing partial solutions by the two translators and suggesting HEINRICH's own approach to translation.

2170. ITO, Setsuko. Summer 1982. "The muse in competition: Uta-awase through the ages." *Monumenta Nipponica* 37(2):201-222. 50 notes. ISSN:0027-0741.

An introduction to the *uta-awase*, or poetry competition (in which women commonly participated), beginning in the Heian Period in the court of the Emperor Uda (867-931), in whose time the opening chapters of *The Tale of Genji* are thought to be set. In the appendix to the article are excerpts from the Records of Uta-awase. Many of the poems (not quoted) were written by women.

2171. KATO, Shuichi. 1979/1981. *A History of Japanese Literature. Volumes One and Two*. [Translated by David CHIBBETT (vol. 1) and Don SANDERSON (vol. 2).] London: MacMillan/Tokyo: Kodansha. Vol. 1 & 2 of a 3 vol. set. Notes. Index. LCCN:77-75967(set). [*Nihon bungakushi*.]

An interesting, somewhat idiosyncratic history by an eminent literary scholar (of German, French, and English as well as Japanese literature) and critic-at-large. Originally written for a Japanese audience and serialized in the *Asahi Journal*. In vol. one ("The First Ten Thousand Years"), an introduction presenting "The Distinctive Features of Japanese Literature" precedes a chronological historical survey from the "seventh or eighth century AD" (p. 29) through the sixteenth century that ranges freely into most areas of Japanese culture. There is considerable treatment throughout of both prose and poetry genres associated with women; one section is devoted to the Aesthetics of the *Kokinshu*, one to Women's Diaries, and one to the *Genji monogatari*. Volume Two ("The Years of Isolation") deals with the Edo Period but lists no women writers in the index. [See #1513 in Modern Prose Criticism for coverage of volume three.]

2172. KEENE, Donald. 1976. *World within Walls: Japanese Literature of the Pre-Modern Era, 1600-1867*. New York: Holt, Rinehart and Winston. Notes/Bibl. Index. LCCN:75-21484.

Part of a planned multi-volume history of Japanese literature by Donald KEENE, this substantial volume is a collection of essays on both major and minor figures and works of poetry, fiction, and drama of the Edo Period. Includes a discussion of the haiku poet Chiyo-jo.

2173. Kokusai Bunka Shinkokai, ed. 1948/1970. *Introduction to Classic Japanese Literature*. Tokyo: Kokusai Bunka Shinkokai/Westport, CT: Greenwood Press. 443p. LCCN:50-31232/72-98847.

The first in a series of books written by committees of eminent Japanese literary scholars and translated into English, containing considerable valuable information but not accessible to the general reader. This volume begins with the earliest times and ends in the Meiji period. Women poets are not especially well represented, but some of the poetry discussed from the *Man'yoshu* and Imperial anthologies is by women.

2174. KONISHI, Jin'ichi. 1958. "Association and progression: Principles of integration in anthologies and sequences of Japanese court poetry, A.D. 900-1350." [Translated by Robert H. BROWER and Earl MINER.] *Harvard Journal of Asiatic Studies* 21:67-127. 26 notes. ISSN:0073-0548.

An important early critical study by the eminent Japanese scholar whose work strongly influenced BROWER and MINER's *Japanese Court Poetry* (#1919). Including poems by six women, treating them in sequentiqal context, KONISHI examines the contradictory trends toward fragmentation and integration and argues that there was a gradual shift in emphasis in integration technique from progression to association during the several centuries of Japanese poetry leading to linked verse (*renga*).

2175. KONISHI, Jin'ichi. 1978. "The genesis of the Kokinshū style." [Translated by Helen McCULLOUGH.] *Harvard Journal of Asiatic Studies* 38(1):61-170. 76 notes. ISSN:0073-0548.

KONISHI provides an excellent scholarly treatment of the influence of Chinese poetic tradition on the formation of the style associated with the *Kokinshū*, the first Imperial anthology of Japanese poetry. The article contains numerous translations of poems, including eight *tanka/waka* by women, most of them by Lady Ise.

2176. KONISHI, Jin'ichi. 1984. *A History of Japanese Literature Volume One: The Ancient and Archaic Ages*. [Translated by Aileen GATTEN and Nicholas TEELE; edited by Earl MINER.] Princeton: Princeton University Press. 475p. Notes/Bibl. Index. LCCN:83-34082. [*Nihon bungeishi.*]

The first of a planned series of five volumes by an eminent scholar of classical Japanese literature, this volume is devoted to a detailed history from prehistory through the ninth century. The work is unusual in that it considers ancient Japanese literature in the context of the rest of Asia and includes Ainu and Ryukyuan literature within its scope. A considerable portion of the study focuses on the *Man'yōshū*, including many women poets.

2177. KONISHI, Jin'ichi. 1986. *A History of Japanese Literature Volume Two: The Early Middle Ages*. [Translated by Aileen GATTEN; edited by Earl MINER.] Princeton: Princeton University Press. 461p. Bibl. LCCN:83-43082. [*Nihon bungeishi.*]

A continuation of #2176; a detailed history by an eminent Japanese scholar, including information and interpretations nowhere else in English, of the history of Japanese literature from the Heian Period. Chapter 8, "Prose in Japanese," offers an excellent articulation and analysis of tale and diary literature of the period, most of which was written by women.

2178. McCULLOUGH, Helen Craig. 1985. *Brocade by Night: Kokin wakashū and the Court Style in Japanese Classical Poetry*. Stanford: Stanford University Press. 591p. Bibl. LCCN:84-50637.

A companion volume to *Kokin Wakashū* [#1942] offering a literary/historical background to 10th-century *tanka/waka* and containing elaborate studies of the three works translated, plus an astounding wealth of information in appendices—including women poets of the *Kokinshū*. Hundreds of poems, translated by McCULLOUGH, are cited in the text.

2179. MINER, Earl Roy. Autumn 1955. "The technique of Japanese poetry." *Hudson Review* 8(3):350-36. No refs. ISSN:0018-702X.

An introduction to *tanka/waka* (touching on versification rules, sound, imagery, metaphor, symbolism) from a Western critical stance, with some consideration of "the literary and philosophical conventions which the poetry assumes" (p. 352). Cites, with romanized texts, many well-known poems, including six by women, five of them by ONO no Komachi.

2180. MINER, Earl. Dec. 1990. "Waka: Features of its constitution and development." *Harvard Journal of Asiatic Studies* 50(2):669-706. 46 notes. ISSN:0073-0548.

A reappraisal of the genre, readdressing basic issues, including comparison of English translations. Cites poems by Princess Shokushi (= Shikishi), Murasaki Shikibu and Lady Ise.

2181. MORRIS, Mark. Jun. 1980. "Sei Shōnagon's poetic categories." *Harvard Journal of Asiatic Studies* 40(1):5-54. 90 notes. ISSN:0073-0548.

A technical article in which MORRIS looks closely at the lists or catalogues that form an important part of the *Pillowbook* [*Makura no sōshi*] (#1766). From the context of traditional Japanese poetics, MORRIS explores "what the catalogues are like, and looking at the . . . scholarly response to them, gauge[s] what sort of materials made their way into them or influenced their form and . . . what SEI Shōnagon achieved with this peculiar, almost subliterary "genre."

2182. OKADA, Richard H. Feb. 1988. "Translation and difference—A review article." *The Journal of Asian Studies* 47(1):29-40. 18 notes & 16 refs. ISSN:0021-9118.

An extremely detailed and controversial critical review of McCULLOUGH's *Kokin Wakashū* [#1942] and *Brocade by Night* [#2178], challenging McCULLOUGH's fundamental principles of translation and analysis.

2183. PAGE, Curtis Hidden. 1923 [rep. 1977]. *Japanese Poetry: An Historical Essay with Two Hundred and Thirty Translations.* Norwood, PA: Norwood Editions. 180p. LCCN:77-12167.

An introduction to Japanese poetry, with translations, sometimes paraphrases, embedded in the text. For the general reader. Includes many women poets. (For example, PAGE dedicates a chapter to the 18th-century haiku poet Chiyo.)

2184. PUTZAR, Edward. 1973. *Japanese Literature: A Historical Outline.* [Adapted from the work by Sen'ichi HISAMATSU.] Tucson: University of Arizona Press. 246p. LCCN:70-189229. [*Nihon bungaku.* Adaptation. 1960.]

A chronological history of Japanese literature, originally intended for a Japanese audience, from 400 to 1945. Women, especially poets, are mentioned throughout, and the discussion of the Heian Period includes sections on Imperial Anthologies, *The Tale of Genji*, and the *Pillow Book*. The modern chapter is organized by groups and movements and focuses on literary ideology and on fiction. Women are mentioned, sometimes discussed, in passing.

2185. RAMIREZ-CHRISTENSEN, Esperanza. 1982. "The operation of the lyrical mode in the *Genji Monogatari*." In: PEKARIK, Andrew, ed. *Ukifune: Love in* The Tale of Genji. New York: Columbia University Press, pp. 21-61. 17 notes. LCCN:82-1157.

An excellent article focusing on specific passages in the "Uji" chapters of *The Tale of Genji* to explicate the relationship of poems to their prose contexts and of descriptive passages to incident, showing that "the *Genji* is a hybrid genre in which narrative is being employed for lyrical or poetic ends" and ". . .[its] climaxes . . .are . . . those moments of heightened emotion in which outer and inner worlds are fused together in a transfiguring metaphor or pattern of images" (p. 21).

2186. RIMER, J. Thomas and Robert E. MORRELL. 1975. *Guide to Japanese Poetry*. Boston: G.K. Hall. 151p. (*Asian Literature Bibliography Series*.) LCCN:74-20610.

A useful handbook providing a historical overview of Japanese poetry from prehistory to the early 1970s, including a wide-ranging, extensively and helpfully annotated bibliography of Japanese poetry translated into English. Includes reviews of many of the items listed here.

2187. WALKER, Janet A. Jun. 1977. "Poetic ideal and fictional reality in the Izumi Shikibu nikki." *Harvard Journal of Asiatic Studies* 37(1):135-182. 47 notes. ISSN:0073-0548.

A scholarly investigation of one of the most important poetic diaries of the Heian Period, finding that "In part, the author adhered to . . . an idealized view of love influenced by the poetic anthology. . . in which ritualized and stylized poetic exchanges play an important role," but that "the author's sense of loyalty to the facts of the affair as she knew them forced her to depart radically from the traditional poetic view. . ." (p. 136). WALKER examines the evidence of a resultant tension in the work.

2188. "The women who wrote classics: Izumi Shikibu, a poet who devoted herself to love." Nov./Dec. 1988. *East* 24(4):12-17. No refs. ISSN:0012-8295.

A brief note introducing the *Diary*, followed by an amusing profile of Izumi Shikibu, "a passionate woman" when "'life' was a synonym for 'love affair'" (p. 13). Part of the series (see #1901-1906). Includes many poems, translated by Edwin A. CRANSTON.

OTHER

18

Non-Japanese Women in Japan

Businesswomen

2189. BIRD, Allan. Jun. 1983. "Wasted talent." *PHP* 14(6):5-7. No refs. ISSN:0030-798X.

Explores the extent of sexual discrimination against foreign businesswomen in Japan. Non-technical, but includes quotations from a variety of women.

2190. BLUMM, Rich. Aug. 1988. "Working Kansai women." *Journal of the American Chamber of Commerce in Japan* 25(Aug. 1988):13-17. No refs. ISSN:0002-7847.

Describes the businesses of three non-Japanese women: Nara FITZWATER's bakery in Kobe, Maureen SUGAI's Galaxy Travel Agency in Osaka, and Holly SIEBERT's intercultural consultant firm in Osaka. All three women discuss how their status as foreign women has helped or hindered their progress.

2191. CARR, Sloan. Jan. 1987. "Teaching 'us' about 'them.'" *Look Japan* 32(370):17. No refs. ISSN:0456-5339.

Interviews Charlotte KENNEDY-TAKAHASHI, president of Oak Associates K.K., a firm which provides cross-cultural training for foreigners coming to Japan and to Japanese going abroad.

2192. MacDONALD, CAROL L. Aug. 1988. "Foreign executive women." *Journal of the American Chamber of Commerce in Japan* 25(8):27-31. No refs. ISSN:0002-7847.

MacDONALD describes the organization, Foreign Executive Women [FEW], and interviews several officers including Charlotte KENNEDY-TAKAHASHI. Discussed are business opportunities, style, effects of being female and foreign, and the probable impact of a "Japan experience" on one's career path. Tightly written and informative.

2193. MacDONALD, CAROL L. Aug. 1988. "An international woman for an international firm." *Journal of the American Chamber of Commerce in Japan* 25(8):47,49-51. No refs. ISSN:0002-7847.

An in-depth profile of SATŌ Kumi, an American citizen and president of Cosmo Public Relations, "the largest independently-owned public relations firm in Japan . . . [which] . . . specializes in bilingual and bicultural communications for international clients."

2194. SCHMITT, Helen and Charlotte KENNEDY-TAKAHASHI. Sep. 1982. "American working women in Japan." *Journal of the American Chamber of Commerce in Japan* 20(9):11-12,15-16. No refs. ISSN:0002-7847.

Survey results provide a profile of American working women in Japan including age, family status, type of work, working conditions, and trends in employment. Notes that most women are involved in education and communication, and that the number of businesswomen is increasing.

2195. "A sweet opportunity." Jul. 1987. *Look Japan* 33(376):20-21. No refs. ISSN:0456-5339.

Interviews Debra FIELDS of the "Mrs. Fields" chain of cookie shops about her entry into the Japanese market.

The Diplomatic Community

2196. ANDERSON, Isabel. 1914. *The Spell of Japan.* Boston: Page Co. 396p. Bibl. Index. LCCN:14-14483.

As the wife of the United States Ambassador, Isabel ANDERSON had a unique position from which to experience the Japan of 1912-1913. She includes a variety of topics, from a description of an Ainu bear hunt (in which she did not participate) to comments on their lives in an official capacity (including pointed remarks about the poor physical condition of the embassy and the dangers of attempting to speak Japanese). A brief description of the position of Japanese women occurs on pp. 108-110.

2197. ANETHAN, Baroness Albert d'. 1912. *Fourteen Years of Diplomatic Life in Japan.* London: Stanley Paul and Co. 471p. No refs. LCCN:12-23677.

E. Mary d'ANETHAN was a British woman married to a Belgian diplomat stationed in Japan from 1893 to 1910. In his forward, the Japanese ambassador to London states: "There was no social or charitable function of any importance . . . in which she did not play an important role," and he calls this diary "a history, social and otherwise, of my country."

2198. ANETHAN, Baroness d'. 1934-1935. "Personal recollections of the court of Japan." *Transactions and Proceedings of the Japan Society of London* 32:1-24. [Title also cited as Japan Society, London. *Transactions and Proceedings.*] No refs. LCCN:08-16048.

The Baroness describes her first audience with Her Majesty the Empress Shōken on 10 October 1893, a farewell visit on 9 April 1901, the silver wedding anniversary celebration of the Imperial couple on 9 March 1894, and the funeral ceremonies held for Her Majesty in 1914.

2199. FRASER, Mary Crawford. 1982. *A Diplomat's Wife in Japan: Sketches at the Turn of the Century.* [Edited by Hugh CORTAZZI.] New York: John Weatherhill. 351p. No refs. LCCN:82-2589.

Originally published in 1899, these memoirs were considered worthy of editing and republication by the British ambassador to Japan in 1980. Included are an introduction setting the larger historical context, and extensive biographical material on the author. Mary FRASER comments about diplomatic life, including interactions with high-ranking Japanese officials, and gives vivid descriptions of the portion of Japan she is able to observe, including the status of women. A strong and readable contribution to this genré of materials.

2200. HODGSON, C. Pemberton. 1861. *A Residence at Nagasaki and Hakodate in 1859-1860.* London: Richard Bentley. 350p. No refs. LCCN:04-24326.

HODGSON, British consul at Nagasaki and Hakodate, includes in his memoirs copies of his wife's letters to her mother describing their stay in Nagasaki as the first British residents there after Japan was "opened." He also describes their relationships with a Hakodate family and includes accounts of the women's conversations during visits.

2201. TERASAKI, Gwen. 1957. *Bridge to the Sun.* Chapel Hill: University of North Carolina Press. 260p. No refs. LCCN:57-3440. [Excerpted in LIVINGSTON, Jon, Joe MOORE, and Felicia OLDFATHER, eds. 1973. *Imperial Japan, 1800-1945.* New York: Pantheon Books, pp. 465-475. (*The Japan Reader*, 1.) LCCN:73-12686.]

In 1930, a 23-year-old woman from Tennessee met and married a young Japanese diplomat stationed in Washington, D.C. After being posted to Asia and Cuba, the TERASAKI's were in Washington once again when war was declared. They were evacuated to Japan. The bulk of the memoir describes their wartime experiences in Tokyo.

Educators and Students

2202. BACON, Alice Mabel. 1900. *A Japanese Interior.* Boston: Houghton-Mifflin. 272p. No refs. LCCN:04-16696.

A collection of letters written in 1888-1889 while the author was an English teacher at the Peeresses' School, a school for noble girls under the sponsorship of the Empress. Her accounts include a brief but interesting description of a ball at the Rokumei-kwan [the Deer-Cry Pavilion], as well as stories of her life among the Japanese where she felt "too Japanese for the foreigners, and too foreign for the Japanese, too worldly for the missionaries and not worldly enough for the rest of the foreign colony." [See also #146.]

2203. "Foreigners living in Japan: Araceli Soriano—Accepted in the family." Mar. 1978. *PHP* 9(3):45-47. No refs. ISSN:0030-798X.

Briefly profiles a Ministry of Education scholarship student from the Philippines.

2204. PHILIP, Leila. 1989. *The Road through Miyama.* New York: Random House. 264p. No refs. LCCN:88-29983. [Title also cited as *The Road to Miyama.*]

A beautifully crafted narrative describing the author's experiences as an apprentice potter in Miyama, a small village on the island of Kyushu. With a perceptive eye, PHILIP describes the life of the pottery town in which she lived for over a year as well as her own accommodations to living in Japan and studying pottery the Japanese way.

2205. VINING, Elizabeth Gray. 1952. *Windows for the Crown Prince.* Philadelphia: J.B. Lippincott. 320p. No refs. LCCN:52-5098.

Elizabeth Gray VINING (a Quaker author) was invited to Japan in 1946 to tutor the Crown Prince in English. Her memoir of her four-year stay covers the Imperial family, her teaching activities, the Occupation (from the situation of Japanese civilians to the war crimes trials) and various Christian endeavors, especially those of Quakers and the American Friends Service Committee. [For the sequel, see #2206.]

2206. VINING, Elizabeth Janet. 1960. *Return to Japan.* Philadelphia: Lippincott. 285p. No refs. LCCN:60-7435.

The sequel to #2205. Covers VINING's subsequent visits in 1957 for the International PEN Conference and for the wedding of the Crown Prince 18 months later.

Entertainers and Musicians

2207. "Foreigners living in Japan: Hide and Rosanna—Veteran entertainment team." Apr. 1978. *PHP* 9(4):45-47. No refs. ISSN:0030-798X.

Describes briefly the lives of an Italian vocalist and her Japanese husband/partner.

2208. "Japan's favorite blond: Joan Shepherd." 1981. *Japan Pictorial* 4(4):20-24. No refs. ISSN:0388-6115.

A profile of an American entertainer married to a Japanese and immensely popular with Japanese audiences. Primarily a singer, she also co-hosts the TV show "Welcome Newlyweds." Includes her philosophy about women's roles.

2209. SASAI, Tsunezō. 1964. "The blue-eyed bride." *East* 1(2):24-28. No refs. ISSN:0012-8295.

Profiles Edith HANSON/TAKAHASHI Yoshiko, an American actress married to TAKAHASHI Teruo (stage name: YOSHIDA Kotama), a Bunraku puppeteer. Extols her traditionally female attitudes toward family and her efforts in preserving Bunraku theater.

Missionaries

2210. ALLEN, Thomasine. 1957. "Two Christmas Trees at Kuji." In: STEVENS, Dorothy A., ed. *Voices from Japan: Christians Speak.* Philadelphia: Judson Press, pp. 65-68. No refs. LCCN:57-8339.

As part of a discussion of the Kuji Center's work by various persons, ALLEN describes the "portable Christmas service" which travels to 20 locations in rural Iwate Prefecture.

2211. BERRY, Katherine F. 1962. *Katie-san, from Maine Pastures to Japan Shores.* Cambridge: Dresser, Chapman, and Grimes. 285p. No refs. LCCN:62-20509.

The story of Katherine Fiske BERRY, born in 1877 to missionary parents on furlough in the United States, who returned to Japan in 1878. The descriptions from her mother's notes and Katie's journals and letters tell of her childhood in Okayama and Kyoto from 1878-1893, and a return visit to Japan in 1919-1920. The emphasis is one of a child growing up in a missionary community.

2212. BROWN, Terry. 1985. "Marjorie and Cyril Powles: A critical biographical sketch." In: LIND, Christopher and Terry BROWN, eds. *Justice as Mission: An Agenda for the Church. Essays in Appreciation of Marjorie and Cyril Powles.* Burlington, Ontario: Trinity Press, pp. 235-245. 4 notes. LCCN:85-177966.

Provides details on the life of Marjorie POWLES (b. 1913), active in the Japanese mission of the Episcopal Church, along with her husband Cyril POWLES (b. 1918), an Anglican priest.

2213. CARROTHERS, Julia D. 1879. *The Sunrise Kingdom; or, Life and Scenes in Japan, and Woman's Work for Women There.* Philadelphia: Presbyterian Board of Publications. 408p. No refs. LCCN:04-28641.

CARROTHERS combines in one volume an introduction to Japan, a memoir of her seven-year service with the Woman's Foreign Missionary Society of the Presbyterian Church, and a lengthy description of mission work to be done by women in Japan. One of the earliest female missionaries in Japan, CARROTHERS began her work before the ban on Christianity was officially lifted in 1873.

2214. CLAPP, Frances Benton. 1955. *Mary Florence Denton and the Dōshisha.* Kyoto: Dōshisha University Press. 439p. No refs. LCCN:75-320300.

A biography of a missionary who served at the Dōshisha School(s) from 1888-1947. Anecdote after anecdote reveals the type of strong-willed personality which resulted in strict but loving teaching and fierce caring for students.

2215. FRANCIS, Mabel with Gerald B. SMITH. 1968. *One Shall Chase a Thousand.* Harrisburg, PA: Christian Publications. 119p. No refs. LCCN:68-3791.

The story of a missionary who spent 55 years in Japan, many of them with her sister Anne DIEVENDORF. She describes her life from 1909-1965, including the war years when she chose to remain in Japan. In 1962, she was awarded the Fifth Order of the Sacred Treasure.

2216. GRANT, Kathryn. Aug./Sep. 1968. "An American in Tokyo: Housewife-Mother-Teacher." *East* 4(5):16-19. No refs. ISSN:0012-8295.

An essay on living in Tokyo by a minister's wife and mother of four children. She mentions the difficulties of reading Japanese and of becoming involved in Japanese community life, and expresses her "greatest concern for Japan [is] that the religious heritage has no meaning for young people."

2217. GRIFFIS, William Elliot. 1913. *Hepburn of Japan and His Wife and Helpmates.* Philadelphia: Westminster Press. 238p. No refs. Index. LCCN:14-2319.

A biography of James Curtis HEPBURN, missionary to Japan (1859-1892). GRIFFIS includes a chapter on HEPBURN's wife, Clarissa [Clara] Leete HEPBURN, who began a school for girls in 1863.

2218. HEMPHILL, Elizabeth Anne. 1964. *A Treasure to Share.* Valley Forge, PA: Judson Press. 160p. No refs. LCCN:64-20501.

The biography of Thomasine ALLEN who went to Japan as an American Baptist missionary in 1915 and spent the majority of her time in the rural regions of Iwate Prefecture. In the town of Kuji, she was instrumental in the establishment of a kindergarten, hospital, church, demonstration farm, and community center.

2219. HILBURN, Samuel M. 1936. *Gaines Sensei: Missonary to Hiroshima.* Kobe: The Friend-sha. 175p. No refs.

A detailed biography of Nannie B. GAINES (1860-1932), a missionary for the Southern Methodist Mission who established the Hiroshima Girls' School and spent 45 years in Japan as an educator.

2220. HITT, Russell T. 1965. *Sensei: The Life Story of Irene Webster-Smith.* New York: Harper and Row. 240p. (*Harper Jungle Missionary Classics.*) No refs. LCCN:65-20452.

The story of Irene WEBSTER-SMITH, an Irish Quaker, who began working in Japan in 1916 under the auspices of the (Anglican) Japan Evangelistic Band and was still active at the time of this biography's publication. The major portion of her life was devoted to founding and running the Sunrise Home, a girls' orphanage (her solution to the problem of government-licensed brothels during the 1920s) and the Ochanomizu Christian Student Center during the early 1960s. Her philosophy: "It would be better to put a fence at the top of a precipice than an ambulance at the bottom."

2221. HOAGLUND, Alan and Betty HOAGLUND. Winter 1978. "Our life and work in Matsuyama." *Japan Christian Quarterly* 44(1):40-42. No refs. ISSN:0021-4361.

A brief description of 17 years of life as a Lutheran pastor's wife in Bofu and Matsuyama, Japan.

2222. KOJIMA, Yoshimi. Sep. 1978. "Kamagasaki and Katmandu: A ministry of motherhood." *Japan Missionary Bulletin* 32(8):486-489. No refs. ISSN:0021-4531.

A brief introduction to Elizabeth STROHM and her work with the homeless and motherless of Kamagasaki district of Osaka.

2223. KRUMMEL, John W. 1977. "Methodist missionary graves in Japan." *Methodist History* 15(2):122-130. 1 note. ISSN:0026-1238.

In his survey of cemeteries and graves of Methodist missionaries, KRUMMEL speaks of many women and their roles in the Church.

2224. KRUMMEL, John W. [ongoing column.] "In memoriam." *Japan Christian Quarterly* [ongoing] ISSN:0021-4361.

Obituaries of missionaries who worked in Japan. A useful way of identifying persons not otherwise discussed in the literature.

2225. LITTLE, Francis. 1906. *The Lady of the Decoration.* New York: Century, 236p. No refs.

A rather appealing collection of letters from an irrepressible and somewhat irreverent missionary/kindergarten teacher. However, this item and its sequel (*The Lady Married/The Lady and Sada San*) appear to be fiction.

2226. MILLER, Basil. 1949. *Twenty Two Missionary Stories from Japan.* Kansas City: Beacon Hill, 107p. No refs.

Included in these anecdotal and inspirational accounts are stories concerning two missionaries, Mrs. Minnie STAPLES and Pearl Wiley HANSON, and a Japanese Christian girl, Toshiko. Other Japanese women are referred to in chapters focusing primarily on men.

2227. OTIS, Clara Paine. 1962. *Sojourn in Lilliput: My Seven Years in Japan.* New York: Carlton Press. 240p. No refs. LCCN:62-5172.

The memoirs of a widow who joined her missionary sister in Japan during the Occupation. She worked primarily in Christian Centers designed to provide "alternatives" for American soldiers and to enable positive interactions among soldiers and Japanese nationals. Unique in subject matter but a personal journal lacking contextual detail.

2228. RICHARDS, Sue. Summer 1984. "Can western women adapt to Japanese society?" *Japan Christian Quarterly* 50(3):159-1. 22 notes. ISSN:0021-4361.

RICHARDS (formerly of the Sapporo Japan Mennonite Mission) details the accommodations she feels a "Western woman" must make to adjust to life in Japan.

2229. SCHROER, Cornelia R. [1979.] "They dared to live their faith: The influence of Christian women in Sendai." In: *Women in Asia: Working together for Christ.* Japan: The Conference, pp. 3-48. 16 ref. (Christian Women's Conference, 1979, Japan.)

Covers the history of Christian churches and schools in Sendai with much information on women missionaries and their educational efforts, as well as on the contributions of Japanese Christian women.

2230. TAKAGI, Takako F. Winter 1985. "Sisters of Notre Dame de Namur in Japan, 1924-1945." *Japan Missionary Bulletin* 39(4):45-52. No refs. ISSN:0021-4531.

A short history of the mission of American Sisters of Notre Dame in Okayama and their school there. Further discusses the "inculturation" of the mission, and the mutual efforts of the Japanese and American educators to keep the school open during World War II.

2231. TAYLOR, Sandra C. Feb. 1979. "The sisterhood of salvation and the Sunrise Kingdom: Congregational women missionaries in Meiji Japan." *Pacific Historical Review* 48(1):27-45. 42 notes. ISSN:0030-8684.

TAYLOR details the type of woman attracted to Congregational missionary service in the late 19th century and the types of services they performed in Japan. Uses as examples of career missionaries Eliza TALCOTT (a single woman) and Elizabeth Starr DeFOREST (mother of Charlotte DeFOREST [see #549]).

2232. TAYLOR, Sandra C. Mar. 1979. "Abby M. Colby: The Christian response to a sexist society." *New England Quarterly* 52(1):68-79. 29 notes. ISSN:0028-4866.

TAYLOR describes the role of female American missionaries in late 19th-century Japan and details the attitudes of Abby M. COLBY (in Japan 1879-1917) toward both the position of Japanese women in their society and female missionaries within their community and its governance structures. Citations are to archival materials only.

2233. TERHUNE, Bob and Hazel TERHUNE. Winter 1978. "Our Tottori experience: Thrills and disappointments." *Japan Christian Quarterly* 44(1):42-46. No refs. ISSN:0021-4361.

The TERHUNES detail their mistakes and successes as missionaries in Tottori. Hazel describes both her initial failure to cope with the combination of isolation, motherhood, and missionary work, and her ultimate growth to enable both family and career roles.

2234. WHITNEY, Clara. 1979. *Clara's Diary: An American Girl in Meiji Japan*. [Edited by M. William STEELE and Tamiko ICHIMATA.] Tokyo: Kodansha. 353p. No refs. Index. LCCN:78-60970.

Selections from a diary written by a daughter of missionary/educator parents living in Japan from 1875-1884, beginning with her arrival at age 15. Includes both detailed descriptions of "scenes of daily life in Meiji Japan" and "the story of her own maturation and accommodation to the Japanese lifestyle." WHITNEY married a Japanese, bore five children, and returned to the United States in her middle age.

Migrant Workers

2235. FRANCIS, Carolyn. Winter 1989. "Asian migrant workers in Japan." *Japan Christian Quarterly* 55(1):19-30. No refs. ISSN:0021-4361.

FRANCIS relates in detail the story of Keri, a Filipina recruited to work as a "plain receptionist" in Japan and discusses the manner in which non-Japanese Asian migrant workers are treated as invisible and disposable. She then goes on both to discuss the mission of HELP, The Asian Women's Shelter, and to question the morality of migrant laborers' treatment.

2236. FRANCIS, Carolyn. Spring 1989. "Helping Asian migrant workers." *Japan Christian Quarterly* 55(2):91-97. No refs. ISSN:0021-4361.

FRANCIS continues her discussion by detailing the recruitment system which brings workers to Japan and the role of HELP Asian Women's Shelter in assisting the same. She then outlines five steps Christians should take to raise their consciousness and that of others concerning the situation.

2237. KAPLAN, David and Alec DUBRO. 1986. *Yakuza: The Explosive Account of Japan's Criminal Underworld*. New York: MacMillan. 336p. Bibl. Index. LCCN:87-9209.

On pp. 206-208, KAPLAN (Center for Investigative Reporting) discusses the involvement of organized crime in the *Japayuki-san* business, i.e. the import of foreign women for bars and brothels in Japan.

2238. MATSUDA, Mizuho. Fall 1989. "Asian perspective: Traded women." *Japan Christian Quarterly* 55(4):245-252. No refs. ISSN:0021-4361.

MATSUDA (Director of the HELP Asian Women's Shelter) defines the four different visas on which female migrant workers are brought to Japan and presents four case studies illustrating situations women face on arrival. She then discusses in detail both context and culpability, exploring the entertainment industry and its demand for female labor.

2239. OHSHIMA, Shizuko. 1988. "Gathering the fires of HELP." *Ampo: Japan-Asia Quarterly Review* 19(4):32-35. No refs. LCCN:77-12830.

Reports on the two-year experience of HELP, a safe-house for women. This article focuses on a number of Asian women brought to Japan under false pretenses who wish to return to their own countries.

2240. OHSHIMA, Shizuko and Carolyn FRANCIS. 1989. *Japan through the Eyes of Women Migrant Workers*. Tokyo: Japan Woman's Christian Temperance Union. 221p. LCCN:91-121339.

A compilation of stories of women who have sought refuge at the HELP Asian Women's Shelter and of the services offered in their aid. Most, but not all, of the stories are about Filipina women.

2241. SAPHIR, Ann. Mar. 1990. "HELP!" *Look Japan* 35(408):48. No refs. ISSN:0456-5339.

An introduction to HELP (House in Emergency of Love and Peace), the Asian Women's Crisis Center and Shelter founded by the Japan Women's Christian Temperance Union. The shelter primarily serves southeast Asian women who have been recruited to Japan to work or as brides; the article briefly summarizes conditions which bring women to the shelter.

2242. SUZUKI, Kazue. Sep. 1987. "Japayuki-san." *PHP Intersect* (Sep. 1987):42-43. No refs. ISSN:0910-4607.

Discusses the problems of Filipina and other Asian women who are recruited to work in Japan under less than desirable circumstances. Includes brief comments from the director of the Asian Women's Shelter [HELP].

2243. TONO, Haruhi. 1986. "The Japanese sex industry: A heightening appetite for Asian women." *Ampo: Japan-Asia Quarterly Review* 18(2/3):70-76. No refs. LCCN:77-12830.

Details the rising number of Asian women, especially Filipina, who are brought to Japan as entertainers and prostitutes. Explains how the procurement system functions, the legal aspects of operations, and provides statistics.

Scientists

2244. "New physics—new frontiers." Oct. 1987. *Look Japan* 33(379):24. No refs. ISSN:0456-5339.

A brief interview with Dr. Jean SWANK (National Aeronautics and Space Administration [NASA]) and her x-ray astronomy work while a guest observer of the Institute for Space and Aeronautical Science [ISAS].

2245. STOPES, Marie C. 1910. *A Journal from Japan: A Daily Record of Life as Seen by a Scientist.* London: Blackie and Son. 274p. No refs. Index. LCCN:10-271.

The personal journal of a female paleontologist working on fossils in Hokkaido coal mines under the auspices of the Royal Society [of London], 1907-1909. Although fairly uneventful, it is an unusual memoir because of STOPES' scientific status.

Travelers/Visitors

2246. ADAM, Evelyn. 1910. *Behind the screens: An Englishwoman's Impressions of Japan.* New York: Putnam's Sons. 277p. No refs. LCCN:10-29714.

An excellent example of the condescension with which many a Westerner saw Japan at the turn of the century. The author spent six years observing "behind the *shōji,*" i.e. at home where people are themselves. She manages, however, to denigrate most of which she sees. Useful for examples of how a Western woman could carry her "cultural baggage" with her for an extended time.

2247. AUMENT, Henrietta. 1964. "Japan is for women, too." *East* 1(3):30-34. No refs. ISSN:0012-8295.

First in a series entitled "Is Japan a Man's Country?" AUMENT, an American writer, describes her two-month stay in glowing terms. [See #274 and #307 for a Japanese woman's and a Japanese man's responses, respectively.]

2248. BACHE, Carol. 1943. *Paradox Isle.* New York: Knopf. 184p. No refs.

A rambling memoir of prewar Japan by a woman who does not identify herself or her reasons for being there.

2249. BIRD, Isabella L. 1880 [rep. 1973]. *Unbeaten Tracks in Japan.* [With an introduction by Terence BARROW.] Rutland, VT: Tuttle. 336p. No refs. Index. LCCN:75-172002. Author also cited as Isabella Lucy Bird BISHOP.]

A "narrative of travels," often in the form of letters, written by a Victorian Britisher traveling for her health in 1878. The frail Isabella BIRD was interested only in "unbeaten" paths and traveled extensively in northern Japan in the company of a Japanese interpreter. A unique woman on a unique journey.

2250. COLLBRAN, Christine. 1900. *An American Girl's Trip to the Orient and around the World.* Chicago: Rand, McNally and Co. 176p. No refs. LCCN:00-5002.

Over half of this memoir/travelogue is based on a three-month stay in Yokohama, but provides only a superficial and "breezy" account of this "girl's" experiences. Her age, reason for the trip, or other personal information are not provided.

2251. EPTON, Nina Consuelo. 1963. *Seaweed for Breakfast.* London: Cassell. 268p. No refs. Index. LCCN:64-14331.

The author of several travelogues, EPTON was invited to Japan by the Japanese Foreign Office; her goal was to find out what the Japanese were like 17 years after the war. She bases her findings on a three-month visit during which she lived and talked with a great variety of Japanese. She is quite perceptive, aware of her limitations, and willing to laugh at herself.

2252. FISHER, Gertrude Adams. 1906. *A Woman Alone in the Heart of Japan.* Boston: L.C. Page. 293p. No refs. Index. LCCN:06-39433.

In general, a very lightweight travelogue with descriptions lacking much insight; another of the "Christian woman traveling in curious Japan" genre. May be useful, however, for a chapter on education which describes two schools for girls and the Women's University, and profiles several major educators.

2253. GEOFFREY, Theodate. [1926.] *An Immigrant in Japan.* London: T. Werner Laurie. 284p. No refs. LCCN:26-7690. [Author also cited as Dorothy Godfrey WAYMAN.]

Stories of four years of travel and interaction with the Japanese based on the experiences of a businessman's wife. A bit unusual because GEOFFREY [WAYMAN's pseudonym] learned Japanese, traveled as much as family life allowed, and when her husband's business went bankrupt leaving them stranded in Japan, lived in a Japanese town in a Japanese-style house, and was adopted by the Japanese mother-in-law next door. A perceptive and balanced portrayal of Westerners and Japanese during the late 'teens.

2254. KEITH, Agnes Newton. 1975. *Before the Blossoms Fall: Life and Death in Japan.* Boston: Little, Brown and Co. 326p. No refs. Index. LCCN:75-12880.

An account of a visit to Japan by a Canadian woman who was held in an internment camp in Borneo during World War II. She includes both her observations on the status of women and accounts of several conversations with Japanese women; material is scattered but accessible through the index.

2255. McCOOEY, Chris. 1984. "Off the beaten track." *Japan Quarterly* 30(3):82-86. No refs. ISSN:0021-4590.

Highlights events in the back-country travels of Isabella L. BISHOP née BIRD in 1878. Taken from letters written to her sister; for the original material see #2249.

2256. MEARS, Helen. 1942. *Year of the Wild Boar: An American Woman in Japan.* Philadelphia: Lippincott, 346p. No refs. LCCN:42-18652.

Based on a visit to Japan in 1935, this memoir by a "writer and editor" is designed to be "a personal record with the emphasis on how the Japanese behave in their daily affairs." Included are descriptions of a textile factory visit, the life of one "modern woman" married to a Communist, and much discussion of the Japanese political scene.

2257. PERRY, Lilla S. 1978. "A treasure hunt in Japan, 1936: Excerpts from the diary of Mrs. Lilla S. Perry." In: KAEMPFER, H.M., ed. *Ukiyo-e Studies and Pleasures: A Collection of Essays on the Art of Japanese Prints.* The Hague: Society for Japanese Arts and Crafts, pp. 68-83. No refs. LCCN:79-322559.

An account of print-hunting in 1936 by an avid collector.

2258. PRIESTOFF, Naomi. 1976. "The gaijin executive's wife—Experiencing Japan with an American family on company assignment abroad. *Conference Board Record* 13(5):51-64. No refs. ISSN:0010-5546.

An insightful record of a three-year stay in Japan as the wife of an American company head. Shows her growth and struggle as she moves through the stages of initial happiness, culture shock and accommodation.

2259. SANSOM, Katharine. 1937. *Living in Tokyo.* New York: Harcourt Brace. 184p. No refs. LCCN:37-5360.

A non-personalized description of living in Tokyo in the 1930s. Discusses Japanese servants, mountain climbing, school girl uniforms, etc.; women are discussed in very general terms.

War and Occupation

2260. ARGALL, Phyllis. 1944. *My Life with the Enemy*. New York: MacMillan. 290p. No refs.

Phyllis ARGALL went to Japan in 1916 as the child of British missionaries, lived in Formosa beginning in 1932 as a principal of a Canadian mission school, and returned to Japan to become managing editor of *Japan News-Week*. By December 1941 she was tried and convicted of being a spy, and sentenced to 18 months hard labor. After six months in prison she was finally released and then evacuated to the United States in June 1942. A unique view of prewar and wartime Japan.

2261. BLAIN, Tats. 1953. *Mother-sir!* New York: Appleton- Century-Crofts. 276p. No refs. LCCN:53-9817. [Author also cited as Mary D. BLAIN.]

A story of a Navy wife based in Sasebo on the island of Kyushu during the early days of the Occupation. She describes an awkward lifestyle in good humor, and while she does not go out of her way to lavish praise on the Japanese, she does not spare the Americans (including herself) either.

2262. BROWN, Margery Finn. 1951. *Over a Bamboo Fence; An American Looks at Japan*. New York: Morrow. 239p. No refs. LCCN:51-13978.

A personal account of the years 1946-1948 by the wife of an Army officer and mother of four children. BROWN joined the staff of the *Mainichi Shimbun*, a Japanese newspaper, as a way of seeing "over the bamboo fence" which separated the Americans and Japanese. Although a bit on the sarcastic side, it could be useful for its insights on how an American woman saw the Occupation affecting the Japanese lifestyle.

2263. CROCKETT, Lucy Herndon. 1949. *Popcorn on the Ginza: An Informal Portrait of Postwar Japan*. New York: William Sloane Associates. 286p. No refs. LCCN:49-7179.

An informal description of occupied Japan based on 18 months of an American Red Cross employee's experiences beginning in December 1945. A refreshing account because the author seems to have a very balanced view of the roles of both sides, and of her opportunity to "participate in our country's first big chance to play God before a conquered nation." Personal reflections are not included, but the memoir will provide insight into the observational powers of an American woman in Japan at a crucial time.

2264. DUUS, Masayo. 1979. *Tokyo Rose, Orphan of the Pacific*. [Translated by Peter DUUS.] Tokyo: Kodansha International. 248p. Notes. Index. LCCN:78-60968. [*Tōkyō Rōzu*. English.]

A well-researched biography of a Nisei woman caught in Japan during World War II, who was the target of the United State's need for a scapegoat after the war. DUUS argues that there was no one Tokyo Rose, and that Ira d'AQUINO was tried and convicted of treason even without compelling evidence. A delineation of post-war pressures on American officials; useful for its exposé of the Tokyo Rose myth.

2265. GUNN, Rex B. 1977. *They Called Her Tokyo Rose*. [Santa Monica, CA]: Gunn. 111p. Notes. LCCN:78-105944.

The story of a Japanese-American woman caught in Japan during World War II who was eventually put on trial in the United States as the Tokyo Rose (when in reality 12 women were broadcasters to the American military). This biography is an "action-packed" version with many quotations from, and references to, primary materials.

2266. HOWE, Russell Warren. 1990. *The Hunt for "Tokyo Rose"*. Lanham, MD: Madison Books. 354p. No refs. Index. LCCN:89-35273.

Another rendition of the Iva d'Aquino story for the general reader. Based heavily on interviews with d'Aquino and other players in the trial, with the intent of encouraging a national apology in the form of a joint resolution of Congress.

2267. PENROSE, Gertrude. 1948. "Reporting on Japan's women." *Independent Woman* 27:322-324. [Title also cited as *National Business Woman*.] ISSN:0027-8831.

Describes the work of Doris COCHRANE, a liaison officer with the U.S. State Department in 1945. COCHRANE conducted leadership training institutes for Japanese women in order to foster democratic participation on a local level.

2268. PHARR, Susan J. 1980. "Weed, Ethel Bernice." In: SICHERMAN, Barbara, ed. *Notable American Women: The Modern Period*. Cambridge: Harvard University Press, pp. 721-723. Bibl. LCCN:80-18402.

A biographical sketch of Ethel B. WEED (1906-1975), Women's Information Officer during the Occupation. WEED was instrumental in promoting women's suffrage, revising the sections of the Civil Code dealing with women, and organizing women's groups to be run by democratic principles.

2269. TAYLOR, Marion. 1956. *American Geisha*. London: G. Bles. 324p. No refs. LCCN:57-993.

The memoir of an American woman whose husband was stationed at Camp Gray, Hokkaido, during the Occupation. A blend of humor, frustration, and understanding; it is the only memoir of this genre found which is set in Hokkaido.

2270. THYSELL, Ellen R. 1956. *The Bride Grew Horns*. New York: Vantage. 151p. No refs. LCCN:56-6840.

The author stayed in Japan from February through May 1951 while her husband testified on a tax case resulting from events during the Occupation. Her letters to her sister during this time show both her excitement and frustrations with being a guest of a Japanese family.

Wives of Japanese Men

2271. BIRMINGHAM, Lucy. Aug. 1988. "Mom, Dad . . . I want you to meet Masayuki." *PHP Intersect* (Aug. 1988):34-40. No refs. ISSN:0910-4607.

Interviews five "international" couples who briefly give their views on their marriages and their children's education. Two of the women are not Japanese.

2272. "Bride hunt." 14 Apr. 1989. *Asiaweek* 15(15):46-50,53-55. No refs. ISSN:1012-6244.

A brief photo-essay on the mixed results of recruiting young Filipina women as wives for rural men in Japan. One photograph shows a portion of the story not usually covered: a crying mother-in-law reacting to a quarrel between her son and daughter-in-law (as her hopes for grandchildren come into question).

2273. CANNON, Peter. 5 Jul. 1990. "Wife shopping." *The Listener* 124(3172):8-9. No refs. ISSN:0024-4392.

The director of a BBC program on the bride importation phenomenon describes the bride selection process in the Philippines. CANNON notes that "President Aquino outlawed the advertising of wives for foreigners and banned matchmaking clubs" in June 1990.

2274. IMAMURA, Anne E. Sep. 1988. "The loss that has no name: Social womanhood of foreign wives." *Gender and Society* 2(3):291-307. 21 refs. ISSN:0891-2432.

In this technical discussion of womanhood and its designation as an ascribed or achieved status, IMAMURA uses data from women who are married to Japanese and Nigerian men, and who reside in those countries. Topics covered include wifehood, kin relations, parenting, work, friendship, and Foreign Wives Associations. IMAMURA concludes that womanhood is socially constructed and achieved and cannot be simply transported from one place to another.

2275. IMAMURA, Anne E. Summer 1990. "Strangers in a strange land: Coping with marginality in international marriage." *Journal of Comparative Family Studies* 21(2):171-191. 28 refs. ISSN:0047-2328.

In this technical discussion focusing on causes of social marginality, IMAMURA continues her work on non-Japanese and non-Nigerian women who are married to Japanese and Nigerian men, respectively, and who reside in their adopted countries. She investigated spousal relations, motherhood, work roles, friendships, and foreign wives associations.

2276. ISSOBE, Mayo. Sep. 1987. "Foreign brides." *PHP Intersect* (Sep. 1987):43. No refs. ISSN:0910-4607.

A short note on the importation of Filipina and other Asian women as brides for farmers in rural areas. The negative reactions of two feminists are quoted briefly.

2277. NAKAMURA, Beverly. Winter 1985. "Inter-cultural marriages." *Japan Christian Quarterly* 51(1):30-36. No refs. ISSN:0021-4361.

Articulates coping strategies for non-Japanese women married to Japanese men, including processes for acclimating to Japanese society and basic survival attitudes.

2278. NAKAMURA, Hisashi. 1988. "Japan imports brides from Sri Lanka: A new poverty discovered." *Ampo: Japan-Asia Quarterly Review* 19(4):26-31. 13 notes. LCCN:77-12830.

Focuses on the phenomenon of bride importation, from not only Sri Lanka but most Asian countries, to meet the needs of males in agricultural and rural areas. The probable loss of the women's human rights and the impact on Japanese society, as well as the structure of the bride import business, are detailed. Includes sample advertisements for potential wives.

2279. NITTA, Fumiteru. 1988. "*Kokusai kekkon*: Trends in intercultural marriage in Japan." *International Journal of Intercultural Relations* 12(3):205-232. 54 refs. ISSN:0147-1767.

A statistically-based study showing that more Japanese men marry non-Japanese women than Japanese women marry foreign men. Discusses reasons for intercultural marriage. Data are from the Ministry of Justice, Association of Foreign Wives of Japanese, and the Kokusai Kekkon o Kangaeru Kai (an association for Japanese women married to non-Japanese men).

2280. SATŌ, Kunio. 1988. "Wives for farmers, a critical import." *Japan Quarterly* 35(3):253-259. No refs. ISSN:0021-4590.

Explores the need for wives for rural men as well as reasons Asian women may be willing to come. Includes some statistics and briefly explains the role of marriage broker businesses.

2281. SHIMIZU, Yasuko. Summer 1988. "Asian perspective—Asian brides for rural Japan." *Japan Christian Quarterly* 54(3):179-181. No refs. ISSN:0021-4361.

Reports on the February 1988 symposium sponsored by the Japan Youth Assembly which focused on the "international arranged marriages practiced in Japanese villages." Questions the moral context of a society which would encourage a phenomenon of this nature.

2282. SUGURO, Suvendrini. Dec. 1988. "Six brides for six villagers." *PHP Intersect* (Dec. 1988):42-43. No refs. ISSN:0910-4607.

SUGURO (a Sri Lankan journalist) describes the cross-cultural difficulties encountered by rural farmers and their imported Asian wives, but is optimistic that these marriages can work given sufficient "compromise, good sense, and affection."

2283. YAMAZAKI, Hiromi. 1988. "Japan imports brides from the Philippines—Can isolated farmers buy consolation?" *Ampo: Japan-Asia Quarterly Review* 19(4):22-25. No refs. LCCN:77-12830.

YAMAZAKI discusses the problems and discrimination many Filipina brides face in their marriages to rural Japanese men. Also describes the "blatant racism and sexism" involved in recruitment and protests government involvement in the "international marriage counseling business."

Other

2284. BARR, Pat. 1968. *The Deer Cry Pavilion: A Story of Westerners in Japan, 1868-1905.* London: MacMillan. 282p. Bibl. Index. LCCN:71-354164.

Although not specifically on women, this work (especially pp. 113-115 and the chapter on diplomats) and BARR's earlier *The Coming of the Barbarians: The Opening of Japan to the West, 1853-1870* (New York: Dutton, 1967. LCCN:67-20534.) describe the context in which foreign women lived, as well as discussing briefly Japanese women—as upper-class ladies at the Deer Cry Pavilion (Rokumeikan) and as ladies of the night in the Yoshiwara District.

2285. "Foreigners living in Japan: Raylene Thompson—Being female is a definite asset." Jan. 1978. *PHP* 9(1):47-49. No refs. ISSN:0030-798X.

A very brief interview with a 14-year resident of Yokohama who enjoys her life in Japan.

2286. SCHULTZE, Emma. 1980. *Letters from Meiji Japan: Correspondence of a German Surgeon's Wife, 1878-1881.* [Translated and edited by Charlotte T. MARSHALL in collaboration with John Z. BOWERS.] New York: Josiah Macy, Jr. Foundation. 160p. Bibl. Index. LCCN:80-83745.

The letters of Emma SCHULTZE, wife of Dr. Wilhelm SCHULTZE, a Prussian military staff sergeant and professor at the Medical College of the University of Tokyo. She relates to her parents the events of their first three years of marriage, focusing primarily on family life and activities of the German community, and indicates (despite her command of Japanese) a strong reliance on news and items from home for emotional and physical comfort.

19

Reviews and Overviews of Scholarship on Women

Commentaries

2287. BESTOR, Theodore C. 1985. "Gendered domains: A commentary on research in Japanese studies." *Journal of Japanese Studies* 11(1):283-287. No refs. ISSN:0095-6848.

Summarizes conclusions drawn at the Workshop on Gender Issues in the Study of Japan (University of Washington, June 1984). Calls for a new emphasis on gender studies focusing on women in areas in which they do not predominate. Also articulates four conceptual themes which emerged in the discussions: "historical transformations [of] gender roles and ideologies," "structured inequalities" including gender, "social and cultural constructions of gender," and "international dimensions of gender."

2288. NAKANO, Ann. Oct. 1986. "Joyce Ackroyd: Grande dame of Japanese studies." *PHP Intersect* (Oct. 1986):40-41. No refs. ISSN:0910-4607.

A biographical sketch of Joyce ACKROYD, long-time scholar of Japan, who wrote one of the earliest scholarly studies in English concerning Japanese women. [See #9.]

2289. NOLTE, Sharon. Sep. 1983. "Report on the Third All-Japan Women's History Conference, Kanagawa Prefecture, Enoshima, August 6-7, 1983." *CWAS: Newsletter of the Committee on Women in Asian Studies of the Association for Asian Studies* 2(1):5-6. No refs. ISSN:0738-3185.

Briefly describes the participants (working women researching in their spare time) and the program of the conference. Although many Japanese women are quite active as non-professional historians, this is the only report found in English on their activities.

2290. NOLTE, Sharon. Feb. 1987. "Gender, status and history: American women as scholars in modern Japan." In: *Eye to Eye: Women Researching Women in Asia.* Minneapolis: Committee on Women in Asian Studies of the Association for Asian Studies, pp. 3-10. (*CWAS Monograph* no.3, ISSN:0743-5762.) 14 notes.

NOLTE reflects on the problems of a female researcher in Japan through both her own experiences and those of four other American women: Alice Mabel BACON, Mary BEARD, Ella Lury WISWELL, and Gail Lee BERNSTEIN. She also notes the difficulties she herself encountered as a married female scholar with an accompanying non-scholar spouse.

2291. SIEVERS, Sharon L. 1984. "The future of feminist scholarship on Japanese women." In: MILLER, Barbara D. and Janice HYDE, eds. *Women in Asia and Asian Studies.* Syracuse:

Committee on Women in Asian Studies of the Association for Asian Studies, pp. 115-121. (*CWAS Monograph* no.1, ISSN:0743-5762.) Bibl.

SIEVERS, an active feminist and Japan scholar, has issued a call for more work on Japanese women, both original scholarship and translations of Japanese works. She outlines problems facing younger scholars, both American and Japanese, and urges tenured professors to foster and protect their efforts.

Bibliographies

2292. FUJITA, Kuniko. 1985. "A bibliographical syllabus of the political economy of women in Japan." *Japan Foundation Newsletter* 13(1):11-17. 176 refs. ISSN:0385-2318.

A list of 176 items divided into the areas of gender relations, state, economy, women's movement, history, and bibliography.

2293. Japan PEN Club, comp. 1990. *Japanese Literature in Foreign Languages, 1945-1990.* [Tokyo]: Japan Book Publishers Association. 383p. LCCN:91-156838.

A somewhat idiosyncratic but extremely valuable resource on Japanese prose and poetry translated into Western languages, plus relevant books, articles, and doctoral dissertations in those languages.

2294. KOH, Hesung Chun, *et al.* 1982. *Korean and Japanese Women: An Analytic Bibliographical Guide.* Westport, CT: HRAF [Human Relations Area Files]/Greenwood Press. 903p. LCCN:81-80305.

A bibliography with a "multidimensional approach to classification and indexing," with 163 references to materials on Japanese women. Includes document analysis and annotations.

2295. Kokusai Bunka Kaikan, Tokyo. Toshoshitsu. 1979. *Modern Japanese Literature in Translation: A Bibliography.* Tokyo: Kodansha International. 311p. [Author also cited as: International House of Japan Library.] LCCN:78-66395.

An invaluable listing, by author, of fiction, drama, poetry, and essays published since 1868, that have been translated into English and many European and Asian languages. Original Japanese titles included.

2296. KRICHMAR, Albert, Virginia Smith CARLSON, and Ann E. WIEDERRECHT. 1977. *The Women's Movement in the Seventies: An International English Language Bibliography.* Metuchen, NJ: Scarecrow Press. 875p. 8637 refs. Index. LCCN:77-21416.

Includes forty annotated references on Japan, all published in the early 1970s. They cover education, politics, work and social roles.

2297. KUNINOBU, Junko Wada. 1984. "Bibliography of contemporary Japanese women (materials in English)." *Women's Studies International Forum* 7(4):307-312. 81 refs. ISSN:0277-5395.

Provides a listing of 81 citations to materials dealing with the status of Japanese women and several more general social issues.

2298. MAMOLA, Claire Zebroski. 1989. *Japanese Women Writers in English Translation: An Annotated Bibliography.* New York: Garland. 469p. 971 refs. Index. LCCN:89-1319.

A listing of 971 items, 583 of them with summaries. MAMOLA restricts her bibliography to materials (both fiction and nonfiction) written by Japanese women.

2299. MARKS, Alfred H. and Barry D. BORT. 1975. *Guide to Japanese Prose*. Boston: G.K. Hall. 150p. (*The Asian Literature Bibliography Series*.) Index. LCCN:74-20608.

A selective annotated bibliography of prose works from earliest times through the early 1970s that have been translated into English. Does not include secondary scholarship. Heian and Kamakura tales and diaries by women are listed and discussed briefly.

2300. SCHIERBECK, Sachiko Shibata. 1989. *Postwar Japanese Women Writers: An Up-to-Date Bibliography with Biographical Sketches*. [Edited by Søren EGEROD.] Copenhagen: University of Copenhagen Press. 196p. (*Occasional Papers of the East Asian Institute, University of Copenhagen*, vol. 5. ISSN:0903-6822.) Bibl. LCCN:90-134286.

A general historical introduction followed by brief portraits (with photographs) of 53 women who have written fiction since World War II, including a short list of "selected" works in Japanese, and in English, French and German translation. Summaries of major, untranslated works are also provided. A numbers of the writers SCHIERBECK includes are not listed in this bibliography since they are not yet represented in English translation.

2301. SHULMAN, Frank Joseph. 1990. *Japan*. Santa Barbara: Clio. (*World Bibliographical Series*, 103.) 873p. Bibl. Index. LCCN:89-70789.

A *tour de force* of annotated bibliographies. A comprehensive treatment of 1,615 English-language books on Japan with thorough and critical annotations. Includes a number of items on women, all of which appear in this bibliography as well.

2302. SIXEL, Nancy and Carol FAIRBANKS. Dec. 1986. "Bibliography of Japanese women poets and fiction writers since 1868." *Bulletin of Bibliography* 43(4):195-220. Bibl. ISSN:0007-4780.

Lists a selection of references for poetry and fiction by Japanese women and also references for criticism and biographical information on the poets and authors.

2303. THOMAS, Roger. 1982. "A *Genji* bibliography: Non-Japanese sources." *Yearbook of Comparative and General Literature* 31:68-75. No refs. ISSN:0084-3695.

A useful annotated bibliography, including entries (in English as well as European langugages) not listed here.

2304. YAMAGIWA, Joseph K. 1959. *Japanese Literature of the Showa Period: A Guide to Japanese Reference and Research Materials*. Ann Arbor: University of Michigan Press. 212p. (*University of Michigan Center for Japanese Studies Bibliographical Series* no. 8.) LCCN:59-62962.

Aimed at an audience reasonably familiar with Japanese literature, this volume contains a wealth of information on almost all recognized twentieth-century groups of writers or poets, with considerable attention to their membership and their publications (journals). Also a valuable, though outdated, bibliographic source for Japanese materials.

Comparative Review Essays on Works Other than Literature

2305. BOOCOCK, Sarane Spence. Sep. 1984. "Japanese women: Shadow or sun?" *Contemporary Sociology* 13(5):551-556. 2 refs. ISSN:0094-3061.

A bibliographic essay covering Gail Lee BERNSTEIN's *Haruko's World* [#782], Liza DALBY's *Geisha* [#922], Dorothy ROBINS-MOWRY's *The Hidden Sun* [#43], Sharon SIEVERS' *Flowers in Salt* [#1167], and James TRAGER's *Letters from Sachiko* [#109].

2306. BUCKLEY, Sandra. Apr./Jun. 1984. "The beginnings of a feminist consciousness: A review essay." *Bulletin of Concerned Asian Scholars* 16(2):63-65. No refs. ISSN:0007-4810.

Compares and contrasts Sharon SIEVERS' *Flowers in Salt* [#1167] and Dorothy ROBINS-MOWRY's *The Hidden Sun* [#43].

2307. LOFTUS, Ronald P. Fall 1980. "Japanese women in history and society." *Journal of Ethnic Studies* 8(3):109-122. 16 notes. ISSN:0091-3219.

Provides a brief overview on women's status historically to introduce a critical and detailed bibliographic essay on approximately 20 English language items dealing with Japanese women.

2308. NOLTE, Sharon. 1983. "Women in a pre-war Japanese village: Suye Mura revisited." *Peasant Studies* 10(3):175-190. 17 refs. ISSN:0149-1547.

In this extensive discussion of *The Women of Suye Mura* [#50], NOLTE provides detailed contextual material and delineates the important issues raised in the work.

2309. TAMANOI, Mariko Asano. 1990. "Women's voices: Their critique of the anthropology of Japan." *Annual Review of Anthropology* 19:17-37. 172 refs. ISSN:0084-6570.

A review article discussing anthropological and sociological research on Japanese women done primarily by women (but not necessarily Japanese women). TAMANOI discusses works on the historical status of Japanese women, women in the larger community including the workplace and religious movements, and briefly, birth control and abortion.

2310. TSURUMI, E. Patricia. Oct./Dec. 1986. "Problem consciousness and modern Japanese history: Female textile workers of Meiji and Taisho." *Bulletin of Concerned Asian Scholars* 18(4):41-48. 27 notes. ISSN:0007-4810.

In this review essay, TSURUMI first severely critiques three English language treatments of female textile workers of the late 19th and early 20th centuries (SAXONHOUSE [#825], KIDD [#815], and HANE [#17]), and commends SIEVERS [#1167] for her feminist approach to questions about textile workers' roles and contributions. She then continues her bibliographic essay by surveying the Japanese primary and secondary sources available.

2311. TSURUMI, E. Patricia. Fall 1987. "Reclaiming the past: Japanese women's history: A review essay." *Atlantis* 13(1):164-168. 9 notes. ISSN:0702-7818.

A detailed review essay covering ISHIMOTO Shidzue's *Facing Two Ways* [#1243] and Sharon SIEVERS' *Flowers in Salt* [#1167].

Chronology of Historical Periods

Conventional Periodization of Japanese History
(Precise dates vary according to source)

Asuka	552-646
Early Nara or Hakuhō	646-710
Nara or Tempyō	710-794
Heian	794-1185
Kamakura	1185-1333
Muromachi or Ashikaga	1333-1568
Momoyama or Azuchi-Momoyama	1568-1600
Tokugawa or Edo	1600-1868
Meiji	1868-1912
Taishō	1912-1926
Shōwa	1926-1989
Heisei	1989-

Author, Editor, Translator, Interviewee Index

Numbers in this index refer to entry numbers, not page numbers

Title Phrase, Series, Proceedings Index

Subject Index

Numbers in this index refer to entry numbers, not page numbers.

About the Authors

KRISTINA RUTH HUBER is an Assistant Professor and Reference and Bibliographic Instruction Librarian at St. Olaf College. She has published several articles in *Research Strategies* and is the compiler of *The Kirtland's Warbler (Dendroica Kirtlandii): An Annotated Bibliography, 1852-1980.*

KATHRYN SPARLING is Professor of Japanese Language and Literature at Carleton College. She has published articles in the *Harvard Journal of Asiatic Studies* and has translated two books from Japanese into English.